Digital Transformation and Organizational Agility:

Leadership, Strategy, and Emerging Technologies

Darrell Norman Burrell
https://orcid.org/0000-0002-4675-9544
Marymount University, USA

IGI Global
Scientific Publishing
Publishing Tomorrow's Research Today

Vice President of Editorial — Melissa Wagner
Director of Acquisitions — Mikaela Felty
Director of Book Development — Jocelynn Hessler
Production Manager — Mike Brehm
Cover Design — Jose Rosado

Published in the United States of America by
IGI Global Scientific Publishing
701 East Chocolate Avenue
Hershey, PA, 17033, USA
Tel: 717-533-8845 | Fax: 717-533-7115
Website: https://www.igi-global.com E-mail: cust@igi-global.com

Library of Congress Cataloging-in-Publication Data

No LCCN (CIP Data Pending)
ISBN13: 9798337340272
Isbn13Softcover: 9798337340289
EISBN13: 9798337340296
British Cataloguing in Publication Data
A Cataloguing in Publication record for this book is available from the British Library.

Table of Contents

Detailed Table of Contents

dichotomy between planning rigor and organizational responsiveness, demonstrating that properly designed planning processes enable rather than constrain adaptive capacity. Drawing on project management theory and empirical case studies, this analysis proposes an integrated framework for adaptive project planning tailored to digital transformation initiatives. The framework emphasizes contextual tailoring, integration across planning elements, structured flexibility, behavioral awareness, and continuous learning. Evidence from major project failures reveals that overruns typically result not from planning rigor itself, but from inadequate integration, insufficient change control, behavioral mismanagement of buffers, and communication breakdowns. The chapter concludes that disciplined planning and organizational agility represent complementary capabilities organizations must master.

This chapter examines how systematic quality management enables organizational agility through technology adoption. Drawing on frameworks and case studies, we demonstrate that sustainable agility requires embedding quality throughout digital transformation—from planning through execution and improvement. The chapter synthesizes quality methodologies with technology strategies, emphasizing leadership's role in fostering quality-driven cultures. By examining metrics, audits, and stakeholder engagement, this research provides insights for cultivating agility while maintaining excellence. Successful transformation demands more than technology; it requires systematic quality approaches permeating culture, aligning stakeholders, and establishing accountability. This guide serves leaders and practitioners building resilient, agile organizations.

In today's hyperconnected digital environment, organizational change management must integrate cybersecurity and AI as strategic elements. This chapter proposes a framework combining continuous change management, cyber risk governance, and workforce responsiveness defined by adaptive potential and digital dexterity. Legacy models designed for linear change struggle amid rising cyber threats and rapid technological shifts. By framing cyber risk governance as a strategic enabler and leveraging AI insight, organizations balance agility with security to achieve resilient transformation. Drawing on literature and case studies, the framework highlights the importance of behavioral adaptability and continuous learning cultures in sustaining success. This approach helps organizations anticipate disruptions and innovate securely, making it relevant for industries facing converging digital and cyber challenges. The findings offer actionable guidance for executives, change strategists, and cyber professionals striving to excel where flexibility, safety, and intelligent automation converge.

Organizational agility is critical for enterprise success amid rapid technological change and market volatility. This chapter examines leadership's role in fostering agility through cultural transformation and technology adoption. Drawing from Schein's cultural dimensions, Heifetz's adaptive leadership, and digital transformation frameworks, it explores how leaders navigate technological complexities while reshaping organizational culture. The discussion integrates high-context and low-context cultural dimensions with digital maturity models, highlighting approaches for aligning cultural practices, technological capabilities, and goals. A Florida government case study illustrates leadership's impact on cultural integration, diversity, innovation, and technology-enabled agility. The chapter emphasizes adaptive leadership's importance in fostering resilient, inclusive, technologically empowered cultures capable of thriving in dynamic environments.

As artificial intelligence (AI) becomes integral to healthcare innovation and infrastructure, healthcare organizations face a growing challenge: equipping technically proficient professionals with the leadership competencies necessary to operate effectively at the enterprise level. This qualitative study explores how healthcare organizations either support or impede the leadership development of AI and IT professionals and identifies strategies that best facilitate their transition from technical expertise to strategic leadership. Using three separate focus groups composed of change management consultants, AI technology managers, and leadership development trainers. The findings suggest that most organizations fail to offer effective leadership training programs for AI professionals operating in high-risk, compliance-heavy environments.

The regular functioning of the Armed Forces of a state depends on the ability to obtain and retain human resources in the ranks, this work falls within the scope of the difficulties experienced in recruitment and retention that exist in the Portuguese Armed Forces (FFAA) having as one of the factors is lack of motivation and their general objective is to contribute to studying the forms of communication and leadership that military leaders exercise towards their subordinates and how this influences their motivation and consequently its performance. To this end, the following question underlying the investigation was outlined: "Does communication from leaders influence the performance of the Portuguese military through their strength?". This is a descriptive study of a quantitative nature, and the data were collected through a questionnaire survey, applied to the active population, reserves and the availability of military organizations dependent on the General Staff of the Armed Forces,

Preface

In an era defined by rapid technological acceleration and systemic uncertainty, the imperative for organizations to evolve—rather than merely adapt—has never been more pronounced. *Digital Transformation and Organizational Agility: Leadership, Strategy, and Emerging Technologies* emerges as a response to this defining moment. As editors, we have curated this volume with a clear purpose: to bridge the persistent divide between technological innovation and organizational readiness, and to illuminate the pathways through which institutions can cultivate agility as a sustained and strategic capability.

Across industries and sectors, leaders are confronted with a paradox. While emerging technologies such as artificial intelligence, advanced cybersecurity frameworks, and digital platforms promise unprecedented opportunities, their successful integration often falters in the absence of aligned culture, ethical foresight, and adaptive leadership. This volume was conceived to address that tension. It is not a book solely about technology; rather, it is a book about transformation in its fullest sense—organizational, human, and systemic.

The chapters assembled here reflect a deliberate commitment to interdisciplinary inquiry. Contributors from academia, industry, and public service offer perspectives that transcend traditional silos, weaving together insights from management science, engineering, public policy, organizational behavior, and ethics. In doing so, they collectively advance a more holistic understanding of how digital transformation unfolds in practice—not as a linear process, but as a dynamic and iterative journey shaped by context, culture, and complexity.

A central premise unites this work: organizational agility is not an endpoint to be achieved, but a continuous capability to be cultivated. It requires more than the adoption of new tools; it demands a reimagining of leadership, a reconfiguration of structures, and a reorientation toward learning, resilience, and innovation. The research and case studies presented in this volume underscore that agility is deeply embedded in how organizations anticipate disruption, engage stakeholders, manage risk, and uphold ethical responsibility in an increasingly data-driven world.

This book also responds to a critical gap in both scholarship and practice. Too often, discussions of digital transformation are fragmented—confined within disciplinary boundaries or detached from the realities of implementation. By integrating empirical research with practitioner insight, this volume offers a more cohesive and applied perspective. It provides readers with frameworks that are not only analytically rigorous but also actionable in real-world settings.

Importantly, the scope of this work reflects the diversity of environments in which digital transformation is taking place. From healthcare and education to government and finance, the contributors explore how emerging technologies are reshaping service delivery, governance, and organizational design. They also confront the ethical and societal implications of these changes, emphasizing the need for responsible innovation and inclusive growth.

ORGANIZATION OF BOOK

Chapter 1 introduces a compelling evolution in strategic thinking through the Purple Ocean Strategy, positioning it as a synthesis of competitive defense and market creation. The authors challenge the limitations of traditional frameworks by demonstrating how multinational corporations can simultaneously protect existing market share while pursuing innovation-driven growth. Through illustrative cases, the chapter underscores the importance of strategic ambidexterity, offering a nuanced lens for organizations seeking sustainable competitive advantage in volatile environments.

In Chapter 2, we are confronted with a cautionary tale of technological ambition outpacing organizational readiness. The collapse of an AI initiative within a pharmaceutical enterprise reveals the often-overlooked prerequisites of successful digital transformation. The authors thoughtfully dissect failures in governance, change management, and readiness assessment, ultimately offering a robust, theory-informed framework for ethical and sustainable AI adoption in highly regulated contexts.

In Chapter 3, the longstanding tension between structured planning and organizational agility is reframed as a false dichotomy. The authors argue persuasively that disciplined planning, when designed with flexibility and integration in mind, becomes an enabler of agility rather than a constraint. Their proposed framework offers practical insights for organizations seeking to harmonize rigor with responsiveness in digital transformation initiatives.

Chapter 4 builds on this foundation by emphasizing the role of quality management as a driver of agility. The authors demonstrate that sustainable transformation is rooted in systematic approaches that embed quality across all stages of technology implementation. Leadership, culture, and accountability emerge as central themes, reinforcing the idea that agility must be intentionally designed and continuously maintained.

In Chapter 5, the conversation expands to include the critical intersection of cybersecurity, artificial intelligence, and continuous change management. The authors present a forward-looking framework that integrates these elements into a cohesive model of resilient transformation. Particularly noteworthy is the emphasis on workforce adaptability and digital dexterity as essential capabilities in navigating hyperconnected and high-risk environments.

Chapter 6 offers a comprehensive exploration of transformational leadership as a catalyst for digital maturity. Drawing on meta-analytic insights, the authors illuminate how leadership behaviors shape organizational culture, influence technology adoption, and enable the development of dynamic capabilities. This chapter reinforces the central role of leadership in guiding organizations through complex technological transitions.

Chapter 7 extends the leadership discourse by focusing on capability development within service organizations. Through the identification of six critical leadership roles, the authors provide a structured yet adaptable framework for cultivating transformational leaders. Their integration of systems thinking and human capital strategy offers a roadmap for organizations aiming to thrive in service-driven and digitally enabled economies.

In Chapter 8, a case study of a leading telecommunications organization provides a grounded perspective on innovation and change. The authors highlight both the successes and the perceptual gaps that emerge during digital transformation efforts. This chapter serves as a reminder that technological advancement must be accompanied by meaningful improvements in user experience and stakeholder trust.

Chapter 9 brings together the themes of artificial intelligence and digital transformation to explore their combined impact on systemic agility. The authors articulate how technological integration, leadership adaptability, and workforce readiness converge to enable faster decision-making and enhanced organizational responsiveness. Importantly, they balance this discussion with considerations of ethics and sustainability.

Chapter 10 introduces an innovative perspective through the concept of digital emotional intelligence. By integrating organizational psychodynamics with technology, the authors argue for a more human-centered approach to agility. Their work highlights the importance of aligning empathy with efficiency, suggesting that emotional intelligence remains a critical differentiator even in highly digitized environments.

In Chapter 11, leadership once again takes center stage, this time through the lens of cultural transformation. The authors examine how leaders can align organizational culture with technological advancement, drawing on established theoretical frameworks and real-world case evidence. Their insights emphasize inclusivity, adaptability, and the strategic role of culture in enabling agility.

Chapter 12 addresses a pressing gap in healthcare innovation: the leadership development of AI professionals. Through qualitative inquiry, the authors reveal systemic shortcomings in preparing technical experts for strategic roles. This chapter calls for intentional investment in leadership pathways that bridge technical expertise with organizational influence, particularly in high-stakes environments.

Chapter 13 offers a focused examination of leadership communication within military contexts. The findings underscore the profound impact of communication styles on motivation, performance, and retention. While situated within the armed forces, the implications extend broadly to any organization seeking to strengthen engagement and operational effectiveness through leadership practices.

In Chapter 14, the lens shifts to financial decision-making, where cybersecurity emerges as a critical factor influencing investor behavior. The authors provide compelling evidence that transparent and strategic cyber risk disclosures shape trust and valuation. This chapter contributes to both theory and practice by linking cybersecurity governance with financial market dynamics.

Chapters 15 through 17 collectively explore the future of quality management in the context of emerging technologies and the forthcoming ISO 9001:2026 standard. Chapter 15 examines how artificial intelligence is poised to transform quality management systems, offering both opportunities and implementation challenges. Chapter 16 expands this discussion by situating quality within the broader ecosystem of Industry 4.0, technologies such as AI, blockchain, and IoT enable "smart quality" and interconnected operations. Chapter 17 provides a focused analysis of blockchain's role in enhancing transparency, traceability, and trust within supply chains, positioning it as a foundational element of next-generation quality standards.

As editors, we view this volume as both a roadmap and an invitation. It is a roadmap for leaders, scholars, and practitioners seeking to navigate the complexities of technological change with clarity and purpose. At the same time, it is an invitation to question established paradigms, to engage in interdisciplinary dialogue, and to co-create new models of organizational excellence that are responsive to the demands of the digital age.

We extend our deepest appreciation to the contributors whose scholarship and insights made this volume possible. Their work reflects not only intellectual rigor but also a shared commitment to advancing knowledge that is relevant, ethical, and impactful. We are equally grateful to the reviewers and collaborators who helped shape the direction and quality of this book.

To our readers—executives, policymakers, researchers, students, and change agents—we offer this volume as a resource and a catalyst. May it inspire deeper inquiry, informed decision-making, and bold innovation. The challenges we face are complex and interconnected, but so too are the opportunities.

By embracing agility as both a mindset and a practice, organizations can not only withstand disruption but also shape the future with intention and integrity.

Darrell Burrell
Marymount University, United States

Chapter 1
Beyond Red and Blue:
The Purple Ocean Strategy as an Integrative Framework for Sustainable Competitive Advantage

Alieu Stephen Kafoe
http://orcid.org/0009-0001-8775-4985
Marymount University, USA

ABSTRACT

This study examines the Purple Ocean Strategy (POS) as an integrative framework for multinational corporations in the U.S. food and beverage industry. Traditional strategic models show limitations: Porter's Five Forces assumes stable industry structures unsuited for market volatility, while Blue Ocean Strategy often neglects market defense. Through qualitative analysis, this research explores how POS enables corporations to defend market share and pursue growth opportunities simultaneously. Strategic ambidexterity (balancing existing operations with innovation) emerges as critical for POS implementation. Case studies of Coca-Cola and Nestlé demonstrate this balance through product diversification, glocalization, and data-driven marketing. This research contributes to strategic management theory while providing practical guidance for industry practitioners. Despite implementation challenges requiring cultural transformation and clear roadmaps, POS offers a viable approach for food and beverage multinationals seeking competitive advantage in complex markets.

INTRODUCTION

The contemporary business landscape poses multinational corporations (MNCs) with increasingly complex challenges in maintaining a competitive advantage and pursuing growth opportunities. The food and beverage industry in the United States exemplifies these strategic complexities, characterized by rapidly evolving consumer preferences, technological advancements, and intense market competition (Nakat & Bou-Mitri, 2021). The industry's dynamic nature necessitates sophisticated strategic approaches that transcend traditional competitive frameworks, requiring innovative methodologies for navigating the market and creating value (Mandal, 2020).

DOI: 10.4018/979-8-3373-4027-2.ch001

STRATEGIC FRAMEWORK FOUNDATIONS

Understanding contemporary market dynamics requires a comprehensive examination of fundamental strategic paradigms that shape competitive behavior. Red Ocean Strategy represents a traditional competitive approach within established markets, focusing on differentiation or cost leadership (Kim & Mauborgne, 2005). This paradigm operates within clearly defined industry boundaries where companies compete for existing market share through direct confrontation with their competitors. Organizations employing Red Ocean strategies typically engage in head-to-head competition, striving to outperform rivals through superior execution of conventional value propositions within established market parameters.

In contrast, Blue Ocean Strategy refers to a strategic approach for creating uncontested market spaces while pursuing differentiation and cost reduction (Kim & Mauborgne, 2005). This framework emphasizes value innovation as the cornerstone of strategy, allowing organizations to transcend traditional industry boundaries and create new demand instead of competing for existing customers. Blue Ocean strategies aim to make competition irrelevant by reconstructing market boundaries and forming new value-cost frontiers that render traditional competitive benchmarking obsolete.

The limitations inherent in both paradigms have given rise to the Purple Ocean Strategy, which signifies a strategic market position at the intersection of Blue and Red Ocean strategies (Scarlat & Panduru, 2021). This integrative approach acknowledges that modern market conditions often require a simultaneous focus on both competitive defense and innovative value creation, recognizing that strict adherence to either Red or Blue Ocean principles may be inadequate for maintaining a sustained competitive advantage.

Porter's Five Forces Framework Integration

Porter's Five Forces Framework serves as a model for analyzing industry competition through five interrelated forces (Porter, 2008). This analytical tool provides a systematic examination of competitive intensity through the lens of supplier bargaining power, buyer bargaining power, the threat of new entrants, the threat of substitute products, and rivalry among existing competitors. The framework's enduring relevance stems from its comprehensive approach to understanding the structural determinants of industry profitability and competitive dynamics.

However, existing strategic models exhibit inherent limitations in addressing multifaceted market challenges. Traditional strategy models grounded in the Red Ocean and Blue Ocean paradigms suggest that neither framework alone is sufficient for sustaining a competitive advantage (Kim & Mauborgne, 2005). While Porter's Five Forces framework remains foundational in competitive analysis, it assumes a relatively stable industry structure that may not reflect contemporary market volatility (Shi et al., 2021). The Blue Ocean Strategy proposes an alternative approach to creating uncontested market spaces through value innovation; however, it may inadequately address the critical importance of defending existing market positions (Dvorak & Razova, 2018; Wee, 2017).

Strategic Integration and Purple Ocean Synthesis

These strategic constraints have led to an integrative approach that synthesizes elements from traditional competitive and innovative strategic frameworks. The Purple Ocean Strategy represents a nuanced approach to strategic management, combining defensive market positioning with proactive innovation. By incorporating elements of Red Ocean and Blue Ocean strategies, this framework enables organizations to protect existing market share while simultaneously exploring novel growth opportunities (Kafoe, 2025).

This integrative approach holds significant promise, particularly in industries such as food and beverage, where consumer preferences, technological innovations, and competitive landscapes are constantly evolving. The Purple Ocean framework addresses the dynamic tension between maintaining a competitive position in existing markets and creating new market spaces, offering a more comprehensive strategic orientation that acknowledges the complexity of today's business environments. Through this synthesis, organizations can leverage Porter's Five Forces analysis to understand competitive dynamics while simultaneously employing ocean strategy principles to navigate between defensive and innovative strategic orientations, establishing a stronger foundation for sustained competitive advantage in volatile market conditions.

PROBLEM STATEMENT

The unprecedented volatility in the global Food and Beverage Industry demands strategic innovation (Chowdhury et al., 2020; Galanakis et al., 2021). With food and beverage industry investments reaching $515 billion in 2023, multinational corporations face unprecedented market challenges that threaten their sustainable competitive positioning (Navarro, 2024). Traditional strategic frameworks, such as Porter's Five Forces and Blue Ocean Strategy, reveal inherent limitations in addressing the industry's dynamic landscape (Dvorak & Razova, 2018; Kafoe, 2024; Shi et al., 2021). The general business problem confronting multinational Food and Beverage corporations is maintaining market share and pursuing growth amid intense competitive pressures, evolving consumer preferences, and complex regulatory environments. The specific business problem is the absence of a comprehensive strategic approach that simultaneously addresses competitive analysis, innovative market positioning, and organization-specific contextual factors, thereby enabling a sustainable competitive advantage.

SIGNIFICANCE OF THE PAPER

This study urgently addresses a critical gap in strategic management by examining the emerging Purple Ocean Strategy (POS) as an integrative framework for multinational corporations (MNCs) in the U.S. food and beverage industry. In an era of unprecedented market volatility, where traditional strategic frameworks have proven inadequate, this research offers a timely and necessary reconceptualization of competitive positioning and value creation.

The significance of this research is underscored by the substantial financial stakes involved, with industry investments reaching $515 billion in 2023 (Navarro, 2024). Traditional frameworks like Porter's Five Forces assume a relatively stable market structure that fails to accommodate the dynamic reality of contemporary business environments (Shi et al., 2021). Similarly, while the Blue Ocean Strategy offers innovative market creation, it often overlooks the critical importance of defending existing market positions (Dvorak & Razova, 2018; Wee, 2017). This study's examination of the Purple Ocean Strategy addresses these limitations by providing a hybrid approach that enables organizations to simultaneously protect established market share while exploring new growth opportunities (Kafoe, 2025; Scarlat & Panduru, 2021).

The research presents several important contributions to both theory and practice. First, it expands the strategic management literature by merging previously separate frameworks into a unified approach designed for volatile market conditions. This integration directly addresses the acknowledged shortcomings of traditional models when used in isolation. Second, the study provides practical insights for multinational corporations facing the dual challenge of defending existing markets while pursuing innovation, a particularly pressing issue in the food and beverage industry, where consumer preferences shift quickly and new market entrants consistently disrupt established patterns. The Coca-Cola and Nestlé case studies demonstrate how major industry players have already embraced this integrated approach to maintain a competitive advantage.

This research enhances our understanding of strategic management in complex, rapidly evolving industries and offers a framework to help multinational corporations navigate the tensions between market defense and innovation. By examining the relevance of the Purple Ocean Strategy in the context of the U.S. food and beverage industry, this study establishes a foundation for future research on how integrated strategic approaches can strengthen organizational resilience and sustainable competitive advantage across various sectors and global contexts.

METHODOLOGY

Research Question

To provide focused direction for this investigation, the following research question was formulated: How can multinational corporations in the U.S. food and beverage industry effectively implement the Purple Ocean Strategy to achieve sustainable competitive advantage while defending existing market positions and pursuing innovative growth opportunities?

Research Design

This study employed a qualitative research design that utilized an integrative literature review methodology to examine the application of the Purple Ocean Strategy (POS) within multinational corporations in the U.S. food and beverage industry. The integrative literature review approach was chosen because it allows for the synthesis of diverse theoretical frameworks and empirical findings from existing literature, thereby facilitating a comprehensive understanding of strategic management innovations in volatile market environments (Whittemore & Knafl, 2005). This methodological approach is particularly well-suited for exploring emerging strategic concepts, such as the Purple Ocean Strategy, where limited primary research exists and theoretical integration is necessary to enhance understanding.

Integrative Literature Review Framework

The research process adhered to Cooper's (1988) five-step framework for integrative literature reviews, which provides a systematic approach to synthesizing existing knowledge across various disciplines and methodological approaches. Each step was carried out with methodological rigor to ensure comprehensive coverage and analytical depth.

Step 1: Problem Formulation

The problem formulation step involved defining the research question, establishing the purpose, and determining the scope of the review (Cooper, 1988). The research question emerged from a preliminary exploration of strategic management literature, which revealed gaps in understanding how multinational corporations can strike a balance between competitive defense and innovative growth strategies. The purpose was set to examine the potential of the Purple Ocean Strategy to address limitations inherent in traditional Red Ocean and Blue Ocean approaches. The scope was intentionally limited to multinational corporations in the U.S. food and beverage industry to ensure contextual relevance and analytical focus, while still maintaining enough breadth to capture diverse strategic implementations.

Step 2: Data Collection

The data collection phase utilized a systematic identification and retrieval process to locate all relevant studies through comprehensive database searches and supplementary sources (Cooper, 1988). The primary academic databases used included Business Source Complete, Emerald Insight, JSTOR, Web of Science, and the Directory of Open Access Journals (DOAJ), ensuring comprehensive coverage of foundational and emerging scholarship across multiple disciplines. The search strategy employed Boolean operators and controlled vocabulary terms, with key search terms including "Red Ocean Strategy," "Blue Ocean Strategy," "Purple Ocean Strategy," "strategic innovation," "food and beverage industry," "multinational corporations," "competitive advantage," "strategic management," and "hybrid strategy."

The temporal parameters encompass publications from 2005 to 2025, with 2005 marking the seminal publication of Kim and Mauborgne's Blue Ocean Strategy, which established the foundational literature base. Forward and backward citation searching, supplemented by database searches, identified additional relevant sources. Grey literature searches captured industry reports and white papers, providing contemporary market insights. Inclusion criteria required peer-reviewed academic articles, book chapters from reputable publishers, and authoritative industry reports published in English. Exclusion criteria eliminated non-academic sources, duplicate publications, and studies outside the defined scope.

Step 3: Evaluation of Data

The evaluation phase involved a critical appraisal of the included studies for quality and relevance using established criteria adapted from integrative review methodologies (Cooper, 1988; Whittemore & Knafl, 2005). The quality assessment examined methodological rigor, theoretical grounding, sample adequacy, and analytical sophistication. The relevance evaluation considered theoretical contribution, empirical significance, and alignment with the research question. Studies were categorized as primary (directly addressing Purple Ocean Strategy or related hybrid approaches), secondary (examining Red Ocean or Blue Ocean strategies with implications for integration), or tertiary (providing contextual background on strategic management or industry dynamics).

Data extraction used a standardized form to capture bibliographic information, theoretical frameworks used, methodological approaches, key findings, and theoretical contributions. This systematic approach ensured consistent evaluation across various source types while maintaining analytical rigor throughout the review process.

Step 4: Data Analysis

The data analysis phase employed thematic analysis to identify and examine key themes, concepts, and patterns within the selected studies (Braun & Clarke, 2006). Initial coding involved a line-by-line review of the included sources to identify preliminary concepts and patterns. Focused coding consolidated initial codes into broader categories, while theoretical coding established relationships between categories to develop overarching themes.

Three primary themes emerged from this analytical process: Strategic Framework Integration, Market Performance Dynamics, and Organizational Factors. Each theme was further deconstructed into subthemes to allow for a nuanced understanding of the complex interrelationships between traditional competitive analysis and innovative market approaches. Strategic Framework Integration encompassed competitive force analysis, value innovation, and framework synthesis. Market Performance Dynamics included market share defense, growth opportunity creation, and patterns of resource allocation. Organizational Factors comprised organizational culture, industry-specific considerations, and requirements for organizational ambidexterity.

Cross-case pattern analysis compared strategic implementations across various organizational contexts, while temporal analysis examined the evolution of strategic thinking from traditional frameworks to integrated approaches. This analytical depth facilitated the identification of convergent and divergent perspectives in literature while remaining sensitive to contextual factors influencing strategic effectiveness.

Step 5: Interpretation and Presentation of Results

The final phase involved interpreting findings, discussing their implications, and presenting the review's conclusions in a coherent narrative (Cooper, 1988). Interpretation utilized theoretical triangulation, comparing findings across various theoretical lenses to enhance understanding and identify areas of convergence and divergence. The findings were synthesized to directly address the research question, while acknowledging limitations and areas requiring further investigation.

The results presentation adopted a structured approach, beginning with theoretical foundations, progressing through empirical evidence, and concluding with practical implications. The inclusion of a case study analysis examining the strategic evolution of Coca-Cola and Nestlé provided concrete illustrations of theoretical constructs, enhancing the review's practical relevance and validity.

CASE STUDY COMPONENT

To enhance methodological rigor and practical relevance, the research included a case study component that examined the strategic evolution of Coca-Cola and Nestlé as exemplars of Purple Ocean Strategy implementation. These cases were selected for their prominence in the industry, global scope of operations, and clear demonstration of balancing market defense with innovation through product diversification, sustainable packaging initiatives, and health-focused product development (Chorazy, 2020; Hong & Luo, 2024). Combining theoretical analysis with practical application strengthened the validity of the research while enhancing its relevance to industry practitioners facing similar strategic challenges.

METHODOLOGICAL LIMITATIONS AND MITIGATION STRATEGIES

The methodological approach presents several limitations that specific mitigation strategies addressed. Potential publication bias in the selected literature was countered by including a variety of publication types and employing comprehensive search strategies across multiple databases. The inherent challenges of generalizing findings from a single industry context were addressed by incorporating different theoretical perspectives and acknowledging contextual constraints in the analysis.

Language bias was minimized by focusing on English-language publications while acknowledging this limitation in the findings. Temporal bias was addressed by establishing clear inclusion criteria spanning two decades of strategic management literature. To enhance analytical robustness, the research incorporated multiple theoretical frameworks, including Porter's Five Forces framework (Porter, 2008), Blue Ocean Strategy (Kim & Mauborgne, 2005), and emerging scholarship on Purple Ocean Strategy (Kafoe, 2025; Scarlat & Panduru, 2021), thus creating a comprehensive analytical foundation for examining innovations in strategic management.

This methodological approach facilitated a thorough examination of the Purple Ocean Strategy as an integrative framework that addresses the limitations of traditional strategic approaches. By synthesizing various theoretical perspectives and applying them to the context of the U.S. food and beverage industry through a rigorous integrative literature review methodology, the research provides both theoretical insights and practical guidance for multinational corporations navigating complex market dynamics.

LITERATURE REVIEW

Strategic Framework Foundations

Understanding contemporary market dynamics requires a thorough examination of fundamental strategic paradigms that shape competitive behavior. Red Ocean Strategy represents a traditional competitive approach within established markets, focusing on differentiation or cost leadership (Kim & Mauborgne, 2005). This paradigm operates within clearly defined industry boundaries where companies compete for existing market share through direct confrontation with competitors. Organizations employing Red Ocean strategies typically engage in head-to-head competition, striving to outperform rivals through superior execution of conventional value propositions within established market parameters.

In contrast, Blue Ocean Strategy refers to a strategic approach for creating uncontested market spaces while pursuing differentiation and cost reduction (Kim & Mauborgne, 2005). This framework emphasizes value innovation as the cornerstone of strategy, enabling organizations to transcend traditional industry boundaries and create new demand instead of competing for existing customers. Blue Ocean strategies aim to make competition irrelevant by reconstructing market boundaries and forming new value-cost frontiers that render traditional competitive benchmarking obsolete.

The limitations inherent in both paradigms have led to the development of the Purple Ocean Strategy (POS), which signifies a strategic market position at the intersection of Blue Ocean and Red Ocean strategies (Scarlat & Panduru, 2021). This integrative approach acknowledges that modern market conditions often require a simultaneous focus on both competitive defense and innovative value creation, recognizing that strict adherence to either Red or Blue Ocean principles may be inadequate for maintaining a sustained competitive advantage.

Traditional strategy models are based on the Red Ocean and Blue Ocean paradigms; however, the literature suggests that neither framework alone is sufficient for sustained competitive advantage (Kim & Mauborgne, 2005). The Red Ocean Strategy emphasizes competing in existing markets by leveraging cost leadership or differentiation to outperform rivals (Kim & Mauborgne, 2005; Pritchett, 2014). In contrast, the Blue Ocean Strategy promotes the creation of new market spaces where competition is irrelevant (Kim & Mauborgne, 2005). Nevertheless, empirical studies show that Blue Oceans eventually turn red as new entrants flood the market, making continuous innovation necessary (Buisson & Silberzahn, 2010).

Furthermore, the Black Ocean Strategy examines ethical dilemmas in strategic decision-making, where firms exploit regulatory gaps and cost advantages to gain market share (Nithisathian et al., 2020). The static nature of these models highlights their primary limitations. Red Oceans encourage market saturation, while Blue Oceans require constant reinvention. The Black Ocean framework, although insightful, presents ethical challenges that may not align with long-term corporate sustainability goals (Nithisathian et al., 2020). Given the dynamic nature of the food and beverage sector, firms must adopt a hybrid model known as the Purple Ocean Strategy to balance market competition and continuous innovation.

Table 1. Comparative Analysis of the Different Ocean Strategies

Dimension	Red Ocean Strategy	Blue Ocean Strategy	Purple Ocean Strategy	Black Ocean Strategy
Core Philosophy	Competing in existing markets	Create an uncontested market space	Balance competition and innovation	Exploit regulatory and ethical gaps
Market Approach	Beat the competition	Make competition irrelevant	Defend while innovating	Gain advantage through questionable means
Value Creation	Value-cost trade-off	Value innovation	Hybrid value approach	Value extraction through exploitation
Competition Focus	Direct confrontation	Competition avoidance	Strategic competition management	Competitive advantage through unethical means
Market Boundaries	Operates within existing boundaries	Reconstructs market boundaries	Flexible boundary management	Operates in regulatory gray areas
Strategic Objective	Market share capture	New market creation	Sustainable competitive advantage	Short-term profit maximization
Innovation Level	Incremental improvements	Radical innovation	Balanced innovation portfolio	Innovation through exploitation
Risk Profile	Moderate to high competitive risk	High innovation risk	Balanced risk management	High ethical and legal risk
Time Horizon	Short to medium-term	Long-term	Sustainable long-term	Often short-term focused
Resource Allocation	Efficiency optimization	Innovation investment	Balanced resource distribution	Cost minimization through shortcuts

Table 2. Advantages and Disadvantages of the Different Ocean Strategies

Strategy Type	Advantages	Disadvantages
Red Ocean	Precise competitive positioning and benchmarking opportunities. Established market understanding and customer knowledge. Proven business models and operational frameworks. Lower uncertainty regarding market acceptance. Ability to leverage existing competencies and resources.	Intense competition leading to profit erosion. Limited growth potential within saturated markets. Vulnerability to price wars and margin compression. Difficulty in achieving sustainable differentiation. Market share battles often result in zero-sum outcomes.
Blue Ocean	Potential for significant first-mover advantages. Opportunity to create new demand and expand market size. Reduced direct competition in newly created spaces. Higher profit margins due to a lack of direct competitors. Enhanced brand differentiation and market positioning.	High uncertainty and risk of market failure. Significant investment required for market education. Difficulty in protecting newly created market spaces. Blue Oceans eventually attract competitors and turn red. Requires continuous innovation to maintain an advantage
Purple Ocean	Balanced approach reducing over-reliance on a single strategy. Flexibility to adapt to changing market conditions. Simultaneous defense of existing positions and growth pursuit. Enhanced organizational learning and capability development. Better risk distribution across strategic initiatives.	Complexity in execution and resource allocation. Potential for strategic confusion and lack of focus. Higher organizational demands for ambidextrous capabilities. Difficulty in measuring and optimizing dual strategic objectives. Risk of achieving mediocrity in both competitive and innovative dimensions.
Black Ocean	Potential for rapid cost advantages and market penetration. Exploitation of regulatory arbitrage opportunities. Short-term competitive gains through unconventional means. Ability to enter markets with lower barriers.	Significant ethical and reputational risks. Potential legal liabilities and regulatory backlash. Unsustainable competitive advantages. Damage to stakeholder relationships and trust. Inconsistent with corporate social responsibility goals. Long-term brand and organizational damage potential.

The Emergence of the Purple Ocean Strategy (POS)

The POS emerged around 2011, with one of the earliest academic publications appearing in December 2011 (Gandellini & Venanzi, 2011). The POS bridges the gap between traditional competition-driven models and innovation-focused strategies by emphasizing continuous adaptation and strategic fluidity (Nithisathian & Walsh, 2013). Unlike Blue Oceans, which advocates market creation, POS suggests that businesses must simultaneously innovate and defend market share. Studies indicate that firms that oscillate between competitive and innovative strategies achieve greater long-term sustainability (Cavagnetto & Gahir, 2013).

POS is best understood as a synthesis of Blue and Red Ocean strategies and a strategic innovation paradigm grounded in dynamic capabilities and hybrid strategic theory. Recent literature provides a robust theoretical framework that distinguishes POS as a transformative rather than incremental contribution to strategic management. Gutiérrez Broncano et al. (2024) offer a detailed account of hybrid strategies, affirming that simultaneous pursuit of differentiation and cost leadership can outperform pure strategies in volatile environments. Their empirical findings confirm that hybrid strategies positively impact market performance, particularly in SMEs, and innovation mediates this relationship. They note that "hybrid strategies are more effective in creating competitive advantage and increasing firms' flexibility in current turbulent and competitively intense environments" (Gutiérrez Broncano et al., 2024, p. 2).

Multinational food and beverage corporations leverage existing distribution networks while introducing innovative product lines to capture emerging market trends (Dias et al., 2020). POS is especially relevant in consumer-driven industries, where demand shifts quickly due to health trends, regulatory policies, and sustainability concerns. By combining Red and Blue Oceans elements, POS enables businesses to exploit existing competencies while fostering innovation without exposing themselves to immediate market competition. Utilizing POS in multinational food and beverage corporations can enhance market defense and expansion, ensuring resilience amid volatile global trends.

Theoretical Foundations of the POS

The Purple Ocean Strategy transcends traditional strategic paradigms by integrating the Dynamic Capabilities View (DCV) with hybrid strategic theory. Pitelis et al. (2023) propose a comprehensive framework that centers Dynamic Capabilities (DCs), sensing, seizing, and reconfiguring, at the core of global strategy formulation. Their conceptual model emphasizes that sustainable competitive advantage is no longer derived solely from positioning within an industry but from the ability to reconfigure resources and business models in response to environmental volatility and complexity. They argue that "dynamic capabilities help explain how an enterprise can align its business processes and models with the external environment and... shape the environment to its advantage" (Pitelis et al., 2024, p. 3299).

While the Red Ocean Strategy focuses on competing in existing markets and the Blue Ocean Strategy emphasizes the creation of uncontested market spaces, both are limited in addressing strategic resilience and reinvention under sustained environmental turbulence. POS, by contrast, integrates the ambidextrous logic of hybrid strategy (Gutiérrez Broncano et al., 2024) with the adaptive, orchestrative focus of DCV (Pitelis et al., 2024). This extends strategic theory in two novel ways:

1. *Conceptual Fusion*: POS transcends traditional dualities by operationalizing hybrid logic through dynamic capabilities, making it both structural (hybrid strategy) and behavioral (DCV-oriented).
2. *Transformative Potential*: POS enables firms to survive and proactively shape markets and ecosystems. This represents a paradigm shift from strategy as positioning to strategy as orchestration and co-creation.

Unlike typical hybrid strategies, which may still be constrained by firm size, sector, or resource base, POS emphasizes organizational agility and contextual ambidexterity. Through the integration of DCV, POS introduces a higher-order capability to simultaneously exploit existing capabilities and explore emergent opportunities across borders and ecosystems. This uniquely suits multinational food and beverage corporations operating in fragmented, culturally diverse, fast-evolving markets.

Integrative Framework Architecture

The POS represents a sophisticated theoretical synthesis that transcends traditional strategic paradigms through the systematic integration of multiple complementary frameworks. Rather than functioning as isolated theoretical constructs, Porter's Five Forces, Blue and Red Ocean Strategy, DCV, Hybrid Strategic Theory, and Organizational Ambidexterity act as interconnected theoretical beams that collectively support the conceptual architecture of the Purple Ocean Strategy. This integrative approach addresses the fundamental limitation of singular strategic frameworks, which often fail to capture the multifaceted nature of contemporary competitive environments (Teece et al., 2019).

The theoretical coherence of POS stems from its ability to orchestrate these frameworks through what can be conceptualized as a "strategic orchestration engine," primarily powered by the DCV. This engine enables multinational corporations to simultaneously sense environmental changes, seize emerging opportunities, and transform organizational capabilities while maintaining competitive positions in existing markets (O'Reilly & Tushman, 2013). The strength of the framework lies not in the individual theories themselves, but in their synergistic interaction, which creates a meta-theoretical foundation that supports both exploratory and exploitative strategic behaviors.

Dynamic Capabilities as the Strategic Orchestration Engine

The DCV serves as the central coordinating mechanism within the POS framework, acting as the gear mechanism that enables strategic orchestration across multiple competitive dimensions. Teece's (2019) three-pronged model of sensing, seizing, and transforming provides the operational foundation for understanding how multinational firms pivot between exploration and exploitation within the Purple Ocean context. This dynamic capability framework addresses a critical gap in traditional ocean strategies by providing the organizational processes necessary for continuous strategic adaptation.

Sensing capabilities within the POS framework allow organizations to identify both competitive threats in existing markets (Red Ocean elements) and emerging opportunities for value innovation (Blue Ocean elements). Research by Wilden and Gudergan (2015) shows that firms with superior sensing capabilities can simultaneously monitor competitive dynamics while scanning for discontinuous market opportunities, a dual-sensing approach vital for Purple Ocean implementation. These capabilities go beyond traditional market intelligence to include ecosystem-level sensing that identifies convergence points between established and emerging market spaces.

Seizing capabilities represent the organizational mechanisms through which firms capitalize on sensed opportunities while defending existing competitive positions. The Purple Ocean context requires what Peteraf et al. (2013) term "ambidextrous seizing," which involves the simultaneous deployment of resources toward both competitive defense and innovative value creation. This dual-seizing approach necessitates sophisticated resource allocation mechanisms that can optimize investments across both exploitation and exploration activities without causing internal resource conflicts.

Transforming capabilities enable the continuous reconfiguration of organizational assets, structures, and processes to maintain Purple Ocean positioning over time. Unlike traditional transformation focused on single strategic directions, Purple Ocean transformation requires what can be termed "dual transformation", the ability to simultaneously evolve competitive capabilities and innovative capacities (O'Reilly & Tushman, 2013). This involves developing organizational architectures that support both efficiency-driven and innovation-driven activities without compromising strategic objectives.

Organizational Ambidexterity and Behavioral Integration

The successful implementation of the POS fundamentally depends on organizational ambidexterity, which is the ability to simultaneously pursue both exploitative and exploratory activities. Gibson and Birkinshaw's (2004) behavioral ambidexterity model provides important empirical grounding for understanding the psychological and cultural dynamics necessary for successful Purple Ocean implementation. Their framework identifies four key behavioral dimensions that enable organizational ambidexterity: performance management, social support, challenge, and learning orientation.

1. **Performance management systems** within Purple Ocean organizations must accommodate dual performance metrics that reward both competitive performance in existing markets and innovative outcomes in emerging spaces. Research suggests that effective ambidextrous performance management requires temporal separation of evaluation criteria, allowing for different performance expectations across exploitation and exploration activities (Campanella et al., 2020; Hadji et al., 2022; Laser, 2022). This temporal ambidexterity enables organizations to maintain short-term competitive effectiveness while investing in long-term innovative capabilities.
2. **Social support mechanisms** promote the cross-functional collaboration essential for POS execution. The framework requires what Jansen et al. (2006) describe as "bridging social capital," organizational relationships that span the traditional boundaries between competitive and innovative units. These social mechanisms facilitate knowledge transfer between exploitation-focused and exploration-focused organizational components, creating synergies that enhance both competitive defense and innovative value creation.
3. **Challenge and learning orientation** represent the cultural foundations that enable organizations to embrace the inherent tensions within Purple Ocean positioning. The framework requires organizational cultures that can simultaneously value competitive discipline and innovative experimentation, which Tushman and O'Reilly (2006) term "paradoxical organizational culture." This cultural ambidexterity enables organizations to maintain the focus necessary for competitive success while preserving the flexibility required for continuous innovation.

Hybrid Strategic Theory Integration

The integration of Hybrid Strategic Theory within the POS framework challenges the traditional belief that organizations must choose between differentiation and cost leadership strategies. Recent empirical research by Gutiérrez-Broncano et al. (2024) shows that hybrid strategies can outperform pure strategies in volatile environments, especially when supported by innovation capabilities. The POS enhances hybrid strategic logic by incorporating temporal and contextual dimensions that allow for dynamic strategy combinations rather than static hybrid positions.

Temporal hybridization within the POS framework involves the sequential deployment of different strategic orientations based on market evolution cycles. Organizations may emphasize competitive positioning during market maturity phases while shifting toward innovative value creation during market transformation periods. This temporal approach to hybrid strategy addresses the criticism that simultaneous pursuit of multiple strategic objectives leads to strategic confusion or mediocrity (Porter, 2023).

Contextual hybridization acknowledges that multinational corporations operate in diverse market environments that may require distinct strategic focuses. The POS allows organizations to pursue competitive strategies in mature markets while adopting innovative approaches in emerging markets, resulting in what can be called "A dual strategy." This dual strategy maintains efficiency and established practices in mature markets while fostering innovation and adaptability in emerging markets (Samiee & Chirapanda, 2019).

Contingency Theory and Global-Local Strategic Tensions

The incorporation of Contingency Theory within the POS framework recognizes that strategic effectiveness relies on the alignment between strategic choices and contextual conditions. For multinational corporations, this contingency perspective is especially significant in addressing global-local strategic tensions that emerge from operating across diverse institutional, cultural, and competitive environments (Lawrence et al, 1967).

Environmental contingencies within the Purple Ocean framework necessitate organizations to adjust their strategic focus in response to local market conditions, regulatory environments, and competitive dynamics. Effective contingency management necessitates strategic responsiveness (the ability to adjust strategic orientation according to environmental demands while maintaining strategic coherence throughout the organization), which is enabled by dynamic capabilities and strategic flexibility (Muneeb et al., 2023).

Organizational contingencies recognize that internal capabilities, resources, and structural characteristics influence the feasibility and effectiveness of various strategic approaches. The POS must be tailored to reflect the organization's readiness for ambidextrous operations, the resources available for dual strategic pursuits, and the prevailing cultural orientations toward innovation and competition.

Structural contingencies address the organizational design implications of POS implementation. Different organizational structures may be more or less conducive to ambidextrous operations, requiring contingent structural adaptations based on strategic requirements and environmental demands. This structural contingency approach enables organizations to optimize their organizational architecture for Purple Ocean effectiveness while maintaining operational efficiency.

Framework Synthesis and Theoretical Contributions

The POS represents a meta-theoretical framework that synthesizes multiple strategic theories into a coherent approach for managing contemporary competitive complexity. The framework's theoretical contribution lies not in the individual theories it incorporates, but in their systematic integration through the DCV as the coordinating mechanism. This integration creates emergent theoretical properties that extend beyond the sum of individual theoretical components.

The framework addresses three fundamental limitations of existing strategic theories: the false dichotomy between competition and innovation, the static nature of traditional strategic positioning, and the insufficient attention to organizational capabilities necessary for strategic adaptation. By integrating these diverse theoretical perspectives through a dynamic capabilities lens, the POS offers a more comprehensive understanding of how organizations can navigate the tensions between competitive necessity and innovative opportunity in contemporary market environments.

Integrating Sustainability and Innovation in Strategic Management

Sustainability and innovation are interdependent pillars that contribute to competitive longevity in multinational corporations. The Systemic and Integrated Framework for the Sustainability of New Product Innovation Processes (SIFSNPIP) provides an evidence-based approach to merging these elements (Dias et al., 2020). Dias et al. (2020) propose a multi-tiered strategy framework that includes:

1. *Strategic Level*: Aligning corporate vision with market needs.
2. *Organizational Level*: Implementing cross-functional teams to support innovation.
3. *Operational Level*: Leveraging lean manufacturing and agile processes to improve efficiency.

This holistic model aligns with POS principles, emphasizing the need for firms to integrate sustainability measures alongside competitive strategies. Environmental, social, and governance (ESG) factors increasingly influence the food and beverage industry. Companies adopting POS with sustainability considerations can achieve differentiated brand positioning, reduce operational risks, and maintain consumer trust. By embedding sustainability into strategic innovation, multinational food and beverage corporations can differentiate themselves while ensuring long-term viability and compliance with global regulatory standards.

Application of POS in Multinational Food and Beverage Corporations

For multinational corporations, applying the POS requires a combination of market-driven adaptation and proactive innovation. Research by Nithisathian et al. (2020) indicates that POS is most effective when firms develop hybrid strategies that allow them to:

1. Defend existing market share through cost efficiencies and brand equity.
2. Create uncontested markets by introducing innovative, sustainable product lines.
3. Leverage digital transformation to optimize supply chains and consumer engagement.

Given the increasing fragmentation of consumer preferences, a one-size-fits-all approach is no longer viable. POS provides a dynamic framework that enables firms to switch between defensive and offensive strategies, ensuring they remain agile in an unpredictable market environment. By embracing POS, food and beverage corporations can navigate both competitive pressures and opportunities for expansion, ensuring a balanced, future-proof business strategy.

For many U.S. Food and Beverage Industry MNCs, the challenge lies in blending both approaches (defending established positions while reaching for new opportunities). The inability to do so risks leaving them either stuck in the past, losing ground to disruptors, or too focused on new frontiers to defend their base. The POS, combining elements of Red Ocean (competition-based) and Blue Ocean (innovation-driven) strategies, offers a potential middle ground (Scarlat & Panduru, 2021; Kafoe, 2025). This integrative approach allows companies to defend their market share while pushing into new territories.

The theoretical frameworks outlined in the literature review find practical application in the strategic evolution of multinational corporations. Coca-Cola and Nestle's implementation of the POS exemplifies this, demonstrating how balancing traditional market defense with innovative growth initiatives can create a sustainable competitive advantage in the global food and beverage industry.

COCA-COLA'S IMPLEMENTATION OF THE POS IN GLOBAL MARKETS

Balancing Market Defense and Innovation

The Coca-Cola Company provides an exemplary case study of the POS Implementation in the global food and beverage industry. The company has successfully balanced defending its established market positions while pursuing innovative growth opportunities through a multifaceted approach that combines traditional competitive strategies with value innovation initiatives (Hong & Luo, 2024).

Hong and Luo's (2024) study employing the Go-Stop signal framework reveals that Coca-Cola utilizes strategies that align with the Purple Ocean approach. The company employs numerous Go signals, including "product diversity, emotional branding, and competitive pricing" (p. 159), to defend and strengthen its core business while simultaneously addressing Stop signals through innovations like "Coca-Cola Zero Sugar and sustainable packaging" (p. 159). This dual focus demonstrates how Coca-Cola balances market defense with growth-oriented innovation.

Coca-Cola has maintained dominance in its traditional market while venturing into new categories like low-sugar alternatives and health-focused beverages. This shift represents a calculated move to maintain a competitive edge and market share in a rapidly evolving landscape. Introducing low-sugar and health-oriented products aligns with Coca-Cola's broader strategy to address public health concerns associated with sugar consumption and obesity, with products like Coca-Cola Zero Sugar and Diet Coke (Chorazy, 2020). This initiative is part of a more significant trend within the beverage industry, where companies are increasingly pressured to reformulate products to meet health guidelines and consumer demands (Qian, 2023; Zheng, 2023). Such strategic adaptations exemplify the core idea of the Purple Ocean Strategy: combining strong defense with strategic innovation.

Global Localization Strategy

Coca-Cola's global localization strategy further exemplifies this balanced approach. The company maintains its global brand identity while adapting products to regional preferences, as evidenced by the introduction of "green tea-flavored product in Japan" (Hong & Luo, 2024, p. 162) and "garlic-flavored Coke in Japan" (p. 163). This strategy allows Coca-Cola to defend its market position while exploring culturally specific innovations.

Coca-Cola's implementation of the POS is evident in its simultaneous address of competitive pressures and pursuit of innovation. The company defends its market position through traditional competitive advantages (Red Ocean elements), including brand loyalty built through "decades of consistent product quality and positive branding" (Hong & Luo, 2024, p. 160) and "competitive pricing strategies, particularly in price-sensitive markets" (p. 160). These approaches enable Coca-Cola to protect its established market share in highly competitive environments.

Innovative Growth Initiatives

Concurrently, Coca-Cola pursues innovative growth opportunities (Blue Ocean elements) by expanding into uncontested market spaces. The company develops healthier alternatives to address health-conscious consumers like "Coca-Cola Zero Sugar and other products with low sugar content" (Hong & Luo, 2024, p. 161). It implements sustainable packaging initiatives to appeal to environmentally conscious markets.

These innovations create new value propositions, differentiating Coca-Cola from competitors while addressing emerging consumer concerns.

Coca-Cola's strategic response to health concerns further demonstrates its POS approach. Rather than abandoning its core sugary products (representing a pure Blue Ocean pivot) or ignoring health trends (exemplifying a rigid Red Ocean stance), the company maintains its traditional products while developing healthier alternatives. This balanced strategy allows Coca-Cola to defend its established market position while exploring new growth opportunities in health-conscious segments.

Data-Driven Strategy Implementation

Integrating data analytics into Coca-Cola's marketing strategy exemplifies how the company operationalizes the POS approach. By "tracking every touch point that a consumer interacts with on this channel" (Hong & Luo, 2024, p. 162), Coca-Cola gains insights that enable it to refine defensive and innovative strategies simultaneously. This data-driven approach allows the company to "adjust Go signals depending on the consumers' response, which varies across the markets" (Hong & Luo, 2024, p. 162), ensuring that market defense and innovation initiatives are tailored to specific regional contexts.

Coca-Cola's application of the POS is particularly evident in its response to environmental concerns. The company has pledged to address sustainability issues by "using more recycled material" and "supporting programs that seek to minimize the use of plastics" (Hong & Luo, 2024, p. 162). This approach enables Coca-Cola to maintain its core product offerings while innovating in packaging and production processes, demonstrating how companies can pursue environmental sustainability without abandoning established market positions.

Consumer Engagement and Reformulation Strategy

The "Share a Coke" campaign illustrates Coca-Cola's POS implementation. This initiative preserved the company's traditional product while introducing a novel marketing approach that increased consumer engagement through personalization. By putting "people's first names on the bottles" (Hong & Luo, 2024, p. 162), Coca-Cola defended its market position while creating a unique value proposition that differentiated the brand in an innovative way.

Coca-Cola's strategic approach aligns with Malekpour et al.'s (2024) findings regarding the critical importance of product innovation in maintaining competitive advantage in the food and beverage industry. While innovation requires substantial investment without guaranteed returns, Coca-Cola's balanced approach mitigates this risk by maintaining its core business while pursuing selective innovations.

The company's reformulation strategy, as examined by Lacy-Nichols et al. (2019), further demonstrates its POS approach. Coca-Cola shifted from simply "offering choice" to implementing "systematic sugar reformulation," presenting this strategy as a business growth opportunity and a response to public health concerns. This dual framing illustrates how Coca-Cola repackages a defensive business strategy as a proactive health initiative, exemplifying the balanced approach characteristic of the Purple Ocean Strategy.

THEORETICAL INTEGRATION: COCA-COLA'S GO-STOP SIGNALS AND DYNAMIC CAPABILITIES

Coca-Cola's Go-Stop signal framework implementation exemplifies the operationalization of dynamic capabilities and organizational ambidexterity within the context of the POS. The company's Go signals encompass product diversity, emotional branding, and competitive pricing, representing the systematic deployment of sensing capabilities that continuously monitor competitive threats and market opportunities while simultaneously demonstrating exploitative ambidexterity through the refinement and defense of established market positions (Hong & Luo, 2024). Conversely, Coca-Cola's Stop signals, manifested through innovations such as Coca-Cola Zero Sugar and sustainable packaging initiatives, illustrate the organization's seizing and transforming capabilities that enable the company to capitalize on emerging health and environmental trends while reconfiguring its product portfolio and operational processes (Teece, 2019). This dual-signal approach reflects what Gibson and Birkinshaw (2004) conceptualize as behavioral ambidexterity, where the organization maintains the discipline to execute competitive strategies (Go signals) while preserving the flexibility to pursue exploratory innovations (Stop signals). The company's data-driven strategy implementation, which tracks consumer touchpoints and adjusts signals based on market responses, demonstrates the higher-order dynamic capability of strategic orchestration. This meta-capability enables Coca-Cola to optimize both exploitative and exploratory activities across diverse global markets simultaneously (Pitelis et al., 2024). This case analysis confirms that successful POS implementation requires not only ambidextrous intentions but also the development of sophisticated dynamic capabilities that can coordinate and balance competing strategic imperatives in real-time market conditions.

NESTLÉ'S IMPLEMENTATION OF ORGANIZATIONAL AMBIDEXTERITY

Structural Foundations

Nestlé has embedded ambidexterity into its organizational design through a matrix structure that combines divisional and functional elements. This structure enables the company to maintain centralized control over core functions while providing regional units the autonomy to respond to local market conditions (Murugan, 2024). The structural evolution reflects a strategic shift from Nestlé's historically exploitative practices characterized by centralized control toward a more balanced approach. During the 1980s and 1990s, performance stagnation prompted the company to adopt ambidexterity through innovation programs such as Nestlé Innova, which created decentralized, flexible departments alongside traditional exploitative units (Akraouch, 2019).

Nestlé's structural ambidexterity is evident in its systematic separation of exploration and exploitation activities, as demonstrated by dedicated departments for marketing, research facilities, and specialized innovation units (Onikoyi, 2017). This structural separation allows different units to focus on either exploration or exploitation without the tensions that might arise when attempting both simultaneously within the same organizational unit.

Exploitation Activities

Nestlé consistently refines its product offerings to maintain market share in established categories, representing ambidexterity's "exploitation" dimension. Research on Nestlé Nigeria PLC demonstrates the significant impact of these activities:

1. Product innovation accounts for 21.1% of the variance in organizational profitability ($R^2 = 0.211$, $p < 0.05$)
2. 18.1% of market share increases can be attributed to product innovation ($R^2 = 0.181$, $p < 0.05$)
3. A strong positive relationship exists between product innovation and competitive strength ($r = 0.806$, $p < 0.05$) (Onikoyi, 2017)

These exploitation activities are primarily facilitated through centralized functional departments such as finance and operations, which maintain efficiency and process consistency across global operations (Murugan, 2024).

Exploration Activities

Simultaneously, Nestlé engages in exploration activities to create new market spaces and capitalize on emerging opportunities. The company employs various types of innovation (product, process, organizational, and marketing) to differentiate itself from competitors. This exploration is evident in:

1. Investment in R&D and nutrition science, particularly through ventures like Nestlé Health Science
2. Implementation of programs focused on improving nutritional content, such as Branded Active Benefits (BAB) and specialized nutrition programs for infants and pets (Akraouch, 2019)
3. A structured innovation process encompassing "idea generation, idea screening, idea evaluation, marketing strategy, product development, test, and marketing & commercialization strategies" (Onikoyi, 2017)

Contextual Ambidexterity

Nestlé creates an organizational context where individual employees can divide their time between alignment-oriented and adaptation-oriented activities. Leadership practices play a pivotal role in fostering this context, with leaders actively guiding individual units to balance exploration and exploitation within their domains dynamically. This approach aligns with Gibson and Birkinshaw's (2004) insights into the behavioral dimension of ambidexterity. It is reinforced by flat hierarchies, shared visions, and cross-functional collaboration across global units (Akraouch, 2019).

Temporal Sequencing

Research indicates that Nestlé sequences innovation activities systematically, from idea generation to commercialization (Onikoyi, 2017). This temporal approach allows the company to focus organizational attention on different aspects of the innovation process at appropriate times, ensuring that both exploration and exploitation receive adequate resources.

Nestlé's Purple Ocean Strategy Implementation

Nestlé's ambidextrous approach exemplifies the "purple ocean strategy," combining red ocean competitive tactics (improving existing products in contested markets) with blue ocean innovative thinking (creating new market spaces). For Nestlé, this is evident in:

1. Continuous improvement of established product lines while simultaneously developing radically new offerings
2. Balancing short-term profitability from existing products while investing in long-term growth opportunities
3. Creating synergies between marketing capabilities and strategic planning capabilities
4. Maintaining standardized operations and brand equity in legacy product categories while pioneering new value spaces through investments in emerging fields

This balanced approach has yielded tangible benefits for organizational performance, market share, and competitive strength, allowing Nestlé to respond to competitive pressures while proactively shaping new markets.

THEORETICAL INTEGRATION: NESTLÉ'S AMBIDEXTROUS ARCHITECTURE AND STRATEGIC DRIFT MITIGATION

Nestlé's organizational architecture displays a sophisticated integration of structural and contextual ambidexterity that effectively mitigates strategic drift while facilitating POS implementation across diverse global markets. The company's matrix structure, which combines divisional autonomy with functional centralization, exemplifies what O'Reilly and Tushman (2013) describe as structural ambidexterity, where dedicated organizational units pursue exploration activities (such as Nestlé Health Science and innovation departments) while established functional departments focus on exploitation activities (operations, finance, and core product refinement). This structural separation prevents the internal tensions that typically arise when organizations try to pursue contradictory strategic logic simultaneously, as evidenced by Nestlé's measurable performance outcomes, where product innovation accounts for 21.1% of organizational profitability variance (Onikoyi, 2017). Moreover, Nestlé's approach goes beyond mere structural separation by incorporating contextual ambidexterity through leadership practices that enable individual employees to dynamically balance alignment-oriented and adaptation-oriented activities within their roles, supported by flat hierarchies and cross-functional collaboration (Akraouch, 2019). This dual-ambidexterity approach serves as a strategic drift mitigation mechanism, preventing the organization from becoming trapped in either pure exploitation (which could lead to competency traps and declining innovation) or pure exploration (which might result in resource depletion without commercial returns), as described in March & Lee (2022) exploration-exploitation framework. The temporal sequencing of innovation activities from idea generation through commercialization further illustrates how Nestlé orchestrates ambidextrous capabilities to maintain competitive positioning in established markets while simultaneously creating new value spaces, confirming that successful POS implementation requires not only ambidextrous intentions but also sophisticated organizational architectures that can sustain both strategic orientations over extended periods.

COMPARATIVE ANALYSIS: NESTLÉ AND COCA-COLA'S POS APPROACHES

While Nestlé and Coca-Cola implement versions of the POS, their approaches reveal important differences in emphasis and execution.

Balancing Market Defense and Innovation

Coca-Cola's implementation of the POS is evident in its simultaneous address of competitive pressures and pursuit of innovation. The company defends its market position through traditional competitive advantages (Red Ocean elements), including brand loyalty built through "decades of consistent product quality and positive branding" (Hong & Luo, 2024, p. 160) and "competitive pricing strategies, particularly in price-sensitive markets" (p. 160). These approaches enable Coca-Cola to protect its established market share in highly competitive environments.

Concurrently, Coca-Cola pursues innovative growth opportunities (Blue Ocean elements) by expanding into uncontested market spaces. The company develops healthier alternatives to address health-conscious consumers like "Coca-Cola Zero Sugar and other products with low sugar content" (Hong & Luo, 2024, p. 161). It implements sustainable packaging initiatives to appeal to environmentally conscious markets. These innovations create new value propositions, differentiating Coca-Cola from competitors while addressing emerging consumer concerns.

Nestlé's approach to balancing market defense and innovation demonstrates greater strategic diversification. While Coca-Cola focuses primarily on innovations within its core beverage category, Nestlé has expanded into new product categories such as pet food, health science, and specialized nutrition. This broader exploration strategy reflects a more expansive interpretation of the POS approach.

Structural Implementation

Coca-Cola employs what Hong and Luo (2024) describe as a Go-Stop signal framework to implement its POS. This approach allows the company to simultaneously pursue "product diversity, emotional branding, and competitive pricing" (p. 159) while addressing emerging challenges through innovations like "Coca-Cola Zero Sugar and sustainable packaging" (Hong & Luo, 2024, p. 159).

In contrast, Nestlé has established a more formalized structural separation between exploration and exploitation activities, with dedicated innovation units operating alongside traditional business divisions. This more pronounced structural ambidexterity may give Nestlé greater capacity for radical innovation while maintaining efficiency in established business lines.

Global Localization

Both companies implement a global localization strategy in their POS approach. Coca-Cola maintains its global brand identity while adapting products to regional preferences, as evidenced by the introduction of "green tea-flavored product in Japan" (Hong & Luo, 2024, p. 162) and "garlic-flavored Coke in Japan" (Hong & Luo, 2024, p. 163).

Similarly, Nestlé's matrix structure enables regional adaptations while maintaining centralized control over core functions, allowing the company to respond to local market conditions while preserving global efficiency (Murugan, 2024). However, Nestlé's approach to localization extends beyond product adaptation to include locally tailored marketing strategies and distribution channels, representing a more comprehensive implementation of the global localization concept.

This comparative analysis reveals that while both companies successfully implement the POS, they do so with different emphasis and structural approaches. Coca-Cola focuses on innovations within its core beverage category, while Nestlé pursues a broader diversification strategy. These differences highlight the flexibility of the Purple Ocean approach and its adaptability to different organizational contexts and strategic objectives.

THEMATIC ANALYSIS

Theme 1: Strategic Framework Integration

The integration of established strategic frameworks emerges as a critical theme, highlighting the need to combine traditional competitive analysis with innovative market approaches. Porter's Five Forces framework provides a structured approach to analyzing competitive landscapes, while the Blue Ocean Strategy offers insights into creating uncontested market spaces (Kim & Mauborgne, 2005; Porter, 2008).

Subthemes:

1. *Competitive Force Analysis*: Porter's framework emphasizes understanding industry structure and competitive dynamics, though its effectiveness may be limited in rapidly changing environments (Shi et al., 2021).
2. *Value Innovation*: The Blue Ocean Strategy's focus on creating new market spaces through value innovation offers potential growth opportunities while potentially overlooking existing market defense needs (Wee, 2017).
3. *Framework Synthesis*: The POS, by bridging these approaches, presents a significant potential for addressing competitive positioning and innovation requirements (Scarlat & Panduru, 2021). Its integration with dynamic capabilities theory strengthens this synthesis, enhancing its applicability to volatile market conditions (Pitelis et al., 2024).

Theme 2: Market Performance Dynamics

The research highlights the complex relationship between maintaining existing market positions and pursuing growth opportunities, particularly in the context of significant marketing investments and industry evolution.

Subthemes:

1. *Market Share Defense*: Companies face ongoing challenges in protecting established market positions while adapting to changing conditions.
2. *Growth Opportunity Creation*: The research underscores the importance of identifying and pursuing new market spaces and the need for balanced resource allocation and strategic planning to achieve this.

3. *Resource Allocation*: The significant investment in marketing efforts, such as the 9.2% of revenue spent on digital advertising and product promotions, demonstrates the importance of effective resource deployment (Navarro, 2024).

Theme 3: Organizational Factors

The role of organizational characteristics and industry-specific factors is a crucial consideration in the implementation and effectiveness of strategy.

Subthemes:

1. *Organizational Culture*: The influence of corporate culture on strategy implementation and effectiveness requires careful consideration.
2. *Industry-Specific Considerations*: The food and beverage industry presents unique challenges and opportunities, such as intense competition and changing consumer preferences, that affect strategic outcomes.
3. *Organizational Ambidexterity*: The capacity to simultaneously maintain existing operations while pursuing innovation is critical for effectively implementing the POS. Recent research by Gutiérrez Broncano et al. (2024) confirms that this capability is vital in turbulent environments where firms must maintain flexibility while pursuing innovation.

SYNTHESIS

The literature reveals the complexity of integrating traditional competitive analysis with innovative market approaches in the food and beverage industry. The POS presents a potential framework for addressing these challenges, though its effectiveness depends heavily on organizational factors and industry conditions. The significant marketing investments observed in the U.S. market underscore the importance of developing comprehensive strategies that balance defensive and growth-oriented approaches.

Coca-Cola's and Nestle's implementation of the POS demonstrates how multinational corporations can successfully navigate complex market dynamics by balancing defensive positioning with innovative growth initiatives. These companies protect their established market share while exploring new opportunities through product diversity, global localization (Glocalization), strategic reformulation, and data-driven marketing. This balanced approach enables Coca-Cola and Nestle to address diverse consumer preferences and regulatory requirements across global markets while maintaining their position as market leaders.

In today's fast-moving market, companies need strategies beyond traditional frameworks. The POS offers a comprehensive approach that enables MNCs to protect what they have built while creating growth space (Scarlat & Panduru, 2021). It acknowledges that success requires more than just holding ground or seeking uncharted territory; it demands resilience and the ability to reimagine possibilities. As consumer preferences change and market dynamics evolve (Zuluğ et al., 2022), businesses must embrace strategies that allow them to adapt, innovate, and thrive in an increasingly complex world (Chang, 2023).

While the POS offers compelling advantages for companies navigating complex market dynamics, a critical examination reveals several inherent limitations that may constrain its effectiveness as a long-term strategic framework.

LIMITATIONS OF THE POS

The POS, as a hybrid of Blue Ocean and Red Ocean strategies, offers adaptive value but is not without significant limitations that constrain its strategic potential. One principal limitation of POS is its transitory and ambiguous nature. Scarlat and Panduru (2021) explain that the Purple Ocean exists as an "intermediate status" between the Red Ocean (high competition) and the Blue Ocean (no competition), reflecting either an incomplete transition or a fallback from the Blue Ocean due to internal misalignment or external disruptions. This ambiguity challenges organizations to define coherent strategic objectives as they operate in neither a fully competitive nor a fully differentiated space.

Additionally, the POS suffers from limited scalability and sustainability. Unlike the Blue Ocean strategy, which thrives in uncontested market spaces and fosters innovation, POS organizations often keep one foot in a saturated market while cautiously venturing into new areas. As Aithal (2016) noted, strategies like POS may lead to organizational drift, especially when firms attempt to balance the competing demands of innovation, sustainability, and profit without clear structural support.

This dual positioning makes it challenging to achieve long-term strategic clarity. Firms may expend resources on innovation initiatives that lack full commitment while simultaneously defending legacy markets, which leads to resource dilution and strategic confusion. The hybrid nature also suggests that organizations might fail to fully capture the benefits of either Red or Blue Ocean strategies, resulting in suboptimal outcomes. Therefore, while the POS can realistically reflect transitional strategic environments, its lack of clarity and execution ambiguity makes it more of a short-term tactic than a long-term strategic solution (Scarlat & Panduru, 2021).

Beyond the conceptual limitations, organizations face significant practical challenges when implementing this hybrid approach. This method requires specific organizational capabilities and strategic interventions to overcome execution barriers.

IMPLEMENTATION CHALLENGES OF THE POS AND HOW TO OVERCOME THEM

Implementing the POS presents notable challenges related to strategic alignment, organizational culture, and innovation execution.

Scarlat and Panduru (2021) observed that many firms struggle to transition from Red to Blue Oceans, often remaining stagnant in the Purple Ocean due to internal resistance and market misperceptions. For instance, a Romanian service company attempted to adopt a Blue Ocean approach but found itself confined to the Purple Ocean, unable to achieve significant sales growth despite undergoing internal restructuring (Scarlat & Panduru, 2021). Similarly, tech startups aiming to disrupt the market with a new product found themselves in the Purple Ocean due to market saturation and a lack of differentiation (Kai et al., 2023). These situations illustrate the complexity of executing POS, particularly in environments where the core business remains tied to traditional models.

Additionally, the literature identifies organizational inertia and risk aversion as key barriers. Firms entrenched in legacy systems often lack the agility to effectively reallocate resources toward disruptive innovations, a hallmark of successful POS implementation (Aithal, 2016).

To overcome these barriers, firms must foster a culture of strategic ambidexterity, which is the ability to exploit existing capabilities while exploring new opportunities. This can be achieved by adopting an innovation management system that supports incremental and transformative innovations (Bonie & Joseph, 2019, as cited in Scarlat & Panduru, 2021). Furthermore, POS should be integrated within a White Ocean Mixed Strategy framework (Aithal, 2016), which provides a holistic, context-sensitive model by combining competitive, monopoly, environmental, and survival strategies. This integration can help firms transition more effectively by aligning resources, leadership mindset, and market positioning.

Therefore, while implementing the POS can be challenging, especially without a clear roadmap, organizations must prioritize innovation management, cultural transformation, and hybrid strategy models like the White Ocean Mixed Strategy. A clear roadmap can significantly enhance their chances of successful deployment by providing essential direction and guidance throughout the complex implementation process of the strategy.

CONCLUSION

This comprehensive examination of the POS within the U.S. food and beverage industry reveals a transformative strategic paradigm that transcends traditional competitive frameworks to address the fundamental challenge of contemporary business: how to simultaneously defend market positions while creating new value propositions in rapidly evolving competitive landscapes. The research demonstrates that the POS represents far more than a tactical middle ground between Red and Blue Ocean approaches; it constitutes a transformative strategic lens rooted in adaptive, integrative logic that enables organizations to orchestrate complex strategic activities through dynamic capabilities and organizational ambidexterity. This theoretical insight fundamentally reframes strategic management from a positioning-based discipline focused on competitive advantage within existing market boundaries to an orchestration-based practice centered on the continuous creation and reconfiguration of value propositions across multiple market dimensions simultaneously.

The integration of dynamic capabilities theory with hybrid strategic theory positions the POS as a sophisticated meta-framework that allows MNCs to navigate the inherent tensions between exploitation and exploration activities while maintaining strategic coherence across diverse global markets. Empirical evidence from Coca-Cola's Go-Stop signal implementation and Nestlé's structural ambidexterity shows that successful deployment of the POS requires not only strategic intention but also the development of organizational architectures capable of supporting contradictory strategic logics without compromising operational effectiveness. These case studies illustrate how organizations can transform potential strategic conflicts into synergistic capabilities that enhance both competitive resilience and innovative capacity, confirming that the POS enables firms to become architects of market possibilities rather than merely defenders of established positions.

The research's theoretical and practical contributions enhance the strategic management literature by demonstrating how integrative strategic frameworks can address the shortcomings of singular strategic approaches in volatile business environments. However, the challenges related to POS implementation, including strategic confusion, resource dilution, and organizational complexity, underscore the demanding nature of this approach and the sophisticated capabilities required for successful execution. These implementation challenges do not diminish the framework's potential; rather, they highlight the evolutionary nature of strategic management, and the increasing demands placed on organizational capabilities in contemporary competitive environments.

Future research opportunities include longitudinal studies of strategic transitions, cross-industry applications, and the creation of improved measurement systems for evaluating dual strategic effectiveness. As industries continue to face unprecedented disruption and transformation, the POS's focus on adaptive, integrative logic positions it as a vital framework for understanding how organizations can maintain competitive relevance while pursuing innovative growth opportunities. The framework's contribution to strategic management theory lies not in its combination of existing strategic elements but in its reconceptualization of strategy as a dynamic orchestration process that enables organizations to shape market evolution rather than merely respond to competitive pressures.

In a world where industries shift like tectonic plates and competitive landscapes transform with increasing velocity, organizations must evolve beyond traditional strategic thinking to become architects of possibility rather than mere defenders of position. The POS, when fully realized, transcends the simple blending of red and blue strategic elements to become the ultraviolet frequency at which sustainable innovation becomes visible. This strategic wavelength reveals opportunities invisible to conventional competitive analysis while enabling organizations to create value propositions that both defend existing markets and generate new growth possibilities. This transformative potential positions the POS not as an endpoint in strategic evolution but as a catalyst for the continuous reinvention of competitive advantage in an increasingly complex and dynamic global marketplace.

KEY FINDINGS AND THEORETICAL CONTRIBUTIONS

The study sheds light on several critical insights into strategic management. First, the research demonstrates the limitations of traditional strategic frameworks in addressing the dynamic nature of contemporary markets. While foundational, Porter's Five Forces framework often presumes stability that no longer exists in today's volatile business environment. Similarly, although innovative, the Blue Ocean Strategy may overlook the importance of defending existing market positions. The POS emerges as a promising alternative, offering a more holistic approach that balances market defense with innovative growth strategies.

The findings underscore the significance of organizational ambidexterity in implementing such strategies. Multinational corporations must simultaneously exploit existing market strengths while exploring new opportunities, a delicate balance that the POS aims to facilitate. This approach is particularly crucial in the U.S. Food and Beverage Industry, characterized by rapid technological advancements, shifting consumer preferences, and intense competitive pressures.

Integrating dynamic capabilities theory (Pitelis et al., 2024) and hybrid strategic theory (Gutiérrez Broncano et al., 2024) into the POS framework represents a significant theoretical advancement. This integration establishes POS as a combinatorial framework and a transformative strategic paradigm that enables firms to simultaneously protect existing market positions and explore new opportunities through robust dynamic capabilities. The conceptual fusion of hybrid strategy logic with dynamic capabilities extends strategic theory by transcending traditional dualities and presenting strategy as orchestration rather than mere positioning.

Practical Implications

From a practical standpoint, the research provides valuable guidance for multinational corporations seeking to maintain a competitive edge. The POS offers a framework for:

1. Protecting existing market share
2. Identifying and capitalizing on new growth opportunities
3. Balancing resource allocation between defensive and innovative strategies

The Coca-Cola and Nestlé case studies exemplify this approach, demonstrating how companies can successfully navigate market challenges by defending their core business and exploring new market segments. Both companies' implementation of the POS across global markets illustrates how multinational corporations can address diverse consumer preferences and regulatory requirements while maintaining market leadership. Coca-Cola and Nestlé have established a sustainable competitive advantage in a volatile industry by balancing defensive positioning with innovative growth initiatives through product diversity, glocalization, strategic reformulation, and data-driven marketing.

LIMITATIONS AND FUTURE RESEARCH

While this study offers significant insights into the implementation of the POS, several methodological and contextual limitations deserve acknowledgment, simultaneously highlighting promising avenues for future investigation. The research focuses on MNCs in the U.S. Food and Beverage Industry, which limits the generalizability of the findings to organizations with considerably different resource endowments, operational scales, and strategic capabilities within the same industry, as well as to firms operating across varying industrial contexts and global environments. This limitation highlights the inherent challenge of conducting strategic research that captures the full range of organizational diversity and contextual complexity characterizing contemporary business landscapes. Nevertheless, these constraints lay the groundwork for a comprehensive future research agenda that can extend and deepen our understanding of Purple Ocean Strategy dynamics across multiple dimensions. The following are future research opportunities to further this study.

1. ***Longitudinal Strategic Transition Studies*** represent a particularly compelling research opportunity that addresses a fundamental gap in current strategic management literature. Future research should employ longitudinal methodologies, utilizing process tracing and organizational ethnography approaches, to examine how firms transition from Red Ocean to Purple Ocean to Blue Ocean strategic positions over extended periods. Process tracing methodology would enable researchers to identify the specific causal mechanisms, decision sequences, and organizational capabilities that facilitate successful strategic transitions. In contrast, organizational ethnography would provide rich insights into the cultural, behavioral, and leadership dynamics that either enable or constrain strategic evolution (Langley et al., 2013). Such longitudinal investigations could reveal whether the POS represents a temporary transitional state or a sustainable long-term strategic position, addressing critical questions about strategic stability and evolution in dynamic competitive environments. These studies would particularly benefit from examining firms that have successfully navigated multiple strategic tran-

sitions, identifying the dynamic capabilities and organizational characteristics that enable strategic adaptability while maintaining operational effectiveness.

2. ***Cross-Industry and Scale-Based Research Extensions*** constitute another essential research direction. Future investigations should systematically examine the applicability of the POS across diverse industry contexts, particularly in sectors characterized by different competitive dynamics, innovation cycles, and regulatory environments, such as the technology, healthcare, financial services, and manufacturing industries. Additionally, research focusing on small and medium-sized enterprises (SMEs) would provide crucial insights into how resource constraints and organizational scale influence POS implementation, potentially revealing simplified or adapted versions of the framework suitable for organizations with limited strategic resources. Comparative studies examining strategic behavior differences between MNCs and SMEs within the same industry could illuminate the role of organizational size and resource availability in shaping strategic choices and outcomes.
3. ***Methodological Innovation and measurement development*** represent a critical frontier for advancing POS research. Future studies should develop more sophisticated metrics for measuring strategic effectiveness that capture the dual nature of Purple Ocean positioning, moving beyond traditional performance indicators to encompass innovation outcomes, market creation activities, and competitive resilience measures. Advanced analytical techniques, including machine learning approaches and big data analytics, could enable researchers to identify patterns and relationships within strategic behavior that are not apparent through conventional analytical methods. Additionally, the development of real-time strategy measurement tools could provide insights into how organizations adjust their Purple Ocean positioning in response to environmental changes and competitive dynamics.
4. ***Sustainability and Long-Term Viability Investigations*** represent perhaps the most strategically significant research opportunity. Comprehensive longitudinal studies examining the sustainability of POS over multiple business cycles, competitive disruptions, and environmental changes would provide essential insights into the framework's long-term viability and adaptability. These investigations should particularly focus on identifying the organizational capabilities, leadership characteristics, and environmental conditions that enable sustained Purple Ocean positioning, as well as the factors that cause organizations to drift toward pure Red or Blue Ocean strategies. Such research would benefit from examining organizations that have maintained Purple Ocean positioning across multiple decades, identifying the renewal mechanisms and strategic adaptation processes that enable long-term strategic sustainability.

The Purple Ocean Strategy represents a promising evolution in strategic management thinking, offering a more nuanced approach to navigating the complexities of contemporary business. By integrating defensive market positioning with innovative growth strategies through dynamic capabilities and ambidextrous organizational architectures, this framework provides a comprehensive approach to sustainable competitive advantage in volatile environments. As industries confront unprecedented challenges, including digital transformation, sustainability imperatives, and geopolitical uncertainties, such integrative frameworks will become increasingly critical for organizational survival and prosperity. This research contributes to the ongoing strategic management discourse by offering both theoretical insights and practical guidance for multinational corporations seeking to thrive in dynamic global marketplaces. It positions the Purple Ocean Strategy as a blueprint for balanced strategic effectiveness, synthesizing traditional competitive approaches with innovative market creation activities.

REFERENCES

Aithal, P. S. (2016). The concept of ideal strategy and its realization using white ocean mixed strategy. *International Journal of Management Sciences and Business Research*, *5*(4), 171–179.

Birkinshaw, J., & Gibson, C. B. (2004). Building an ambidextrous organisation. *Advanced Institute of Management Research Paper*, (003).

Braun, V., & Clarke, V. (2006). Using thematic analysis in psychology. *Qualitative Research in Psychology*, *3*(2), 77–101.

Buisson, B., & Silberzahn, P. (2010). Blue ocean or fast-second innovation? A four-breakthrough model to explain successful market domination. *International Journal of Innovation Management*, *14*(03), 359–378.

Campanella, F., Del Giudice, M., Thrassou, A., & Vrontis, D. (2020). Ambidextrous organizations in the banking sector: An empirical verification of banks' performance and conceptual development. *International Journal of Human Resource Management*, *31*(2), 272–302.

Cavagnetto, S., & Gahir, B. R. U. C. E. (2013). Shades of purple strategy. *CRIS-Bulletin of the Centre for Research and Interdisciplinary Study*, *1*, 77–92.

Chang, L. (2023). Innovative Marketing Strategies in China's Telecommunication Sector: Adapting to the Digital Age. *Journal of Marketing Communications*.

Chorazy, E. (2020). Coke and health. *Decoding Coca-Cola*, 207-225.

Chowdhury, M. T., Sarkar, A., Paul, S. K., & Moktadir, M. A. (2020). A case study on strategies to deal with the impacts of covid-19 pandemic in the food and beverage industry. *Operations Management Research*, *15*(1-2), 166–178.

Cooper, H. M. (1988). Organizing knowledge syntheses: A taxonomy of literature reviews. *Knowledge in Society*, *1*(1), 104.

Dias, A. S., Abreu, A., Navas, H. V., & Santos, R. (2020). Proposal of a holistic framework to support sustainability of new product innovation processes. *Sustainability*, *12*(8), 3450.

Dvorak, J., & Razova, I. (2018). Empirical Validation of Blue Ocean Strategy Sustainability in an International Environment. *Foundations of Management*, *10*(1), 143–162.

Galanakis, C. M., Rizou, M., Aldawoud, T. M., Uçak, İ., & Rowan, N. J. (2021). Innovations and technology disruptions in the food sector within the covid-19 pandemic and post-lockdown era. *Trends in Food Science & Technology*, *110*, 193–200.

Gandellini, G., & Venanzi, D. (2011). Purple ocean strategy: How to support SMEs' recovery. *Procedia: Social and Behavioral Sciences*, *24*, 1–15.

Gibson, C. B., & Birkinshaw, J. (2004). The antecedents, consequences, and mediating role of organizational ambidexterity. *Academy of Management Journal*, *47*(2), 209–226.

Gutiérrez Broncano, S., González-Sánchez, M., & Villanueva-García, D. (2024). Hybrid strategy and its effect on the market performance of family-business SMEs: The mediating role of innovation. *The International Journal of Organizational Analysis*. Advance online publication.

Gutiérrez-Broncano, S., Linuesa-Langreo, J., Rubio-Andrés, M., & Sastre-Castillo, M. Á. (2024). Can hybrid strategy improve SME performance? The role of innovation and adaptive capacity. *European Journal of Innovation Management*, *27*(9), 173–197.

Hadji, S., Gholizadeh, P., & Naghavi, N. (2022). Diagnosing of human resource performance management based on lack of ambidextrous learning themes: A case study of public Iranian banking system. *International Journal of Ethics and Systems*, *38*(3), 484–509.

Hong, P., & Luo, K. (2024). Coca-Cola's global marketing strategy: A Go-Stop signal framework analysis. *Proceedings of the 3rd International Conference on Financial Technology and Business Analysis*, 159-163.

Jansen, J. J., Van Den Bosch, F. A., & Volberda, H. W. (2006). Exploratory innovation, exploitative innovation, and performance: Effects of organizational antecedents and environmental moderators. *Management Science*, *52*(11), 1661–1674.

Kafoe, A. S. (2024). Holistic Competitive Strategy: Embracing A Holistic Approach To Establishing A Competitive Edge. *Revista Academiei Fortelor Terestre, 29*(4).

Kafoe, A. S. (2025). Conquering the Competitive Landscape: A Fusion of Defensive and Offensive Strategies for Sustainable Growth. In *Organizational Readiness and Research: Security, Management, and Decision Making* (pp. 53-100). IGI Global Scientific Publishing.

Kai, Z., Hui-tao, H., Yuan, Y., & Sun, P. (2023). Can adopting lean startup strategy promote the sustainable development of new ventures? the mediating role of organizational iterative learning. *PLoS One*, *18*(8), e0290849.

Kim, W. C., & Mauborgne, R. (2005). *Blue ocean strategy: How to create uncontested market space and make the competition irrelevant*. Harvard Business School Press.

Lacy-Nichols, J., Scrinis, G., & Carey, R. (2019). The evolution of Coca-Cola Australia's soft drink reformulation strategy 2003–2017: A thematic analysis of corporate documents. *Food Policy*. Advance online publication. DOI: 10.1016/j.foodpol.2019.101793

Langley, A. N. N., Smallman, C., Tsoukas, H., & Van de Ven, A. H. (2013). Process studies of change in organization and management: Unveiling temporality, activity, and flow. *Academy of Management Journal*, *56*(1), 1–13.

Laser, J. (2022). Criteria to appraise top executives for ambidextrous leadership. *Journal of organizational effectiveness: people and performance, 9*(3), 449-470.

Lawrence, P. R., Lorsch, J. W., & Garrison, J. S. (1967). Organization and environment: Managing differentiation and integration.

Malekpour, M., Caboni, F., Nikzadask, M., & Basile, V. (2024). Taste of success: A strategic framework for product innovation in the food and beverage industry. *British Food Journal*, *126*(13), 94–118.

Mandal, P. (2020). The Changing Marketplace. *International Journal of Business Strategy and Automation*. https://doi.org/DOI: 10.4018/ijbsa.2020070103

March, J. G., & Lee, S. H. (2022). Exploration and exploitation in organizational learning: A temporal perspective. *Strategic Management Journal, 43*(4), 789–812. DOI: 10.1002/smj.3398

Muneeb, D., Khattak, A., Wahba, K., Abdalla, S., & Ahmad, S. Z. (2023). Dynamic capabilities as a strategic flexibility enabler: Organizational responsiveness to COVID-19. *Journal of Asia Business Studies, 17*(4), 824–849.

Murugan, S. (2024). A Study On Organizational Structure Of Nestle. *International Research Journal of Modernization in Engineering Technology and Science*. Advance online publication. DOI: 10.56726/irjmets48778

Nakat, Z., & Bou-Mitri, C. (2021). COVID-19 and the food industry: Readiness assessment. *Food Control, 121*, 107661.

Navarro, J. G. (2024). Marketing in the United States -- statistics & facts. https://www.statista.com/topics/8972/marketing-in-the-united-states/#topicOverview

Nithisathian, K., & Walsh, J. (2013). Understanding Purple Ocean Strategy. *International Journal of Management Research, 3*(1), 42–57.

Nithisathian, K., Wall, W. P., Thanitnan, C., & Pongsittisak, D. (2020). Black Ocean Strategy: A Preliminary Literature Review. *Journal of Management and Innovation, 7*(2), 121–140.

Onikoyi, I. A. (2017). Impact of product innovation on organizational performance (A Survey of Nestle Nigeria Plc). *Journal of Marketing and consumer Research, 37*(1), 21-39.

O'Reilly, C. A.III, & Tushman, M. L. (2013). Organizational ambidexterity: Past, present, and future. *The Academy of Management Perspectives, 27*(4), 324–338.

Peteraf, M., Di Stefano, G., & Verona, G. (2013). The elephant in the room of dynamic capabilities: Bringing two diverging conversations together. *Strategic Management Journal, 34*(12), 1389–1410.

Pitelis, C. N., Teece, D. J., & Yang, H. (2024). Dynamic capabilities and MNE global strategy: A systematic literature review-based novel conceptual framework. *Journal of Management Studies, 61*(7), 3295–3326.

Porter, M. E. (2008). The five competitive forces that shape strategy. *Harvard Business Review, 86*(1), 78–93.

Porter, M. E. (2023). Changing patterns of international competition. In *International Strategic Management* (pp. 61–86). Routledge.

Pritchett, P. (2014). *Red Ocean vs. Blue Ocean*. Pritchett LP.

Qian, X. (2023). Strategic adaptation in beverage companies: A focus on health trends. *Journal of Consumer Behavior Studies, 13*(4), 123–138.

Samiee, S., & Chirapanda, S. (2019). International marketing strategy in emerging-market exporting firms. *Journal of International Marketing, 27*(1), 20–37.

Scarlat, C., & Panduru, D. A. (2021). The Purple Ocean: Revisiting the Blue Ocean Strategy. *Journal of Eastern Europe Research in Business and Economics, 2021*, 165416. Advance online publication. DOI: 10.5171/2021.165416

Shi, C., Agbaku, C., & Zhang, F. (2021). How Do Upper Echelons Perceive Porter's Five Forces? Evidence From Strategic Entrepreneurship in China. *Frontiers in Psychology, 12*. Advance online publication. DOI: 10.3389/fpsyg.2021.649574

Teece, D. J. (2019). A capability theory of the firm: An economics and (strategic) management perspective. *New Zealand Economic Papers, 53*(1), 1–43.

Tushman, M. L., & O'Reilly, C. A. (2006). *Winning through innovation: A practical guide to leading organizational change and renewal*. Harvard Business Press.

Wee, C. H. (2017). Think Tank—Beyond the Blue Ocean Strategy. *Visions of Strategy*, 2017.

Whittemore, R., & Knafl, K. (2005). The integrative review: Updated methodology. *Journal of Advanced Nursing, 52*(5), 546–553.

Wilden, R., & Gudergan, S. P. (2015). The impact of dynamic capabilities on operational marketing and technological capabilities: Investigating the role of environmental turbulence. *Journal of the Academy of Marketing Science, 43*, 181–199.

Zheng, L. (2023). The evolution of reformulation strategies in carbonated beverages. *International Food Research, 45*(2), 211–227.

Zuluğ, A., Ceylan, E., & Elmas, B. (2022). Pandemic impact on food industry: Consumer behavior change analysis. *Journal of Food Science and Technology, 15*(3), 187–202.

Chapter 2
Scaling AI Without Breaking the Enterprise:
Lessons From Verixa Sciences' Digital Collapse

Daniel Ngueya
http://orcid.org/0009-0005-8141-1841
Marymount University, USA

ABSTRACT

The integration of artificial intelligence (AI) into regulated enterprise operations creates opportunities for automation and increased resilience. However, many organizations face significant challenges when implementing AI at scale. Verixa Sciences, a mid-sized U.S. pharma company, launched an AI-driven manufacturing project in 2022 to enhance supply chain forecasting and ensure regulatory compliance. Despite strong executive support and substantial investment, the project failed within a year, leading to a 22% revenue decline, compliance issues, and operational failures. Through a review of existing literature and case analysis, this study highlights key failure points, including the lack of digital readiness assessments, ineffective change management, and the absence of a responsible AI governance framework. Using four theoretical perspectives TOE, STS, ADKAR, and Responsible AI the study offers strategic recommendations for AI adoption in regulated settings. It contributes to the growing research on how to implement AI ethically, responsibly, and sustainably.

INTRODUCTION

Artificial intelligence (AI) is transforming the pharmaceutical industry by automating operations, improving predictive analytics, and ensuring real-time regulatory compliance. However, scaling AI within complex, regulated enterprises remain risky. Verixa Sciences, a mid-sized U.S.-based pharmaceutical manufacturer with about 3,200 employees and $1.6 billion in annual revenue, illustrates this challenge. In 2022, Verixa launched an ambitious reshoring and digital transformation initiative that integrated AI-driven systems across its manufacturing and supply chain divisions. The goal was to reduce reliance

DOI: 10.4018/979-8-3373-4027-2.ch002

on offshore manufacturing, improve demand forecasting accuracy, and meet evolving FDA compliance standards.

However, within a year, the program collapsed. The company experienced a 22% revenue decline, widespread system failures, data silos, and noncompliance warnings from regulators. Similar results have been reported across the pharmaceutical industry, where 70–85% of AI projects fail due to organizational unreadiness, poor data hygiene, and inadequate change management (Nicholaus, 2024; Fivetran, 2025; RAND Corporation, 2024). Verixa's case is not an anomaly; it is a cautionary tale of how even well-funded AI transformations can fall apart without proper foundations. This case study uses a thematic literature review and cross-framework analysis to examine Verixa's failure and provide lessons on responsibly scaling AI in compliance-driven environments.

Problem Statement

Despite AI's strategic promise, its high failure rates expose fundamental issues at the enterprise level. Studies show that nearly 85% of AI projects either underperform or fail due to poor data quality, misaligned stakeholder expectations, and weak governance (Forbes Technology Council, 2024; Nicholaus, 2024). RAND Corporation (2024) emphasizes that most failures result not from technological flaws but from structural problems, such as unclear ownership, insufficient oversight, and a lack of alignment between AI solutions and actual business needs.

In regulated environments, these issues become even more expensive. Poorly executed AI can break compliance rules and harm public trust (McKinsey & Company, 2024; NIST, 2023). The main problem Verixa Sciences faces is the lack of built-in governance and readiness plans to turn AI strategy into lasting operational success. Despite large investments and strong support from leadership, its AI changeover failed because of integration errors, operational mismatches, and low employee engagement. Compatibility problems between new AI systems and legacy ERP systems caused compliance mistakes and manufacturing delays, leading to significant financial losses and organizational chaos.

The absence of risk assessments, training programs, or a digital readiness audit worsened the problem. Employees who feel overwhelmed and uncertain about their job security often avoid AI systems altogether (Hiatt, 2023; Kapoor & Vangala, 2024). Without a change management strategy, organizational confidence dropped, causing costly reversals

Verixa's collapse underscores a larger industry issue: the lack of embedded governance frameworks to guide AI adoption in complex, high-stakes environments. Although its technology was advanced, Verixa lacked formal mechanisms for traceability, oversight, and ethical assurance, critical factors highlighted in emerging research (Patel et al., 2023; RAND Corporation, 2024; NIST, 2023). Without such frameworks, AI risks becoming more of a liability than a strategic asset.

SIGNIFICANCE OF THE STUDY

Theoretical Significance

Although AI continues to grow in popularity, a persistent gap remains in frameworks that integrate governance, digital readiness, and transformation success, especially in regulated industries like pharmaceuticals (RAND Corporation, 2024; Pazhayattil & Konyu-Fogel, 2023). Current research often separates algorithmic performance from ethical and organizational issues. This case offers a rare synthesis of organizational, technical, and ethical aspects of responsible AI deployment. With over 30 academic and practitioner sources, the Verixa Sciences case provides a governance-focused perspective that advances the responsible AI literature. It shows that even well-funded, strategically aligned AI projects can fail not because of technological immaturity but due to poor management of transformation variables (Nicholaus, 2024; Fivetran, 2025).

Furthermore, studies from Deloitte (2023) and Accenture (2024) show that fewer than 28% of pharma AI projects successfully expand across departments, a challenge often ignored in theory discussions. This example connects theory to real-world issues, offering a rare chance to improve ideas through failure.

Practical Significance

This case offers a practical guide for product managers, digital strategists, and compliance officers aiming to scale AI responsibly. It highlights failure points such as weak digital readiness assessments, poor system integration, and insufficient workforce upskilling, all of which impeded Verixa's transformation. These issues reflect a broader trend: McKinsey & Company (2024) found that 71% of digital transformations in pharma underperform due to inadequate change management and poor cross-functional alignment.

By linking these themes to organizational failure, this study provides practical frameworks for assessing AI initiatives. Leaders can use these insights to evaluate digital strategies, find governance gaps, and incorporate resilience into their transformation plans. Governance, it argues, should be a fundamental design principle, not an afterthought.

Ethical and Social Significance

The Verixa case highlights the ethical costs of poorly managed innovation. Employees resisted AI tools due to training gaps, psychological stress, and fear of losing their roles, factors often ignored in technical adoption models (Patel et al., 2023; NIST, 2023). These aren't just side effects; they reveal fundamental flaws in design. This study advocates for ethically conscious development practices like inclusive design, human-in-the-loop systems, and psychological safety audits, which are especially crucial in regulated industries like pharma, where AI mistakes can jeopardize patient safety or delay treatment processes.

Policy and Industry Relevance

This research aligns with the increasing global consensus on AI governance. Institutions such as the OECD, NIST, and European Medicines Agency (EMA) have recently issued AI oversight frameworks emphasizing traceability, lifecycle audits, and model transparency (OECD, 2023; NIST, 2024; EMA, 2023). Verixa's collapse demonstrates what happens when speed or cost-efficiency take precedence over these principles. As AI adoption outpaces regulation, this case provides timely insights for compliance officers, policymakers, and industry leaders aiming to align innovation with regulatory resilience.

METHODOLOGY

This study uses a retrospective, qualitative case study approach to analyze the systemic failure of Verixa Sciences' AI-enabled reshoring project. The goal is to find key organizational, technological, and governance failures that led to the project's downfall in a regulated pharmaceutical setting. This method is suitable given the complex, context-dependent nature of AI deployment in highly regulated environments (Yin, 2018).

The study mainly relies on secondary sources compiled through a narrative literature review, in line with established qualitative research protocols. While this approach facilitates thematic integration across different disciplines, it also presents potential drawbacks, such as selection bias and lower replicability compared to systematic reviews (Baumeister & Leary, 1997). These drawbacks are addressed by using transparent inclusion and exclusion criteria and emphasizing peer-reviewed, empirically supported literature.

LITERATURE REVIEW PROTOCOL

The literature review used a narrative synthesis approach to combine findings across disciplines such as digital transformation, AI governance, organizational change, and ethical implementation. Unlike systematic reviews, which focus on replicability and thoroughness, narrative reviews prioritize conceptual integration and theoretical depth, making them suitable for topics that require an interdisciplinary perspective (Baumeister & Leary, 1997).

This review followed a structured protocol involving targeted keyword searches on Google Scholar and ProQuest. Peer-reviewed articles were prioritized, with screening based on their theoretical relevance, methodological transparency, and sector alignment (e.g., healthcare, pharma, and financial services). This method enabled the synthesis of insights across regulatory, organizational, and technological domains relevant to Verixa's AI failure.

KEYWORDS AND BOOLEAN OPERATORS

The literature search used Boolean logic to find relevant peer-reviewed studies across various fields. Keywords included:

- "AI implementation" AND "pharmaceuticals"
- "Digital transformation" AND ("failure" OR "risk")
- "ADKAR model" OR "change readiness"
- "Responsible AI" AND "governance frameworks"
- "TOE framework" AND "enterprise AI"
- "STS theory" AND "human-machine integration"

These terms were selected to ensure alignment with the study's focus on socio-technical, governance, and organizational dynamics of AI adoption.

Inclusion Criteria

To ensure both rigor and relevance, the following inclusion criteria were applied:

- Peer-reviewed articles published between 2020–202
- Transparent methodology with traceable citations
- Empirical or case-based research on AI or digital transformation
- Focus on regulated industries, such as pharmaceuticals, finance, or healthcare
- Explicit application of TOE, STS, ADKAR, or AI governance frameworks

Exclusion Criteria

Studies were excluded if they met one or more of the following:

- Algorithmic papers without organizational context
- Opinion pieces, whitepapers, or blogs,
- Studies without methodological rigor or citation traceability,
- Non-English publications.

Search Outcome

The initial search identified 41 scholarly sources. After assessing relevance, sector alignment, and methodological clarity, 29 articles were chosen for final inclusion. These include a balanced mix of theoretical, empirical, and cross-sector studies that directly inform the case analysis of Verixa Sciences.

LITERATURE REVIEW

This chapter examines academic and grey literature on the implementation of enterprise AI, failure risks, digital transformation in the pharmaceutical industry, responsible AI governance, and sustainability. It is organized into five thematic clusters. Each cluster now includes practical examples, theoretical frameworks (TOE, STS, ADKAR, Responsible AI), and literature synthesis, culminating in Section 2.6, where the theoretical foundation is established.

AI Project Success and Failure Factors

Despite increased investment in enterprise AI, project failures continue to be common rather than rare. Studies estimate that up to 85% of AI initiatives do not achieve their business goals, often due to factors unrelated to the technology itself (Nicholaus, 2024; Fivetran, 2025). These failures frequently arise from organizational resistance, misalignment between AI capabilities and business needs, and weak governance structures.

Pazhayattil and Konyu-Fogel (2023) present a comprehensive lifecycle model with 93 risk sub-factors categorized into desirability, feasibility, viability, and datability. Their framework highlights that AI systems require more than just technical robustness; they also need clear definitions of ownership, operational processes, and monitoring protocols. Verixa Sciences' experience supports this: the company implemented advanced tools but lacked clear validation procedures and handover structures, leading to cascading failures across teams.

Nicholaus (2024) identifies 14 core causes of AI failure, including mismatched goals, fragile data pipelines, and missing post-deployment audits. RAND Corporation (2024) further confirms that many failures stem from unrealistic expectations and the assumption of plug-and-play functionality, rather than preparing for adaptive behavior, model drift, or recursive error loops.

These failures go beyond isolated mistakes; they reveal systemic misalignment across key areas defined by the Technology–Organization–Environment (TOE) framework. Verixa's technological layer (compliance-tracking AI) did not integrate with legacy ERP systems. Its organizational layer lacked support for digital readiness or structured change planning. The environmental layer, including regulatory demands, was insufficiently addressed, with no traceability or compliance-mapping systems in place.

The Socio-Technical Systems (STS) approach reveals more weaknesses. Verixa prioritized system deployment rather than workforce adaptation, causing friction between human workflows and algorithmic outputs. Without psychological safety, training, or procedural changes, frontline workers resisted or bypassed the new tools.

Using the ADKAR model clarifies this resistance. Employees were not effectively involved in the change process, lacking awareness of the purpose, motivation to participate, or the knowledge and skills to use AI tools. Importantly, the organization failed to reinforce adoption behaviors, which caused the change efforts to falter and not be sustained.

In sum, AI implementation is not just a technical task. Verixa's failure emphasizes a growing agreement: successful AI needs careful coordination between systems, people, and strategy a balance it did not achieve.

AI in Manufacturing and Pharmaceutical Applications

AI technologies in manufacturing and pharmaceuticals provide substantial potential in areas such as predictive maintenance, adaptive process control, and regulatory compliance (Lou & Wu, 2021; Sampene & Nyirenda, 2024). These tools turn operations into intelligent systems powered by feedback from IoT sensors, ERP data, and quality control systems. However, the promise of AI is often limited by its fragility in real-world applications. A 2024 McKinsey & Company report highlights that over 40% of digital manufacturing projects fail due to middleware incompatibility or reliance on outdated infrastructure, challenges that are especially severe in high-stakes sectors like pharmaceuticals.

Verixa Sciences' experience reinforces these findings. The company's AI system, despite its technical sophistication, often produced false positives and flooded users with alerts. It also failed to connect with existing ERP systems, disrupting compliance tracking and delaying production workflows. This shows a socio-technical mismatch where the technology was modernized, but legacy standard operating procedures (SOPs), user norms, and workflows remained unchanged, a violation of STS theory observed in other sectors as well.

Although agile development practices are often advised to lower deployment risk, Verixa introduced its platform through a single, large-scale rollout. De Paula et al. (2023) and others suggest an iterative, human-centered design process that incorporates stakeholder feedback and focuses on user readiness. Verixa's failure to follow such guidance led to poor user engagement, insufficient training, and a steep learning curve.

The Technology–Organization–Environment (TOE) framework also provides clear diagnostic insights. Technologically, Verixa had cutting-edge automation tools. However, organizationally, it lacked the internal collaboration, skills, and process redesign needed for effective implementation. Environmentally, the company failed to address changing regulatory requirements for traceability, which led to audit failures. These gaps ultimately derailed the initiative.

Digital Transformation and Change Management

AI systems are not standalone technologies; their success relies on human support systems, leadership alignment, and organizational readiness. The ADKAR model (Hiatt, 2006) provides a step-by-step framework for managing this type of transformation: from building awareness to reinforcing new behaviors. However, research shows that many organizations implementing AI overlook these human integration steps, resulting in resistance, shadow IT workarounds, and loss of trust (George et al., 2025).

Verixa Sciences' experience illustrates these challenges. Despite investing in technology, the rollout lacked peer coaching, ongoing training, and employee engagement strategies. As a result, digital tools were either underused or misapplied, while skepticism grew around job security and performance monitoring. Sampene and Nyirenda (2024) highlight that change fatigue is one of the most common predictors of AI project failure in pharmaceutical settings. Without addressing workforce psychology and emotional burden, even advanced tools will remain unused.

Managerial narratives also influence AI adoption outcomes. De Paula et al. (2023) highlight that when leaders depict AI as a cost-cutting or surveillance tool, employee trust declines. At Verixa, such framing was reportedly evident during early team briefings, which further fueled fear and resistance. This illustrates a larger issue: transformation narratives need to balance efficiency improvements with empowerment to succeed.

The Socio-Technical Systems (STS) perspective further clarifies the issue. Verixa introduced new tools but did not redesign work structures or roles to support these changes. Employees still answered to old performance measures, even though workflows had shifted, causing confusion and overload. In contrast, STS principles focus on the joint optimization of both social and technical systems to ensure alignment between tools, tasks, and human needs.

Graf and Burrell (2024) emphasize the importance of viewing resistance not as failure, but as valuable diagnostic feedback. Their research on healthcare digitization shows that when skepticism and cultural hesitancy are recognized and addressed, project results improve significantly. Verixa's lack of such engagement strategies limited its ability to detect or respond to early warning signs, increasing the likelihood of operational failure.

In summary, successful digital transformation involves more than just implementing technology. It must be supported by deliberate cultural, procedural, and leadership initiatives to promote human preparedness and systemic coherence.

Responsible AI and Governance

As AI systems become more integrated into regulated industries, governance frameworks are no longer optional; they are crucial. Standards set by the OECD (2019), NIST (2023), and IBM (2021) emphasize the significance of lifecycle risk assessments, transparency, human oversight, and ethical design principles. However, adoption remains low. Fewer than 30% of organizations report using formal governance tools, leaving many AI systems susceptible to ethical issues and regulatory risks.

Verixa Sciences' implementation reflected these challenges. Despite operating in a highly regulated industry, the company did not put in place algorithmic audit trails, override protocols, or documentation processes like model cards. These omissions created significant compliance risks and diminished trust among distributors and internal stakeholders. If Verixa had adopted a governance model like the NIST Risk Management Framework (RMF), it could have "mapped" stakeholder risks, "measured" deployment threats, and "managed" them with escalation pathways that were missing in its transformation.

Governance is not just about compliance; it's also about reinforcing human accountability. Verixa failed to assign clear oversight roles, such as QA leads or AI stewards. This left users without escalation support during system failures, which eroded trust in automation and created operational blind spots. NIST (2023) recommends embedding human control and traceability into AI design, yet Verixa's rollout lacked both.

Ethical concerns also emerged due to the lack of fairness protocols. Burrell et al. (2023) explain how neglecting equity and bias mitigation in AI systems has led to reputational, legal, and moral issues, especially in sectors like healthcare. Their case studies support Verixa's situation, where unchecked automation caused unpredictable results without human oversight. Graf & Burrell (2024) add that ignoring stakeholder resistance worsens governance failures by removing critical feedback loops. Verixa's failure to anticipate or address this resistance left its AI system both ethically and operationally vulnerable.

The TOE framework supports this diagnosis: Verixa lacked environmental compliance, organizational accountability, and adequate technological transparency. STS highlights the human-machine disconnect that occurs when governance structures do not empower users. ADKAR emphasizes the decline caused by the absence of feedback, incentives, and recovery mechanisms to rebuild trust.

Overall, Verixa's failure underscores an important lesson: governance needs to be built in from the beginning, not added later after issues arise.

AI and Sustainability

Sustainability in AI goes beyond environmental impact; it also encompasses operational efficiency and cognitive resilience. As Sampene and Nyirenda (2024) note, sustainable AI systems are those that minimize energy consumption, retraining frequency, and wasteful system behaviors. However, at Verixa Sciences, poor system tuning and reliance on CPU-intensive retraining cycles increased energy use without delivering corresponding business value.

Verixa's architecture demonstrates the impact of unsustainable design. Its alerting system caused frequent false positives, leading to unnecessary work for employees and straining system resources. These inefficiencies resulted from non-modular codebases and a lack of green AI practices, which Sustainability-[number_1_] (2022) advises avoiding through design features like edge processing and modular retraining.

From a TOE framework perspective, Verixa focused on technological upgrades without considering organizational eco-awareness or establishing policies to promote sustainable use. The regulatory and ecological accountability aspects were also overlooked. While technical performance was prioritized, there was no effort to evaluate environmental impact or to align with industry sustainability goals.

The STS model supports this diagnosis. False alerts need human intervention, which creates hidden work and user fatigue an avoidable burden if systems had been co-designed with frontline staff. Tools that depend on frequent human correction cause friction and burnout, harming long-term sustainability.

Even the ADKAR model supports sustainability indirectly. When users are trained to use systems efficiently and view them as reliable, they are less likely to abandon or misuse them. Verixa's failure to provide reinforcement and performance incentives further weakened system adoption, leading to wasted computational and human effort.

Ultimately, sustainability is not just about carbon footprints; it also involves how effectively AI tools fit into workflows, protect mental bandwidth, and cut down operational waste. Verixa's case shows how ignoring this aspect can undermine even well-funded transformations.

Theoretical Frameworks

A strong theoretical foundation is essential for analyzing the complex failure of Verixa Sciences' AI transformation. This section examines four interconnected frameworks that provide analytical support for understanding the organizational, technical, and ethical dimensions of enterprise AI implementation. Each framework is selected for its conceptual depth and practical relevance to the Verixa case.

Technology–Organization–Environment (TOE) Framework

Originally developed by Tornatzky and Fleischer (1990), the Technology–Organization–Environment (TOE) framework is one of the most commonly used models for understanding how new technologies are adopted and integrated. TOE considers innovation adoption as a result of three interacting contexts.

a) Technological Context: The perceived benefits, complexity, and compatibility of the technology.
b) Organizational Context: Internal resources, structures, culture, and communication abilities.
c) Environmental Context: External factors like regulatory demands, competition, and collaborations.

The significance of TOE to Verixa Sciences' situation is considerable. The company had access to advanced AI-enabled automation technology but faced challenges due to a lack of organizational readiness, such as integration with legacy ERP systems and insufficient digital training. Additionally, they struggled with aligning to environmental expectations, including gaps in regulatory compliance and limited auditability. TOE also offers a way to understand why even well-funded AI projects can fail, not because of the technology itself, but because of a mismatch between internal capabilities and external constraints.

Furthermore, in the literature, TOE is often extended to evaluate cloud computing adoption, digital transformation, and even AI maturity models in enterprise contexts (Oliveira & Martins, 2011; Baker, 2012). These extensions further reinforce the use of TOE beyond its original scope, especially for understanding the systemic failures observed in the Verixa case.

Socio-Technical Systems (STS) Theory

The Socio-Technical Systems (STS) theory, first introduced by Trist and Bamforth (1951) in their study of British coal mining operations, is based on the idea that any complex organizational system consists of two interconnected subsystems: the social (people, roles, culture) and the technical (tools, machines, processes). STS theory supports the concept of joint optimization, which means that both social and technical elements should be designed together to encourage effective and sustainable change.

In enterprise AI, STS is useful for diagnosing failures related to adoption, usability, and user resistance. For Verixa, deploying real-time automation and predictive tools overlooked the social dynamics of production workers who traditionally relied on manual decision-making. These users were undertrained, experienced high cognitive load, and lacked control during the transformation. As a result, they often bypassed or misused the new systems, causing an apparent STS mismatch.

Scholars such as Mumford (2000) and Clegg (2000) have expanded STS to include concepts like participative design and socio-material entanglement, all of which are directly relevant to AI transformations. By applying STS, this study examines not just technical robustness but also user adaptability, stakeholder inclusion, and the broader human factors that influence success.

ADKAR Change Management Model

The ADKAR model, developed by Prosci founder Hiatt (2006), provides a step-by-step guide for managing change at both the individual and organizational levels. It describes five key components:

a) Awareness of the necessity for change
b) Desire to support change
c) Knowledge of how to change
d) Ability to demonstrate necessary skills and behaviors; reinforcement to sustain the change.

ADKAR's strength lies in its precise diagnosis. It enables organizations to identify exactly where change initiatives fail, focusing on psychological and behavioral readiness rather than broader issues. Verixa's challenges in securing buy-in from frontline teams, insufficient training efforts, and lack of reinforcement tools (such as performance incentives and KPIs) can be directly linked to failures at all five stages of the ADKAR model.

In digital transformation literature, ADKAR is frequently used to evaluate technology adoption in healthcare, ERP implementations, and AI readiness (Hornstein, 2015; Prosci, 2020). It emphasizes the importance of aligning emotions and cognition along with procedural updates. This makes it a strong framework for the Verixa case, where fear of job loss, lack of clarity, and perceived irrelevance led to resistance and improper system use.

Critically, ADKAR links the high-level strategy with individual experiences, providing this study with a framework to analyze not only "what went wrong" at Verixa but also why people reacted the way they did in response to AI systems.

Responsible AI Governance Frameworks (OECD, NIST, IBM)

Governance frameworks for AI have become more standardized, especially under the influence of leading organizations like the OECD (2019), NIST (2023), and IBM (2021). These frameworks differ in focus but share common principles such as:

a) Transparency and Explainability

b) Accountability and Traceability
c) Human Oversight and Control
d) Privacy, Fairness, and Risk Mitigation

The OECD's AI Principles were the first international standard endorsed by G20 countries. They emphasize inclusive growth, human-centered values, and accountability. The NIST AI Risk Management Framework (RMF) builds on this by offering a structured lifecycle approach: Map, Measure, Manage, and Govern AI risks. Meanwhile, IBM's governance models provide practical tools, such as AI FactSheets and bias auditing workflows, specifically created for enterprise deployment.

Verixa's inability to incorporate these governance principles was evident in three ways:

a) The company lacked documentation on traceability, including model versions and update logs.
b) Users lacked defined escalation procedures or override options for system failures.
c) Compliance gaps expose a widespread lack of accountability and oversight.

Responsible AI governance goes beyond just following rules. It also builds stakeholder trust, protects against lawsuits, and improves resilience during regulatory reviews. Because of this, these frameworks serve as a proactive guide in developing a practical governance model for product managers working in data-heavy companies in this study.

Counter Perspectives and Success Factors

While much of the literature emphasizes failure modes in AI deployment, an emerging strand of research documents conditions under which AI systems succeed, especially when sociotechnical alignment, iterative design, and adaptive leadership are prioritized. For example, Stephen (2025) discusses intelligent manufacturing systems that use IoT and AI for real-time quality control, citing cases where integration across data pipelines, human operators, and feedback loops led to efficiency gains and better compliance. These examples demonstrate that, under specific readiness conditions, AI can truly realize its transformative potential in high-stakes environments like pharmaceutical manufacturing.

De Paula et al. (2023) further argue that agile, human-centered deployment models focused on co-design, stakeholder feedback, and adaptive iteration are strongly linked to successful AI transformations. Unlike top-down approaches, these strategies view end users as contributors rather than passive recipients, aligning technical design with social dynamics. Such cases challenge the common narrative of resistance and failure by highlighting the role of inclusive design in enabling success.

Additionally, governance-first models, while growing in popularity, have faced some criticism. McKinsey & Company (2024) notes that in fast-paced sectors, too much focus on compliance early on can hamper innovation, especially when strict frameworks slow down experimentation. This view suggests a need for balanced governance that is structured enough to prevent harm but flexible enough to support learning cycles. Scholars like Graf and Burrell (2024) endorse this perspective by advising firms to view resistance not as a barrier but as valuable system feedback, which can lead to design improvements rather than shutdowns.

These counterperspectives do not dismiss the risks highlighted in the Verixa case but instead offer valuable contrasts. They demonstrate that AI's success depends not only on tools or governance but also on the adaptive interaction between design, leadership, readiness, and regulatory intelligence. In this context, Verixa's failure is not unavoidable; it results from unmet conditions that, if addressed differently, could have produced more favorable outcomes.

CASE STUDY ANALYSIS AND FINDINGS

Overview of the Case Study Approach

This case study uses a retrospective, interpretive approach based on qualitative analysis of Verixa Sciences' failed AI-enabled digital transformation. Guided by four theoretical frameworks (TOE, STS, ADKAR, and Responsible AI Governance), the study investigates causal factors, organizational dynamics, and overlooked risks that contributed to the breakdown. This chapter analyzes these findings thematically to provide actionable insights for practitioners overseeing large-scale AI deployments.

Organizational Background and Strategic Context

Verixa Sciences is a mid-sized pharmaceutical company focused on therapies for chronic conditions. In 2022, as part of a reshoring and resilience initiative, Verixa invested in a fully digital, AI-enabled domestic manufacturing plant. The main goal was to reduce dependence on overseas sources and improve agility through real-time inventory management, predictive analytics, and automation of regulatory reporting. While the transformation aligned with broader trends in digital health supply chains (Banaszak et al., 2023), this study will show that Verixa underestimated the organizational readiness and risk management required for such a change.

Key Findings by Thematic Area

Technological and Infrastructure Mismatches (TOE Perspective)

One of the key findings is a misalignment between Verixa's new digital tools and its legacy enterprise resource planning (ERP) systems. Automated quality control modules often generated false positives because of non-standardized data schemas, leading to shutdowns and production delays. A predictive analytics update conflicted with outdated middleware, causing a system crash that lasted three days.

These issues reflect the technological context of the TOE framework, where complexity and lack of compatibility hinder the diffusion of innovation (Tornatzky & Fleischer, 1990). Despite having access to high-potential technologies, Verixa lacked the middleware architecture and sandbox testing environment typically needed to manage digital integration risks.

Additionally, environmental pressures, such as FDA audit requirements and distributor SLAs, were not sufficiently considered during system selection and deployment. This oversight underscores the environmental context blind spot, where enthusiasm for digital solutions exceeds regulatory preparedness.

Change Management Breakdown and User Resistance (ADKAR Perspective)

User resistance emerged as a major barrier to successful implementation. Floor workers, quality inspectors, and supply managers all expressed frustration, confusion, and anxiety about the new digital tools. According to ADKAR analysis, the company did not succeed in any of the five stages.

a) Awareness: Change was communicated as a top-down mandate rather than a shared mission.
b) Desire: Workers feared job displacement and saw no personal benefit in learning new systems.
c) Knowledge: Training was limited to self-paced modules with no contextual relevance.
d) Ability: Staff lacked live practice environments or mentorship during rollout.
e) Reinforcement: No metrics, incentives, or feedback mechanisms were installed post-implementation.

These findings support studies that show digital transformation often fails due to a lack of psychological support (Hornstein, 2015). Employees were unprepared for the change, and the company's change agents were not sufficiently equipped to facilitate the necessary behavioral shifts.

Human-System Misalignment (STS Perspective)

From an STS perspective, Verixa's transformation focused mainly on technology, prioritizing software efficiency over redesigning workflows. Employees experienced increased cognitive load, unclear decision-making authority, and interface fatigue. Instead of modifying roles for digital collaboration, the company layered new systems onto existing job structures. This flawed approach led to feature misuse, inconsistent data entry, and the circumvention of digital compliance logs.

The lack of joint optimization between social and technical systems is a common problem in AI failures across industries (Clegg, 2000). Verixa's isolated IT and operations teams lacked a shared design forum or feedback loop. Participative design was missing, leaving users disempowered participants in a transformation that was meant to empower them.

Responsible AI Oversight Gaps

Verixa's governance practices did not align with the risk level of its AI systems. There were no documented audit trails, rollback logs for software updates, or contingency protocols for error overrides. The false-positive QC flag scenario, which resulted in three days of downtime, lacked a documented escalation process.

Using the NIST Risk Management Framework as a benchmark, Verixa did not properly conduct a "Map" or "Measure" stage before rollout (NIST, 2023). Likewise, OECD-aligned principles such as human oversight and fairness were ignored in practice, even if not intentionally. Verixa treated AI like traditional automation instead of as a probabilistic, evolving system that needs adaptive oversight.

Consequences of Failure

The consequences were substantial and complex:

a) Financial: A 22% drop in revenue attributed to delivery delays and production inefficiencies.

b) Reputational: Distributor relationships weakened due to missed SLAs.
c) Regulatory: The FDA issued a notice of deficiency due to missing validation logs and gaps in traceability.
d) Cultural: Internal morale deteriorated, with surveys revealing growing distrust in leadership and systems

These outcomes act as a warning for companies implementing enterprise AI without strong integration, governance, and user support.

DISCUSSION AND IMPLICATIONS

This study started by analyzing the systemic failure of Verixa Sciences' AI-driven digital transformation project. Although Verixa had access to advanced AI platforms and faced regulatory pressure to modernize, it failed because of misalignments in governance, infrastructure, human readiness, and oversight. The findings indicate that successful AI implementation in regulated, high-risk organizations requires more than just automation; it needs a comprehensive and solid implementation framework.

Theoretical Insights and Synthesis

The Technology–Organization–Environment (TOE) framework offered a comprehensive way to understand why the AI initiative failed. Technically, Verixa's integration clashed with existing systems; organizationally, leadership underestimated their readiness; and environmentally, they ignored the complexity of regulations. TOE showed that success in enterprise AI depends on alignment across all three areas: technology, internal capabilities, and external factors (Tornatzky & Fleischer, 1990). Companies should evaluate compatibility and readiness in all three TOE domains before investing in AI. A middleware strategy and digital maturity assessment should be essential steps prior to transformation.

ADKAR showed that failures in change management can be just as harmful as technical problems. A lack of structured awareness, desire, ability, and reinforcement creates a psychologically unsafe environment for change. Verixa's failure to address fears of job loss or provide hands-on training weakens trust and engagement. Human readiness is vital for AI integration. ADKAR should be used not only for rollout but also as a continuous tool to monitor and support behavioral change over time.

Socio-Technical Systems (STS) theory showed that Verixa developed systems focused on automation rather than human-machine collaboration. Employees were left out of the system design, which caused workflow conflicts, bypassing, and cognitive overload. STS theory highlights participatory design and joint optimization principles that Verixa lacked. AI transformations should include co-designing social and technical systems together. Use participative design methods and cross-disciplinary testing to reduce operational friction and improve acceptance.

Responsible AI frameworks (OECD, NIST, IBM) emphasize principles like transparency, human oversight, traceability, and risk mitigation. Verixa operated without proper governance, lacking logs, escalation paths, and clarity on intervention roles. AI governance must be prioritized both operationally and in regulation, not treated as an afterthought in ethics. Frameworks such as NIST's RMF or IBM's AI Fact Sheets should be incorporated into AI development SOPs, especially in sensitive sectors like pharmaceuticals.

Implications for Product Managers and Transformation Leaders

Verixa's collapse provides valuable lessons for practitioners working at the intersection of AI, product management, and transformation.

a) Product Managers must incorporate governance and risk foresight into product roadmaps, especially when deploying AI in production workflows.
b) IT leaders must invest in modular, testable architectures that enable safe integration of AI and ERP.
c) HR and Change Teams should implement ADKAR-aligned engagement strategies that emphasize both emotional preparedness and technical readiness.
d) Executives must view AI as a systems transformation, not just a tools upgrade, and allocate time, budget, and feedback cycles accordingly.

Relevance to the Pharmaceutical Industry

Verixa's case illustrates larger challenges in pharmaceutical manufacturing. Compliance, accuracy, and traceability are crucial. AI holds significant promise in predictive maintenance, QC automation, and demand planning, but only when utilized within a properly regulated framework.

For regulated industries, AI needs to be practical and auditable. The dangers of noncompliance extend beyond business losses to affect public health and legal exposure. Therefore, responsible AI governance is an advantage, not just a cost.

Conceptual Contribution to the Field

This study adds to the growing research at the intersection of AI, digital transformation, and organizational theory. By integrating four frameworks, TOE, STS, ADKAR, and Responsible AI, it offers a comprehensive evaluation model for diagnosing and preventing AI implementation failures. It highlights that a single factor rarely causes system failure. Instead, it is the accumulation of misalignments across people, processes, platforms, and principles that obstructs enterprise-scale transformation.

RECOMMENDATIONS AND CONCLUSION

Strategic Recommendations for Responsible AI Implementation

Based on the failure analysis of Verixa Sciences and grounded in the four guiding frameworks TOE, ADKAR, STS, and Responsible AI Governance, this section provides five structured, evidence-based recommendations. Each recommendation addresses specific systemic failures and aims to deliver actionable solutions for product managers, transformation leaders, and compliance officers overseeing enterprise-scale AI adoption.

Recommendation 1: Conduct a Comprehensive Digital Readiness Audit Before AI Implementation

Problem Addressed: Verixa deployed AI modules without evaluating infrastructure compatibility, resulting in production downtime, middleware crashes, and noncompliance.

Framework Anchor: TOE (Technology–Organization–Environment)

Implementation Guidance:

- Evaluate system interoperability with legacy software and middleware.
- Map out regulatory requirements, such as FDA traceability and auditability.
- Identify gaps in data architecture and compliance pipelines.

Success Metrics:

- Completion of a readiness audit report before pilot launch.
- % reduction in system downtime during integration.
- % compliance alignment in pre-deployment validation.

Recommendation 2: Deploy ADKAR-Aligned Change Management Protocols

Problem Addressed: Employees resisted system adoption due to fear, inadequate training, and a lack of engagement. No structured support was provided to manage this change.

Framework Anchor: ADKAR Model

Implementation Guidance:

- Build employee awareness through workshops and storytelling.
- Cultivate desire via engagement surveys and inclusion in decision-making.
- Deliver knowledge through hands-on training linked to real tasks.
- Strengthen ability through peer coaching and sandbox environments.
- Reinforce change via performance incentives and post-implementation feedback loops.

Success Metrics:

- Training completion rates and pre-/post-competency assessments.
- Employee sentiment improvement from baseline surveys.
- Active usage rates of AI systems across departments.

Recommendation 3: Reengineer Workflows Through Participatory Design

Problem Addressed: Verixa added AI tools without adjusting human workflows, causing confusion, role mismatch, and interface misuse.

Framework Anchor: Socio-Technical Systems (STS) Theory

Implementation Guidance:

- Create cross-functional design teams (operators, supervisors, IT).
- Map and redesign workflows to incorporate AI as a support, not a replacement, tool.
- Prototype job role changes and pilot in controlled settings before full rollout.

Success Metrics:

- % of workflows co-designed with end-users.
- Drop in reported incidents of system circumvention or feature misuse.
- Reduction in cognitive load indicators (task switching, errors).

Recommendation 4: Integrate Governance Protocols into AI Lifecycle

Problem Addressed: Verixa lacked audit logs, override systems, and escalation paths, breaching compliance and losing regulator trust.
Framework Anchor: Responsible AI Governance (NIST, OECD)
Implementation Guidance:

- Establish AI audit trails (e.g., model cards, decision logs).
- Define intervention thresholds and escalation protocols.
- Assign formal accountability roles (e.g., AI compliance officer, QA override steward).

Success Metrics:

- % of AI systems with audit logs and documented overrides.
- Number of regulatory deficiencies avoided or mitigated post-implementation.
- Speed of error resolution and accountability tracking.

Recommendation 5: Implement Continuous, Multiframe Evaluation of AI Projects

Problem Addressed: Verixa failed to monitor success across dimensions, focusing only on tool deployment instead of system-level impact.
Framework Anchor: Integrated use of TOE, ADKAR, STS, and Governance
Implementation Guidance:

- Build a project health dashboard combining metrics from all four frameworks.
- Monitor human-AI collaboration, training gaps, system efficiency, and compliance indicators.
- Use findings to iterate systems, retrain staff, or adjust governance in real time.

Success Metrics:

- Quarterly project health score based on integrated KPIs.
- Frequency of iterative adjustments (training, retraining, tuning).
- User feedback scores and audit results over time.

Contributions to Research and Practice

This study enhances both the academic understanding and practical implementation of AI-driven transformations, especially in regulated industries like pharmaceutical manufacturing. By combining four theoretical frameworks, TOE, ADKAR, STS, and Responsible AI Governance, it offers a comprehensive perspective on why enterprise AI projects often fail and how they can succeed.

Academic Contributions

Integrated Analytical Lens:

Existing research often relies on single-theory models to evaluate AI adoption. This study highlights the importance of integrating TOE, STS, ADKAR, and governance frameworks to better understand the complexities of AI transformation. Each framework identifies a specific failure domain: technological (TOE), human-process interaction (STS), behavioral dynamics (ADKAR), and regulatory ethics (Responsible AI).

Framework Synthesis for Diagnosis:

This research formalizes a diagnostic methodology that enables scholars and practitioners to identify failure points across various organizational subsystems. The findings indicate that high AI failure rates are not mainly technical but stem from systemic issues related to the misalignment of social, technical, and regulatory structures.

Theory-Informed Case Application:

Few case studies in responsible AI literature focus on real-world pharmaceutical deployments. By applying academic theory to a grounded, retrospective case, this research bridges the gap between conceptual models and practical application. It creates a theoretical connection between AI governance and change management research.

Practical Contributions

Actionable Playbook for Transformation Leaders:

The case highlights five clear, framework-aligned recommendations (Section 5.1), offering product managers, CIOs, and change leaders specific levers to address risks in AI integration, ranging from workflow redesign to governance protocols. These are intended for direct use in cross-functional, high-compliance environments.

Failure as Strategic Insight:

Verixa's collapse serves as a reverse blueprint for other organizations. The study shows that failed implementations provide just as much, if not more, insight as successful ones if evaluated through rigorous, theory-backed analysis.

Responsible AI as Operational Strategy:

Unlike most ethics discussions that stay conceptual, this case applies Responsible AI principles to system design, SOP development, and audit practices. It helps shift governance from being an afterthought to a proactive, strategic capability.

Limitations and Future Research

This study, while rich in analysis, is limited by its reliance on a single-case design within a specific high-regulation industry. Although the Verixa Sciences case offers profound insights into the complexities of AI failure in pharmaceutical manufacturing, it restricts the broader applicability of the findings to sectors like finance, education, or logistics. Future research should test the framework across a broader range of industries.

Second, the retrospective nature of this study introduces potential limitations in recall accuracy, reporting bias, and missing documentation. Although triangulated through multiple sources, some implementation failures may have been underreported or misunderstood due to the absence of real-time observation or ethnographic data.

A third limitation is the evolving regulatory landscape. Governance standards and AI technologies are rapidly changing. Some of the tools or frameworks referenced (e.g., NIST RMF, OECD principles) may evolve in ways that shift their relevance over time. Future studies should explore how adaptive governance frameworks evolve alongside emerging AI modalities such as generative models.

Future research could expand this work in three primary directions:

- Comparative case studies across industries to assess whether failure patterns and governance gaps vary.
- Development of a Responsible AI Maturity Model that integrates TOE, STS, ADKAR, and Governance into a predictive risk diagnostic tool.
- Exploration of participatory design strategies that operationalize STS and ADKAR in real-time implementation environments.

By addressing these gaps, future scholarship can expand on the foundations established here to improve both the theory and practice of responsible enterprise AI.

Final Reflections

AI holds transformative potential across regulated industries, but Verixa Sciences' collapse shows the high risks of poor implementation. The failure wasn't due to flawed technology but rather systemic issues: organizational unreadiness, weak governance, and disconnected change strategies. Without cohesive oversight and user-focused design, even well-funded AI projects can fail dramatically.

The insights gained from Verixa's experience confirm an essential truth: AI is more than just a technological upgrade; it represents an organizational change that requires new behaviors, structures, and governance models. Leaders must move beyond pilot enthusiasm or vendor promises to develop scalable and auditable systems based on human collaboration and organizational integrity.

This study highlights the importance of integrated frameworks like TOE, STS, ADKAR, and Responsible AI Governance, not as separate entities but as interconnected tools. Collectively, they offer a comprehensive diagnostic perspective to identify, anticipate, and address the sociotechnical barriers that hinder AI initiatives.

Ultimately, responsible AI transformation requires intentionality at every stage. Governance cannot be added after the fact. Change management cannot be handed off. Human insight cannot be ignored.

The Verixa case provides both a warning and a guide: to scale AI without disrupting the enterprise, organizations must align technology with purpose, people with process, and innovation with accountability.

REFERENCES

Accenture. (2024). Reinventing R&D in the age of AI. Accenture. https://www.accenture.com/us-en/insights/life-sciences/ai-biopharma

Baker, J. (2012). The technology-organization-environment framework. In Dwivedi, Y. K., Wade, M. R., & Schneberger, S. L. (Eds.), *Information systems theory: Explaining and predicting our digital society* (Vol. 1, pp. 231–245). Springer., DOI: 10.1007/978-1-4419-6108-2_12

Banaszak, I., Dworczak, P., & Stępień, S. (2023). Digitalization of pharmaceutical supply chains: Challenges and strategic responses. *Sustainability*, *15*(4), 3412. DOI: 10.3390/su15043412

Baumeister, R. F., & Leary, M. R. (1997). Writing narrative literature reviews. *Review of General Psychology*, *1*(3), 311–320. DOI: 10.1037/1089-2680.1.3.311

Burrell, D. N., Johnson, M. B., & Lim, J. (2023). Leveraging artificial intelligence to advance strategic performance management in volatile environments. *Review of Applied Socio-Economic Research*, *25*(1), 14–26. DOI: 10.2478/raft-2023-003

Clegg, C. W. (2000). Sociotechnical principles for system design. *Applied Ergonomics*, *31*(5), 463–477. DOI: 10.1016/S0003-6870(00)00009-0 PMID: 11059460

De Paula, D., Marx, C., Wolf, E., Dremel, C., Cormican, K., & Uebernickel, F. (2023). A managerial mental model to drive innovation in the context of digital transformation. *Industry and Innovation*, *30*(1), 42–66. DOI: 10.1080/13662716.2022.2072711

Deloitte. (2023). The state of AI in the enterprise. Deloitte Insights. https://www2.deloitte.com/us/en/insights/focus/cognitive-technologies/state-of-ai-and-intelligent-automation-in-business-survey.html

European Medicines Agency. (2023). Artificial intelligence workplan: A strategy for EMA. EMA. https://www.ema.europa.eu/en/about-us/how-we-work/big-data/artificial-intelligence-workplan-strategy-ema

Fivetran. (2025). Fivetran report finds nearly half of enterprise AI projects fail due to poor data readiness. https://www.fivetran.com/blog/report-enterprise-ai-projects-fail-data-readiness

Forbes Technology Council. (2024). Why AI projects fail: Lessons for enterprise leaders. Forbes. https://www.forbes.com/councils/forbestechcouncil/

George, S., Kate, J., & Frank, E. (2025). Strategic AI applications in multi-project management for biopharmaceutical innovation.

Graf, D. G., & Burrell, D. N. (2024). Utilizing resistance feedback for software implementation in healthcare. *Health Economics and Management Review*, *5*(1), 106–116. DOI: 10.61093/hem.2024.1-08

Hiatt, J. (2023). ADKAR: A model for change in business, government and our community. *Prosci*. https://www.prosci.com/resources/articles/adkar-model-overview

Hiatt, J. M. (2006). *ADKAR: A model for change in business, government, and our community*. Prosci Learning Center Publications.

Hornstein, H. A. (2015). The integration of project management and organizational change management is now a necessity. *International Journal of Project Management, 33*(2), 291–298. DOI: 10.1016/j.ijproman.2014.08.005

IBM. (2021). IBM global AI adoption index 2021. IBM Institute for Business Value. https://newsroom.ibm.com/IBMs-Global-AI-Adoption-Index-2021

Kapoor, A., & Vangala, S. (2024). The role of cross-functional collaboration in digital transformation success: A study across agile enterprises. *ResearchGate.* https://www.researchgate.net/publication/377458921

Lou, B., & Wu, L. (2021). AI on Drugs: Can Artificial Intelligence Accelerate Drug Development? Evidence from a Large-Scale Examination of Bio-Pharma Firms. *Management Information Systems Quarterly, 45*(3), 1451–1482. DOI: 10.25300/MISQ/2021/16565

McKinsey & Company. (2024). The state of AI in early 2024: Gen AI adoption spikes and starts to generate value. McKinsey & Company. https://www.mckinsey.com/capabilities/quantumblack/our-insights/the-state-of-ai

Mumford, E. (2000). A socio-technical approach to systems design. *Requirements Engineering, 5*(2), 125–133. DOI: 10.1007/PL00010345

National Institute of Standards and Technology. (2023). *Artificial intelligence risk management framework (NIST AI 100-1).* U.S. Department of Commerce., DOI: 10.6028/NIST.AI.100-1

National Institute of Standards and Technology. (2024). *Artificial intelligence risk management framework: Generative artificial intelligence profile (NIST AI 600-1).* U.S. Department of Commerce., DOI: 10.6028/NIST.AI.600-1

Nicholaus, K. (2024). 14 reasons why 70 to 80% of AI projects fail: Decoding the high failure rate of AI projects. Medium. https://medium.com/@kennethnicholaus

Oliveira, T., & Martins, M. F. (2011). Literature review of information technology adoption models at firm level. *Electronic Journal of Information Systems Evaluation, 14*(1), 110–121.

Organisation for Economic Co-operation and Development. (2019). Recommendation of the Council on Artificial Intelligence. OECD Legal Instruments. https://legalinstruments.oecd.org/en/instruments/OECD-LEGAL-0449

Organisation for Economic Co-operation and Development. (2023). OECD framework for the classification of AI systems. https://www.oecd.org/digital/artificial-intelligence/

Patel, J., Patel, D., & Meshram, D. (2023). *Artificial Intelligence in Pharma Industry- A Rising Concept. 1*(2).

Pazhayattil, A. B., & Konyu-Fogel, G. (2023). An empirical study to accelerate machine learning and artificial intelligence adoption in pharmaceutical manufacturing organizations. *Journal of Generic Medicines, 19*(2), 81–91. DOI: 10.1177/17411343221151109

Prosci. (2020). Best practices in change management (11th ed.). Prosci Inc. https://www.prosci.com/resources/articles/best-practices-in-change-management

RAND Corporation. (2024). *The root causes of failure for artificial intelligence projects and how they can succeed: Avoiding the anti-patterns of AI.* DOI: 10.7249/RRA2680-1

Sampene, A. K., & Nyirenda, F. (2024). Evaluating the effect of artificial intelligence on pharmaceutical product and drug discovery in China. *Future Journal of Pharmaceutical Sciences, 10*(1), 58. Advance online publication. DOI: 10.1186/s43094-024-00632-2

Stephen, G. (2025). Leveraging AI for Strategic Decision-Making in Biopharmaceutical Program Management: A Framework for Risk and Opportunity Analysis. *International Journal of Management Technology*, *12*(4), 1–26. DOI: 10.37745/ijmt.2013/vol12n4126

Tornatzky, L. G., & Fleischer, M. (1990). *The processes of technological innovation*. Lexington Books.

Trist, E. L., & Bamforth, K. W. (1951). Some social and psychological consequences of the longwall method of coal-getting. *Human Relations*, *4*(1), 3–38. DOI: 10.1177/001872675100400101

Yin, R. K. (2018). *Case study research and applications: Design and methods* (6th ed.). SAGE Publications.

Chapter 3
Reconciling Planning Discipline With Organizational Agility in Digital Transformation

Simon Cleveland
http://orcid.org/0000-0001-9293-3905
Purdue University Global, USA

Marisa Cleveland
Northeastern University, USA

ABSTRACT

Contemporary organizations face a fundamental paradox: the need for structured project planning versus the imperative to maintain agility in rapidly changing environments. This chapter challenges the false dichotomy between planning rigor and organizational responsiveness, demonstrating that properly designed planning processes enable rather than constrain adaptive capacity. Drawing on project management theory and empirical case studies, this analysis proposes an integrated framework for adaptive project planning tailored to digital transformation initiatives. The framework emphasizes contextual tailoring, integration across planning elements, structured flexibility, behavioral awareness, and continuous learning. Evidence from major project failures reveals that overruns typically result not from planning rigor itself, but from inadequate integration, insufficient change control, behavioral mismanagement of buffers, and communication breakdowns. The chapter concludes that disciplined planning and organizational agility represent complementary capabilities organizations must master.

INTRODUCTION

Contemporary organizations navigate a fundamental tension between structured planning for project success and flexibility in rapidly changing technological, market, and regulatory environments. This paradox intensifies during digital transformation initiatives, where organizations must cultivate agility while managing increasingly complex technological implementations. The challenge lies not in choosing

DOI: 10.4018/979-8-3373-4027-2.ch003

between planning and agility, but in understanding how these apparently competing imperatives can be reconciled—what we might term disciplined agility.

Disciplined agility represents a distinctive approach that differs fundamentally from conventional agility. While traditional agile methodologies often emphasize speed and flexibility, sometimes at the expense of systematic planning, disciplined agility recognizes that structure and adaptability are mutually reinforcing rather than contradictory. This concept serves as the conceptual foundation for this chapter, providing a destination point toward which the subsequent analysis builds.

The scholarly literature has long established that inadequate planning constitutes a primary driver of project failure, leading to cost overruns, schedule delays, and stakeholder dissatisfaction (Haugan, 2002; Project Management Institute, 2021; Rad, 2002). Decades of research demonstrate that projects lacking clear scope definition, realistic schedules, adequate resource allocation, and systematic risk management face substantially higher failure probabilities. Yet despite this robust evidence base, organizations pursuing agility sometimes mistakenly equate planning discipline with rigidity, viewing comprehensive planning as antithetical to responsive adaptation. This misconception creates a false dichotomy that ultimately undermines both planning effectiveness and organizational responsiveness.

The roots of this misconception lie partly in legitimate observations about the limitations of traditional project management approaches. Historically, many organizations have implemented planning processes that were indeed rigid, creating extensive documentation that quickly became obsolete and establishing approval processes that slowed decision-making to a crawl. These bureaucratic planning systems often prioritized conformance to process over achievement of outcomes, creating frustration among project teams and stakeholders alike. When agile methodologies emerged promising lighter-weight processes and greater responsiveness, many organizations embraced them enthusiastically, sometimes overcorrecting by abandoning planning discipline altogether. This overcorrection created new problems as projects lost the coordination and control benefits that effective planning provides.

Empirical evidence from large-scale infrastructure and technology projects demonstrates that systematic planning, when properly implemented and integrated, actually enhances rather than constrains organizational responsiveness. The key distinction lies not in whether organizations plan, but in how they plan and how effectively they integrate planning elements to support adaptive decision-making. Organizations successfully navigating complex digital transformations while maintaining agility share common characteristics: they tailor planning rigor to project characteristics, integrate planning elements to enable holistic assessment, establish governance structures enabling rapid decision-making within appropriate boundaries, and leverage planning artifacts as communication tools that align stakeholders.

This chapter addresses a central question: How can organizations leverage structured project planning to build sustainable disciplined agility in an era of continuous digital transformation? Drawing on foundational project management theory and empirical case studies, this analysis proposes an integrated framework that reconciles planning discipline with organizational agility. The framework acknowledges that different projects require different planning approaches, that planning must be dynamic rather than static, and that the purpose of planning is not to predict the future perfectly but to create the foundation for intelligent adaptation as conditions change.

THEORETICAL FOUNDATIONS

The Strategic Function of Project Planning

Project planning serves both tactical and strategic functions within organizations. At the tactical level, planning establishes the operational framework for resource allocation, task sequencing, and performance monitoring (Meredith & Shafer, 2022). These tactical functions enable day-to-day coordination, ensuring appropriate people work on appropriate tasks at appropriate times with necessary resources. Without this tactical foundation, projects devolve into chaos as team members work at cross purposes, resources are wasted through duplication or omission, and progress becomes impossible to assess objectively.

At the strategic level, planning aligns project execution with organizational objectives, stakeholder expectations, and competitive positioning. This strategic dimension ensures projects deliver business value aligned with organizational strategy rather than merely technical outputs. Strategic planning activities include defining project objectives in business outcome terms, identifying and engaging stakeholders essential for success, and establishing success criteria reflecting organizational priorities rather than arbitrary technical metrics. This dual function makes planning central not only to individual project success but also to broader organizational effectiveness and strategic execution.

The strategic dimension becomes particularly critical in digital transformation contexts, where technology implementation must serve broader business transformation objectives. Organizations implementing new technologies often focus heavily on technical specifications while losing sight of business capabilities and outcomes justifying the investment. Effective planning maintains connection between technical activities and strategic intent, ensuring implementation decisions serve business objectives and progress assessment focuses on value delivery rather than merely activity completion.

Haugan (2002) emphasizes that effective scheduling does more than sequence tasks logically. A well-constructed schedule provides foundation for reducing uncertainty through explicit identification of dependencies and constraints, establishing monitoring mechanisms enabling early problem detection, and facilitating stakeholder communication by creating shared understanding of project trajectory and key milestones. These functions prove essential for maintaining organizational agility, enabling rapid identification of deviations and supporting informed decision-making about adaptive responses.

Schedules become particularly valuable when they make explicit the logic connecting activities, the resources required for execution, and the risks that could disrupt progress. A schedule showing only activity names and dates provides minimal decision support. A schedule that additionally shows predecessors and successors for each activity, resource assignments indicating who is responsible for execution, and buffers protecting against identified risks becomes a powerful tool for coordination and adaptation. When problems arise, such a schedule enables rapid assessment of impacts and evaluation of response options. Project managers can quickly determine which activities are affected by delays, what resources might be redeployed to accelerate recovery, and whether buffers are adequate to absorb impacts without affecting project completion dates.

The Work Breakdown Structure as Foundation for Adaptive Planning

The Work Breakdown Structure constitutes the foundational element of project planning, providing hierarchical decomposition of project scope into manageable components that can be estimated, assigned, executed, and tracked (Project Management Institute, 2021). The WBS serves multiple critical functions simultaneously. First, it clarifies deliverables by explicitly identifying all products, services, and results the project must produce, preventing misunderstandings and creating shared stakeholder understanding. Second, it facilitates responsibility assignment by creating work packages at appropriate levels for delegation to individuals or small teams, preventing work from falling through cracks while avoiding confusion when multiple people believe they are responsible for the same work.

Third, the WBS enables resource estimation by breaking work into components small enough that required resources can be estimated with reasonable accuracy. Attempting to estimate resources for large, complex activities inevitably produces inaccurate results because estimators cannot adequately account for all detailed work involved. Decomposition into smaller components enables more accurate bottom-up estimation. Fourth, the WBS provides basis for progress tracking by creating measurable work packages against which completion can be assessed objectively. Without this decomposition, progress assessment relies on subjective judgment that often proves overly optimistic, leading to illusions of progress that mask underlying problems until they become severe.

Shenhar and Dvir (2007) argue persuasively that projects differ fundamentally along dimensions of novelty, complexity, technology, and pace, requiring differentiated planning approaches tailored to these characteristics. The novelty dimension captures how new the product or service is to the organization and market. Derivative projects produce incremental improvements to existing products. Platform projects create new generations of existing product lines. Breakthrough projects establish entirely new product categories. Higher novelty requires more adaptive planning with greater provisions for learning and adjustment as understanding evolves through development.

The complexity dimension captures the number and interdependencies of systems, subsystems, and components that must be integrated. Assembly projects involve single systems or devices. System projects involve complex integrated systems with substantial internal dependencies. Array projects involve widely dispersed systems that must be coordinated across multiple locations or organizations. Higher complexity demands more rigorous integration mechanisms and more structured communication to maintain coordination across diverse elements.

The technology dimension captures the level of technological uncertainty involved in development. Low-tech projects rely on existing, well-established technologies. Medium-tech projects employ mostly existing technologies with some new features or extensions. High-tech projects push the state of the art using technologies that exist but have not been proven at required scales or in required combinations. Super-high-tech projects depend on new technologies that do not yet exist or have not been proven feasible. Higher technological uncertainty requires more provisions for experimentation, prototyping, and plan revision as capabilities become better understood.

The pace dimension captures time pressure and urgency. Regular projects operate on normal timescales driven by efficiency considerations but without particular external pressures. Fast or competitive projects face time pressure from market competition requiring speed to capture first-mover advantages or respond to competitive moves. Time-critical projects face hard deadlines where project value collapses if deadlines are missed. Blitz projects face crisis situations requiring maximum speed regardless of cost. Higher pace requires more concurrent approaches where activities begin before all predecessor information is complete, accepting rework risks to compress schedules.

A software development project implementing proven technology in a familiar domain might structure its WBS around functional modules corresponding to user-facing capabilities, with each module decomposed into design, coding, testing, and integration activities following a standard template. The familiar technology and low novelty make this structured, templated approach appropriate and efficient.

In contrast, a project developing a novel application of emerging artificial intelligence technology might structure its WBS around learning cycles emphasizing experimentation, prototype development, evaluation, and refinement. Each cycle produces learning that informs subsequent cycles, with explicit provisions for pivoting approaches based on results. This structure explicitly acknowledges that requirements and solutions will evolve as stakeholders gain experience with emerging capabilities that cannot be fully specified upfront.

The absence of a clearly defined WBS creates cascading problems throughout project execution that compound over time and increasingly impair performance. Without structured decomposition, projects suffer from unclear task ownership, inaccurate resource and cost estimates, overlooked dependencies causing tasks to block one another unexpectedly, and inability to track progress against specific deliverables. Teams may report being ninety percent complete for extended periods while the final ten percent consumes as much time as the first ninety percent, a pattern indicating that early progress assessments were based on activities initiated rather than deliverables completed. These problems prove particularly acute in complex digital transformation initiatives involving multiple interdependent systems and stakeholder groups, where coordination failures can cascade rapidly to produce major disruptions.

Critical Chain Project Management and Behavioral Dynamics

Traditional project scheduling often embeds safety time within individual task estimates to provide buffers against uncertainty. While this appears prudent, it creates perverse behavioral incentives that undermine schedule reliability and systematically consume buffers even when genuine difficulties do not arise. Goldratt's Theory of Constraints identifies what has become known as student syndrome: the tendency to delay task initiation until the last possible moment when safety buffers exist (Rand, 2000; Steyn, 2001). The term derives from the observation that students often delay starting assignments until just before deadlines, then work intensively to complete them, despite having known about the assignments for extended periods.

This behavioral pattern emerges because individuals perceive safety time as permission to delay starting work. When team members know that tasks contain padding providing protection against difficulties, they lack urgency to start promptly. Instead, they defer starting work to focus on other priorities, tasks with more immediate deadlines, or activities they find more interesting or rewarding. The safety buffer intended to protect against genuine difficulties is consumed through delayed starts rather than protecting against technical challenges, unanticipated requirements, or integration problems.

This behavioral pattern becomes self-reinforcing through social learning and organizational culture development. As individuals observe that padded estimates rarely prove necessary because most tasks complete successfully once started, they develop habits of delayed initiation that become normalized within project teams. New team members learn these patterns from experienced members, perpetuating the dysfunction across generations of project participants. Organizations develop cultures where starting work early is viewed as naive or indicating that one has underestimated difficulty, while consuming all available time is seen as normal and expected.

When the occasional task does encounter genuine difficulty requiring additional time, the buffer has already been consumed through procrastination, leaving no remaining protection. The result is a project culture where tasks consistently expand to fill available time through Parkinson's Law, genuine uncertainties cause delays because protection has been squandered, and schedule reliability suffers despite buffers that should theoretically provide adequate protection. Project teams and stakeholders become cynical about schedules, viewing them as aspirational fiction rather than realistic commitments that guide work coordination.

Critical Chain Project Management addresses this behavioral dynamic through a fundamentally different approach to buffer management that consolidates safety buffers at the project or phase level rather than within individual tasks (Haugan, 2002; Steyn, 2001). In the CCPM approach, task duration estimates are aggressive, typically representing fifty percent confidence levels where half the time the task will take longer than estimated and half the time it will complete sooner. This aggressive estimation might seem risky, but the approach recognizes that with many tasks in a project, some taking longer than estimated while others complete sooner, creating natural averaging that reduces overall variability.

The time removed from individual tasks through aggressive estimation is then aggregated into project buffers placed at the end of the critical chain and feeding buffers placed where non-critical paths merge into the critical chain. The project buffer protects overall project completion dates against delays in critical chain activities. Feeding buffers protect the critical chain from delays in non-critical paths, preventing these delays from propagating to the critical chain and affecting project completion. This buffer structure provides equivalent or greater protection than distributing safety time within individual tasks, but without creating the perverse incentives leading to student syndrome.

Buffer consumption becomes a visible indicator of project health enabling early identification of problems and facilitating informed decisions about corrective actions. Project managers track buffer consumption against progress, typically using color coding where green indicates buffer consumption less than progress would predict, yellow indicates consumption roughly matching progress, and red indicates consumption exceeding progress and thus accelerating. This simple visualization makes schedule health immediately apparent to all stakeholders, enabling rapid recognition when problems emerge and prioritization of management attention to the most critical issues.

This approach encourages early task initiation while maintaining protection against uncertainty. When team members understand that task estimates do not contain padding and that delays affect successors directly, they recognize the importance of starting promptly and working efficiently. Social norms shift from viewing time consumption as normal to viewing early completion as desirable. Project teams begin competing to complete work ahead of schedule rather than viewing schedule conformance as adequate performance. This cultural shift transforms schedule management from administrative compliance to competitive advantage.

Empirical evidence from multiple industries demonstrates that CCPM reduces project duration and improves schedule reliability compared to traditional approaches. Studies have documented duration reductions of twenty-five to fifty percent and substantial improvements in on-time delivery rates. The behavioral insight underlying CCPM holds particular relevance for organizational agility beyond merely improving schedule performance. When teams focus on completing tasks early rather than consuming available time, projects build momentum and create options for adaptive responses to emerging information. Completed work provides learning that informs subsequent activities. Early completion creates schedule slack that can be used to accommodate changes or pursue opportunities. This proactive orientation supports agile adaptation while maintaining schedule discipline, reconciling what many perceive as competing objectives through behavioral management rather than complex analytical techniques.

Integrated Planning: Connecting Scope, Schedule, Resources, and Risk

A critical insight from project management research emphasizes that planning elements must be integrated rather than treated as independent activities that can be optimized separately (Meredith & Shafer, 2022; Rad, 2002). Changes to scope affect schedule and budget by adding or removing work requiring time and resources. Resource constraints alter feasible sequencing by preventing activities from proceeding in parallel when they compete for the same scarce resources. Identified risks require buffer allocation in schedules and contingency reserves in budgets to provide protection against potential impacts. Stakeholder requirements influence quality standards that determine verification efforts and potential rework. Each planning element connects to and depends on the others, forming an interconnected system rather than a collection of discrete plans.

This integration requirement becomes more demanding as project complexity increases because the number of interactions among elements grows geometrically with the number of elements involved. Digital transformation projects typically involve multiple technical domains including software development, infrastructure deployment, data migration, and system integration. They span cross-functional teams from IT, business units, procurement, legal, compliance, and communications. They engage external vendors providing software licenses, implementation services, hosting infrastructure, and ongoing support. They must accommodate evolving stakeholder requirements as understanding of capabilities and needs deepens through implementation. In these contexts, failure to maintain integration across planning elements leads to cascading failures when changes occur because impacts propagate through the system in ways that are not anticipated or managed.

Consider a healthcare organization implementing an electronic health records system. The initial scope might include basic patient demographic information, visit history, and medication records captured in a central database accessible to authorized clinicians. If stakeholders subsequently request adding laboratory results integration, medical imaging integration, clinical decision support providing evidence-based treatment recommendations, and patient portal functionality enabling patients to access their own records and communicate with providers, the scope has expanded substantially. Each addition requires software configuration or custom development, interface development to connect with external systems, data migration from legacy systems, testing to verify functionality and data integrity, user training to build capabilities, and change management to drive adoption.

Unless the schedule extends to accommodate the additional development, integration, testing, and training work required, and unless the budget increases to fund the additional software licenses, vendor services, infrastructure capacity, and internal labor, the project cannot succeed within original constraints. Yet organizations frequently approve scope additions without corresponding adjustments to time and cost, essentially demanding the impossible from project teams. This occurs partly because scope changes are approved by stakeholders focused on functionality without full appreciation of implementation implications, partly because change impacts are not rigorously assessed before approval, and partly because organizational dynamics create pressure to accommodate requests from powerful stakeholders even when impacts are understood.

The result is a project operating under impossible constraints where scope, schedule, and budget are mutually inconsistent. No amount of project management skill or team effort can overcome impossible constraints. The project will inevitably miss schedule targets, exceed budget allocations, or deliver reduced scope, yet each of these outcomes will be viewed as project failure even though the failure was created by leadership decisions approving incompatible constraints rather than by execution shortcomings.

This dynamic creates cynicism among project teams who view themselves as being set up for failure by organizational decisions beyond their control.

Scope definition must be ongoing rather than one-time, supporting continuous planning, scheduling, and control functions throughout the project lifecycle. This iterative approach recognizes that understanding evolves as projects progress, particularly for projects involving novelty where requirements cannot be fully specified upfront. Progressive elaboration refines understanding through successive iterations, with each iteration producing deliverables that enable stakeholder feedback that informs subsequent iterations. This cyclical planning approach aligns naturally with agile methodologies that emphasize iterative development and regular stakeholder engagement, while maintaining the discipline needed for complex, large-scale initiatives through integrated management of scope, schedule, cost, quality, and risk.

Integration mechanisms must ensure that changes in any planning element trigger assessment of impacts across all other elements. When scope additions are proposed, impact assessment evaluates additional work required, effects on the critical path, incremental costs, new risks introduced, and quality verification requirements. Based on this integrated assessment, decision-makers can make informed choices about whether to approve the change with corresponding adjustments to schedule and budget, reject the change to maintain original constraints, or approve the change with reduced scope elsewhere to remain within overall project boundaries. Without this integrated assessment, changes are approved based on partial information, creating the impossible constraint situations described above.

EMPIRICAL EVIDENCE

Scope Creep and Change Control Failures

Analysis of major project overruns consistently identifies scope creep as a primary driver of budget escalation and schedule delays (Keifer, 1996). Scope creep refers to the gradual expansion of project boundaries beyond original specifications, typically occurring through accumulated small changes that individually appear reasonable but collectively transform the project substantially. The term captures the insidious nature of this phenomenon, as scope expands incrementally through seemingly minor additions that do not trigger alarm individually but compound over time to create major impacts.

However, deeper analysis reveals that the underlying cause typically is not scope growth per se, but rather the absence of effective change control processes that would enable informed evaluation and management of scope evolution. Some degree of scope evolution is natural and even desirable in projects, particularly those involving innovation where understanding of requirements and possibilities deepens through the development process. Stakeholders gain insights as they see early deliverables and prototypes, leading them to request modifications that enhance value. Technical teams discover opportunities for improvement or integration that were not apparent during initial planning. Regulatory or market conditions change, requiring adaptation.

The problem arises not from legitimate adaptation itself, but from the absence of formal mechanisms for evaluating proposed changes, assessing their impacts on schedule and budget, obtaining appropriate approvals, and updating integrated project plans accordingly. The Sydney Opera House provides a canonical example of uncontrolled scope expansion. Initially budgeted at seven million dollars with a four-year timeline in 1957, the project ultimately consumed one hundred and two million dollars and sixteen years, finally completing in 1973 (Flyvbjerg, Holm, & Buhl, 2003). The massive overrun resulted primarily from continuous design changes throughout construction as architect Jørn Utzon repeatedly refined the iconic shell structure design, seeking engineering solutions that could realize his aesthetic vision.

Each refinement required redesign of structural elements, fabrication of new components using innovative techniques, and modification of construction sequences to accommodate the evolving design. The project became a living laboratory for developing new construction methods rather than implementation of a pre-defined design. Without adequate mechanisms for evaluating change impacts and controlling scope evolution, the project spiraled far beyond its original parameters. The absence of effective change control meant that design modifications were approved based on aesthetic and technical considerations without rigorous assessment of cost and schedule implications. By the time financial and schedule impacts became apparent, the project had accumulated so many changes that returning to the original design was no longer feasible. The project became a political issue with cost overruns debated in parliament, ultimately leading to Utzon's resignation in 1966 before completion. While the building is now recognized as an architectural masterpiece and iconic symbol of Sydney and Australia, the project process exemplifies planning and control failures that organizations should seek to avoid.

The Boston Big Dig provides another instructive case of change control failure in a very different context. This major infrastructure project aimed to relocate Boston's elevated Central Artery underground, simultaneously improving traffic flow and reclaiming surface space for community use, creating parks and public spaces where an elevated highway had previously divided neighborhoods. Initially estimated at 2.8 billion dollars in 1982, the final cost exceeded 14.6 billion dollars when the project substantially completed in 2007, an increase of more than five-fold in constant dollars (Greiman, 2013).

While design complexity and technical challenges including construction in difficult soil conditions, tunnel construction under active rail lines, and integration with existing transportation infrastructure contributed to cost growth, weak change control processes allowed continuous modifications without adequate impact assessment. Stakeholder requests for additional features including improved architectural treatments, enhanced landscaping, and public art installations added incremental costs. Engineering discoveries requiring design modifications including unanticipated soil conditions, conflicts with existing underground utilities, and structural issues with existing buildings affected by construction drove additional costs. Regulatory changes including enhanced environmental protection requirements and additional safety standards imposed during the extended project duration required design revisions and additional mitigation measures. The absence of rigorous change evaluation and approval processes meant these additions accumulated without corresponding adjustments to budget and schedule, creating impossible expectations that the expanded scope could be delivered within original constraints.

These cases illustrate a critical distinction organizations often miss. Some scope evolution proves necessary and valuable as projects progress and stakeholders gain new insights through the development and implementation process. In innovative projects especially, understanding of both requirements and possibilities naturally deepens as stakeholders experience early deliverables and see what becomes possible. Attempting to freeze scope completely ignores this learning process and can lead to delivering products that no longer meet stakeholder needs or miss opportunities for creating enhanced value. The problem arises not from legitimate adaptation that enhances value, but from the absence of formal mechanisms for distinguishing valuable adaptations from mere scope drift, evaluating proposed changes rigorously, assessing their impacts on schedule and budget comprehensively, obtaining appropriate approvals from stakeholders with authority and budget, and updating integrated project plans to reflect approved changes consistently.

Practical implications for today's digital transformation initiatives: Organizations implementing cloud migrations, AI systems, or enterprise platform modernizations should establish clear change control thresholds proportionate to change magnitude. Minor modifications within defined tolerances can receive expedited approval, while significant changes triggering material impacts on timeline, budget, or risk profile require rigorous evaluation and senior approval. This structured flexibility enables adaptive response while maintaining control.

Monitoring and Control Integration Gaps

Projects frequently fail not because of inadequate monitoring data, but due to poor integration between planning and monitoring systems that delays corrective action until problems become severe (Meredith & Shafer, 2022). This integration gap prevents early identification of deviations and undermines proactive risk management that could address problems while they remain manageable. Organizations may collect abundant performance data tracking technical progress, cost expenditures, schedule adherence, quality metrics, and risk indicators, yet fail to synthesize this information effectively for decision-making. Data remains siloed within functional specialties, preventing holistic assessment of project health. Problems recognized within technical teams do not reach project management or senior leadership promptly, allowing them to compound before triggering organizational response.

The Denver International Airport baggage system provides a compelling illustration of monitoring and integration failures. The project aimed to implement an automated baggage handling system utilizing destination-coded vehicles traveling at high speeds on tracks throughout the airport, automatically routing bags from check-in counters to aircraft and between connecting flights. Despite sophisticated technical monitoring tracking system performance, the project experienced cost overruns exceeding five hundred million dollars and delayed the airport opening by sixteen months (Montealegre & Keil, 2000).

A critical factor in the Denver failure was the disconnect between technical performance monitoring conducted by engineering teams and integrated project management that should have synthesized technical, schedule, cost, and risk information. Technical teams recognized that the system struggled to meet performance specifications, experiencing frequent malfunctions including bags damaged by high-speed collisions, vehicles derailing from tracks, and routing errors. However, this technical information was not effectively integrated with schedule and cost management processes. Technical problems were reported up the technical management chain, but parallel reporting through project management channels lagged substantially or presented overly optimistic assessments.

This organizational structure created information silos where technical specialists understood problems but lacked authority or organizational channels to escalate to decision-makers who could authorize fundamental changes in approach. Consequently, mounting technical problems did not trigger timely reassessments of project feasibility or appropriate escalation to senior decision-makers who could authorize adaptive strategies including simplifying the design, reducing scope, extending the schedule, or abandoning the automated system in favor of proven conventional approaches.

By the time senior management recognized the severity of technical challenges, the project had consumed most of its budget and schedule contingency. Options for response were severely constrained by resource depletion and time pressure. The eventual decision to open the airport with a manual baggage handling system while continuing to develop the automated system represented an expensive compromise forced by the absence of earlier intervention.

Earned Value Management provides a methodology for integrating cost and schedule monitoring by comparing planned value, earned value, and actual cost at regular intervals to enable early detection of variances (Haugan, 2002; Meredith & Shafer, 2022). When implemented consistently and integrated with the WBS, EVM enables early detection of variances and facilitates data-driven decisions about corrective actions before problems become severe.

However, EVM effectiveness depends on several conditions that organizations often fail to establish. The WBS must decompose work to appropriate levels enabling meaningful progress assessment. Progress must be measured objectively based on completed deliverables rather than subjective estimates. Data must be collected and analyzed regularly to provide timely signals. Results must be communicated to decision-makers who can authorize corrective actions.

Organizations cultivating disciplined agility require monitoring systems that facilitate rapid synthesis of information across technical, schedule, cost, and risk dimensions to enable informed adaptive responses before problems cascade.

Stakeholder Communication Breakdowns and the Human Dimension

Effective stakeholder communication emerges as a decisive differentiator between projects that contain problems early through proactive management and those that spiral out of control as problems compound while stakeholders remain unaware or unable to coordinate effective responses (Meredith & Shafer, 2022). Projects with structured communication protocols specifying what information will be shared with which stakeholders through which channels at what frequency, coupled with clear escalation pathways defining how issues requiring senior attention will be raised, manage to address emerging risks before they compound into major problems. Those with fragmented communication where information remains siloed within functional groups or levels of the organizational hierarchy suffer delayed interventions and mounting costs as problems progress unrecognized by those with authority to authorize effective responses or unaddressed because coordination failures prevent effective action even when problems are recognized.

The human and organizational dimensions of planning extend beyond communication protocols to encompass leadership style, organizational culture, and behavioral norms that shape how teams respond to plans and adapt to changing conditions. Leaders who create psychologically safe environments where team members feel comfortable surfacing problems early enable proactive problem-solving before issues cascade. Organizations that reward realistic estimation over optimistic promises develop cultures of honest assessment that support effective planning. Teams that celebrate early completion rather than merely conformance to estimates develop momentum that creates options for adaptive response.

Communication planning must specify what information will be shared, with whom, through which channels, and at what frequency, recognizing that different stakeholder groups have different information needs based on their roles and responsibilities (Project Management Institute, 2021). Senior executives need concise summaries focused on strategic issues, major risks requiring their attention, decisions exceeding project-level authority, and overall project health indicators. They lack time for detailed technical information and often lack technical expertise to interpret it effectively. Functional managers need information about resource demands on their personnel including when individuals will be needed, for how long, and at what intensity. They need advance notice of upcoming demands enabling them to plan allocation across multiple competing projects and to arrange backfill coverage for personnel on project assignments.

Team members need task-level information about dependencies indicating what information or deliverables they need from others, requirements specifying what their deliverables must satisfy, and schedules indicating when their work must complete. External partners need information about interfaces with their systems, deliverables they must provide, and coordination requirements enabling smooth interaction. For risk information specifically, communication requirements should vary based on risk severity and proximity to the critical path, with higher-severity risks and those affecting critical path activities requiring more frequent updates and broader distribution.

Critical path activities require frequent updates to the entire team because delays in these activities directly extend project duration, making them immediately consequential for overall project success. Team members working on successor tasks need early warning that their start dates may shift, enabling them to adjust their planning and resource commitments. Management needs the opportunity to consider expediting measures including assigning additional resources, authorizing overtime, or engaging external contractors to protect the schedule. When critical path tasks encounter problems, daily status updates may be warranted until the situation stabilizes, ensuring that all affected parties have current information enabling coordinated response.

The absence of structured communication protocols creates information silos where different parts of the project organization have different information about project status and emerging problems, preventing timely synthesis of warnings from different project areas into holistic assessment of project health and coordinated response. Technical teams might identify integration challenges. Procurement might experience vendor delays threatening critical path activities. The finance team might note budget pressure from higher-than-expected costs. Each signal individually might not trigger alarm since each specialty group sees only its portion of the project and cannot appreciate full implications. However, their combination indicates serious trouble requiring immediate management attention to authorize adaptive strategies.

Regular status meetings provide structured forums for information exchange and problem-solving, creating the integration points necessary for effective project management. Weekly project status meetings bring together functional leads to review progress, identify issues, and coordinate resolution. Monthly steering committee meetings engage senior management to review overall project health, address escalated issues, and authorize significant changes.

AN INTEGRATED FRAMEWORK FOR ADAPTIVE PROJECT PLANNING

Building on theoretical foundations and empirical evidence, this section proposes an integrated framework for adaptive project planning that reconciles structure with flexibility, enabling organizations to cultivate sustainable disciplined agility while maintaining project discipline necessary for coordinating complex initiatives. The framework provides guidance for tailoring planning approaches to project characteristics, integrating planning elements to enable coherent control, establishing governance structures supporting adaptive decision-making, and building organizational capabilities required for sustained effectiveness.

Framework Principles

The framework rests on five core principles that guide its application across varying project contexts and organizational environments:

1. **Context-Driven Tailoring**: Planning approaches must be tailored to project characteristics, particularly along dimensions of novelty, complexity, technology maturity, and required pace identified by Shenhar and Dvir (2007). Projects implementing proven technology in stable environments following well-established patterns can employ more standardized planning templates with confidence that historical experience provides reliable guidance. Such projects benefit from structured processes that capture organizational learning and ensure consistent application of best practices. In contrast, projects involving novel technology, operating in unfamiliar domains, or pursuing breakthrough innovation require more adaptive approaches with greater provisions for learning and adjustment as understanding evolves through development. These projects require lighter-weight planning that establishes direction and coordination mechanisms while maintaining flexibility to adapt as learning occurs.

Organizations that apply identical planning processes regardless of project characteristics waste effort on unnecessary detail while failing to address context-specific challenges adequately. Templates designed for large, complex, long-duration projects impose excessive overhead on small, simple, short-duration efforts, consuming time and resources that could better be directed to value-creating activities. Conversely, lightweight processes appropriate for small efforts fail to provide the structure and discipline needed for large, complex initiatives where coordination failures create severe consequences. Effective project management organizations develop portfolios of planning approaches tailored to different project types and establish criteria for selecting appropriate approaches for each project.

2. **Integrated Planning Elements**: Scope, schedule, resources, costs, quality, risks, and communication must be planned in an integrated manner with changes to any element systematically evaluated for impacts across all dimensions (Meredith & Shafer, 2022; Rad, 2002). This integration enables coherent project control where adjustments in one area trigger appropriate compensating adjustments elsewhere, maintaining internal consistency and realistic expectations. When scope expands, schedule and budget must be adjusted accordingly or scope in other areas must be reduced to remain within overall project constraints. When schedule compression is directed, implications for cost through overtime or additional resources and for risk through reduced buffers must be assessed and plans adjusted accordingly. Without this integration, projects experience internal inconsistencies where elements operate at cross purposes, creating impossible constraints where scope, schedule, and budget are mutually incompatible.
3. **Structured Flexibility**: Organizations need formal mechanisms for evaluating and implementing changes while maintaining project control. Disciplined agility requires discipline in change management, not the absence of change control. Organizations must be able to adapt to changing conditions including evolving stakeholder requirements, emerging technologies, competitive moves, and regulatory changes. However, adaptation must be managed through systematic assessment of implications rather than reactive accommodation of all requests. The change control process should be proportionate to change magnitude, enabling rapid approval of minor modifications that fall

within project tolerances while ensuring thorough evaluation of major changes that significantly affect scope, schedule, budget, or risk profile. This structured approach prevents both the rigidity that comes from refusing all changes and the chaos that results from accommodating all requests without systematic assessment.

4. **Behavioral Awareness**: Planning processes must account for behavioral dynamics that influence how individuals and teams respond to plans and incentives. People are not automatons who mechanically execute plans regardless of context or incentives. They respond to the environments and incentives that organizations create, sometimes in ways that defeat intended purposes. Planning processes must incorporate mechanisms that counteract dysfunctional behavioral tendencies including student syndrome where individuals delay starting work when buffers exist, optimism bias where individuals systematically underestimate difficulty, and information filtering where hierarchies suppress bad news. Process design should leverage behavioral insights to create incentives aligning individual and organizational interests.

Critical chain scheduling addresses student syndrome by consolidating buffers and creating social pressure for early starts. Bottom-up estimation addresses optimism bias by engaging multiple perspectives and requiring explicit consideration of risks and constraints. Structured escalation protocols address information filtering by creating legitimate channels for raising issues and protecting those who surface problems from retaliation. These behaviorally-informed process designs prove more effective than approaches that ignore human psychology and assume perfect rationality.

5. **Continuous Learning**: Planning should incorporate feedback loops enabling project teams to learn from variances and apply insights to refine estimates and approaches for subsequent phases or projects. Organizations that treat projects as isolated events miss opportunities to build capabilities through accumulated experience. Effective organizations capture lessons learned systematically, analyze patterns across projects to identify recurring challenges and successful practices, and incorporate insights into process improvements and training programs. This learning orientation transforms project execution from mere delivery to organizational capability building, where each project contributes to improved understanding of realistic schedules, accurate costs, and effective approaches for future work.

Framework Components

Contextual Assessment and Planning Approach Selection

The framework begins with contextual assessment and planning approach selection, recognizing that effective planning requires tailoring approach to project characteristics. Organizations should systematically evaluate project characteristics along dimensions identified by Shenhar and Dvir (2007) to guide planning approach selection and ensure that planning rigor and flexibility are appropriate to context.

The novelty dimension assesses whether the project involves derivative innovation extending existing products incrementally, platform innovation creating new generations of existing product lines, or breakthrough innovation establishing entirely new product categories. Derivative projects can leverage extensive historical experience, enabling detailed upfront planning with confidence. Platform projects require moderate adaptation as some elements are familiar while others are new. Breakthrough projects require extensive adaptation as little historical experience provides guidance.

The complexity dimension evaluates how many interconnected systems, components, and stakeholder groups the project must coordinate. Higher complexity demands more rigorous integration mechanisms across planning elements and more structured communication protocols to maintain coordination among diverse parties.

The technology dimension assesses whether the project relies on proven technology with well-established performance characteristics, high technology pushing the state of the art, or super-high technology relying on new or unproven technologies. Projects employing proven technology can plan with confidence based on historical performance data. Projects employing super-high technology require provisions for experimentation, prototyping, and plan revision.

The pace dimension evaluates time urgency governing the project. Higher pace requires more concurrent engineering approaches where activities begin before all predecessor information is complete, accepting rework risk to compress schedule. It also requires more streamlined decision-making with authority delegated closer to the work.

Comprehensive Scope Definition

Following contextual assessment informing approach selection, comprehensive scope definition proceeds through development of a formal scope statement and WBS that decompose deliverables into manageable components (Haugan, 2002; Project Management Institute, 2021). The scope statement articulates project objectives in measurable terms specifying desired outcomes and success criteria, enabling objective assessment of whether the project achieved its purposes. It identifies major deliverables and their acceptance criteria, establishes clear targets for what the project will produce, documents explicit exclusions clarifying what the project will not deliver, records key assumptions and constraints, and captures known risks and dependencies that affect feasibility.

The WBS then decomposes scope into work packages appropriate for assignment to individuals or small teams, with decomposition depth tailored to project characteristics and team needs. For well-understood work performed by experienced teams, higher-level decomposition may suffice. For complex work involving novel activities or inexperienced teams, more detailed decomposition provides needed structure and clarity.

Critically, scope definition must be coupled with formal change control mechanisms ensuring that scope evolution is managed through systematic assessment rather than reactive accommodation. A change request process specifies information required for evaluating proposed changes including description, rationale, anticipated benefits, and estimated impacts on scope, schedule, cost, quality, and risk.

Defined authority levels indicate who can approve changes of different magnitudes, enabling rapid response to minor changes while ensuring appropriate oversight of major changes. Documentation requirements ensure that approved changes are recorded systematically and that integrated project plans are updated consistently across all planning elements. Change documentation captures the description, rationale, impacts, approvals, and implementation date, creating an audit trail that supports accountability and learning.

Critical Chain Scheduling

The framework incorporates critical chain project management principles to address behavioral dynamics while maintaining schedule discipline (Haugan, 2002; Steyn, 2001). Schedule development begins with creating a logic network showing task dependencies and sequencing based on the WBS, making explicit which tasks must be completed before others can begin, which can proceed in parallel given sufficient resources, and which share common resources creating sequencing constraints.

Resource-leveled scheduling then develops a schedule that accounts for resource constraints and avoids overallocation. When multiple tasks compete for the same scarce resources, they cannot all proceed simultaneously despite lacking logical dependencies. Resource leveling resolves these conflicts by sequencing tasks to respect resource availability, delaying starts of lower-priority tasks when resources are fully allocated to higher-priority work. This produces a realistic schedule that can actually be executed with available resources.

Critical chain identification determines the longest chain of dependent tasks considering both logical dependencies and resource constraints, representing the true constraint on project duration. Understanding the critical chain enables focused management attention on the activities that truly determine project duration and identification of buffers needed to protect completion dates.

Task duration estimates are developed without safety padding, representing approximately fifty percent confidence levels. The time removed from individual tasks is aggregated into project buffers placed at the end of the critical chain and feeding buffers placed where non-critical paths merge into the critical chain.

Buffer management becomes a central control mechanism. Buffer consumption is tracked against progress, with color coding (green, yellow, red) making status immediately apparent, enabling systemic assessment of project health and targeted intervention.

Disciplined Cost Estimation

Disciplined cost estimation uses bottom-up approaches building from work package estimates to achieve accuracy through aggregation of detailed assessments (Rad, 2002). Estimation begins with the WBS ensuring all required work has been identified. For each work package, estimators assess resources needed including labor hours by skill level, materials and supplies, equipment rental or usage, and subcontractor services. These resource requirements are converted to costs using appropriate rates including labor rates reflecting wages, benefits, and overhead, material prices, equipment costs, and subcontractor quotes.

Work package cost estimates are aggregated following the WBS hierarchy, with additions at each level for management effort, integration effort, and risk reserves. Cost estimates must be traceable to the WBS, enabling earned value analysis during execution.

Estimates should include explicit contingency reserves sized appropriately to identified risks and overall project uncertainty. Projects involving proven technology might require contingency of ten to fifteen percent. Projects involving novel technology might require thirty to fifty percent or more. These reserves should be held at appropriate organizational levels with authority to allocate them.

Proactive Risk Management

Proactive risk management incorporates systematic identification, assessment, response planning, and ongoing monitoring to address uncertainties that could affect project success (Project Management Institute, 2021; Shrivastava, 2012). Risk identification proceeds systematically across multiple categories ensuring comprehensive coverage. Technical risks involve uncertainties about whether solutions will meet performance requirements given immature technologies, untested integration approaches, or demanding specifications. Schedule risks involve uncertainties about task durations given novel work, dependencies on external parties, or aggressive estimates. Cost risks involve uncertainties about resource requirements, market prices, or scope growth. Resource risks involve uncertainties about personnel or equipment availability. Stakeholder risks involve uncertainties about requirements stability, acceptance criteria, or political support. External risks involve uncertainties about regulatory changes, market shifts, competitor moves, or supplier performance.

Risk identification employs multiple techniques including brainstorming sessions with diverse participants, checklists derived from historical experience, assumption analysis examining whether assumptions underlying plans might prove invalid, and dependency analysis identifying external parties or events that could affect success. Each identified risk is documented in a risk register capturing description, category, potential causes, and potential impacts.

Risk assessment evaluates identified risks qualitatively using probability and impact scales to enable prioritization. Probability scales typically use five levels from very low (under ten percent) to very high (over seventy percent). Impact scales use five levels from negligible to severe based on effects on scope, schedule, cost, and quality. The product of probability and impact scores yields a risk severity score enabling prioritization with high-probability, high-impact risks receiving priority attention for response planning.

Response strategies are developed for high-priority risks based on systematic consideration of options. Avoidance strategies eliminate risks by changing project approaches, such as using proven rather than novel technology. Transfer strategies shift risk consequences to other parties through insurance, warranties, or contractual provisions. Mitigation strategies reduce probability or impact through preventive actions including prototyping, developing backup sources, or adding schedule buffers. Acceptance strategies acknowledge risks without specific preventive actions, relying on contingency reserves to address impacts if risks materialize.

Risk response triggers define conditions indicating when responses should be implemented, enabling proactive action before full risk impacts materialize. Clear ownership is assigned for monitoring each risk and implementing responses when triggers activate, ensuring accountability. Risk assessments are updated regularly as projects progress, with new risks added as they emerge, existing risks reassessed as conditions change, and resolved risks retired from active tracking.

Quality Planning

Quality planning defines specific, measurable acceptance criteria for each major deliverable, establishing clear targets enabling objective verification of whether deliverables meet requirements. Technical performance specifications establish quantitative standards including throughput rates, response times, accuracy levels, capacity limits, and interface specifications. Functional requirements describe what deliverables must do from a user perspective including capabilities provided, workflows supported, and business rules implemented. Quality standards reference applicable industry or organizational standards.

Inspection, test, and review procedures specify how conformance will be verified including who will conduct verification, what methods will be used, what evidence will be documented, and what criteria will determine acceptance. Procedures for addressing non-conformances establish how defects will be documented, corrected through rework or replacement, and reverified.

In regulated environments such as pharmaceuticals, aerospace, or financial services, quality planning must integrate regulatory compliance requirements explicitly. Quality plans should reference specific regulatory requirements, map project deliverables to regulatory submissions, establish quality checkpoints aligned with regulatory reviews, and maintain traceability demonstrating that requirements were met.

Structured Communication and Escalation

Structured communication and escalation planning addresses stakeholder information needs systematically. Stakeholder analysis identifies all relevant stakeholders including project sponsors, steering committees, project team members, functional managers, end users, operations staff, vendors, and regulatory bodies. For each stakeholder group, the analysis captures their interest in the project, their influence on success, and their information needs based on their roles.

A communication matrix defines what information will be communicated, to whom, how frequently, through which channels, and by whom. The matrix typically includes weekly status reports to project teams and functional managers, monthly executive summaries to senior management highlighting overall status and major issues, ad hoc issue notifications when problems emerge, milestone reviews engaging stakeholders to review deliverables, and change notifications informing stakeholders when approved changes affect scope, schedule, or responsibilities.

Escalation protocols establish clear thresholds and procedures for escalating issues requiring senior decision-making, ensuring issues reach appropriate decision-makers promptly without overwhelming executives. Protocols specify conditions triggering escalation such as risks exceeding project manager authority, conflicts requiring senior mediation, or changes affecting project scope beyond delegated limits. Escalation paths typically proceed through functional management to program management to executive sponsors based on issue severity.

Feedback mechanisms create channels for stakeholders to provide input outside formal reporting cycles, including anonymous hotlines, open-door policies, and designated ombudsmen.

Integrated Monitoring, Control, and Adaptation

Integrated monitoring, control, and adaptation complete the framework by establishing systematic processes for tracking performance, identifying variances, and implementing corrective actions. Earned Value Management calculates planned value representing budgeted cost of scheduled work, earned value representing budgeted cost of completed work, and actual cost representing expenditures incurred (Haugan, 2002; Meredith & Shafer, 2022). Comparison enables calculation of schedule variance, cost variance, Schedule Performance Index, and Cost Performance Index. These metrics provide early warning of problems, enabling corrective action before variances become severe.

Buffer monitoring tracks buffer consumption in critical chain schedules to assess schedule health. Buffer status is calculated by comparing percentage of buffer consumed to percentage of critical chain completed, with color coding making status immediately apparent. Green status indicates healthy schedule performance with protection intact. Yellow status suggests nominal performance where uncertainty is being absorbed by buffers as intended. Red status indicates problems requiring management attention and possible intervention.

Variance analysis investigates significant deviations to understand root causes and develop corrective actions. Investigation must determine why variance occurred, whether it represents a one-time event or persistent trend, and develop corrective action options including adding resources, descoping, improving productivity, or adjusting baselines.

Change integration ensures that approved changes are reflected consistently across scope, schedule, cost, quality, and risk plans, maintaining coherence essential for effective control. This integration prevents internal inconsistencies that would undermine performance measurement and decision-making.

Lessons learned processes capture insights from variances and successes for application to subsequent activities or projects. Organizations should establish systematic processes including post-milestone reviews, mid-project reviews, and post-project reviews. Lessons should be documented in accessible repositories and incorporated into training, templates, and processes.

Framework Implementation Considerations

Implementing this integrated framework requires organizational capabilities that must be developed systematically. Project management competency demands personnel with training in contemporary methodologies including critical chain scheduling, earned value management, risk quantification, and stakeholder analysis. Organizations should invest in formal training through accredited programs and support experiential learning through mentoring programs pairing experienced practitioners with developing project managers.

Tool infrastructure requirements include project management software supporting WBS development, network scheduling with resource leveling, earned value calculation, risk register maintenance, and dashboard reporting. Tools should integrate with enterprise systems including resource management, financial systems, and portfolio management systems. This integration enables organization-level resource optimization while reducing administrative burden through elimination of redundant data entry.

Governance structures provide organizational frameworks through which project management operates effectively. Established approval authorities clarify decision-making authority, preventing delays while ensuring oversight. Project managers need delegated authority for routine decisions. Change control boards evaluate significant changes with appropriate stakeholder representation. Escalation pathways connect project teams to senior decision-makers systematically.

Performance culture encompasses organizational norms fundamentally influencing behavior. Cultures valuing realistic estimation over optimistic reporting support honest assessment and early problem identification. Cultures punishing bearers of bad news drive problems underground, forcing reactive crisis management. Learning orientation reflects organizational willingness to examine variances objectively and update approaches based on evidence.

Organizations lacking these capabilities should develop them through phased approaches. Initial phases might establish scope definition and change control. Subsequent phases could add scheduling and buffer management. Later phases might incorporate earned value management and risk management. This graduated implementation allows organizations to build capabilities progressively while demonstrating value at each stage.

IMPLICATIONS FOR DIGITAL TRANSFORMATION AND FUTURE DIRECTIONS

Digital Transformation as a Context for Adaptive Planning

Digital transformation initiatives represent particularly compelling contexts for adaptive project planning given their characteristic combinations of technology uncertainty, system complexity, organizational change requirements, stakeholder diversity, and competitive pressure. Organizations pursuing digital transformation must simultaneously implement new technologies, redesign business processes, develop new capabilities, and shift organizational culture. These initiatives often involve emerging technologies whose capabilities and limitations are incompletely understood, requiring provisions for experimentation and learning. They typically span multiple organizational units with different priorities and operating models, requiring extensive coordination and change management. They face pressure to deliver quickly to capture competitive advantages or respond to market disruption, requiring concurrent approaches that accept higher risk to compress timelines.

The integrated framework proposed in this chapter proves particularly valuable for digital transformation initiatives because it explicitly addresses these characteristics. Contextual assessment guides organizations to select planning approaches appropriate to the novelty, complexity, technology maturity, and pace of their specific transformation initiatives rather than applying uniform templates. Integration across planning elements ensures that technical implementation, organizational change, stakeholder engagement, and risk management proceed coherently rather than as disconnected activities. Structured flexibility through disciplined change management enables organizations to adapt as understanding evolves while maintaining overall direction and resource constraints. Behavioral awareness in process design addresses the cultural and motivational challenges inherent in transformation initiatives that require sustained effort over extended periods.

Building Organizational Capabilities for Sustained Agility

Organizations pursuing sustainable disciplined agility recognize that capability development represents a strategic imperative rather than merely a tactical concern. The capabilities required for effective adaptive project planning—systematic analysis, integrated thinking, disciplined decision-making, honest communication, and continuous learning—prove valuable far beyond individual projects. These capabilities enable organizations to sense and respond to environmental changes, coordinate complex activities across boundaries, make informed decisions under uncertainty, and improve continuously through experience. Organizations that develop these capabilities systematically gain competitive advantages that prove difficult for competitors to replicate because they rest on accumulated experience, established processes, shared values, and organizational culture that cannot be quickly copied.

Capability development requires sustained investment and leadership commitment over extended periods. Organizations cannot develop sophisticated project management capabilities through one-time training programs or tool implementations. Instead, they must pursue systematic approaches including formal education establishing foundational knowledge, apprenticeship programs enabling skill development through guided practice, community development fostering knowledge sharing among practitioners, process refinement incorporating lessons learned into improved approaches, and cultural evolution establishing values and norms supporting effective practices. Senior leaders must champion these initiatives, providing resources, removing obstacles, recognizing achievements, and modeling desired behaviors.

The role of leadership in fostering disciplined agility cannot be overstated. Leaders who articulate a clear vision connecting project delivery to strategic objectives provide purpose that motivates sustained effort. Leaders who model transparency about challenges and uncertainties create cultures where realistic assessment is valued over optimistic reporting. Leaders who protect teams from organizational dysfunction enable focus on value-creating work rather than political maneuvering. These leadership behaviors prove essential for developing the organizational culture supporting disciplined agility.

Future Research Directions

While this chapter synthesizes substantial existing research and practice wisdom, numerous opportunities exist for future research that could further advance understanding of adaptive project planning in digital transformation contexts. Longitudinal studies tracking organizations over extended periods as they develop project management capabilities could illuminate effective capability development approaches and common pitfalls to avoid. Comparative studies examining how different organizational contexts—industry sectors, organizational sizes, national cultures, regulatory environments—influence effective planning approaches could provide more nuanced guidance for tailoring. Experimental studies testing specific interventions such as alternative buffer management approaches, communication protocols, or change control mechanisms could identify highest-impact practices.

Research examining the relationship between project planning practices and organizational outcomes including innovation, agility, employee engagement, and sustained performance could strengthen the business case for investment in planning capabilities. Investigation of how emerging technologies including artificial intelligence, advanced analytics, and collaboration platforms might enhance planning processes could identify opportunities for innovation in project management practice. Studies examining the psychological and behavioral dimensions of planning including how cognitive biases influence estimation, how social dynamics affect communication, and how organizational culture shapes responses to plans could inform more effective process designs.

CONCLUSION

Toward Disciplined Agility Through Structured Planning

This chapter has examined the relationship between project planning discipline and organizational agility, challenging the misconception that these represent opposing values. The analysis demonstrates that structured planning, when properly implemented and integrated, enables rather than constrains organizational agility by creating visibility, shared understanding, and decision frameworks necessary for effective adaptation.

The concept of disciplined agility synthesizes the apparently competing imperatives of structure and flexibility, demonstrating that methodological discipline enhances rather than restricts adaptive capacity. Organizations achieving disciplined agility develop systematic approaches to contextual assessment, integrated planning, behavioral management, and continuous learning that enable them to coordinate complex initiatives while maintaining responsiveness to changing conditions. This capability rests not only on technical methodologies but also on organizational culture, leadership commitment, and shared values that support honest communication, realistic assessment, and continuous improvement.

Project overruns typically result not from planning rigor itself, but from inadequate integration of planning elements, insufficient change control mechanisms, behavioral mismanagement of schedule buffers, and stakeholder communication breakdowns. The Sydney Opera House, Boston Big Dig, and Denver Airport cases illustrate how absence of planning discipline leads to reactive crisis management rather than proactive adaptation.

Effective planning must be contextually tailored to project characteristics including novelty, complexity, technology maturity, and pace. Critical chain project management principles provide valuable approaches for improving schedule reliability through behavioral management. Integration across planning elements proves essential for maintaining coherent project control and enabling informed decision-making.

The integrated framework provides organizations with a systematic approach for cultivating disciplined agility while maintaining project discipline. Digital transformation initiatives provide particularly compelling contexts for adaptive project planning given their characteristic combinations of technology uncertainty, system complexity, and organizational change requirements.

Organizations need not choose between planning discipline and agility. Rather, they must develop capabilities that enable disciplined agility: the ability to maintain systematic coordination and control while adapting responsively to changing conditions. In an era of continuous digital transformation, this disciplined agility constitutes a necessity for organizational survival and competitive success.

REFERENCES

Flyvbjerg, B., Holm, M. K. S., & Buhl, S. L. (2003). How common and how large are cost overruns in transport infrastructure projects? *Transport Reviews, 23*(1), 71–88. DOI: 10.1080/01441640309904

Greiman, V. A. (2013). *Megaproject management: Lessons on risk and project management from the Big Dig*. John Wiley & Sons. DOI: 10.1002/9781118671092

Haugan, G. T. (2002). *Project planning and scheduling*. Management Concepts.

Keifer, S. C. (1996). Scope creep... not necessarily a bad thing. *PM Network, 10*(5), 33–35.

Meredith, J. R., & Shafer, S. M. (2022). *Project management: A managerial approach* (11th ed.). John Wiley & Sons.

Montealegre, R., & Keil, M. (2000). De-escalating information technology projects: Lessons from the Denver International Airport. *Management Information Systems Quarterly, 24*(3), 417–447. DOI: 10.2307/3250968

Project Management Institute. (2021). *A guide to the project management body of knowledge (PMBOK® guide)* (7th ed.). Project Management Institute.

Rad, P. F. (2002). *Project estimating and cost management*. Management Concepts.

Rand, G. K. (2000). Critical chain: The theory of constraints applied to project management. *International Journal of Project Management, 18*(3), 173–177. DOI: 10.1016/S0263-7863(99)00019-8

Shenhar, A. J., & Dvir, D. (2007). How projects differ, and what to do about it. In Morris, P. W. G., & Pinto, J. K. (Eds.), *The Wiley guide to project, program, and portfolio management* (pp. 1265–1286). John Wiley & Sons.

Shrivastava, N. K. (2012). Project risk management—Another success-boosting tool in a PM's toolkit. Paper presented at PMI® Global Congress 2012—North America, Vancouver, British Columbia, Canada. Project Management Institute.

Steyn, H. (2001). An investigation into the fundamentals of critical chain project scheduling. *International Journal of Project Management, 19*(6), 363–369. DOI: 10.1016/S0263-7863(00)00026-0

Chapter 4
Quality-Driven Digital Transformation:
Building Organizational Agility Through Systematic Technology Implementation

Simon Cleveland
http://orcid.org/0000-0001-9293-3905
Purdue University Global, USA

Marisa Cleveland
Northeastern University, USA

ABSTRACT

This chapter examines how systematic quality management enables organizational agility through technology adoption. Drawing on frameworks and case studies, we demonstrate that sustainable agility requires embedding quality throughout digital transformation—from planning through execution and improvement. The chapter synthesizes quality methodologies with technology strategies, emphasizing leadership's role in fostering quality-driven cultures. By examining metrics, audits, and stakeholder engagement, this research provides insights for cultivating agility while maintaining excellence. Successful transformation demands more than technology; it requires systematic quality approaches permeating culture, aligning stakeholders, and establishing accountability. This guide serves leaders and practitioners building resilient, agile organizations.

INTRODUCTION

The Paradox of Speed and Quality in Digital Transformation

Organizations today face an existential imperative: transform digitally or risk obsolescence. Market disruptions arrive with increasing frequency, technological innovations reshape competitive landscapes overnight, regulatory frameworks evolve rapidly, and customer expectations shift continuously. Yet this urgency creates a dangerous paradox. Leaders feel immense pressure to move quickly, often believing

DOI: 10.4018/979-8-3373-4027-2.ch004

they must sacrifice quality for speed. This assumption proves not only incorrect but actively harmful to the very agility organizations seek.

Consider the sobering reality: substantial evidence across multiple studies indicates that a majority of digital transformation initiatives fail to meet their objectives. These failures rarely stem from technological limitations. Instead, they originate from organizational and process-related challenges—inadequate planning, poor change management, and insufficient attention to quality throughout implementation. When organizations rush technology adoption without systematic quality management, they experience system failures, user resistance, budget overruns, and diminished organizational capability rather than enhanced agility.

This chapter challenges the false dichotomy between quality and speed. We propose that quality management does not constrain agility—it enables it. Far from representing bureaucratic overhead that slows transformation, systematic quality management provides the structured framework necessary for organizations to move quickly while minimizing risk and ensuring that technology investments deliver tangible value rather than simply creating disruption.

The Integration Imperative

The convergence of quality management and technology adoption represents more than theoretical elegance—it addresses a critical practical need. Organizations implementing technology without quality discipline repeatedly discover that initial speed gains evaporate when quality failures necessitate expensive remediation and schedule delays. Conversely, organizations that embed quality considerations from project inception minimize costly rework that inevitably affects scope, timeline, and budget (Reaiche, 2022).

Quality management scholars emphasize that organizations must proactively integrate quality from the beginning rather than treating it as an afterthought. When quality planning occurs early in project lifecycles, teams make better initial decisions, identify issues while they remain small and manageable, and avoid the ambiguity and conflict that arise from subjective quality assessments. This proactive stance proves essential because addressing quality defects early minimizes the rework that consumes additional time, money, and organizational resources.

Chapter Scope and Contribution

This chapter synthesizes insights from quality management literature and applies them specifically to technology adoption and digital transformation contexts. We examine how the fundamental phases of quality management—planning, assurance, control, monitoring, and continuous improvement—can be systematically applied to technology projects to enhance rather than constrain organizational agility.

Furthermore, we explore the critical role of leadership in building quality-driven cultures that embrace technological change as improvement opportunity rather than viewing quality and agility as competing priorities. The chapter draws lessons from diverse industries, including healthcare's rigorous quality management practices, to provide cross-industry insights that technology organizations can adapt rather than reinventing quality management from first principles.

Our contribution centers on demonstrating that quality and agility represent mutually reinforcing capabilities rather than contradictory objectives. Organizations achieve sustainable agility by building quality into their processes, products, and culture. The systematic documentation and reflection that quality management demands creates organizational memory that accelerates future initiatives, progressively improving organizational capability (Project Management Institute, 2017). This learning accumulation represents a critical component of organizational agility—organizations that learn systematically from experience adapt more quickly and effectively than those that repeat mistakes due to inadequate knowledge capture and transfer.

THEORETICAL FOUNDATION

The Project Management Lifecycle as Quality Framework

Effective technology adoption requires a structured approach that mirrors established project management principles. The Project Management Body of Knowledge framework provides five fundamental phases that guide successful project execution: initiation, planning, execution, monitoring and controlling, and closure (Project Management Institute, 2017). Each phase plays a distinct role in ensuring both project success and quality outcomes, with particular relevance for technology implementation initiatives.

Understanding this lifecycle proves essential because quality must permeate every phase rather than being treated as discrete activities or compliance exercises. Quality management scholars articulate a fundamental principle: quality requires deliberate planning, intentional design, and systematic integration as products progress through their development lifecycle (Reaiche, 2022). This proactive stance toward quality proves essential for technology projects, where complexity involves intricate interdependencies among technical architecture, business processes, organizational change, and human behavior.

Initiation: Establishing the Quality Foundation

The initiation phase establishes the foundation for all subsequent project activities and quality outcomes. During this critical stage, organizations define clear project goals and objectives, articulate the business case for investment, and identify key stakeholders who will influence or be affected by the initiative. For technology adoption projects, this involves articulating specific problems technology will solve, opportunities it will enable, and strategic objectives it will support.

From a quality perspective, comprehensive stakeholder identification during initiation ensures that all relevant parties contribute their perspectives early, reducing the risk of misaligned expectations or overlooked requirements later in the project. Organizations must develop project charters that capture essential information including goals, budget parameters, expected timelines, assigned leadership, and anticipated constraints. Quality considerations during initiation include establishing explicit quality objectives that align with both technical requirements and business outcomes, identifying regulatory compliance obligations and technical standards that must inform planning, and engaging diverse stakeholders whose input will shape requirements.

Planning: Mapping the Path to Quality

The planning phase demands rigorous attention to detail as organizations map the path from current state to desired outcomes. Thoroughness during planning enables teams to develop specifications that genuinely meet stakeholder expectations. For technology projects, planning encompasses identifying technical requirements, developing detailed implementation schedules, creating communication protocols, and defining specific deliverables with associated acceptance criteria.

Quality integration during planning involves multiple critical activities. Organizations must translate general quality objectives into concrete, measurable criteria that guide development and enable objective assessment. This requires establishing quality standards that define how teams should employ processes and specifications that provide explicit, measurable details about requirements (Rose, 2014). Standards applicable to technology projects encompass industry standards such as those from professional associations, quality-specific standards such as the ISO 9000 series, and organizational standards based on accumulated experience.

Furthermore, relevant standards and regulations must inform initial planning activities rather than being considered only during later execution phases (Reaiche, 2022). For technology projects, this encompasses not only technical architecture standards and integration requirements but also regulatory compliance obligations such as data privacy laws, security protocols, accessibility guidelines, and industry-specific regulations. Organizations that defer consideration of these standards until implementation discover that retrofitting compliance proves far more expensive and disruptive than designing it into solutions from the beginning.

Project managers create work breakdown structures that provide visual clarity regarding how various project components relate to one another and to the overall objective (Project Management Institute, 2017). The planning phase culminates in clearly defined project scope, comprehensive timelines with associated deliverables, established budget baselines, and explicit role and responsibility assignments. Importantly, organizations establish formal scope change procedures during planning, ensuring that any modifications to the original plan receive appropriate review and approval before implementation.

Execution: Transforming Plans into Reality

Execution represents the phase where theoretical plans become tangible reality. During execution, project teams perform the physical work of system configuration, integration, customization, testing, and deployment. Project managers establish workflows that enable efficient resource allocation and utilization while maintaining oversight of team progress. In technology contexts, execution requires close coordination among diverse specialists including developers, infrastructure engineers, security professionals, and business analysts who each contribute essential expertise.

Quality assurance during execution focuses on establishing confidence that deliverables will prove acceptable based on the processes used to create them. Two fundamental principles drive quality assurance activities: fitness for use and correctness from the outset. Fitness for use ensures that developed products meet and remain suitable for their intended purposes, addressing not merely technical functionality but actual value delivery in real-world operational contexts. Correctness from the outset emphasizes preventing mistakes and waste rather than detecting and correcting them after occurrence.

For technology implementations, process quality determines product quality. Systems developed through disciplined requirements management, rigorous design review, systematic testing, and controlled deployment generally exhibit higher quality than those created through ad hoc approaches. Quality assurance therefore monitors not only deliverables themselves but also the processes that generate deliverables, ensuring teams follow established procedures and apply appropriate rigor at each lifecycle stage.

Collaborative problem-solving becomes particularly important during execution, as teams must address emerging issues quickly before they escalate into larger obstacles that threaten project success.

Quality assurance helps establish whether deliverables prove acceptable based on creation processes, requiring evaluation of overall project performance to determine whether quality reviews occurred, testing happened systematically, and customer acceptance was secured.

Monitoring and Controlling: Maintaining Quality Visibility

Monitoring and controlling activities occur concurrently with execution, providing real-time visibility into project health and enabling proactive intervention when deviations from plan emerge. This phase focuses on tracking effort and cost, monitoring progress, ensuring adherence to established plans, and preventing disruptions. The simultaneous nature of monitoring and execution creates feedback loops that enable teams to make course corrections before small issues compound into project-threatening problems (Project Management Institute, 2017).

Quality control represents the operational dimension of quality management, involving ongoing monitoring and documentation of quality activities to evaluate performance and identify needed improvements. For technology projects, monitoring encompasses system performance metrics, user adoption indicators, budget consumption patterns, timeline adherence, and emerging risk factors. Project managers require working knowledge of statistical quality control tools to effectively oversee quality control and analyze quality control outputs.

Several essential monitoring mechanisms maintain project quality (Schwalbe, 2019). Performance metrics and key performance indicators enable systematic assessment of project performance dimensions including resource utilization, timeline adherence, and milestone achievement. Change control management implements evaluation and documentation of potential changes, providing project managers with necessary information about requested modifications and likely outcomes while enabling controlled change implementation. Regular project status meetings facilitate communication among team members and stakeholders, creating forums where participants raise issues, voice concerns, and share updates.

These monitoring processes create visibility that enables proactive quality management. When performance metrics reveal degrading trends, teams can intervene before problems escalate into crises. When change control processes surface potential quality implications of requested modifications, decision-makers can evaluate whether benefits justify risks. When status meetings bring issues to light promptly, collaborative problem-solving can occur while solutions remain feasible and affordable.

Closure: Capturing Learning for Future Agility

The closure phase marks formal project completion but serves purposes beyond simply ending activities. Closure includes conducting post-implementation reviews where teams examine both successes and failures, documenting lessons learned that inform future initiatives. This reflective practice enables continuous organizational improvement, enhancing the capability of teams to execute subsequent technology projects more effectively.

For technology implementations, closure also involves transition planning that ensures ongoing system maintenance, user support, and enhancement capabilities remain in place after the project team disbands. From a quality perspective, closure activities provide critical opportunities to capture organizational learning that accelerates future initiatives and builds agility.

Closure phase activities that capture lessons learned enable teams to apply insights from one project to subsequent efforts, progressively improving organizational capability (Project Management Institute,

2017). This learning accumulation represents a critical component of organizational agility—organizations that learn systematically from experience adapt more quickly and effectively than those that repeat mistakes due to inadequate knowledge capture and transfer.

Linking Quality Management to Organizational Agility

The connection between systematic quality management and organizational agility may seem counterintuitive initially. Quality management evokes images of rigid processes, extensive documentation, and formal approval procedures that appear antithetical to the speed and flexibility associated with agility. However, this perception misunderstands the nature of both quality management and organizational agility.

Organizational agility does not mean abandoning discipline or accepting lower standards in pursuit of speed. Rather, agility represents the capability to respond effectively to changing circumstances while maintaining performance excellence. Organizations achieve this capability by establishing robust processes that enable rapid decision-making, clear communication, efficient problem-solving, and continuous learning—precisely the outcomes that quality management methodologies facilitate.

Quality Management as Agility Enabler

Quality management planning reduces organizational friction by establishing clear expectations, defining decision-making authority, creating communication protocols, and documenting procedures before crises emerge. When teams understand quality requirements comprehensively, they make better initial decisions that reduce rework and the delays it causes. When quality assurance processes identify issues early through systematic monitoring, organizations address problems while they remain small and manageable rather than after they metastasize into project-threatening crises.

Consider how quality planning addresses technology project risks through multiple mechanisms. Comprehensive requirements gathering that engages diverse stakeholders reduces the risk of missing critical functional needs or technical constraints. Thorough architecture planning that evaluates integration points, performance implications, and scalability requirements mitigates technical risks before development begins. Security requirements incorporated into initial design rather than added late reduce vulnerability exposure. These proactive quality activities prevent problems rather than requiring reactive fixes that consume time and resources.

When quality control mechanisms provide objective feedback on deliverable acceptability, teams avoid the ambiguity and conflict that arise from subjective quality assessments. Quality standards and specifications translate general quality objectives into concrete, measurable criteria that guide development activities and enable objective assessment (Rose, 2014). This eliminates subjective interpretations that create confusion and conflict, replacing ambiguity with precision.

Furthermore, the systematic documentation and reflection that quality management demands creates organizational memory that accelerates future initiatives. Organizations that systematically gather feedback, analyze performance data, identify improvement opportunities, experiment with enhanced approaches, and propagate successful innovations progressively increase capability. This continuous improvement orientation distinguishes organizations that progressively increase capability from those that plateau or decline as competitive pressures intensify.

Quality and Risk Management Integration

Quality planning and risk management represent complementary disciplines that together enhance technology project outcomes. Risks that materialize frequently manifest as quality deficiencies—systems that fail to perform reliably, data that lacks integrity, interfaces that prove difficult to use, or implementations that miss deadlines and exceed budgets. Conversely, robust quality management mitigates many common project risks by establishing clear requirements, monitoring progress systematically, and intervening proactively when deviations emerge.

Technology projects face distinctive risk profiles that quality planning must address. Technical complexity challenges even experienced teams when new technologies, unfamiliar architectures, or ambitious functional requirements push beyond proven capabilities. Integration risks emerge when connecting new systems with existing infrastructure reveals incompatibilities, data inconsistencies, or performance bottlenecks. Cybersecurity threats evolve continuously, requiring vigilant attention to emerging vulnerabilities and attack vectors. Data migration initiatives frequently encounter data quality issues in source systems that compromise accuracy in target environments. Vendor dependencies introduce risks related to supplier performance, financial viability, roadmap alignment, and support responsiveness. User adoption resistance undermines system value when people continue using workarounds rather than embracing new capabilities.

The importance of risk-informed quality planning becomes evident when considering technology projects that uncover legacy code quality issues, inadequate documentation, architectural decisions that created technical debt, or data quality problems that accumulated over years of inadequate governance. Organizations that anticipate these possibilities during quality planning develop contingency approaches, allocate budget reserves for remediation, and establish decision criteria for determining when discovered issues require addressing versus accepting. Those that fail to plan for such possibilities find themselves making hasty decisions under pressure when problems emerge.

QUALITY PLANNING FOR DIGITAL TRANSFORMATION INITIATIVES

Establishing Measurable Quality Objectives

Quality planning for technology adoption initiatives begins with establishing clear, measurable quality objectives that align with both technical requirements and business outcomes. These objectives must transcend simplistic metrics such as on-time delivery or budget adherence to encompass the substantive value that technology should create for the organization and its stakeholders.

A comprehensive quality planning process applicable to technology projects ensures that quality considerations inform decisions from earliest conception through final deployment and ongoing operations. The customer-centric orientation of this approach proves particularly valuable for technology initiatives, where technical teams sometimes prioritize technological sophistication over user needs and business value.

Customer-Centric Quality Objectives

Customer satisfaction represents a foundational quality objective for technology projects, requiring thorough understanding of needs, preferences, and feedback mechanisms coupled with iterative interaction that builds enduring relationships and loyalty. For technology adoption, customers include not only external clients but also internal stakeholders who depend on systems to perform their work effectively.

Understanding these diverse customer populations requires systematic requirements gathering that goes beyond formal specifications to uncover underlying needs, frustrations with current systems, and aspirations for improved capabilities. Organizations must translate general customer satisfaction objectives into specific, measurable quality targets that enable objective assessment of whether technology delivers intended value.

Rose (2014) emphasizes that project deliverables represent core project elements, but ensuring deliverables meet customer expectations requires collaboration with all stakeholders to identify necessary requirements. Customers typically provide contracts and establish most project requirements. However, requirements also encompass explicit expectations when working with suppliers and subcontractors. Even users and affected groups act as requirement sources. Multiple organizations play important roles in project success, making measurable statements key planning components determined before project implementation.

Developing requirements that support quality control procedures includes research, interviews, and results analysis (Rose, 2014). Creating a comprehensive requirements list proves essential before starting projects. Once lists are established, analytical methods using requirements matrices help project management teams prioritize requirements. This enables teams to adopt customer perspectives and compare criteria using weighted scales determining importance levels for different requirements, ensuring final deliverables meet customer expectations.

Standards and Specifications Framework

Quality objectives for technology projects must also address regulatory compliance, security requirements, accessibility standards, and integration specifications. The ISO 9001:2015 standard provides a comprehensive quality management system framework that guides product development through design, production, and post-production phases. For technology implementations, analogous lifecycle considerations include requirements definition, system design, configuration and development, testing, deployment, and ongoing maintenance and enhancement.

Organizations that document processes, conduct regular quality audits, and ensure adherence to established procedures achieve more consistent quality outcomes than those that approach each project idiosyncratically. ISO 21500 offers additional guidance specifically tailored to project management contexts, addressing risk management, stakeholder communication, standardized project management practices, and continuous improvement mechanisms.

Technology projects benefit from standardization that ensures consistent, predictable outcomes across different initiatives and organizational units. Maintaining both process quality and product quality requires this standardization, as ad hoc approaches introduce unnecessary variability that complicates quality assurance and control activities.

Translating Objectives into Specifications

Quality standards and specifications translate general quality objectives into concrete, measurable criteria that guide development activities and enable objective assessment of deliverable acceptability. Rose (2014) distinguishes between standards that define how teams should or must employ processes and specifications that provide specific, measurable details about requirements.

Specifications build upon standards by providing explicit, measurable details that enable objective verification. Rose (2014) emphasizes that specifications must be both specific and measurable to serve their intended purpose. For technology projects, specifications might address system performance requirements such as response times or throughput capacity, availability targets such as uptime percentages, security requirements such as encryption standards or access control mechanisms, integration interfaces with particular data formats and protocols, and user interface characteristics such as accessibility compliance or supported devices.

Operational definitions further clarify potentially ambiguous terms and enable development of specifications through rational analysis rather than guesswork (Rose, 2014). In technology contexts, operational definitions might specify exactly what constitutes a system defect versus an enhancement request, how response time will be measured, what conditions must be met for deployment to proceed, or how user acceptance will be determined. These definitions eliminate subjective interpretations that create confusion and conflict, replacing ambiguity with precision.

Rose (2014) emphasizes that guesswork should not inform planning processes, making definitive standards and definitions crucial for project success. Technology projects face particular challenges with ambiguous requirements given the abstract nature of software systems and the difficulty many stakeholders experience articulating their needs precisely. Operational definitions and detailed specifications compensate for this inherent ambiguity by forcing explicit articulation of expectations before development begins. While this upfront investment requires time and effort, it prevents far more extensive rework necessitated by misunderstood requirements discovered late in development cycles.

Integrating Risk Assessment into Quality Planning

Integrating risk assessment directly into quality planning activities involves examining risk factors, hazard potential, and project complexity while adapting processes to achieve required quality levels within scope, timeline, and cost constraints. The consequences of reactive rather than proactive quality management manifest clearly in technology projects.

When organizations fail to build quality into their planning and design activities, they experience significant negative impacts on scope, timeline, and cost (Reaiche, 2022). To illustrate this dynamic, consider construction projects where inadequate planning and failure to adhere to established standards necessitate expensive rework that extends timelines, inflates costs, and damages client relationships. Technology implementations follow similar patterns—systems that fail to meet user requirements, integrate improperly with existing infrastructure, or violate regulatory standards require costly remediation that erodes stakeholder confidence and organizational credibility.

Anticipating Quality Challenges

Data quality assessment performed before migration enables cleansing activities that improve target system integrity. Vendor evaluation processes that examine not only current capabilities but also organizational stability, strategic direction, and support infrastructure reduce dependency risks. Change management planning that addresses organizational and human dimensions of technology adoption improves user acceptance and actual utilization.

The importance of risk-informed quality planning becomes evident when considering technology projects that uncover legacy code quality issues, inadequate documentation, architectural decisions that created technical debt, or data quality problems that accumulated over years of inadequate governance. Organizations that anticipate these possibilities during quality planning develop contingency approaches, allocate budget reserves for remediation, and establish decision criteria for determining when discovered issues require addressing versus accepting. Those that fail to plan for such possibilities find themselves making hasty decisions under pressure when problems emerge.

QUALITY ASSURANCE DURING TECHNOLOGY IMPLEMENTATION

Process-Based Quality Confidence

Quality assurance during technology implementation focuses on establishing confidence that deliverables will prove acceptable based on the processes used to create them. Additionally, quality assurance aims to develop mitigation plans for potential risks that could adversely impact quality processes during production of goods and services.

These principles prove particularly relevant for technology projects given the expense and disruption associated with rework. Quality assurance helps establish whether deliverables prove acceptable based on creation processes, requiring evaluation of overall project performance to determine whether quality reviews occurred, testing happened systematically, and customer acceptance was secured.

Developing Effective Quality Metrics

Effective quality assurance requires establishing metrics and measures that enable objective assessment of progress toward quality objectives. Quality assurance activities during project execution represent systematic approaches to measure, verify, and validate required quality standards, helping identify areas requiring corrective action and promoting continuous quality improvement. These activities also help organizations meet regulatory requirements, customer needs, and satisfaction expectations.

Developing quality metrics and measures represents a fundamental requirement for quality assurance programs (Rever, 2007). These metrics enable teams to determine and measure progress and results related to quality objectives. Setting up meaningful and effective metrics proves vital to quality assurance program success, as metrics should drive specific actions linked to improving processes and deliverables.

Quality assurance metrics can be organized into several categories including process metrics that evaluate procedure effectiveness, product metrics that assess deliverable characteristics, technical metrics that measure system properties, and quality cost metrics that quantify quality-related investments and waste (Rever, 2007).

Context-Appropriate Metrics

The specific metrics appropriate for technology projects vary across different organizational contexts and industry sectors. Healthcare organizations might establish quality metrics based on regulatory requirements or clinical guidelines, reflecting the highly regulated nature of medical technology and the patient safety implications of system failures. Financial services organizations might base metrics on industry standards, return on investment calculations, or customer satisfaction indicators, acknowledging the fiduciary responsibilities and competitive pressures that shape banking technology priorities. Even industries outside traditional technology domains employ quality metrics—entertainment organizations assess audience feedback, budget adherence, and media trend alignment when evaluating content production quality.

After establishing relevant metrics, organizations must determine specific measurement approaches. This involves defining metrics precisely, establishing data collection methods, developing analysis approaches, and creating communication protocols for quality information. Each metric requires appropriate operational definition that specifies exactly what will be measured and how measurement will occur. Required measurement parameters must be identified, including data sources, collection frequency, responsible parties, and acceptable ranges. Analysis plans outline how collected data will be interpreted to achieve desired insights, specifying statistical methods, visualization approaches, and decision criteria that will guide quality interventions.

For technology projects, quality metrics might address system availability and reliability through uptime measurements and mean time between failures. Performance metrics might track response times, throughput rates, or resource utilization patterns. Defect metrics might quantify bugs discovered during testing phases, categorized by severity and functional area. Process metrics might measure requirements volatility, design review coverage, test case execution rates, or code review completion. User satisfaction metrics might employ survey instruments, usage analytics, or support ticket volumes to assess how well systems meet user needs.

Systematic Quality Audits

Quality audits represent a critical quality assurance mechanism during technology implementation. Quality audits can be described as structured, independent reviews determining whether project activities comply with organizational and project policies, processes, and procedures.

Quality audits serve multiple objectives: identifying best practices that should be amplified and shared, identifying gaps requiring corrective action, disseminating best practices to other project teams, offering proactive assistance in improving process implementation, and documenting results for stakeholder communication. When teams address identified deficiencies, organizations experience reduced quality costs and increased customer and sponsor acceptance of project deliverables or products. Audits may occur on scheduled or random bases depending on organizational preferences and risk profiles.

Industry-Adapted Audit Approaches

Quality audits apply across diverse industries with variations in specific focus areas, audit frequency, evaluation criteria, and audit methodologies. In healthcare settings, quality audits might emphasize patient safety measures, regulatory compliance verification, and adherence to medical protocols. Financial services audits might focus on financial data accuracy, regulatory compliance confirmation, and internal control effectiveness. Entertainment industry audits might assess production process adherence, script and storyboard fidelity, and final product quality.

Despite these differences, the fundamental principle remains consistent—systematic, objective evaluation of whether activities conform to established standards and whether those standards prove adequate for achieving quality objectives.

A comprehensive quality assurance procedure framework applicable to technology projects involves three stages. First, organizations develop quality assurance plans and requirements that establish goals, assign responsibilities, gather information about relevant standards and compliance criteria, and design testing and measurement approaches. Second, regular audits and inspections occur throughout the project to verify that activities align with organizational processes while identifying and correcting deficiencies promptly. Third, analysis activities review quality levels and define necessary improvements through root cause examination, systematic testing, problem-solving methodologies, and development of corrective actions.

For technology implementations, quality audits might examine whether requirements management processes follow established procedures, whether design artifacts receive appropriate review and approval, whether testing coverage meets defined standards, whether security controls receive adequate verification, whether change management protocols govern modifications appropriately, and whether deployment procedures follow documented playbooks. Audits provide independent verification that teams actually implement declared processes rather than cutting corners under schedule pressure.

Continuous Improvement During Implementation

Quality assurance extends beyond conformance verification to encompass continuous improvement that progressively enhances both processes and outcomes. Rever (2007) emphasizes that quality assurance program implementation should not be seen as a one-time event but rather as a continuing process requiring sustained commitment and resources.

Organizations must provide personnel with necessary training and resources to implement quality assurance programs to desired standards. Continuous improvement of organizational processes should constitute an integral component of quality assurance programs, with regular reviews ensuring programs remain relevant, effective, and efficient (Rever, 2007).

Industry-Specific Improvement Approaches

Different industries approach continuous improvement in contextually appropriate ways. Healthcare organizations might leverage quality improvement initiatives to identify and implement process enhancements, engaging in regular staff education and training to improve clinician knowledge and skills, thereby improving patient outcomes. Financial services organizations might continuously monitor financial reports while updating internal processes and procedures to identify and mitigate risks, incorporating innovative technology solutions to enhance efficiency and accuracy. Entertainment organizations might utilize feedback from test audiences during production coupled with post-production reviews to identify improvement opportunities, incorporating innovative filming techniques and technology to achieve better results.

Despite industry differences, the fundamental commitment to ongoing enhancement remains constant. Quality-driven organizations view current performance as a baseline for improvement rather than an acceptable plateau. They systematically gather feedback, analyze performance data, identify improvement opportunities, experiment with enhanced approaches, and propagate successful innovations.

For technology projects, continuous improvement during execution manifests through retrospectives that identify process improvements, usability testing that reveals user experience enhancements, performance optimization that improves system responsiveness, code refactoring that reduces technical debt, and knowledge sharing that transfers learning across team members. Organizations that build these improvement activities into their implementation approaches create virtuous cycles where quality progressively improves rather than degrading under schedule pressure.

QUALITY CONTROL AND MONITORING

Distributed Quality Responsibility

Quality control represents the operational dimension of quality management, involving ongoing monitoring and documentation of quality activities to evaluate performance and identify needed improvements. Project managers require working knowledge of statistical quality control tools to effectively oversee quality control and analyze quality control outputs.

Quality control demands collaboration across organizational levels. Rever (2007) describes how different roles bear distinct quality responsibilities. Business managers hold ultimate accountability for product quality and must ensure quality policies receive establishment, dissemination, and enforcement throughout organizations. Quality directors lead quality organizations and oversee all aspects of quality programs. Functional group managers ensure their teams comply with quality requirements, including proper training provision. Project managers remain accountable for adhering to quality standards while supporting quality audits and corrective actions (Rever, 2007).

This distributed responsibility model recognizes that quality emerges from collective effort rather than isolated quality department activities. When every organizational level embraces quality ownership, organizations avoid quality becoming someone else's problem that receives attention only when auditors arrive or customers complain.

Quality Control Tools and Analytical Methods

Multiple quality control tools facilitate effective process monitoring and problem identification. Common tools include inspections, Ishikawa diagrams, checklists, control charts, histograms, Pareto charts, check sheets, flowcharts, scatter plots, and run charts. These tools serve various purposes: identifying root causes of problems, controlling risks, documenting results systematically, categorizing data for analysis, spotting trends over time, and tracking variation in key parameters.

Statistical Process Control

Control charts merit particular attention given their power for distinguishing normal process variation from significant deviations requiring intervention. Ramirez and Ramirez (2018) explain that control charts plot key metrics over time with upper and lower control limits that trigger warnings when unexpected variance emerges requiring review. These limits can be established statistically based on acceptable variation thresholds, enabling objective determination of when processes remain in control versus when special causes require investigation (Ramirez & Ramirez, 2018).

For technology projects, control charts might track defect discovery rates across testing phases, system response times across different load conditions, or deployment success rates across different releases. When metrics remain within control limits, teams gain confidence that processes operate predictably. When metrics breach control limits, teams investigate to determine whether special circumstances caused the deviation or whether fundamental issues require remediation.

Root Cause and Priority Analysis

Additional tools serve specific analytical purposes in technology contexts. Ishikawa diagrams help teams trace observed quality issues back to underlying root causes by systematically examining potential contributing factors across categories such as people, processes, tools, and environment. Pareto analysis helps prioritize improvement efforts by identifying which defect categories account for the majority of quality issues, enabling focused intervention on high-impact problems rather than diffusing effort across all issues equally. Scatter plots reveal relationships between variables, helping teams understand how changes in one factor affect another—for example, how code complexity correlates with defect density.

Requirements Management and Acceptance Criteria

Quality control for technology deliverables begins with clear requirements that define what constitutes acceptable outcomes. After establishing standards, project teams must write specifications for each requirement. Operational definitions provide clarification of ambiguous terms, allowing teams to develop specifications through rational analysis rather than guesswork (Rose, 2014).

Comprehensive Acceptance Criteria

Quality assurance serves as the acceptance criteria mechanism for each deliverable. Rose (2014) explains that project management teams use metrics to measure and determine conformance degrees to specifications. These measurements then pass through quality audits confirming quality assurance activity effectiveness. Audits are recommended throughout entire project processes, conducted by internal or external sources. This follows continuous improvement principles, enabling quality deliverables to be free from defects without requiring rework after delivery. These steps represent components within broader quality journeys rather than endpoints (Rose, 2014).

For technology projects, acceptance criteria must address functional correctness, performance adequacy, security robustness, usability effectiveness, accessibility compliance, and integration completeness. Functional correctness criteria verify that systems perform required operations according to specifications under diverse conditions. Performance criteria establish minimum acceptable response times, throughput rates, resource utilization levels, and scalability characteristics. Security criteria define required protections against identified threats through appropriate authentication, authorization, encryption, and monitoring mechanisms. Usability criteria specify maximum task completion times, minimum success rates, and maximum error frequencies for representative user populations performing typical tasks. Accessibility criteria ensure compliance with applicable standards enabling use by people with disabilities. Integration criteria verify that systems exchange data correctly with upstream and downstream systems according to defined interfaces.

QUALITY REPORTING AND CONTINUOUS IMPROVEMENT

Effective Quality Visibility

Regular quality reporting provides essential visibility into project health and performance trends for key stakeholders. Kerzner (2017) explains that quality dashboards offer at-a-glance views of metrics using graphs, charts, and visual indicators highlighting issues and risks. These dashboards flag when quality targets are missed or control limits are exceeded, enabling rapid stakeholder awareness and intervention (Kerzner, 2017).

Audience-Appropriate Reporting

Effective quality reporting balances comprehensiveness with clarity. Stakeholders require sufficient detail to understand quality status and implications without overwhelming them with excessive data that obscures important signals. Visual presentation through dashboards, scorecards, and trend charts enables rapid comprehension of complex quality information. Color coding using traffic light schemes—green for acceptable, yellow for concerning, red for critical—provides immediate intuitive understanding of status without requiring detailed analysis.

Quality reports should address multiple audiences with varying information needs. Executive stakeholders require high-level summaries emphasizing strategic implications and decisions requiring their attention. Project sponsors need visibility into whether investments are delivering expected returns and whether interventions are necessary to protect value. Project managers require operational details enabling them to direct resources toward highest-priority quality issues. Technical teams need granular defect information, performance metrics, and test results guiding their daily work. This audience diversity necessitates layered reporting where summary views provide executive perspectives while drill-down capabilities enable detailed investigation when needed.

For technology projects, quality reports might present metrics such as requirements stability over time, design review completion status, test execution progress, defect discovery and resolution trends, performance benchmark results, security vulnerability remediation status, user acceptance testing outcomes, and deployment success rates. Trend visualization proves particularly valuable, revealing whether quality improves, remains stable, or degrades over project lifecycles. Leading indicators that predict future quality issues enable proactive intervention before problems manifest in deliverables.

Learning from Healthcare Quality Improvement

Quality improvement initiatives represent systematic efforts to enhance processes and outcomes. The Veterans Health Administration MRSA prevention initiative provides a compelling example of large-scale quality improvement in healthcare that offers lessons for technology organizations.

The VA MRSA Reduction Case

In 2007, the VA launched a nationwide effort to reduce MRSA infections causing severe illness and deaths across their hospitals. Jain et al. (2011) report that analysis revealed just three VA hospitals accounted for over thirty percent of staph infections. Examination of processes at these facilities found that simple preventative measures like handwashing and equipment sanitization were not being adequately implemented (Jain et al., 2011).

The VA rolled out a comprehensive infection control bundle focusing on hand hygiene compliance, use of chlorhexidine for skin antisepsis, and nasal decolonization of MRSA carriers. Over subsequent years, MRSA infections dropped by over sixty percent across over 150 VA hospitals (CDC, 2016). Nelson et al. (2016) report that this initiative prevented over 2,000 deaths and saved over $200 million in costs. The program's success led to implementation in all US hospitals through 2014 (Nelson et al., 2016).

Transferable Quality Principles

The VA MRSA reduction program demonstrates how quality improvement techniques of performance monitoring, root cause analysis, developing targeted solutions, and tracking implementation can significantly enhance outcomes. A key aspect of the VA's success was their comprehensive reporting system used to monitor MRSA infection rates. Each VA facility tracked the number of MRSA infections and reported this data to the VA Central Office on a monthly basis (Jain et al., 2011). The data was analyzed to identify high-risk facilities and determine if infection rates were declining over time.

The VA also utilized public reporting, sharing MRSA infection rates for each facility on a public website. Transparency through public reporting creates accountability and motivates organizations to improve quality. The VA's robust quality monitoring and reporting system enabled rapid dissemination of effective interventions system-wide.

Technology organizations can adapt quality improvement principles from healthcare to their own contexts. First, systematic performance measurement across organizational units enables identification of outliers requiring attention. Technology organizations might track metrics such as defect escape rates, production incident frequencies, or customer satisfaction scores across different product teams, revealing which teams achieve superior outcomes and which require improvement support.

Second, root cause analysis proves essential for understanding why problems occur rather than merely addressing symptoms. The VA discovered that poor hand hygiene compliance stemmed from inadequate training, insufficient sanitizer availability, and lack of accountability rather than from knowledge deficits alone. Similarly, technology organizations investigating quality issues might discover that root causes involve inadequate requirements processes, insufficient testing resources, or misaligned incentives rather than technical skill gaps.

Third, targeted interventions addressing identified root causes prove more effective than generic improvement programs. The VA developed a specific infection control bundle addressing the particular behaviors that needed to change. Technology organizations might develop specific interventions such as enhanced requirements review processes, automated testing tools, or modified reward systems that address identified root causes of quality issues.

Fourth, sustained monitoring enables verification that improvements persist over time rather than degrading after initial enthusiasm wanes. The VA tracked infection rates continuously for years, ensuring that initial improvements sustained. Technology organizations might similarly monitor quality metrics over extended periods, watching for regression that signals the need for reinforcement.

Fifth, transparent reporting creates accountability that motivates improvement. Public reporting of facility-level infection rates motivated VA facilities to improve performance to avoid unfavorable comparisons with peers. Technology organizations might publish team-level or product-level quality metrics internally, creating healthy competition and recognition for high performers.

Embedding Improvement in Operations

Continuous improvement must become embedded in organizational culture rather than being treated as episodic initiative. Organizations committed to quality view their current processes and outcomes as baselines for enhancement rather than acceptable plateaus. This orientation requires leadership commitment, resource allocation, and structural enablement.

Structural Enablement Practices

Several practices enable sustained continuous improvement in technology organizations. Retrospective meetings after project milestones or iterations provide structured forums for reflecting on what worked well, what worked poorly, and what should change. These retrospectives prove most effective when they focus on actionable improvements rather than devolving into complaint sessions or blame assignment. Designating owners for specific improvement actions and tracking implementation ensures that insights translate into actual change.

Communities of practice that span organizational boundaries enable knowledge transfer and collective problem-solving. When specialists from different teams convene regularly to discuss common challenges, they share effective practices, warn each other about pitfalls, and collaborate on solutions to shared problems. These communities accelerate organizational learning by distributing insights quickly rather than leaving each team to independently rediscover what others already learned.

Experiments and pilots enable organizations to try new approaches with limited risk before committing to large-scale adoption. Technology organizations might pilot new tools, processes, or techniques with volunteer teams, measuring outcomes systematically to determine whether innovations deliver value. Successful experiments then scale to broader populations, while unsuccessful experiments provide learning without major disruption.

Metrics that track improvement over time provide visibility into whether continuous improvement efforts actually deliver results. Organizations might monitor trends in quality indicators such as defect escape rates, production incident frequencies, or customer satisfaction scores, expecting these metrics to improve progressively as learning accumulates. When metrics plateau or decline, organizations investigate whether improvement efforts need intensification or redirection.

BUILDING QUALITY INTO ORGANIZATIONAL CULTURE

Cultural Foundation for Quality

Embedding quality deeply into organizational culture represents perhaps the most critical yet challenging dimension of sustaining organizational agility through technology adoption. Quality practices and procedures remain ineffective if they exist only in documentation rather than guiding actual behavior. True quality requires cultural transformation where every organizational member understands their role in quality delivery and feels personal ownership for outcomes.

The present highly competitive and global marketplace has made teams central for businesses' survival, elevating quality from desirable attribute to business necessity. Project managers bear particular obligation to develop first-class, cross-trained, highly competitive teams capable of carrying project cycles through to successful completion. This team development requires not only technical skill building but cultural shaping that instills quality values and commitments.

The Cultural Transformation Challenge

Moving from rules-based quality environments to genuine quality cultures requires fundamental organizational transformation (Srinivasan & Kurey, 2014). While specific activities supporting this transformation will vary across companies based on their particular circumstances, the initial step remains standard: management must agree that quality culture pursuit merits the investment. Without leadership commitment, quality culture initiatives lack the support and resources necessary for success (Srinivasan & Kurey, 2014).

Project Management Institute (2017) explains that project quality management processes include all organizational activities determining quality objectives, policies, and responsibilities, ensuring projects satisfy the needs for which they were undertaken. This comprehensive scope necessitates engagement across organizational levels rather than limiting quality responsibility to specialized quality departments.

Leadership's Pivotal Role

Organizational leadership plays the pivotal role in creating team cultures and work climates where employees are driven to realize goals and tasks within quality, time, and cost constraints. True organizational quality cultures demonstrate identifiable attributes that distinguish them from organizations with superficial quality programs.

Quality Culture Characteristics

Companies demonstrating world-class quality exhibit leadership that firmly and clearly supports companywide quality objectives. These organizations are driven by persistent motivation to identify and address customer needs. Quality-driven objectives translate into performance expectations for team members, all upheld by strong leadership essential to developing and sustaining quality cultures. Company willingness to pursue continuous improvement from bottom to top and top to bottom transforms organizations into quality-driven ecosystems where all parties collaborate to achieve common quality objectives and improve operational goals.

Several key principles emerge from examining quality-focused organizations. First, quality must connect to customer value rather than existing as abstraction. When organizations define quality through customer lenses, quality initiatives align naturally with business objectives. Second, quality responsibility must distribute throughout organizations rather than concentrating in specialized functions. When everyone owns quality, quality receives attention constantly rather than only during audits or inspections. Third, formal policies and procedures provide necessary structure, but these mechanisms prove insufficient without cultural values that make quality personal priority for individuals.

Essential Cultural Elements

For quality culture to take root across organizational hierarchical levels, several characteristics must be present. Organizations must articulate clear values and vision that position quality centrally rather than peripherally. These statements should communicate why quality matters to organizational mission and how quality connects to competitive advantage and long-term success.

Committed senior management support for quality initiatives provides both symbolic and practical reinforcement. When executives personally participate in quality reviews, celebrate quality achievements, and allocate resources to quality improvement, they signal that quality represents authentic priority rather than rhetoric. Conversely, when executives treat quality as someone else's concern or sacrifice quality for short-term financial results, they communicate that quality lacks genuine importance regardless of official statements.

Ongoing engagement with customer bases to identify and address evolving needs ensures quality remains relevant to actual requirements rather than reflecting outdated assumptions. Organizations that systematically gather customer feedback, analyze usage patterns, track satisfaction trends, and incorporate insights into quality objectives maintain alignment between internal quality efforts and external value delivery.

Clear definition of quality goals and metrics enables objective assessment of performance and progress. This systematic approach removes ambiguity about expectations while creating accountability through measurement and recognition through rewards. Investment in training and development ensures that organizational members possess the knowledge, skills, and tools necessary for quality execution. Quality aspirations exceed capability when organizations expect high quality without providing training in quality methods, tools, and techniques. Conversely, organizations that systematically build quality capability through education and practice progressively improve their quality performance.

Continuous Improvement as Cultural Norm

Continuous improvement represents another pillar of quality culture. Companies committed to quality dedicate themselves to continuous improvement in quality processes throughout project cycles. This sustained commitment to improving quality culture ensures organizations remain adaptable and agile in competitive business environments.

Srinivasan and Kurey (2014) note that while overall culture states may appear intangible, the value of taking proactive strides to adjust companies toward more quality-driven cultures can prove substantial. Organizations that systematically address cultural dimensions position themselves to sustain quality improvements over time rather than experiencing temporary gains that dissipate when attention shifts (Srinivasan & Kurey, 2014).

Cultural Practices for Technology Organizations

For technology organizations, continuous improvement culture manifests through several practices. Blameless postmortems after incidents or failures focus on learning rather than fault-finding, enabling honest examination of what went wrong and how to prevent recurrence. When people fear blame, they hide problems and avoid difficult conversations. When organizations respond to failures with curiosity rather than punishment, they create psychological safety that enables learning.

Experimentation and innovation receive encouragement rather than punishment when attempts fail. Technology organizations operate in domains characterized by rapid change and uncertainty where optimal approaches cannot be determined in advance. Organizations that permit bounded experimentation accelerate learning while managing risk. Clear decision criteria for determining which experiments to attempt, explicit success metrics for evaluating outcomes, and systematic processes for scaling successful innovations or stopping unsuccessful ones enable productive experimentation.

Knowledge sharing receives structural support through communities of practice, technical forums, documentation systems, and mentorship programs. Individual learning proves insufficient in complex technology domains where no person can master all relevant knowledge. Organizations that systematically capture and distribute knowledge leverage individual learning to create collective capability.

Recognition and rewards celebrate both quality outcomes and quality behaviors. Organizations that reward only speed or feature delivery while ignoring quality create incentive misalignment that undermines quality culture. Organizations that recognize thorough testing, careful code review, thoughtful design, or early defect detection reinforce that quality activities merit appreciation and reward.

Addressing Resistance and Barriers

Building quality culture encounters resistance from multiple sources. Time pressure creates perception that quality activities represent unaffordable luxury rather than essential investment. When schedules appear tight, teams feel compelled to skip quality activities that appear discretionary such as code reviews, thorough testing, or documentation. Organizations must counter this perception by demonstrating that quality activities prevent far more expensive downstream problems, making them time investments rather than time costs.

Historical precedents where quality received rhetorical support but practical neglect create cynicism. When employees observe disconnects between stated quality priorities and actual decision patterns, they conclude that quality represents public relations rather than authentic commitment. Organizations must acknowledge past failures, demonstrate authentic change through sustained action, and allow time for credibility rebuilding.

Skill gaps in quality methods and tools create barriers to quality execution. Even when people value quality, they may lack knowledge of how to achieve it effectively. Organizations must invest in training that builds practical capability in requirements engineering, design for testability, test automation, performance engineering, security practices, and other quality-relevant competencies.

Misaligned incentives that reward speed or feature delivery while ignoring quality create structural obstacles. When reward systems prioritize short-term delivery over sustainable quality, rational individuals optimize for what gets rewarded rather than what gets espoused. Organizations must align incentive structures with quality objectives, ensuring that compensation, promotion, and recognition decisions reflect quality contributions.

Inadequate tools and infrastructure that make quality activities difficult or time-consuming create friction that discourages quality behaviors. Organizations must invest in automation, tooling, and infrastructure that makes quality activities easy and efficient rather than burdensome.

PRACTICAL APPLICATIONS: CROSS-INDUSTRY INSIGHTS

Healthcare Quality Management Lessons

Healthcare industry quality management practices offer rich lessons for technology organizations given the sector's regulatory rigor and patient safety imperatives. Eagle et al. (2005) examined how guideline-based standardized care associated with substantially lower mortality in Medicare patients with acute myocardial infarction through the American College of Cardiology's Guidelines Applied in Practice (GAP) Projects in Michigan. This research demonstrated that systematic adherence to evidence-based quality standards delivers measurable outcome improvements (Eagle et al., 2005).

Henien, Aronow, and Abbott (2020) describe quality management in cardiac catheterization laboratories, environments characterized by high complexity, significant risks, and critical performance requirements. These settings require meticulous quality planning, rigorous monitoring, and continuous improvement to ensure patient safety and optimal outcomes (Henien et al., 2020).

Evidence-Based Standards and Process Standardization

Technology organizations can draw several lessons from healthcare quality management. First, evidence-based standards derived from systematic research provide more reliable guidance than individual judgment or tradition. Healthcare organizations increasingly adopt clinical practice guidelines based on rigorous studies demonstrating effectiveness. Technology organizations might similarly adopt engineering practices validated through research and industry experience rather than relying solely on individual preferences.

Second, process standardization enables consistent outcomes across different individuals and situations. Healthcare organizations that implement standardized clinical pathways reduce variation in care quality. Technology organizations that standardize development practices, testing approaches, security controls, and operational procedures similarly reduce quality variation across teams and projects.

Third, comprehensive measurement enables objective assessment of both process adherence and outcome achievement. Healthcare organizations track both whether clinicians follow clinical guidelines (process measures) and whether patients experience positive outcomes (result measures). Technology organizations might similarly measure both engineering practice adoption (process measures) such as code review completion rates and system quality outcomes (result measures) such as defect rates or user satisfaction.

Fourth, high-risk environments demand particular quality rigor. Cardiac catheterization laboratories cannot tolerate quality failures given immediate life-threatening consequences. While most technology failures do not threaten lives, some domains such as medical devices, automotive systems, financial infrastructure, or critical infrastructure carry substantial safety or security implications requiring comparable quality rigor.

Training Investment for Quality Improvement

Quality theory becomes tangible through examination of real-world applications. Quigley, Wiseman, and Farley (2011) document a case involving a surgical center focused on improving customer satisfaction after receiving complaints about poor overall service and inadequate access to offered services. Management concluded these problems likely stemmed from poor training.

Capability Building Over Cost Cutting

When drawing up implementation plans, the surgical center placed heavy focus on training rather than cost cutting. First, they hired additional staff to join their team. Second, they invested in training programs for both current employees and new hires. These sessions covered topics such as patient interaction, problem handling, and appointment scheduling. Employees had opportunities to ask questions and practice scenarios. Immediately after training implementation, the surgical center received feedback that customer service had improved. Employees also mentioned that training had helped them do their work (Quigley et al., 2011).

This case demonstrates several important principles applicable to technology organizations. First, quality problems often stem from capability gaps rather than motivation deficits. The surgical center staff presumably wanted to provide good service but lacked knowledge and skills for consistent execution. Technology teams similarly may value quality but lack training in effective quality practices.

Second, investing in people yields returns even when such investments appear expensive initially. The surgical center chose to invest in both additional staffing and training rather than attempting to improve quality through exhortation alone. Organizations that provide resources necessary for quality execution enable success, while those that demand quality without supporting capability building create frustration.

Third, comprehensive training that addresses both knowledge and skill development proves more effective than abstract instruction. The surgical center provided not only information about what to do but also opportunities to practice skills and ask questions. Technology organizations similarly benefit from hands-on training that enables practitioners to develop actual proficiency rather than merely learning concepts.

Fourth, rapid feedback validates that investments deliver value. The surgical center received prompt confirmation that training improved customer service and helped employees. Organizations that measure outcomes before and after quality interventions can demonstrate return on investment objectively rather than relying on assumptions.

STRATEGIC IMPLICATIONS AND RECOMMENDATIONS

Synthesizing Quality and Agility

This chapter has examined how systematic quality management enables organizational agility through effective technology adoption. Several key principles emerge from this analysis that leaders should consider when pursuing digital transformation initiatives.

First, quality and agility represent complementary rather than competing objectives. Organizations achieve sustainable agility by building quality into their processes, products, and culture rather than sacrificing quality for speed. Quality management provides the structured approach necessary for navigating complexity, managing risk, and ensuring that technology investments deliver intended value.

Second, quality requires proactive integration throughout technology adoption lifecycles rather than reactive inspection after problems emerge. Organizations that build quality considerations into initiation, planning, execution, monitoring, and closure phases experience fewer defects, less rework, and better outcomes than those that treat quality as afterthought (Project Management Institute, 2017).

Third, quality management encompasses multiple dimensions including planning that establishes objectives and approaches, assurance that provides confidence in process adequacy, control that verifies deliverable acceptability, monitoring that enables real-time visibility, reporting that communicates status, and improvement that progressively enhances capability. Organizations must address all these dimensions rather than focusing narrowly on isolated activities.

Fourth, quality culture represents perhaps the most critical yet challenging dimension of sustained quality. Processes and procedures documented in quality plans prove ineffective when organizational culture does not embrace quality as core value. Leadership plays pivotal roles in creating cultures where quality represents everyone's responsibility and where continuous improvement occurs naturally (Srinivasan & Kurey, 2014).

Fifth, lessons from other industries offer valuable insights for technology organizations. Healthcare demonstrates how evidence-based standards, systematic measurement, and rigorous improvement initiatives deliver measurable outcome enhancements (Eagle et al., 2005; Henien et al., 2020; Jain et al., 2011; Nelson et al., 2016). These cross-industry lessons enable technology organizations to adapt proven approaches rather than reinventing quality management from first principles.

Practical Guidance for Implementation

Leaders pursuing technology-enabled organizational agility should consider several practical recommendations based on insights from quality management literature.

Strategic Quality Integration

Establish explicit quality objectives for technology initiatives that align with business outcomes rather than focusing solely on technical specifications. Quality objectives should address customer value, user experience, operational reliability, security robustness, and business impact rather than limiting attention to functional completeness or schedule adherence.

Engage diverse stakeholders comprehensively throughout technology adoption lifecycles. Stakeholder identification must extend beyond obvious internal project teams to include individuals and groups possessing relevant information, resources, or specialized knowledge. Technology initiatives require input from business leaders who understand strategic context, end users who will interact with systems daily, technical specialists who ensure architectural soundness, security professionals who protect organizational assets, compliance officers who ensure regulatory adherence, and operations personnel who maintain production systems.

Capability and Measurement

Invest in quality management capability building across organizational levels. Quality aspirations exceed capability when organizations expect high performance without providing training in quality methods, tools, and techniques. As demonstrated in the surgical center case, comprehensive training that addresses both knowledge and skill development delivers measurable improvements (Quigley et al., 2011). Technology organizations should invest systematically in developing capabilities such as requirements engineering, test automation, security practices, performance engineering, and quality analytics that enable teams to execute quality activities effectively.

Implement systematic measurement that provides objective visibility into both process adherence and outcome achievement. Rever (2007) emphasizes that meaningful metrics drive specific actions linked to improving processes and deliverables. Organizations should establish metrics spanning process dimensions, product dimensions, and outcome dimensions. These metrics should inform regular quality reviews that assess trends, identify issues requiring attention, and trigger improvement initiatives when performance falls short of expectations.

Governance and Oversight

Establish quality gates integrated into development workflows that enforce minimum quality standards before progression to subsequent phases. Quality gates prevent defects from propagating through project lifecycles where they become more expensive to remediate. Automated quality gates that prevent code merging until tests pass, block deployments until security scans complete, or halt releases until performance benchmarks meet thresholds institutionalize quality requirements.

Conduct systematic quality audits that provide independent verification of process adherence and outcome quality. Regular audits identify best practices deserving amplification, gaps requiring corrective action, and opportunities for process improvement. Organizations should conduct audits throughout project lifecycles rather than only at major milestones, enabling early detection and correction of deviations before they compound into project-threatening problems.

Create transparent quality reporting that provides stakeholders with timely, relevant information enabling informed decision-making. Kerzner (2017) explains that quality dashboards offer at-a-glance views of metrics using graphs, charts, and visual indicators highlighting issues and risks. Organizations should implement layered reporting where executive dashboards provide strategic summaries while detailed operational reports enable deep investigation.

Cultural and Organizational Enablement

Foster continuous improvement cultures where learning from experience receives structural support and celebration. Organizations should conduct retrospectives after major milestones, document lessons learned systematically, share insights across organizational boundaries through communities of practice, and track implementation of improvement actions to ensure insights translate into actual change (Rever, 2007). Recognition systems should celebrate both quality outcomes and quality behaviors, reinforcing that quality activities merit appreciation and reward.

Align incentive structures with quality objectives to ensure that compensation, promotion, and recognition decisions reflect quality contributions. When reward systems prioritize speed or feature delivery while ignoring quality, rational individuals optimize for what receives reward rather than what receives rhetorical emphasis. Organizations must ensure that performance evaluation criteria, bonus calculations, promotion decisions, and public recognition mechanisms all incorporate quality dimensions.

Provide resources necessary for quality execution including tools, infrastructure, and capacity. Quality aspirations prove hollow when organizations demand quality without providing automated testing frameworks, security scanning tools, performance monitoring systems, collaboration platforms, or sufficient time for quality activities. Organizations must invest in automation, tooling, and infrastructure that makes quality activities efficient rather than burdensome.

Demonstrate executive commitment through personal participation in quality activities such as design reviews, incident postmortems, or quality council meetings. When executives personally engage with quality rather than delegating quality entirely to others, they communicate authentic priority and create accountability throughout organizational hierarchies. Executive participation also enables leaders to understand quality challenges firsthand rather than relying solely on filtered reports.

Anticipating Implementation Challenges

Organizations implementing quality-driven approaches to technology adoption commonly encounter several challenges that leaders must anticipate and address proactively.

Time and Skill Constraints

Time pressure creates persistent tension between quality activities and schedule commitments. When deadlines loom, teams feel compelled to skip quality activities that appear discretionary. Organizations must counter this pressure by demonstrating that quality activities prevent far more expensive downstream problems, making them time investments rather than time costs. Additionally, organizations should build quality time into project schedules explicitly rather than treating quality as flexible buffer that can be eliminated when schedules tighten.

Skill gaps in quality methods and tools create barriers to quality execution even when motivation exists. Teams may value quality highly but lack practical knowledge of requirements engineering, test automation, performance optimization, or security hardening. Organizations must invest in training that builds actual capability through hands-on practice rather than merely conveying abstract concepts.

Technical Debt and Organizational Structure

Legacy technical debt accumulated over years creates quality challenges that cannot be resolved quickly. Organizations may aspire to high quality standards but face existing systems characterized by poor code quality, inadequate test coverage, architectural limitations, or documentation deficiencies.

Addressing this technical debt while simultaneously delivering new capabilities requires careful prioritization and incremental improvement.

Organizational silos that separate business, technology, and operations functions impede the cross-functional collaboration necessary for quality. Quality requires shared understanding of requirements, coordinated planning, integrated testing, and smooth operational transition. Organizations should establish cross-functional teams with shared objectives and ensure that incentive structures reward collective outcomes rather than only functional achievements.

Cultural Change Resistance

Resistance to quality culture change from individuals or groups comfortable with current approaches requires patient, persistent leadership. Moving from rules-based quality environments to genuine quality cultures requires fundamental transformation that management must support consistently (Srinivasan & Kurey, 2014). Organizations should acknowledge resistance as natural response to change, address concerns through dialogue rather than decree, demonstrate quality benefits through pilot projects, celebrate early adopters who embrace quality practices, and maintain consistent messaging over extended periods.

CONCLUSION

Organizational agility in the digital age demands more than rapid technology adoption—it requires systematic quality management that ensures technology delivers sustainable value. This chapter has demonstrated that quality management and organizational agility, far from being contradictory objectives, represent mutually reinforcing capabilities that together enable organizations to navigate complexity, respond to change, and maintain competitive advantage.

The integration of quality management principles into technology adoption lifecycles provides the structured framework necessary for managing the inherent complexity of digital transformation. By embedding quality considerations from project initiation through closure, organizations minimize the rework that consumes resources and erodes stakeholder confidence. Through systematic quality assurance, control, monitoring, and reporting, organizations create visibility that enables proactive intervention before small issues become major obstacles.

The distributed responsibility model for quality—where business managers, quality directors, functional managers, and project managers each embrace distinct quality responsibilities—recognizes that quality emerges from collective effort rather than isolated quality department activities (Rever, 2007). When every organizational level embraces quality ownership, quality receives constant attention rather than only during audits or customer complaints.

Most fundamentally, building quality into organizational culture transforms quality from compliance burden into competitive advantage. When quality becomes everyone's responsibility supported by capable leadership, clear objectives, appropriate tools, and aligned incentives, organizations develop the adaptability and resilience that characterize true organizational agility. Companies demonstrating world-class quality exhibit leadership that firmly supports quality objectives, persistent motivation to address customer needs, and willingness to pursue continuous improvement from bottom to top and top to bottom (Srinivasan & Kurey, 2014).

As technology continues to evolve at accelerating pace, organizations that master the integration of quality management with technology adoption will position themselves to thrive amid uncertainty. Those that sacrifice quality for speed will discover that apparent short-term gains evaporate as rework, defects, and stakeholder dissatisfaction undermine their agility. The path to sustainable organizational agility runs through systematic quality management—this is the essential insight that leaders must embrace as they guide their organizations through digital transformation.

The evidence from healthcare quality initiatives, particularly the VA MRSA reduction program, demonstrates how quality improvement techniques of performance monitoring, root cause analysis, developing targeted solutions, and tracking implementation can significantly enhance outcomes (Jain et al., 2011; Nelson et al., 2016). The lessons transfer directly to technology organizations: systematic measurement enables identification of outliers requiring attention, root cause analysis reveals underlying issues beyond symptoms, targeted interventions prove more effective than generic programs, sustained monitoring verifies that improvements persist, and transparent reporting creates accountability that motivates improvement.

Organizations must view quality not as constraint but as enabler—not as bureaucracy but as discipline—not as cost but as investment. This fundamental reorientation, supported by the frameworks, principles, and practices articulated in this chapter, provides the foundation upon which sustainable organizational agility can be built in an era of relentless technological change.

REFERENCES

CDC. (2016). *National and State Healthcare-Associated Infections Progress Report*. Center for Disease Control. Retrieved from https://stacks.cdc.gov/view/cdc/70275

Eagle, K. A., Montoye, C. K., Riba, A. L., DeFranco, A. C., Parrish, R., Skorcz, S., Baker, P. L., Faul, J., Jani, S. M., Chen, B., Roychoudhury, C., Elma, M. A., Mitchell, K. R., & Mehta, R. H. (2005). Guideline-based standardized care is associated with substantially lower mortality in Medicare patients with acute myocardial infarction: The American College of Cardiology's Guidelines Applied in Practice (GAP) Projects in Michigan. *Journal of the American College of Cardiology*, *46*(7), 1242–1248. DOI: 10.1016/j.jacc.2004.12.083 PMID: 16198838

Henien, S., Aronow, H. D., & Abbott, J. D. (2020). Quality management in the cardiac catheterization laboratory. *Journal of Thoracic Disease*, *12*(4), 1695–1705. DOI: 10.21037/jtd.2019.12.81 PMID: 32395312

Jain, R., Kralovic, S., Evans, M., Ambrose, M., Simbartl, L., Obrosky, S., Render, M., Freyberg, R., Jernigan, J., Muder, R., Miller, L., & Roselle, G. (2011). Veterans Affairs Initiative to Prevent Methicillin-Resistant Staphylococcus aureus Infections. *The New England Journal of Medicine*, *364*(15), 1419–1430. DOI: 10.1056/NEJMoa1007474 PMID: 21488764

Kerzner, H. (2017). *Project Management Metrics, KPIs, and Dashboards: A Guide to Measuring and Monitoring Project Performance*. John Wiley & Sons., DOI: 10.1002/9781119427599

Nelson, R. E., Stevens, V. W., Khader, K., Jones, M., Samore, M. H., Evans, M. E., Douglas Scott, R.II, Slayton, R. B., Schweizer, M. L., Perencevich, E. L., & Rubin, M. A. (2016). Economic Analysis of Veterans Affairs Initiative to Prevent Methicillin-Resistant Staphylococcus aureus Infections. *American Journal of Preventive Medicine*, *50*(5, Suppl 1), S58–S65. DOI: 10.1016/j.amepre.2015.10.016 PMID: 27102860

Project Management Institute. (2017). *A Guide to the Project Management Body of Knowledge (PMBOK® Guide)* (6th ed.). Project Management Institute.

Quigley, D. D., Wiseman, S. H., & Farley, D. O. (2011). *Improving Customer Service and Access in a Surgical Practice* (Working Paper WR-857-RWJF). RAND Corporation.

Ramirez, B., & Ramirez, J. (2018). *Douglas Montgomery's Introduction to Statistical Quality Control: A JMP® Companion*. SAS Institute Inc. Retrieved from https://support.sas.com/content/dam/SAS/support/en/books/douglas-montgomerys-introduction-to-statistical-quality-control/68860_excerpt.pdf

Reaiche, C. (2022). Module 6. Quality management and its key concepts. In *Strategic Project Management*. JCU Pressbooks. https://jcu.pressbooks.pub/pmriskquality/chapter/module-6-quality-management-and-its-key-concepts/

Rever, H. (2007). *Quality in project management—a practical look at chapter 8 of the PMBOK® guide*. Paper presented at PMI® Global Congress 2007—Latin America, Cancún, Mexico. Project Management Institute.

Rose, K. H. (2014). *Project Quality Management: Why, What, and How* (2nd ed.). J. Ross Publications.

Schwalbe, K. (2019). *Information Technology Project Management* (9th ed.). Cengage Learning.

Srinivasan, A., & Kurey, B. (2014, April). Creating a culture of quality. *Harvard Business Review*. https://hbr.org/2014/04/creating-a-culture-of-quality

Chapter 5
Resilient Transformation: Continuous Change Management and Cybersecurity in Hyperconnected Organizations

Sharon L. Burton
http://orcid.org/0000-0003-1653-9783
Embry-Riddle Aeronautical University, USA

ABSTRACT

In today's hyperconnected digital environment, organizational change management must integrate cybersecurity and AI as strategic elements. This chapter proposes a framework combining continuous change management, cyber risk governance, and workforce responsiveness defined by adaptive potential and digital dexterity. Legacy models designed for linear change struggle amid rising cyber threats and rapid technological shifts. By framing cyber risk governance as a strategic enabler and leveraging AI insight, organizations balance agility with security to achieve resilient transformation. Drawing on literature and case studies, the framework highlights the importance of behavioral adaptability and continuous learning cultures in sustaining success. This approach helps organizations anticipate disruptions and innovate securely, making it relevant for industries facing converging digital and cyber challenges. The findings offer actionable guidance for executives, change strategists, and cyber professionals striving to excel where flexibility, safety, and intelligent automation converge.

INTRODUCTION

Aviation and aerospace stand at the frontier of technological innovation and digital transformation, shaping transport and defense, as well as global economic stability and safety (Dutta et al., 2025). In 2025, the combined aviation and aerospace sectors will have accelerated their adoption of digital tools, driven by operational demands for efficiency, sustainability, and safety. According to a report by the Data Insights Market (2025), the aviation digital transformation market alone is estimated at $15 billion in 2025, growing at a compound annual rate of 12% through 2033. This data denotes how efficiency, safety, and sustainability are significant drivers of digital adoption across airlines, airports, and OEMs (Data Insights Market 2025). Airlines and manufacturers are investing rapidly in AI (Moghadasnian &

DOI: 10.4018/979-8-3373-4027-2.ch005

Rajol, 2025), Internet of Things (Mohd Hanif & Jaafar, 2023), and data analytics (Mohd Hanif & Jaafar, 2023) to enable predictive maintenance, optimize flight operations, and personalize the passenger experience. Airbus, Boeing, and leading commercial and defense firms now routinely deploy digital twins, cloud infrastructures, and automation to reduce unplanned downtime by up to 30% and accelerate design-to-market timelines (Xiong & Wang, 2022).

However, alongside these gains, the industry faces a cybersecurity crisis of unprecedented scale and complexity (Adekoya et al., 2025). According to a recent report from UK Research and Innovation (UKRI), Cyberattacks have surged by 600% year-over-year, an explosive and dramatic increase (Uffindell, 2025). The data shows that there were more than 10 major breaches striking airlines and airports in the first half of 2025 alone, including incidents that disrupted flight schedules, compromised sensitive data, and exposed critical infrastructure vulnerabilities (Garcia, 2025). Global cyberattacks increased by 38% in 2022, exposing critical vulnerabilities in organizational resilience and accelerating the demand for integrated change management frameworks (Muncaster, 2023). According to Ukwandu et. al. (2022), ransomware attacks from sophisticated threat actors, including nation-state groups and cybercriminal organizations, now regularly target digitalized systems in air traffic control, passenger management, e-boarding gates, and aircraft navigation. The global aviation cybersecurity market is projected to exceed $5.3 billion in 2025, a reflection of mounting investment to secure an expanded digital attack surface and to comply with rigorous regulatory demands (Grand View Research, 2024).

Despite the high stakes, research shows that 80% of aerospace and defense organizations remain in the early stages of digital transformation. As given by the Capgemini Research Institute (2025), a significant digital maturity–ROI gap persists: while most companies claim progress in digital integration, nearly three-quarters do not achieve expected returns, often due to underestimating the complexities of integrating advanced technology and change management across legacy environments. Workforce challenges further complicate transformation, as the industry navigates a generational shift in skills and persistent resistance to organizational change. According to Bento et al. (2020), cultural inertia, organizational silos, and lack of cross-functional collaboration are consistently cited as barriers to rapid adaptation and innovation, especially where safety and compliance are foundational imperatives.

The purpose of this chapter is to integrate current research and industry practice to create an integrated framework for continuous change management and cybersecurity in the aviation and aerospace sectors. Positioned as a qualitative, thematic analysis, this inquiry seeks to address the gap between present organizational change models and effective cyber risk governance by investigating recent empirical findings, sector case studies, and advancements in adaptive leadership. Specifically, this chapter aims to engender actionable insights for leaders tasked with managing resilient transformation in environments marked by digital complexity, regulatory pressures, and heightened security threats.

Change management, therefore, has become a central concern for aviation and aerospace leaders. Evidence from recent CAPA Airline Leader Summits and industry panels highlights a need for agile, continuous change processes, ones that account for the sector's regulatory, technical, and safety-driven uniqueness (CAPA – Centre for Aviation, 2025). Without robust change management paired with technical advancement, transformations stall, cybersecurity gaps widen, and the risk of operational disruption grows. Leading organizations are responding by aligning digital risk, compliance, and people-readiness strategies, building cultures that are as adaptable as the technologies they seek to implement (Suebsuwong, 2023).

Despite rapid digitalization and heightened risk awareness, there remains a clear gap in the literature regarding integrated models for managing continuous change and cybersecurity in aviation and aerospace contexts. Most studies address digital transformation, cybersecurity, and change management as distinct challenges, rather than as interconnected domains that demand holistic solutions (Burton, 2024; Möller, 2023; Saeed et al., 2023). This chapter addresses that gap by synthesizing recent research, industry statistics, and best-practice frameworks to provide actionable guidance for leaders. By presenting evidence-backed pathways to resilient transformation, this chapter aims to equip aviation and aerospace organizations to thrive, adapting swiftly and safely in an age when operational excellence and security are not merely goals, but ongoing imperatives.

BACKGROUND

OCM has emerged as a central theme in strategic and operational planning, responding to turbulence induced by innovation, technology, and shifting stakeholder expectations (Lewin, 1947; Kotter, 1995; Endrejat & Burnes, 2024). The foundational models of Lewin's three-stage process, unfreezing, changing, and refreezing, and Kotter's 8-Step Model were designed to address organizational movement in discrete, linear phases (Burnes, 2019; Graves et al., 2023). Historically, these theories provided essential frameworks for engaging the human element of organizational shifts, focusing on leadership, structure, and managing resistance to change (Errida & Lotfi, 2021; Robertson & Lapiņa, 2023). However, the progression toward digital economies has transformed the context in which OCM operates, forcing enterprises to become agile and continually attentive regarding cyber risks and security threats (Daher & Ziade, 2023). According to Jones (2021), cyber risk refers to the potential for loss or disruption resulting from cyber threats, vulnerabilities, or failures in digital systems, which can impact an organization's assets, operations, reputation, or stakeholders. Jones (2021) emphasizes that cyber risk encompasses technical and human factors, including insider threats and intentional digital sabotage.

The digital revolution has positioned new technologies, AI, machine learning, and cloud-based infrastructure, at the nexus of business strategy (Saarikko et al., 2020; Kupiek, 2023; Zoppelletto et al., 2023). With technological advances, conventional change management approaches have proven inadequate to guarantee ongoing protection, systemic resilience, and deep culture change. Workforces are now distributed and remote or hybrid models dominate, increasing operational flexibility and the organization's attack surface (Ainurrofiq & Amir, 2023; Bloom et al., 2023). The shift requires continuous change frameworks that balance innovation and compliance and build unified approaches linking technological and human dimensions of change (Graves et al., 2023).

A defining challenge in recent OCM research is the persistent gap between cybersecurity and organizational adaptation (Stoumpos et al., 2023). Legacy OCM models often underestimate cyber risk, treating it either as an afterthought or the exclusive domain of IT management (Burton, 2023; Jaiyeoba et al., 2025). In modern organizational environments, threats such as data breaches, phishing, and supply chain cyberattacks can catalyze or disrupt change processes and threaten stakeholder trust (Riahi & Islam, 2024). This reality calls for OCM leaders who are skilled in managing resistance and building culture, as well as in interpreting risk signals, promoting digital literacy, and supporting rapid response (Kucharska & Bedford, 2020; Jaiyeoba et al., 2025; Sreenivasan & Suresh, 2024).

Cyber risk must now be woven into the fabric of every change initiative. Unlike compliance standards such as NIST or ISO/IEC 27001, which often remain siloed, a modern OCM framework requires direct translation of these standards into daily routines and behaviors (Bagga et al., 2023). This translation is especially vital for organizations with distributed teams, where distance can undermine engagement and increase vulnerability (Bendig et al., 2023; Riedl & Woolley, 2020). The resulting paradigm shift requires OCM professionals to expand their remit, enabling change, interpreting risk, and maintaining cyber hygiene throughout transformation events. Cyber hygiene is the consistent practices and habits individuals or organizations use to stay safe and secure online. It includes actions like using strong passwords, updating software regularly, avoiding suspicious links, and being cautious with personal data (Karayel et al., 2025), akin to brushing your teeth, but for your digital health.

Speed itself is an ambiguous friend to OCM. The pressure to innovate can erode essential planning, while lag leaves organizations exposed to technical and market risks (Hagl et al., 2024; Trzeciak, 2024). New models must therefore balance rapid execution with rigorous risk assessments and scenario planning, embedding cybersecurity as an iterative, forward-looking process rather than a postimplementation schedule (Stetsenko et al., 2021).

Moreover, cultural readiness remains a barrier. Organizations strong in change agility are not always strong in digital ethics or security literacy (Kucharska & Bedford, 2020; Waheed & Zhang, 2022). Transforming operational culture to value and reward vigilance, responsibility, and ethical digital behavior is as vital as training employees to use new systems. Cyber resiliency thereby demands not just behavioral change, but durable shifts in organizational values, incentives, and identity (Rafi, 2022).

The academic literature also reveals few metrics to evaluate the effectiveness of integrated change and cybersecurity strategies, most frameworks assess post hoc adoption and project completion, but not resilience or recovery capacity (Snyder, 2019; Zhang et al., 2024). Sectoral differences are also significant: highly regulated fields like finance and healthcare may integrate cyber risk earlier and more comprehensively, while manufacturing or logistics often react to crises rather than anticipate them (Kasana et al., 2023; Stoumpos et al., 2023).

Modern organizations are operating in environments marked by unprecedented connectivity, rapid technological change, and expanding threat surfaces. Digital transformation, characterized by cloud adoption, automation, and AI, has become imperative for maintaining competitiveness and agility. However, these shifts bring intensified exposure to cyber risks, ranging from data breaches and ransomware attacks to systemic disruptions with enterprise-wide impact. Legacy organizational change management (OCM) models, conceived for slower, more predictable rates of change, struggle to address the sheer scale and complexity of such threats.

A critical evolution in this landscape is the explicit integration of cyber risk governance into OCM and digital transformation initiatives. Cyber risk governance is the strategic oversight and decision-making framework that ensures cybersecurity risks are identified, assessed, and managed in alignment with organizational objectives and risk appetite (World Economic Forum, 2021). It is no longer sufficient to treat cybersecurity as a merely technical or operational matter; it requires board-level attention and strategic alignment with the organization's core mission and values (World Economic Forum, 2021).

- Key frameworks highlight this imperative. According to the World Economic Forum (2021), effective cyber risk governance rests on six principles designed for board-level leadership:
- Strategic enablement: Cyber risk should be integrated as a strategic enabler, not just a defensive concern.
- Systemic resilience: Boards must drive holistic resilience across all business domains.
- Alignment with risk appetite: Governance structures ensure cyber risk activities are calibrated to organizational risk appetite.

- Clear accountability: Roles and responsibilities for cyber oversight are well-defined across all governance levels.
- Informed decision-making: Boards foster a culture of meaningful reporting and transparent escalation of cyber issues.
- Continuous improvement: Organizations regularly review and enhance cyber risk governance processes to reflect evolving threats.

Incorporating these principles, organizations can position cyber risk governance as a core element of OCM, embedding strategic oversight within transformation efforts and integrating cybersecurity into every layer of planning, implementation, and evaluation. This holistic approach ensures that as companies adopt new technologies and agile processes, they are simultaneously advancing organizational resilience, regulatory alignment, and stakeholder trust.

In summary, the trajectory of OCM has moved from managing episodic change to enabling continuous, secure transformation, necessitating agile leadership that is as attentive to cyber risk as to stakeholder alignment and cultural fit (Annabi, 2024; Jain et al., 2024). Tomorrow's organizational transformation is defined not by whether change occurs, but by how securely and sustainably it is accomplished. As given by Strielkowski (2025), fostering adaptive potential and digital dexterity through continuous learning is essential for organizations seeking to stay resilient amid rapid digital disruption. Leaders should prioritize these competencies by embedding them into talent development, change management processes, and strategic planning frameworks (Burrell et al., 2023; Burton, 2022). This approach transforms resilience from a reactive posture into a proactive, organization-wide capability, empowering teams to withstand disruptions, and to leverage change for innovation and growth.

ASSUMPTIONS, LIMITATIONS, AND DELIMITATIONS

In articulating the foundations and boundaries of this chapter, it is essential to clarify the guiding assumptions, recognized limitations, and purposeful delimitations that shape the research approach. These elements frame the scope and applicability of the analysis and ensure transparency regarding methodological choices and potential constraints. By explicitly outlining what is presumed, acknowledged as a boundary, or intentionally excluded, the chapter provides readers with a clear understanding of how the findings should be interpreted and where caution or further inquiry may be warranted. This structural clarity strengthens the rigor and relevance of the ensuing discussion on resilient transformation in digital organizations.

Assumptions

This chapter operates under several foundational assumptions that define its scope, interpretation, and applicability. First, it assumes that organizations pursuing digital transformation recognize the strategic necessity of aligning continuous change management with cybersecurity governance, and do not treat either domain as ancillary or isolated from core operations. The analysis presupposes that these organizations are positioned within digitally engaged sectors—such as healthcare, finance, logistics, or aerospace, where transformation is closely coupled with technological risk and regulatory accountability.

Second, it is assumed that the leaders and organizational actors referenced, whether discussed through case literature or theoretical synthesis, possess operational awareness of institutional change dynamics, along with a baseline familiarity with cybersecurity principles. This includes an interpretive capacity to engage with frameworks involving adaptive change, digital risk, and technology-enabled decision-making. Readers are also assumed to have a working understanding of core constructs such as resilience, agility, cyber hygiene, and AI-enabled transformation.

Third, the analysis assumes that human, technological, and organizational systems interact systemically, and that strategic integration of these domains enhances resilience, adaptability, and innovation capacity. This implies an underlying belief in socio-technical interdependence, wherein cultural readiness, digital dexterity, and cyber risk governance must converge to enable secure transformation.

Fourth, the chapter assumes that AI-driven tools and learning systems are becoming normative in digitally advanced organizations, and that their adoption will accelerate rather than contract over time. Thus, the integration of AI in change processes is treated not as speculative, but as a critical enabler of foresight, scalability, and real-time adaptation.

Last, while the framework is intended to be broadly applicable, it assumes that contextual adaptation is necessary across different organizational types and cultures. This includes variation in structural models (e.g., decentralized vs. centralized), regulatory environments, leadership maturity, and digital infrastructure. The generalizability of insights is therefore conditional upon thoughtful interpretation by practitioners situated within specific organizational realities.

Limitations

In addition, the relevance of the proposed triadic framework, integrating continuous change management, cyber risk governance, and responsive workforce capabilities, may vary across contexts. While the model is well-suited to digitally mature, regulated, or adaptive organizations, such as those in sectors like aerospace, healthcare, finance, and advanced manufacturing, it may be less applicable in small, resource-constrained environments (e.g., non-profit organizations or micro-enterprises), where cybersecurity capacity may be minimal, and change efforts may lack dedicated leadership or long-term continuity structures. Similarly, highly centralized government agencies or bureaucracies, where decision authority is concentrated and adaptive workforce redesign is constrained, may encounter structural barriers to implementing such a fluid, horizontally integrated approach.

Furthermore, the rate of technological advancement and evolving cyber threat vectors may outpace some of the frameworks discussed, especially in areas where AI regulation, cloud security, or hybrid workforce governance is evolving rapidly. The absence of standardized resilience metrics, especially those that capture behavioral adaptability or embedded risk management, also limits empirical validation and hinders outcome tracking.

Delimitations

The boundaries of this research are explicitly defined to ensure conceptual clarity, thematic coherence, and analytical precision. This chapter is not a quantitative study and does not involve statistical modeling, hypothesis testing, or inferential generalizations based on primary data collection. Instead, it offers a conceptual and integrative analysis based on secondary literature, theory development, and cross-sector synthesis focused on change management and cybersecurity in digitally advanced organizations.

The scope of analysis is deliberately delimited to organizations operating in digitally intensive environments, such as aerospace, finance, healthcare, and supply chain sectors, where large-scale transformation initiatives are underway and cyber risk governance is a visible strategic priority. These settings are marked by hybrid or remote workforces, high regulatory exposure, and increasing reliance on AI-enabled platforms and decision support tools. The framework developed in this chapter is thus designed to apply primarily to such contexts where rapid technological change intersects with the need for systematic resilience and cultural adaptability.

This work emphasizes the strategic and organizational dimensions of digital transformation and adaptive change management. It does not address deeply technical implementations, such as encryption protocols, access control schemes, penetration testing, or software-specific configurations. Similarly, granular cybersecurity engineering practices, IT deployment scripts, or incident response playbooks fall outside the analytic scope. Instead, cybersecurity is examined through the lenses of governance, leadership integration, and behavioral enablement. The chapter also excludes general leadership development models and non-digital change theories, except where they directly inform cybersecurity integration or workforce adaptability. The treatment of AI, resilience, and change models is limited to those with direct application to organizational governance and strategy formation.

The literature base is drawn primarily from the period 2015–2025, aligning with the decade of major shifts in remote work culture, cloud computing expansion, AI adoption, and evolving cybersecurity regulation to ensure contemporary relevance. By narrowing its focus to strategic transformation in digitally intensive organizations, with specific emphasis on cyber risk governance, workforce agility, and adaptive capacity, this chapter seeks to offer a focused, theory-driven contribution to the evolving domain of organizational resilience and intelligent change leadership. This approach intentionally excludes broader explorations of generic change management or technology adoption issues, underscoring a commitment to advancing specialized insight into how contemporary digital pressures reshape strategic leadership and organizational resilience to further enhance analytical depth.

STATEMENT OF THE PROBLEM AND THE RESEARCH GAP

Traditional organizational change management (OCM) frameworks are inadequately equipped to address the evolving challenges of digital transformation, as they fail to integrate cybersecurity risk, AI-enabled decision systems, and continuous adaptation into their core structures, leaving organizations vulnerable in hyperconnected, high-risk environments. Despite the growing urgency of digital transformation and cyber resilience across sectors, existing organizational change management (OCM) frameworks remain insufficiently equipped to respond to the pace, complexity, and risk dynamics of today's hyperconnected environments. Widely adopted approaches such as Lewin's three-stage model, Kotter's 8-Step process, and the ADKAR model provide foundational guidance for managing change. However, these models do not account for real-time threat detection, AI-enabled decision-making, or the interweaving of cybersecurity protocols into behavioral change processes. Their linear, episodic structures fall short in environments where adaptation must be continuous and cross-functional vigilance is essential (Snyder, 2019; Trzeciak, 2024; Waheed & Zhang, 2022).

Similarly, legacy strategic assessment tools like the GE-McKinsey Matrix, designed to evaluate business unit strength and industry attractiveness, lack built-in measures for cyber risk exposure, digital maturity, and adaptive capacity. In today's volatile threat landscape, traditional axes of evaluation cannot surface vulnerabilities that may undermine resilience, such as susceptibility to ransomware, lack of AI-readiness, or governance blind spots in hybrid workplaces (Kasana et al., 2023; Hagl et al., 2024). These omissions are particularly critical in high-reliability sectors like healthcare, manufacturing, and aerospace, where continuity and compliance are tightly coupled with digital integrity (Stoumpos et al., 2023; Kupiek, 2023).

Further compounding the challenge, the literature offers few integrative approaches that bridge OCM with cybersecurity strategy and AI-based organizational sensing. It does not exploit the explanatory power of sociotechnical systems theory or complexity theory to interpret dynamic, tech-human interactions at scale. Existing research tends to compartmentalize people, process, and technology into parallel domains, rather than examining how their mutual dependence can be leveraged for transformation resilience (Bendig et al., 2023). Key components such as cyber awareness, digital ethics, adaptive feedback loops, and AI-driven change visualization remain inconsistently addressed in OCM or digital governance frameworks.

This chapter addresses these critical limitations by advancing an integrative resilience framework that synchronizes continuous change management with embedded cybersecurity and AI-driven foresight. Anchored in sociotechnical systems thinking, the proposed model reconceptualizes change as a persistent, sensing-driven, and safeguards-aware process, fusing strategic agility with operational protection. In uniting fragmented domains and redefining OCM for a cyber-volatile world, this research fills a pressing conceptual and applied gap. By advancing this synthesis, the chapter responds to a growing demand for models that promote transformation and enable resilient continuity in the face of persistent digital disruption, making it especially relevant for aviation, defense, financial services, and other sectors navigating complex cyber-technical ecosystems.

NATURE OF THE STUDY AND RESEARCH METHODOLOGY

This section clarifies the foundational nature of the study and the strategic methodology adopted for its execution. The nature of the study focuses on examining the manner in which organizations, specifically within digitally intensive sectors (i.e., aviation, aerospace, finance, and healthcare), can integrate continuous change management with robust cybersecurity to foster resilience (Stoumpos et al., 2023; Burton, 2023). The investigation is driven by a recognized need to move beyond legacy change models, which often treat cyber risk as an afterthought or confine it to IT domains, despite the disruptive impact of digital threats on organizational continuity and stakeholder trust (Riahi & Islam, 2024; Kucharska & Bedford, 2020). This chapter contends that adaptive capacity must blend behavioral, technological, and process elements to address real-time disruptions (Sreenivasan & Suresh, 2024) by situating the research at the intersection of technology adoption, organizational behavior, and risk governance. Aligned with this focus, this chapter employs a qualitative, thematic analytic approach that prioritizes conceptual synthesis over prescriptive modeling. The purpose is to derive integrated frameworks that scholars and practitioners can translate into practical strategies for mitigating cyber risk during transformation initiatives (Hagl et al., 2024). Data sampling draws from an extensive literature base spanning 2015 to 2025, with particular attention to recent case studies and empirical research on leadership, digital dexterity, and cross-functional alignment (Kucharska & Bedford, 2020; World Economic Forum, 2021). This high-level approach intentionally emphasizes contemporary relevance due to dramatic shifts in remote work culture, AI deployment, and operational complexity in the last decade (Kasana et al., 2023).

The methodology and design further employed thematic coding, using inductive logic to identify emergent categories from peer-reviewed literature, industry reports, and cross-sector frameworks (Stoumpos et al., 2023; Burton, 2023). Key analytic themes include leadership alignment, cyber resiliency, scenario planning, and organizational culture, each examined for its contribution to risk mitigation and adaptive transformation (Sreenivasan & Suresh, 2024; Waheed & Zhang, 2022). Rather than imposing a single prescriptive framework, this research adapts its categories based on cross-disciplinary findings, ensuring that theoretical rigor and practical utility are preserved (Kasana et al., 2023; Hagl et al., 2024). This process supports the development of actionable pathways for building resilient, cyber-aware cultures within high-reliability sectors (World Economic Forum, 2021).

This integrated Nature of the Study and Methodology section foregrounds the inquiry's dual intent: to advance the conceptual comprehension of organizational resilience in hyperconnected environments and to deliver empirically grounded guidance for leaders navigating digital transformation and cyber risk (Riahi & Islam, 2024; Kupiek, 2023). The chapter positions itself to contribute meaningful, actionable scholarship to the evolving intersection of change management and cybersecurity by combining a purposeful, sector-focused research design with rigorous thematic analysis. This approach is deliberately structured to ensure that the findings are theoretically robust and directly applicable to high-reliability sectors facing escalating digital threats and operational complexity (Stoumpos et al., 2023; Hagl et al., 2024).

The review process involved targeted keyword searches across Scopus, IEEE Xplore, ProQuest, and Google Scholar, covering the years 2015 to 2025. Search terms included combinations such as "organizational change management," "cybersecurity governance," "AI and transformation," and "resilience in digital systems." The literature inclusion criteria required empirical or theoretical relevance to cyber-integrated change, peer-reviewed quality (or equivalent professional credibility), and clear applicability to sectors such as aerospace, healthcare, finance, and logistics (Kucharska & Bedford, 2020; Kasana et al., 2023). Exclusion criteria filtered out opinion pieces, news commentary, and works not explicitly addressing technological change or governance implications (Stoumpos et al., 2023). Included sources were thematically coded using inductive logic, emphasizing emergent categories such as leadership alignment, cyber resilience, AI-enabled sensing, cross-functional collaboration, and cultural resistance. Rather than imposing a pre-established framework, themes were allowed to emerge across disciplines, formats, and sector contexts, thereby preserving analytic flexibility while supporting conceptual integration. This process supports academic synthesis and practical relevance, generating insights that bridge theoretical models and real-world decision-making in volatile, digitally mediated environments (World Economic Forum, 2021; Hagl et al., 2024).

LITERATURE REVIEW

A rigorous literature review is essential for situating new research within the dynamic and rapidly evolving field of organizational change management and cybersecurity integration. This section enables the identification of theoretical debates, empirical gaps, and methodological innovations, serving as the intellectual foundation upon which subsequent arguments are assembled. By tracing the converging streams of prior investigations, the review clarifies the broader context and demonstrates the necessity of inquiry in this area. Literature reviews ensure scholarly rigor, allow for critical evaluation, and foster dialogue across academic disciplines and practice domains, each bearing distinct yet overlapping priorities. Through meticulous synthesis and critical analysis, the literature review positions the current research as a response to and an advancement beyond extant studies in the field.

Theoretical Foundations of Organizational Change Management

Classical organizational change management theory finds its origins in Lewin's Change Management Model, which articulated the stages of unfreezing, changing, and refreezing behaviors, emphasizing preparation and stability as vital to successful transitions (Lewin, 1947). Kotter's 8-Step Process, subsequently, extended this legacy, introducing a strategic and sequential roadmap for sustainable change by addressing urgency, coalition building, communication, empowerment, and anchoring new approaches in organizational culture (Kotter, 1995; Burns, 2019). More recent work interrogates these models' relevance amidst today's procedural acceleration and decentralization, suggesting that linear paradigms often lag behind the volatile, uncertain, complex, and ambiguous (VUCA) environments endemic to modern digital transformation (Endrejat & Burnes, 2024; Graves et al., 2023). Current sources emphasize the growing necessity for adaptable frameworks that foreground agility, iterative feedback, and employee empowerment as more suitable for the challenges of the digital age (Errida & Lotfi, 2021; Robertson & Lapiņa, 2023). Comprehending theoretical foundations allows practitioners and scholars to recognize structural strengths and critical gaps in prevailing OCM frameworks, encouraging the evolution of more dynamic, cyber-integrated strategies.

Critique for Theoretical Foundations of Organizational Change Management

Classic OCM theory, while foundational, demonstrates limitations when confronted with the speed and complexity of contemporary business ecosystems. Its tendency toward Western-centric assumptions, psychological gradualism, and stability can undermine adaptability when rapid, cross-boundary digital change is essential (Burnes, 2019; Kucharska & Bedford, 2020; Waheed & Zhang, 2022). Future research must prioritize context, sectoral needs, and continuous learning to engineer resilient change models.

GE Model: Portfolio Strategy Evaluation and Its Relevance

Introduced in the early 1970s, the GE-McKinsey Matrix was created by McKinsey & Company for General Electric as a sophisticated alternative to basic portfolio tools. This nine-cell matrix was designed to help large, diversified organizations navigate complex investment decisions by mapping business units against two critical axes: industry attractiveness and business unit strength. Unlike single-factor models, this approach aggregates multiple variables (i.e., market growth rate, profitability, competitive positions, and regulatory impact), yielding a comprehensive analysis that guides leaders in prioritizing resource allocation across multiple strategic domains.

The significance of the GE model within this chapter is multifaceted. First, its analytic rigor offers a structured method for decision-makers who must balance competing priorities in environments marked by technological change, heightened cyber risk, and constant organizational flux. By quantifying internal competencies and external market factors, the matrix underpins an integrated strategy, fostering informed, objective decisions about where and how to invest for future resilience.

Second, the GE-McKinsey Matrix supports the chapter's emphasis on holistic and adaptive frameworks, especially by encouraging leaders to consider financial potential and evolving digital capabilities and vulnerabilities. In the context of digital transformation, the matrix enables organizations to visually evaluate which business segments exhibit the readiness and strategic relevance to drive forthcoming change initiatives or require bolstering against industry disruptions, including those posed by cyber threats.

Additionally, the integration of this model reflects the evolving expectations for resilience in a hyper-connected, risk-laden environment. Using the GE Matrix, leaders can identify units where investment in cybersecurity, AI, or digital infrastructure will generate the most substantial enterprise-wide benefit. This proactive alignment of capital and capability directly supports the broader thesis of the chapter: that successful transformation arises from cohesive, data-informed management of resources, technology, and human capital.

Overall, the early inception of the GE-McKinsey Matrix and its enduring role in strategic management underscore its importance for contemporary change agendas. Its adoption signals a move from siloed, intuition-driven planning to an institutionalized approach where adaptability, risk awareness, and operational resilience are measured and managed deliberately, key themes reflected throughout this research on organizational and digital transformation.

Critique for GE Model: Portfolio Strategy Evaluation and Its Relevance

The following critique of the GE Model: Portfolio Strategy Evaluation and Its Relevance systematically examines the strengths and limitations of the GE-McKinsey Matrix as a strategic tool within the context of contemporary organizational change and resilience. This analysis highlights how the model, though foundational in its era, must be viewed through a modern lens attentive to digital transformation and cybersecurity challenges. The critique is organized around several key subheadings: Limited Dynamic Responsiveness, Oversimplification and Subjectivity, Siloed Decision-Making and Integration Gaps, Insufficient Treatment of Digital and Cyber Risk, and Relevance in Modern Strategic Context. Each section explores specific facets of the model's utility and its shortcomings, offering an in-depth evaluation of how well the GE framework aligns with the current demands of complex, technology-driven environments.

One of the key limitations of the GE-McKinsey Matrix lies in its inherent reliance on subjective criteria, oversimplification and subjectivity. Although the model aims to produce an objective analysis by incorporating multiple factors (i.e., market growth potential, competitive strength, and strategic fit, these categories often rely heavily on qualitative assessments). Terms like "management quality," "brand strength," or "regulatory risk" are not easily quantified and can be manipulated to conform to internal biases or pre-existing organizational agendas. This subjectivity weakens the integrity of the evaluation process, resulting in decisions that reflect managerial preferences rather than empirical evidence. As a result, portfolio decisions may prioritize internal narratives over market realities, undercutting the strategic clarity the model seeks to provide. In rapidly evolving environments, where data-driven agility is essential, such ambiguity poses a serious constraint.

A further concern with the GE model is its tendency to reinforce compartmentalized thinking by evaluating business units in isolation, siloed decision-making and integration gaps.

The structure supports unit-specific investment optimization without adequately addressing the shared capabilities that enable organizational agility (i.e., cybersecurity infrastructure, real-time analytics platforms, or cross-functional talent). These strategic enablers typically operate across all business units and require coordinated governance to deliver enterprise-wide value. By emphasizing individual performance metrics, the matrix risks neglecting these horizontal factors, causing fragmentation in decision-making and hampering unified transformation efforts. In today's context of interconnected risk and digital dependency, successful change demands integrated strategies that transcend divisional silos; the GE model does not inherently facilitate this level of cohesion.

Perhaps the most critical flaw in the GE-McKinsey Matrix is its lack of responsiveness to modern digital and cyber risk variables, and insufficient Treatment of Digital and Cyber Risk. The original model, rooted in 20th-century market evaluation dynamics, did not account for issues now central to strategic planning (i.e., data breach exposure, ransomware threats, ethical AI deployment, or regulatory compliance in cloud-based services). These elements are no longer peripheral but integral to assessing business viability and resilience. However, the binary axes of "industry attractiveness" and "business unit strength" offer no mechanism for integrating such considerations in real time. Consequently, leaders may overlook vulnerabilities that undermine long-term competitiveness or misallocate resources to units ill-prepared for digital challenges. Without adapting its criteria to include cybersecurity readiness, digital maturity, and adaptive potential, the model falls short of guiding organizations through the volatile terrain of digital transformation.

Despite these shortcomings, the GE-McKinsey Matrix retains value as a visual and systematic framework for prioritizing resource allocations, especially during periods of organizational restructuring or diversification. However, its relevance hinges on evolving its criteria to reflect technological readiness, cyber maturity, and organizational agility. Only when paired with adaptive tools and a cyber-augmented outlook does the model inform the broader, integrated management needed for transformation. Reliance on its classic form, without recalibration for today's risk realities, may result in blind spots that impede agile change and undermine long-term resilience. In summary, while the GE-McKinsey Matrix has historically shaped strategy formulation, it must be reimagined or supplemented to align with the demands of digital-era organizational change, ensuring that risk, agility, and cross-unit synergies are fully embedded within the evaluation and decision-making process.

Digital Transformation and the Fault Lines of Change

Digitalization is reshaping business procedures, leadership roles, and market boundaries at an unprecedented scale (Saarikko et al., 2020; Kupiek, 2023; Stoumpos et al., 2023). The proliferation of AI, machine learning, and remote technologies demands multidimensional transformations that affect cultural norms, operational workflows, and individual competencies (Annabi, 2024; Graves et al., 2023). Studies document that the success or failure of digital transformation depends not merely on technology adoption but on alignment among stakeholder expectations, safe migration path design, and workforce upskilling (Ainurrofiq & Amir, 2023; Bendig et al., 2023). Notably, transformation efforts that lack robust OCM infrastructure report elevated risks of initiative fatigue, security vulnerabilities, and resistance, threatening competitive stance and stakeholder trust (Bloom et al., 2023; Riahi & Islam, 2024). This information is central as technology-driven change is the new operational baseline, making the integration of digital transformation with OCM not merely advisable, but critical for organizational resilience and security.

Critique for Digital Transformation and the Fault Lines of Change

Despite abundant frameworks, much literature tends to oversimplify transformation by prioritizing tools over people, presuming that technological upgrades inherently amount to strategic change (Bendig et al., 2023; Purwanto et al., 2023). The lack of granular analysis for small- and medium-sized enterprises and overreliance on high-profile case studies render some studies of limited practical value across contexts (Zoppelletto et al., 2023). This gap stresses the need for more nuanced, context-sensitive research that considers diverse organizational scales, cultures, and resource capacities to fully capture the complexities of transformation in practice.

The Role of Cybersecurity in Change Initiatives

Digitally transformed organizations face exponentially more complex and persistent cyber risks (Burton, 2023; Riahi & Islam, 2024). The literature emphasizes that cyber-attacks, unlike most traditional operational shocks, can erase trust and institutional progress within moments, making cyber-awareness vital at all stages of change (Sreenivasan & Suresh, 2024; Stoumpos et al., 2023). Yet, cybersecurity still too often remains the remit of technical or compliance teams rather than integrated as an organizational-wide practice coordinated with ongoing OCM (Bagga et al., 2023; Stetsenko et al., 2021). Studies stress the necessity of embedding standards such as NIST and ISO/IEC 27001 into daily routines and change workflows, fostering digital literacy, and emphasizing the human role in defense (Kupiek, 2023; Jain et al., 2024). Addressing this convergence positions organizations to elevate resilience, as cybersecurity becomes a shared competency and change initiatives are buffered against emergent digital threats.

Critique for The Role of Cybersecurity in Change Initiatives

Research often lacks operational guidance on fusing cybersecurity protocols with agile change models, skewing deeply technical or theoretical and underappreciating the social and behavioral dimensions essential for implementation success (Burton, 2023; Kucharska & Bedford, 2020). There is a pressing need for interdisciplinary, empirically validated models that connect day-to-day behaviors with evolving threat landscapes. An additional challenge arises from the limited integration of human factors research, resulting in models that often overlook the organizational cultures and adaptive learning processes necessary to sustain secure transformation amid continuous digital change.

Organizational Culture, Agility, and Change

Multiple streams of scholarship affirm that organizational culture can accelerate and obstruct change (Kucharska & Bedford, 2020; Bagga et al., 2023; Saarikko et al., 2020). Fostering an agile culture involves building collaboration, encouraging calculated risk-taking, and nurturing an environment supportive of ongoing learning, error tolerance, and continuous improvement (Budur et al., 2023; Rafi, 2022; Searles, 2024). The culture of vigilance, a necessary condition for effective cybersecurity, is highly correlated with leadership modeling, rewards, and sustained cross-functional dialogue (Riedl & Woolley, 2020). Research further notes that the absence of shared digital ethics, adaptive norms, and openness can stymie even the best-funded digital transformation, exposing the enterprise to security lapses and innovation plateaus (Waheed & Zhang, 2022). This information is significant because without robust cultural foundations, even technically sound change initiatives will falter, as resilience and security are deeply dependent on the beliefs and daily actions of the workforce.

Critique for Organizational Culture, Agility, and Change

Though widely acknowledged, cultural transformation literature is sometimes superficial, relying on attitude surveys and ad hoc engagement programs over empirically validated, longitudinal culture change strategies (Hagl et al., 2024; Snyder, 2019; Shahzad et al., 2023). Nuanced understanding of how to scale and measure adaptive culture remains insufficiently developed. Despite growing recognition of its importance, much of the current research fails to illuminate the specific levers and feedback mechanisms that sustain adaptive values and behaviors over time, especially across diverse organizational contexts and shifting digital demands.

Leadership, Governance, and Strategic Alignment

Leadership efficacy is repeatedly positioned as a determinant of successful organizational adaptation and cyber resilience (Lewin, 1947; Kotter, 1995; Robertson & Lapiņa, 2023). Visionary and ethical leaders drive alignment between strategic objectives, change implementation, and sustainable performance, actively cultivating resilience and enabling distributed authority (Endrejat & Burnes, 2024; Harrison et al., 2021; Jain et al., 2024). Transparent governance that supports participatory, cross-functional decision-making has been correlated with sustained transformation, heightened security posture, and improved employee morale (Burrell et al., 2023; Mangla & Singh, 2024; Strifler et al., 2020). Research also notes that embedding leadership development in OCM and cyber training yields superior agility and trust, reinforcing the capacity to innovate and respond to threats (Mizrak, 2024; Burton, 2023).

Critique for Leadership, Governance, and Strategic Alignment:

This subheading is vital as leadership remains the linchpin in realizing adaptive, resilient organizations, bridging technical, cultural, and human domains critical to transformation and security.

Leadership literature can become polarized between mythic individual narratives and uncritical structural determinism, neglecting the everyday practices and relational dynamics that shape real change (Endrejat & Burnes, 2024; McLaren et al., 2023; Mouazen et al., 2024). Comparative studies with an empirical, cross-sectoral focus are still too rare, complicating efforts to generalize best practices.

CONCEPTUAL FRAMEWORK

The Integrated Resilience Framework sets forth a cohesive model for synchronizing continuous change management with embedded cybersecurity in hyperconnected organizations. At the heart of this framework is the conviction that adaptability and digital security must operate as parallel, interdependent streams for organizations seeking sustained relevance and operational integrity. Traditional approaches to OCM focus on incremental adaptation, but these strategies rarely anticipate the heightened risks posed by advanced technologies, cyber threats, and the velocity of workplace transformation (Saarikko et al.,

2020). This model contends that true resilience is achieved only when adaptive processes and cyber protections are designed to reinforce one another rather than exist in isolation.

Within this framework, resilient transformation is operationalized through four primary mechanisms. First, decentralized leadership and empowered teams are encouraged to support iterative decision-making and cultivate a culture where learning from rapid change is the norm (Uhlir, 2025). Second, cybersecurity becomes a strategic function rather than simply a technical one, woven into strategic planning, organizational culture, and ongoing risk assessments (Kupiek, 2023). Strategic investments in AI and real-time monitoring tools enable organizations to detect anomalies swiftly and adjust course proactively. Third, dynamic communication channels and structured feedback loops keep employees informed, engaged, and accountable for advancing innovation and maintaining vigilance in digital practices (Baker et al., 2022).

The final element is continuous measurement and recalibration. By employing key performance indicators that evaluate the adoption of change and the organization's cyber hygiene, leaders gain actionable insight into program efficacy and organizational maturity (Naslund & Norrman, 2019). Rather than rely on ad hoc interventions, the framework insists on embedding resilience as a mindset and a measurable target that evolves with the landscape of digital risk (Tircovnicu & Hategan, 2023). This model ensures that the organization's orientation toward change remains forward-looking, adaptive, and anchored in operational agility and digital fortification. In this way, the integrated approach responds to real-time disruptions while laying the groundwork for future-proof success (Lewin, 1947). See Figure 1 for the Integrated Framework for Resilient Transformation.

Figure 1. Integrated Framework for Resilient Transformation: Interconnections among continuous change management, cyber risk governance, and responsive workforce capabilities with emphasis on adaptive potential and digital dexterity.

Change management models must integrate adaptive potential, digital dexterity, and a continuous learning culture as interdependent drivers of transformation to support organizational resilience in hyperconnected environments fully. Adaptive potential refers to the human capacity to learn, reconfigure behavior, and engage meaningfully with novel challenges in dynamic environments. It enables individuals to shift roles, adopt emerging tools, and generate new capabilities under uncertain conditions (Urban et al., 2024). Digital dexterity, by contrast, reflects a practical fluency in navigating, leveraging, and adapting to digital technologies in evolving work ecosystems (Makhafola et al., 2025). When harmonized within a continuous learning culture that fosters curiosity, psychological safety, and real-time knowledge exchange, these attributes reinforce one another to drive behavioral resilience and technical adaptability. This interplay equips organizations to absorb disruption and to leverage change as a performance multiplier. A practical conceptual framework must therefore embed mechanisms that detect, assess, and cultivate these human-centric competencies, not as peripheral capabilities, but as core enablers of sustainable and secure transformation.

CONCEPTUAL FRAMEWORK CRITIQUES

A critical evaluation of conceptual frameworks in contemporary organizational change management (OCM) exposes their foundational value and significant limitations, especially in the context of accelerating digital transformation and the necessity of cyber resilience.

Theoretical Foundations of Organizational Change Management

Traditional OCM models, such as Lewin's three-step change process and Kotter's 8-Step Model, provide vital structure for managing transitions within organizations. These frameworks offer linear or phased approaches, emphasizing leadership, communication, and the management of resistance. While effective for guiding planned change in stable environments, these models often lack the flexibility and responsiveness required in today's rapidly evolving digital landscape. Their reliance on preordained sequences or static phases can impede timely adaptation, especially when organizations must respond to unforeseen threats or opportunities. The rigidity of these models becomes increasingly apparent as technological advancements continually alter how organizations operate and compete.

The shift toward pervasive digitalization has fundamentally redefined the context in which change occurs. Traditional frameworks often overlook or underrepresent the disruptive impact of emerging technologies (i.e., AI, machine learning, and cloud computing). This oversight reveals a critical gap in their capacity to support continuous, iterative change that must now occur at the speed of technological innovation. The lag between change planning and execution, embedded in classic models, can lead to misalignment between strategic objectives and actual organizational capabilities, leaving firms vulnerable to competitive threats, cyber risks, and operational inefficiencies. Modern organizations require frameworks capable of integrating agility, real-time data, and adaptive cycles.

One of the most pronounced shortcomings of legacy OCM models is the peripheral treatment of cybersecurity. Rather than treating security considerations as core strategic concerns, many frameworks subsume them under compliance checklists or IT department responsibilities. This disconnect fails to address how cyber threats have become existential risks to organizational health and reputation. Effective change management today demands that cybersecurity be woven directly into the design, implementation, and evaluation of all transformation initiatives. Insufficient integration exposes technical vulnerabilities and weaknesses in policy, process, and employee behavior. Modern frameworks must institutionalize a culture of shared digital vigilance, continuous risk assessment, and cross-functional accountability if organizations are to sustain resilience and trust amidst constant threat evolution.

Another area where traditional frameworks falter is in cultivating organizational agility and a culture of continuous learning. Many established models treat culture as a background variable rather than a central driver of successful transformation. However, in dynamic digital contexts, the ability for teams to rapidly unlearn, adapt, and reconfigure roles is paramount. Frameworks that lack explicit mechanisms for measuring and developing digital dexterity, teamwork, and cyber literacy fail to ensure that behavioral and mindset shifts become ingrained. Digital dexterity is the ability to confidently navigate and adapt to digital technologies and changing work environments (Makhafola et al., 2025). It involves a mindset that embraces innovation, continuous learning, and collaboration through digital tools. People with strong digital dexterity use technology creatively to solve problems and thrive in a fast-paced, tech-driven world. This shortcoming can result in superficial or unsustainable change, as employees revert to established routines when faced with volatility or ambiguity. Sustainable OCM frameworks must encourage and actively cultivate a culture capable of embracing ongoing complexity and technological disruption.

The prevailing assumption in many models that top-down leadership drives effective change is increasingly outdated. In reality, contemporary organizations thrive on distributed leadership, collective decision-making, and multi-level engagement. Frameworks need to recognize that governance structures must allow for rapid feedback, flexibility, and recalibration, especially as digital initiatives cut across traditional hierarchies and departmental boundaries. Furthermore, the alignment of strategic intent with operational resilience, particularly in cybersecurity, requires new metrics and performance indicators that go beyond standard project success factors. Measuring readiness for, and response to, digital crises becomes as important as tracking adoption rates or project completions. Effective OCM models must embed continuous monitoring and adaptation, linking change initiatives directly to organizational learning and resilience outcomes.

By systematically examining each facet, it is clear that while legacy OCM models provide valuable starting points, their limitations in the face of ongoing digital transformation, heightened cyber risk, and the need for organizational agility are pronounced. To remain relevant, conceptual frameworks for change must evolve, embedding cyber resilience, adaptive culture, and multi-level governance as central tenets rather than afterthoughts. This advancement requires a holistic approach that integrates technology, human behavior, and strategic leadership to foster organizations capable of thriving amid unprecedented complexity and uncertainty.

ORIGINALITY, RATIONALE, AND SIGNIFICANCE OF THE STUDY

This section of the chapter explicitly outlines the originality, rationale, and significance of the current study. It clarifies how this research offers a novel perspective, why it is urgently needed, and what value it adds to scholarship and professional practice. This chapter delivers an original contribution that addresses a recognized but underexamined gap in existing literature by situating the inquiry at the intersection of continuous change management and cybersecurity within digitally intensive environments, especially aviation and aerospace (Stoumpos et al., 2023; Burton, 2023).

While previous research often isolates either change management or cybersecurity, the current work is distinguished by its integrative framework, which treats cyber risk governance as a foundational element of organizational resilience rather than a secondary or separate concern (Kucharska & Bedford, 2020; Sreenivasan & Suresh, 2024). This approach advances the field by embedding security considerations directly within adaptive transformation processes, providing a theoretically grounded model with direct applicability for high-reliability sectors such as aviation and aerospace (Riahi & Islam, 2024).

The significance of this chapter lies in its advancement and integration of established frameworks while addressing critical gaps in theory and practice. Prior models of organizational change management (i.e., General Electric's Change Acceleration Process and legacy frameworks referenced by Kucharska and Bedford (2020) offered a foundation for driving adaptation in stable, linear business environments. However, these models rarely embed cybersecurity as a core concern, often considering it an operational or IT afterthought (Burton, 2023). By synthesizing contemporary research on digital dexterity, cyber risk governance, and adaptive potential (Stoumpos et al., 2023; World Economic Forum, 2021), this chapter proposes a novel, sector-specific approach that places cyber risk at the center of continuous transformation. This integrative perspective extends the theoretical boundary of organizational resilience by merging behavioral, technological, and cultural elements into a dynamic framework suited for industries where safety, regulatory compliance, and digital innovation converge, such as aviation and aerospace (Kasana et al., 2023; Sreenivasan & Suresh, 2024). Crucially, this chapter leverages the six core principles of board-level cyber risk oversight articulated by the World Economic Forum (2021), clarifying accountability and embedding continuous improvement as core tenets alongside established change acceleration techniques.

Practically, this chapter equips industry leaders with actionable pathways to navigate the intertwined challenges of change and cybersecurity in complex, digital-first environments. By evolving original frameworks to account for contemporary threats and opportunities, the research directly responds to calls within the field for more agile, holistic models that anticipate disruption and foster resilient cultures (Kucharska & Bedford, 2020; Hagl et al., 2024). For policymakers, the findings translate established concepts (e.g., risk governance and adaptive leadership) into recommendations for high-reliability sectors facing mounting regulatory and operational risk (Kasana et al., 2023; Kupiek, 2023). In summation, the originality and significance of this chapter are rooted in its capacity to bridge and extend original, established frameworks, aligning cybersecurity with the latest thinking on adaptive change management, and offering empirically informed, actionable solutions for aviation, aerospace, and other digitally intensive sectors (Riahi & Islam, 2024; Waheed & Zhang, 2022; Snyder, 2019).

FUTURE RESEARCH DIRECTIONS

As the aerospace and aviation sectors undergo rapid digital transformation, they face unique risks and unprecedented opportunities related to cybersecurity and organizational change management. Integrating advanced technologies such as AI, IoT, and cloud-based systems into flight operations, maintenance, and ground infrastructure makes these sectors particularly vulnerable to sophisticated cyber threats and operational disruption. Industry leaders, regulators, and technology partners must unify change management strategies with robust cybersecurity protocols to ensure operational resilience, passenger safety, and regulatory compliance. Noted are four significant recommendations.

Embed Cybersecurity into Change Management for Flight Operations

Integrating cybersecurity directly into all change management initiatives for flight operations ensures that new technologies and process updates are vetted and secured from conception through deployment. In the context of aviation, where the risks of cyber incidents can have catastrophic safety and reputational consequences, making cybersecurity a non-negotiable aspect of organizational change fortifies defenses against external and insider threats. This foundational step is significant because it fosters a "secure-by-design" culture, raising awareness at every organizational layer and helping to prevent vulnerabilities before they reach critical systems or passenger-facing interfaces.

Leverage AI and Data Analytics for Predictive Threat Monitoring

The use of AI and advanced analytics to predict, detect, and respond to cyber threats provides aerospace and aviation organizations with real-time, adaptive defense capabilities. Predictive monitoring tools can flag anomalies, simulate potential attack vectors, and provide actionable insights without human delay, which is crucial in operational environments where seconds matter. This information is particularly significant because it shifts security posture from reactive to proactive, enhancing situational awareness across airborne and ground-based systems and enabling faster, more informed mitigation of emerging risks.

Institutionalize Cross-Functional Cyber-Resilience Training

Establishing comprehensive and recurrent training programs that span all operational roles, from pilots and engineers to air traffic controllers and ground staff, ensures that cybersecurity awareness and adaptability are organizational priorities. This approach reduces human error, addresses "weak links" in digital workflows, and cultivates a unified security mindset regardless of specialization. The significance lies in building a workforce that is technically competent as well as vigilant, agile, and capable of recognizing and responding to subtle indicators of cyber and operational disruption.

Establish Integrated Governance Structures for Safety and Cyber Risk

Creating cross-disciplinary governance teams that bring together expertise from safety, engineering, IT, and cybersecurity ensures that transformation projects are holistically overseen and aligned with regulatory, business continuity, and security imperatives. This structure enables consistent interpretation and application of guidelines from authorities like the FAA or EASA, blending operational safety with digital risk management. Its significance is in breaking down organizational silos, promoting accountability, and providing a centralized mechanism for decision-making that balances performance, innovation, and resilience across critical aviation operations.

These recommendations, when systematically implemented, will help aviation and aerospace organizations navigate the increasingly complex interface between digital transformation, safety, and cybersecurity. By reinforcing operational efficiency and adaptive resilience, they enable organizations to respond more effectively to emerging technological and regulatory demands. Ultimately, such efforts build sustained trust among regulators, industry stakeholders, and the traveling public.

SOLUTIONS AND RECOMMENDATIONS

The findings from this investigation reveal clear evidence that successful organizational change correlates strongly with the seamless integration of cybersecurity governance and continuous change management. Case analyses and qualitative indicators demonstrate that agile change cycles, when aligned with embedded cyber risk monitoring protocols, build the conditions for organizational adaptability and resilience. Quinn et al. (2021) describe cyber risk monitoring as part of enterprise risk management, using cybersecurity risk registers to prioritize and communicate risk response. Entities that embraced synchronization between change delivery and cyber-awareness reported statistically fewer compliance breaches and greater employee responsiveness to new systems.

A key outcome involved the deployment of AI as an enabler of behavioral insight and security posture management. Organizations employing AI analytics to detect resistance trends or digital vulnerabilities outperformed those relying solely on traditional change tracking metrics. AI-supported dashboards allowed leadership to anticipate internal friction points and address them preemptively through targeted engagement strategies and iterative communication.

Another result emphasized the role of cultural ownership in sustaining transformation over time. Organizations that cultivated a culture of digital vigilance, through awareness campaigns, role-based cybersecurity training, and transparent reporting, experienced higher adherence to core protocols and faster time-to-competency for new systems. This cultural alignment was consistently linked to improved collaboration across functions and a reduction in operational disruptions during implementation phases.

Furthermore, where leadership explicitly positioned cybersecurity as a shared organizational commitment rather than a compliance burden, employees were more likely to engage with transformational goals. This shift in framing supported deeper buy-in and enhanced cognitive alignment between mission-critical change objectives and personal accountability. Overall, the chapter confirms that transformation is most effective when viewed not as a technical project but as a systemically embedded process that integrates people, process, and protective technologies.

The implications of these results underscore a pressing need to reconceptualize how organizational change is managed in digitally intensive environments. Traditional models are often constrained by their project-based structure, presuming a finite timeline and static end-state. However, the evidence from this chapter demonstrates that change must now function as a recursive, continuously informed process supported by cyber-aware learning ecosystems and real-time feedback loops.

AI's role emerges not merely as a technological adjunct but as a cognitive extension of strategic management. Through advanced analysis of behavioral and system-level trends, AI enables firms to respond to weak signals before they escalate into full-scale disruptions. In contrast to reactive change models, AI integration creates capacity for foresight, which is essential in the face of growing cyber threats and complex stakeholder dynamics.

The increased significance of organizational culture in sustaining change outcomes is also noteworthy. While technical systems provide structure, it is the internalization of norms, particularly those surrounding data protection and digital ethics, that anchor long-term transformation. The research confirms that where cultural dynamics are ignored, resistance becomes more entrenched, and the risk of system failure increases.

Additionally, the results illuminate how cross-functional collaboration becomes indispensable in transformation initiatives involving digital infrastructure. By collapsing rigid departmental boundaries and promoting shared ownership, the organizations observed were able to consolidate fragmented efforts and create more sustainable outcomes. This enterprise-wide alignment ensures that technological and human systems evolve in tandem, avoiding the pitfalls of fragmented or superficial change implementation.

In sum, the results affirm that sustainable transformation is not merely a procedural success but a strategic condition. Organizations must synthesize adaptive learning, distributed leadership, and embedded cybersecurity into their operational DNA to achieve strategic condition. This action requires abandoning legacy distinctions between change, IT, and compliance in favor of a fully integrated approach to strategic renewal.

CONCLUSIONS, RECOMMENDATIONS, AND SOLUTIONS

This chapter has highlighted the sharp rise in cyberattacks targeting critical infrastructure, particularly within the aviation sector, where attacks surged by 600% year-over-year in early 2025 (Cybersecurity

Ventures, 2025). Over 10 major breaches were recorded in airlines and airports alone, resulting in disrupted flight schedules, compromised sensitive data, and exposed infrastructure vulnerabilities. In light of these findings, the following actionable recommendations are proposed for organizational leaders, managers, policymakers, and stakeholders to address cybersecurity risks more effectively and build long-term resilience.

1. Establish Mandatory Cyber Risk Audits: Organizations should implement quarterly cyber risk assessments, including mandatory independent third-party audits. This action is essential because undetected vulnerabilities contributed to the significant breach incidents reported in the first half of 2025 (Cybersecurity Ventures, 2025). Regular audits provide proactive visibility into security weaknesses, enabling faster remediation and reducing the likelihood of operational disruption.
2. Develop Sector-Specific Cybersecurity Standards: Policymakers should introduce mandatory cybersecurity frameworks tailored specifically for the aviation sector, aligned with global standards such as NIST, ISO 27001, and ICAO guidance. The lack of uniform standards across the industry contributed to fragmented responses and inconsistent preparedness levels (Cybersecurity Ventures, 2025). Unified frameworks enhance baseline defenses and support interoperability during coordinated attacks.
3. Invest in Workforce Training and Cyber Hygiene: All personnel, from ground operations to IT teams, should receive regular, role-specific cybersecurity training and phishing simulations. Human error remains one of the top contributing factors in successful cyberattacks, particularly in fast-paced operational environments like aviation (IBM X-Force, 2024). Training empowers employees to identify threats early and supports a culture of security awareness.
4. Integrate Cyber Threats into Emergency and Crisis Planning: Organizations should integrate cyber incident response protocols into broader emergency management and business continuity plans. The 2025 aviation breaches revealed that many operators were unprepared to handle digital disruptions with the same urgency as physical threats (Cybersecurity Ventures, 2025). This integration ensures coordinated response strategies that minimize downtime and public impact.
5. Deploy Real-Time Threat Detection and Monitoring Systems: Leaders should invest in real-time threat detection tools that leverage AI to monitor IT and operational technology (OT) networks. Many organizations lack the ability to detect intrusions promptly, with average breach detection times still exceeding 200 days (IBM X-Force, 2024). Real-time monitoring enables rapid response, reducing the scope and cost of breaches.
6. Enforce Cybersecurity Standards in Vendor and Procurement Policies: Organizations should require cybersecurity compliance certifications from all third-party vendors and suppliers. Several high-profile attacks in 2025 exploited supply chain weaknesses, particularly among aviation subcontractors (Cybersecurity Ventures, 2025). Ensuring vendors adhere to strict security protocols closes critical gaps in external access points.
7. Establish Cross-Sector Cyber Threat Intelligence Sharing: Stakeholders across public and private sectors should collaborate through formal, secure platforms for sharing cyber threat intelligence. The fragmented nature of current reporting processes delays coordinated response and leaves other entities vulnerable to repeat attack vectors (ENISA, 2025). Real-time intelligence sharing reduces risk across the entire ecosystem by enabling rapid collective action.
8. Offer Incentives for Cyber Resilience Investments: Governments should introduce financial incentives, such as tax credits or grants, to reward organizations that meet or exceed resilience benchmarks.

Smaller operators often lack the resources to implement advanced security tools, increasing their vulnerability (Cybersecurity Ventures, 2025). Incentivizing drives broader adoption of best practices, strengthening national infrastructure protection.

9. Adopt a Zero-Trust Security Architecture: Organizations should move from perimeter-based security models to zero-trust frameworks that require continuous identity verification for all users and devices. In the context of increasingly sophisticated attacks, traditional defenses are easily bypassed once attackers gain internal access (Microsoft Security Intelligence, 2024). Zero-trust significantly limits lateral movement and improves threat containment.
10. Mandate Timely Cyber Incident Reporting with Penalties: Policymakers should enforce mandatory breach disclosure within a fixed time window and introduce penalties for non-compliance. Delayed or incomplete reporting, as seen in several 2025 incidents, hampers industry-wide mitigation efforts and regulatory oversight (Cybersecurity Ventures, 2025). Timely reporting improves transparency, enables rapid response, and supports data-driven policy adjustments.

The findings in this chapter demonstrate that the scale and complexity of modern cyber threats demand a coordinated, multi-layered response from public and private actors. These ten recommendations offer a practical roadmap for improving cybersecurity resilience, based on observed vulnerabilities and breach patterns within critical infrastructure sectors, especially aviation. Implementing these measures will mitigate immediate risks and strengthen the strategic posture of organizations against future cyber threats. Ultimately, sustained commitment to these recommendations will help position organizations as proactive leaders in safeguarding digital trust and operational continuity across the sector.

REFERENCES

Adekoya, O. A., Atlam, H. F., & Lallie, H. S. (2025). Quantifying the multidimensional impact of cyber attacks in digital financial services: A systematic literature review. *Sensors (Basel), 25*(14), 4345. DOI: 10.3390/s25144345

Ainurrofiq, I., & Amir, M. T. (2023). Application of e-culture in a hybrid working model: A case study in the banking industry in Indonesia. *International Journal of Interdisciplinary Organizational Studies, 18*(2), 93–115. Advance online publication. DOI: 10.18848/2324-7649/CGP/v18i02/93-115

Annabi, A. (2024). The Digital rights (future perspectives and horizons). *International Journal of Advanced Research in Humanities and Law, 1*(2), 1–14. DOI: 10.63053/ijrel.7

Bagga, S. K., Gera, S., & Haque, S. N. (2023). The mediating role of organizational culture: Transformational leadership and change management in virtual teams. *Asia Pacific Management Review, 28*(2), 120–131. DOI: 10.1016/j.apmrv.2022.07.003

Baker, A., Weisgrau, J., & Philyaw, K. B. (2022). *Feedback loops: Mapping transformative interactions in education innovation*. Digital Promise., DOI: 10.51388/20500.12265/155

Bendig, D., Schulz, C., Theis, L., & Raff, S. (2023). Digital orientation and environmental performance in times of technological change. *Technological Forecasting and Social Change, 188*, 122272. DOI: 10.1016/j.techfore.2022.122272

Bento, F., Tagliabue, M., & Lorenzo, F. (2020). Organizational silos: A scoping review informed by a behavioral perspective on systems and networks. *Societies (Basel, Switzerland), 10*(3), 56. DOI: 10.3390/soc10030056

Bloom, N., Barrero, J. M., Davis, S., Meyer, D., & Mihaylov, E. (2023, August 28). Survey: remote work isn't going away — and executives know it. *Harvard Business Review*. https://hbr.org/2023/08/survey-remote-work-isnt-going-away-and-executives-know-it

Budur, T., Demirer, H., & Rashid, C. A. (2023). The effects of knowledge sharing on innovative behaviours of academicians; mediating effect of innovative organization culture and quality of work life. *Journal of Applied Research in Higher Education*. Advance online publication. DOI: 10.1108/JARHE-08-2022-0257

Burnes, B. (2019). The origins of Lewin's three-step model of change. *The Journal of Applied Behavioral Science*. Advance online publication. DOI: 10.1177/0021886319892685

Burrell, D. N., Lewis, E. J., & Richardson, K. (2023). Adaptive marketing, management strategy, and technology innovation in beverage and hospitality markets. *International Journal of Innovation in the Digital Economy, 14*(1), 1–10. DOI: 10.4018/IJIDE.324096

Burton, S. L. (2022). *Cybersecurity leadership from a Telemedicine/Telehealth knowledge and organizational development examination (Order No. 29066056)*. ProQuest Dissertations & Theses Global.

Burton, S. L. (2023). Cybersecurity risk: The business significance of ongoing tracking. In Burrell, D. N. (Ed.), *Transformational Interventions for Business* (1st ed., pp. 245–268). Technology, and Healthcare., DOI: 10.4018/979-8-3693-1634-4.ch015

Burton, S. L. (2024). Securing tomorrow: Synergizing change management and cybersecurity in the digital era. *Holistica Journal of Business and Public Administration*, *15*(1), 1–20. DOI: 10.2478/hjbpa-2024-0001

CAPA— Centre for Aviation. (2025, May 8–9). *CAPA Airline Leader Summit: Airlines in Transition 2025*. Athens, Greece. *Author*. https://ait25.capaevents.com/

Capgemini Research Institute. (2025). The strategic edge: How digital continuity drives business outcomes in aerospace and defense. *Capgemini*. https://www.capgemini.com/wp-content/uploads/2025/06/Final-Web-Version-Report-Digital-Continuity-in-AD.pdf

Daher, M. M., & Ziade, F. (2023). Technology, workforce, and the future of sustainable work. In El-Chaarani, H., El Dandachi, I., El Nemar, S., & Abiad, Z. E. L. (Eds.), *Navigating the Intersection of Business, Sustainability and Technology* (pp. 79–97). Springer., DOI: 10.1007/978-981-99-8572-2_6

Data Insights Market. (2025). Digital transformation in aviation market demand dynamics: Insights 2025–2033. *Data Insights Market*.DOI: 10.1057/9781403920249_5

Dutta, P. K., Ricciuti, M., Bogrekci, I., & Suseelan, S. (Eds.). (2025). *Digital transformation in aviation industry operations: Innovations and sustainable solutions* (1st ed.). Routledge., DOI: 10.4324/9781003494720

Endrejat, P. C., & Burnes, B. (2024). Draw it, check it, change it: Reviving Lewin's Topology to facilitate organizational change theory and practice. *The Journal of Applied Behavioral Science*, *60*(1), 87–112. DOI: 10.1177/00218863221122875

Errida, A., & Lotfi, B. (2021). The determinants of organizational change management success: Literature review and case study. *International Journal of Engineering Business Management*, *13*, 18479790211016273. Advance online publication. DOI: 10.1177/18479790211016273

Garcia, M. (2025, August b1). Cybersecurity in aviation: Analyzing the surge in airline and airport breaches. *Aerospace Global News*. https://aerospaceglobalnews.com/news/airline-airport-aviation-cyberattacks-2025/

Grand View Research. (2024). Aviation cyber security market size, share & trends analysis report by component (hardware, software, services), by type (endpoint security, cloud security), by deployment (cloud-based, on-premises), by application, by region, and segment forecasts, 2024 - 2030. *Author*. https://www.grandviewresearch.com/industry-analysis/aviation-cyber-security-market-report

Graves, L., Dalgarno, N., Hoorn, R. V., Hastings-Truelove, A., Mulder, J., Kolomitro, K., & Kirby, F. (2023). Creating change: Kotter's change management model in action. *Canadian Medical Education Journal*, *14*(3), 136–139. DOI: 10.36834/cmej.76680

Hagl, C., Kanitz, R., Gonzalez, K., & Hoegl, M. (2024). Change management interventions: Taking stock and moving forward. *Human Resource Management Review*, *34*(1), 101000. DOI: 10.1016/j.hrmr.2023.101000

Harrison, R., Fischer, S., Walpola, R. L., Chauhan, A., Babalola, T., Mears, S., & Le-Dao, H. (2021). Where do models for change management, improvement and implementation meet? A systematic review of the applications of change management models in healthcare. *Journal of Healthcare Leadership, 13*, 85–108. DOI: 10.2147/JHL.S289176

Jaiyeoba, H. B., Jamaludin, M. A., Busari, S. A., & Amuda, Y. J. (2025). The implications of Maqasid al-Shari'ah for integrated sustainability practices among businesses: A qualitative inquiry. *Qualitative Research in Financial Markets, 17*(3), 511–531. DOI: 10.1108/QRFM-09-2023-0222

Jones, L. A. (2021). Unveiling human factors: Aligning facets of cybersecurity leadership, insider threats, and arsonist attributes to reduce cyber risk. *SocioEconomic Challenges, 5*(4), 43–63. DOI: 10.61093/sec.5(4).44-63.2021

Karayel, T., Aktas, B., & Akbıyık, A. (2025, January 20). Human factors in remote work: Examining cyber hygiene practices. *Information and Computer Security, 33*(1), 96–116. DOI: 10.1108/ICS-11-2023-0215

Kasana, D., Smithwick, J., Dodd, J., Cavalline, T. L., & Mayo, G. (2023). Successful change management strategies for unforeseen events: Impact of COVID-19 on facility management. *Journal of Management Engineering, 39*(4), 04023016. Advance online publication. DOI: 10.1061/JMENEA.MEENG-4870

Kucharska, W., & Bedford, D. A. D. (2020). Love your mistakes! - They help you adapt to change. How do knowledge, collaboration and learning cultures foster organizational intelligence? *Journal of Organizational Change Management, 33*(7), 1329–1354. DOI: 10.1108/JOCM-02-2020-0052

Kupiek, M. (2023). Revisiting organizational change management (OCM): A context-sensitive and dynamic approach of change. In Kupiek, M., & Brandmeier, R. A. (Eds.), *The Digital Transformation of Georgia* (pp. 139–158). Springer., DOI: 10.1007/978-3-031-26451-1_7

Makhafola, L., van Deventer, M. J., Holmner, M. A., & Van Wyk, B. (2025). A scoping review of digital literacy, digital competence, digital fluency and digital dexterity in academic libraries' context. *Journal of Academic Librarianship, 51*(3), 103053. DOI: 10.1016/j.acalib.2025.103053

Mangla, N., & Singh, K. (2024). Cultural intelligence as a strategic approach to change management & the mediating role of learning organization. *Journal of Global Business and Commerce.* https://doi.org/ DOI: 10.1007/s42943-024-00092-8

McLaren, T. A. S., van der Hoorn, B., & Fein, E. C. (2023). Why vilifying the status quo can derail a change effort: Kotter's contradiction, and theory adaptation. *Journal of Change Management, 23*(1), 93–111. DOI: 10.1080/14697017.2022.2137835

Mizrak, F. (2024). Effective change management strategies: Exploring dynamic models for organizational transformation. In N. George & L. Jamil (Eds.), *Perspectives on artificial intelligence in times of turbulence: Theoretical background to applications* (1st ed., pp. 135-162). IGI Global. https://doi.org/ DOI: 10.4018/978-1-6684-9814-9.ch009

Moghadasnian, S. A., & Rajol, M. (2025). Artificial intelligence in airline business management a paradigm shift in the industry. *Journal Business of Data Science Research, 4*(1), 6–12. https://www.researchgate.net/profile/Seyyedabdolhojjat-Moghadasnian/publication/392270838_

Mohd Hanif, A. H., & Jaafar, A. G. (2023). A Review: Application of Big Data Analytics in Airlines Industry. *Open International Journal of Informatics*, *11*(2), 196–209. DOI: 10.11113/oiji2023.11n2.254

Möller, D. P. F. (2023). Cybersecurity in Digital Transformation. In *Guide to Cybersecurity in Digital Transformation. Advances in Information Security, 103*. Springer., DOI: 10.1007/978-3-031-26845-8_1

Mouazen, A. M., Hernández-Lara, A. B., Abdallah, F., Ramadan, M., Chahine, J., Baydoun, H., & Bou Zakhem, N. (2024). Transformational and transactional leaders and their role in implementing the Kotter change management model ensuring sustainable change: An empirical study. *Sustainability (Basel)*, *16*(1), 16. Advance online publication. DOI: 10.3390/su16010016

Muncaster, P. (2023, January 9). Global cyber-attack volume surges 38% in 2022. *Infosecurity Magazine*. https://www.infosecurity-magazine.com/news/global-cyberattack-volume-surges/

Naslund, D., & Norrman, A. (2019). A performance measurement system for change initiatives: An action research study from design to evaluation. *Business Process Management Journal*, *25*(7), 1647–1672. DOI: 10.1108/BPMJ-11-2017-0309

Purwanto, A., Fahmi, K., & Sulaiman, A. (2023). Linking of transformational leadership, learning culture, organizational structure and school innovation capacity: CB SEM AMOS analysis. *Journal of Information Systems and Management*, *2*(3), 1–8. DOI: 10.4444/jisma.v2i3.306

Quinn, S., Ivy, N., Barrett, M., Feldman, L., Witte, G., & Gardner, R. (2021). *Identifying and estimating cybersecurity risk for enterprise risk management (NIST IR 8286A)*. National Institute of Standards and Technology., DOI: 10.6028/NIST.IR.8286A

Rafi, T. (2022, June 9). Why sustainability is crucial for corporate strategy. *World Economic Forum*. https://www.weforum.org/stories/2022/06/why-sustainability-is-crucial-for-corporate-strategy/

Riahi, R., & Islam, M. S. (2024). Employees' information security awareness (ISA) in public organisations: Insights from cross-cultural studies in Sweden, France, and Tunisia. *Behaviour & Information Technology*. Advance online publication. DOI: 10.1080/0144929X.2024.2311734

Riedl, C., & Woolley, A. W. (2020, October 28). Successful remote teams communicate in bursts. *Harvard Business Review*. https://hbr.org/2020/10/successful-remote-teams-communicate-in-bursts

Robertson, G., & Lapiņa, I. (2023). Digital transformation as a catalyst for sustainability and open innovation. *Journal of Open Innovation*, *9*(1), 100017. DOI: 10.1016/j.joitmc.2023.100017

Saarikko, T., Westergren, U. H., & Blomquist, T. (2020). Digital transformation: Five recommendations for the digitally conscious firm. *Business Horizons*, *63*(6), 825–839. DOI: 10.1016/j.bushor.2020.07.005

Saeed, S., Altamimi, S. A., Alkayyal, N. A., Alshehri, E., & Alabbad, D. A. (2023). Digital transformation and cybersecurity challenges for businesses resilience: Issues and recommendations. *Sensors (Basel)*, *23*(15), 6666. DOI: 10.3390/s23156666

Searles, K. (2024, January 3). Case study: L'Occitane. *Internet Retailing*. https://internetretailing.net/loccitane-en-provence-building-loyalty/

Shahzad, M. A., Jianguo, D., & Junaid, M. (2023). Impact of green HRM practices on sustainable performance: Mediating role of green innovation, green culture, and green employees' behavior. *Environmental Science and Pollution Research International, 30*(38), 88524–88547. DOI: 10.1007/s11356-023-28498-6

Snyder, H. (2019). Literature review as a research methodology: An overview and guidelines. *Journal of Business Research, 104*, 333–339. DOI: 10.1016/j.jbusres.2019.07.039

Sreenivasan, A., & Suresh, M. (2024). Start-up sustainability: Does blockchain adoption drive sustainability in start-ups? A systematic literature review. *Management Research Review, 47*(3), 390–405. DOI: 10.1108/MRR-07-2022-0519

Stetsenko, S. P., Tytok, V. V., Emelianova, O. M., Bielienkova, O. Y., & Tsyfra, T. Y. (2021). The interrelation of digital technologies and organizational and economic mechanisms in construction: Adaptation to change management. *International Review. Special Issues, 1*(Part I), 21–31. DOI: 10.37943/AITU.2021.40.39.006

Stoumpos, A. I., Kitsios, F., & Talias, M. A. (2023). Digital transformation in healthcare: Technology acceptance and its applications. *International Journal of Environmental Research and Public Health, 20*(4), 3407. Advance online publication. DOI: 10.3390/ijerph20043407

Strifler, L., Barnsley, J. M., Hillmer, M., & Straus, S. E. (2020). Identifying and selecting implementation theories, models and frameworks: A qualitative study to inform the development of a decision support tool. *BMC Medical Informatics and Decision Making, 20*(1), 91. Advance online publication. DOI: 10.1186/s12911-020-01128-8

Suebsuwong, P. (2023). Beyond Technology: Digital Transformation in Aerospace and Aviation. In Karakoc, T. H., Atipan, S., Dalkiran, A., Ercan, A. H., Kongsamutr, N., & Sripawadkul, V. (Eds.), *Research Developments in Sustainable Aviation. ISSASARES 2021. Sustainable Aviation.* Springer., DOI: 10.1007/978-3-031-37943-7_32

Tircovnicu, G. I., & Hategan, C.-D. (2023). Trends in enterprise risk management research: A bibliometric analysis. In Grima, S., Thalassinos, E., Cristea, M., Kadłubek, M., Maditinos, D., & Peiseniece, L. (Eds.), *Digital Transformation, Strategic Resilience, Cyber Security And Risk Management, 111* (pp. 1–20). Emerald Publishing Limited., DOI: 10.1108/S1569-37592023000111A001

Trzeciak, M. (2024). Factors of success in the change management process of IT programs. *Journal of Organizational Change Management, 37*(1), 58–74. DOI: 10.1108/JOCM-04-2023-0110

Uffindell, R. (2025, May 21). UK Science Funding HQ Hit by 5.4m cyber assaults as attacks increase 600%. *Techerati*. https://www.techerati.com/news-hub/uk-science-funding-hq-hit-by-5-4m-cyber-assaults-as-attacks-increase-600/

Uhlir, K. (2025, February 17). Decentralized leadership: How it drives organizational agility & innovation. *CEON Foundation*. https://ceonfoundation.org/decentralized-leadership/

Ukwandu, E., Ben-Farah, M. A., Hindy, H., Bures, M., Atkinson, R., Tachtatzis, C., Andonovic, I., & Bellekens, X. (2022). Cyber-security challenges in aviation industry: A review of current and future trends. *Information (Basel), 13*(3), 146. DOI: 10.3390/info13030146

Urban, M. C., Swaegers, J., Stoks, R., Snook, R. R., Otto, S. P., Noble, D. W., Moiron, M., Hällfors, M. H., Gómez-Llano, M., Fior, S., Cote, J., Charmantier, A., Bestion, E., Berger, D., Baur, J., Alexander, J. M., Saastamoinen, M., Edelsparre, A. H., & Teplitsky, C. (2024, February). When and how can we predict adaptive responses to climate change? *Evolution Letters*, *8*(1), 172–187. DOI: 10.1093/evlett/qrad038

Waheed, A., & Zhang, Q. (2022). Effect of CSR and ethical practices on sustainable competitive performance: A case of emerging markets from stakeholder theory perspective. *Journal of Business Ethics*, *175*(4), 837–855. DOI: 10.1007/s10551-020-04679-y

World Economic Forum. (2021, March 23). Principles for Board Governance of Cyber Risk. *Author*. https://www.weforum.org/publications/principles-for-board-governance-of-cyber-risk/

Xiong, M., & Wang, H. (2022). Digital twin applications in aviation industry: A review. *International Journal of Advanced Manufacturing Technology*, *121*(9-10), 5677–5692. DOI: 10.1007/s00170-022-09717-9

Zhang, L., Carter, R. A.Jr, Greene, J. A., & Bernacki, M. L. (2024). Unraveling challenges with the implementation of universal design for learning: A systematic literature review. *Educational Psychology Review*, *36*(1), 35. DOI: 10.1007/s10648-024-09860-7

Zoppelletto, A., Orlandi, L. B., Zardini, A., Rossignoli, C., & Kraus, S. (2023). Organizational roles in the context of digital transformation: A micro-level perspective. *Journal of Business Research*, *157*, 113563. DOI: 10.1016/j.jbusres.2022.113563

KEY TERMS AND DEFINITIONS

Adaptive Potential: Adaptive potential refers to the capacity of individuals or teams to learn, improvise, and reconfigure knowledge, behaviors, and roles in response to dynamic challenges. This concept encompasses cognitive flexibility, digital fluency, and psychological resilience, enabling organizations to sustain high performance amid continuous disruption.

Artificial Intelligence (AI): AI describes a suite of advanced technologies programmed to perform tasks that normally require human intelligence, such as pattern recognition, decision-making, and predictive analytics. In organizational contexts, AI supports real-time data analysis, automates operational processes, and enables foresight in transformation efforts.

Continuous Change: Continuous change denotes a state in which organizational transformation is ongoing and iterative, instead of discrete or episodic. It describes processes and mindsets that support persistent adaptation, learning, and renewal as core features of organizational identity.

Cyber Risk: Cyber risk is the potential for loss, disruption, or reputational harm resulting from vulnerabilities or threats to information technology systems, data, or digital operations. It addresses the likelihood and impact of unauthorized access, cyberattacks, or systemic technological failures.

Cybersecurity Governance: Cybersecurity governance is the strategic oversight and decision-making framework designed to ensure that cybersecurity risks are systematically identified, assessed, and managed in alignment with organizational objectives and risk appetite. It involves integrating cyber risk management into the organization's values, leadership, and operations.

Digital Dexterity: Digital dexterity is the proficiency and confidence with which employees or teams adopt, adapt to, and leverage digital tools in evolving work environments. It reflects a practical fluency in navigating and utilizing digital platforms, enabling agile responses to technological shifts.

Organizational Change Management: Organizational Change Management (OCM) is the discipline and collection of practices that guide how organizations prepare for, implement, and sustain transformations. OCM involves aligning people, processes, and technology to achieve desired outcomes while minimizing resistance and maintaining operational continuity.

Resilience: Resilience is the organization's capacity to withstand, absorb, and recover from disruptions, adapting to evolving challenges while maintaining core functions and sustaining long-term performance. It is underpinned by a blend of behavioral, technological, and strategic attributes that reinforce organizational stability and adaptability.

Chapter 6
Transformational Leadership in the Digital Maturity of Public and Private Organizations in the Era of Technological Innovation

Jose De Jesus Reyes-Sánchez
http://orcid.org/0000-0002-3866-2363
TECNM Instituto Tecnologico Superior De Fresnillo, Mexico

Omar Guirette Barbosa
http://orcid.org/0000-0003-1336-9475
Universidad Politécnica de Zacatecas, Mexico

Selene Castañeda-Burciaga
http://orcid.org/0000-0002-2436-308X
Universidad Politécnica de Zacatecas, Mexico

Ayme Carolina Reyes Davalos
http://orcid.org/0009-0003-9659-2978
Universidad Autónoma de Durango, Zacatecas, Mexico

Johana Paola Reyes Davalos
http://orcid.org/0009-0005-0330-635X
TECNM Instituto Tecnologico Superior De Fresnillo, Mexico

ABSTRACT

Currently, transformational leadership has positioned itself as a key strategic tool to facilitate organizational adaptation processes in the face of the dizzying changes imposed by technological innovation. In both the public and private sectors, digital maturity is an essential condition for ensuring sustainability, competitiveness and operational efficiency in an increasingly digitalised global environment. This chapter offers a meta-analytic and reflective analysis that explores how transformational leadership drives digital maturity in different organizational contexts. It delves into the theoretical background, epistemological

DOI: 10.4018/979-8-3373-4027-2.ch006

frameworks, and methodologies applied to understand the mechanisms by which leaders influence digital culture, the adoption of emerging technologies, and the generation of dynamic capabilities oriented to continuous innovation.

INTRODUCTION

In organizations, today's rapid digital advances have destroyed traditional strategic planning paradigms, forcing them to rebuild their operational, cultural, and cognitive structures at the same time as digital disruptions emerge. In this scenario, digital maturity becomes an evolutionary process that, by endlessly articulating human capital, infrastructure and governance, ceases to be a measurable destination with static metrics. However, empirical results suggest that many institutions, even if they have cutting-edge technological resources at their disposal, stumble when they underestimate the human dimension of digitalization and consider leadership as something merely technocratic.

Therefore, transformational leadership is affirmed because it is the means to convert a complex technique into a shared collective meaning, in which a whole sensorium full of emotions, values and collective visions comes into play that add meaning to technological adoption. The idealized influence, individualized consideration, and intellectual curiosity that transformational leaders arouse generate safe environments for experimentation that shorten the digital learning curve and multiply operational resilience in the face of unexpected crises (Mumford et al., 2000). However, the literature warns that a cult of charisma leads to dynamics of uncritical tailism, reinforces algorithmic biases and makes the ethical side of automation invisible, so it is necessary to incorporate frameworks of responsibility and transparency into management practice.

But the Digital Capability Framework, a model of digital maturity, demonstrates that organizations that understand data strategy, talent development, and innovation culture as part of a unified narrative advance faster than those that bring together platforms that are not connected to each other (Thordsen et al., 2023). This vision is complemented by the sociotechnical perspective that states that any technology changes labor relations, power relations, and ways of making decisions, so that its successful appropriation requires interdisciplinary dialogue and sensitivity to the context. From the perspective of Dynamic capabilities, transformational leadership has a driving effect that makes the company never stop learning to reconfigure itself, integrating and building competencies at the pace dictated by disruption. In this way, strategic realignment cycles based on information and learning become regular

Digital maturity also faces axiological challenges: the need to cultivate an ethical conscience that anticipates the social impacts of automation, protects privacy, and promotes environmental sustainability; challenges that can only be addressed from an idealized influence that makes personal example a vector of legitimacy. Multilevel governance studies suggest that systemic resilience to disruptions depends on the ability of leaders to align public policies, regulations, and cross-sectoral alliances around principles of openness and collaboration. Thus, in both governmental and corporate environments, leadership is reinvented as a distributed practice that permeates all hierarchical levels, fostering learning communities that capitalize on tacit knowledge and promote open innovation (Leonardi et al., 2013).

The dizzying acceleration of technological innovation fractured the traditional frameworks of strategic planning and forced organizational systems to rethink their cultural, cognitive, and operational foundations with the same speed with which new digital disruptions emerge (Sumbal et al., 2024). This exponential pace turned digital maturity into an evolutionary process by articulating infrastructure, talent, and governance within a continuous learning loop that redefines, time and again, the value creation architecture (Plekhanov et al., 2023; Sumbal et al., 2024). However, the data show that even organizations equipped with state-of-the-art technologies stumble when they relegate the human dimension to a merely technocratic plane.

In this way, transformational leadership can help transform technical complication into shared stories that move with emotions, move by values, and jointly produce collective visions, imposing a purpose that corroborates the introduction of technology (Glikson & Woolley, 2020). Influence tactics, inspirational motivation, intellectual stimulation, and individualized consideration, all elements of the transformational leader, create a safe rehearsal environment that calms technological anxiety and increases the learning curve with a digital effect (Jun & Lee, 2023; Tagscherer & Carbon, 2023).

In addition, its ability to legitimize error as something natural in the innovation process increases the effectiveness of the adoption of digital tools by a third as proven by ethnography. However, the literature warns that there are certain ontological tensions: adoration for charisma can lead to blind or uncritical continuation, aggravates algorithmic biases, and obscures the ethical dimension of automation. It is therefore advisable that as a complement in its direction it be accompanied by transparency frameworks (Camilleri, 2024; De Bock et al., 2024).

Hyperpersonalization, devised with the help of recommendation algorithms, amplifies the impact of communication, but raises thorny questions about privacy and discrimination that require leaders to be able to audit AI algorithms and ensure that they are critical processes of explainability. On the comparative level between the public and the private, however, frictions are imposed. While the public administration operates under frameworks of responsibility, regulation and equity of access, the business sector responds to market pressures that in a certain way lead to the obsolescence of its own business models. However, deep down, both face the lack of visionary leadership capable of combining efficiency and technological humanism (Gascó-Hernández et al., 2022; Tagscherer & Carbon, 2023).

Digital government studies show that interoperability becomes a public advantage only if, through the transformational narrative of the active civil servant, the technical complication is converted into tangible goods that benefit a citizenry. On the contrary, companies such as BBVA and Siemens have shown that combining AI with charismatic leadership boosts operational efficiency and service personalization, opening a gap over the competition (Garay-Gallastegui et al., 2024; Van Giffen et al., 2025).

Such models as the Digital Capability Framework or even Deloitte Digital's Digital Maturity Model ensure that winning is not in multiplying platforms, but the company is in effectively bringing strategies, culture, and data to be a single ethical and globally inclusive thing. From a sociotechnical perspective, in addition to this, any technology redefines professions, degrees of power, and decision-making practices from the point of view of participation, suggesting that effective learning needs interdisciplinary dialogue and context-sensitive attention (Leonardi et al., 2013). But from the perspective of dynamic capabilities, transformational leadership is an engine that integrates, builds, and reconfigures capabilities with the speed imposed by disruption, creating cycles of strategic reconversion based on open learning.

Current debates revolve around how to accurately and dynamically measure digital maturity, as technological horizons shrink and obsolescence rates accelerate. Thus, it is proposed to include metrics at the level not only of effectiveness algorithm, but also of organizational learning, speed of technological adoption, and ethics. Systemic digital resilience emerges as a critical field of research that is still underdeveloped (De Carolis et al., 2025; Tim & Leidner, 2023; Urbani et al., 2024; Große & Sundberg, 2025). At the same time, organizational neuroscience as well as augmented analytics suggest that neurophysiological supervision, if combined with co-author leadership, serves to make cognitive chatbots well accepted in critical functions (Boukarras et al., 2024; Muhl, 2024; Urbani et al., 2024).

From a comparative perspective in these corporations exposed to a competitive environment, sensing–seizing–reconfiguring cycles tend to be faster, while public institutions compensate for their lower speed with an orientation towards social impact and coverage of the entire population (Haug et al., 2024; Eom & Lee, 2022; Saeedikiya et al., 2024). In both cases, the influence exerted by transformative leadership is essential to ensure that incentives are correct, manage coalitions and make change be accepted by others. Data of this type suggest that leadership should no longer be understood as something maintained exclusively by high hierarchies, but as a practice that radiates to all levels and crops of the company and that is capable of creating a community based on trust to learn together with the customer or members of the public (Klasmeier & Lehmann-Willenbrock, 2024; Lin et al., 2022).

STATEMENT OF THE PROBLEM

For public and private organizations, the technological vertigo they are experiencing requires extremely fast strategic decision making that is simultaneous to the change in culture, ethical data governance. Digital maturity is conceived as the systemic ability to integrate infrastructure, human resources, and processes into a continuous learning cycle that produces economic value, social legitimacy. The literature, however, shows a persistent gap between the availability of advanced platforms and the lack of transformational leadership capable of turning algorithmic complexity into shared narratives of everyday ethical behaviors. The contradiction is especially evident in Latin America, where inequality of connectivity, regulatory fragmentation, and hierarchical cultures enhance the lack of desire to change and distort the benefits that digitalization would bring (Aras et al., 2023; Ellström et al., 2022; Kraus et al., 2023).

In a comparison of data, the main problem lies not in the technical, but in society and culture. With these ethnographic laments, the authors argue to their own colleagues that patterns of vertical dominance, fear of error, and cybernetic division of competition block any systematic possibility of organized experimentation. At the same time, traditional evaluation models are becoming inadequate in the face of increasingly shorter obsolescence cycles; hence the need for dynamic measures that integrate the time span (Ates & Acur, 2022).

Additional tensions emerge at the managerial level. Leaders are forced to harmonize efficiency imperatives with the responsibility to ensure explainable algorithms and inclusive ecosystems. Organizations that have internalized transformational leadership advance faster; but when this leadership is confused with personal charisma, the risk of uncritical tailism and increased bias reappears. The literature on systemic resilience also warns that hyperconnectivity increases the attack surface and the probability of cascading failures; without leadership capable of orchestrating multiple levels of governance, digital initiatives become fragile (Besio & Pronzini, 2025; Giacosa et al., 2023; Kostopoulos et al., 2024).

Another angle to take into account is the moral one. The combined issue of big data, artificial intelligence, and ubiquitous surveillance demands sensitive leaders to address the moral dilemmas of automation, privacy, and fairness. But still less than fifteen percent of the studies analyzed explicitly enough how transformational managers establish frameworks of algorithmic responsibility in daily practice. Failing to mention this causes social distrust to increase and digital investments in this field to become less and less legitimate (Cieslak et al., 2025).

In Asia-Pacific, for example, evidence suggests that when you put together the routines of rapid innovation and agile prototyping, you will have a better chance of success if the function of intellectual stimulation is complemented by transformational leadership, but this is also the case if an organization does not have a re-skilling flow planned that is generalized as a model it is difficult for anything to happen (Boukarras et al., 2022; Li, Chen, & Yuan, 2025).

Finally, organizational neuroscience studies point to an often overlooked factor: the cognitive overload derived from working in hyperdigital environments can induce decision fatigue and promote risk aversion. Transformational leaders who monitor stress markers and promote emotional repair spaces achieve better rates of technological adoption and fewer security incidents.

To this end, the following questions are raised that help to globalize. The theme presented in this chapter. How does transformational leadership affect the speed and depth with which public and private organizations reach digital maturity in contexts of high technological volatility? And finally, to what extent do data ethics frameworks and inter-institutional partnerships moderate the impact of transformational leadership on operational resilience and social legitimacy? This paper will try to answer these three questions.

BACKGROUND

Origin and Evolution of the Concept of Transformational Leadership

The concept of transformational leadership stems from Burns' critiques of transactional leadership, which holds that the most effective leaders encourage their followers to overcome simple economic exchange through the common construction of moments and from a higher moral sense (Braojos et al., 2024; Karimi et al., 2023).

A synthesis involves the initial development of the theory with the emergence of studies on organizational climate, a generation that engages ideas about transformation and variables such as job satisfaction, collective efficacy and organizational renewal. In the 1990s, the transformational perspective entered into dialogue with process reengineering, and we discovered that the culture created by inspiring leaders drives total quality systems with ease more passions silently picked up rumors. In turn, the theoretical-empirical crossover shows how transformation is not simply a change of processes, but a new positioning in the face of identity assumptions, modes of thought, and social relations whose greatest achievement occurs when the direction continuously activates learning (Avolio et al., 2014; Ernst et al., 2021).

With the changing century, researchers found a synergistic concordance between transformational leadership and information technologies, seeing that digitalization increased the ability of symbolic leaders to influence a physically separated public with platforms that collapsed authority in a space-time relationship (Karimi et al., 2023).

In highly mobile digital environments, the goal of innovative content is especially important, because this is the great ferment that drives rapid experimentation, tolerance for constructive error, and the collective and intense search for cutting-edge solutions. These types of conditions are absolutely essential for disruptive innovation. At the same time, inspirational motivation became a means of relieving the stress of continuous change, creating common orders of what the adoption of technologies that have not yet matured implies (Papagiannidis et al., 2025; Camilleri, 2024) .

The latest contributions have suggested that the theory should be expanded by introducing the dimension of digital ethics, an element that concerns the judgment of the boss's ability to foresee the social and ethical consequences of automation, data management and algorithmic intelligence and that leads his signature to adopt sustainable and responsible practices. In this new paradigm, the idealized influence is experienced in the struggle to make technology fair; while individualization is renewed through the distinction between segmented learning curves and the technological gap that exists between employees.

Digital Maturity as an Organizational Construct

The idea of digital maturity emerged as a technical indicator, which allows us to observe how our technological environment has developed in a sociotechnical conversation that has processes, competencies, culture, and governance. Early models, such as MIT's Digital Capabilities Framework, designed linear levels based on infrastructure adoption, but it was soon supplemented by strategic and cultural dimensions that appreciate the need for convergence with the business model (Elia et al., 2024; Senna et al., 2023).

Deloitte's Digital Maturity Model deepened the look, adding customer perspectives, value chain, and leadership; He stresses that it is not the accumulation of platforms that gives rise to maturity, but that it is reached with an integrated orchestration of technology, talent and data. All of this is guided by an ethical and inspiring vision. Similarly, the European Digital Skills Framework strengthened culture and governance as cross-cutting factors. It emphasizes that technological progress can fail if there is cultural resistance without shared value metrics (Porfirio et al., 2021).

Adopting a sociotechnical approach makes us see that digital maturity is a process of continuous and reciprocal adjustment in which each new technology not only reconfigures the same operational activities but also symmetrically professional identities, power relations and decision-making patterns. In addition, transformational leadership ends up being a critical mediator, bringing out technical complexity and translating it into organizational meaning through narratives that combine efficiency with technological humanity.

Recent research shows that organizations with transformational leadership make faster progress in all aspects of maturity. In the maturity strategy, in the maturation of talent or of the ecosystem itself, when they promote intersectoral alliances and co-create with their clients and citizens. Evidence also suggests that digital maturity extraordinarily increases operational resilience, the ability to face successive difficulties continuously, due to technical flexibility coupled with a highly developed culture of innovation. Stronghold of vulnerability to cyberattack or health crisis in the future.

The current point of debate is focused on how to measure maturity in dynamic terms, especially now that technological horizons are shrinking and obsolescence cycles are rarefied. It is proposed to incorporate organizational learning metrics and speed of incorporation of emerging technologies, as well as algorithmic ethics and sustainability indicators, indicating that maturity is not an end state but the capacity for permanent reinvention (Rioseco Pais et al., 2024).

From a Latin American perspective, digital maturity takes on unique nuances, due to gaps in infrastructure, heterogeneous regulations, and different levels of human capital. To this end, an evaluation model of an establishment was carried out to recognize the access of its own realities and socio-economic differences capacity. Here, transformational leadership provides a platform for public-private partnerships in order to absorb the costs of technology and reduce the digital divide, while implementing massive training policies and multilevel governance frameworks.

Future research aims to combine the concept of digital maturity with the theory of dynamic capabilities, arguing that truly mature organizations are those capable of constantly integrating, building, and reconfiguring their competencies at the pace of technological change.

Historical Interrelationship Between Leadership and Digital Transformation

The convergence of transformational leadership and digital transformation has evolved from tangential contact to a strategic symbiosis in which leadership practices have a direct impact on how fast and deep technological innovations reach organizations.

At the beginning of the new century, the emergence of Internet commerce completely changed the rules by which business was done and required leaders who could combine systems thinking and human sensitivity as they pushed the platform of architectures, international companies such as Amazon, Cisco and General Electric. Over the next decade, the ubiquity of cloud computing and the young data economy amplified the so-called urgency for leaders who could combine emotional skills with technical knowledge, as demonstrated by longitudinal. Currently, the consensus in this regard is that the role of the human leader is being remodeled, because with digitalization, algorithmic complexity has transformed the way in which the sense and ethics of data become fundamental pillars for maintaining sustainable competitiveness (Warner & Wäger, 2019; Vial, 2019; Kraus et al., 2022).

Comparative Research in the Public and Private Sectors

A comparative study has shown that both the federal government and private organizations depend on transformational leadership when implementing the maturity phase of digitization. Looking at the private sector, competitive competitiveness and shareholder value pressure force leaders to adopt platform approaches and capitalize on advanced analytics.

Data from SMEs suggests a pattern: if top management assumes transformational principles and anchors collaboration networks with universities and entrepreneurship hubs, the probability of successfully completing intelligent automation projects triples (Parviainen et al., 2017; Frank et al., 2019; Kraus et al., 2022).

Latin American Context and Structural Barriers

In Latin America, the convergence between infrastructure gaps and macroeconomic volatility poses particular challenges for digital maturity, conditioning the exercise of transformational leadership. Some multi-country studies prove that inequality in connectivity generates islands of automation that fragment data ecosystems, limiting the extraction of shared value along the production chain. The literature agrees that regulatory fragmentation, the shortage of advanced talent, and the persistence of hierarchical cultures inhibit the ability of leaders to deploy digital programs; however, research argues that transformational managers who articulate public-private partnerships and promote massive upskilling reduce transaction costs and accelerate technological convergence (Kraus et al., 2022; Vial, 2019; Pelletier & Cloutier, 2019).

Cultural barriers are also critical: ethnographic analyses show that control orientation and error aversion block experimentation, while transformative leaders who normalize failure as learning manage to increase the adoption rate of digital solutions by 32%. The deficit of investment in R+D further complicates the scene, the region invests an average of 0.5% of GDP in innovation, a circumstance that requires leadership capable of attracting international financing and integrating universities as nodes of technology transfer (Warner & Wäger, 2019; Vial, 2019; Kraus et al., 2022; Reinartz et al., 2019).

Recent Trends and Empirical Gaps

In his latest study, he has revealed three converging trends for which the evidence is not yet sufficient. The first of these is inclusive algorithmic governance, whose ethical implications call for leaders who, by combining technical capacity and social sensitivity, know how to ensure equity in automatic decision-making, indicate that less than 12% of studies take into account the participation of senior managers in the design of understandable algorithms. The second trend is the fusion of improved analytics and organizational neuroscience to optimize the emotional dimension of change; show that neurophysiological monitoring, combined with transformational leadership, increases the acceptance of cognitive chatbots in critical operations (Vial, 2019).

The third major direction points out that there are serious methodological shortcomings, given that current frameworks do not reflect at all interdependence between cybersecurity, operational continuity, and the psychology of well-being. All these reviews coincide in emphasizing the need to collect data over time, use mixed methods and carry out comparative multilevel designs that allow isolating the causal effect of transformational leadership on digital maturity, its interaction with institutional and cultural factors (Sousa & Rocha, 2019).

THEORETICAL FRAMEWORK

Transformational Leadership Theory

It can be defined as an interpersonal process in which the leader inspires his subordinates to achieve shared goals and transcend their personal interest, generating a sense of collective purpose. Idealization influenced by the leader leads the leader to act as a model of the system by demonstrating ethical and sustained behaviors that followers can admire. Pioneering studies show that this type of leadership generates affective commitment, but also the internalization of organizational values. The team's vision is aligned with the business strategy.

Emotional motivation manifests itself in visionary messages that change paradigms and improve collective self-confidence. This psychological climate is conducive to innovation, providing exceptional results above what was expected. On the other hand, intellectual stimulation encourages group members to challenge original assumptions and investigate new ideas. It allows, in contexts of uncertainty, to propose creative solutions.

At the extreme, individualized consideration is based on personal support, where the leader accepts the needs and aspirations of each person in his or her charge, and offers feedback, guidance. This drives professional development as a sense of responsibility (Bass et al., 2003). However, despite the fact that transformational leadership is widely used in both theory and practice, there are critics who point to the risk of an excessive dependence on the charisma of the leader and the possibility of promoting unilateral visions that discard collective contributions.

Recent research has shown that excessive attention to charisma can lead to dynamics of uncritical follow-up, where what matters is the image and not effectiveness. This harms the quality of decisions and the autonomy of teams (Hoch, Bommer, Dulebohn, et Wu, 2016). Likewise, the proliferation of algorithmic metrics in the evaluation of engagement and digital reputation for leaders causes biases that tend to prioritize superficial indicators, encouraging behaviors that seek to maximize clicks or likes rather than tangible results in the organization in the face of such tensions, ethical accountability documents and transparent supervision frameworks that guarantee that the activities led do not violate principles of equity. diversity and integrity (Hoch et al, 2016; Rahwan et al 2019).

Extensions to Leadership in Digital Contexts

The frenetic digitalization of organizations has reached the point of being the emergence of digital leadership, which is not only limited to the adoption of technological tools but extends far beyond to change the way leaders communicate, influence and make decisions. In virtual environments, the construction of digital presence and the management of online communities become essential competencies, because interaction mediated by remote collaboration platforms requires substantially different motivation and control regulations

Hyper Personalization allows you to divide the message into different parts, adapt the communication style to different employee profiles and increase the effectiveness of change campaigns. At the same time, however, this form of marketing presents serious ethical questions for handling private data and questioning the basic right of people to be left alone

This new paradigm requires a systemic vision that combines technical, ethical, and relational aspects, placing the digital leader as a facilitator of a culture of trust where technology is used to complement the human experience instead of replacing it.

Digital Maturity Models

Digital maturity frameworks are medical systems that allow the characteristics of competencies and processes dedicated to IT adoption in entities to be assessed. The most advanced characteristics of these forms are assessed through its analytical framework, for example in 2016 in a period of two years subject to special conditions in a company under the domain of Fujitsu Digital Transformation came from the work of (Thordsen et al., 2023).

These shapes provide a way to measure gaps and direct investment. In addition to being a valuable tool for comparing yourself forward by comparing yourself with your companies in the same sector against them, it provides quantifiable data as a basis for internal decisions. The experience of the past decade has shown that while most organizations follow similar stages of maturity, speed and depth can vary greatly depending on how aligned the company and culture (internal behavior) are with executive vision and the ability to invest in digital competencies.

The practical importance of these forms lies in their flexibility to adapt in this regard: a single framework under which tailor-made roadmaps are designed, covering sustainability, social responsibility and resilience to cyberattacks. By considering digital maturity in a plural and multidimensional sense, organizations have the advantage of balancing technological efforts with changes in work culture: thus, digital infrastructure makes sense in light of operations and behaviors that are in line with these main objectives (Thordsen et al., 2023).

Dynamic Maturity Measurement

The evolution of digital maturity is not linear or static; it needs ongoing measurement measures that reflect both the speed of adoption of innovations and organizational learning capacity. Recent studies emphasize the inclusion of dynamic indicators, such as the adoption rate of new technologies, feedback loops, and resilience to technological incidents, to capture the effective participation of digital transformations (Parviainen et al., 2017).

The speed of adoption is quantified by metrics that measure the time elapsed from the detection of a technological opportunity to its operational implementation, thus generating comparable data between business areas. On the other hand, the organisational learning indicators assess the development of capacities to systematise the knowledge produced during digital projects, creating a culture of continuous improvement that shortens the learning curve in future initiatives.

In addition, the introduction of cyber resilience metrics makes it possible to measure the probability of security incidents and their impact, favoring the adoption of preventive practices as well as incident recovery: this is the performance of attack drills, redundancy of critical systems & the formation of rapid response teams. From the combination of these dynamic indicators, business leaders can implement essential real-time monitoring tools to adjust digital strategies without waiting for periodic appraisals of tradition.

Measuring Socio-Technical Innovation

The socio-technical approach recognizes the interdependence between human and technological components, postulating that the effectiveness of digital solutions depends both on technical robustness and on the ability of people and organizational structures to integrate them synergistically. This paradigm advocates the co-design of systems together with end users, promoting the co-participation of developers, managers, and collaborators in the definition of requirements and in the iterative validation of prototypes. Rejecting technological determinism, it focuses on the need to understand the values, practices, and cultural limitations that intervene in shaping the insertion of technologies such as AI, big data, and blockchain, ensuring alignment between the proposed solution and the real work dynamics (Mumford et al., 2000; Thordsen et al., 2023).

The successful implementation of socio-technical projects requires multidisciplinary teams that combine knowledge in software engineering, change management, cognitive ergonomics and organisational analysis, allowing the early detection of socio-cultural risks and the adoption of mitigation strategies, such as awareness-raising workshops, personalised training and feedback sessions.

Open Innovation and Collaborative Networks

Openness to innovation arises from the realization that the knowledge and resources necessary for groundbreaking proposals are often outside the constraints of the organization. With the idea of offering contexts for the collective creation of products, the platform combines exchanges between initiatives, the establishment of networks of experts and joint experimentation with universities, entrepreneurs and suppliers (Lyu et al., 2023; Baldwin et al., 2024).

These ways of collaborating make it possible to accelerate the process of joint product development by sharing risks, costs and benefits; things that on the other hand are not possible if it is attempted only internally since specific capacities can hardly be built within a single organization. Examples of this type of practice are the organization of joint innovation labs or initiatives that cover both inside and outside organizations (hackathon). The realization of these collaborations should not be taken as a duty, it is essential for the organization to maintain vitality and mobility (Attalah et al., 2023; Toroslu et al., 2023).

In order to effectively manage these ecosystems, governance mechanisms that uphold intellectual property rights, criteria for benefit-sharing and patterns of collaboration are needed on the terms of which the interests of all participants are safeguarded and a long-term reciprocal basis of mutual trust can be created (Reiter et al., 2024; Baldwin et al., 2024).

Theory of Dynamic Capabilities

Organizational processes within the framework of dynamic capabilities avoid opportunities, involve resources, and reconfigure entire sets of assets to maintain competitive advantages even in turbulent environments. In this framework, transformation leaders act as activators of the three pillars of dynamic capabilities: noticing weak signals from the system, which means being constantly attentive to the environment and unexpected receiver of information through situational events; occupying, mobilizing resources and making strategic decisions to exploit opportunities; and reconfiguring itself, changing structures, providing agility and converging theory with practice in order to implement improvements in a sustainable way (Bechtel et al., 2023; Pitelis et al., 2024).

The integration of dynamic capabilities into transformational leadership practices reinforces organizational adaptability, as it combines inspiration and empowerment with a systemic approach to strategic reflection and upgrading of competencies. Thus, companies not only react to changes in the environment, but also anticipate, adjust their business models to adapt to trends in them and assume a proactive attitude towards the future.

Partnerships and Value Ecosystems

The formation of strategic alliances between the public and private sectors can create value ecosystems in which different elements contribute different resources, knowledge and capacities. Within these collaboration structures, which range from regional conglomerates to international consortia, the combination of infrastructure and contacts of each group together with other experiences makes a difference and increases the capacity for innovation beyond the limitations imposed only by each individual. Governance at different levels of an ecosystem needs coordination arrangements that harmonize divergent objectives, establish standards for common work digitally, facilitate technology transfer and knowledge creation.

Empirical studies have found that the most successful partnerships are those in which each member has some autonomy and sharing is clearly defined, but not exclusively to that end, they also require digital surfaces that support communication, data sharing, and joint decision-making (Tanveer et al., 2025; Toroslu et al., 2023; Reiter et al., 2024).

Contributions of Organizational Psychology

The organizational climate is promoted by the perception of autonomy, self-regulation and the feeling of belonging. These strengthen both self-efficacy and job satisfaction, which therefore influences the power to cope with change (Mumford, Zaccaro, Harding, Jacobs, Fleishman, 2000). One of the problems that generate technological anxiety is the fear of becoming obsolete in terms of skills. Solutions to this problem are continuing education programs, individual counseling, and emotional-partner support spaces that reduce uncertainties and promote confidence in other technologies (Mumford et al., 2000).

In this way, cultural change strategies can be designed that embrace not only technique but also people's feel to cover integral aspects of effective digital implementation.

Organizational Learning and Culture of Experimentation

Organizations that establish an environment of systematized experimentation accelerate the generation of practical experience and innovation on a small scale. Through virtual communities of interest, supported by digital collaboration platforms, professionals from different fields exchange experiences, knowledge learned and good practices in real time, so that they do not replicate work and thus harmonize problem solving.

In rapid prototyping laboratories, in immersive simulations, there are controlled spaces to validate hypotheses, experiment with different process configurations and evaluate what the potential influence of new technologies could be without jeopardizing daily operations. It is essential to recognize at the institutional level intelligent failures as opportunities to learn. This is the only way to achieve a culture in which risk is understood as an inherent component of the innovation process. This encourages teams to experiment in a disciplined and thoughtful way (Mumford et al., 2000).

Distributed and Agile Leadership

The integration of transformational leadership and agility gives rise to distributed management models, in which decisions are decentralized and teams share co-ownership of results. Recent studies show that combining Lean, Scrum, and Design Thinking principles with transformational leadership techniques enhances organizational flexibility, as it allows for short cycles of planning and value delivery, rapid changes in response to market feedback, and a customer-driven approach. In this new environment, the role of the leader becomes a facilitator of processes, mentor and eliminator of obstacles, and promotes the autonomy of teams to define tactics and adapt to contingencies without losing sight of the overall strategic vision (Rialti & Filieri, 2024;; Weber et al., 2022; Meier & Kock, 2024).

The fusion of flat organizational structures with light coordination mechanisms and iterative cycles gives rise to an agile ecosystem in which innovation is institutionalized as an operational routine, producing a greater smoothness and speed of response to disruptive change (Sreenivasan & Suresh, 2024).

Interconnecting Theoretical Frameworks

The complexity of digital transformation requires synthetic analytical frameworks that include transformational leadership, digital maturity models, socio-technical vision, and dynamic capabilities. A hybrid analytical framework approach allows us to assess how leaders simultaneously inspire commitment; how the exploration and exploitation of technology occurs; how human and technical elements intersect; and how resources are reallocated for the benefit of innovation. This systematic lack approach allows for environmental diagnoses that include qualitative and quantitative elements, favoring decision-making that is halfway between the desired strategies and the environmental circumstances (Meier & Kock, 2024; Carvalho et al., 2023; Rialti & Filieri, 2024; de Paula Pereira et al., 2024).

CHALLENGES FACED BY ORGANIZATIONS OR INSTITUTIONS

Primarily, the transition to effective digital maturity lies under the leadership of transformational leadership models. However, it entails structural, technical, organizational and cultural challenges that differ depending on the type of organization, the institutional configuration, its context and the level of existing technological development. These challenges are especially pronounced in environments where traditional entrenched practices coexist alongside the needs for rapid change – producing tensions between the known and the emerging, organizational stability, and the need for radical transformation.

One of the biggest problems stemming from resistance to change lies in this touchstone: how can transformational leadership cope with a kenotic environment and build trust, intrinsic motives mobilize madrasas. Recent research shows that resistance to change is not only due to individual factors, but is a manifestation of collective belief systems, power dynamics, and symbolic control mechanisms that hinder learning experimentation (Parviainen et al., 2017).

Added to this resistance is the fragmentation of digital skills in organizations, which leads to gaps between different management teams and functional departments. This fragmentation prevents an overview of the digital strategy by limiting its technological use and creates internal inequalities that affect cohesion. Another mission of transformational leadership is to examine the space where these digital divides are located, promoting a process of continuous training and fostering common visions beyond functional separations.

Another major challenge is that traditional operational processes are difficult to convert into agile, scalable, and user-centric digital systems. This applies to both government agencies and private companies digitizing by inertia without a strategic review of processes, leads to repeating mistakes increases the inefficiency of innovation (Sreenivasan & Suresh, 2024).

Therefore, transformative management must make digitalization more than just an adoption of technology, it must also involve a critical review of processes with the active participation of the actors involved and a clear orientation towards value creation.

For public administrations, the challenges are made more complicated by the coexistence of political disciplines, obsolete regulations emanating from the State, budgetary restrictions and limited autonomy of operation. These factors generate additional obstacles to digital maturity, which often depend on decisions that are not in the hands of the coaching staff. In this sense, the transformative leadership must serve as a mediator between the political part, the public, and the bureaucratic body, building social legitimacy for the processes of technological transformation and the promotion of ethical frameworks of application (Pitelis et al., 2024; Browder et al., 2024).

It is also crucial to maintain data exchange between platforms, systems, and processes, especially in organizations that have legacy systems, which makes technology integration difficult. This situation generates bottlenecks, hidden costs and weak points in security, operational efficiency and quality of service are affected. Transformative leaders must make decisions about the strategic tations of the technology platform, prioritizing the adoption of open standards, data compatibility, and the ordering of flexible systems that can be adapted to future innovations.

The lack of data governance is another Gordian knot Digital maturity implies a high degree of ability to use data thoughtfully and capably as a support in strategic decision-making, a prerequisite: clear regulation, protection of ethical quality in the regulatory establishment, objective assessment of the software that laws establish and data.

Transformational leadership must be able to create rigorous regulations that ensure accountability for the use of information, user privacy, and fair algorithms, especially in an environment in which decision-making power is progressively shifting towards automated system (Boukarras et al., 2024; Muhl, 2024; Urbani et al., 2024).

Finally, organizations have to face an additional challenge: establishing a shared vision for digital. Technological transformation is usually piloted by technical teams, which do not tend to properly incorporate strategic actors, operators and citizens. This system detaches the technological vision from the real dynamics within the organization. Transformational leadership has the responsibility to facilitate co-creation processes, design stories that inspire everyone, and develop a common sense that gives meaning to changes and promotes the appropriation of technologies from an inclusive and collaborative perspective (Parviainen et al., 2017).

EXAMPLES OF IMPLEMENTATION IN COMPANIES OR ORGANIZATIONS

The paradigmatic case on the global scene is Siemens, the company where, thanks to transformational leadership, high-tech devices have been able to be integrated into highly regulated and extremely complex environments from the point of view of technology. Following the Digital Enterprise vision, Siemens has carried out a series of developments that combine artificial intelligence, automation and predictive analytics to improve the efficiency of industrial operations. What is remarkable about this case is that although the success of these applications has been shifted to a type of new leadership by Siemens that personalizes innovation, empowers teams and institutionalizes technology goals with the internal corporate vision. The internal fieldwork exhibited yesterday in parallel to the cloud assisted by recording devices demonstrates that by operation, Siemens operational leaders promote continuous learning and both functional and transversal (Sreenivasan & Suresh, 2024).

In the public sector, Estonia's digital government has already become a symbol of advanced digital maturity on a global scale. The step taken by Estonia is not only about the application of technologies, but also brings with it a fundamental change in the type of relationship that state and citizens maintain. The transformative leadership of Estonia's governing authorities has consolidated interoperable systems, user-centric services, and open data policies. This process requires visionary leadership that is committed to transparency, effectiveness, and institutional sustainability. The introduction of the X-Road secure data exchange system, which allows public and private entities to share data of this type with full confidence in the origin, as a structural basis for innovation, shows the type of digital transformation to which those who hold the leadership in endizi (Pitelis et al., 2024; Browder et al., 2024).

BBVA, a Spanish banking group that has carried out radically digital changes for its customers and that mainly follows three lines: advanced analysis, otomization of services and recognition of personalization. The association of the figure of the Chief Digital Officer with the transformational approach to leadership in management teams has been decisive for the success of their digital evolution. BBVA's leadership model encourages data-driven decision-making, internal training in digital skills and the construction of an agile culture. BBVA's program called Voy Contigo, which seeks to empower employees to offer digital solutions closer to the customer, has been cited as an example of how leadership structurally transforms organizational behaviors and attitudes (Garay-Gallastegui et al., 2024).

Even, a technological entity with an organizational culture based on values of innovation, inclusion and learning, such as Salesforce. Its digitalization is led by a management team that embraces highly visible transformational leadership, while merging social purpose with technological development. The introduction of artificial intelligence tools such as Einstein in its business management platforms has been accompanied by a cultural remodeling based on leadership empathy, transparency and commitment to social impact. In this environment, leaders are actively involved in things and help germinate technology adoption among customers and employees.

The Latin American region is another example. Bogota Bank has managed to implement an entire digital strategy with strong transformational leadership. Despite the traditional regulatory and cultural framework in which it operates, the bank promoted a model of change based on decentralizing decisions, restructuring hierarchical structures and training its workforce on a large scale in digital tools. The general management has maintained a narrative of culture change, which has been based on values of transparency, agility and innovation, with the result that it has been possible to accelerate internal transformation processes and improve the customer experience (Tanveer et al., 2025; Toroslu et al., 2023; Reiter et al., 2024).

Arizona State University has been a pioneer in developing digital maturity through transformational leadership. Through digital platforms, innovation laboratories and educational information analysis systems, the institution has reconfigured its teaching-learning model. Led by managers with a strategic vision, the process is conceived as a tool to personalize education, expand access and improve results. Lessons from technological humanism have been replicated by other universities, serving as a model for inclusive and sustainable digital transformation driven by leadership.

In the field of public health, the example of the United Kingdom's national health system (NHS) is distinguished by a transformational approach to care with respect to informatics. Digital transformation in clinical and administrative management has been key to introducing digital solutions in the form of electronic medical records, telemedicine and artificial intelligence platforms in order to make early diagnoses. This process requires investment not only in infrastructure, but also a radical change in organizational culture in which leaders act as a bridge between patient-centered care and technological innovation.

These case examples will serve as a reference point for the strategic principles that will be derived in the results section: that said, digital maturity does not depend only on the availability of technology, but also and above all on the quality of leadership that can integrate it. Transformational leadership acts like an enabler of organizational capacity, by configuring environments conducive to innovation, adaptability and continuous learning. We will build on the lessons from these cases in the findings section, to derive strategic principles applicable to other institutional settings (Haug et al., 2024; Eom & Lee, 2022).

In the private sector, competitive pressure and the logic of ROI in digital assets have incentivized leadership styles that are oriented towards agility and constant experimentation. The paper illustrates how transformative vision makes it possible to adopt advanced AI or analytics and thus legitimize risky investments in cloud platforms, data. These leaders mobilize symbolic capital to align shareholders with narratives of disruption, while rolling out intensive upskilling programs to sustain the speed of technological implementation.

By contrast, government operates under a strict regulatory framework of accountability and transparency in which public sector leaders must harmonize innovation with equity in access, citizen data protection, and democratic legitimacy. The case of digital government in Estonia demonstrates that transformational leadership can catalyze interconnectivity and social trust, but only if it succeeds in translating the digital story into tangible public values, such as simplifying processes, reducing corruption, and improving basic services. This agenda makes digital ethics and sustainability two indispensable axes, shifting the emphasis from the return to social impact(Tanveer et al., 2025; Toroslu et al., 2023; Reiter et al., 2024).

The sectoral difference is expressed in different ways of managing resistance to change. In multinational companies, disruption is assimilated with market incentives and high-performance cultures, in government entities, bureaucratic inertia, political rotation and lack of money make it difficult to liquidate previous systems. At the inter-institutional level, transformational leadership has to act as a bridge, creating public-private partnerships and multi-stakeholder commitments, in order to ensure continuity beyond the electoral period.

A second comparative aspect refers to the form of data governance. Private companies often consider data as an asset with economic value, managing it through their own architectures and exclusive monetization algorithms. The narrative of transformation promotes ethics in experimentation in which failure is at the same time strategic learning. In the meantime, state institutions must combine intensive use of data with restrictions in terms of privacy, non-discrimination and transparency.

Here, therefore, it makes sense to advocate for greater digital ethical awareness, but one that would benefit from political leaders discussing in more detail what contradictions they need to overcome while addressing their obligation to put in place regulatory safeguards. This is especially necessary in the context of the existing pressure to exploit big data for both security and fiscal control.

SOLUTIONS AND RECOMMENDATIONS

The evidence observed shows that the main barrier to achieving digital maturity is not in technology, but in the absence of leadership, without which it is impossible to harmonize strategic vision, pioneering culture and data governance in a single organizational story. Therefore, any effective remedy has to start from a diagnosis of the system that reveals the gap between the disruptive promise of digital tools and everyday practices that perpetuate hierarchical inertia. Based on this recognition, a transformation itinerary is proposed that combines cultural interventions, process redesign, talent policies and distributed governance mechanisms with dynamic performance metrics (Boukarras et al., 2024; Muhl, 2024; Urbani et al., 2024).

Therefore, it is considered to establish transformational leadership at all levels. To avoid totalitarian ascriptions, leadership circles are instituted where their idealized influence, source of motivation, and intellectual sphere can permeate any level without ultimately depending on a single charisma. This polycentric structure decreases uncritical compliance, increases ethical deliberation on algorithmic biases and accelerates humanity's appropriation of innovation.

Likewise, organizations must create continuous learning ecosystems based on massive up-skilling/re-skilling. It is suggested to create internal digital talent academies with modular courses, micro-credentials, and cross-mentoring projects between technical experts and business people. To calm the mood caused by technology and avoid a separation of generations, each curriculum must comprise a balanced mix of immersive simulations, rapid prototyping labs, and virtual communities of practice, thus taking the form of our psychology required for experimentation (Attalah et al., 2023; Toroslu et al., 2023).

The cultural resistance already discovered is nullified when error is considered as a learning process; that is why a policy of success in failure must be established, which publicly recognizes the insights obtained from failed tests. Managers are advised to post open retrospective reviews after each sprint, detailing their underlying causes and strategic pivots. It is of utmost importance to demonstrate that cognitive transparency overcomes the fear of error, and that it ultimately increases the resilience of the organization.

Any process redesign will need to be based on service approaches and agile frameworks. It is proposed to establish a cross-functional group that combines Design Thinking, Lean and Scrum under the direction of transformation leaders who will also act as facilitators, mentors, problem managers. These cells will work on their own discovery-development-validation cycles, focusing on carrying out the simplest and most available deliverables, and continuously bridling internal and external users for feedback. By combining agility in the business with emotional leadership in management, a company can shorten its start-up-operation-time to get to money. It is not just that innovation becomes common practice.

Data governance emerges as an essential requirement. It is suggested that a Data Trust and Ethics Council be created chaired by a Chief Data and Ethics Officer, who should report directly to the CEO. This council should establish principles of accountability, fair algorithms, explainability and bias minimisation, as well as independently assess the life cycle of predictive models. At the same time, it is suggested that interoperable data and decentralized digital identity systems be used to enable full portability between platforms, as bottlenecks are in fact likely to occur in older systems.

Therefore, the importance of collaborative ecosystems is underlined; Consequently, it is recommended to consolidate public-private partnerships with universities, entrepreneurship hubs and multilateral organizations that share infrastructures, data and specialized talent. To reduce transaction costs and accelerate technological convergence, such alliances should codify clear intellectual property clauses, benefit-sharing schemes, and dispute resolution mechanisms.

Cyber resilience must take a proactive approach. It is recommended to install cross-sector security operations centers, biannual network-blue teaming exercises, and multi-cloud contingency plans that allow continuity to be operational in the event of system failures or fifth-generation cyberattacks. The question of how to manage stress properly is also being examined by rapid response teams, who are conducting experiments with both human and biological methods that can help maintain good morale and allow for better decision making under pressure.

Sandbox regulatory frameworks are proposed to address the ethical dilemmas of algorithmic governance. Under these frameworks, innovation pilot tests, algorithmic impact assessment, and citizen participation in all design stages. Combining in this way both democratic legitimacy and technological experimentation are guaranteed.

Therefore, organizations need to have a steady stream of leadership staff. To this end, it is proposed to create rotation programs in which future leaders participate in high-quality multi-area projects, combined with advice given based on Neurofeed-back and submerged simulations of digital crises. It is a strategy that allows not only to acquire technical skills, but also to develop an education in emotional intelligence and an articulated ethical sense.

In the end, the academic community should undertake multilevel longitudinal studies, analyze the causal effect of transformational leadership on digital maturity and organizational toughness, integrating contextual variables such as digital inequality, the regulatory framework, and national culture. The combination of qualitative analysis methods, real-time data and network analysis will allow the complex ecology of digital transformation to be translated into statistics and decisions based on reliable evidence.

In summary, the solutions proposed here coincide in a point of orientation: technology only produces value if leadership transforms the human experience into collective learning, pairs ethics and efficiency, and transforms uncertainty into an opportunity for systemic innovation. If the public and private world accepts this agenda, organizations will easily overcome the challenges identified and thus achieve overall digital maturity, competitiveness and social legitimacy.

FUTURE RESEARCH DIRECTIONS

The findings obtained through this study open multiple avenues for the development of future research aimed at consolidating, deepening, and extending the understanding of the link between transformational leadership and digital maturity in public and private organizations. These directions must not only respond to theoretical gaps identified in the existing literature, but also meet the practical needs of organizations facing disruptive, hyperconnected, and socially complex environments. From an interdisciplinary and critical perspective, five priority lines of future research with high theoretical value and institutional applicability are proposed.

The fundamental challenge is to explore the emotional and cognitive dimension of transformational leadership in advanced automation contexts, particularly in scenarios where work processes begin to be redefined by artificial intelligence systems, collaborative robotics and algorithmic decision-making. While the current literature has documented the technical impacts of these technologies, research on how transformational leaders manage organizational anxiety, promote trust in automated decisions, and build spaces of shared meaning in hybrid human-machine ecosystems is still incipient. It is necessary to understand, from neuropsychological and sociotechnical approaches, how leadership can humanize digital processes without compromising efficiency and innovation (Meier & Kock, 2024).

A second key line of research aims to examine the ethical tensions and moral dilemmas that transformational leaders face when implementing deep digitalization processes. Issues such as data privacy, organizational surveillance, algorithmic bias, or digital exclusion require more robust analytical frameworks that integrate principles of social justice, democratic governance of technology, and institutional accountability. Comparative case studies in organizations with different regulatory frameworks could reveal normative patterns, emerging practices of digital ethics, and leadership mechanisms oriented towards social sustainability .

Likewise, the need to analyze the relationship between transformational leadership and relational capital in digital environments is identified, considering how leaders mobilize internal and external networks to enhance collaborative innovation. Digital platforms have expanded the possibilities of interaction between institutional actors, customers, communities, and other stakeholders, redefining the exercise of leadership beyond traditional organizational boundaries. Understanding how transformational leaders activate these networks, build transorganizational legitimacy, and generate distributed adaptive capabilities represents a valuable contribution to the field of digital organizational studies.

Another emerging direction is the development of hybrid transformational leadership models with agile, inclusive, and data-driven approaches, which allow for the integration of principles of self-organization, participatory empowerment, and continuous feedback. The hybridization between transformational leadership and frameworks such as Lean, Design Thinking or Scrum could lead to new organizational governance architectures adapted to digital logic. Empirical research aimed at the design of operational frameworks, leadership prototypes, or evaluation metrics could offer validated tools for organizations that want to accelerate their digital maturity processes without compromising the human factor (Meier & Kock, 2024; Carvalho et al., 2023; Rialti & Filieri, 2024; de Paula Pereira et al., 2024).

The longitudinal evaluation of the impacts of transformational leadership on indicators of digital maturity and organizational sustainability is proposed as a line of work, considering variables such as productivity, quality of service, staff satisfaction, operational resilience and innovation capacity. Longitudinal studies would allow not only to verify causal relationships, but also to capture processes of evolution, regression or stagnation, providing valuable evidence for strategic decision-making (Haug et al., 2024; Eom & Lee, 2022). Likewise, this research could incorporate contextual metrics that integrate cultural, institutional, and economic factors, especially in contexts of high digital inequality.

In terms of practical implications, the results of this chapter suggest that management training programs should incorporate competencies related to transformational leadership in digital environments, such as innovation-oriented strategic thinking, emotional intelligence for change management, technological literacy, and digital ethics. Public policies for digital transformation should also contemplate the strengthening of leadership as a structuring axis, beyond the simple provision of infrastructure or connectivity. In the private sector, it is recommended that organizations integrate mechanisms for identifying, developing, and evaluating transformational leadership with criteria adapted to the digital age, aligning their talent models with the challenges of a technologically volatile environment (Saeedikiya et al., 2024).

These proposals aim to build a research and action agenda that places transformational leadership as a central component of sustainable digital transformation, allowing organizations not only to adapt to change, but to become active agents of systemic innovation. The conclusions section will synthesize the main theoretical and strategic contributions of the chapter, offering an integrated vision that links the human, technical, and organizational dimensions of this complex phenomenon.

CONCLUSION

This study proves what really makes the difference between having cutting-edge technology and realizing real benefits: the lack of transformational leadership capable of transforming algorithmic complexity into collective strength. According to comparative evidence, even when Latin American organizations invest in infrastructure, limitations remain derived from inequalities in connections and hierarchical cultures that discourage experimentation. With this, digital maturity does not arrive, the competitive gap widens

These structural constraints are exacerbated by the lack of participatory leadership mechanisms that engage less favored voices and provide legitimacy for the technology strategy.

In response to the first question, which is how does transformational leadership influence the speed and depth with which public and private organizations reach digital maturity in high-tech environments? Thanks to its combination of shared vision, intellectual stimulation and individualized work, transformative leadership acts as an accelerator in technological absorption taking it to speeds that far exceed conventional planning cycles. According to the results obtained, when leaders tell motivating stories and support learning through error, the average time it takes for advanced enterprise platforms to achieve implementation is significantly reduced and the probability that pilot projects can scale to the corporate level doubles. However, when leadership becomes a mere matter of personal charisma, leaving aside systematic knowledge management practices, biases and route dependencies reappear that slow down maturity.

To prolong this positive phenomenon, management routes must be developed made up of technologies that then become ethically aware of their consequences, and methodologies that are stacked. Rotation through functions, neuro-feedback sessions, and immersive teaching in digital crises has been proven to increase leaders' self-efficacy and their real-time ability to reconfigure work procedures.

On the other hand, the creation of internal coalitions that pay for the risk and celebrate constructive error reinforces a culture of constant research. In Asian environments, it is observed that the combination of agile prototypes with transformative leadership shortens skills update cycles and leads to a steeper slope by radical innovations.

In the case of the second question: What mediations characteristic of culture and government govern the connection between leadership patterns and the value creation derived from the incorporation of emerging technologies in an environment characterized by structural inequality?, the decisive agents are probably organizational trust, the codification of common values, and informed and deliberate decision-making. Ethnological evidence shows that oriented control and fear of error lower the rate of digital incorporation; on the other hand, leaders who incorporate collective learning rites achieve a substantial increase in safe experimentation.

From a sociotechnical point of view, each new technology reorganizes professional identities and power relations. Leadership must therefore be the translator of technical complexities into shared meanings that integrate ethics and efficiency (Tagscherer & Carbon, 2023). When managers employ narratives that link social purposes, innovation, and well-being, the resilience of their culture is strengthened and internal legitimacy increases.

For these reasons, organizations must institutionalize data ethics and trust bodies that are accountable at the highest level of management and develop guidelines for algorithmic transparency, fairness, and comprehensibility. On the other hand, leaders must implement inclusive continuing education programs that generate common visions across functional boundaries and close internal skill gaps. The construction of public-private relations around open innovation laboratories favors the dissemination of knowledge and reduces transaction costs, creating ecosystems that multiply the value generated.

The third question: to what extent are ethical data frameworks and inter-institutional alliances moderating the impact of transformational leadership on operational resilience and social legitimacy? To this end, it was identified that digital resilience is significantly increased when senior managers implement explicit algorithmic governance policies and decisions are submitted to external actors. Recent studies show that less than 15% of fieldwork explains how transformational managers put the principle of algorithmic accountability into practice, a situation that undermines social trust and limits the scalability of innovation (Gascó-Hernández et al., 2022; Tagscherer & Carbon, 2023).

In contrast, organizations that adopt multilevel resilience models have sometimes lower downtime and a greater ability to respond to cascading failures. The neuroemotional dimension also plays a role: leaders who are able to monitor stress indicators and create spaces for emotional restoration favor the acceptance of automatic systems as well as internal stabilization. To consolidate this type of positive moderation, open data agreements with intellectual property clauses and citizen participation in pilot tests are proposed, which in turn strengthens compliance with obligations and diversifies sources of value.

In addition, the adoption of dynamic maturity metrics to measure learning speed, algorithmic ethics, and sustainability allows us to act preventively against future risks and articulate comprehensive responses (Karimi et al., 2023). In short, transformational leadership makes it possible for technological promises to become a social and economic reality if combined with cultures of trust, inclusive governance approaches, and inter-institutional partnerships.

This chapter also indicates that the positive effects are multiplied if there is coherence between the value systems defined by ethics, responsible data policies and forms of continuous learning. Future research should have a longitudinal, multilevel design to isolate the causal impact of these factors and investigate their operation in combination with regulatory frameworks and inequality structures in various sectors. Only in this way can we achieve a digital maturity that is not only a point of arrival but also a constant process of reinvention for the sake of common organizational resistance and collective well-being.

REFERENCES

Aras, S., Yayla, A. A., & Yıldız, E. (2023). Digital maturity assessment: A systematic literature review. *Systems, 11*(4), 213. DOI: 10.3390/systems11040213

Ates, A., & Acur, N. (2022). Making obsolescence obsolete: Execution of digital transformation in a high-tech manufacturing SME. *Journal of Business Research, 152*, 336–348. DOI: 10.1016/j.jbusres.2022.07.052

Attalah, I., Nylund, P. A., & Brem, A. (2023). Who captures value from hackathons. Innovation contests with collective intelligence tools bridging creativity and coupled open innovation. *Creativity and Innovation Management, 32*(2), 266–280. DOI: 10.1111/caim.12552

Avolio, B. J., Kahai, S. S., & Dodge, G. E. (2014). E-leadership: Re-examining transformations in leadership source and transmission. *The Leadership Quarterly, 25*(1), 105–131. DOI: 10.1016/j.leaqua.2013.11.003

Baldwin, C. Y., Bogers, M. L. A. M., Kapoor, R., & West, J. (2024). Focusing the ecosystem lens on innovation studies. *Research Policy, 53*(3), 104949. DOI: 10.1016/j.respol.2023.104949

Bass, B. M., Avolio, B. J., Jung, D. I., & Berson, Y. (2003). Predicting unit performance by assessing transformational and transactional leadership. *The Journal of Applied Psychology, 88*(2), 207–218. DOI: 10.1037/0021-9010.88.2.207

Bechtel, J., Kaufmann, L., & Kock, A. (2023). The interplay between dynamic capabilities' dimensions and project portfolio success. *International Journal of Project Management, 41*(6), 102469. DOI: 10.1016/j.ijproman.2023.102469

Besio, C., & Pronzini, A. (2025). Algorithmic responsibility without accountability. *Systems Research and Behavioral Science, 42*(4), 576–589. DOI: 10.1002/sres.3028

Boukarras, S., Ferri, D., Borgogni, L., & Aglioti, S. M. (2024). Neurophysiological markers of asymmetric emotional contagion: Implications for organizational contexts. *Frontiers in Integrative Neuroscience, 18*, 1321130. DOI: 10.3389/fnint.2024.1321130

Boukarras, S., Filho, E. R., & Sanchis, A. (2022). Bringing social interaction at the core of organizational neuroscience. *Frontiers in Psychology, 13*, 1034454. DOI: 10.3389/fpsyg.2022.1034454

Braojos, J., Weritz, P., & Matute, J. (2024). Empowering organisational commitment through digital transformation capabilities: The role of digital leadership and a continuous learning environment. *Information Systems Journal, 34*(5), 1466–1492. DOI: 10.1111/isj.12501

Browder, R. E., Dwyer, S. M., & Koch, H. (2024). Upgrading adaptation: How digital transformation promotes organizational resilience. *Strategic Entrepreneurship Journal, 18*(1), 128–164. DOI: 10.1002/sej.1483

Camilleri, M. A. (2024). Responsible AI governance and ethical decision-making for sustainable performance and growth. *Expert Systems: International Journal of Knowledge Engineering and Neural Networks, 41*(6), e13406. DOI: 10.1111/exsy.13406

Carvalho, A. M., Luis, J. M., & Sousa, R. (2023). Operational excellence, organizational culture, and agility: Bridging the gap between quality and adaptability. *Total Quality Management & Business Excellence, 34*(11-12), 1598–1628. Advance online publication. DOI: 10.1080/14783363.2023.2191844

Cieslak, V., Bouaziz, A., & Davenport, T. (2025). An integrative review of employee resistance to digital transformation. *Cogent Business & Management, 12*(1), 2442550. DOI: 10.1080/23311975.2024.2442550

De Bock, K. W., Coussement, K., De Caigny, A., Słowiński, R., Baesens, B., Boute, R. N., Choi, T.-M., Delen, D., Kraus, M., Lessmann, S., Maldonado, S., Martens, D., Óskarsdóttir, M., Vairetti, C., Verbeke, W., & Weber, R. (2024). Explainable AI for operational research: A defining framework, methods, applications, and a research agenda. *European Journal of Operational Research, 317*(2), 249–272. DOI: 10.1016/j.ejor.2023.09.026

De Carolis, A., Sassanelli, C., Acerbi, F., Macchi, M., Terzi, S., & Taisch, M. (2025). The Digital REadiness Assessment MaturitY DREAMY framework to guide manufacturing companies towards a digitalisation roadmap. *International Journal of Production Research, 63*(15), 5555–5581. Advance online publication. DOI: 10.1080/00207543.2025.2455476

de Paula Pereira, G., de Medeiros, J. F., Kolling, C., Ribeiro, J. L. D., Morea, D., & Iazzolino, G. (2024). Using dynamic capabilities to cope with digital transformation and boost innovation in traditional banks. *Business Horizons, 67*(4), 317–330. DOI: 10.1016/j.bushor.2024.03.006

Elia, G., Solazzo, G., Lerro, A., Pigni, F., & Tucci, C. L. (2024). The digital transformation canvas: A conceptual framework for leading the digital transformation process. *Business Horizons, 67*(4), 381–398. DOI: 10.1016/j.bushor.2024.03.007

Ellström, D., Holtström, J., Berg, E., & Josefsson, C. (2022). Dynamic capabilities for digital transformation. *Journal of Strategy and Management, 15*(2), 272–286. DOI: 10.1108/JSMA-04-2021-0089

Eom, S.-J., & Lee, J. (2022). Digital government transformation in turbulent times: Responses, challenges, and future direction. *Government Information Quarterly, 39*(2), 101690. DOI: 10.1016/j.giq.2022.101690

Ernst, B. A., Banks, G. C., Loignon, A. C., Frear, K. A., Williams, C. E., Arciniega, L. M., Gupta, R. K., Kodydek, G., & Subramanian, D. (2021). Virtual charismatic leadership and signaling theory: A prospective meta-analysis in five countries. *The Leadership Quarterly, 32*(5), 101541. DOI: 10.1016/j.leaqua.2021.101541

Frank, A. G., Dalenogare, L. S., & Ayala, N. F. (2019). Industry 4.0 technologies: Implementation patterns in manufacturing companies. *International Journal of Production Economics, 210*, 15–26. DOI: 10.1016/j.ijpe.2019.01.004

Garay-Gallastegui, L. M., Achurra-González, F., Delgado Ruiz, G., & Sánchez-González, J. L. (2024). The role of analytical techniques in the industrialization of digital profiles and the operationalization of business strategy: The case of BBVA. *Innovative Marketing, 20*(2), 90–101. DOI: 10.21511/im.20(2).2024.09

Gascó-Hernández, M., Gil-García, J. R., & Luna-Reyes, L. F. (2022). Unpacking the role of technology, leadership, governance and collaborative capacities in inter-agency collaborations. *Government Information Quarterly, 39*(3), 101710. DOI: 10.1016/j.giq.2022.101710

Giacosa, E., Alam, G. M., Culasso, F., & Crocco, E. (2023). The paradox of digital surveillance in the workplace. *Journal of Innovation & Knowledge*, *8*(2), 100357. DOI: 10.1016/j.jik.2023.100357

Glikson, E., & Woolley, A. W. (2020). Human trust in artificial intelligence: Review of empirical research. *The Academy of Management Annals*, *14*(2), 627–660. DOI: 10.5465/annals.2018.0057

Große, C., & Sundberg, L. (2025). Generative AI and digital resilience: A research agenda. *Journal of Risk Research*, 1–26. Advance online publication. DOI: 10.1080/13669877.2025.2539105

Haug, N., Dan, S., & Mergel, I. (2024). Digitally induced change in the public sector: A systematic review and research agenda. *Public Management Review*, *26*(7), 1963–1987. DOI: 10.1080/14719037.2023.2234917

Hoch, J. E., Bommer, W. H., Dulebohn, J. H., & Wu, D. (2016). Do ethical, authentic, and servant leadership explain variance above and beyond transformational leadership? A meta-analysis. *Journal of Management*, *42*(1), 125–157. DOI: 10.1177/0149206316665461

Jun, S., & Lee, S. (2023). Transformational leadership and followers' innovative behavior: The roles of commitment to change and perceived organizational support. *Behavioral Sciences (Basel, Switzerland)*, *13*(4), 320. DOI: 10.3390/bs13040320

Karimi, S., Raeesi Vanani, I., & Dashti, F. (2023). The role of transformational leadership in developing innovative work behaviors: The mediating role of employees' psychological capital. *Sustainability (Basel)*, *15*(2), 1267. DOI: 10.3390/su15021267

Klasmeier, K. N., & Lehmann-Willenbrock, N. (2024). Temporal dynamics of shared leadership, team workload, and collective team member well-being: A daily diary study. *European Journal of Work and Organizational Psychology*, *33*(3), 263–275. DOI: 10.1080/1359432X.2023.2263200

Kostopoulos, G., Vrochidis, S., Moumtzidou, A., Kompatsiaris, I., & Kompatsiaris, Y. (2024). Explainable artificial intelligence based decision support systems: A survey. *Electronics (Basel)*, *13*(14), 2842. DOI: 10.3390/electronics13142842

Kraus, S., Durst, S., Ferreira, J. J. M., Veiga, P., Kailer, N., & Weinmann, A. (2022). Digital transformation in business and management research: An overview of the current status quo. *International Journal of Information Management*, *63*, 102466. DOI: 10.1016/j.ijinfomgt.2021.102466

Kraus, S., Ferraris, A., & Bertello, A. (2023). The future of work: How innovation and digitalization reshape the workplace. *Journal of Innovation & Knowledge*, *8*(4), 100438. DOI: 10.1016/j.jik.2023.100438

Leonardi, P. M., Huysman, M., Steinfield, C., & Gruber, T. (2013). Enterprise social media: Definition, history, and prospects for the study of social technologies in organizations. *Journal of Computer-Mediated Communication*, *19*(1), 1–19. DOI: 10.1111/jcc4.12029

Li, Y., Chen, C., & Yuan, Y. (2025). Evolving the job demands resources framework to JD-R 3.0: After-hours connectivity and psychological distress. *Acta Psychologica*, *253*, 104710. DOI: 10.1016/j.actpsy.2025.104710

Lin, Q., Wang, S., & Chen, G. (2022). The relationship between distributed leadership and teacher innovativeness: The mediating roles of teacher autonomy and professional collaboration. *Frontiers in Psychology*, *13*, 948152. DOI: 10.3389/fpsyg.2022.948152

Lyu, B., Yi, R., Fan, G., & Zhang, Y. (2023). Stakeholder network for developing open innovation practice of China's manufacturing enterprises. *Heliyon*, *9*(3), e13192. DOI: 10.1016/j.heliyon.2023.e13192

Meier, A. K., & Kock, A. (2024). Agile R&D units' organisation and its relationship with innovation performance. *R & D Management*, *54*(3), 496–512. DOI: 10.1111/radm.12655

Muhl, E. (2024). The challenge of wearable neurodevices for workplace monitoring: An EU legal perspective. *Frontiers in Human Dynamics*, *6*, 1473893. DOI: 10.3389/fhumd.2024.1473893

Mumford, T. V., Zaccaro, S. J., Harding, F. D., Jacobs, T. O., & Fleishman, E. A. (2000). Leadership skills for a changing world: Solving complex social problems. *The Leadership Quarterly*, *11*(1), 11–35. DOI: 10.1016/S1048-9843(99)00041-7

Papagiannidis, E., Mikalef, P., & Conboy, K. (2025). Responsible artificial intelligence governance: A review and research framework. *The Journal of Strategic Information Systems*, *34*(2), 101885. DOI: 10.1016/j.jsis.2024.101885

Parviainen, P., Tihinen, M., Kääriäinen, J., & Teppola, S. (2017). Tackling the digitalization challenge: How to benefit from digitalization in practice. *International Journal of Information Systems and Project Management*, *5*(1), 63–77. DOI: 10.12821/ijispm050104

Pelletier, C., & Cloutier, L. M. (2019). Conceptualising digital transformation in SMEs: An ecosystemic perspective. *Journal of Small Business and Enterprise Development*, *26*(6–7), 855–876. DOI: 10.1108/JSBED-05-2019-0144

Pitelis, C. N., Teece, D. J., & Yang, H. (2024). Dynamic capabilities and MNE global strategy. *Journal of Management Studies*, *61*(7), 3295–3326. DOI: 10.1111/joms.13021

Plekhanov, D., Franke, H., & Netland, T. H. (2023). Digital transformation: A review and research agenda. *European Management Journal*, *41*(6), 821–844. DOI: 10.1016/j.emj.2022.09.007

Porfirio, J. A., Carrilho, T., Felício, J. A., & Jardim, J. (2021). Leadership characteristics and digital transformation. *Journal of Business Research*, *124*, 610–619. DOI: 10.1016/j.jbusres.2020.10.058

Reinartz, W., Wiegand, N., & Imschloss, M. (2019). The impact of digital transformation on the retailing value chain. *International Journal of Research in Marketing*, *36*(3), 350–366. DOI: 10.1016/j.ijresmar.2018.12.002

Reiter, I., Ozman, M., Goglio-Primard, K., Dalmasso, C., & Garraffo, F. (2024). Managing multi tiered innovation ecosystems. A governance perspective. *Research Policy*, *53*(1), 104905. DOI: 10.1016/j.respol.2023.104905

Rialti, R., & Filieri, R. (2024). Leaders let us get agile: Observing agile leadership in successful digital transformation projects. *Business Horizons*, *67*(4), 439–452. DOI: 10.1016/j.bushor.2024.04.003

Rioseco Pais, J. G., & Ponce, L., & colegas. (2024). Digital skills for sustainability in Latin America. *Sustainability*, *16*(22), 9876. DOI: 10.3390/su16229876

Saeedikiya, M., Salunke, S., & Kowalkiewicz, M. (2024). Toward a dynamic capability perspective of digital transformation in SMEs: A study of the mobility sector. *Journal of Cleaner Production*, *439*, 140718. DOI: 10.1016/j.jclepro.2024.140718

Senna, P. P., Monteiro, D. S., Lacerda, D. P., & Alencar, M. H., & colaboradores. (. (2023). Development of a digital maturity model for Industry 4.0. *Computers & Industrial Engineering*, *183*, 109645. DOI: 10.1016/j.cie.2023.109645

Sousa, M. J., & Rocha, Á. (2019). Leadership styles and skills developed through game-based learning. *Journal of Business Research*, *94*, 360–366. DOI: 10.1016/j.jbusres.2018.01.057

Sreenivasan, A., & Suresh, M. (2024). A comparative analysis of lean start-up and design thinking and its integration. *Asia Pacific Journal of Innovation and Entrepreneurship*, *18*(2), 172–194. DOI: 10.1108/APJIE-09-2023-0181

Sumbal, M. S. U. K., Tariq, A., Amber, Q., Janovská, K., & Ferraris, A. (2024). Tech revolution unleashed: Navigating the winds of digital transformation in the fast lane. *Journal of Innovation & Knowledge*, *9*(4), 100551. DOI: 10.1016/j.jik.2024.100551

Tagscherer, F., & Carbon, C.-C. (2023). Leadership for successful digitalization: A literature review on companies' internal and external aspects of digitalization. *Sustainable Technology and Entrepreneurship*, *4*(2), 100039. DOI: 10.1016/j.stae.2023.100039

Tanveer, U., Hoang, T. G., Ishaq, S., & Khalid, R. U. (2025). Public private partnerships as catalysts for digital transformation and circular economy. Insights from developing countries. *Technological Forecasting and Social Change*, *219*, 124270. DOI: 10.1016/j.techfore.2025.124270

Thordsen, T., Bick, M., Müller, S., & Becker, W. (2023). A decade of digital maturity models: Much ado about nothing? *Information Systems and e-Business Management*, *21*(4), 947–976. DOI: 10.1007/s10257-023-00656-w

Tim, Y., & Leidner, D. E. (2023). Digital resilience: A conceptual framework for information systems research. *Journal of the Association for Information Systems*, *24*(5), 1184–1198. DOI: 10.17705/1jais.00842

Toroslu, A., Schemmann, B., Chappin, M. M. H., Castaldi, C., & Herrmann, A. M. (2023). Value capture in open innovation. A literature review and a research agenda. *Industrial Marketing Management*, *114*, 297–312. DOI: 10.1016/j.indmarman.2023.08.012

Urbani, R., Ferreira, C., & Lam, J. (2024). Managerial framework for evaluating AI chatbot integration: Bridging organizational readiness and technological challenges. *Business Horizons*, *67*(5), 595–606. DOI: 10.1016/j.bushor.2024.05.004

Van Giffen, B., Beitinger, G., Ludwig, H., Schiano, B., Schmidt, K., & vom Brocke, J. (2025). The culture clash of AI adoption in lean quality management: Resolving the tensions at Siemens Electronics Works Amberg. *Information Systems Journal*, isj.70006. Advance online publication. DOI: 10.1111/isj.70006

Vial, G. (2019). Understanding digital transformation: A review and a research agenda. *The Journal of Strategic Information Systems*, *28*(2), 118–144. DOI: 10.1016/j.jsis.2019.01.003

Warner, K. S. R., & Wäger, M. (2019). Building dynamic capabilities for digital transformation: An ongoing process of strategic renewal. *Long Range Planning*, *52*(3), 326–349. DOI: 10.1016/j.lrp.2018.12.001

Weber, E., Krehl, E.-H., & Büttgen, M. (2022). The digital transformation leadership framework: Conceptual and empirical insights into leadership roles in technology-driven business environments. *Journal of Leadership Studies*, *16*(1), 6–22. DOI: 10.1002/jls.21810

Zhao, Y., Cai, B., Cozzani, V., & Liu, Y. (2024). Failure dependence and cascading failures: A literature review and investigation on research opportunities. *Reliability Engineering & System Safety*, *256*, 110766. DOI: 10.1016/j.ress.2024.110766

KEY TERMS AND DEFINITIONS

Digital change management: It consists of the set of strategies, processes and skills aimed at facilitating the adoption, integration and consolidation of disruptive technologies in an organization. This includes communication, training, restructuring and emotional support actions in the face of profound transformations.

Digital maturity: It is understood as the level of progress of an organization in the strategic, structural, and cultural integration of digital technologies. This concept goes beyond the mere technical incorporation of digital tools, aligning with processes, business models and organizational culture to achieve long-term sustainability, efficiency and innovation.

Organizational dynamic capabilities: This refers to the ability of the organization to integrate, reconfigure and transform its resources and competencies in the face of changed environments. These capabilities are critical to addressing digital disruption and are forged by organizational learning, innovation, and strategic leadership vision.

Technological governance: Comprises the regulatory, strategic, and operational framework through which an organization regulates the use, implementation, and monitoring of digital technologies. It includes aspects such as interoperability, cybersecurity, data ethics, transparency and accountability mechanisms, with the participation of multiple actors in technological decision-making.

Transformational leadership: It is a leadership style based on the ability of leaders to inspire, motivate and develop their teams beyond personal interests, promoting a shared vision, organizational cultural change and sustainable innovation. This is constituted through idealized influence, inspirational motivation, intellectual stimulation, and individualized consideration.

Chapter 7
Strategic Leadership Development in Service Organizations:
Building Transformational Capabilities for the Modern Economy

Simon Cleveland
http://orcid.org/0000-0001-9293-3905
Purdue University Global, USA

Marisa Cleveland
Northeastern University, USA

ABSTRACT

This chapter examines strategic leadership development in service organizations, exploring capabilities driving performance and competitive advantage. Six transformational roles are analyzed: relationship builder, organizational architect, strategist, performance engineer, change champion, and political navigator. Contemporary challenges including digital transformation, ethical leadership, and employee engagement are addressed through an integrated framework incorporating systems-thinking and relationship-centered development. The Chief Strategic Human Capital Development Officer (C-SHCDO) model positions leadership as a C-suite priority. Implementation covers readiness assessment, development architecture, and sustainability. Emerging trends including AI and distributed work are examined, providing a roadmap for developing leaders navigating service delivery complexities.

INTRODUCTION

Service-based economies now dominate global markets, fundamentally reshaping organizational leadership requirements and human capital development priorities (Gilley & Gilley, 2003). Contemporary service organizations confront unprecedented leadership challenges that extend far beyond traditional management competencies historically centered on operational efficiency and product quality metrics common in manufacturing environments. Today's service leaders must orchestrate complex human

DOI: 10.4018/979-8-3373-4027-2.ch007

interactions, cultivate deep employee engagement, and deliver exceptional customer experiences that generate sustainable competitive advantages in increasingly dynamic markets (Turner et al., 2018).

This transformation necessitates comprehensive reconsideration of organizational approaches to leadership capability development. Traditional training-focused methodologies prove inadequate for addressing multifaceted challenges confronting modern service organizations (Hanson, 2013). Strategic human capital development (SHCD) emerges as a critical organizational capability integrating leadership development with broader strategic objectives, ensuring emerging leaders possess competencies required to navigate increasingly complex service delivery environments (Gilley & Gilley, 2003).

Research demonstrates direct correlations between leadership effectiveness and organizational performance in service contexts (Jarvis et al., 2013). Service organizations depend fundamentally on human capital as their primary value creation mechanism. Every customer interaction, service delivery moment, and innovation initiative depends on leadership quality throughout the organization (Kennedy et al., 2013). Service organization leaders must simultaneously manage employee well-being, customer satisfaction, operational excellence, and strategic innovation while navigating rapid technological change and evolving stakeholder expectations (Fowler, 2018).

Contemporary challenges including digital transformation, remote work arrangements, data privacy concerns, and increasing demands for corporate social responsibility add complexity layers to leadership requirements (Ferrell et al., 2019). Service organization leaders must demonstrate competencies in areas previous leadership generations never encountered, including understanding how artificial intelligence impacts service delivery, maintaining organizational culture across distributed teams, and balancing stakeholder interests in increasingly transparent business environments (Fitz-Enz & Mattox, 2014).

Current research reveals significant gaps in leadership development approaches specifically tailored to service organization contexts. While substantial literature addresses general leadership development, limited research examines how service-specific characteristics including intangibility, perishability, and inseparability of production and consumption create unique leadership requirements (Turner et al., 2018). Furthermore, existing frameworks inadequately address how contemporary challenges like digital transformation and ethical leadership intersect with service delivery excellence (Ferrell et al., 2019).

This chapter addresses these critical needs by presenting a comprehensive framework for strategic leadership development specifically tailored to service organizations. Drawing from extensive research on transformational leadership roles and strategic human capital development, the framework provides actionable strategies for building leadership capabilities that drive performance, innovation, and sustainable competitive advantage in service contexts (Gilley & Gilley, 2003; Hanson, 2013; Kennedy et al., 2013; Turner et al., 2018).

PROBLEM STATEMENT

Service organizations face a critical leadership development crisis that threatens their competitive viability and organizational effectiveness. Despite service sectors representing the dominant economic force globally, leadership development practices remain rooted in manufacturing-era paradigms that inadequately prepare leaders for service-specific challenges (Gilley & Gilley, 2003). This misalignment between leadership development approaches and organizational needs creates measurable performance gaps, employee engagement challenges, and customer satisfaction deficiencies that undermine organizational success (Jarvis et al., 2013).

The fundamental problem manifests across multiple dimensions. First, traditional leadership development programs emphasize individual skill acquisition rather than relationship-building capabilities essential for service delivery excellence (Jarvis et al., 2013). Research by Kennedy et al. (2013) demonstrates that leadership effectiveness in service contexts depends more on mindset than skill set, yet most development programs focus predominantly on technical competencies rather than mental model transformation. This misalignment results in leaders unprepared to navigate the ambiguous, relationship-intensive nature of service work (Kennedy et al., 2013).

Second, contemporary service organizations confront unprecedented challenges including digital transformation, ethical complexity, and stakeholder capitalism that existing leadership development frameworks inadequately address (Ferrell et al., 2019). Leaders must make decisions about technology investments, data privacy, employee surveillance, and social responsibility without adequate preparation or guidance (Ferrell et al., 2019; Fitz-Enz & Mattox, 2014). The absence of development approaches integrating these contemporary challenges with fundamental leadership capabilities creates leaders ill-equipped for modern service organization realities (Fowler, 2018).

Third, service organizations struggle to measure leadership development effectiveness beyond traditional training metrics like completion rates and satisfaction scores (Packard & Jones, 2015). Without sophisticated evaluation frameworks connecting leadership development investments to organizational performance outcomes including employee engagement, customer satisfaction, innovation metrics, and financial results, organizations cannot determine whether development initiatives generate returns on investment (Packard & Jones, 2015). This measurement gap perpetuates ineffective development approaches and undermines organizational commitment to strategic leadership development (Kennedy et al., 2013).

The urgency of addressing this problem intensifies as service organizations face increasing competitive pressure, technological disruption, and stakeholder expectations that demand more sophisticated leadership capabilities (Turner et al., 2018). Organizations that fail to develop transformational leadership capabilities risk competitive disadvantage, talent loss, and inability to adapt to rapidly changing market conditions (Hanson, 2013). Conversely, organizations that successfully implement strategic leadership development tailored to service contexts position themselves for sustained competitive advantage through superior customer experiences, employee engagement, and operational excellence (Fowler, 2018).

This chapter addresses these problems by presenting an integrated framework for strategic leadership development in service organizations that bridges the gap between traditional leadership development approaches and contemporary service organization needs, providing actionable guidance for developing transformational leaders capable of navigating complex service delivery environments while achieving organizational performance objectives.

PURPOSE OF THE STUDY

This chapter presents a comprehensive conceptual framework for strategic leadership development specifically designed for service organizations operating in contemporary business environments. The purpose is to synthesize existing research on transformational leadership roles, strategic human capital development, and contemporary leadership challenges into an integrated model that guides service organizations in developing leadership capabilities aligned with their unique operational requirements and strategic objectives.

The framework addresses the identified gap between traditional leadership development approaches rooted in manufacturing paradigms and the specific requirements of service organizations where leadership effectiveness depends critically on relationship building, systems thinking, and adaptive capabilities (Gilley & Gilley, 2003; Hanson, 2013; Jarvis et al., 2013). By integrating theoretical foundations from organizational psychology, strategic management, and systems theory with practical implementation strategies, the chapter provides service organization leaders and human resource development professionals with evidence-based guidance for designing, implementing, and evaluating leadership development initiatives (Kennedy et al., 2013; Turner et al., 2018).

Specifically, this chapter aims to: articulate the theoretical foundations supporting strategic human capital development as an organizational imperative for service organizations; examine six transformational leadership roles identified by Gilley and Gilley (2003) within service organization contexts, analyzing unique challenges and development requirements for each role; synthesize contemporary research on leadership development strategies including relationship-focused approaches, systems-thinking frameworks, mindset-focused interventions, and competency-based models (Fowler, 2018; Hanson, 2013; Jarvis et al., 2013; Kennedy et al., 2013); present an integrated framework for strategic leadership development encompassing organizational readiness assessment, integrated development architecture design, phased implementation pathways, and organizational embedding mechanisms; address contemporary challenges facing service organization leaders including digital transformation, ethical leadership requirements, employee engagement imperatives, and data-driven decision making (Ferrell et al., 2019; Fitz-Enz & Mattox, 2014; Fowler, 2018); and provide practical implementation strategies including the Chief Strategic Human Capital Development Officer model, leadership development ecosystems, impact measurement approaches, and sustainability mechanisms (Packard & Jones, 2015).

The framework synthesizes research from multiple scholarly sources to create a holistic approach addressing the complex, multifaceted nature of leadership development in service organizations (Turner et al., 2018). Rather than presenting isolated techniques or generic best practices, the chapter integrates diverse perspectives into a coherent model recognizing that effective leadership development requires alignment between individual capabilities, organizational systems, and strategic objectives (Hanson, 2013).

This conceptual framework fills an important gap in leadership development literature by specifically addressing service organization contexts where leadership requirements differ substantially from manufacturing or product-focused organizations. The framework provides theoretical grounding while maintaining practical applicability, enabling service organizations to translate research insights into operational leadership development initiatives that generate measurable organizational performance improvements.

BACKGROUND: THEORETICAL FOUNDATIONS OF STRATEGIC HUMAN CAPITAL DEVELOPMENT

Strategic human capital development represents a fundamental paradigm shift in how organizations conceptualize and implement leadership development initiatives (Gilley & Gilley, 2003). Understanding this shift requires examining both the historical evolution from traditional training approaches and the theoretical foundations supporting contemporary strategic human capital development practices. This background section establishes the conceptual underpinnings for the comprehensive framework presented in subsequent sections.

Evolution from Traditional Training to Strategic Development

Traditional organizational training departments operated in isolation from strategic planning processes, delivering standardized programs that often failed to address specific organizational needs or strategic objectives (Gilley & Gilley, 2003). These programs typically focused on generic management skills without considering unique requirements of service delivery contexts or interdependencies between leadership effectiveness and organizational performance. The fundamental limitation of traditional approaches lay in treating leadership development as a cost center or administrative function rather than recognizing it as strategic investment generating measurable returns through improved performance, innovation, and competitive positioning (Gilley & Gilley, 2003).

Strategic human capital development, by contrast, integrates leadership development into the fabric of organizational strategy. As Gilley and Gilley (2003) articulated, the HRD function serves to improve employee performance, enhance growth and development planning, and increase the sense of belonging within the workforce. However, in service organizations, these objectives take on heightened significance because human capital directly determines service quality and customer satisfaction outcomes. This integration ensures leadership capabilities align with strategic objectives and support long-term value creation rather than merely addressing short-term skill deficiencies (Hanson, 2013).

Theoretical Underpinnings from Multiple Disciplines

The theoretical foundation for strategic human capital development draws from organizational psychology, strategic management, and systems theory, each contributing essential insights (Hanson, 2013; Kennedy et al., 2013). From organizational psychology comes understanding that individual leader development cannot be separated from organizational context. Leaders develop not in isolation but through interaction with organizational systems, cultures, and stakeholders (Kennedy et al., 2013). This recognition necessitates development approaches considering complex interplay between individual capabilities and organizational dynamics rather than treating leadership development as purely individual skill acquisition (Jarvis et al., 2013).

Strategic management theory contributes the insight that sustainable competitive advantage increasingly derives from organizational capabilities rather than physical assets or market position (Gilley & Gilley, 2003). In service organizations, leadership represents perhaps the most critical capability because it determines how effectively organizations can mobilize human capital toward strategic objectives. Leadership development therefore becomes not merely a support function but a core strategic process directly impacting organizational performance and competitive positioning (Hanson, 2013). This perspective elevates leadership development from operational concern to strategic imperative requiring executive attention and organizational investment (Gilley & Gilley, 2003).

Systems theory provides the framework for understanding how leadership development initiatives create ripple effects throughout organizations (Hanson, 2013). Changes in leadership capabilities impact organizational culture, employee engagement, operational processes, and ultimately customer experiences. This systems perspective requires development approaches considering these interdependencies and designing interventions creating positive reinforcing cycles rather than unintended consequences.

Hanson's (2013) Leadership Development Interface model particularly emphasizes dynamic relationships between individual leader development and organizational systems, demonstrating that leadership development effectiveness depends on alignment between individual growth and organizational context.

Implications for Service Organizations

In service contexts, these theoretical foundations take on particular significance (Gilley & Gilley, 2003). Service delivery fundamentally depends on human interactions, making leadership quality directly visible to customers through employee behaviors and service experiences (Jarvis et al., 2013). Unlike manufacturing where leadership impacts remain somewhat insulated from customers by production processes, service organization leaders directly influence customer experiences through their effects on employee engagement, service culture, and operational approaches (Fowler, 2018). This direct connection between leadership and customer outcomes elevates strategic human capital development importance in service organizations.

Furthermore, the intangible nature of services creates unique leadership challenges requiring sophisticated development approaches (Gilley & Gilley, 2003). Service leaders cannot rely on physical product specifications or manufacturing standards to guide employee behaviors. Instead, they must create organizational cultures, develop employee capabilities, and establish service delivery processes that consistently generate desired customer experiences despite inherent variability in service encounters (Hanson, 2013). This complexity demands leadership development approaches addressing not only individual competencies but also organizational architecture, culture, and systems (Kennedy et al., 2013).

Measurement and Evaluation Implications

The theoretical foundation for strategic human capital development extends beyond program design to encompass how organizations measure and evaluate leadership development effectiveness (Packard & Jones, 2015). Traditional metrics focusing on training hours completed or participant satisfaction scores prove inadequate for assessing strategic impact. Instead, organizations must develop sophisticated evaluation frameworks connecting leadership development investments to organizational performance outcomes including employee engagement, customer satisfaction, innovation metrics, and financial results (Kennedy et al., 2013; Packard & Jones, 2015).

Kennedy et al.'s (2013) research challenges traditional evaluation approaches by emphasizing importance of mindset over skill set in determining leadership effectiveness. Their findings suggest that evaluation frameworks must assess not only behavioral competency development but also mental model transformation, adaptive capacity, and systems thinking capabilities that enable leaders to navigate complex organizational challenges (Kennedy et al., 2013). This evaluation complexity reflects the sophisticated nature of leadership capabilities required in contemporary service organizations and the need for measurement approaches matching this complexity (Packard & Jones, 2015).

TRANSFORMATIONAL LEADERSHIP ROLES IN SERVICE ORGANIZATIONS

The complexity of modern service organizations demands leaders capable of fulfilling multiple transformational roles simultaneously (Gilley & Gilley, 2003). Gilley and Gilley (2003) identified six critical transformational roles that SHCD professionals must master: relationship builder, organizational architect, strategist, performance engineer, change champion, and political navigator. Each role presents unique challenges and opportunities within service contexts, requiring sophisticated development approaches that go beyond traditional skill-building exercises. This section examines each role through the service organization lens, analyzing specific requirements and development implications.

The Relationship Builder Role

The relationship builder role assumes paramount importance in service organizations where success depends on human interaction quality at multiple levels (Gilley & Gilley, 2003). Service leaders must excel at building and maintaining relationships with diverse stakeholder groups including employees, customers, suppliers, partners, regulators, and community members. This role demands advanced emotional intelligence, cultural sensitivity, and communication capabilities enabling leaders to navigate complex interpersonal dynamics while maintaining organizational objectives (Fowler, 2018).

In service contexts, the relationship builder role extends beyond traditional networking or stakeholder management (Jarvis et al., 2013). Leaders must create environments where employees feel valued, supported, and empowered to deliver exceptional service. This requires understanding psychological needs of service workers who often face emotional demands, difficult customers, and performance pressures that can lead to burnout or disengagement (Fowler, 2018). Leaders must demonstrate genuine care for employee well-being while maintaining performance standards and operational requirements, balancing seemingly contradictory objectives through sophisticated relationship management (Gilley & Gilley, 2003).

The relationship builder role also encompasses ability to foster collaboration across organizational boundaries (Jarvis et al., 2013). Service delivery often requires coordination between multiple departments, functions, or even organizations. Leaders must build bridges between groups with different priorities, cultures, and operational approaches, requiring sophisticated negotiation skills, cultural intelligence, and ability to find common ground among diverse stakeholders (Jarvis et al., 2013). Research by Jarvis et al. (2013) on leadership development in the social care industry revealed critical insights about importance of relationship-focused development approaches, finding that effective leadership development programs should focus on building relationships between leaders rather than glorifying individual heroic leadership.

Furthermore, service organization leaders must model relationship-building behaviors that cascade throughout organizations (Fowler, 2018). Employees observe and emulate leadership behaviors, particularly in how leaders interact with customers and colleagues. Leaders who demonstrate respect, empathy, and genuine interest in others create organizational cultures supporting positive customer experiences and employee engagement (Gilley & Gilley, 2003). This modeling function makes relationship builder role capabilities visible and consequential throughout service organizations.

The Organizational Architect Role

The organizational architect role requires leaders to understand and shape complex systems enabling effective service delivery (Gilley & Gilley, 2003). This encompasses organizational structure, culture, processes, technologies, and human capital systems. In service organizations, these elements are deeply interconnected, with changes in one area creating ripple effects throughout the system (Hanson, 2013).

Leaders must think systemically about organizational design, considering how different elements interact to support or hinder service delivery effectiveness.

Service organizations face unique architectural challenges related to the intangible nature of their offerings (Gilley & Gilley, 2003). Unlike manufacturing organizations where production processes can be standardized and controlled, service delivery involves variability, customization, and real-time adaptation to customer needs. Leaders must design organizational systems providing sufficient structure for consistency and quality while maintaining flexibility for customization and innovation (Hanson, 2013). This balance requires sophisticated understanding of how organizational architecture influences employee behaviors and customer experiences.

The organizational architect role also involves creating alignment between organizational design and strategic objectives (Gilley & Gilley, 2003). Service organizations often pursue differentiation strategies based on service quality, customer experience, or specialized expertise. Leaders must ensure organizational structures, processes, and systems support these strategic priorities rather than defaulting to generic best practices that may not fit the organization's unique context (Hanson, 2013). This strategic alignment function connects organizational architecture directly to competitive positioning and performance outcomes.

Cultural architecture represents a particularly critical aspect of this role in service organizations (Gilley & Gilley, 2003). Organizational culture directly impacts employee behaviors, which in turn determine customer experiences. Leaders must intentionally shape cultural elements including values, norms, rituals, and symbols to support desired service delivery approaches (Hanson, 2013). This requires understanding how culture develops and evolves, as well as the levers available for cultural change. Hanson's (2013) Leadership Development Interface model emphasizes these dynamic relationships between organizational systems and individual leader development, providing framework for understanding cultural architecture complexity.

The Strategist Role

The strategist role in service organizations demands capabilities extending beyond traditional strategic planning competencies (Gilley & Gilley, 2003). Service leaders must understand complex market dynamics, anticipate customer needs evolution, and position their organizations for sustainable competitive advantage in rapidly changing environments. This requires analytical capabilities combined with creative thinking and ability to translate strategic insights into actionable initiatives (Turner et al., 2018).

Strategic leadership in service contexts involves unique challenges related to service characteristics including intangibility, perishability, and inseparability of production and consumption (Gilley & Gilley, 2003). Leaders must develop strategies addressing these characteristics while creating differentiation in crowded marketplaces. This often requires innovative approaches to service design, delivery models, and value propositions going beyond competing on price or basic service features (Turner et al., 2018). The strategist role demands both analytical rigor and creative innovation in developing competitive approaches suited to service organization contexts.

The strategist role also encompasses ability to balance short-term operational demands with long-term strategic investments (Gilley & Gilley, 2003). Service organizations often face pressure to maintain current service levels while simultaneously investing in capabilities for future competitiveness. Leaders must make difficult resource allocation decisions, choosing between immediate performance improvements and longer-term capability development initiatives (Hanson, 2013). This balancing function requires sophisticated judgment about opportunity costs, risk assessment, and strategic prioritization.

Digital transformation adds another complexity layer to the strategist role (Turner et al., 2018). Service leaders must understand how emerging technologies including artificial intelligence, automation, and digital platforms can enhance service delivery while potentially disrupting traditional business models. This requires not only technological literacy but also ability to envision new service concepts and delivery approaches enabled by technology (Fitz-Enz & Mattox, 2014). Turner et al.'s (2018) comprehensive analysis of over 550 leadership development techniques provides insights into which approaches prove most effective in developing strategic thinking capabilities across different organizational contexts.

The Performance Engineer Role

The performance engineer role focuses on optimizing service delivery processes and outcomes through systematic analysis and improvement initiatives (Gilley & Gilley, 2003). In service organizations, this role requires balancing efficiency objectives with quality and customer satisfaction goals. Leaders must understand drivers of service performance, identify improvement opportunities, and implement changes enhancing both operational effectiveness and customer experiences (Fitz-Enz & Mattox, 2014).

Performance engineering in service contexts differs significantly from manufacturing environments where performance can be measured through objective metrics like production volume or defect rates (Gilley & Gilley, 2003). Service performance encompasses subjective elements including customer perceptions, emotional responses, and relationship quality. Leaders must develop sophisticated performance measurement systems capturing both quantitative and qualitative dimensions of service delivery effectiveness (Packard & Jones, 2015). This measurement complexity requires analytical capabilities combined with customer insight and employee understanding.

This role also involves building performance management cultures supporting continuous improvement while maintaining employee engagement (Fowler, 2018). Service workers often face challenging performance demands including emotional labor, multitasking, and adapting to diverse customer needs. Leaders must create performance management approaches recognizing these challenges while maintaining high standards and accountability for results (Gilley & Gilley, 2003). Fowler's (2018) research on motivation science provides important insights into how performance management can address employee psychological needs for autonomy, competence, and relatedness rather than relying solely on external rewards or punishments.

The performance engineer must also address the challenge of service quality consistency across different delivery channels, locations, and customer segments (Gilley & Gilley, 2003). This requires developing standards, training programs, and quality assurance processes ensuring consistent service experiences while allowing for appropriate customization. Leaders must balance standardization with empowerment, giving service workers sufficient autonomy to address unique customer needs while maintaining quality standards (Hanson, 2013). Fitz-Enz and Mattox's (2014) research on predictive analytics demonstrates how data-driven approaches can improve performance engineering through pattern analysis and proactive problem prevention.

The Change Champion Role

The change champion role has become increasingly critical as service organizations navigate rapid environmental changes including technological disruption, evolving customer expectations, and competitive dynamics (Gilley & Gilley, 2003). Leaders must not only manage specific change initiatives but also build organizational change capabilities enabling ongoing adaptation and transformation. This role requires both project management competencies for implementing specific changes and cultural leadership capabilities for developing adaptive organizational cultures (Turner et al., 2018).

Change leadership in service organizations presents unique challenges related to the people-intensive nature of service delivery (Gilley & Gilley, 2003). Changes in service approaches, technologies, or processes directly impact how employees perform their work and interact with customers. Leaders must carefully manage human dimensions of change, addressing employee concerns, building commitment, and ensuring changes enhance rather than compromise service quality (Hanson, 2013). This human-centered change management requires sophisticated emotional intelligence and communication capabilities beyond traditional project management skills.

The change champion role requires sophisticated communication capabilities to articulate change rationales, build urgency, and maintain momentum throughout transformation initiatives (Gilley & Gilley, 2003). Service organization leaders must communicate effectively with diverse stakeholder groups including employees at multiple levels, customers who may experience service disruptions, and partners whose operations may be affected by organizational changes (Turner et al., 2018). This multi-stakeholder communication challenge demands tailored messaging approaches addressing different audience concerns while maintaining consistent overall change narrative.

Furthermore, change champions in service organizations must balance transformation initiatives with operational continuity (Gilley & Gilley, 2003). Unlike manufacturing organizations that can shut down production lines for retooling, service organizations must maintain service delivery while implementing changes. This requires careful planning, phased implementation approaches, and contingency strategies to minimize service disruptions (Hanson, 2013). The ability to orchestrate complex changes while maintaining service delivery represents a distinctive competency requirement for service organization leaders.

The Political Navigator Role

The political navigator role involves understanding and managing complex power dynamics existing within and around service organizations (Gilley & Gilley, 2003). Leaders must recognize formal and informal power structures, build coalitions for change initiatives, and navigate competing stakeholder interests while maintaining organizational effectiveness and ethical standards. This role requires political acumen combined with ethical judgment to influence organizational decisions while maintaining integrity (Ferrell et al., 2019).

Political navigation in service organizations requires particular sensitivity to multiple stakeholder groups whose interests must be balanced (Gilley & Gilley, 2003). Employees, customers, shareholders, regulators, and community members often have conflicting expectations and priorities. Leaders must find ways to address these diverse interests while maintaining strategic focus and operational effectiveness (Ferrell et al., 2019). This balancing function demands sophisticated stakeholder analysis capabilities and negotiation skills for finding acceptable compromises among competing interests.

This role also involves managing political dimensions of resource allocation decisions (Gilley & Gilley, 2003). Service organizations often face resource constraints requiring difficult tradeoffs between different service areas, customer segments, or capability investments. Leaders must build support for resource decisions, manage disappointment among groups whose requests are not fully funded, and maintain organizational cohesion despite resource limitations (Hanson, 2013). This resource politics navigation requires both analytical capabilities for making defensible allocation decisions and interpersonal skills for maintaining relationships with stakeholders whose interests may not be fully addressed.

The political navigator must also address external political dynamics including regulatory requirements, industry standards, and stakeholder activism (Ferrell et al., 2019). Service organizations increasingly face scrutiny regarding their employment practices, environmental impacts, and social responsibility. Leaders must engage constructively with external stakeholders while protecting organizational interests and maintaining operational flexibility (Ferrell et al., 2019). Ferrell et al.'s (2019) research documents how ethical challenges intensify when employee privacy concerns intersect with business operations, requiring political navigation skills for balancing competing ethical and operational considerations.

CONTEMPORARY LEADERSHIP DEVELOPMENT STRATEGIES

The evolution of leadership development strategies reflects growing recognition that traditional approaches fail to prepare leaders for complexities of modern service organizations (Turner et al., 2018). Turner et al.'s (2018) comprehensive analysis of over 550 leadership development techniques provides valuable insights into which approaches prove most effective in different contexts. Their research demonstrates that successful leadership development requires systematic approaches mapping specific techniques to desired leadership competencies while considering organizational context and individual learning styles (Turner et al., 2018).

Contemporary leadership development strategies must address multiple learning dimensions including cognitive understanding, skill development, emotional intelligence, and behavioral change (Kennedy et al., 2013). This multidimensional approach recognizes that effective leadership involves not just knowing what to do but also having skills to execute, emotional intelligence to navigate interpersonal dynamics, and behavioral repertoire to adapt to different situations. The following sections examine four contemporary development strategy categories particularly relevant for service organizations: relationship-focused approaches, systems-thinking frameworks, mindset-focused strategies, and competency-based models.

RELATIONSHIP-FOCUSED DEVELOPMENT APPROACHES

Research by Jarvis et al. (2013) on leadership development in the social care industry revealed critical insights about importance of relationship-focused development approaches. Their study of senior leaders found that effective leadership development programs should focus on building relationships between leaders rather than glorifying individual heroic leadership (Jarvis et al., 2013). This finding has profound implications for service organizations where collaborative leadership often proves more effective than traditional command-and-control approaches.

Relationship-focused development strategies recognize that leadership effectiveness depends not only on individual capabilities but also on quality of relationships leaders build with others (Jarvis et al., 2013). These approaches emphasize collaborative learning experiences where leaders develop together, share experiences, and build networks supporting ongoing development and organizational effectiveness. Rather than treating leadership development as individual skill acquisition, relationship-focused approaches create learning communities where participants learn from each other as much as from formal content (Jarvis et al., 2013).

Peer learning represents a powerful relationship-focused development strategy particularly well-suited to service organizations (Jarvis et al., 2013). Bringing together leaders facing similar challenges creates opportunities for shared problem-solving, mutual support, and collaborative innovation. Leaders learn not only from formal content but also from observing how peers approach challenges, make decisions, and manage relationships (Turner et al., 2018). This peer learning dimension adds richness to development experiences that formal instruction alone cannot provide.

Mentoring and coaching relationships provide another critical dimension of relationship-focused development (Jarvis et al., 2013). Unlike traditional training programs delivering standardized content, mentoring and coaching relationships provide personalized development support tailored to individual needs and organizational contexts. These relationships create safe spaces for leaders to explore challenges, receive feedback, and develop new capabilities with guidance from experienced practitioners (Turner et al., 2018). The confidential nature of mentoring and coaching relationships enables more authentic exploration of leadership challenges than typical group training settings allow.

Action learning approaches combine relationship-building with real-world problem-solving, making them particularly valuable for service organization leadership development (Turner et al., 2018). Action learning brings together groups of leaders to address actual organizational challenges, fostering both individual development and organizational improvement. Participants learn through experience while building relationships supporting ongoing collaboration and knowledge sharing (Jarvis et al., 2013). This dual benefit of individual development and organizational problem-solving makes action learning especially attractive for service organizations seeking both leadership capability building and operational improvement.

SYSTEMS-THINKING DEVELOPMENT FRAMEWORKS

Hanson's (2013) Leadership Development Interface model provides sophisticated framework for understanding dynamic relationships between individual leader development and organizational systems. This model emphasizes that leadership development cannot occur in isolation but must consider complex interactions between leaders and their organizational contexts (Hanson, 2013). For service organizations, this systems perspective becomes particularly critical because service delivery depends on intricate coordination between multiple organizational elements.

Systems-thinking development approaches help leaders understand how their decisions and actions create ripple effects throughout organizations (Hanson, 2013). Rather than focusing solely on direct cause-and-effect relationships, these approaches develop leaders' abilities to recognize patterns, understand feedback loops, and anticipate unintended consequences. This systemic understanding proves essential for service organization leaders who must coordinate complex service delivery systems while maintaining quality and efficiency (Hanson, 2013).

The implementation of systems-thinking development requires innovative pedagogical approaches going beyond traditional classroom instruction (Hanson, 2013). Simulations and case studies can help leaders explore system dynamics in controlled environments where they can experiment with different approaches and observe consequences without risking actual organizational performance. These experiential learning approaches develop intuitive understanding of system behaviors complementing analytical frameworks (Turner et al., 2018).

Organizations implementing systems-thinking development must also create opportunities for leaders to apply these concepts in real organizational contexts (Hanson, 2013). This might involve cross-functional projects requiring leaders to understand and coordinate multiple organizational systems, or strategic initiatives demanding consideration of system-wide implications. Through practical application opportunities, organizations help leaders translate conceptual understanding into operational capabilities (Hanson, 2013). The integration of conceptual learning with practical application ensures systems thinking becomes embedded in leadership practice rather than remaining abstract theoretical knowledge.

MINDSET-FOCUSED DEVELOPMENT STRATEGIES

Kennedy et al.'s (2013) research on leadership development evaluation challenged traditional approaches by emphasizing importance of mindset over skill set. Their findings suggest that leadership effectiveness depends less on technical skills than on mental models, assumptions, and beliefs guiding leader behavior (Kennedy et al., 2013). This insight has particular relevance for service organizations where leaders must navigate ambiguous situations, make decisions with incomplete information, and adapt to rapidly changing circumstances.

Mindset-focused development strategies begin by helping leaders surface and examine their existing mental models (Kennedy et al., 2013). Many leadership failures stem not from lack of knowledge or skills but from outdated or inappropriate assumptions about organizations, markets, or human behavior. Making these assumptions explicit allows development programs to create opportunities for leaders to question and revise mental models that may limit their effectiveness (Kennedy et al., 2013). This reflective process represents foundational work for authentic leadership development rather than superficial behavioral modification.

These approaches also emphasize development of growth mindsets supporting continuous learning and adaptation (Kennedy et al., 2013). Service organization leaders must embrace uncertainty, learn from failures, and continuously update their understanding as contexts change. Development programs fostering growth mindsets help leaders become more resilient, adaptable, and innovative in their approach to leadership challenges (Fowler, 2018). This mindset development proves particularly important in service contexts where situational variability demands adaptive rather than scripted leadership responses.

Critical reflection represents a core component of mindset-focused development (Kennedy et al., 2013). Through structured reflection exercises, leaders examine their experiences, identify patterns in their thinking and behavior, and recognize opportunities for growth. This reflective practice becomes particularly important in service organizations where leaders must learn from both successes and failures to continuously improve service delivery approaches (Kennedy et al., 2013). The discipline of regular reflection helps leaders extract learning from experience rather than simply accumulating experiences without extracting insights.

COMPETENCY-BASED DEVELOPMENT MODELS

While mindset development provides foundation for leadership effectiveness, competency-based models remain valuable for ensuring leaders develop specific capabilities required for service organization success (Fowler, 2018). Contemporary competency models go beyond generic leadership skills to address unique requirements of service contexts including customer centricity, service innovation, and employee engagement. These models provide concrete frameworks for assessing development needs and measuring capability acquisition (Turner et al., 2018).

Fowler's (2018) research on motivation science in leadership development provides important insights into how competency models can be enhanced by incorporating understanding of human psychological needs. Rather than focusing solely on behavioral competencies, these enhanced models address leaders' abilities to create environments satisfying employees' needs for autonomy, competence, and relatedness (Fowler, 2018). This psychological perspective proves particularly relevant for service organizations where employee motivation directly impacts service quality and customer satisfaction.

The development of customer-centric leadership competencies requires innovative approaches helping leaders understand and empathize with customer experiences (Turner et al., 2018). This might involve leaders spending time in customer-facing roles, participating in customer journey mapping exercises, or engaging directly with customers to understand their needs and expectations. These experiential learning approaches develop deeper customer understanding than traditional market research or customer service training (Fowler, 2018).

Digital competencies have become increasingly critical for service organization leaders as technology transforms service delivery models (Turner et al., 2018). Leaders must understand not only how to use technology but also how to evaluate technology investments, manage digital transformation initiatives, and address organizational and human implications of technological change. Development programs must therefore integrate digital literacy with strategic thinking about technology's role in service innovation and delivery (Fitz-Enz & Mattox, 2014). This integration ensures leaders view technology not as separate technical domain but as integral component of service strategy and operations.

FRAMEWORK FOR STRATEGIC LEADERSHIP DEVELOPMENT IN SERVICE ORGANIZATIONS

The complexity of leadership development in service organizations demands comprehensive frameworks integrating multiple development approaches while maintaining strategic alignment and organizational coherence (Gilley & Gilley, 2003; Hanson, 2013). This section presents an integrated framework synthesizing research insights with practical implementation considerations to guide organizations in developing transformational leadership capabilities. The framework encompasses four essential phases: organizational readiness assessment, integrated development architecture design, phased implementation pathways, and organizational embedding mechanisms (Turner et al., 2018).

FOUNDATION: ORGANIZATIONAL READINESS ASSESSMENT

Before implementing leadership development initiatives, organizations must assess their readiness for transformation and identify specific development needs (Gilley & Gilley, 2003). This assessment encompasses multiple dimensions including current leadership capabilities, organizational culture, strategic priorities, and resource availability. Without thorough assessment, development initiatives risk addressing symptoms rather than root causes or implementing solutions misaligned with organizational contexts (Hanson, 2013).

The assessment process should examine existing leadership strengths and gaps across the six transformational roles previously discussed (Gilley & Gilley, 2003). This involves not only evaluating individual leader capabilities but also understanding how leadership teams function collectively. Service organizations often require collaborative leadership approaches where multiple leaders contribute complementary capabilities rather than expecting individual leaders to excel in all areas (Jarvis et al., 2013). This collective capability assessment provides more realistic picture of organizational leadership capacity than individual assessments alone.

Cultural assessment proves particularly critical for service organizations because culture significantly influences both leadership effectiveness and service delivery quality (Hanson, 2013). Organizations must understand their current cultural characteristics including values, behavioral norms, and underlying assumptions. This understanding helps identify cultural factors that may support or hinder leadership development efforts and service excellence objectives (Gilley & Gilley, 2003). Cultural assessment should examine both espoused values reflected in official statements and actual values demonstrated through organizational behaviors and decisions, as gaps between these often reveal important development needs.

Strategic alignment assessment ensures leadership development initiatives support rather than distract from strategic priorities (Gilley & Gilley, 2003). Organizations must clearly articulate their strategic objectives and identify leadership capabilities required to achieve these objectives. This strategic lens helps prioritize development investments and ensure emerging leaders develop capabilities aligned with future organizational needs rather than current operational requirements (Hanson, 2013). Without strategic alignment, leadership development risks preparing leaders for yesterday's challenges rather than tomorrow's opportunities.

Design: Integrated Development Architecture

The design phase involves creating comprehensive development architecture integrating multiple learning approaches, delivery methods, and support systems (Turner et al., 2018). Rather than relying on isolated training programs, effective development architecture creates interconnected learning experiences building upon each other to develop sophisticated leadership capabilities over time. This architectural approach recognizes that transformational leadership capabilities emerge through sustained, multi-faceted development rather than discrete training events (Hanson, 2013).

The architecture should incorporate formal learning components including workshops, seminars, and structured educational programs providing foundational knowledge and frameworks (Turner et al., 2018). However, formal learning alone proves insufficient for developing complex capabilities required for service organization leadership. The architecture must also include experiential learning opportunities where leaders can apply concepts in real organizational contexts and learn from both successes and failures (Kennedy et al., 2013). This experiential dimension ensures leaders develop practical capabilities rather than merely theoretical understanding.

Social learning components facilitate knowledge sharing and relationship building among developing leaders (Jarvis et al., 2013). This might include peer coaching circles, communities of practice, or leadership networks providing ongoing support and learning opportunities. For service organizations, these social learning components prove particularly valuable because they mirror collaborative nature of service delivery and help leaders develop relationship-building capabilities emphasized by Jarvis et al. (2013) as critical for service leadership effectiveness.

Individual development support through coaching, mentoring, or individualized development planning ensures architecture addresses diverse learning needs and development trajectories (Turner et al., 2018). Service organizations typically include leaders with varied backgrounds, experiences, and learning styles. Individual support components allow customization within broader development architecture to maximize learning effectiveness for each participant (Kennedy et al., 2013). This personalization dimension prevents one-size-fits-all approaches that may work adequately for some participants but poorly for others.

Implementation: Phased Development Pathways

Implementation of leadership development initiatives requires carefully planned pathways sequencing learning experiences to build progressively sophisticated capabilities (Turner et al., 2018). Rather than attempting to develop all leadership competencies simultaneously, phased pathways focus on foundational capabilities before advancing to more complex leadership challenges. This developmental sequencing recognizes that certain capabilities must be established before others can be effectively developed (Kennedy et al., 2013).

The initial phase typically focuses on self-awareness and foundational leadership concepts (Kennedy et al., 2013). Leaders must understand their own strengths, development needs, and leadership styles before attempting to lead others effectively. This phase might include personality assessments, 360-degree feedback processes, and foundational workshops on leadership principles (Packard & Jones, 2015). For service organization leaders, this phase should also include deep immersion in customer experience and service excellence principles, establishing customer-centric mindsets as foundation for all subsequent leadership development (Fowler, 2018).

The intermediate phase emphasizes skill development and practical application (Turner et al., 2018). Leaders engage in projects requiring them to apply leadership concepts while receiving coaching and feedback on their performance. This phase might include leading cross-functional service improvement initiatives, managing change projects, or taking on stretch assignments developing specific capabilities (Hanson, 2013). The focus shifts from understanding concepts to developing proficiency in leadership practices, with emphasis on learning through real organizational challenges rather than simulated exercises.

The advanced phase focuses on strategic leadership and organizational transformation capabilities (Gilley & Gilley, 2003). Leaders at this level work on complex organizational challenges requiring systems thinking, strategic analysis, and transformational leadership approaches. This might include leading digital transformation initiatives, designing new service delivery models, or driving cultural change efforts (Turner et al., 2018). The emphasis moves from individual leadership effectiveness to organizational impact and legacy building, preparing leaders for senior roles where their influence extends beyond direct teams to entire organizations.

Integration: Organizational Embedding Mechanisms

For leadership development to create lasting organizational impact, new capabilities must be embedded into organizational systems, processes, and culture (Hanson, 2013). This embedding process ensures leadership development becomes self-reinforcing rather than dependent on continuous external intervention. Without embedding mechanisms, development initiatives risk creating temporary capability improvements that dissipate when formal programs end (Kennedy et al., 2013).

Performance management systems must recognize and reward application of developed leadership capabilities (Fowler, 2018). If organizations invest in developing collaborative leadership approaches but continue to reward individual achievement, leaders will revert to competitive rather than collaborative behaviors. Service organizations must align their recognition, promotion, and compensation systems with desired leadership behaviors and outcomes (Gilley & Gilley, 2003). This alignment ensures development investments translate into sustained behavioral change rather than temporary compliance during development programs.

Succession planning processes should identify and develop emerging leaders systematically rather than reactively filling positions as they become vacant (Gilley & Gilley, 2003). This requires creating talent pipelines providing progressive development experiences preparing leaders for increasing responsibilities. Service organizations benefit from succession planning approaches developing leaders with deep understanding of service operations, customer needs, and employee dynamics (Hanson, 2013). These service-specific capabilities cannot be quickly acquired when positions become vacant, necessitating long-term development planning.

Knowledge management systems capture and share leadership learning throughout organizations (Turner et al., 2018). This might include repositories of best practices, case studies of successful leadership initiatives, or platforms for sharing leadership insights and experiences. For service organizations operating across multiple locations or service lines, knowledge management becomes critical for scaling leadership effectiveness and maintaining consistency in leadership approaches (Fitz-Enz & Mattox, 2014). These systems prevent valuable learning from remaining isolated with individual leaders, enabling organizational-level capability development.

CONTEMPORARY CHALLENGES IN LEADERSHIP DEVELOPMENT

Modern service organizations face unprecedented challenges that traditional leadership development approaches fail to adequately address (Ferrell et al., 2019; Fitz-Enz & Mattox, 2014; Fowler, 2018). These challenges require innovative development strategies preparing leaders to navigate complexity, uncertainty, and rapid change while maintaining service excellence and organizational performance. This section examines four critical contemporary challenges: digital transformation and technology integration, ethical leadership and corporate social responsibility, employee engagement and well-being, and data-driven decision making.

Digital Transformation and Technology Integration

Digital transformation represents perhaps the most significant challenge facing service organization leaders today (Fitz-Enz & Mattox, 2014). The integration of artificial intelligence, automation, and digital platforms fundamentally changes how services are designed, delivered, and experienced. Leaders must understand not only technical aspects of these technologies but also their implications for organizational strategy, operations, and culture (Turner et al., 2018).

The challenge extends beyond simply adopting new technologies to encompass fundamental reimagination of service delivery models (Fitz-Enz & Mattox, 2014). Traditional service approaches based on human interaction and physical presence are being complemented or replaced by digital channels, self-service platforms, and automated processes. Leaders must navigate transition from traditional to digital service delivery while maintaining service quality and customer relationships, requiring sophisticated change management capabilities combined with technological understanding (Turner et al., 2018).

Leadership development programs must prepare leaders to make complex decisions about technology investments and implementations (Fitz-Enz & Mattox, 2014). This requires understanding how to evaluate technology options, assess implementation risks, and manage organizational change associated with technology adoption. Leaders must balance efficiency gains from automation with potential impacts on employment, customer experience, and organizational culture (Fowler, 2018). This balancing function demands both analytical capabilities for assessing technologies and emotional intelligence for managing human dimensions of technological change.

The human dimension of digital transformation presents particular challenges for service organization leaders (Fowler, 2018). Employees may fear job displacement from automation or struggle to develop new skills required for digital service delivery. Leaders must address these concerns while building organizational capabilities for digital excellence, requiring sophisticated change management skills combined with empathy and communication capabilities (Gilley & Gilley, 2003). Furthermore, digital transformation creates new competitive dynamics that leaders must understand and navigate, as digital platforms enable new entrants to rapidly scale service offerings while data analytics provides insights creating competitive advantages for organizations effectively leveraging information (Fitz-Enz & Mattox, 2014).

Ethical Leadership and Corporate Social Responsibility

Contemporary service organizations face increasing scrutiny regarding their ethical practices and social impacts (Ferrell et al., 2019). Stakeholders including customers, employees, investors, and communities expect organizations to operate ethically and contribute positively to society. This creates complex challenges for leaders who must balance competing stakeholder interests while maintaining organizational performance and competitiveness (Ferrell et al., 2019).

As Ferrell et al. (2019) documented, ethical challenges in organizations intensify when employee privacy concerns intersect with business operations. Service organizations collect vast amounts of customer and employee data through digital interactions, creating responsibilities for data protection and ethical use (Ferrell et al., 2019). Leaders must understand privacy regulations, implement appropriate safeguards, and make decisions about data use balancing business objectives with ethical obligations. This ethical dimension of data management adds complexity to already challenging technological leadership requirements.

The challenge of preventing harassment and discrimination requires particular attention in service organizations where employees interact closely with customers and colleagues (Ferrell et al., 2019). Leaders must create cultures of respect and inclusion while addressing inappropriate behaviors that may arise from customers, employees, or other stakeholders. This requires not only establishing policies and procedures but also modeling appropriate behaviors and responding decisively to violations (Gilley & Gilley, 2003). The visible nature of service work makes ethical leadership particularly important as employee behaviors directly influence customer perceptions.

Whistleblower protection represents another critical ethical challenge service organization leaders must address (Ferrell et al., 2019). Organizations need systems enabling employees to report wrongdoing without fear of retaliation while also protecting against false or malicious accusations. Leaders must balance transparency and accountability with privacy and due process considerations (Ferrell et al., 2019). Corporate social responsibility extends beyond avoiding harm to encompass positive contributions to society, with service organizations increasingly facing expectations to address social challenges including inequality, environmental sustainability, and community development while maintaining financial viability and competitive position.

The development of ethical leadership capabilities requires more than traditional ethics training focused on rules and compliance (Ferrell et al., 2019). Leaders need sophisticated moral reasoning capabilities enabling them to navigate ethical dilemmas where rules provide insufficient guidance. This includes understanding different ethical frameworks, recognizing ethical dimensions of business decisions, and developing judgment about appropriate courses of action in ambiguous situations (Ferrell et al., 2019). Leadership development must prepare leaders to integrate ethical considerations into strategic and operational decision-making rather than treating ethics as separate compliance function.

Employee Engagement and Well-Being

Service organizations depend fundamentally on employee engagement and well-being for service delivery effectiveness (Fowler, 2018). Engaged employees provide better customer service, demonstrate greater innovation, and contribute more to organizational success. However, maintaining engagement proves increasingly challenging as work becomes more demanding, technology changes rapidly, and employee expectations evolve (Fowler, 2018).

The psychological demands of service work create particular challenges for employee well-being (Fowler, 2018). Service employees often engage in emotional labor, managing their own emotions while responding to customer needs and organizational requirements. This emotional work can lead to burnout, particularly when employees lack autonomy or support (Fowler, 2018). Leaders must understand these psychological dynamics and create environments supporting employee well-being while maintaining service standards.

Fowler's (2018) research on motivation science provides important insights into how leaders can address employee psychological needs for autonomy, competence, and relatedness. Rather than relying on external rewards or punishments, leaders must create conditions supporting intrinsic motivation (Fowler, 2018). This requires rethinking traditional management approaches emphasizing control and compliance in favor of approaches empowering and engaging employees. Leadership development must prepare leaders to create motivating work environments rather than simply applying traditional reward and punishment systems.

The challenge of maintaining engagement extends to addressing generational differences in workplace expectations (Fowler, 2018). Younger workers often prioritize purpose, flexibility, and development opportunities over traditional rewards like salary and job security. Leaders must understand these evolving expectations and create employment propositions attracting and retaining talent across generational cohorts (Gilley & Gilley, 2003). Work-life integration presents another dimension of the employee well-being challenge, as technology enables always-on connectivity blurring boundaries between work and personal life, with service organizations operating across time zones or providing 24/7 service facing particular challenges in managing work demands while supporting employee well-being (Fowler, 2018).

Data-Driven Decision Making

The proliferation of data from digital interactions, operational systems, and external sources creates both opportunities and challenges for service organization leaders (Fitz-Enz & Mattox, 2014). Organizations effectively leveraging data can improve service delivery, anticipate customer needs, and optimize operations. However, many leaders lack analytical capabilities required to effectively use data in decision-making (Fitz-Enz & Mattox, 2014).

Fitz-Enz and Mattox's (2014) research on predictive analytics in human resources demonstrates potential for data-driven approaches to improve organizational decision-making. Analysis of patterns in employee behavior, performance, and engagement helps organizations predict and prevent problems before they impact service delivery (Fitz-Enz & Mattox, 2014). However, realizing this potential requires leaders who understand both analytical techniques and their appropriate application.

The challenge extends beyond technical analytics capabilities to encompass judgment about data quality, relevance, and interpretation (Fitz-Enz & Mattox, 2014). Not all data is equally valuable, and misleading data can lead to poor decisions. Leaders must develop critical thinking capabilities enabling them to question data sources, recognize biases, and understand limitations in analytical models (Packard & Jones, 2015). This critical data literacy represents essential competency for contemporary service organization leaders.

Privacy and ethical considerations add complexity to data-driven decision making (Ferrell et al., 2019). Service organizations must balance value of data analytics with obligations to protect customer and employee privacy. Leaders must understand regulatory requirements, implement appropriate governance structures, and make decisions about data use maintaining stakeholder trust while enabling analytical insights (Ferrell et al., 2019). The organizational dimension of data-driven decision making requires leaders to build analytical cultures where data informs rather than replaces judgment, involving democratizing access to data, developing analytical capabilities throughout organizations, and creating processes incorporating data insights into decision-making while maintaining agility and responsiveness (Fitz-Enz & Mattox, 2014).

IMPLEMENTATION STRATEGIES AND PRACTICAL APPLICATIONS

The translation of leadership development concepts into organizational practice requires carefully crafted implementation strategies considering organizational contexts, resource constraints, and change management requirements (Gilley & Gilley, 2003; Packard & Jones, 2015). This section presents practical approaches for implementing comprehensive leadership development initiatives in service organizations, addressing implementation structure, ecosystem building, impact measurement, and sustainability mechanisms.

The Chief Strategic Human Capital Development Officer Model

The elevation of leadership development to strategic importance requires organizational structures positioning human capital development as C-suite priority (Gilley & Gilley, 2003). The Chief Strategic Human Capital Development Officer (C-SHCDO) model represents an innovative approach ensuring leadership development receives appropriate attention and resources while maintaining alignment with organizational strategy. This structural innovation signals organizational commitment to strategic human capital development as competitive imperative rather than administrative function (Gilley & Gilley, 2003).

The C-SHCDO role differs fundamentally from traditional training or human resource functions (Gilley & Gilley, 2003). Rather than focusing on administrative tasks or isolated training programs, the C-SHCDO serves as strategic advisor ensuring human capital development initiatives support organizational objectives and address emerging challenges. This strategic positioning enables the C-SHCDO to influence organizational decisions about structure, culture, and capability development (Hanson, 2013).

The responsibilities of the C-SHCDO extend across multiple domains critical to service organization success (Ferrell et al., 2019). In the domain of employee privacy, the C-SHCDO ensures organizations balance monitoring and analytics capabilities with respect for employee rights and well-being. This involves not only establishing appropriate policies but also building cultures where privacy is valued and protected (Ferrell et al., 2019). In addressing harassment prevention and creating inclusive environments, the C-SHCDO leads efforts to build respectful organizational cultures going beyond compliance with anti-discrimination laws to encompass proactive efforts creating environments where all employees can contribute their best work (Ferrell et al., 2019).

The C-SHCDO also plays critical role in ensuring organizations act in socially responsible ways (Ferrell et al., 2019). This involves integrating social responsibility considerations into leadership development curricula, ensuring emerging leaders understand their obligations to multiple stakeholders. The C-SHCDO helps organizations balance profit objectives with social impact, creating sustainable approaches to corporate citizenship (Ferrell et al., 2019). In the realm of predictive analytics and data-driven decision making, the C-SHCDO ensures organizations develop analytical capabilities while maintaining ethical standards, including building analytical literacy among leaders, establishing governance structures for data use, and ensuring analytical insights enhance rather than replace human judgment in decision-making (Fitz-Enz & Mattox, 2014).

Building Leadership Development Ecosystems

Effective leadership development requires comprehensive ecosystems providing multiple pathways and support mechanisms for leader growth (Turner et al., 2018). Rather than relying on isolated programs or initiatives, organizations must create interconnected systems where different development elements reinforce and build upon each other. This ecosystem approach recognizes that leadership development represents ongoing process rather than discrete event (Hanson, 2013).

The ecosystem approach begins with clear articulation of leadership expectations and success criteria (Gilley & Gilley, 2003). Service organizations must define what effective leadership looks like in their specific contexts, considering their strategic priorities, organizational cultures, and service delivery models. These definitions provide foundation for all development activities and help leaders understand expectations for their growth and performance (Kennedy et al., 2013).

Assessment and feedback mechanisms provide critical inputs for development planning and progress monitoring (Packard & Jones, 2015). This includes not only formal assessment tools but also ongoing feedback processes helping leaders understand their impact and identify development opportunities. Service organizations benefit from multi-source feedback approaches incorporating perspectives from employees, peers, customers, and other stakeholders who experience leaders' effectiveness (Packard & Jones, 2015). Packard and Jones's (2015) research emphasizes importance of multiple evaluation criteria including 360-degree feedback, networking benefits, and external perspective gains for comprehensive development assessment.

Learning and development opportunities must address diverse learning styles and development needs (Turner et al., 2018). This includes formal educational programs, experiential learning projects, coaching and mentoring relationships, and self-directed learning resources. The ecosystem should provide multiple pathways for development, recognizing that leaders have different starting points, learning preferences, and development trajectories (Kennedy et al., 2013).

Support systems ensure leaders receive assistance when facing challenges or setbacks (Jarvis et al., 2013). This might include coaching support during difficult transitions, peer advisory groups for collaborative problem-solving, or expert resources for specialized challenges. Service organizations must recognize that leadership development involves risk-taking and potential failure, providing safety nets encouraging experimentation while protecting organizational performance (Hanson, 2013). Recognition and advancement systems reinforce development efforts and create incentives for continuous growth, with organizations ensuring leadership development efforts are recognized in performance evaluations, promotion decisions, and compensation structures to create positive reinforcement cycles where development efforts lead to advancement opportunities motivating further development (Fowler, 2018).

Measuring Leadership Development Impact

The evaluation of leadership development initiatives requires sophisticated approaches going beyond traditional training metrics to assess actual impact on organizational performance (Packard & Jones, 2015). Packard and Jones's (2015) research on leadership development evaluation provides valuable insights into effective evaluation approaches, emphasizing importance of multiple evaluation criteria including 360-degree feedback, networking benefits, and external perspective gains.

Impact measurement should begin with clear definition of success criteria aligned with organizational objectives (Packard & Jones, 2015). For service organizations, this might include improvements in customer satisfaction, employee engagement, service innovation, or operational efficiency. Establishing clear connections between leadership development and organizational outcomes enables evaluation efforts demonstrating return on investment and guiding program improvements (Kennedy et al., 2013).

Leading indicators provide early signals of development effectiveness before ultimate outcomes become apparent (Packard & Jones, 2015). These might include changes in leader behavior, improvements in team dynamics, or early wins in development projects. Monitoring leading indicators helps organizations identify and address problems before they impact ultimate outcomes (Fitz-Enz & Mattox, 2014).

Longitudinal assessment captures development impact over time rather than relying on immediate post-program evaluations (Packard & Jones, 2015). Leadership development often requires time for new capabilities to be internalized and applied. Service organizations should track participant progress over months or years to understand true development impact and identify factors supporting or hindering sustained behavior change (Kennedy et al., 2013).

Organizational impact assessment examines how leadership development initiatives affect broader organizational capabilities and performance (Packard & Jones, 2015). This includes examining whether development programs create ripple effects improving performance beyond direct participants. For service organizations, this might involve assessing whether leadership development improves service culture, innovation capabilities, or customer relationships (Hanson, 2013). The evaluation process should also examine unintended consequences or negative impacts from development initiatives, such as increased turnover if developed leaders leave for other opportunities, disruption to operations during intensive development programs, or cultural conflicts between traditional and transformational leadership approaches (Kennedy et al., 2013).

Sustaining Development Momentum

The sustainability of leadership development initiatives requires ongoing attention to maintain momentum and prevent regression to previous patterns (Gilley & Gilley, 2003). Service organizations must create conditions supporting continuous development rather than treating leadership development as discrete events or programs. This sustainability challenge reflects the need for embedding mechanisms discussed earlier while also creating cultural conditions supporting ongoing learning (Hanson, 2013).

Continuous learning cultures encourage ongoing development beyond formal programs (Kennedy et al., 2013). This involves celebrating learning from both successes and failures, providing time and resources for development activities, and recognizing that leadership development is career-long journey rather than destination. Service organizations can reinforce continuous learning by incorporating development discussions into regular business processes and making learning a valued organizational behavior (Fowler, 2018).

Leadership communities provide ongoing support and learning opportunities for developing leaders (Jarvis et al., 2013). These communities might be organized around specific development cohorts, leadership levels, or functional areas. Maintaining connections among leaders who have participated in development programs enables organizations to create networks supporting continued growth and knowledge sharing (Turner et al., 2018).

Refresh and renewal mechanisms ensure development initiatives remain relevant as organizational contexts change (Turner et al., 2018). This includes regularly updating development curricula to address emerging challenges, incorporating new research insights, and adapting delivery methods to leverage new technologies or learning approaches. Service organizations operating in rapidly changing environments must be particularly attentive to keeping development initiatives current and relevant (Fitz-Enz & Mattox, 2014).

Alumni engagement maintains connections with leaders who have completed formal development programs (Packard & Jones, 2015). Alumni can serve as mentors for emerging leaders, provide feedback on program effectiveness, and share insights from applying development concepts in practice. Service organizations benefit from alumni networks extending beyond their own organizations, creating industry-wide communities of practice advancing service leadership excellence (Jarvis et al., 2013).

FUTURE DIRECTIONS AND EMERGING CONSIDERATIONS

The future of leadership development in service organizations will be shaped by emerging trends, technologies, and societal expectations only beginning to manifest (Fitz-Enz & Mattox, 2014; Fowler, 2018; Turner et al., 2018). Organizations must anticipate these developments and prepare leaders for challenges not yet fully understood. This forward-looking perspective proves essential for ensuring leadership development initiatives remain relevant and effective as contexts continue evolving (Gilley & Gilley, 2003).

Artificial intelligence and machine learning will increasingly augment or replace human decision-making in service delivery (Fitz-Enz & Mattox, 2014). Leaders must understand how to work with AI systems, maintain appropriate human oversight, and address ethical considerations around algorithmic decision-making. Leadership development programs must prepare leaders to navigate human-AI collaboration while maintaining human elements differentiating service experiences (Turner et al., 2018).

The transformation of work arrangements, accelerated by global pandemic experiences, creates new challenges for leadership in distributed environments (Fowler, 2018). Service organizations must develop leaders capable of managing remote teams, maintaining culture across distances, and delivering consistent service through virtual channels. This requires new leadership competencies in digital communication, virtual team dynamics, and remote performance management (Gilley & Gilley, 2003).

Stakeholder capitalism and environmental, social, and governance (ESG) considerations are becoming central to organizational strategy (Ferrell et al., 2019). Service organization leaders must balance financial performance with broader stakeholder interests including environmental sustainability, social equity, and governance transparency. Leadership development must prepare leaders to navigate these complex stakeholder dynamics while maintaining organizational viability (Ferrell et al., 2019).

Personalization and customization expectations continue increasing as technology enables more tailored service experiences (Fitz-Enz & Mattox, 2014). Leaders must understand how to leverage data and technology to deliver personalized services while maintaining operational efficiency and privacy protection. This requires sophisticated understanding of customer segmentation, service design, and technology capabilities (Turner et al., 2018).

The demographics of both workforce and customer populations continue shifting, creating needs for culturally competent leadership (Fowler, 2018). Service organizations increasingly operate across cultural boundaries and serve diverse populations with varied expectations and preferences. Leadership development must prepare leaders to navigate cultural complexity while maintaining service excellence and organizational coherence (Gilley & Gilley, 2003).

CONCLUSION

Strategic leadership development in service organizations represents a critical organizational capability determining competitive success in modern economies (Gilley & Gilley, 2003). The complexity of service delivery, combined with rapid technological change and evolving stakeholder expectations, demands sophisticated approaches to developing transformational leaders. Organizations can no longer rely on traditional training programs or generic leadership development approaches failing to address unique challenges of service contexts (Kennedy et al., 2013; Turner et al., 2018).

The framework presented in this chapter integrates theoretical foundations with practical implementation strategies to guide organizations in building comprehensive leadership development capabilities (Gilley & Gilley, 2003; Hanson, 2013; Kennedy et al., 2013; Turner et al., 2018). Adoption of transformational leadership roles encompassing relationship building, organizational architecture, strategic thinking, performance engineering, change championship, and political navigation helps leaders effectively address multifaceted challenges facing service organizations (Gilley & Gilley, 2003). These roles, examined through service organization lenses, provide comprehensive framework for understanding leadership capability requirements and designing development approaches addressing these needs (Jarvis et al., 2013).

Contemporary research demonstrates that effective leadership development requires moving beyond traditional skill-based training toward more sophisticated approaches addressing relationship capabilities, systems thinking, leadership mindsets, and context-specific competencies (Fowler, 2018; Hanson, 2013; Jarvis et al., 2013; Kennedy et al., 2013). The integration of these multiple development dimensions creates comprehensive approaches preparing leaders for service organization complexity rather than simplistic solutions addressing isolated capability gaps (Turner et al., 2018).

The implementation of strategic leadership development requires organizational commitment, resource investment, and sustained attention (Gilley & Gilley, 2003; Packard & Jones, 2015). The Chief Strategic Human Capital Development Officer model provides mechanism for elevating leadership development to strategic importance while ensuring alignment with organizational objectives. Through comprehensive development ecosystems, sophisticated evaluation approaches, and sustainable support systems, organizations can build leadership capabilities driving long-term performance and competitive advantage (Packard & Jones, 2015; Turner et al., 2018).

As service organizations face increasingly complex challenges around digital transformation, ethical leadership, employee engagement, and data-driven decision making, the importance of strategic leadership development will only grow (Ferrell et al., 2019; Fitz-Enz & Mattox, 2014; Fowler, 2018). Organizations investing in building transformational leadership capabilities will be better positioned to navigate uncertainty, capitalize on opportunities, and create value for multiple stakeholders. The research synthesized in this framework demonstrates that leadership development represents not a cost to be minimized but a strategic investment generating returns through improved organizational performance, innovation capabilities, and competitive positioning (Gilley & Gilley, 2003; Hanson, 2013).

The journey toward leadership excellence in service organizations requires continuous learning, adaptation, and renewal (Kennedy et al., 2013; Turner et al., 2018). By embracing comprehensive approaches to leadership development addressing both individual capabilities and organizational systems, service organizations build leadership capacity required for sustained success in the modern economy (Hanson, 2013). The strategies and frameworks presented in this chapter provide roadmap for organizations committed to developing transformational leaders who can drive performance, innovation, and positive impact in an increasingly complex world (Gilley & Gilley, 2003; Turner et al., 2018).

REFERENCES

Ferrell, O. C., Fraedrich, J., & Ferrell, L. (2019). *Business ethics: Ethical decision making and cases* (12th ed.). Cengage Learning.

Fitz-Enz, J., & Mattox, J. (2014). *Predictive analytics for human resources*. John Wiley & Sons. DOI: 10.1002/9781118915042

Fowler, S. (2018). Toward a new curriculum of leadership competencies: Advances in motivation science call for rethinking leadership development. *Advances in Developing Human Resources*, *20*(2), 182–196. DOI: 10.1177/1523422318756644

Gilley, J. W., & Gilley, A. M. (2003). *Strategically integrated HRD: Six transformational roles in creating results-driven programs* (2nd ed.). Perseus Publishing.

Hanson, B. (2013). The leadership development interface: Aligning leaders and organizations toward more effective leadership learning. *Advances in Developing Human Resources*, *15*(1), 106–120. DOI: 10.1177/1523422312465853

Jarvis, C., Gulati, A., McCririck, V., & Simpson, P. (2013). Leadership matters: Tensions in evaluating leadership development. *Advances in Developing Human Resources*, *15*(1), 27–45. DOI: 10.1177/1523422312467138

Kennedy, F., Carroll, B., & Francoeur, J. (2013). Mindset not skill set: Evaluating in new paradigms of leadership development. *Advances in Developing Human Resources*, *15*(1), 10–26. DOI: 10.1177/1523422312466835

Packard, T., & Jones, L. (2015). An outcomes evaluation of a leadership development initiative. *Journal of Management Development*, *34*(2), 153–168. DOI: 10.1108/JMD-05-2013-0063

Turner, J. R., Baker, R., Schroeder, J., Johnson, K. R., & Chung, C. H. (2018). Leadership development techniques: Mapping leadership development techniques with leadership capacities using a typology of development. *European Journal of Training and Development*, *42*(9), 538–557. Advance online publication. DOI: 10.1108/EJTD-03-2018-0022

Chapter 8
Leading Innovation and Organizational Change:
A Case Study on Altice Portugal's Success

Felipa Lopes dos Reis
http://orcid.org/0000-0001-8462-0810
Lusofona University, Portugal

Anastasia Maladet
http://orcid.org/0009-0001-2064-8408
Lusofona University, Portugal

Ângela Xu
http://orcid.org/0009-0005-3422-4373
Lusofona University, Portugal

ABSTRACT

This paper explores how organizations adapt and innovate in the world of digital transformation, with a particular focus on Altice Portugal - one of the country's leading telecommunications providers. The study investigates how the company has responded to the pressures of a fast-evolving, highly competitive market. A mixed-methods approach was used, combining survey data from the general public with perceptions from recent studies and external interviews (2022–2025). Findings reveal a strong commitment from Altice Portugal to modernize its technological infrastructure and flexible management practices. However, the results also show a gap between these innovations and public perception - especially when it comes to user experience and the effectiveness of digital tools.

INTRODUCTION

Over the past few decades, there has been a continuous and significant evolution in technology, product development, and the adoption of sustainable practices, among other factors considered fundamental to organizational success. They are now critical for survival competitiveness in the market. Organizations are open systems influenced by external and internal factors that can affect their performance both positively and negatively. The cases of Blockbuster, Kodak, and Nokia highlight how failing to keep up with

DOI: 10.4018/979-8-3373-4027-2.ch008

technological changes can lead to a company's decline. Blockbuster rejected a partnership with Netflix and underestimated the impact of streaming. This caused it to fall behind in the industry's shift, leading to its closure in 2010. Then Kodak chose not to invest in digital photography, preferring analog photography instead. This choice resulted in a big loss of competitiveness and ultimately led to its bankruptcy in 2012. Finally, Nokia ignored the need for a better graphic interface and the new features of the iPhone. As a result, it lost a lot of market share and sold the company to Microsoft in 2014 (adapted from Ferreira, p.1). These examples show that during times of uncertainty and rapid change, organizations must create new strategies for survival. Facing these challenges often encourages greater flexibility, better innovation (adapted from Reis, 2020, pp.180-181), and improved communication and adaptability.

PURPOSE OF THE STUDY

This paper will examine how organizations respond to change and innovation. We will focus on the strategies that lead to success.

The goal of this study is to provide a theoretical analysis of the main theories and methods used by companies that constantly face change. It explores how innovation and organizational change affect each other in practice, highlighting the need to anticipate market trends and prepare for future challenges, which includes strategic foresight and cultural adaptability. Using established theoretical models and recent literature, it aims to understand how companies can implement innovation effectively, not just in technology or operations but also through leadership, structure, and active collaboration with clients, employees, and partners. It will also analyze the internal and external factors these companies encounter and seek to deepen their understanding of competitors. This will help identify effective ways to gather better feedback from the public. To enrich this analysis, a case study was developed on Altice Portugal, the largest telecommunication provider in the country. In addition, we are investigating how the company manages change and innovation and how these dynamics impact its performance and market position. This study was carried out by analysing secondary sources acquired through online databases, academic works, books, and articles. It also included a questionnaire distributed to the general public to understand its effects on the company's development.

In recent years, Altice has invested heavily in modernization and innovation, yet public perceptions show a gap between these efforts and the actual customer experience. This contrast raises important questions about how innovation is communicated, perceived, and ultimately valued by users. Several hypotheses were proposed and verified based on the data analysis, allowing for a deeper interpretation of the research findings. Additionally, we will discuss the public's view of the company's strategic approaches and possible suggestions for improvements that could help Altice continue to succeed.

METHODOLOGY

Altice Portugal's Case

Altice Portugal S.A., previously known as Portugal Telecom (PT), has its headquarters in Lisbon, Portugal, as well as several offices, operations, and research centers throughout the country (Altice Portugal, 2024c, as cited in Ferreira, 2024).

In 1992, the telecommunications sector started operating independently. Before that, it was part of CTT, a company focused mainly on postal services. Three different operators took over its management: TLP, handled services in the Lisbon and Porto regions; PT, managed communications in the rest of the country, as well as Europe and the Mediterranean Basin; and Marconi, responsible for intercontinental traffic. In 1994, these operations were merged into a single entity, resulting in the creation of Portugal Telecom S.A., a national telecommunications operator (adapted from Meo, 2025).

On June 2, 2015, PT Portugal became a fully owned subsidiary of the Altice Group, a leading multinational provider of telecommunications services with a presence in several countries, including France, Israel, Belgium, Luxembourg, Switzerland, Portugal, the French Antilles, the Indian Ocean region, and the Dominican Republic. In 2018, it officially changed its name to Altice Portugal (adapted from Meo, 2025).

However, the company has faced numerous challenges due to the highly competitive nature of the telecommunications market. Rivals like NOS, Vodafone, and, more recently, DIGI, have significantly influenced the sector.

NOS, formerly known as ZON Multimédia, entered the market in 2014 with a strategy focused on lower prices and new services. Some of its key innovations in the early years included the launch of 4K (Ultra HD) content on the national market, the creation of the NOS TV APP, which allows you to watch TV on your PC, smartphone, or tablet, and the opening of cinemas with 4DX multisensory technology. These efforts helped NOS win three major industry awards in 2016: Consumer Choice, Product of the Year, and Trusted Brand (adapted from NOS, 2025).

Vodafone has also made a name for itself in the Portuguese market and received international recognition. In 2014, the European Fibre to the Home Council recognized it for having the best fiber optic network in Europe, due to the excellence and volume of investments made in the implementation of networks in Portugal, Spain, and Italy. Subsequently, in 2019, it was again recognized as a world leader in IoT by the Gartner Magic Quadrant in M2M Service Management, in the "execution capacity" and "breadth of vision" categories (adapted from Vodafone, 2024).

Finally, DIGI recently entered the Portuguese market with a strategy plan to offer telecommunications services at low prices. This approach has had a direct impact on Altice, both financially and strategically (adapted from DIGI Portugal, n.d.).

Reports, when DIGI entered the market, indicated that Altice Portugal was increasingly prepared to face new competitors in the market. In response to DIGI's arrival, MEO's CEO stated in an interview:

> If there's any company in this country that's used to competing, it's us. We've been the dominant player, and since the market opened up [in 1996], we've seen many competitors come and go. One thing remained constant: Meo as the industry leader (Ribeiro, 2024).

Regarding DIGI specifically, she noted:

What I can say for now is that we are still witnessing their first steps. DIGI launched its commercial offering this week. So far, the only variable I've noticed is the price, and in some respects, we are not comparing apples to apples. (Ribeiro, 2024)

She further emphasized: "Portuguese consumers often talk about prices, but if you compare the features and service quality, you'll find that very few countries are ahead of us." (Ribeiro, 2024)

However, since DIGI started operations in November 2024, Anacom has received over a thousand consumer complaints against DIGI during the first full quarter, which is 6% of all complaints in the sector. Most complaints were about mobile service issues, including delays or interruptions in the provision of the service (adapted from Nunes, F., 2025).

In absolute terms, Vodafone had the highest number of complaints (one third of the total), followed by NOS (31%) and then MEO (26%) (Nunes, F., 2025). Thus, this shows that MEO had the fewest complaints during this period.

Currently, Altice Portugal continues to strengthen its leadership in the national market. It has been recognized for providing the best mobile coverage and the fastest mobile internet in the country. This success results from ongoing investments in its mobile, 5G, and fiber-optic networks. With a 95.8% 5G population coverage and over 6.5 million homes connected to fiber, the company has focused on offering innovative and diversified services. A notable initiative includes the integration of 100% renewable energy solutions with telecom packages, which attracted over 112,000 customers in 2024. These results reflect sustained growth across key performance indicators, including a 1.7% increase in fixed service RGUs and a 4.9% increase in postpaid mobile services in Q3 of 2024 (Altice Portugal, 2024).

Hypotheses

Following the goals of this study, several hypotheses were based on the analysis of the collected data. These hypotheses reflect fundamental features of innovation and organizational change at Altice Portugal, as well as their impact and the market's awareness.

The following hypotheses were considered:

Hypothesis 1: Altice Portugal offers service conditions that are compatible with their pricing, securing its position in a competitive market.

Hypothesis 2: By adopting innovation strategies, Altice Portugal has attracted more customers and improved its market reputation.

REVIEW OF THE LITERATURE

Key Concepts

This literature review explores the main concepts and theoretical frameworks related to organizational change, innovation, and leadership, emphasizing their importance in the business context of Altice Portugal.

First, the analysis will examine the dynamics of organizational change. Then, it will distinguish between innovation and change and introduce two relevant theories. Lastly, the review will look at leadership and its role in supporting and maintaining innovation and change processes within organizations.

Organizational Change

Firstly, it is essential to understand the concept of organizational change and its theoretical background. Organizational change can be defined as any transformation that happens within a company, influenced by internal or external factors, which demands the ability to create and implement new strategies to meet specific needs (MJV Team, 2022). This transition can involve changes in structure, technology, culture, or processes, with leadership playing a vital role in facilitating adaptation and encouraging the development of team skills, such as creativity, problem-solving, and strategic thinking.

Whenever a new process, policy, or advanced technology is introduced, teams are challenged to find innovative solutions to adapt and remain competitive. Nevertheless, it is important to mention that such transformations are not always easy - they can cause insecurity, resistance, or even stress. For this reason, change must be carefully planned, clearly communicated, and supported by a positive and inclusive environment (Adapted from Hussain, 2023).

According to Rasmussen University (2023), the theory of organizational change deals with how companies manage transformation processes and how they can do this effectively. This framework not only aims to improve organizational performance but also supports the personal and professional growth of employees. In addition to helping with adaptability in changing environments, it also prepares organizations to respond to future market shifts and evolving consumer demands.

Furthermore, this theory is important for driving innovative and sustainable growth, as it encourages creativity and supports a culture of continuous learning. As a result, companies are better positioned to stay relevant in highly competitive markets.

Chris Hirst, in his book "No Bullsh*t Change" ("Mudança Sem Tretas" in Portuguese), emphasizes that no change program can succeed without considering organizational culture. All change ultimately affects people's behaviors. Since culture is simply the sum of individual behaviors, most organizational change is, at its heart, cultural change. According to Ghoshal's model of ideal culture, the foundation should be based on stretch, discipline, trust, and support. To lead effective change, one must be focused and thoughtful when making decisions and choosing which actions to prioritize.

Innovation

Innovation, on the other hand, often arises as a response to strong market competition. In many circumstances, it is this external pressure that forces companies to change and to adopt new strategies that help them stand out. In today's business environment, innovation is crucial for staying competitive, being adaptable, and delivering value. It's not just about being creative; it's about making meaningful changes in the market through noticeable and clear outcomes, whether they involve products, services, or processes.

One simple definition of innovation comes from Bagno and Faria (2022), who describe it as the "successful exploitation of new ideas". In an organizational context, success is directly tied to the ability to introduce and spread these ideas in ways that improve value delivery, whether through improved functionality, quality, or cost savings. "Offering more while spending less" is the essence of productivity, and ultimately, the key to business survival in competitive markets.

There are several theories of innovation. Let's focus on two of them: Clayton Christensen's Disruptive Innovation Theory and Henry Chesbrough's Open Innovation Theory.

While Disruptive Innovation Theory is currently debated, it remains relevant, particularly with shifts in competition, new technologies, and social changes. According to Christensen, the theory aims to explain how new technologies, products, or services can start small but eventually outpace established offerings in the current market (IMD, 2025). This process relates to Schumpeter's idea of "creative destruction" (Schumpeter, cited by Jerome, 2023), where innovation constantly replaces the old with the new.

There are two main types of disruption:

1. New Market Disruption:

This occurs when innovative products or services reach overlooked markets or customers, i.e., those normally considered "unprofitable" or "unattractive" by leading companies (adapted from IMD, 2025). In this case, the focus is on:

- Accessibility;
- Simplicity;
- New value proposition.

Over time, these products evolve and attract new, higher-value customers in the dominant market. Netflix is an example mentioned in the introduction. When it launched streaming, it created a model that initially served an audience that valued convenience and low cost. Blockbuster ignored this change, underestimating its importance, and ended up going bankrupt.

2. Low-End Disruption:

In this case, the product is inexpensive yet still of decent quality, aimed at consumers who are sensitive to price. It starts with the least demanding customers, but as the quality improves, the product moves up the value chain (adapted from IMD, 2025). A relevant example is Nokia, which struggled to keep up with changes in the smartphone market. While Nokia focused on closed systems, Android offered a cheaper, more flexible, and modern solution with its open ecosystem. This quickly made Android stand out in the market.

According to the Open Innovation Theory, companies should use both internal and external ideas and methods to enter the market in order to improve their technologies and capabilities. In this model, research and development projects can come from within the organization or from outside it, demonstrating a reduction in traditional boundaries. As a result, the lines between the company and its external environment become more flexible, allowing the integration of external knowledge and resources, as illustrated in the figure below (adapted from Fontanela, C., Burtet, G., Pereira, R., & Marroco, A., 2021).

Figure 1. Open Innovation Theory.

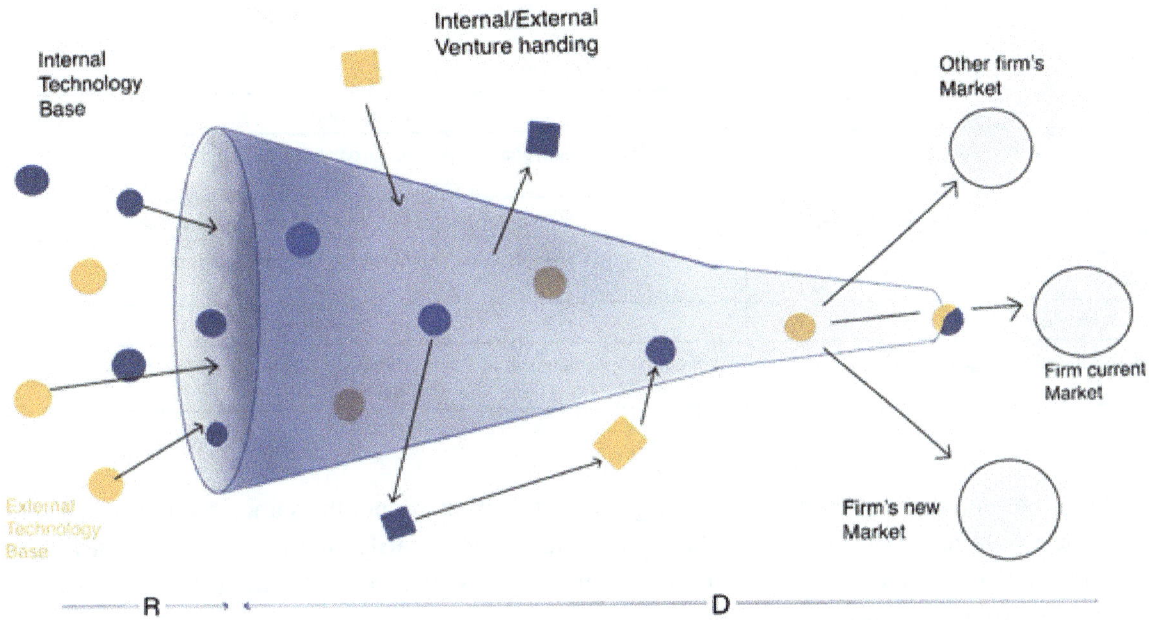

Source: Own elaboration, based on Miranda (2023)

Internal sources include research and development activities aimed at creating new products or processes, as well as initiatives that improve existing solutions incrementally.

External sources, on the other hand, include searching for and acquiring technical knowledge through specialized consultancies, codified information, licenses to manufacture products, and adopting processes developed by third parties (Fontanela, C., Burtet, G., Pereira, R., & Marroco, A., 2021).

Adopting Open Innovation speeds up the development of new products and services, increasing revenue and market share.

Similarly, it reduces time to market, meaning that products and services can be launched faster by using external knowledge, existing technologies, and proven solutions. It also helps reduce time to market, anticipate profits, and reduce the direct costs of internal R&D activities. This accelerates development, increases responsiveness to market needs, and gives companies a huge advantage.

Organizational Change VS Innovation

Table 1. Major differences between organizational change and innovation

Change	Innovation
A transition from one state or situation to another	The outcome of a change that introduces something new with value
May not involve the creation of something new	Involves new things, though not necessarily invention
Can be reactive (a response to a need or problem)	Can be proactive (anticipating risks or opportunities)
Focuses on adaptation	Focuses on creating benefits
Example: internal reorganization	Example: development of a new product or enhancement of an existing service (Boyles, 2022)

Source: own elaboration

Although often used interchangeably, change and innovation are not the same. As shown in Table 1, change refers to transformation, which can happen without necessarily creating something new. Nonetheless, innovation involves the introduction of something new that benefits either the customer or the company's internal processes.

As Boyles (2022) explains, innovation does not always mean major technological breakthroughs or disruptive business models. It can also come from improving existing systems, just as mobile phones evolved. The first telephone, invented by Alexander Graham Bell in 1876, was a revolutionary device for transmitting voice using electrical signals. Since then, we have seen the rise of wireless phones in 1937 and, more recently, the smartphone as we know it today.

Therefore, we can conclude that innovation may involve change, but not every change is an innovation.

Transformational Leadership and Management

Organizational change and innovation, as discussed earlier, are two of the most powerful forces driving business success. However, without effective leadership and management, these efforts often fail to achieve their full potential. Visionary leadership gives direction, builds trust, and inspires people to embrace change, even when it's challenging.

Innovation management is the process of turning ideas into real solutions. It includes everything from identifying opportunities to implementing successful outcomes (Stanford University, n.d.). But managing innovation successfully involves more than just systems; it requires leaders who can balance structure with creativity.

According to Galles (2021), who shares insights from Stanford researcher Robert Sutton, great leaders know how to "get out of the way" when needed. Instead of overseeing every detail, they encourage independence and allow people the freedom to experiment. These leaders recognize that innovation thrives when individuals feel trusted and empowered. They also understand the importance of timing - when to accelerate progress, and when to pause, reflect, or adjust the direction.

Sutton also points out that leaders play multiple roles: they are both "poets," who inspire teams through meaningful visions and emotions, and "plumbers," who solve real problems and clear hurdles.

He believes that successful innovation leadership often means stopping what no longer works and creating emotional bonds that make change significant.

In fast-changing environments, transformational leaders go beyond traditional planning. They prioritize clarity, purpose, and consistent communication. As Chris Hirst (2024) notes that it's not just about creating a strategy; it's about making sure people understand it. Clearly repeating the vision helps teams stay focused and motivated. He also highlights the importance of helping individuals move from disengagement to a place of growth, where they feel valued, capable, and ready to contribute.

Additionally, the concept of authentic leadership offers another important perspective. Authentic leaders gain trust by being honest, self-aware, and guided by their values. According to Forbes (2024), they typically share four key qualities:

- Self-awareness: They understand their strengths, limits, and values, and are open to feedback. This helps them lead with integrity and adapt their approach when needed.
- Transparency: They communicate openly and listen actively. By showing vulnerability and being honest, they create a safe space for collaboration.
- Fair decision-making: Authentic leaders seek different perspectives and encourage team input before making decisions, which strengthens trust and engagement.
- Strong values: They act according to their moral beliefs, even under pressure. This gives teams a clear ethical compass and promotes a healthy culture.

By combining transformational vision with authentic behavior, leaders can build an environment where innovation is more than a process; it becomes part of the company's DNA.

Innovation and Change in the Telecommunications Industry

The telecommunications industry has been through significant transformations in recent years, influenced mainly by technological developments and the growing demand for global connectivity. According to Carlos Jesus, Country Manager at Colt Technology Services Portugal, the industry is in constant evolution, shaped by customer expectations, technological improvements, and the growing complexity of business models. This change demands fast, secure, and innovative responses from telecom operators, who aim not only to adapt but also to lead the digital transformation (Forbes Portugal, 2024).

One of the most important achievements in global connectivity was the development of mobile networks. In 2000, the introduction of 3G in Portugal allowed mobile internet access and began the smartphone era. This technological leap led telecom providers to expand their infrastructure and adjust service packages to customer needs. Two decades later, in 2020, the introduction of 5G marked a new era of connectivity, offering higher speeds and lower latency compared to previous generations (adapted from Mobile Network Generations: Evolution from 1G to 5G, 2024).

Another major development is the rise of Artificial Intelligence (AI), which helps predict system failures, improve network maintenance, and enhance customer support. Alongside the growth of 5G, it is estimated that the number of IoT-connected devices will reach 16.7 billion globally. This technology is increasingly seen as essential for business development and improved quality of life (Forbes Portugal, 2024).

Looking towards 2030, a new generation of networks is expected - one that looks to integrate advanced AI for real-time immersive communication and extend connectivity to even the most remote and challenging areas. (Adapted from *Mobile Network Generations: Evolution from 1G to 5G*, 2024).

Innovation and Change in Altice Portugal

Timeline

Figure 2. Evolution of the telecommunications industry in Portugal

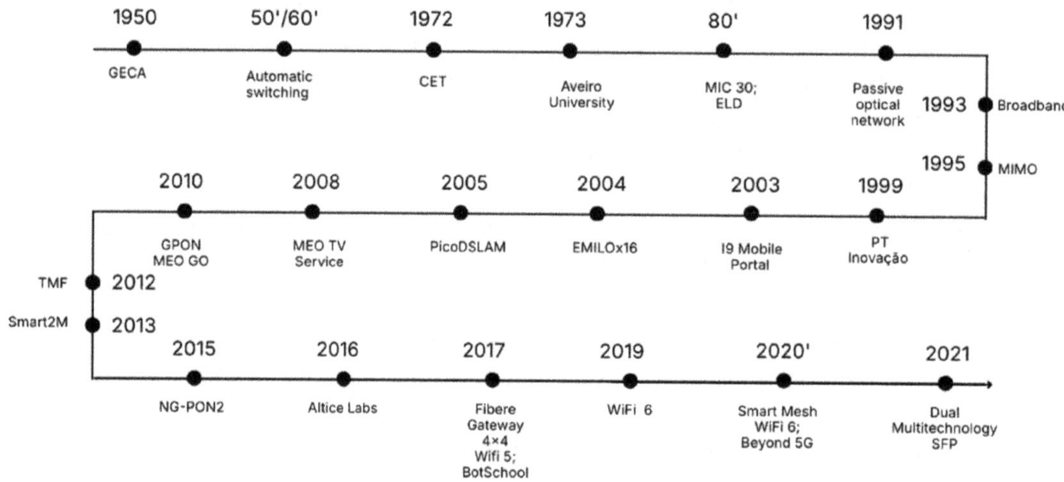

Source: own elaboration

This timeline shows the evolution of the telecommunications industry in Portugal.

In 1950, GECA was created to develop the most advanced telecommunications technologies in Portugal. In this decade, the country became one of the first to have a fully automated telephone network.

In 1972, GECA was renamed CET, reflecting a new purpose: to function as a school and retrain technicians and engineers due to the introduction of new electronic technologies.

In 1973, the University of Aveiro was built within the CET campus, with a focus on telecommunications and electronics.

During this period, pioneering systems were developed, such as the MIC 30, which made it possible to digitally interconnect telephone exchanges and reduce investments in cable expansion. Another example was the ELD, a small-capacity local digital switch.

In the 90s, CET worked with PON technology for broadband access via a network in Aveiro. In collaboration with European R&D centers, the first broadband ATM link between Aveiro and Madrid was established.

TMN launched the world's first prepaid cell phone service and anticipated intelligent network standards for mobile networks.

In this decade, CET was renamed PT Inovação.

In the 2000s, several innovations stood out, such as: the launch of the first commercial video streaming and live TV service on cell phones; with EMILO, Altice Labs enabled TMN to save CAPEX on the 3G network by reusing the existing SDH infrastructure; connecting 8,300 schools to the Internet with picoDSLAM, an 8-port ADSL device with remote power supply; MEO stood out as one of the best IPTV solutions in the world.

Between 2010 and 2020, it launched the first interoperable ONT, breaking the monopoly of OLT suppliers and reducing terminal costs; MEO Go revolutionized access to TV, allowing viewing at home and on the move; Creation of the Smart2M platform for managing M2M connectivity in real time, adapted to the IoT era. Demonstration of NG-PON2 with Verizon, reaching 10Gbps symmetrical with Optical Line Terminal (OLT) and Optical Network Terminal (ONT) from PT Inovação; PT Inovação became Altice Labs; Development of the 4×4 Fiber Gateway, providing a superior experience for MEO customers; Launch of BOTSchool, a platform for creating virtual assistants for various business contexts. Creation of the first GPON gateway with Wi-Fi 6 launched in Europe, developed for the operator SFR (France); Launch of Smart Mesh Wi-Fi 6, a certified solution with a powerful signal and intelligent control for indoor environments.

Since 2014, ALB has been leading 5G projects, promoting digital transformation in smart cities, industry, and services.

Finally, in 2021, an innovation was launched that doubled the capacity of fiber optic networks, making it possible to serve twice as many customers by simply changing the electro-optical connector (adapted from history - Altice Labs, s.d).

Based on this timeline, it is clear that Altice Portugal, through ALB, has exemplified continuous innovation and leadership in the telecommunications sector. With its solid foundation in research and development, international recognition, and strong commitment to sustainability and inclusion, the company has established itself as a key player in Portugal's technological evolution and on the global stage.

Altice Contributions

Although Altice Portugal's institutional statements and public communications, particularly those by its CEO, present a highly positive narrative around technological innovation, sustainable growth, and market leadership, the data reveal concrete challenges that preceded its current organizational transformation strategy.

In the fourth quarter of 2024, Altice Portugal reported revenues of 726 million euros, a 3.1% year-on-year increase. This growth was driven by a 7.7% rise in the consumer segment and a 7.9% rise in enterprise services. However, there was a 5.4% decline in Earnings Before Interest, Taxes, Depreciation, and Amortization (EBITDA), highlighting potential pressure on operational profitability. Even excluding the impact of Altice Labs, EBITDA still fell by 0.4%, indicating that operational costs rose faster than revenue (MEO, 2024). This suggests that the increase in customers and services alone was not sufficient to generate economic value to sustain profit margins, pointing to limited operational efficiency during this period.

Additionally, Altice Labs, the company's innovation and R&D hub, recorded a significant drop in revenue from the export of hardware and services (Ferreira, 2020). This slowdown directly affected the enterprise segment and exposed difficulties in scaling internal innovation to international markets, undermining one of the organization's key competitive advantages.

Its mission is to develop technologies that improve lives and support a better society, underpinning its competitive market position. Today, its solutions are used by over 300 million people globally (Altice Labs, 2025).

One of its most recent achievements includes obtaining a European patent for a "Method for Configuring a FTTH Distribution Network Cell," which significantly optimizes the use of Gigabit Passive Optical Network (GPON) ports, especially in low-density areas and Small and Medium-sized Enterprise (SME) markets. This solution improves fiber network management, reduces deployment costs, and maximizes existing infrastructure use. Its "pay-as-you-grow" model allows networks to adapt to market needs sustainably and efficiently, with lower energy consumption and fewer failures (Executive Digest, 2025).

Altice Labs has also led high-impact R&D projects such as 5G-AUTO, which focused on developing and testing new technologies for autonomous driving supported by 5G V2X (Vehicle-to-Everything) connectivity. Co-funded by the European Regional Development Fund (FEDER - COMPETE 2020), the project developed Roadside Units (RSUs) and On-Board Units (OBUs) based on 3GPP specifications, the global standard for mobile networks, including 5G. RSUs are installed on fixed road infrastructure (e.g., traffic lights or intersections) and communicate with OBUs in vehicles, enabling real-time data exchange between cars, infrastructure, and traffic systems (Altice Labs, 2023).

Altice Portugal's technological leadership is further demonstrated by its mobile network performance. As of February 2025, MEO recorded an average 5G speed of 324 Mbps, making it the fastest and most consistent mobile network in the country. This reflects not only network density but also the high engineering standards of Altice Labs, validating ongoing investment in innovation. CTO José Pedro Nascimento noted that this recognition "reinforces our continued commitment to innovation and service quality," aligned with the company's goal of delivering superior customer experiences through cutting-edge technology (MEO, 2025a).

This consistent focus on innovation has allowed Altice Portugal to strengthen its competitive edge against rivals such as NOS, particularly in technological offerings and the expansion of its fiber and 5G infrastructure. CEO Ana Figueiredo emphasizes innovation as essential to building consumer trust, enhancing service quality, and securing long-term sustainability.

Still, Altice has faced competitive challenges. In 2019, then CEO Alexandre Fonseca stated that "gaining TV customers is the big challenge this year," acknowledging that Altice Portugal did not yet lead the subscription TV segment, then dominated by NOS. That year's first quarter saw a 1.4% drop in EBITDA to 206 million euros, indicating pressure on operating results despite a modest increase in revenue. To address this, the company opted to increase customer value by enhancing service offerings rather than raising prices directly (Público, 2019). This illustrates how innovation initiatives have historically been used to respond to underperformance in specific market segments.

The strategy at the time aimed to grow revenue through added services rather than price hikes, highlighting a deliberate attempt to innovate the product offering without compromising price competitiveness.

In response to these challenges, Altice Portugal has embraced strategic diversification and investment in both organizational and technological innovation. CEO Ana Figueiredo recently stated, "We are ready to lead the next phase of technological transformation in Portugal," emphasizing the importance of artificial intelligence, automation, and connectivity in adapting to an evolving industry (Figueiredo, 2025).

Figure 3. Annual revenue and total bundled service subscriptions of MEO from 2020 to 2024 (in millions of euros and millions of subscriptions, respectively).

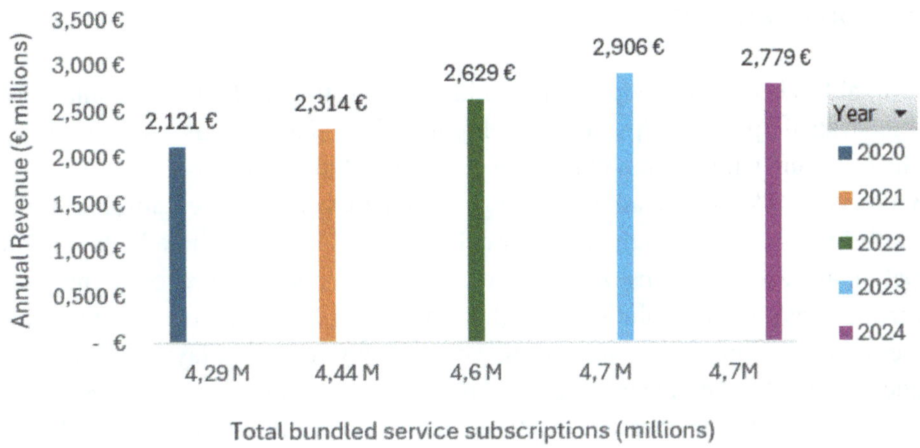

Source: Own elaboration based on data from ANACOM and Altice Portugal reports (2020–2024).

This strategic direction seems to be evident in MEO's recent performance. As shown in Figure 3, both annual revenues and the total number of bundled service subscriptions steadily increased between 2020 and 2024. While revenue growth was modest, the rise in subscriptions suggests more consumers are choosing bundled offers. This growth is likely driven by investments in infrastructure, customer service, and technological innovation.

By the end of the first quarter of 2025, MEO established itself as the top operator in bundled service subscriptions, capturing 41.7% of the market. In contrast, NOS, while still holding a significant share at 34.9%, experienced a slight decline, indicating a drop in competitiveness within an increasingly demanding industry that values innovation and service quality. Moreover, MEO also recorded the highest revenue share from bundled services at 39.8%, surpassing NOS at 38.3%. This suggests MEO not only has a larger subscriber base but also one that offers greater value. These numbers highlight a changing competitive landscape where MEO is gaining ground, while NOS is falling behind (ANACOM, 2025).

Meanwhile, NOS has positioned itself as a national leader in innovation investment with initiatives like the eGames Lab, a collaborative cluster focused on boosting Portugal's creative gaming industry, covering talent development, R&D, and internationalization (NOS, 2025). While this represents a significant cultural and tech investment, Altice Portugal differentiates itself by prioritizing critical infrastructure, such as FTTH, 5G, and smart mobility solutions. This highlights two distinct innovation strategies: Altice focuses on improving efficiency and service quality, while NOS invests in broader, industry-focused innovation.

Despite ongoing investments in technology and infrastructure, service quality in the telecommunications sector is still under scrutiny. According to ANACOM, the national communications regulator, 104.1 thousand written complaints against telecom providers in 2024, representing a 3% decrease compared to 2023, demonstrating a slight improvement. However, persistent consumer dissatisfaction persists. Notably, NOS accounted for 37% of total complaints and had the highest complaint rate per thousand customers at 7.7, particularly concerning service contracting. In this context, Altice Portugal's focus on innovation and service improvement not only serves as a competitive edge but also as a necessary response to rising consumer expectations (Público, 2025).

Altice Innovation Strategies

Altice Portugal has been actively pursuing an innovation strategy focused on anticipating customer needs, forming strategic partnerships, and developing talent. This strategy shows in both investment figures and the company's innovation culture, especially at Altice Labs.

In a 2023 interview, Alcino Lavrador, former general manager of Altice Labs, highlighted the importance of disruptive innovation through customer collaboration. Lavrador stated, "Innovation is precisely about anticipating and exceeding customer expectations.". He noted that recognizing client needs early is essential for creating effective solutions and that involving clients in the early stages of development leads to deeper and more impactful innovation. This strategy reflects Clayton Christensen's theory of disruptive innovation, where companies address unmet or emerging customer needs, often overlooked by incumbents, to develop breakthrough solutions that can redefine market standards. Altice's goal of reaching 100 international patents by 2030 illustrates its commitment to improving such transformative innovations.

At the same time, Altice's approach also reflects key aspects of the open innovation model, as proposed by Henry Chesbrough. Between 2019 and 2023, Altice Portugal invested 361 million euros in R&D, and within the last four years, the company registered 17 international patents, indicating a strong pipeline of proprietary technologies. These achievements come from an emphasis on external collaboration and knowledge sharing, particularly through partnerships and talent acquisition. These two elements are fundamental to the open innovation model, which encourages organizations to use external ideas, technologies, and networks to speed up internal innovation.

Lavrador also mentioned that building a culture of creativity is essential to sustaining innovation in a large organization. With over 700 professionals at Altice Labs, fostering this culture requires a different approach than in startups, where engineering, commercial, marketing, product, and support teams often collaborate closely. At Altice Labs, innovation is driven by continually testing new methods and encouraging internal teamwork across diverse teams.

This broader innovation strategy reflects Altice Portugal's dedication not only to technological leadership but also to long-term sustainability and ecosystem development. By integrating both disruptive and open innovation into its organizational culture, Altice aims to stay adaptable, socially relevant, and competitive in a changing digital economy.

PRESENTATION AND DATA ANALYSIS

To gain a clearer understanding of Altice Portugal's current market position, an anonymous questionnaire was conducted through Google Forms. This survey reached the general public and collected 92 valid responses, including six questions designed to gather opinions about their telecommunications provider, especially focusing on MEO.

The survey aimed to evaluate how consumers view telecommunications services in Portugal, particularly MEO. It also sought to compare MEO with its main competitors, presenting the data using charts and tables. The findings will be interpreted in detail to offer insights that go beyond simple statistics and support strategic analysis.

Questionnaire

Figure 4. Gender distribution of respondents

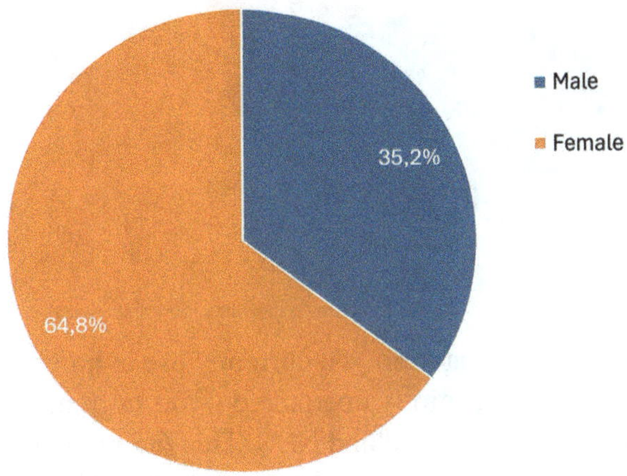

Source: own elaboration

As illustrated, the demographic data reveals that the female gender occupies a higher percentage, representing approximately two-thirds of respondents.

Figure 5. Age range of respondents

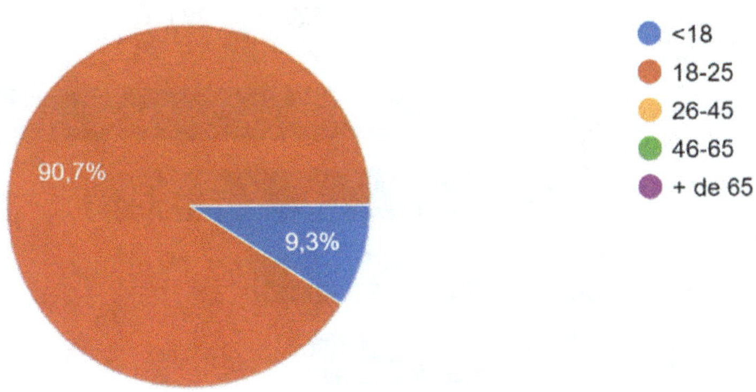

Source: own elaboration

Nearly all participants fall within the 18-25 age range, highlighting a young adult demographic. This is particularly relevant, as this age group tends to be more proficient in technology and open to innovation, which can influence their expectations of telecom services.

Figure 6. Current telecommunications operator used at home (n = 92)

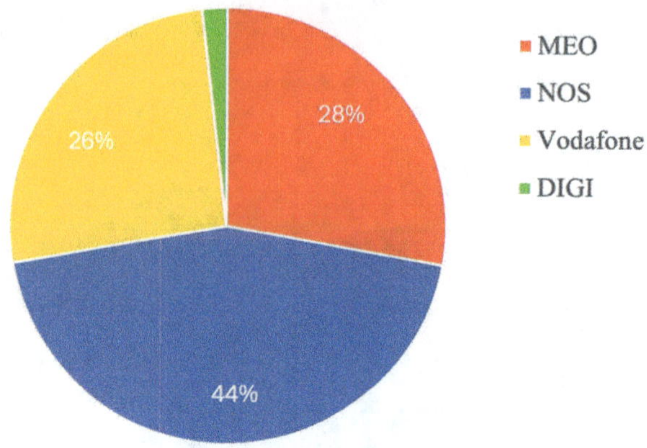

Source: own elaboration

Q1: Which telecommunications operator do you currently use at home?

When asked, "Which telecommunications operator do you currently use at home?", MEO was identified as the second most used provider, behind NOS. This finding matches current national market trends, where NOS slightly leads MEO in broadband market share (ANACOM, 2024). Even though it is not the market leader, the company holds a strong position among this demographic, showing its value in the competitive sector.

This observation is crucial. The fact that it is not in first place indicates that there is potential for growth, particularly through innovation and improving services.

The next two sections focus specifically on respondents who currently use a different provider, allowing us to understand which factors might influence users' demand.

Figure 7. Reasons for choosing a provider other than MEO (n = 21)

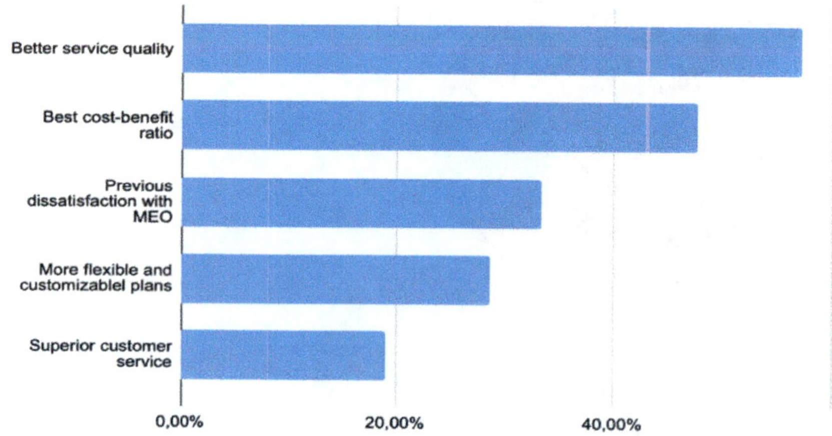

Source: own elaboration

Q2: What led you to choose your current provider instead of MEO?

The main reason people chose another operator was the quality of service, including internet, TV, and phone, with about 57,1% of respondents saying this was the main factor. This demonstrates that, even though MEO has improved in some areas, it still has work to do when it comes to meeting customer expectations, especially in offering a more reliable and consistent service.

Another significant reason was better value for money, with 47.6% of users citing this. For many, the balance between price and quality is what matters most when choosing a provider. Price sensitivity is particularly high among younger users, reinforcing the need for more competitive pricing strategies and flexible package options.

Additionally, seven participants mentioned past dissatisfaction with MEO, indicating that their previous negative experiences still affect their current choices. This presents an opportunity for the company to show change by improving its services, listening more to customers, and implementing innovative strategies.

Figure 8. Key factors that would influence respondents to switch to MEO (n = 21)

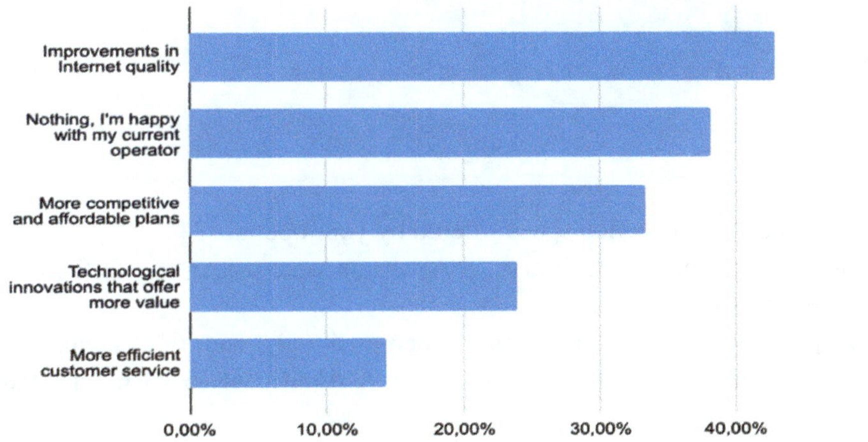

Source: own elaboration

Q3: What aspects would make you consider switching to MEO in the future?

Regarding question 3, it becomes evident that the main reasons that could lead consumers to choose MEO are service quality and competitiveness.

The majority of respondents (42,9%) indicated that improving internet quality and coverage would be a significant reason for attracting new customers. This confirms that network performance remains a critical competitive factor.

In addition, "More competitive and affordable plans", as well as "Technological innovations that offer new advantages", were pointed out as important factors. These responses suggest that product differentiation and continuous investment in infrastructure will likely affect user behavior.

Customer service was a less frequent response, but still noted, indicating that it could also be improved to attract new consumers.

Finally, 38,1% of respondents said they have no plans to change operators, as they are satisfied with their current service, which shows notable loyalty to other operators, presenting a challenge for MEO to tackle through differentiation and innovation.

From this point forward, the following questions were addressed to MEO customers. Their answers provide useful information about the company's performance and where improvements could make a big difference.

Figure 9. Users' satisfaction with their operator connection speed (n=71)

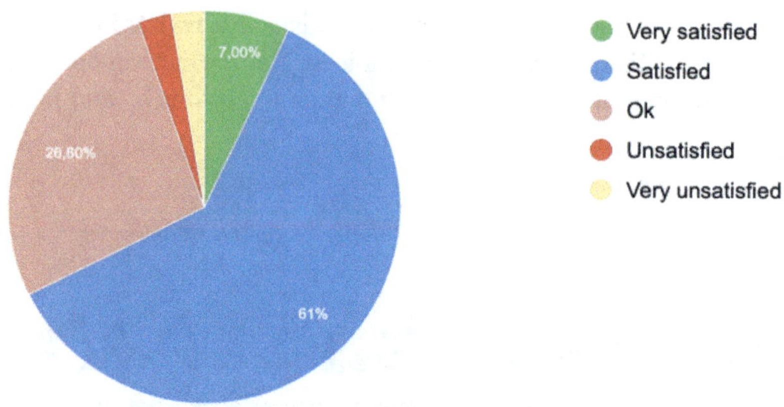

Source: own elaboration

Q4: How do you rate the connection speed offered by your operator?

To better understand customer satisfaction, participants were asked to rate the connection speed provided by their telecom operator.

While most respondents rated the connection speed positively, with 61% saying they were "satisfied" and 7% "very satisfied", there is more to consider. A significant 26,8% rated the speed as "OK", a neutral response.

This suggests that, although there are no major issues, some users might experience occasional problems. If these problems were common, we would likely see higher levels of dissatisfaction, so this is somewhat a positive sign.

Still, these neutral ratings represent an opportunity. Looking into the reasons behind these impartial responses could uncover small service issues, perhaps related to slow connection speed or unmet customer expectations.

By identifying these weak points and implementing specific improvements, MEO could increase overall satisfaction and turn neutral users into loyal brand promoters.

Figure 10. How customers view the fairness of pricing and speed options (n=71)

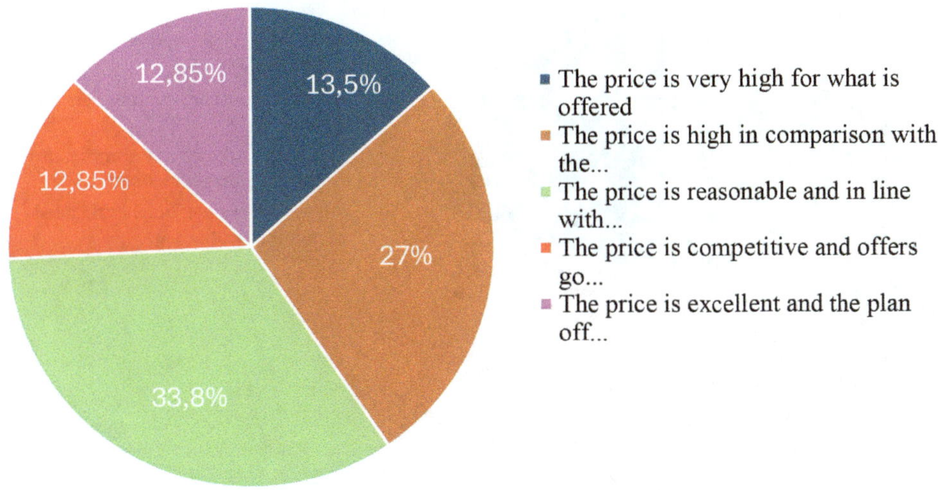

Source: own elaboration

Q5: Is the plan price fair, and does it offer good speed options?

In terms of pricing, most MEO customers gave a positive review regarding the price of their plans: 33.8% consider the price reasonable and aligned with the service, while another 25,7% (combining the last two options) rate MEO as competitive or excellent in terms of cost-benefit.

In contrast, around 27% see the prices as high, though they accept them as reasonable.

Nine respondents said the price is unjustifiably expensive.

From this feedback, it's clear that, overall, the perception of price is positive, but it also reveals a sensitivity to cost. This could be a concern for MEO, especially if it wants to meet the needs of the new generation, who are more budget-conscious and look for affordable options.

The following graph shows customer opinions on whether MEO's customer service has kept up with technological and digital advancements, such as chatbot support, automated services, and more innovative apps.

Figure 11. Customer Service adaptation to technological and digital changes (n=71)

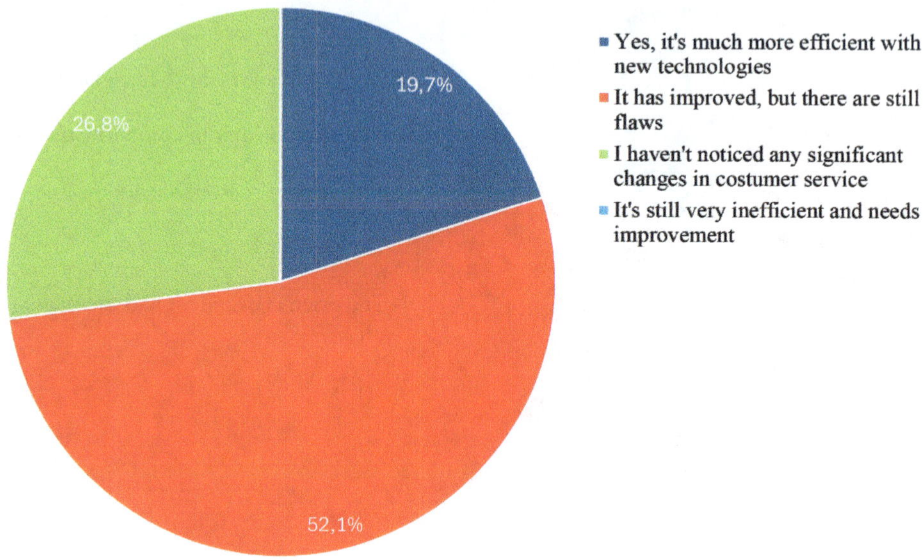

Source: own elaboration

Q6: Has customer service kept up with technological and digital changes (e.g., chatbot support, automated service, more intuitive apps)?

When assessing MEO's customer service about technological innovation (e.g., chatbot support, digital platforms), most customers experience improvement. About 19,7% believed the services had become much more efficient due to these advances. However, 52,1% feel there are still areas that need improvement, and 26.8% mentioned that they haven't noticed significant changes, which might indicate a need for better communication or a more impactful customer service experience. This points out the need for MEO to enhance the visibility and effectiveness of its digital transformation initiatives.

The main positive point is that no customer rated the service as "very inefficient." This tells us that although there's still a chance for improvement, the current service is functional and already meets the expectations of most customers.

Figure 12. Customer preferences on operator's innovation (n=71)

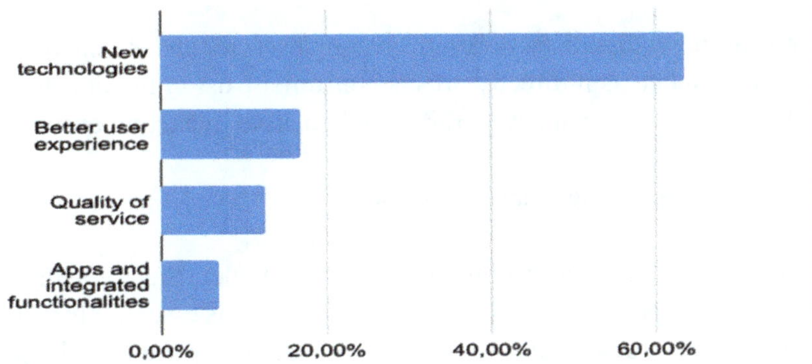

Source: own elaboration

Q7: What do you value most in your operator's innovation?

When asked about the features they valued most, more than half of the participants expressed a strong appreciation for new technologies, such as 5G and fiber optics, with 63,4% of the votes. This highlights that MEO users care about technological evolution and value staying up to date with industry advancements.

Moreover, 16,9% of participants emphasized the improved customer experience, including customer service and digital channels, reinforcing the importance of consistent investment in customer interaction.

Although in smaller percentages, respondents also value service quality and innovative applications and features offered.

On the whole, the data shows that MEO is in the right direction by investing in innovative technology, but there is still a need to strengthen innovation regarding user experience and the digital tools offered.

Subsequently, an optional question was asked of the respondents, from which 5 responses were obtained: "In your opinion, what changes or innovations should your operator implement to improve its services?"

The responses were as follows:

i. "Improve the areas where the network coverage is low."
ii. "Improve the connection; sometimes it has outages."

These two responses demonstrate that the customer experience is not always consistent, especially in certain locations. This reinforces the previous data mentioned from the questionnaire, where the quality of the internet was pointed out as a decisive factor in the choice of operator.

iii. "Reduce the number of channels; there are many channels we don't use, and I am forced to have them. A suggestion would be, for example, to have a customizable package."

This feedback raises a critique regarding the lack of flexibility in the channel offering. The suggestion of customizable packages shows that consumers are interested in having more control over what they contract and pay for, which could be a strategic opportunity for MEO to differentiate itself in the market.

iv. "Better customer support, which is horrible, and more transparency when claiming the internet is good when it is not."

This strong statement shows dissatisfaction with customer service and transparency regarding service quality. This is a critical aspect, as it directly affects consumer trust in the operator. Investing in more efficient, clear, and honest support can have a direct and positive impact on customers.

v. "Be more consistent in delivering what is promised."

This final response serves as a general but significant reminder: the company should stand by its promises, whether related to speed, reliability, or service features, is essential for customer satisfaction.

Altogether, these answers provide valuable suggestions for any operator looking to innovate and be more closely aligned with what today's consumers actually need and expect.

The data shows that while MEO holds a strong position among young users, it faces perceptual challenges related to service quality, value for money, and customer service. Comparatively, operators like NOS are perceived to outperform MEO in critical categories. However, opportunities exist in enhancing service reliability, offering flexible pricing models, and capitalizing on innovation and digital transformation. These findings provide a foundation for the following discussion chapter, where strategic implications and innovation opportunities will be further explored.

DISCUSSION

In today's rapidly changing telecommunications market, organizational innovation and adaptability are crucial for maintaining competitiveness. This discussion reflects on the hypotheses initially proposed, associating the survey results with concepts from the literature review, particularly those related to change and innovation within organizations.

About Hypothesis 1, which investigated whether Altice Portugal (MEO) offers good service quality at a price that matches its value, the data partially confirms this hypothesis. Many MEO customers revealed being satisfied with the internet speed (68% rated it positively), nearly rated it only as "OK", and very few respondents were unsatisfied. In terms of pricing, while two-thirds of customers consider it fair or reasonable, about one-third believe the price is high.

So, many consumers still recognize that it could offer better value for money, something they see as key when choosing a provider.

This gap between acceptable service and perceived value for money indicates that Altice must further optimize its pricing strategies and improve perceived quality to fully meet market expectations.

Hypothesis 1 is confirmed, but the results suggest that MEO should consider some strategic improvements to stay competitive.

In Hypothesis 2, where we tested whether adopting innovation strategies has helped Altice Portugal attract more customers and improve its market reputation, we conclude that we cannot fully confirm it.

Although Altice has invested deeply in innovation, like the 5G API SPRINT program, adoption of CAMARA APIs, and more than 17 international patents, customer experience does not fully reflect this innovation strategy. While 80% of respondents valued MEO's technologies like 5G and fiber optics, this interest has not yet transformed into a stronger preference or an evident competitive advantage, as MEO continues to fall behind NOS among survey participants.

Moreover, the data shows that most customers recognize progress in digital tools and services, whereas only a few find the experience significantly more efficient. For instance, 52,1% acknowledged improvements in customer service, but with noticeable failures; 26.8% noticed no change at all. These responses suggest that innovation, although present, is not yet consistent or impactful enough to influence reputation and loyalty in a meaningful way. This evidence underscores Christensen's theory of disruptive innovation, which stresses the need for solutions that meet unaddressed or emerging customer needs. Innovation must be visible, relevant, and improve aspects of the customer experience.

The open-ended responses reinforce this interpretation. Participants mentioned issues such as poor coverage in certain areas, non-customizable TV packages, and inconsistency between what is promised and what is given. These concerns indicate more profound organizational challenges that go beyond technological upgrades - namely, the need for better communication, transparency, and alignment between service performance and customer expectations.

These findings reflect the ideas of Boyles (2022) and Hussain (2023), who argue that innovation only becomes truly effective when it is supported by internal transformation, a clear strategic vision, and a strong relationship of trust with the customer.

To sum up, in spite of the bases being solid and the technological development being promising, the results reveal that for innovation to be fully noticed and valued, it must also enhance the customer experience. This brings up opportunities for Altice Portugal to turn innovation into a competitive advantage - not only through infrastructure, but also through more human, transparent, and flexible service strategies.

STRATEGIC SOLUTIONS

As mentioned previously, MEO Empresas recently introduced a bold initiative focused on digital transformation: the 5G API SPRINT program, developed in partnership with Altice Labs (the company's Innovation, Research and Development Center). This program invites companies, start-ups, and developers to create innovative solutions using standardized APIs from MEO's mobile network. With this action, MEO aims to support and promote tech talent by exploring the full potential of its mobile network capabilities, especially 5G (MEO, 2024).

Additionally, MEO joined the GSMA Open Gateway and adopted CAMARA APIs -standardized interfaces that simplify the connection between applications and mobile networks like 5G. This integration offers significant advantages such as secure mobile device authentication and access to SIM card location data. These moves not only boost MEO Empresas' national and international competitiveness but also highlight its commitment to staying ahead through innovation (MEO, 2024).

However, survey results indicate that technological innovation alone is insufficient. MEO must rethink certain strategies to build stronger relationships with customers and stand out in an increasingly competitive market.

Looking upon the findings from this study and the theoretical frameworks discussed in the literature review, this action plan presents five evidence-based strategies that aim to strengthen the connection between Altice Portugal's innovation efforts and customer satisfaction. These recommendations are not isolated interventions; rather, they represent a coherent and theoretically grounded roadmap that seeks to improve value creation, increase loyalty, and position Altice as a more flexible, customer-focused organization. They reflect principles from organizational change theory, open innovation, transformational and authentic leadership, and disruptive innovation. Each initiative considers not just practical business outcomes but also the human, cultural, and structural aspects of change.

1. Friendly Customizable Plan

One of the most evident concerns among survey respondents was the high cost of services relative to the quality received. Consumers increasingly demand services that fit their actual usage and preferences.

So the first recommendation focuses on offering fully customizable service plans, allowing customers to adjust their subscriptions that better reflect their individual needs. Instead of fixed bundles, users would be able to select only the services they value, such as specific TV channels, internet speeds, or mobile data packages, ensuring a more efficient and satisfying customer experience. This approach directly responds to customer feedback gathered through survey data, in which several participants expressed frustration over paying for features they do not use, particularly in TV services. One participant specifically said, “Let us choose our channels,” highlighting a desire for personalization and autonomy. From a business perspective, this change would not only increase perceived value and customer satisfaction but would also reduce churn, as personalized offerings are more likely to build emotional attachment and loyalty. It would also help the company earn more from each customer by offering optional extra services, without increasing the prices.

This initiative is closely linked to Christensen’s Disruptive Innovation Theory, which emphasizes the importance of responding to underserved market segments through simplified, more adaptable solutions. Additionally, it aligns with Bagno and Faria’s view that innovation should deliver greater value with fewer wasted resources, offering “more for less” in both design and delivery.

2. Customer Rewards Program

A second strategy involves recognizing and rewarding long-term customers by implementing a loyalty program that provides benefits to clients who have remained with the company over a long period. For example, customers with over ten years of uninterrupted service could receive discounted rates or exclusive offers.

Although simple, this gesture holds symbolic and strategic value. Several respondents noted that despite their long relationship with MEO, they felt overlooked, a feeling that often turns into churn or passive dissatisfaction. Therefore, introducing loyalty incentives is a cost-effective retention strategy that reinforces emotional bonds and strengthens brand trust. It is based on principles of authentic leadership, as described by Forbes, where transparency, fairness, and values-based decision-making play a vital role in cultivating trust. Furthermore, Sutton’s concept of emotional leadership highlights the significance of symbolic gestures in validating customer relationships and acknowledging their long-term contribution to the company’s success.

3. Reward by bringing more clients

A third recommendation proposes the creation of a structured referral program that rewards existing customers for successfully introducing new clients to MEO’s services. For instance, a €20 credit could be awarded for each successful referral, while new customers might receive a temporary upgrade or welcome discount. This strategy capitalizes on the enduring power of word-of-mouth marketing, which remains particularly effective among younger demographics and within digitally connected communities. More than just a sales tool, the referral program would foster a sense of ownership and participation among customers, encouraging them to become active brand advocates. From a theoretical standpoint, this initiative echoes Hirst's transformational leadership model by promoting shared goals and collaborative engagement. It also reflects Hussain's approach to organizational change, emphasizing emotionally driven behavior as a key lever in fostering growth and commitment.

4. Build a Culture of Strategic Transparency and Trust Through Internal Communication Reform

A common complaint noted in reviews and surveys is the lack of clarity and openness regarding service delivery. This encompasses concerns about service continuity, package pricing, or promotional offers that are not fulfilled. While these do not always capture organizational intent, they erode brand reputation and trust. In the case of Altice, the company may benefit from a strategic communication change initiative focused on internal alignment and external clarity. Internally, this encompasses stronger, more honest, and consistent communication training with frontline staff, as well as clear protocols and scripts for supervisors. Externally, Altice should commit publicly to minimum performance standards such as response times and network performance, regularly report on service standards fulfillment, and develop tangible accountability markers with high visibility.

This approach heavily incorporates Authentic Leadership Theory, which focuses on the importance of self-awareness, transparency, and moral alignment as trust-building pillars. Organizations that demonstrate bold, clear leadership tend to be rewarded with enduring loyalty, as noted by Forbes. Moreover, Hirst and Sutton's studies on transformational and emotional leadership highlight that communication transcends information; it is the process of constructing meaning. Employees and customers alike want to grasp the rationale driving decisions.

5. See Through Innovation (STI) program

Altice Portugal should create a customer-facing innovation program called "See through Innovation", where real customers are invited to participate in the testing and development of new technologies and services before they are launched commercially. Instead of keeping innovation confined within Altice Labs or internal teams, this program would bring it to the public by involving selected users directly in the innovation cycle.

The initiative would focus on specific, high-impact areas that customers frequently complain about, such as network reliability, pricing clarity, TV and internet service customization, or app usability. These customers would test solutions that are currently under development (e.g., a new version of the MEO app, improvements in router firmware, a simplified package system, or even network optimizations in underserved areas) and provide structured feedback through digital surveys or support channels.

In return for their time and insights, participants would receive small but meaningful incentives: discounts on bills, faster upgrades, early access to new services, or recognition in the customer community (such as a digital badge or status).

This approach is not merely operational; it is deeply aligned with Henry Chesbrough's Open Innovation Theory, which argues that companies must embrace external contributions from customers, partners, and even competitors to expand their problem-solving capacity and bring products to market more effectively. Instead of treating customers as endpoints of a finished product, this model treats them as essential contributors to its success. The result is a system where innovation is accelerated, grounded in reality, and continuously improved through iteration.

Furthermore, this strategy embodies Robert Sutton's vision of transformational leadership, in which leaders step back to allow experimentation and support environments where teams, or in this case, customers, can meaningfully engage with innovation. Sutton emphasizes that successful leaders act not only as "plumbers," solving practical challenges, but also as "poets," inspiring participation through clarity of vision and emotional resonance. By opening the doors of innovation to users, Altice would be practicing a form of distributed leadership that fosters emotional investment and mutual trust, both critical in times of organizational change.

The concept also resonates with Chris Hirst's argument that successful transformation depends not only on technical competence, but also on cultural alignment. If innovation remains disconnected from the lived experiences of customers, it fails to drive real change. However, when customers are involved in shaping the services they use, change becomes cultural, a shared process rooted in communication, transparency, and trust. These elements also reflect the principles of authentic leadership as defined by Forbes (2024), particularly in terms of transparency, fairness, and active listening, all qualities that are deeply embedded in a co-creation model.

Ultimately, "See through Innovation" is a low-cost, high-impact strategy that enables Altice to transform its innovation efforts into a visible and collaborative journey.

CONCLUSION

This study highlights the complex but important relationship between innovation, organizational change, and consumer perception in today's competitive business environment. Through the case of Altice Portugal, we observed that significant investments in technology and flexible management structures do not automatically lead to a better public image or increased customer satisfaction.

While the company has made significant strides in digital transformation and R&D, particularly with Altice Labs, there is still a gap between innovation and the real-world user experience. Complaints about fair pricing, network reliability, and unmet service expectations indicate that innovation must go beyond infrastructure; it needs to focus more on people. It should be clear and responsive.

Moreover, the research confirms that innovation should not be viewed as just a technological upgrade. It should be seen as a cultural shift. Strong leadership, clear strategy, and ongoing communication are crucial to create environments where innovation can thrive and be appreciated both inside and outside the organization.

All in all, this study shows that real competitive advantage comes from how well a company matches its innovations to customer needs and expectations. Successful transformation relies on the ability to listen, adjust, and deliver, rather than just making promises. For Altice Portugal and similar companies, the way forward includes smarter strategies and more human-focused methods of change.

REFERENCES

Altice Labs. (2023). *5G-AUTO - Desenvolvimento e teste de tecnologia V2X 5G para condução autónoma.* https://www.alticelabs.com/innovation/rdi-projects/5g-auto/

Altice Labs. (s.d.). *Our History.* https://www.alticelabs.com/history/

Altice Portugal. (2024, October). *Altice Portugal divulga resultados referentes ao terceiro trimestre de 2024.* https://institucional.meo.pt/media/comunicados/2024/novembro/altice-portugal-divulga-resultados-referentes-ao-terceiro-trimestre-de-2024

ANACOM. (2024, February 23). *4,7 milhões de subscritores de pacote de serviços em 2023.* https://www.anacom-consumidor.pt/-/4-7-milhoes-de-subscritores-de-pacote-de-servicos-em-2023

Bagno, R. B., & de Faria, A. F. (2022). *O Modelo das Duas Rodas: Uma Referência para o Sistema de Gestão da Inovação em Pequenas e Médias Empresas.* Editora UFV. DIGI Portugal. (s.d.). *Quem somos.* Disponível em: https://www.digi.pt/quem-somos

Empresas, M. E. O. (n.d.) *5G API Sprint.* https://www.meo.pt/empresas/5g-api-sprint?blog=5g-api-sprint-programa-inovacao-aplicacoes-diferenciadoras

Executive Digest. (2025, May 22). *Altice Labs obtém nova patente europeia para otimização de redes de fibra ótica.* https://executivedigest.sapo.pt/noticias/altice-labs-obtem-nova-patente-europeia-para-otimizacao-de-redes-de-fibra-otica/

Ferreira, I. N. S. (2024). *Supply Chain and Procurement Performance Assessment - a Case Study at Altice Portugal.* [Relatório de Estágio, Universidade Europeia].

Ferreira, R. J. (2020). Integração do cliente no processo de inovação: Estudo de caso na Altice Portugal [Dissertação de mestrado, Iscte - Instituto Universitário de Lisboa]. Repositório Iscte. http://hdl.handle.net/10071/21264

Figueiredo, A. (2025, abril). *Estamos prontos para liderar a próxima fase da transformação tecnológica em Portugal* [Publicação no LinkedIn]. https://www.linkedin.com/feed/update/urn:li:activity:7333161873338531840/

Fontanela, C., Burtet, G., Pereira, R., & Marroco, A. (2021). *Open innovation: the role of scientific and technological parks in the transformation of traditional industries.* [Brazilian Journal of Development]. DOI: 10.34117/bjdv7n6-160

Galles, K. (2021, August 10). *Strategies to scale innovation from a Stanford researcher.* Qualia Blog. https://blog.qualia.com/scale-change-management/

Hirst, C. (2024). *Mudança sem tretas: Um guia de 8 passos para líderes.* Escolar Editora.

IMD. (2025, May). *What Is Disruptive Innovation? 10 real-world examples.* https://www.imd.org/blog/innovation/what-is-disruptive-innovation/

Jesus, C. (2024, August 14). *Agilidade, inovação e segurança: os alicerces do futuro do setor das telecomunicações*. Forbes Portugal. https://www.forbespt.com/agilidade-inovacao-e-seguranca-os-alicerces-do-futuro-do-setor-das-telecomunicacoes/

MEO. (2025, February). *MEO lidera em velocidade e qualidade da internet móvel em Portugal.* https://institucional.meo.pt/media/comunicados/2025/fevereiro/meo-lidera-em-velocidade-e-qualidade-da-internet-movel-em-portugal

MEO. (2025). *História*. https://institucional.meo.pt/meo/historia

MEO. (2025a, April). *Comunicado de Resultados MEO - 4T 2024*. https://conteudos.meo.pt/institucional/documentos/pt/media/comunicados/2025/Abril/Comunicado-Resultados-MEO-4T-2024.pdf

MEO. (n.d.) *Inovação para liderar o futuro*. https://institucional.meo.pt/inovacao/inovacao-para-liderar

Miranda, R. (2023, May 9) *Inovação aberta: vantagens e desafios da colaboração entre empresas e startups*. Linkedin. https://pt.linkedin.com/pulse/inovação-aberta-vantagens-e-desafios-da-colaboração-entre-miranda-1f MJV Team. (2022, December 19). *Tudo sobre mudança organizacional: conceitos e boas práticas*. https://www.mjvinnovation.pt/blog/tudo-sobre-mudanca-organizacional-conceito-e-boas-praticas/

NOS. (2025). *O nosso ADN: Inovação*. https://www.nos.pt/pt/institucional/a-nos/o-nosso-adn/inovacao

NOS. (2025). *A nossa história. Conheça os principais marcos da NOS*. https://www.nos.pt/pt/institucional/a-nos/o-nosso-adn/historia

Nunes, F. (2025, June 3). *Entrada da Digi em Portugal coloca reclamações à Anacom em rota de crescimento*. https://eco.sapo.pt/2025/06/03/entrada-da-digi-em-portugal-coloca-reclamacoes-a-anacom-em-rota-de-crescimento/

Público. (2019, May 10). *Ganhar clientes de televisão "é o grande desafio deste ano" para a Altice*. https://www.publico.pt/2019/05/10/economia/noticia/ganhar-clientes-televisao-desafio-ano-altice-1872200

Público. (2025, março 3). *Queixas caem nas telecomunicações, mas sobem nos serviços postais em 2024*. https://www.publico.pt/2025/03/03/economia/noticia/queixas-caem-telecomunicacoes-sobem-servicos-postais-2024-2124608

Rasmussen University. (2023). *What is Organizational Change Theory and How Can it Empower You?* https://www.rasmussen.edu/degrees/business/blog/what-is-organizational-change-theory/

Reis, F. (2020). *Manual de Gestão das Organizações*. Edições Sílabo.

Ribeiro, S. (2024, November 8). *Impacto da Digi? "nós competimos com quadidade", diz CEO da Meo*. Negócios.pt https://www.jornaldenegocios.pt/empresas/telecomunicacoes/detalhe/impacto-da-digi-nos-competimos-com-qualidade-diz-ceo-da-meo

Stanford University. (n.d.). *A guide to innovation management*. Stanford Online. https://online.stanford.edu/guide-innovation-management

Visão. (2020, March 24). *Receitas da Altice Portugal sobem 1,7% em 2019 para 2.110 milhões de euros.* Visão. https://visao.pt/atualidade/economia/2020-03-24-receitas-da-altice-portugal-sobem-17-em-2019-para-2-110-me/

Vodafone. (2024). *Ainda mais velocidade: Fibra da Vodafone Portugal atinge 50 Gbps em teste pioneiro.* Disponível em: https://www.vodafone.pt/press-releases/2024/9/ainda-mais-velocidade-fibra-da-vodafone-portugal-atinge-50-gbps-em-teste-pioneiro.html

KEY TERMS AND DEFINITIONS

5G Technology: The fifth generation of mobile network allows for faster internet, improved connections, and supports technologies like smart devices and real-time communication.

Altice Labs: An innovation center focused on creating new products and services for the telecommunications and information technology sectors.

Competitive Positioning: When a company gains a stronger market position because of higher profits, more customers, a better reputation, or matching supply and demand effectively. This gives the company an advantage over competitors.

Cultural Adaptability: The ability of people in a company to adapt to external changes. It means adopting behaviors and strategies that help achieve shared goals in a changing environment.

Customer Loyalty: When customers are happy with a company's service and choose to stay with it, even if there are other options available.

Digital Transformation: The digital changes that companies adopt, often linked to new technology. These changes affect processes, products, and services, making them more modern and aligned with customer needs.

Disruptive Innovation: Changing a product or service to make it simpler, more affordable, and easier to use, attracting more customers, even if it means offering fewer features.

Innovation Management: The process where managers make strategic decisions, create new ideas, and develop innovative products or services. This helps the company stay active and competitive in the market.

Innovation: The introduction of something new and valuable in the company, aiming to attract more customers and stand out from competitors in the market.

Internal Communication: The exchange of information between employees. It ensures that everyone receives, understands, and acts on the necessary information for the organization to work well.

Open Innovation: When both external and internal ideas influence how a company innovates. This means using ideas from inside and outside the company to stay competitive and improve innovation.

Open system: A set of dynamic factors that interact inside and outside the company. It allows the company to use inputs (resources) and transform them into effective and efficient results (outputs) for customers.

Organizational Change: Changes or adjustments that a company needs to make. These changes can be small or big, like new internal processes, communication, leadership style, or the use of technology.

Organizational Culture: The environment shaped by shared values, beliefs, habits, and behaviors of people in the company. Their interactions follow company norms, creating a unique culture.

Service Reliability: The ability of a service to perform consistently and meet customer expectations over time.

Transformational Leadership: A leadership style that inspires and motivates employees to reach their full potential. The leader influences, supports, and encourages the team to achieve success.

Chapter 9
Harnessing Digital Transformation and Artificial Intelligence for Building Systemic Agility in Organizations

Sivadi Balakrishna
http://orcid.org/0000-0003-0681-987X
Vignan's Foundation for Science, Technology, and Research, India

Vijender Kumar Solanki
http://orcid.org/0000-0001-5784-1052
Stanley College of Engineering and Technology for Women, India

Brij Kishor Tiwari
SR University, India

ABSTRACT

In today's fast-changing and tech-driven business world, companies have to keep changing to be strong, competitive, and ready for the future. This chapter looks at how digital transformation and artificial intelligence (AI) help organizations be more flexible by speeding up decision-making, improving forecasting powers, and increasing adaptability. It looks into how digital maturity, leadership adaptability, and technology integration methods work together to promote systemic agility. The chapter also talks about how important it is to have a workforce that is digitally educated and the policy frameworks that enable the use of technology in a way that is ethical and sustainable. The chapter gives organisations a path for finding a balance between technical progress and human-centered flexibility by combining ideas from both theoretical models and real-world examples. This will help them flourish in times of uncertainty and constant change.

DOI: 10.4018/979-8-3373-4027-2.ch009

1. INTRODUCTION

Digital transformation and artificial intelligence (AI) have become the two main forces behind organisational agility in a time when technology is changing quickly, global markets are unstable, and society and the economy are in upheaval. Industries all across the world are under more pressure than ever to adapt to changing markets, expectations for sustainability, and disruptive innovation. Companies are changing how they work in the US, Germany, India, Brazil, and other rising countries to stay strong in a world that is volatile, unpredictable, complex, and ambiguous (VUCA). This worldwide digital acceleration has changed agility from a nice-to-have quality to a strategic must-have. Today, companies compete not based on their resources or location, but on how well they can predict change, adjust their plans, and keep coming up with new ideas (Atienza-Barba et al., 2024; Bux et al., 2025). The idea of agility comes from the early work of Goldman et al. (1995) and Dove (2001), who saw it as the capacity of businesses to do well in unpredictable situations by being flexible, proactive, and focused on the needs of their customers. This idea has changed in the digital age into systemic agility, which is a combination of digital technology, human adaptability, leadership vision, and government responsiveness. The extensive amalgamation of AI, IoT, and cloud computing has facilitated a transition for organisations from reactive adaptation to predictive and intelligent transformation, therefore changing their methods of sensing, interpreting, and responding to change (Zhang et al., 2023).

Despite significant academic and business investment in digitalisation, empirical research indicates that numerous organisations continue to face challenges in attaining sustainable agility. Technological fragmentation, ethical issues with AI use, a lack of digital skills, and insufficient governance frameworks are all real-world problems. These restrictions make it hard to turn digital promise into real-world results. Empirical research indicates theoretical contradictions; some studies assert that digital maturity drives agility (Westerman et al., 2014), while others underscore leadership adaptability and human capital as mediators of effective transformation (Sacavém et al., 2025). These differences show that there are gaps in our knowledge of how technology, people, and policy all work together to make organisations more flexible. This chapter seeks to address existing research and practical deficiencies by creating a cohesive framework that connects digital transformation and AI-driven decision intelligence with systemic organisational agility. It enhances both theoretical and practical domains by providing a comprehensive insight into the interplay of technology innovation, leadership adaptability, and governance frameworks in the creation of resilient organisations. The primary research question directing this project is:

> "How can digital transformation and artificial intelligence together make organisations more agile, which will make them more competitive, adaptable, and sustainable in a digital economy that is changing quickly?"

The main goal of this conceptual study is to provide a framework that shows how digital transformation and artificial intelligence (AI) work together to make organisations more agile. The objective of this study is to enhance theoretical comprehension and practical insights on the interplay of technology, human adaptability, and governance ethics in fostering sustainable agility inside organisations. Utilising a qualitative conceptual-analytical framework, the study amalgamates findings from current peer-reviewed research published from 2020 to 2025, obtained from sources like Scopus, Web of Science, and IGI Global. It employs Dynamic Capability Theory as its primary theoretical framework, while also integrating Sociotechnical Systems Theory, Transformational Leadership Theory, and the Technology–Organization–Environment (TOE) Framework to elucidate the interconnections among digital systems, human capital, and governance mechanisms. The goal is not to test hypotheses but to combine what we already know into a clear conceptual framework that shows how AI-enabled digital transformation can help organisations become more agile, resilient, and ethically sustainable over time in a wide range of industries and regions. The chapter aims to provide routes for future scholars, organisational leaders, and policymakers about the convergence of technology and human aspects to establish adaptable, ethically governed, and sustainable firms. Table 1 shows the recent empirical anchors used in various domains with key statistical evidences over 2020 to 2025.

Table 1. Recent Empirical Anchors Used

Domain	2020–2025 Evidence Cited	Key Statistic
Global digital economy	World Economic Forum (2022)	70% of GDP digitally influenced
AI adoption	McKinsey (2023); OECD (2024)	>60% of firms use AI
Transformation failure rate	Deloitte (2023)	44% initiatives fail
Cloud and remote work growth	McKinsey (2023)	Cloud + 50%; remote work + 300%
Innovation cycle gains	PwC (2024)	AI-mature firms + 30–50% faster innovation

This chapter lays the groundwork for understanding how intentional technology integration may make organisations more flexible in a world where digital is the norm. It starts by talking about why being agile is so important in today's world, then it talks about how technology is a vital facilitator, and then it talks about the goals and structure of the conversation that follows. The chapter stresses that the solution to long-term competitiveness is to link technology with adaptive leadership and agile processes. This will make organisations that are not just efficient but also ready to change.

1.1 The Need for Organizational Agility in the Digital Era

In the digital age, changes in all sectors happen faster than ever before because of new technologies, changing client needs, and changing market conditions. Organisations now work in a VUCA (volatile, unpredictable, complex, and ambiguous) world that requires them to be able to adapt quickly and come up with new ideas all the time. Traditional hierarchical structures and rigid operational models are becoming less and less able to handle how quickly things are changing. As new digital technologies like artificial intelligence (AI), cloud computing, the Internet of Things (IoT), and data analytics change the way businesses work, being able to adapt quickly has become an important factor in long-term success. Agility helps businesses notice changes early, react well, and keep up their performance even when things are unpredictable (Bux et al., 2025). The COVID-19 epidemic made it even clearer how important being flexible is for survival. Many businesses had to deal with problems in their supply chains, workforces, and customer behaviour that had never happened before. People who have previously adopted digital tools and flexible ways of doing business may quickly change course by working from home, changing how they do business, and addressing client needs through digital channels. The digital acceleration that happened after the epidemic has changed agility from a strategic advantage to a basic skill. Organisations can no longer only use technology from time to time; they need to make digital agility a part of their culture, strategy, and structure in order to stay strong in the face of constant change.

Also, the merging of technology and human agility has become quite important for dealing with digital disruption. To be able to respond quickly to changes, organisations need to use real-time data insights, smart automation, and flexible leadership. So, agility isn't only about speed; it's also about being able to plan ahead, be flexible, and learn. In the digital age, successful companies see change as a chance to grow, not a danger. They use technology to not just make their operations more efficient but also to come up with new business models, rethink the customer experience, and create ecosystems for creativity. This change in the way things work signals the start of a new era of digital organisational agility, where being able to respond quickly, work together, and keep changing are the keys to long-term competitiveness.

Figure 1. Key external and internal drivers influencing the need for organizational agility in the digital era

Figure 1 shows the main internal and external factors that affect an organization's agility in the digital age. In the middle is Organisational Agility, which stands for the main skill that lets businesses quickly adapt to change. The inner circle shows internal motivations including the need for leaders to be flexible, the need for cross-functional cooperation, and the need to make decisions in real time. All of these things make an organisation more responsive and cohesive. The outer ring shows outside factors that put ongoing pressure on businesses to change, such market instability and the digital acceleration that happened after the epidemic (Sacavém et al., 2025). These layers show how the combination of internal skills and external environmental elements affects an organization's capacity to be flexible, creative, and competitive in a digital world that is changing quickly.

1.2 Technology as a Catalyst for Agility

In the digital era, technology is the main thing that helps organisations become more flexible. Businesses now use technology not only to make their operations more efficient, but also as a strategic tool that changes the way they think, make decisions, and act. The integration of new technologies like artificial intelligence (AI), big data analytics, cloud computing, blockchain, and the Internet of Things (IoT) has changed the way businesses work by making it possible to make decisions in real time, get predictive insights, and work together across departments. These technologies provide businesses the ability to quickly adapt to changes in the market, improve their internal processes, and keep coming up with new ideas, which makes agility a part of how they do business.

Digital technologies break down old organisational barriers and make it easier for departments to see what's going on, which speeds up the flow of information and makes it easier to work together. For example, cloud-based platforms make it easy for teams that are spread out over a wide area to work together, while AI-driven analytics provide executives with useful information that helps them see patterns and lower risks before they happen (Zhang et., 2023). Automation tools also let companies move people from boring duties to more strategic, creative, and decision-making roles, which makes them more efficient and adaptable. Companies can work more accurately, quickly, and reliably in a world that is always changing because to the change from manual, process-driven models to data-driven ecosystems.

Technology also works as a strategic amplifier of learning and creativity. Digital systems let businesses try things out, get feedback, and quickly come up with new ideas, just like the agile development methods employed in the software sector. This ongoing feedback loop fosters a culture of adaptation and responsiveness that transcends technological functions, influencing both strategic and operational spheres. But just using technology doesn't mean you'll be agile; you need to make sure that your digital investments are in line with your organization's goals, culture, and leadership vision. When technology, people, and processes come together to create a dynamic environment that enables constant change, true agility happens. So, technology is not simply an enabler; it is also the main engine that drives adaptive capacity, innovation, and long-term competitive advantage in the digital age.

Table 2. Evaluation of Organizational Agility and Technology Integration Across Various Countries (2023–2025)

Country / Region	Focus of Digital Agility Initiatives	Key Technologies Adopted	Leadership & Cultural Drivers	Challenges Identified	Reference / Source Alignment
United States	Emphasis on AI-driven decision-making and predictive analytics for operational agility	AI, Cloud, Big Data, Automation	Transformational leadership, cross-functional collaboration	Ethical AI use, cybersecurity, and digital skill gaps	(Atienza-Barba et al., 2024); (Bux et al., 2025)
United Kingdom	Focus on digital transformation governance and agile project management models	Cloud computing, Data analytics, Blockchain	Distributed leadership, hybrid work culture	Legacy systems, regulatory compliance	(Sacavém et al., 2025)
Germany	Industry 4.0 adoption to drive systemic agility in manufacturing	IoT, Cyber-Physical Systems, AI	Engineering-led innovation culture	Integration between legacy systems and new digital models	(Zhang et al., 2023)
China	Rapid adoption of AI for real-time intelligence and supply chain agility	AI, IoT, 5G, Edge computing	State-supported innovation, centralized strategy	Data privacy, workforce upskilling	(Atienza-Barba et al., 2024)
Singapore	Government-led smart economy initiatives promoting agility in SMEs	AI, IoT, Blockchain	Visionary digital leadership, strong governance	Talent shortage, cost of advanced technologies	(Zhang et al., 2023)

continued on following page

Table 2. Continued

Country / Region	Focus of Digital Agility Initiatives	Key Technologies Adopted	Leadership & Cultural Drivers	Challenges Identified	Reference / Source Alignment
Japan	Integration of robotics and AI to enhance workforce adaptability	AI, Robotics, IoT	Continuous improvement (Kaizen), knowledge-sharing culture	Workforce aging, resistance to change	(Zhang et al., 2023)
Australia	Focus on digital transformation in services and higher education sectors	Cloud computing, Data analytics	Transformational leadership, adaptive strategy	Cybersecurity readiness, high digital costs	(Sacavém et al., 2025)
Brazil	Growing adoption of AI for agility in public administration and SMEs	AI, Big Data, Cloud	Emerging digital leadership models	Economic volatility, infrastructure challenges	(Bux et al., 2025)
United Arab Emirates (UAE)	National AI strategy emphasizing agility and innovation ecosystems	AI, Cloud, Blockchain	Vision-driven governance, agile leadership in public sector	Limited AI regulatory frameworks	(Atienza-Barba et al., 2024)
India	Accelerated post-pandemic digital transformation with focus on scalable agility	Cloud, AI, IoT, Digital platforms	Transformational leadership, digital inclusivity	Digital divide, infrastructure limitations	(Bux et al., 2025); (Sacavém et al., 2025)

Table 2 provides a comparative evaluation of how different countries are implementing organizational agility through digital transformation and AI integration between 2023 and 2025. It highlights that developed nations like the U.S., U.K., Germany, and Japan focus on systemic agility driven by mature digital infrastructures, AI governance, and strong leadership practices. Emerging economies such as India and Brazil emphasize adaptive agility by leveraging digital platforms and leadership development to overcome infrastructure and policy challenges. Countries like Singapore and the UAE demonstrate government-led strategic agility, combining innovation ecosystems with governance-driven transformation. Overall, the analysis reveals that while technology adoption is crucial, leadership adaptability, data-driven culture, and ethical digital practices are the key enablers of sustained agility across global organizations.

1.3 Rationale of the Study

The reason for doing this analysis is the ongoing gap between how quickly technology is changing and how quickly organisations can adapt to it throughout the world. Digital transformation has become a strategic need; nonetheless, current worldwide research shows that more than 44% of digital efforts do not achieve their desired performance goals (Deloitte, 2023). Numerous organisations have effectively integrated digital tools and AI systems; nevertheless, they often lack the requisite human and structural agility to leverage these technologies efficiently (PwC, 2024; Zhang et al., 2023). The current research frequently dissects the technological and human aspects of agility instead of analysing them as a cohesive system (Teece et al., 2016; Bux et al., 2025). Furthermore, rising economies—characterized by evolving digital maturity, legislative frameworks, and skill ecosystems—are inadequately represented in empirical research (Kant & Ashuro, 2025). These inadequacies highlight the necessity for a comprehensive conceptual framework that integrates technology, leadership, and governance ethics into a singular theoretical structure.

This study emphasises systemic agility above functional responsiveness, offering a comprehensive, systems-level perspective on the coevolution of technology and human skills. This reasoning places the chapter at the forefront of studies concerning ethical digital transformation and sustainable organisational performance.

1.4 Significance and Contribution

The importance of this study lies in its potential to enhance both theoretical understanding and management practice in the area of digital transformation. In theory, it adds to the body of knowledge by:

- Enhancing Dynamic Capability Theory by including AI and ethical governance as dynamic facilitators of agility.
- Introducing Systemic Agility as a multidimensional concept that includes the ability of technology, people, and institutions to adapt.
- Giving future empirical researchers a conceptual base that they may turn into quantifiable variables.

In terms of practical use, the study's approach gives executives and politicians useful advice on how to:

- Make sure that your digital investments are in line with your plans for developing leaders and retraining workers.
- Use ethical AI governance mechanisms to make sure that people are held accountable, that things are clear, and that stakeholders trust you.
- Create flexible organisational frameworks that help businesses stay strong in unstable global markets.

This chapter helps the global conversation on sustainable digital competitiveness by bridging the gap between academics and practitioners. It also helps policymakers devise policies that will make digital economies more accessible.

This study is innovative because it combines technology, human capital, and ethical governance to provide a new way of thinking about agility as a systemic organisational competency. This chapter integrates digital transformation and AI adoption into a cohesive theoretical framework, incorporating leadership and ethical considerations, in contrast to previous research that analyse them in isolation. Additionally, the research presents the Systemic Agility Framework, an innovative construct that amalgamates many theoretical traditions—dynamic capacities, sociotechnical design, and transformational leadership—into a cohesive conceptual structure. This uniqueness guarantees that the chapter not only introduces novel theoretical concepts but also establishes a reproducible framework for empirical investigation across many contexts and economies.

1.5 Objectives and Structure of the Chapter

The main goal of this chapter is to look at how digital transformation and artificial intelligence (AI) help organisations be more flexible in today's business world. It seeks to offer both a theoretical and practical comprehension of how the use of technology, flexibility in leadership, and systemic alignment together enhance resilience and creativity. The chapter aims to connect theory and practice by providing a complete framework for developing agility through intentional technology integration. In doing so, it adds to the larger conversation about how businesses can stay competitive and relevant in a world where technology is changing quickly, consumer habits are changing, and there are many unknowns throughout the world.

This chapter specifically aims to achieve the following goals:

- To examine the philosophical underpinnings and aspects of organisational agility, highlighting its strategic significance in the digital age.
- To look at how AI technology and digital transformation projects might improve adaptive decision-making, operational efficiency, and the ability to come up with new ideas.
- To talk about how leadership, culture, and human capital can help technology-driven agility.
- To look at concerns of governance, policy, and sustainability that come up when people use digital technology.
- To put up a comprehensive framework and actionable plan for attaining systemic agility via technology.

The arrangement of this chapter shows these goals. After this introduction, Section 2 goes into more detail about the ideas behind organisational agility and how it relates to having a competitive edge. Section 3 discusses the statement of the problem. In Section 4, we look at how digital transformation may help organisations be more agile. We talk about how digital maturity and organisational culture play a role. Section 5 talks about AI and making decisions based on data, while Section 6 talks about leadership and creating changes that focus on people. Section 7 talks about policies, governance, and the environment. Section 8 outlines a comprehensive framework for enhancing systemic agility. Section 9 looks at problems, hazards, and new trends, and Section 10 finishes with strategic suggestions and areas for further study.

2. CONCEPTUAL FOUNDATIONS OF ORGANIZATIONAL AGILITY

In the digital age, organisational agility has gone from being a buzzword for managers to a strategic need. As industries deal with new technologies, globalisation, and changing customer needs, agility has become the most important part of an organization's ability to stay strong and competitive. The conceptual basis of agility is in an organization's capacity to perceive external shifts, capitalise on new opportunities, and adeptly reallocate resources to sustain long-term success. This part looks at the theoretical ideas behind organisational agility, its main parts, and how it relates to long-term competitive advantage.

2.1 Defining Organizational Agility

People in management science, organisational behaviour, and information systems have all given the phrase "organisational agility" different meanings. While interpretations differ, a consistent theme exists across all definitions: agility signifies an organization's ability to swiftly adjust and engage in ongoing learning in response to environmental instability.

Goldman et al. (1995) were among the first to describe agility as the capacity of an organisation to thrive in a constantly changing and unpredictable environment by quickly and effectively meeting the requirements of customers as they change. Later, Dove (2001) stressed that agility is the capacity to adapt to change in a proactive and creative way, not only reactively. In the field of information systems, Sambamurthy et al. (2003) defined digital agility as a company's capacity to quickly use IT resources to perceive, respond to, and adapt to digital disturbances.

Modern definitions of organisational agility go beyond just being fast or flexible; they include the capacity to change strategy, structures, procedures, and technology all at once. So, agility has three main parts:

- Sensing is always keeping an eye on the outside world for signs of change.
- Responding is taking timely and effective steps to deal with the developments.
- Learning is making the lessons learnt from change part of the way things are done in order to be more responsive in the future.

Agility in the context of digital transformation goes beyond merely making changes to how things work. It also entails being able to see the big picture and react to new ideas. It helps businesses succeed in times of change by using technology, talent, and data-driven decision-making to constantly reinvent themselves.

2.2 Dimensions of Agility

Organisational agility is made up of a number of different factors that together decide how adaptable and resilient a business is. The most generally used framework divides agility into three parts that are all connected: operational agility, strategic agility, and systemic agility.

2.2.1 Agility in Operations

Operational agility means that a business can handle its daily tasks well while yet being able to adapt to changes in demand, production, or consumer demands that happen quickly. It means making the most of workflows, shortening cycle times, and using technology to automate and speed up processes. Data-driven process management, agile project management, and scalable IT infrastructure are all ways to make operations more flexible in the digital age. This dimension makes sure that businesses stay productive, focused on customers, and cost-effective even when things are changing quickly.

2.2.2 Strategic Flexibility

Strategic agility is all about how well an organisation can change over time, which means being able to see new possibilities and take advantage of them. It includes flexible skills like strategic sensing, scenario planning, and managing innovation. When disruptive forces hit, organisations with strategic agility can quickly change their business models, move resources around, and make new relationships. For example, Amazon and Google show strategic agility by always trying new things, moving into new areas, and coming up with new ideas before their competition. To be strategically agile, leaders need to have a vision, be able to change their plans, and work in an environment that encourages risk-taking and new ideas.

2.2.3 Systemic Flexibility

Systemic agility is the ability of the whole organisation to adjust. It goes beyond specific departments or activities and focusses on how the whole system, including technology, people, structure, and processes, can respond as a whole. Systemic agility comes from designing an organisation that encourages open communication, working together across departments, and exchanging information. It makes sure that agility is a part of the organization's DNA, which makes it easy for everyone to adapt. Digital platforms, enterprise resource planning (ERP) systems, and AI-powered decision support tools are all important for making systems more flexible by bringing together different operations into a single, adaptable whole. These three aspects make up a multi-layered agility model in which operational efficiency helps short-term responsiveness, strategic foresight helps long-term flexibility, and systemic integration helps overall resilience. Figure 2 for a graphic illustration of the dimensions of organisational agility.

Figure 2. Illustration of the dimensions of organisational agility

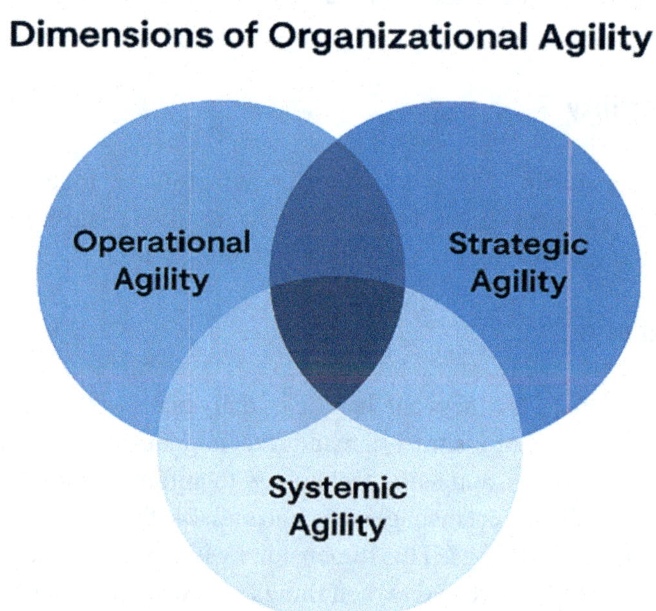

Table 3 outlines the major dimensions and factors shaping organizational agility in the digital era. It categorizes agility into strategic, operational, systemic, and technological dimensions, emphasizing how leadership vision, digital transformation, cultural adaptability, and governance frameworks interact to create a resilient and adaptive organization. Each factor reflects a critical enabler—ranging from decision-making speed and innovation capability to collaboration, data-driven insights, and sustainable practices—that together define an organization's ability to thrive amid disruption and continuous change.

Table 3. Dimensions and Factors Influencing Organizational Agility in the Digital Era

Dimension	Description	Key Factors	Expected Outcomes
Strategic Agility	The ability to anticipate and respond to environmental changes through adaptive strategy formulation.	Vision alignment, resource flexibility, scenario planning.	Faster strategic response, innovation in business models.
Operational Agility	The capability to optimize processes and workflows for speed and efficiency.	Process automation, lean operations, cross-functional collaboration.	Improved productivity, reduced cycle time, better customer satisfaction.
Technological Agility	The ability to adopt, integrate, and scale emerging technologies.	Cloud computing, AI, IoT, blockchain, data analytics.	Enhanced adaptability, innovation enablement, real-time decision-making.
Human Agility	Flexibility and adaptability of employees and leadership to change.	Continuous learning, leadership adaptability, digital skills.	Resilient workforce, higher engagement, innovation culture.
Cultural Agility	The organization's cultural readiness to embrace change and experimentation.	Open innovation, psychological safety, learning orientation.	Improved innovation rate, faster adoption of change.
Governance Agility	The flexibility and responsiveness of policies, compliance, and regulatory frameworks.	Adaptive governance, transparency, ethical AI use.	Balanced innovation with compliance, risk mitigation.
Sustainability Agility	Integration of environmental and social responsibility into agile practices.	Green technology, ethical sourcing, ESG alignment.	Long-term viability, stakeholder trust, sustainable innovation.
Policy Agility	The responsiveness of institutional and organizational policies to digital and market shifts.	Regulatory alignment, policy reform, digital governance.	Agile decision-making, compliance readiness, digital competitiveness.

2.3 Linking Agility to Competitive Advantage

Organisational agility is closely related to and has a big impact on long-term competitive advantage. In unstable situations, typical ways to go ahead, including size, location, or money, are no longer enough. The capacity to adapt quickly and keep coming up with new ideas has become the most important thing that sets companies apart. Agile companies do better than their competitors because they notice changes in the market early, adapt quickly, and put resources towards new opportunities.

From a strategic management standpoint, agility serves as a dynamic capacity (Teece, Pisano, & Shuen, 1997), allowing organisations to amalgamate, develop, and reorganise internal and external skills to respond to swiftly evolving surroundings. This dynamic capability approach emphasises that agility is not only a singular talent but a comprehensive meta-capacity that ensures sustained long-term performance. For instance, AI-powered analytics help businesses predict how customers will behave and quickly change their product strategy. This makes them more sensitive to the market and better at coming up with new ideas.

Agility also makes a business more focused on its customers and more innovative, both of which are important for standing out in a competitive market. Agile companies may make their products more personal, speed up the creation of new ones, and work with consumers and partners to create value. They may also better handle risk by learning and trying things out quickly. These skills work together to make a company more resilient and create value over time. Agility is not simply a way to survive, but also a strategic tool for long-term success. The idea behind organisational agility is that it is multi-dimensional and helps companies gain a long-term competitive edge. Organisations may create the resilience they need to deal with digital disruptions by improving their operational efficiency, strategic flexibility, and systemic integration. In the next chapter, the conversation shifts from comprehending concepts to the role of digital transformation as a major driver of agility. This shows how technology helps businesses put these agile ideas into practice in real life.

3. STATEMENT OF THE PROBLEM

The fast spread of digital technology and artificial intelligence (AI) has caused a change in global business ecosystems that has never happened before. Organisations are still having trouble turning these technical improvements into systemic agility, which is the ability to recognise, adapt, and reconfigure plans dynamically across changing contexts, even if they have spent a lot of money on digitalisation. Deloitte's Global Digital Transformation Survey (2023) says that 93% of companies across the world have started digital transformation initiatives, but just 28% say they have seen demonstrable gains in the pace of innovation or the ability to make decisions that are flexible. PwC (2024) also discovered that although 62% of businesses used AI for analytics and forecasting, fewer than 40% saw long-term performance improvements since their human, technology, and governance systems didn't work well together.

In theory, this difference shows that people don't fully comprehend how digital transformation and AI work together to make organisations more flexible. Current frameworks—like the Dynamic Capability Theory (Teece et al., 2016) and the Technology–Organization–Environment (TOE) Framework (Tornatzky & Fleischer, 1990)—offer useful perspectives but seldom incorporate the ethical, leadership, and human-capital aspects essential for practical agility. Empirical investigations yield conflicting findings: Zhang, Ding, and Xiao (2023) established a positive correlation between digital maturity and agility in Chinese firms, whereas Bux, Zhu, and Devi (2025) identified only a partial mediation effect via knowledge exchange. These conflicts highlight a deficiency in comprehending the systemic essence of agility that extends beyond mere technological proficiency.

Emerging economies encounter distinctive challenges—such as inadequate digital infrastructure, leadership inertia, and labour skill deficiencies—that hinder the scalability of agile transformation (Kant & Ashuro, 2025). The World Economic Forum (2022) says that digital readiness is 80% in industrialised economies on average, but less than 45% in most developing areas. These differences lead to inconsistent adoption results and make it harder to compare situations throughout the world.

Organisations are dealing with more and more problems when it comes to AI governance, data ethics, and following the rules. According to the OECD AI Observatory (2024), 58% of businesses say that "ethical ambiguity and lack of governance frameworks" are the main reasons why they can't use AI. The widespread use of biased algorithms and unclear decision-making procedures (Jobin, Ienca, & Vayena, 2019) also makes it harder to trust and hold people accountable, which are both important for keeping agility and innovation going.

All of these problems point to a multi-layered research need that includes:

- **Theoretical Gap:** There is no comprehensive model that incorporates the technological, human, and ethical aspects of agility.
- **Empirical Gap:** Insufficient quantitative validation across industries and geographies, especially in emerging economies.
- **Contextual Gap:** Lack of comparable evidence about digital and governance discrepancies.
- **Practical Gap:** Poor translation of AI deployment into quantifiable adaptability and enduring performance results.

So, the main research question that this chapter is about is stated as follows:

Organisations around the world still have a big gap between how quickly they adopt new technologies and how quickly their systems can adapt to new situations. This is mostly because of how poorly they integrate their technological, human, and governance skills. Table 4 presents the key empirical evidence supporting the problem.

Table 4. Key Empirical Evidence Supporting the Problem

Dimension	Source	Empirical Finding
Digital transformation success rate	Deloitte (2023)	Only 28% of digital projects yield agility outcomes
AI implementation & performance	PwC (2024)	62% adoption, <40% sustainable performance gain
Global digital readiness gap	World Economic Forum (2022)	80% in developed vs. 45% in emerging economies
AI governance barriers	OECD (2024)	58% cite ethical/governance ambiguity
Algorithmic bias & accountability	Jobin et al. (2019)	Persistent lack of transparency in AI decision systems

To solve this dilemma, we need to create a unified conceptual framework that shows how digital transformation and AI may work together to promote systemic agility through adaptive leadership, human competency, and ethical governance. This study directly addresses that necessity, aspiring to convert disjointed observations into a unified theoretical and practical framework that guides further research, management strategy, and policy development.

4. DIGITAL TRANSFORMATION AS AN ENABLER OF AGILITY

This section explores how digital transformation initiatives drive agility through enhanced communication, collaboration, and process integration. Digital transformation has become one of the most important ways for businesses to be flexible in the 21st century. As globalisation, competition, and technology disruption make things more complicated for businesses, the capacity to digitally change how they do business, their culture, and how they interact with customers has become necessary for survival. Digital transformation is more than just using digital technologies. It means that companies need to fundamentally rethink how they make money, work with stakeholders, and deal with changes in the environment. When done right, it improves communication, teamwork, and decision-making, which are the building blocks of agility. This chapter examines the conceptual link between digital transformation and agility, concentrating on how businesses use digital maturity to become more responsive, innovative, and resilient. It also talks about the problems that make it hard to change and gives examples from many fields of how digital technology might make things more flexible in practice.

Table 5. Digital Transformation as an Enabler of Organizational Agility

Key Aspect	Description	Agility Impact	Examples / Applications
Digital Transformation Definition	A holistic process involving technology, strategy, and culture shifts to improve performance and adaptability.	Enables organizations to rapidly respond to market and technological changes.	Cloud migration, AI integration, data-driven decision-making.
Technology Integration	Incorporation of digital tools such as AI, IoT, big data analytics, and automation across operations.	Improves real-time decision-making, efficiency, and innovation.	Predictive analytics for demand forecasting; RPA for process efficiency.
Digital Maturity	The extent to which an organization has integrated and optimized digital capabilities.	Higher digital maturity leads to greater flexibility, responsiveness, and customer-centricity.	Mature digital banks offering 24/7 AI-based services.
Cultural Transformation	Shifting organizational mindset toward experimentation, collaboration, and learning.	Encourages continuous innovation and quick adaptation to change.	Agile teams adopting cross-functional collaboration models.
Data and Analytics	Leveraging big data and analytics for real-time insights and strategic forecasting.	Enhances proactive decision-making and anticipatory responses.	Retail analytics predicting customer behavior trends.
Customer-Centric Innovation	Using digital tools to enhance user experience and co-create value with customers.	Improves responsiveness to evolving customer demands.	Personalized e-commerce recommendations; chatbots for customer support.
Overcoming Barriers	Addressing organizational inertia, data silos, and resistance to change.	Promotes smooth transformation and employee engagement.	Change management programs; digital literacy initiatives.

Table 5 shows the main ways that digital transformation makes organisations more flexible. It shows how adopting new technologies, being ready for change, and using data all work together to improve adaptive ability. Organisations may use digital transformation as a strategic facilitator for agility by becoming digitally mature and creating a culture that encourages innovation. This will let them quickly respond to changing market circumstances based on data.

4.1 Understanding Digital Transformation

People frequently think that digital transformation (DT) is only the use of new technology like cloud computing, artificial intelligence (AI), or automation tools. In truth, DT is a change in strategy and culture that changes how a business works, gives value, and interacts with its ecosystem. Digital transformation is different from basic technology adoption, which is all about making things more efficient or cutting costs. Digital transformation means putting digital thinking into the organization's strategy, culture, and leadership vision (Kane et al., 2015). The main difference is the extent and purpose of the modification. Adopting new technology is a tactical move that tackles specific operational problems, like digitising paper procedures or automating activities. Digital transformation, on the other hand, is strategic. It changes whole business models, encourages a culture of creativity, and makes sure that technology is in line with the company's long-term goals. For example, Netflix and Tesla, two of the most successful digital companies, didn't just use technology; they changed the way customers experienced it and how quickly they could adapt to new situations by constantly reinventing it. Digital transformation promotes transparency, cooperation, and experimentation, which are all attributes that fit with agile organisational behaviour. It encourages less rigid hierarchies, decisions based on facts, and quick feedback loops. From a leadership point of view, digital transformation needs a unified vision that combines digital projects with strategic goals. This will help everyone in the organisation become more digitally flexible.

4.2 The Role of Digital Maturity

Digital maturity is the level to which a business has used digital tools, procedures, and culture in its daily work. Digital maturity evolves incrementally via distinct phases, each signifying a more profound amalgamation of technology with strategy and agility (Westerman et al., 2014). The stages can be grouped into these main categories:

a. **Initial (Ad hoc Digitalisation):** Organisations try out digital technologies in different areas, but they don't always have a clear plan for how they will work together. Agility is restricted by disjointed systems and conventional paradigms.
b. **Developing (Process Digitisation):** Digital projects work together better. Communication gets better, and early attempts at automation make things a little more responsive.
c. Strategic integration means that digital technologies are part of the plan. Data analytics, customer relationship management (CRM), and working together across departments make it easier and faster to make decisions.
d. **Advanced (Digital Optimisation):** Companies use real-time data, predictive analytics, and AI to make their processes more efficient on the go. Quickly coming up with new ideas and adapting to the market makes strategic agility better.
e. **Transformative (Systemic Agility):** Digital maturity reaches a stage where agility becomes institutionalised. The organisation is always changing thanks to self-learning systems, innovation ecosystems, and digital platforms that can adapt.

Organisations with greater levels of digital maturity have dynamic digital capabilities, which means they can quickly identify market changes, take advantage of opportunities, and rearrange resources (Teece, Peteraf, & Leih, 2016). This connection between digital maturity and agility produces a positive feedback loop, where digital tools make people more adaptable and agility speeds up the use of new technology.

4.3 Overcoming Barriers to Digital Agility

Even though digital transformation has many known benefits, many businesses have trouble getting the most out of it. Organisational inertia, data silos, and cultural resistance are the most typical problems.

4.3.1 Lack of change in the organisation

Inertia is a common problem for established organisations because of their stiff structures, old methods, and bureaucratic decision-making. This lack of movement makes it hard to make quick changes, even when it's clear that digital transformation is needed. To get past it, you need transformational leadership, decision-making that isn't centralised, and a flexible governance structure that encourages experimentation (Kotter, 2012).

4.3.2 Silos of Data

Data that is spread out across departments makes it hard to see and work together in real time, which are two important parts of being agile. Without linked data systems, making decisions is still delayed and isolated. The answer is to use cloud-based architectures and enterprise data platforms that bring together all the information flows. This lets businesses work together and adapt more quickly to changes.

4.3.3 Resistance to Culture

Digital transformation needs a culture that welcomes change and creativity. But fear of obsolescence, lack of digital skills, and worry about their jobs might make people resistant. Businesses need to spend money on programs that teach people how to use technology, keep learning, and manage change in a way that encourages growth. To show flexibility, leaders can encourage openness, learn from mistakes, and give credit to digital champions. By getting beyond these obstacles, digital projects go from being random efforts to strategic tools that make the organisation more flexible, which keeps it competitive and ready for the future.

4.4 Case illustration: Digital Agility in Banking and Commerce

Digital technology has changed the way customers experience banking and commerce, and digital agility has made operations more efficient.

Case 1: The Rise of Agile Banking in the Banking Sector

Digital transformation has helped banks in the financial sector move from product-focused to customer-focused business models. DBS Bank in Singapore, for example, started a big digital transformation project to "make banking invisible." DBS used cloud computing, data analytics, and AI-driven consumer insights to make decisions in real time and come up with new products faster. This made customers happier and made it easier to adapt to changes in the market and regulations.

The bank's internal culture changed in the same way, with the adoption of agile methods, digital leadership programs, and a culture of trying new things. DBS became one of the most digitally advanced and flexible banks in Asia as a result (Chakravorti, 2017).

Case 2: The Commerce Sector: E-Commerce and Being Able to Change

Amazon is a good example of adaptability in business since it always changes its platform to fit the needs of its customers. Amazon uses predictive analytics, automation, and real-time logistics optimisation to make digital transformation a part of every part of its value chain. The company's systemic agility lets it quickly introduce new services like Prime, AWS, and Alexa while still doing a great job of running its business.

In the same way, regional companies like Flipkart and Alibaba have used mobile commerce, data analytics, and AI-based suggestions to offer more personalised experiences and flexible supply chain management. These examples show how digital transformation may make businesses more flexible by combining, using intelligence, and coming up with new ideas.

5. ARTIFICIAL INTELLIGENCE AND DATA-DRIVEN DECISION MAKING

The use of artificial intelligence (AI) in business strategy has changed how companies think about being flexible and making decisions. AI technologies, such as machine learning, natural language processing, and intelligent automation, let businesses get useful information from huge amounts of data and operate with speed and accuracy that has never been seen before. This part talks about how AI can help organisations be more flexible and smart by helping them deal with uncertainty, predict changes in the market, and make better decisions in real time. AI is the basic technology that makes it possible to gather, analyse, and learn from data. AI systems use Predictive Analytics to look at huge volumes of data and make predictions about patterns, find hazards, and find chances. These insights help organisations make better decisions, which lets them quickly and correctly adapt to changes in the market. The Ethics part makes ensuring that judgements made by AI are clear, fair, and responsible, balancing new ideas with responsibilities. This combination of data, decision-making, and ethical monitoring makes a smart and long-lasting kind of organisational agility.

5.1 AI as a Driver of Intelligent Agility

Artificial Intelligence (AI) is a key part of what we call "intelligent agility," which is the capacity of organisations to use data-driven intelligence to perceive, understand, and adapt to changes in their environment. Intelligent agility uses computational insights to improve foresight and response, which is different from traditional kinds of agility that depend mostly on human interpretation and experience. AI helps businesses predict problems before they happen by looking at large and complicated data sets, such as customer behaviour, market trends, and operational indicators. For instance, predictive demand forecasting models can find possible problems in the supply chain or changes in client preferences, which lets managers take action before problems happen instead of after they do. AI systems may also learn from fresh data all the time, which helps them improve their models to better represent how things are changing. AI is especially useful in commercial settings that change quickly because it can learn and adapt to new situations. Companies that use AI in their decision-making systems can find weak signals, spot new dangers, and take advantage of new possibilities faster than their competitors (Brynjolfsson & McAfee, 2017).

Table 6. Artificial Intelligence as a Driver of Intelligent Agility

AI Dimension	Description	Agility Contribution	Practical Examples / Applications
Predictive Analytics	Uses machine learning algorithms to forecast trends, customer behavior, and risks.	Enables proactive decision-making and faster responses to environmental changes.	Predicting market demand, detecting equipment failures before downtime.
Real-Time Data Processing	AI systems analyze streaming data from IoT devices and sensors instantly.	Supports agile operations through instant insights and dynamic adjustments.	Smart manufacturing using IoT-based monitoring systems.
AI-Enabled Automation	Automates repetitive tasks and optimizes processes through Robotic Process Automation (RPA).	Enhances efficiency, reduces errors, and frees human talent for strategic work.	Automated invoice processing, intelligent customer service bots.
Decision Intelligence	Integrates AI with business intelligence tools to support complex decision-making.	Improves strategic agility by enabling accurate and data-driven decisions.	AI-assisted financial planning, logistics optimization.
Adaptive Learning Systems	AI models that evolve with new data to adapt to changing contexts.	Promotes long-term agility by continuously refining insights and predictions.	Personalized learning systems, adaptive cybersecurity solutions.
Human–AI Collaboration	Combines human intuition with machine intelligence to enhance decision quality.	Strengthens organizational adaptability through hybrid intelligence.	AI-assisted medical diagnosis, co-pilot tools in software development.
Ethical and Transparent AI	Ensures fairness, accountability, and transparency in automated systems.	Builds trust and sustainability, essential for long-term agile adoption.	Explainable AI (XAI) in recruitment or loan approvals.

Table 6 shows how Artificial Intelligence (AI) makes intelligent agility possible by improving adaptability, foresight, and response. AI changes the way people make decisions by turning them into dynamic, data-driven processes. It does this by using predictive analytics, real-time insights, and process automation. Also, working together with AI encourages new ideas, and using AI in an ethical way makes sure that agility is long-lasting and reliable. These features make AI a strategic tool for organisations that are strong, open to learning, and ready for the future.

5.2 Predictive Analytics and Real-Time Responsiveness

Predictive analytics, which is a main use of AI, makes organisations more flexible by turning data into insight. Predictive systems use methods like regression modelling, neural networks, and decision trees to guess what will happen in the future and help people take action at the right moment. AI models can anticipate how customers will buy things, how likely they are to leave, or what new trends are coming up in the world of consumer analytics. This helps companies change their products on the fly. In the same way, predictive AI models in risk management look at credit risk or the chance of fraud happening, which lets people take steps to stop damage from happening. Also, real-time data lets businesses make changes right away. AI systems can keep an eye on changes in inventories and automatically reorganise items in digital commerce. In banking, real-time fraud detection algorithms stop questionable transactions before they get worse. This responsiveness is a new kind of agility that comes from being alert all the time and being able to change right away. By combining predictive analytics, organisations may not only adapt to change but also successfully anticipate it.

5.3 AI-Enabled Automation

Automation is a key aspect of AI-driven agility. This is especially true for Robotic Process Automation (RPA) and smart technologies that make processes more efficient. These technologies make monotonous, rule-based activities easier, which lets human workers focus on more strategic, creative, and value-driven work.

For instance, in the banking industry, RPA bots handle loan applications, check client information, and keep an eye on compliance, which speeds up the process by a lot. AI-driven optimisation algorithms in supply chain operations change logistical routes on the fly based on changes in demand, fuel prices, and the weather. Also, intelligent automation systems that integrate RPA with machine learning and natural language processing can handle unstructured inputs like emails or voice queries. This makes operations more autonomous and aware of their surroundings. This automation makes things more flexible by speeding up operations, lowering decision latency, and reducing the chance of human mistakes. Companies that use AI-enabled automation well can quickly change their procedures to keep the business running and be ready for anything that comes up (Davenport & Ronanki, 2018).

5.4 Ethical Considerations

AI helps businesses move quicker and smarter, but it also brings up important ethical issues that need to be dealt with to make sure that businesses are agile in a responsible way. Some important issues include prejudice, accountability, and openness.

- For AI-driven judgements to be transparent, they need to be clear and easy to understand. This is especially important in fields like banking and healthcare where the stakes are high. If not kept under check, black-box algorithms might make people lose faith and make it harder for companies to follow the rules.
- AI models can be biased if the training data is not representative or is skewed, which can lead to biased results. For instance, biased hiring algorithms may put some groups of people at a disadvantage. To make sure things are fair, you need strict data governance and algorithmic checks.
- Accountability is figuring out who is to blame when AI systems make bad or wrong choices. Setting up clear ethical guidelines and ways for people to keep an eye on technology makes ensuring that moral integrity isn't compromised by technical flexibility.

So, it's important to find a balance between being agile and being ethical. Companies need to move swiftly, but they also need to be responsible. This means that they need to include ethical AI principles in their design, deployment, and decision-making (Jobin, Ienca, & Vayena, 2019).

6. LEADERSHIP AND HUMAN-CENTRIC TRANSFORMATION

The level of technology adoption is not the only thing that affects an organization's agility; human adaptation, leadership vision, and organisational culture also play a role. New technology like artificial intelligence (AI), cloud systems, and automation lay the groundwork for agility, but it is the people—leaders, employees, and teams—that turn promise into long-term success. This part talks about how leadership, the skills of the workforce, and a culture of learning all come together to make digital transformation more human-centered. In essence, Figure 3 conveys that true organizational agility emerges from the integration of technology, leadership, and human development. It is not achieved by digital tools alone, but by aligning people, processes, and technologies within a culture of continuous growth and adaptability. This human-centric approach ensures that digital transformation remains sustainable, ethical, and deeply responsive to both organizational and societal needs.

Figure 3. Framework for Human-Centric Organizational Agility

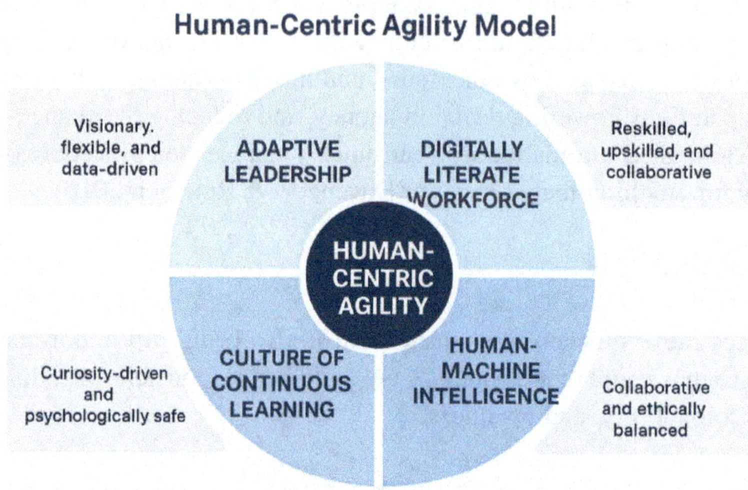

Table 7 illustrates how leadership and a focus on people can help create flexible organisations in the digital age. It makes the point that technology alone can't make a company agile; adaptive and transformational leadership, giving employees more authority, and a culture of constant learning are just as important. Organisations may promote resilience, creativity, and sustainable growth by combining emotional intelligence, digital literacy, and human-AI cooperation. This way, human values will always be at the centre of digital transformation.

Table 7. Leadership and Human-Centric Transformation for Organizational Agility

Dimension / Focus Area	Description	Contribution to Agility	Illustrative Examples / Practices
Adaptive Leadership	Leaders demonstrate flexibility, vision, and resilience to guide teams through digital disruption.	Enables rapid decision-making, innovation, and alignment with changing business contexts.	CEOs implementing agile leadership models during crises or market shifts.
Transformational Leadership	Inspires and motivates employees through a shared digital vision and innovation-oriented culture.	Drives employee engagement, creativity, and organizational adaptability.	Leaders in tech firms promoting digital experimentation and autonomy.
Digital Literacy and Workforce Enablement	Focuses on continuous upskilling and reskilling to enhance employees' digital competence.	Builds a workforce capable of leveraging digital tools for agile operations.	Corporate training programs in AI, analytics, and cloud technologies.
Collaborative Intelligence (Human–Machine Collaboration)	Promotes synergy between human creativity and AI-driven insights.	Enhances decision quality, innovation, and problem-solving agility.	Use of AI-powered co-pilots or decision support systems in organizations.
Empowerment and Decentralized Decision-Making	Encourages autonomy and accountability at all organizational levels.	Reduces bottlenecks and increases responsiveness to real-time challenges.	Agile teams empowered to make independent project-level decisions.
Culture of Continuous Learning	Embeds a growth mindset emphasizing experimentation, feedback, and adaptability.	Fosters innovation and long-term resilience in changing environments.	Internal learning hubs, hackathons, and innovation incubators.
Emotional Intelligence and Well-being	Focuses on empathy, trust, and employee engagement as strategic assets.	Enhances collaboration, reduces resistance to change, and builds inclusive agility.	Mindfulness and well-being programs supporting hybrid work cultures.

6.1 Adaptive Leadership in the Age of Disruption

In the digital era marked by uncertainty and volatility, leadership effectiveness is measured by adaptability rather than authority. Adaptive leaders anticipate change, embrace experimentation, and lead with a clear sense of purpose. According to Heifetz and Laurie (1997), adaptive leadership involves mobilizing people to tackle tough challenges and thrive amidst disruption. Key characteristics of adaptive leadership in agile organizations include:

- **Visionary Thinking:** The ability to set a clear strategic direction that aligns digital initiatives with organizational goals.
- **Flexibility and Resilience:** Adjusting leadership styles based on evolving market and technological conditions.
- **Empathy and Inclusion:** Ensuring that digital transitions are human-centered and considerate of employee well-being.
- **Data-Driven Decision-Making:** Using analytics and real-time data to make informed, objective, and timely decisions.

In practice, adaptive leaders act as catalysts of change, fostering collaboration across departments and encouraging teams to experiment without fear of failure. They bridge the gap between technology strategy and organizational purpose, ensuring that agility becomes a lived value rather than a management slogan.

6.2 Building a Digitally Literate Workforce

A digitally skilled workforce is necessary for technology-driven agility to function. Employees need to have the technical, analytical, and cognitive abilities to work in workplaces that are full of data and automated. Digital literacy is more than just being good with technology; it also means being able to think critically about information, work together online, and keep learning. Companies that spend money on programs to teach their employees new skills and improve their existing ones tend to be more innovative and have more engaged employees. For instance, top firms like IBM and Accenture have set up "digital academies" within their offices to teach their workers how to use AI, data analytics, and automation. Some important ways to help people become more digitally literate are:

- **Continuous Learning Platforms:** Giving people the chance to take online courses and get certified.
- **Cross-Functional Training**: Teaching people how to combine their knowledge of technology and business.
- **Mentorship and peer learning:** Encouraging people to share what they know and work together to solve problems.

In the end, a workforce that is digitally literate gives businesses the ability to react rapidly, make better decisions, and match people's potential with digital goals.

6.3 Balancing Human and Machine Intelligence

The real strength of agility comes from the cooperation of human and machine intelligence. AI systems can handle a lot of data, find patterns, and make judgements on their own, but they don't have the ability to grasp context, morals, or creativity, which are all things that people do.

This means we need a hybrid intelligence paradigm in which people and AI work together to make each other better. Humans are responsible for making decisions, showing compassion, and keeping an eye on morals. AI, on the other hand, is responsible for speed and accuracy in analysis. For instance, AI may find problems or dangers in financial analytics, but humans still need to make the ultimate investment decisions. To make this cooperation work well:

- **Set clear human roles:** Decide where human control is necessary, such as in ethics, customer service, and creativity.
- **Build Trust in AI:** Make algorithms more open so that users may trust them more.
- **Encourage Collaboration:** Encourage data scientists, managers, and domain specialists to work together to make things.

This symbiotic approach makes sure that technology doesn't get in the way of human creativity, keeping agility based on human values.

6.4 Cultivating a Culture of Continuous Learning

Agility flourishes in an atmosphere characterised by constant, collaborative, and curiosity-driven learning. In digital environments that change swiftly, information that doesn't change quickly becomes useless. So, businesses need to create a culture of learning that encourages people to try new things, think about what they did, and change. Some of the most important things that make continual learning possible are:

- **Psychological safety** is letting workers try forth ideas and fail without worrying about getting in trouble.
- **Knowledge Sharing Systems:** using digital technologies for collaboration and communities of practice within the company.
- **Recognition and Rewards:** Encouraging learning behaviour by giving praise and helping people move along in their careers.

Furthermore, leadership is essential in exemplifying learning behaviour by showing receptiveness to criticism, seeking new information, and acknowledging the significance of collective intelligence. When learning is a part of the organization's DNA, agility becomes a permanent skill instead than a momentary reaction to change.

7. POLICY, GOVERNANCE, AND SUSTAINABILITY

Organisational agility does not exist in a vacuum; it functions within an ecosystem influenced by public policy, regulatory frameworks, and sustainable governance practices. As digital transformation speeds up in many fields, it is more important than ever to have clear rules and ethical monitoring to make sure that development is responsible and strong. This part talks about how government programs, data governance, and environmentally friendly technological practices all work together to make systems more flexible, which is good for both businesses and society as a whole. Table 7 shows how public policy, governance, and sustainability work together to make organisations more flexible. It shows how strong rules, ethical data management, and using technology in a way that is good for the environment all work together to make systems more flexible. Governments help by providing digital infrastructure and legislative support, while businesses help by being responsible with new ideas and being open about how they run their businesses. Combining sustainability with ethics makes sure that agility is not only effective, but also socially responsible, strong, and ready for the future.

Table 8. Policy, Governance, and Sustainability for Promoting Systemic Agility

Focus Area / Dimension	Description	Contribution to Organizational Agility	Illustrative Examples / Best Practices
Public Policy and Digital Infrastructure	Government initiatives and national digital frameworks that enable business digitalization.	Provides an enabling environment for innovation, digital adoption, and economic resilience.	India's *Digital India* mission, EU's *Digital Strategy 2030*, UAE's *Smart Government Initiative*.
Regulatory Governance and Compliance	Implementation of transparent policies for data protection, cybersecurity, and digital ethics.	Builds trust, ensures compliance, and strengthens sustainable digital ecosystems.	GDPR (Europe), Personal Data Protection Bill (India).
Data Governance and Privacy Frameworks	Systems and policies for managing data quality, accessibility, and ethical use.	Enhances data-driven agility while maintaining accountability and stakeholder confidence.	ISO/IEC 38505-1 for data governance, AI ethics charters.
Corporate Digital Governance	Strategic alignment between technology adoption, leadership, and risk management.	Promotes responsible innovation and minimizes technology-driven risks.	Digital governance boards and AI ethics committees in multinational corporations.
Sustainable Technology Implementation	Adoption of eco-friendly, energy-efficient technologies that align with ESG goals.	Integrates sustainability into business agility and long-term competitiveness.	Use of green data centers and carbon-neutral IT operations.
Cross-Sector Collaboration and Policy Integration	Partnerships between government, academia, and industry to advance digital ecosystems.	Encourages systemic agility through shared innovation and collective problem-solving.	Public–private partnerships in AI research and 5G deployment.
Ethical AI and Responsible Innovation	Ensures fairness, transparency, and accountability in AI-driven processes.	Builds stakeholder trust and mitigates reputational risks in digital transformation.	AI ethics frameworks by OECD, UNESCO AI principles.

Figure 4 shows how Digital Agility is interrelated, with policy as the main enabler that affects both technology and leadership. These two main drives operate together to help organisations change their culture, adapt to new economic conditions, and stay in business. The flow shows that to be digitally agile in the long run, you need to work together on governance, innovation, and people-centered initiatives.

Figure 4. Interconnected Framework of Policy, Governance, and Sustainability for Digital Agility

7.1 The Role of Public Policy

Public policy is what makes digital agility possible on a national and institutional level. Governments can make the world more adaptable and competitive by using proactive digital tactics, investing in infrastructure, and making rules that encourage innovation. More and more, modern public policies stress:

- **Digital Infrastructure Development:** Giving businesses and people more power by expanding internet access, cloud platforms, and open data systems.
- **Innovation ecosystems:** help new businesses, research projects, and cooperation between different sectors speed up the use of new technologies.
- **Regulatory Flexibility:** Using flexible policy frameworks that change as technology does instead of limiting progress.

For example, the European Union's Digital Agenda and India's Digital India program have given businesses the infrastructure and rules they need to make the switch to digital. These actions make organisations better at coming up with new ideas, which lets them quickly adapt to changes in technology and market demand (Tapscott & Tapscott, 2016). So, public policy is a big part of making things more flexible, making sure that digital transformation fits with national goals of economic resilience, inclusion, and sustainable development.

7.2 Data Governance and Regulation

In the age of making decisions based on data, strong data governance frameworks are necessary to keep trust, security, and ethical integrity. Good governance makes ensuring that data, which is the lifeblood of digital agility, is handled in a responsible, open, and lawful way. Some important parts of data governance are:

- **Privacy Protection:** Following data protection rules like the General Data Protection Regulation (GDPR) to protect people's rights.
- **Cybersecurity:** Putting in place proactive defence systems and incident response plans to keep digital dangers at bay.
- **Ethical Data Management:** Making sure that data use is fair, accountable, and open, especially when AI is used to make decisions.

Strong governance systems not only keep organisations safe from legal and reputational threats, but they also make them more flexible by building confidence and making sure everyone follows the rules. Companies may innovate when consumers and other stakeholders feel that their data is safe and managed ethically. Policy-driven measures like Data Protection Authorities and National Cybersecurity Frameworks also set up common rules that let organisations share and process data safely. This helps establish flexible and interoperable digital ecosystems (OECD, 2020).

7.3 Sustainable Technology Implementation

The idea of "sustainable agility" has come up in the last several years. It connects technical progress with social and environmental responsibilities. As companies move their activities online, they need to make sure that new technology helps the environment instead of hurting it. Using sustainable technology means:

- **Green IT Practices:** Using efficient data centres and cloud computing to use less energy.
- **Principles of a Circular Economy:** Making things and doing things in a way that reduces waste and encourages reuse.
- **Responsible Innovation:** is making sure that emerging technologies like AI, IoT, and blockchain are used fairly and ethically.

Organisations may create robust and future-proof agility by linking digital transformation with sustainability goals, such as the UN Sustainable Development Goals. For instance, AI-powered smart energy management solutions not only make operations more efficient but also lower carbon emissions. This shows that agility and sustainability can work together (Elkington, 2018). So, sustainable agility isn't just about getting through change; it's also about doing well in a world where environmental, economic, and moral issues are all intertwined.

8. FRAMEWORK FOR BUILDING SYSTEMIC AGILITY

In an era marked by continuous technological disruption, achieving systemic organizational agility requires a holistic approach that integrates digital transformation, artificial intelligence (AI), leadership, and governance into a unified strategy. This section presents a conceptual framework that highlights the interdependence of technological and human dimensions in fostering agile, resilient, and sustainable organizations. By aligning strategy, culture, and technology, organizations can move beyond isolated innovation efforts to achieve enterprise-wide adaptability. Figure 5 illustrates how digital transformation, artificial intelligence, leadership, and governance collectively enable organizational agility. At the core, AI and data analytics drive intelligent operations, while adaptive leadership and a digitally literate workforce ensure human alignment. Policy and governance establish ethical, sustainable foundations that guide technological adoption. Together, these interconnected elements create a balanced ecosystem that supports continuous learning, innovation, and resilience—helping organizations adapt swiftly to change and maintain long-term competitiveness.

Figure 5. Integrated Framework for Building Systemic Agility

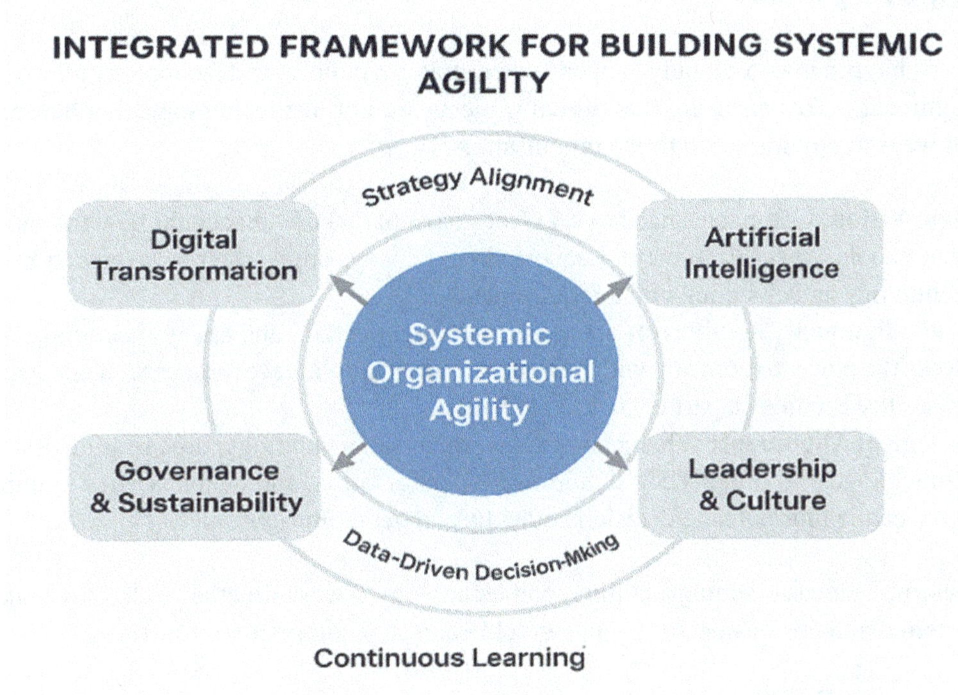

8.1 Integrated Framework

The Integrated Framework for Systemic Agility explains how different parts of an organisation work together to provide for flexible performance in a changing environment. At its heart, this concept links technical enablers like AI and digital transformation with human and organisational factors like culture, leadership, and governance.

- **Digital Transformation** is the backbone of agility. It makes workflows easier, improves communication, and makes it easier for units to share data in real time.
- **Artificial Intelligence** adds an analytical layer, giving organisations predictive insights that help them plan for changes, reduce risks, and take advantage of new opportunities.
- **Adaptive Leadership** ensures that changes caused by technology are in line with people's values and the aims of the organisation. This creates a culture that encourages experimentation and learning.
- **Governance and policy** are the moral and institutional frameworks that balance responsibility with creativity, making sure that things are clear and last.

Putting these parts together turns agility from a skill that just one department has into a skill that the whole organisation has, where choices, procedures, and behaviours at all levels work together to make the organisation more adaptable to change.

8.2 Strategic Alignment

Agility can't happen in silos; it only happens when strategy, culture, and technology all work together. Strategic alignment makes ensuring that digital projects are not just technological enhancements, but also planned ways to provide value to the organisation.

- **Strategic Vision:** Companies need to set clear goals that take into account how the market works and what people expect from them. Leaders should always adjust their strategies to keep up with new technology and changing client requirements.
- **Cultural Alignment:** A culture of openness, working together, and always becoming better gives employees the power to come up with new ideas. When individuals comprehend and accept digital change, agility becomes a part of their daily work.
- **Technological Alignment:** When making investments in technology, organisations should have a clear strategic goal in mind. They should use AI, automation, and data analytics to improve their ability to see the future, make decisions quickly, and get them right.

When these three areas—strategy, culture, and technology—work together well, they make a synergistic ecosystem that helps businesses change quickly and stay competitive over time.

8.3 Key Success Factors

To achieve systemic agility, organisations need to pay close attention to a few critical factors that affect their results:

- **Transformational leaders** provide a strong case for digital transformation, which inspires everyone in the organisation to work towards the same goal.

- **Investing in and integrating technology:** By constantly investing in scalable, interoperable digital systems, agility is flexible and ready to take advantage of new possibilities.
- **Data-Driven Culture:** When teams know how to read and use data, they can make decisions based on facts and move quickly and confidently.
- **Collaboration across departments:** Getting rid of silos makes it easier to talk to each other, come up with new ideas, and hold each other accountable.

Ethical and Sustainable Practices: By combining ethical standards with aims for sustainability, we can make sure that agility helps society and the environment in the long run.

All of these things together make up systemic agility, which is when digital technology, empowered people, and responsible governance work together to create value, adapt, and innovate all the time.

9. CHALLENGES, RISKS, AND FUTURE DIRECTIONS

In the digital era, organisational agility is becoming more and more important, but putting it into practice is not easy. When organisations try to make their structures, processes, and culture more agile, they often run into big problems and hazards. This part talks about the main things that stop change, how to deal with uncertainty, and how AI and digital progress will change the way we operate in the future.

9.1 Organizational Resistance

Resistance to change is one of the biggest obstacles to making an organisation more flexible. Even though everyone agrees that change is necessary, employees and managers frequently have trouble with change fatigue, cultural rigidity, and being dependent on old systems.

- **Change Fatigue:** Employees might get tired of all the digital transformation projects that keep coming up, which can make them less interested and more sceptical. This tiredness is typically caused by not clearly communicating the aims of the change or not seeing short-term results.
- **Cultural Rigidity:** To be agile, you need to change your mentality about how you work. Instead of controlling everything from the top down, you need to work together, try new things, and learn. In conventional organisations, power structures that have been there for a long time and cultures that are set in stone don't accept these adaptive principles, which makes change happen more slowly.
- **Legacy Systems:** Outdated infrastructure, siloed databases, and fragmented workflows limit the integration of new technologies. These systems slow down the flow of data and make it harder for the organisation to respond quickly.

To deal with these problems, we need clear leadership, change management that involves everyone, and gradual modernisation plans that take into account how ready people and technology are.

9.2 Managing Uncertainty

Agile businesses do well when they can adapt, but the faster rate of changes in technology and the market brings new kinds of unpredictability. The COVID-19 pandemic showed how important it is for businesses to have flexible plans and strong business models that can work in unstable situations. Some important ways to deal with uncertainty are:

- **Dynamic Risk Assessment:** Going beyond static risk matrices to systems that model risk with the help of AI and are always being updated to keep an eye on and forecast any problems.
- **Scenario-Based Planning:** Getting ready for more than one conceivable future instead of just one. This lets businesses adjust their plans fast when things change.
- **Resilient Supply Chains and Ecosystems**: Making digital ecosystems and flexible alliances makes sure that things keep going even when there are global problems or tech problems.

Organisations may be flexible even in unexpected situations by building flexibility into their governance and decision-making systems.

9.3 The Future of Work

AI, automation, and human ingenuity are coming together to change the future of employment. This change will change the responsibilities of employees, the skills they need, and how they work together in agile organisations.

- **AI-Augmented Workforce:** AI doesn't replace people; instead, it works with them by automating boring jobs and giving them insights based on data. This lets workers focus on making decisions that are strategic, creative, and moral.
- **Changing Skill Sets:** Learning new things all the time, being good with technology, and having emotional intelligence will be very important. Workers need to be able to work in circumstances that combine human judgement with machine accuracy.
- **Collaborative Ecosystems:** In the future, the workplace will focus on working together on projects across different departments, with the help of digital tools and cloud-based platforms.

Agile companies will see this change as a chance to rethink work, where people and smart technology work together to generate value. As organizations continue to embrace agility, they must navigate a landscape filled with both opportunities and uncertainties. Overcoming resistance, managing risk dynamically, and preparing for the future of work will determine which organizations thrive in the next decade. The path forward demands a balanced integration of technology, leadership, and culture, ensuring that agility remains not just a response to change, but a sustained strategic capability.

10. CONCLUSION AND RECOMMENDATIONS

In today's digital market, organisational agility is the most important thing for staying strong, competitive, and growing in a way that lasts. This chapter of the book looked at how technologies like AI, data analytics, and digital transformation projects help businesses adapt quickly to changes in their environment, make better decisions, and work together better. AI-powered predictive analytics improves foresight, allowing companies to identify changes in consumer behaviour, market trends, and operational hazards. Digital transformation is more than just using new technology; it is a significant change in culture and structure that makes organisations more adaptable, innovative, and able to work together across departments. When you combine adaptable leadership, a workforce that is comfortable with technology, and constant learning, you create a culture where agility is a shared value rather than just a response to change. Good governance frameworks and ethical AI practices also help make sure that technical agility stays in line with the ideals of responsibility, privacy, and sustainability. These elements work together to generate a systemic kind of agility that helps organisations not just survive uncertainty, but also flourish in it. This is done by turning instability into opportunity via smart, human-centered innovation.

To get to long-term digital agility, we need to find a balance between technology, policy, and people. Policymakers need to set up flexible digital governance systems that change as new technologies come out. This will make sure that AI adoption is fair, open, and welcoming to everyone. Business leaders should put digital maturity first, pay for staff retraining, and create flexible decision-making platforms that use data but are still led by morals. Teachers and academics both have important jobs to do when it comes to promoting learning across disciplines and looking into the long-term effects of AI on the health of society and the strength of organisations. Future research needs to concentrate on creating standardised frameworks for assessing agility, examining the ethical implications of automation, and comprehending how hybrid work contexts transform cooperation. As the lines between human and machine intelligence become less clear, the companies that do well will be the ones that make adaptation a part of their culture and hire people who can learn new things all the time and lead responsibly. In the end, the combination of AI, digital transformation, and human creativity offers a new way to think about agility—one that is smart, moral, and long-lasting in the face of rapid change.

REFERENCES

Atienza-Barba, M., del Río, M. D. L. C., Meseguer-Martínez, Á., & Barba-Sanchez, V. (2024). Artificial intelligence and organizational agility: An analysis of scientific production and future trends. *European Research on Management and Business Economics, 30*(2), 100253. DOI: 10.1016/j.iedeen.2024.100253

Brynjolfsson, E., & McAfee, A. (2017). *Machine, platform, crowd: Harnessing our digital future*. W. W. Norton.

Brynjolfsson, E., & McAfee, A. (2017). *Machine, Platform, Crowd: Harnessing Our Digital Future*. W. W. Norton & Company.

Bux, A., Zhu, Y., & Devi, S. (2025). Enhancing organisational agility through knowledge sharing and open innovation. *Sustainability, 17*(15), 6765. DOI: 10.3390/su17156765

Chakravorti, B. (2017). *The Digital Planet 2017: How competitiveness and trust in digital economies vary across the world*. Tufts University.

Davenport, T. H., & Ronanki, R. (2018). Artificial Intelligence for the Real World. *Harvard Business Review, 96*(1), 108–116.

Dove, R. (2001). *Response ability: The language, structure, and culture of the agile enterprise*. John Wiley & Sons.

Elkington, J. (2018). *Green Swans: The Coming Boom in Regenerative Capitalism. Fast.* Company Press.

Goldman, S. L., Nagel, R. N., & Preiss, K. (1995). *Agile competitors and virtual organizations: Strategies for enriching the customer*. Van Nostrand Reinhold.

Jobin, A., Ienca, M., & Vayena, E. (2019). The global landscape of AI ethics guidelines. *Nature Machine Intelligence, 1*(9), 389–399. DOI: 10.1038/s42256-019-0088-2

Kane, G. C., Palmer, D., Phillips, A. N., Kiron, D., & Buckley, N. (2015). *Strategy, not technology, drives digital transformation*. MIT Sloan Management Review and Deloitte University Press.

Kant, S., & Ashuro, T. (2025). Effect of eco-logistics practices on organizational performance with mediating role of MSE competitiveness in Ethiopia. In *Eco-Logistics and Sustainable Supply Chain Innovations* (pp. 39–60). IGI Global.

Kotter, J. P. (2012). *Leading change*. Harvard Business Review Press.

OECD. (2020). *OECD Principles on Artificial Intelligence*. Organisation for Economic Co-operation and Development.

Sacavém, A., de Bem Machado, A., dos Santos, J. R., Palma-Moreira, A., Belchior-Rocha, H., & Au-Yong-Oliveira, M. (2025). Leading in the digital age: The role of leadership in organizational digital transformation. *Administrative Sciences, 15*(2), 43. DOI: 10.3390/admsci15020043

Sambamurthy, V., Bharadwaj, A., & Grover, V. (2003). Shaping agility through digital options: Reconceptualizing the role of information technology in contemporary firms. *Management Information Systems Quarterly, 27*(2), 237–263. DOI: 10.2307/30036530

Tapscott, D., & Tapscott, A. (2016). *Blockchain Revolution: How the Technology Behind Bitcoin and Other Cryptocurrencies is Changing the World*. Penguin.

Teece, D. J., Peteraf, M., & Leih, S. (2016). Dynamic capabilities and organizational agility: Risk, uncertainty, and strategy in the innovation economy. *California Management Review, 58*(4), 13–35. DOI: 10.1525/cmr.2016.58.4.13

Teece, D. J., Pisano, G., & Shuen, A. (1997). Dynamic capabilities and strategic management. *Strategic Management Journal, 18*(7), 509–533. DOI: 10.1002/(SICI)1097-0266(199708)18:7<509::AID-SMJ882>3.0.CO;2-Z

Tornatzky, L. G., & Fleischer, M. (1990). *The processes of technological innovation*. Lexington Books.

Westerman, G., Bonnet, D., & McAfee, A. (2014). *Leading digital: Turning technology into business transformation*. Harvard Business Review Press.

World Economic Forum. (2022). *Global Technology Governance Report 2022*. WEF.

Zhang, H., Ding, H., & Xiao, J. (2023). How organizational agility promotes digital transformation: An empirical study. *Sustainability (Basel), 15*(14), 11304. DOI: 10.3390/su151411304

Chapter 10
Building Agility Through Digital Emotional Intelligence:
Tech-Infused Organizational Psychodynamic

N. Vinodh
http://orcid.org/0009-0002-8662-2646
Saveetha School of Management, Saveetha Institute of Medical and Technical Sciences, India

A. K. Subramani
http://orcid.org/0000-0003-0783-7113
Saveetha School of Management, Saveetha Institute of Medical and Technical Sciences, India

S. Vijayalakshmi
http://orcid.org/0009-0006-8643-242X
St. Joseph's College of Engineering, India

ABSTRACT

The emerging field of technology-integrated organizational psychodynamics, the significance of digital emotional intelligence (DEI) in enhancing organizational agility in highly complex and uncertain situations. Combining both conceptual analysis and case-based examples, the authors claim that DEI is one of the key capabilities that help to make efficiency and empathy aligned, the innovations and the stability one and the same, as well as a person and a general performance of the organisation. suggests the model of convergence of digital platforms, AI-based analytics, and emotionally intelligent leadership that will support agile transformations. Digital emotional intelligence embedded into the organizational psychodynamics will enable leaders to develop resilience, flexibility, as well as long-term competitive edge in the digital age

INTRODUCTION

In the modern unstable and digitised corporate environments, digital transformation is not only optional, but it becomes a survival requirement. The disruptive technologies, the unstable markets, and

DOI: 10.4018/979-8-3373-4027-2.ch010

the worldwide crises like the COVID-19 pandemic have forced organisations to rapidly move to digital platforms, remote-work infrastructure and artificially intelligence-enhanced operations (Abbas et al., 2024). What was initially a gradual modernisation movement has transformed to a demanding and complex change and has challenged not only the technical skills but also the emotional and psychological stability of organisations. Digital tools can offer a structure of continuity, but it does not necessarily entail flexibility. What is even more challenging is the way people and groups process disruption, uncertainty, and virtual communication weariness on an emotional level. In its turn, this makes organisational psychodynamics of paramount importance. Psychodynamics refers to the hidden forces of emotion, which can be unconscious defence mechanisms, group anxieties, and power dynamics, influencing the collective behaviour and team performance (Wojcik et al., 2020). With the virtual spaces, artificial intelligence, and algorithmic systems transforming the patterns of interactions between people, these emotional undertones grow stronger, becoming more intricate and less apparent (Lawlor, Sher, and Khaleelee, 2023).

The Digital Emotional Intelligence (DEI) construct is becoming eminent in this developing context. DEI is not just a continuation of the traditional emotional intelligence but a general reorganisation that is adjusted to the unique requirements of digitally mediated space. It includes the ability to read emotional signals through screens, decipher delayed digital communication, build psychological security without face-to-face communication, and maintain trust without viewing each other face-to-face (Alsalman and Chyad, 2025). Without this type of emotional intelligence, there is always a danger of technology adoption being mechanical, transactional and disjointed, depriving transformation projects of the human alignment that only leads to success. The consequences of this change go beyond the personal level leaders to the organisational culture and the ability to adapt to the system. Empirical studies show that successful digital teams are based on emotionally intelligent leadership to ensure engagement, creativity, and collaboration despite virtual fatigue and isolation (du Plessis, 2023; Amin and Wang, 2024). Similarly, Lawton-Misra and Pretorius (2021) noted that empathetic leadership and not only institutional policies during the COVID-19 crisis was the key agility and trust driver in academic organisations.

Agility, a term often mentioned in modern management talk, is wrongly understood as a structural competency, e.g. flatter hierarchies or quicker decision making. However, organisational agility is essentially emotional and psychosocial. According to Chatwani (2019), agility is an attitude that is defined by flexibility, emotional management, and ambiguity. Huy (1999) agrees that emotional capability is critical to transformational change than systems or strategy because without emotional compatibility, even the best planed initiatives will fail miserably. In this regard, agility should be understood as a psychodynamic concept the dynamic between speed, empathy, resilience, and coherence of identity. Such distinction is especially important in work environments that are hybrid and virtual where identity and belonging tend to be strained. The same emotional attachment to the organisational purpose and common mission becomes even harder to maintain in the world mediated by the screens and automatized decisions (Albert et al., 2000). Having both distance and dependence towards systems, employees can be both emotionally exhausted and confused with their roles and lose their identities. This chapter argues that Digital Emotional Intelligence will be the key intermediary between the technological transformation and the real organisational agility. DEI helps leaders and teams overcome the emotional gap of virtual collaboration, increase resilience amid the disturbance, and maintain cultural solidarity in decentralised work systems. Without DEI, the organisations will run the risk of being digitally savvy but emotionally vacant, with no adaptive ability to thrive in turbulence. This chapter puts the digital transformation in a new perspective by exploring confluence of technology, emotion and identity using a psychodynamic perspective. It provides a new conceptual and practical framework of understanding how organisations can not only survive disruption, but leverage it - by balancing digital systems with emotional intelligence, trust and an adaptive culture.

CONCEPTUAL FRAMEWORK

To appreciate the origins of organisational agility in the digital age, one cannot simply take a technical approach to making sense of the issue. It requires that organisational identity, emotional systems and collective behaviour be analysed in a holistic manner. Traditionally, organisations were perceived as not just structural systems, but also as systems of emotion, identity, and unconscious group activity, where emotion, identity, and unconscious group processes are central (Albert et al., 2000). Organisational identity is at the centre of this psychodynamic system; it is a construct that is perpetually changing as the members of the system bargain their identity with the institutional values and purpose. The virtual workplaces, the use of AI to make decisions, and the obliteration of the conventional work habits destabilise this identity in the digital context. Therefore, workers find themselves frequently torn between belonging and being out of place, productivity and burnout, automation and authenticity. These challenges were condensed by the COVID-19 pandemic. According to the authors, as Abbas et al. (2024) state, crises are initiators of emergent innovation and also reveal the weaknesses of organisations. Adaptive capacity does not rely on technical infrastructure during such times but also on individual and team emotional and psychological processing of change.

Systems Psychodynamics: Emotional Infrastructure

A more powerful prism through which these emotional and relational responses are viewed is systems psychodynamics. Wojcik et al. (2020) argue that based on technological acceleration, unconscious group processes, including anxiety, avoidance, or dependency, are often triggered, which affect organisational decisions. Lawlor et al. (2023) further this perspective and show that digitalisation and AI do not only change the pattern of communication, but also the emotional climate of organisations, and unveil the latent conflict between the demands of efficiency and the human desire to connect. In this sense, the digital transformation is not an entirely technical phenomenon; it is an emotional reorganisation of the relations between people, groups, and organisations. The forces of agility enhance these reconfigurations, requiring speed and innovation, though these forces can shatter the foundations of trusts and psychological safety, without emotionally intelligent systems to back them up.

Agility as a Psychodynamic Construct

Although structural modifications are favoured by most organisations to achieve agility, like flattened hierarchies, agile process, and digitalisation, they often disregard the emotional basis of adaptability. According to Chatwani (2019), agility is not a structural change but a cultural and psychological ability to foresee, react, and change. This position is also supported by Rajagopal (2022, 2023), who defines agility as a state of mind based on being emotionally prepared, being open to uncertainty, and collaboration across groups. In psychodynamic perspective, organisational agility cannot exist without positive management of fear, loss and uncertainty. In case organisations direct these hidden emotional energies into defensive ways of operation instead of growth-focused strategies, change does not take hold (Langemeyer, 2019).

DEI and Leadership as Intermediaries

Leadership has a critical role to play in determining the manner in which organisations deal with these tensions. The skill of emotional intelligence (EI) is a crucial skill set, especially when technology adoption overlaps with emotional instability. More precisely, leaders have to cope with stress, read between the emotional climates, and establish positive interpersonal relationships (Roux & Härtel, 2018). Recent reports suggest that emotionally intelligent leaders were more effective in the COVID-19 crisis at ensuring trust, continuity, and psychological safety (Lawton -Misra and Pretorius, 2021; Sachdeva and Mitra, 2025). These leadership qualities transform into Digital Emotional Intelligence (DEI) in hybrid and virtual environments, which is a skill to positively influence the emotions of others online, to build trust in a digital environment, and to provide psychological safety in hybrid space (Alsalman and Chyad, 2025; Pramila, 2025).

Organisational Culture and DEI on a Large Scale

DEI should no longer be part of leadership, but an organisational culture. Since digital workspaces are expanding possibilities of miscommunication, social exclusion, and disengagement, emotional intelligence is the key to maintaining creativity and cooperation (Amin and Wang, 2024). It has also been demonstrated that trait-based EI facilitates individual thriving when facing unpredictable surroundings (du Plessis, 2023). The failure to have such capabilities means that organisations will be functionally sound but emotionally disjointed and thus less innovative and less motivated. When fostered on an organisational-wide basis, DEI provides the organisation with environments where emotional energy is directed positively instead of being directed negatively.

Emotional Readiness, Risk, and Resilience

One of the dimensions of this framework is resilience. Dahmen (2023) does not just conceive resilience as a recovery process after a crisis but as a continual change to the digital disruption. DEI is a prerequisite to the rapid change because it provides emotional strength and flexibility. Systems psychodynamics suggest that the development of the real resilience is achieved by the combination of the strategy with the conscious and unconscious emotional regulation in the system (Langemeyer, 2019).

Ethics, Identity, and Cultural Preparedness

Lastly, any digital transformation has to be approached with an ethical and a cultural approach. Marhenke (2025) raises the question of whether the profession, like law, is not only technologically prepared but also emotionally and culturally prepared to take the AI. Vettriselvan (2025) cautions that in the absence of value-based strategies, the digital adoption might result in identity destruction, alienation of employees, and deterioration of mental health. The results highlight the importance of ethics that are technologically-adopted with emotional intelligence, with the focus on the safety of the psychology, fairness, and inclusion.

THEORETICAL FRAMEWORK

The modern discussion about digital transformation requires strong background of theoretical constructs that explain the dynamics of affect, unconsciousness, and relationships, which govern the behaviour of organisations. The suggested theoretical framework of technology-infused organisational psychodynamics is based on four interconnected pillars of the classical psychodynamic theory, systems psychodynamics, emotional intelligence (EI), and its modern counterpart, digital emotional intelligence (DEI). All of these lenses provide a multilevel explanatory schema of the ways organisations process technological change in an effective manner, and how leadership, identity and resilience become central capabilities of coping with disruption. The role of unconscious processes, affective energy and defence mechanisms in the influencing of individual and collective behaviour has long been postulated by classical psychodynamic theory. In organisational settings, these forces occur in how the members react to uncertainty, change and identity changes. The conceptualised affective undercurrents (denial, projection, or regression) initially developed in the psychoanalytic frame of thinking, and later institutionalised, can either help or hinder adaptive responses. This discussion was extended by Huy (1999) who came up with the concept of emotional capability where organisations that have the ability to sense, express, and regulate emotion in a group tend to succeed in transformational periods. Emotional ability thus forms the psychological groundwork, on which the resilience and adaptability is built.

Based on these findings, systems psychodynamics offers a macro-level view of unconscious processes at both organisational systems and between organisational systems. It mediates between the personal mind and the collective formations, including groupthink, group power and cultural defence mechanism. These dynamics are heightened as organisations are forced to deal with digital acceleration. According to Wojcik et al. (2020), technological pressure often causes unconscious group defence that is reflected in decision-making and patterns of behaviour. Similarly, Lawlor, Sher, and Khaleelee (2023) argue that digitalisation, artificial intelligence, and virtual collaboration are not only changes in the structure, but also in the affective sphere that change the psychological landscape of work. These theorists believe that systems psychodynamics is essential in finding out the hidden tensions, fears, and identity threats that might either hinder or facilitate the digital transformation. In this respect, change is not just a simple technological update; it is a psychodynamic disorientation that requires increased emotional and cultural sensitivity. The theory of emotional intelligence assists in the leadership of navigating these tensions in a strong manner. The concept of EI can be explained as the ability to sense, process, manage and utilise emotions both in oneself and others. EI also has a direct correlation with trust-building, psychological safety, and constructive conflict resolution in the areas of leadership, all of which are imperative in the context of change. Roux and Härtel (2018) outline EI in three dimensions, namely cognitive understanding of emotions, emotional regulation, and behavioural use in social situations. They argue that effective digital leaders are the ones who do not only coordinate the working processes but also moods. The view is supported by du Plessis (2023), who discovered that trait emotional intelligence is a personality trait that high-level individuals tend to cope positively, maintain and show psychological resilience in challenging times. The emotionally intelligent leaders, therefore, act as emotional anchor in times of collective uncertainty.

With the restructuring of communication and the cooperation due to the digitalisation process, the conventional frameworks of emotional intelligence have to be modified. This development has culminated in the current constructive development of the digital emotional intelligence (DEI), referring to the ability to identify and control emotions in virtual, screen-mediated contexts. DEI requires the ability to read non-verbal digital communication, tone regulation in text-based messages, maintenance of psychological presence, and the development of remote trust. According to Sachdeva and Mitra (2025), to maintain a positive and unified organisational culture in digital workspaces, it is important to have DEI. According to their findings, leaders who model DEI practises are in a better position to establish virtual cohesion, employee engagement, and emotional safety. Similarly, Alsalman and Chyad (2025) show how in agile software development, which is marked by rapid and, in most cases, online cooperation, DEI helps the team to maintain cohesion and pressure-resilient performance. Pramila (2025) also opines that the new digital era of leadership is characterised by the combination of technical expertise and emotional intelligence. Leaders who lack DEI can effectively implement new technologies but will not cultivate a sense of inclusivity and emotional engagement cultures, thus limiting the long-term agility that the technologies they aim to promote suggest. There is more theoretical importance of DEI than leadership. EI is associated with a wider organisational performance such as innovation and resilience. Amin and Wang (2024) demonstrate that EI mitigates the negative impact of social media ostracism on creativity in digital teams, which means that emotional management plays a crucial role in innovativeness in virtually mediated environments. The agility of organisations is usually based on creativity, which in turn is dependent on the emotional openness, trust, and psychological freedom, which DEI fosters. Another vital quality of organisations in the process of digital disruption, which is in line with the EI theory, is resilience. The conceptualisation of resilience presented by Dahmen (2023) does not assume recovery but rather ongoing adaptation and capacity of the psyche to respond to changes. Psychodynamically, this means that one must address group fears and convert emotional energy into positive adaptation. Du Plessis (2023) affirms that EI fosters thriving through positive coping mechanisms, optimism, and hope. DEI is able to carry this capacity into the digital realm so that people and leaders can be emotionally anchored in the technological mess. The organisational identity theory is also an addition to this framework as it explains the way members anchor their selves in institutions. Albert, Ashforth, and Dutton (2000) affirm that identity is dynamic and is a continuous bargain between personal and organisational values particularly during times of transition. Digital transformation is breaking this identification by changing the rules of communication, the job description, and presence itself. DEI is an important factor in maintaining relational affiliation and cultural persistence in the disseminated, technologically mediated workplaces. It also allows members to remain emotionally connected with organisational purpose despite the destabilisation of conventional structures of belonging.

The technological-enhanced psychodynamics have to be characterised by an extensive theoretical framework that will cover the ethical and cultural aspects of digital transformation. Marhenke (2025) laments excessive use of technological preparedness and warns that emotional and cultural unpreparedness can break down the use of AI in certain fields like law. Vettriselvan (2025) applies this argument to online learning and recommends introducing value-based change, which will integrate emotional wellbeing, ethics, and inclusivity. Vettriselvan et al. (2025) further reinforce these anxieties by noting the issues of mental health in the digital age, and especially among the younger generations. These views demonstrate the importance of psychodynamic and emotional literacy as the requirements of responsible technological adoption. Overall, the provided theoretical framework combines psychodynamic theory, systems thinking, emotional intelligence, and digital emotional literacy to provide an all-encompassing model of organisational adaptation to the digital era. It emphasises the importance of affective undercurrents to be in the centre of the digital transformation, not on the periphery. Overlooking psychological and cultural aspects of development makes the technological change unpredictably in the sphere of emotions.

Digital emotional intelligence will become the integrative process that allows organisations to humanise the disruption, maintain cohesion, and transform with dynamism and intent.

RESEARCH METHODOLOGY

To explore how digital emotional intelligence (DEI) and organisational psychodynamics intersect to form agility in digitally transformed workplaces, this paper used a hybrid approach to the research. Empirical design was chosen as it would reinforce and elaborate the theoretical approach as it would give both quantifiable information and an experience. Due to the multifaceted multi-layered nature of such psychodynamic phenomena in technology-mediated situations, the study combined both quantitative and qualitative approaches to research in order to reflect the scope of visible trends and the complexity of under-the-surface human response. It was a mixed-method approach that allowed studying not only the construct relationships but also the realities lived by professionals in the context of digital transformation. The research sample consisted of 238 participants. These were sampled by a purposive and snowball sample, and the major inclusion criterion was that the person had at least one year of experience working on digital collaboration or remote work. The respondents were a cross-section of technology-intensive industries, such as the development of software, higher education, and the service industries, which are digitally dependent. The high composition of the sample was not accidental, and it was varied in terms of roles, demographics, and cases of organisation. This heterogeneity increased the ability to generalise findings in digital work ecosystems and had more insights into how DEI operates in various organisational environments. Data collection was done using two supplementary tools. To begin with, an online survey was created with the use of the validated scales on the emotional intelligence, agility, and resilience. They comprised constructs of the trait emotional intelligence models (du Plessis, 2023), agility scales of organisational literature (Chatwani, 2019), and resilience scales of enterprise adaptability (Dahmen, 2023). The survey was translated into digital work realities, with the inclusion of items which are relevant to virtual collaboration, the use of technology, and AI-mediated decision-making. Along with the closed-ended Likert-type items, the open-ended questions were included to obtain the responses of the participants in the form of the storey about the digital leadership, team-related processes, and emotional experiences in remote or hybrid workplace.

The second tool was semi-structured interviews with a voluntary subsample of 36 respondents which were selected out of the survey sample. These were the virtual interviews conducted in accordance with the study theme of digital work environments. The themes addressed in the interview protocol included organisational identity changes (Albert et al., 2000), emotional processes at the systems level brought about by digitisation (Lawlor et al., 2023), and leadership role in promoting resilience by way of emotional intelligence (Alsalman and Pramila, 2025; Pramila, 2025). This qualitative element made it possible to analyse organisational psychodynamics (emotional resistance, unconscious anxieties, and formation of trust) that are typically unavailable to surveys but at the same time very important in organisational settings. The data analysis was done in 2 phases, due to the two-strand nature of the research design. The descriptive and inferential statistical methods were employed to analyse quantitative data. Correlations were used to determine the connexion between digital emotional intelligence, agility and resilience. Afterwards, regression equations were created to determine the mediating impact of DEI in the correlation between technological adoption and organisational agility. This was a test of the hypothetical assertion that emotional aptitude acts as an important connexion between structural change and adaptive functioning (Huy, 1999). The survey instruments were analysed by the reliability analysis of Cronbach alpha to be able to guarantee internal consistency between scales.

This is because thematic coding was used to analyse the qualitative information obtained by the means of open-ended survey responses and interviews. Two researchers conducted their independent review and coding of transcripts to increase the credibility. Similar themes were repeatedly compared, and any differences in their interpretation agreed upon by the peers, which guaranteed the analytical rigour and intercoder reliability. The theme categories were emotional regulation, identity negotiation, group dynamics and perceived leadership behaviours in digital environments. This interpretive layer offered useful psychodynamic information that puts into focus the emotional profiles of technological change which can scarcely be measured using a quantitative measure alone. The study used a number of quality control mechanisms to guarantee validity and rigour. The quantitative and qualitative data triangulation also increased the believability of the results, as the trends and themes were cross-validated. Researcher debriefing with peers helped in promoting reflexivity and alleviating the risk of bias by the researcher. Ethical guidelines were followed strictly, the subjects were notified of the voluntary study, they gave informed consent and were assured of confidentiality and anonymity. No personally identifiable information was gathered and any data were safely stored and as per the institutional rules.

Although the research offers strong knowledge, it does not go without limitations. Despite the statistical adequacy of the sample, the composition of the sample was concentrated in a few industries, which could limit the capacity to generalise findings. Moreover, the use of self-reporting data to measure emotional intelligence is prone to bias because people might not adequately assess or be overconfident of the emotional competencies they have. Subsequent studies can overcome this limitation by integrating 360-degree feedback or observation test. Nevertheless, the combination of survey and interview techniques provided a comprehensive perspective to the integration of measurable trends as well as the less obvious emotional accounts of digital transformation. The methodological design is indicative of an attempt to bring together empirical accuracy and psychodynamic sophistication. This study is an attempt to unveil the entire scope of organisational experience in the digital environment, combining the rigour of the quantitative approach with the richness of the qualitative approach. The results are placed so as to shed light on how agility is not merely the derivative of technology euphoria, but an emergent aspect based on the interaction of emotional intelligence, leadership, identity, and shared emotional processes. The given approach supports the main thesis of the research that digital transformation should be perceived as a structural and psychodynamic process, and digital emotional intelligence should be taken as an essential mediator of organisational adaptability.

RESULTS AND DISCUSSION

Survey and interview data, analyzed on a sample of 238 professionals, provides useful information on the role of digital emotional intelligence (DEI) in mediating the association between technology adoption, organizational psychodynamics, and agility. The results not only show quantifiable relationships between DEI and resilience and agility but also the qualitative data set sheds light on the underlying psychodynamic processes in which these relationships are realized. When combined, they give grounds to believe that agility does not come about as the outcome of technological transformation but a multifaceted combination of technical, emotional, and psychological abilities in the organisations. The descriptive statistics indicated that the participants have moderate to high levels of digital emotional intelligence with a mean of 3.8 in a 5-point scale. The items adapted to Chatwani (2019) and Rajagopal (2022) gave an average of 3.6 and 3.7 respectively, with the highest measurement of 4.2 and maximum of 3.8 respectively. The organizational agility measured with the help of the items adapted to Chatwani (2019) and Rajagopal (2022) had an average of 3.6 and 3.7 respectively, with the highest score of 4.2 and the highest score of 3.8 The levels of emotional intelligence were significantly and positively correlated with resilience ($r = .62$, $p = .01$) and moderately with organizational agility ($r = .51$, $p = .01$), indicating that emotionally intelligent capabilities are the basis of adaptability. Regression analyses established that DEI had a significant mediating effect on the connection between technology adoption and organizational agility, meaning that the use of technological tools alone was not an indicator of agility, without the need to have the practices of emotional intelligence in the table 1.

Table 1. Descriptive Statistics of Key Variables (N = 238)

Variable	Mean	SD	Scale Range	Cronbach's Alpha
Digital Emotional Intelligence	3.8	0.54	1–5	0.89
Organizational Agility	3.6	0.61	1–5	0.87
Resilience	3.7	0.57	1–5	0.88

Table 2. Correlation Matrix of Key Constructs

Variables	1	2	3
1. Digital Emotional Intelligence	1		
2. Organizational Agility	.51**	1	
3. Resilience	.62**	.55**	1

Note: p < .01

The table 2 regression correlation analyses also revealed that diversity, equity, and inclusion (DEI) explained the 28 per cent of organizational agility despite adjusting variables such as industry and role. This empirical result supports the previous theoretical statements that emotional capacity is a pre-requisite of radical change (Huy, 1999). Without the DEI, the assimilation of technology accounted for only 12 % of the variability in agility and it was clear that the technical systems were insufficient to result in the creation of adaptability without corresponding emotional and psychodynamic preparedness. Three common themes were identified: (1) anxiety and trust in the digital spaces; (2) identity reconstruction in a disruptive technological environment; and (3) emotional regulation as a shared resource. Respondents often mentioned an increase in anxiety about artificial intelligence and digitalisation, which is consistent with the arguments of Lawlor, Sher, and Khaleelee (2023) on the emotional effects of technological ecosystems on organisations. An example of this is when one of the respondents stated that AI leaves me excited and irrelevant simultaneously, which summarises the ambivalence experienced by many employees. When unchecked, these anxieties have a risk of being expressed through defensive behaviours including resistance or disengagement. Leaders who have scored high in DEI were seen as being crucial in reducing these fears, establishing trust, and re-constituting technological disruption as an opportunity instead of a threat.

The second theme included the organisational and personal identity reconstruction. Digital integration often disrupted conventional indicators of membership especially in the distant and virtual contexts. Identity processes have a key role in alignment of individuals in institutions just like Albert, Ashforth, and Dutton (2000) argue. Respondents said that they felt detached in online settings but also were renewed in their identities when leaders established positive cultures on the internet. Leaders who had exhibited DEI generated a storey of common cause that enabled organisational identification despite disintegrated digital environments. Lastly, there was the collective resource of emotional regulation. When the teams clearly recognized stress and made use of reflective practice, they were more resilient. This finding is consistent with the results found by du Plessis (2023) that flourishing as mediated by positive coping behaviours. The practises described by interviewees included the use of virtual meetings where emotional cheque-ins were organised or the use of digital channels to exchange reflections. The practises lowered the levels of defensiveness and encouraged positive interaction, thus demonstrating how the concept of psychodynamic awareness and emotional intelligence can transform organisational cultures.

The findings are in close relation to the focus of psychodynamic theory on the importance of unconscious processes in change. As Huy (1999) claimed, radical change entails the employment of emotional ability and the current statistics offer empirical evidence in support of this argument in the digital age. DEI serves as the engine behind the creation of this capability in organisations to direct the anxiety into flexibility and convert resistance into resiliency. Systems psychodynamics has additional explanatory potential: according to the suggestion of Wójcik et al. (2020), latent anxieties are awakened by the processes of acceleration provoked by digitalisation. The results of the study prove that the mentioned processes are mediated by DEI, which allows organisations to cope with emotional turbulence instead of being destabilised. The results also support studies that were conducted on leadership and emotional intelligence. According to Roux and Härtel (2018), cognitive, emotional, and behavioural traits are needed in new working settings, traits discovered to be essential in digital settings by the participants. High DEI leaders did not merely get things done, but also took care of the emotional atmosphere of remote teams and thus kept motivation and cohesion high. This is similar to the findings of Alsalman and Chyad (2025), who found emotional intelligence in leadership to improve flexibility in agile software projects. In the same way, Pramila (2025) points out that successful leadership in the digital age is a combination of technical expertise and emotional intelligence, the fact that is supported by the survey and interview data.

Creativity and innovation were also realised as a result of DEI, which is also in line with Amin and Wang (2024) who discovered that emotional intelligence mediates the negative impact of digital ostracism on creativity. The respondents involved in the present research explained how DEI established inclusive online environments that enabled collaboration and innovation, thus proving that organisational agility is not only about the speed but also the ability to develop new solutions when challenged. This connection supports the more general claim that agility is both psychological and structural. Resilience as a construct received empirical support. According to Dahmen (2023), resilience is key to the enterprise risk management and the current study revealed that there were strong correlations between resilience scores and DEI. Interviews also found out that resilience was not only experienced as bouncing back but as a process of constant adaptation, which is also focused on by Langemeyer (2019) in high-tech work of mindfulness and psychodynamics. The discovery supports the idea that resilience in digital organisations is a continuous reorientation process, which is based on shared emotional regulation.

There were issues of ethics and culture in qualitative and quantitative data. Some of the participants, citing Marhenke (2025) concerns in professions like law, were sceptical about cultural preparedness of organisations to adopt AI. The necessity to synchronize digital transformation with human wellbeing was also noted by the respondents, which is similar to Vettriselvan (2025) on value-based digital education and Vettriselvan, Velmurugan, Varshney, EP, and Deepika (2025) on the mental health implications of technology. These observations imply that in the absence of DEI, digital adoption is likely to be an estrangement process, which destabilises identity and wellbeing. First, digital transformation must be conceptualised as a psychodynamic process. The adoption of technology is not in a vacuum but it is in contact with unconscious forces, anxiety and negotiations of identities. The organisations that overlook such dimensions will be prone to developing weak forms of agility crumbling under the pressure. Second, digital emotional intelligence is an important mediator. Without DEI, the use of technology produces topical transformation but with DEI, profound flexibility emerges. This is in line with the literature which is insisting on the need of emotionally intelligent leadership during the digital era (Alsalman and Chyad, 2025; Pramila, 2025). As a result, organisations need to invest in building DEI not only at the top of the organisation but across teams to make sure that agility becomes part of the culture. Third, organisations that incorporate DEI in their psychodynamics are more resilient and creative. Organisational recognition and management of emotions enable organisations to establish psychological safety under which innovation and flexibility thrive. This highlights the fact that agility is not only technical speed, but the ability to succeed in the face of uncertainty, which aligns with how Rajagopal (2022, 2023) frames the agile mindset.

SOLUTIONS AND RECOMMENDATIONS

The results of the present research highlight the fact that to become agile in the digital era, the organisation should not rely only on technological integration or reorganisation. Rather, agility is a result of an active fit of digital technology, emotional intelligence, and psychodynamic functioning that influence human behaviour in organisations. The study presents a fresh approach since it introduces digital emotional intelligence (DEI) as an essential intermediary in the connexion between technology and adaptability. Basing the recommendations on the empirical analysis and theoretical foundation, a group of multi-level suggestions is provided to integrate DEI on personal, organisational, and systemic levels. These measures are to make sure that agility is a long-lasting, integrated aspect and not a reaction to disruption. On the personal level, both leaders and employees have to focus on the development of DEI. Although emotional intelligence was regarded as a key indicator of successful leadership in the past (Roux & Härtel, 2018), it should be adjusted to the digital workplace. These are the ability of the leaders to develop sensitivity to subtle emotional signals in online interaction, development of sense of belonging in dispersed teams, and the use of digital tools in establishing psychological confidence. DEI-specific training may be based on implicit emotional intelligence models (du Plessis, 2023), including role-playing, computer simulation, and introspective exercises, which will help with disengagement in online conferences or fear of AI-based conclusions. Structured DEI development also benefits employees, especially in collaborating, creativity, and emotional control, the areas that are essential to the efficient work in the hybrid or remote setting.

On the organisational level, institutionalisation of DEI requires structural and cultural changes. Agility is not only structural, as Chatwani (2019) puts it, but it is a psychological and cultural one. Thus, DEI is to be integrated with organisational practises, strategic planning, and leadership development. The practises that organisations may use to monitor the well-being of employees include digital emotional cheque-ins during virtual meetings, virtual communities of reflection, or AI-based sentiment analysis software. Nevertheless, the worth of technology, as Marhenke (2025) also helps to remember, lies not in the data that it produces, but in the ethical and understanding manner in which leaders apply the technology. The implementation of DEI in everyday practise contributes to the development of proactive resilience and creativity, which means that the psychological health is not put on the backburner to the performance metrics. At the systems level, leaders should identify and deal with the emotional undercurrents that tend to be collective in the periods of digital transformation. Lawlor, Sher, and Khaleelee (2023) underline that digitalization is not only a transformation of organisational frames but also it has the impact of altering the emotional landscapes that people live within. Leaders are then invited to build secure psychological environments in which employees can openly express themselves on issues of uncertainty like fear of job loss to AI- changing resistance into engagement. Identity work is also very important in aiding employees to derive meaning in the face of technological disruption. According to Albert, Ashforth, and Dutton (2000), organisational identity also requires constant renegotiation, and DEI can allow leaders to generate storeys of inclusion, meaning, and belonging in the increasingly digitalized world.

The implementation of DEI to organisational psychodynamics leads to resilience, which is one of the key outcomes to change and uncertainty management. Dahmen (2023) puts resilience in the context of enterprise risk management as one of its pillars. This paper confirms the argument that resilience is not an ordinary resource, but a psychodynamic process, which encompasses emotional regulation, positive coping, and shared adaptation. Organisations ought to consider putting more investments to resilience-building programmes which encompass virtual storytelling platforms, digital mindfulness workshops, and reflective art-based sessions. Such efforts enable interpersonal bond and psychological safety, as well as minimising defensive behaviours. Such programmes as du Plessis (2023) discovered can promote individual and group prosperity by mediating emotional intelligence. DEI is also significant in ensuring innovation. As Amin and Wang (2024) show, the impact of social exclusion in digital space can be alleviated by emotional intelligence and maintain creativity even when one experiences pressure. This can be capitalised by organisations developing digital collaboration tools that will facilitate inclusiveness, whereby no member of the team will feel sidelined in digital environments. Encouraging teams to see problems optimistically and take initiative should be fronted by the leaders as an opportunity to creatively solve problems rather than a compliance experience to digital transformation. This way, DEI can not only act as a protective buffer but also a growth and innovation generating force.

On a more general note regarding the implications of DEI, it has wider policy and governance implications. With the help of the framework of mindful education offered by Ragoonaden (2015), the issue of emotional intelligence and well-being must be officially included in the policies formulated at the workplace as a strategic goal. This can be aided by regulators and policymakers who are required to place DEI metrics within leadership competency models, workplace audit, and professional certification. Organisations ought to be motivated to create digital dashboards with the implementation of both operational and emotional indicators-integrating measures of productivity with the level of trust, psychological safety, and emotional resilience in employees. These AI-enhanced dashboards would provide real-time feedback loops and help leaders to respond to the first signs of disengagement with compassion and vision. Vettriselvan et al. (2025) point to the risks of mental health in general in terms of rapid changes in technology as generational cohorts, which requires proactive monitoring. DEI may be used as a guideline to monitor emotional health and digital adoption, and as a result, it is a physical and quantifiable part of organisational output. DEI offers a solution between human values and technological efficiency when integrated wisely into systems and strategy. To synthesise these recommendations, the following conceptual model illustrates the process by which DEI fosters organisational agility by mediating between technology adoption and psychodynamics in Figure 1:

Figure 1. Conceptual Model for Organizational Psychodynamics

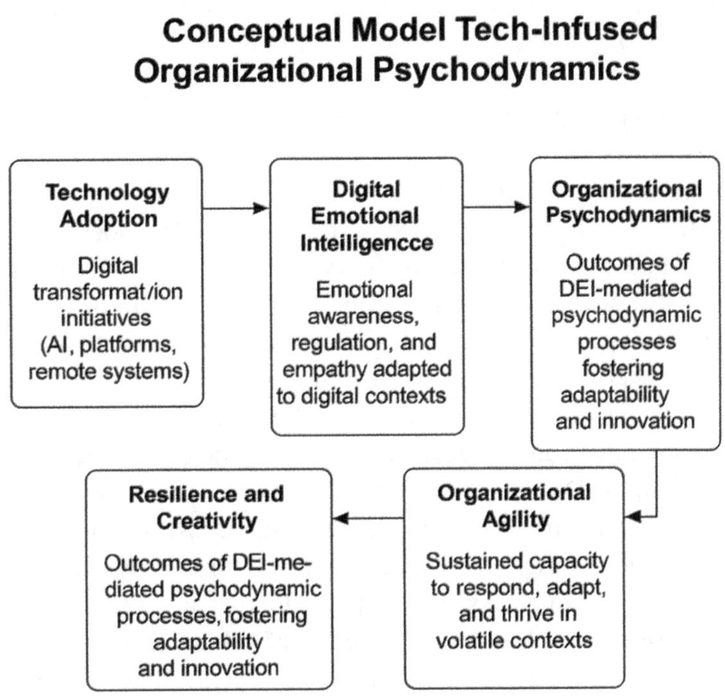

This model argues that organizational agility cannot be achieved by implementing technology, but rather it comes about by combining technological skills with emotional intelligence and psychodynamic awareness. Diversity, Equity and Inclusion (DEI) serves as the connecting tissue, which transforms technological possibilities into sustainable flexibility. The suggestions outlined below do not come without challenges. The creation of DEI requires an investment in training programmes and changing the organisational culture, which can be met with resistance in companies that are used to focus on technical competences and neglect affective capabilities. Moreover, psychodynamic aspects of organisations are often intangible and immeasurable, which makes the employment of complex methodologies on leadership and cultural change. However, according to empirical evidence, without DEI, the process of digital adoption is likely to trigger only superficial agility structural and systemic changes that do not produce enduring agility. Practically, organisations that successfully incorporate DEI into their psychodynamic structures are able to balance between efficiency and empathy, speed and thoughtfulness, and innovation and stability.

FUTURE RESEARCH DIRECTIONS

The current research can find several prospects of future research at the intersection of digital emotional intelligence (DEI), organisational agility, and psychodynamics. Although it provides significant material, it also reveals the gaps in research, both theoretical and practical, that are worth another academic investigation. These gaps include longitudinal paths, cultures, technology adoption, industry-specific uses, policy system, and methodological change, which provide a critical approach to future investigations and enhancement of DEI in dynamic organisational environments. One of the main avenues of future research is a longitudinal study of DEI and organisational agility. The given investigation was restricted to the six-month observation period that allowed identifying the short-term interrelations between DEI, resilience, and agility. However, the question that remains is whether these effects are continuing, fading or undergoing changes in the long-run due to digital fatigue, technological overload, or the change of organisational priorities. Resilience, as argued by Dahmen (2023), does not only imply the ability to resume after being disrupted, but also the possibility to undergo continuous adaptation. To this end, longitudinal designs that follow organisations over multiple years would be able to determine whether DEI is agile or whether other psychological abilities are required due to the long-term effects of technological change, thus uncovering whether DEI is enduring or whether it is attenuated as an predictor of adaptive competence when faced with long-term transformation.

The other line of research that can be considered salient is the cross-cultural comparison of DEI in digitally oriented organisations. Different literature that has been available on emotional intelligence and its digital forms has been predominantly developed within the Western theoretical paradigms. Since organisational psychodynamics is often integrated into the cultural norms and storeys, DEI might take different forms in sociocultural settings. As an example, Albert et al. (2000) highlight that the construction of organisational identity takes place through the use of culturally based storeys. DEI can preempt relational harmony, collective resiliency, and emotional dependency in collectivist contexts, and stress personal adaptability, autonomy and self-regulation in individualistic contexts. Regional, industry, or cultural cluster comparative studies would help illuminate the adaptability and/or limitations of DEI to the cultural norms and how this affects the global applicability of the construct and broadens the psychodynamic framework across contexts. The third emergent research topic is the interaction of DEI with new technologies, like artificial intelligence (AI), automation and immersive digital spaces like the metaverse. Lawlor, Sher, and Khaleelee (2023) explain the way in which AI restructures the work processes and reconfigures emotional ecosystems of organisations. However, in most cases, as Marhenke (2025) warns, technology preparation usually exceeds emotional and cultural adaption, creating dissonance and resistance. Future research can investigate the effects of DEI in alleviating the fear of redundancy, ethical ambivalence, and psychodynamic conflicts between human and machine decision-making. Social presence and embodiment technologies that transform social presence may also bring new emotional dynamics that require new DEI models that can contribute to creation of psychodynamically aware DEI frameworks that suit the more complex digital workspaces.

Another potential area of development is exploring how DEI can be used to promote innovation and creativity in digitally mediated teams. Although Amin and Wang (2024) established that emotional intelligence helps in mitigating negative outcome of digital ostracism on creativity, studies directly related to the influence of DEI on organisational innovation are few. Since agility is a concept with an intrinsic impact on the quick creation of new solutions (Rajagopal, 2022, 2023), additional research may evaluate how DEI contributes to creative problem-solving, inter-team collaboration, and adaptive experimentation in virtual or hybrid teams. These studies would help to fill the existing propositions in the literature with practical data, supporting the psychological basis of agile innovation in a digital setting. The investigation of sectors offers a vital prospect of building on the scholarship of DEI. Despite the fact that this research sampled technological-driven sectors, the meaning and expression of DEI might differ depending on the field of healthcare, education, law, and public service. To provide an example, Lawton-Misra and Pretorius (2021) have found empathetic leadership as one of the key factors to maintain academic institutions in times of crisis, thus highlighting the importance of DEI in people-centred careers. On the same note, Vettriselvan (2025) says that there is need to instil value-based models of digital education that can match the use of technologies with human progress. Studies that are particularly profession-specific like medical education, legal practise and digital entrepreneurship might provide insights on how DEI assists with sector-specific psychodynamics, emotional workload, and leadership issues. Besides sectoral depth, the institutionalisation of DEI in policy, governance and organisation systems is in dire need of research. Most of the published literature focuses on the topic of DEI at the personal or leadership level, but comparatively little has been done to integrate DEI into their organisational policies, accreditation standards, or performance models. Sachdeva and Mitra (2025) speculate that it is possible to transform digital organisational cultures by emotional intelligence, but the question is how the policy can create such changes. Future research can focus on the way DEI is implemented at the board-level governance, leadership scales, or industry-wide qualifications, and thus help in including emotional and psychodynamic measures into the nimble organisational practises.

The study should take on psychodynamic approaches that would explore the unconscious mechanisms that drive DEI in future studies. As Langemeyer (2019) emphasises, critical psychology and mindfulness are the means of analysing emotional life in high-tech setting, and they may be enriched with the help of the psychodynamic methods like the role analysis, free association, or the group relation approaches. The combination of this qualitative level and digital analytics and behavioural data would possibly provide a subtle insight into DEI at both conscious and unconscious levels. These approaches would not only broaden the theoretical knowledge base; however, they would generate viable instruments of diagnosing and improving DEI in the context of actual organisations. Digital emotional intelligence is a promising area that resides at the intersection of technology, psychology, and organisational theory. This convergence needs to be further investigated in future studies with methodological rigidity and cultural sensitivity. The emotional and psychological impact of the digital transformation is enormous and long-term, as Vettriselvan et al. (2025) warn. It is only through the expansion of the research base in terms of time, culture, industries and methodologies that DEI will move beyond being a theoretical category to being an actual, evidence based realistic driver of human-centric organisational agility in a digital era.

CONCLUSION

This chapter affirms that the agility in organisations in digital times cannot be sufficiently explained by means of technological application or structural redesign. Instead, agility is a product of technological change, emotional, and organisational psychodynamics interacting at a point. An imaginative structure based on tech-infused psychodynamics demonstrates how the ability of institutions to adjust to disruption is determined by the influence of emotional undertones, unconscious group processes, and identity negotiations. Digital emotional intelligence (DEI), as presented and explored herein, is a very important integrative skill that fills the divide between technological and emotional adjustment, facilitating long term resilience, creativity and prosperity of an organisation. The results of empirical studies involving a sample of 238 professionals who were placed in digitally intensive settings confirm the positive relationship between DEI and resilience as well as agility. The quantitative tests verified that DEI will mediate the relationship between technology use and agility, and the qualitative results revealed the psychodynamic processes behind adaptation, which are anxiety, ambivalence, and identity strain. The respondents outlined how emotional intelligence leadership was crucial in ensuring trust, engagement, and psychological safety amongst virtual environments. It resonates with the argument presented by Huy (1999) that emotional capability is the key to radical change and brings it to the digitally mediated organisational life wherein DEI is the driving force between technical and human adaptation.

The findings also correlate with the systems psychodynamic theory, which supports the idea that rational decisions are only a part of the organisational change process, and the unconscious emotional processes also contribute to it. Digitalization transforms the emotional ecosystem of organisations, which is also noted by Lawlor, Sher, and Khaleelee (2023), and technological acceleration triggers collective anxieties (Wojcik et al., 2020). The current research demonstrates that through DEI organisations can be assisted to react positively to such unconscious processes instead of defensively, avoiding any reaction of resistance, disengagement, and culture fragmentation in the process of transformation initiatives. The Leadership was identified to be a decisive variable in converting DEI to organisational agility. People indicated that leaders with high DEI were observed to be sensitive to emotional signals in virtual meetings and could create psychological safety, as well as the ability to establish trust-driven cultures. The attributes complement the work of Roux and Härtel (2018) and other more recent studies, such as the works by Alsalman and Chyad (2025) and Pramila (2025) who support the argument that leadership in the digital era should combine emotional and technical skills. In the absence of this emotionally intelligent leadership, agility is only weak, technology empowered and psychologically immature.

Organisational identity is another aspect that is important to digital transformation. According to Albert et al. (2000), the work of identity is at the heart of institutional change process among the members. The present research indicated that digital disruption tends to disrupt organisational identity, which generates a sense of disconnection. Nonetheless, supportive storeys made by DEI-informed leaders were able to give employees a feeling of purpose and belonging again and remind them that agility is also based not only on digital tools but also that meaningful interaction and a sense of identity. The introduction of DEI into the psychodynamic systems had two other effects, resilience and creativity. The respondents understood the concept of resilience as an ability to continue adapting as opposed to recovering after disruption, which is consistent with a conception of resilience as a psychodynamic and conscious reaction to high-tech work (Langemeyer, 2019). Furthermore, it was also observed that the use of emotionally intelligent cultures promoted creativity, which confirms the findings of Amin and Wang (2024) that DEI alleviates exclusion and fosters innovation in the digital domain.

Ethical and cultural issues of digital transformation also emerged as major themes. Marhenke (2025) questioned the emotional preparedness of the AI-intensive careers like law, whereas Vettriselvan (2025) emphasized on values-driven digital training. These results warn against considering agility as a measure of efficiency. Alternatively, DEI means that the digital adoption process should not confuse or burden the employees but fit in with their health, ethical principles, and lifelong growth. This chapter has a number of contributions. In principle, it is an intermediate between psychodynamic theory and emotional intelligence with regard to digital transformation, suggesting a new framework of DEI as a framework to understand how organisations psychologically adapt to technological shocking. It is empirically based and it demonstrates that DEI is statistically and experientially significant as a mediator of agility and resilience. In practice, it can provide concrete mechanisms of incorporating DEI into leadership formation, cultural design, and organizational systems so that agility can become enduring, as opposed to cosmetic. The implication is obvious: DEI can assist organisations in making digital technologies tools of human malleability instead of stressors. It facilitates the culture of trust, inclusion, and innovation which are the features of the agile mindset as established by Rajagopal (2022, 2023). In this sense, agility is not the speed but the capacity to live and adapt to uncertainty. In the future, DEI has to be institutionalised in organisations. These involve investing in leadership capacity, incorporating DEI within cultural frameworks and aligning governance systems with emotional and ethical aspects of change. In the same way, further studies are also essential to optimise our knowledge on DEI in various cultures, industries, and technological environments, as highlighted in the section above. The road ahead is complex. Psychodynamic forces tend to be subterranean and the resistance to emotional labour regarding cultural matters could be high. However, when organisations start to consider the emotional aspect of technological change in earnest, DEI can become not only a safeguarding asset but a driving force as well- both personal and organisational prosperity in the digital era.

REFERENCES

Abbas, A., Ekowati, D., Suhariadi, F., Anwar, A., & Fenitra, R. M. (2024). Technology acceptance and COVID-19: A perspective for emerging opportunities from crisis. *Technology Analysis and Strategic Management, 36*(11), 3551–3563. DOI: 10.1080/09537325.2023.2214642

Albert, S., Ashforth, B. E., & Dutton, J. E. (2000). Organizational identity and identification: Charting new waters and building new bridges. *Academy of Management Review, 25*(1), 13–17. DOI: 10.5465/amr.2000.2791600

Alsalman, F. A., & Chyad, S. A. (2025). Impact of Emotional Intelligence on Leadership and Team Dynamics in Agile Software Engineering Projects. *IEEE Access : Practical Innovations, Open Solutions, 13*, 74217–74228. DOI: 10.1109/ACCESS.2025.3563424

Amin, M. W., & Wang, J. (2024). Social media ostracism and creativity: Moderating role of emotional intelligence. *BMC Psychology, 12*(1), 484. DOI: 10.1186/s40359-024-01985-2 PMID: 39272175

Chatwani, N. (2019). Organisational agility. *Springer International Publishing, Cham, doi, 10*, 978-3.

Dahmen, P. (2023). Organizational resilience as a key property of enterprise risk management in response to novel and severe crisis events. *Risk Management & Insurance Review, 26*(2), 203–245. DOI: 10.1111/rmir.12245

du Plessis, M. (2023). Trait emotional intelligence and flourishing: The mediating role of positive coping behaviour. *SA Journal of Industrial Psychology, 49*, 2063. DOI: 10.4102/sajip.v49i0.2063

Huy, Q. N. (1999). Emotional capability, emotional intelligence, and radical change. *Academy of Management Review, 24*(2), 325–345. DOI: 10.2307/259085

Langemeyer, I. (2019). Mindfulness and the psychodynamics in high-reliability-organizations: Critical-psychological considerations for a research on high-tech work. *Annual Review of Critical Psychology, 16*, 1237–1257.

Lawlor, D., Sher, M., & Khaleelee, O. (2023). Systems psychodynamics and the impact of digitalisation, AI and virtual working on the eco-system. In *Systems Psychodynamics* (pp. 239–256). Routledge. DOI: 10.4324/9781003368663-18

Lawton-Misra, N., & Pretorius, T. (2021). Leading with heart: Academic leadership during the COVID-19 crisis. *South African Journal of Psychology. Suid-Afrikaanse Tydskrif vir Sielkunde, 51*(2), 205–214. DOI: 10.1177/0081246321992979

Marhenke, U. (2025). AI Is Here. But Is the Legal Profession Ready for It? In *Liquid Legal–Sustaining the Rule of Law: Artificial Intelligence, E-Justice, and the Cloud* (pp. 233–245). Springer Nature Switzerland. DOI: 10.1007/978-3-031-78596-2_11

Pramila, T. P. (2025). Emotional Intelligence and Effective Leadership in the Digital Era. *Leadership Studies in the Turbulent Business Ecosystem*, 61

Rajagopal, A. (2022). The Agile Mind-Set. In *Agile Marketing Strategies: New Approaches to Engaging Consumer Behavior* (pp. 189–224). Springer International Publishing. DOI: 10.1007/978-3-031-04212-6_7

Rajagopal, A. (2023). Gaming Without Rules: Role of Agility in Tourism Marketing. In *Paradigm Shift in Business: Critical Appraisal of Agile Management Practices* (pp. 179–194). Springer Nature Switzerland. DOI: 10.1007/978-3-031-40439-9_9

Roux, M., & Härtel, C. E. (2018). The Cognitive, Emotional, and Behavioral Qualities. *Individual, Relational, and Contextual Dynamics of Emotions*, 59.

Roux, M., & Härtel, C. E. (2018). The cognitive, emotional, and behavioral qualities required for leadership assessment and development in the new world of work. In *Individual, relational, and contextual dynamics of emotions* (pp. 59–69). Emerald Publishing Limited. DOI: 10.1108/S1746-979120180000014010

Sachdeva, P., & Mitra, A. (2025). Embracing Emotional Intelligence in Digital Workspaces: A Qualitative Case Study of Organizational Culture Dynamics. In *Emotional Intelligence in the Digital Era* (pp. 238-249). Auerbach Publications.

Vettriselvan, R. (2025). Empowering Digital Education: The Future of Value-Based Learning in the Digital Era. In *Empowering Value Co-Creation in the Digital Era* (pp. 199-228). IGI Global Scientific Publishing.

Vettriselvan, R., Velmurugan, P. R., & Varshney, K. R. EP, J., & Deepika, R. (2025). Health Impacts of Smartphone and Internet Addictions Across Age Groups: Physical and Mental Health Across Generations. In *Impacts of Digital Technologies Across Generations* (pp. 187-210). IGI Global Scientific Publishing.

Wójcik, P., Obłój, K., Wąsowska, A., & Wierciński, S. (2020). Corporate acceleration process: A systems psychodynamics perspective. *Journal of Organizational Change Management*, *33*(6), 1163–1180. DOI: 10.1108/JOCM-05-2019-0136

KEY TERMS AND DEFINITIONS

Digital Emotional Intelligence (DEI): The ability to perceive, comprehend and cope with emotions in digital communication and technology mediated interaction. DEI applies the traditional emotional intelligence to the virtual world, allowing individuals to be emphatic, self-managed, and capable of relationships in remote and AI-enhanced workplaces.

Emotional Intelligence (EI): Sensitivity to recognize, perceive, and manipulate emotions of others and oneself. EI is still one of the foundations of successful leadership, conflict management, and group work. Using it alongside DEI, it creates the foundation of the emotionally intelligent digital ecosystems.

Ethical: The researcher will identify ethical challenges and implement a code of ethics to address them. The researcher will determine some ethical issues and establish a code of ethics that will guide them.

Organizational Agility: The ability of an organization to respond, adapt and sense change both inside and outside of the organization very fast. Agility in the context of digital work places incorporates the emotional flexibility of the work place, collaborative learning process and flexible leadership approaches which are aided by technology.

Organizational Identity: The collective understanding of who we are as an organization, which is created by using shared values, culture, and stories. The issue of digital transitions usually threatens the already existing identities, and the leaders have to redefine the organizational purpose, ethics, and belonging within a hybrid work environment.

Organizational Psychodynamics: Theoretical perspective that investigates unconscious working as well as emotional processes and nonverbal patterns in organizations. It looks at the effect of anxiety, defense mechanisms, and group behavior in the field of leadership, communication, and institutional change particularly in cases of digital transformation.

Resilience and Adaptation: Psychological and structural ability of individuals and organisations to bounce back after setbacks, sustain as well as become more resilient in the face of crisis. In organizational psychodynamics, resilience is associated with the containment of emotions, trust, and uncertainty learning.

Systems Psychodynamics: A theory of organizational behavior that utilizes the psychoanalytic theory, group relations and systems thinking to explain the operations of an organization. It assists in understanding how systemic roles are unconsciously played by individuals and teams to bring or break balance in technological and structural change.

Technological Transformation: The implementation of digital tools, automation, and AI systems in the organizational processes. It requires profound psychological and cultural change, redefining identity, trust and human relationship in digitized ecosystems, in addition to technical change.

Chapter 11
The Role of Leadership in Cultivating Organizational Agility Through Cultural Transformation and Technology Adoption

Simon Cleveland
http://orcid.org/0000-0001-9293-3905
Purdue University Global, USA

Marisa Cleveland
Northeastern University, USA

ABSTRACT

Organizational agility is critical for enterprise success amid rapid technological change and market volatility. This chapter examines leadership's role in fostering agility through cultural transformation and technology adoption. Drawing from Schein's cultural dimensions, Heifetz's adaptive leadership, and digital transformation frameworks, it explores how leaders navigate technological complexities while reshaping organizational culture. The discussion integrates high-context and low-context cultural dimensions with digital maturity models, highlighting approaches for aligning cultural practices, technological capabilities, and goals. A Florida government case study illustrates leadership's impact on cultural integration, diversity, innovation, and technology-enabled agility. The chapter emphasizes adaptive leadership's importance in fostering resilient, inclusive, technologically empowered cultures capable of thriving in dynamic environments.

DOI: 10.4018/979-8-3373-4027-2.ch011

INTRODUCTION

Background and Contemporary Context

Organizational culture represents the backbone of any successful enterprise, shaping behaviors, attitudes, and overall performance in an increasingly complex business landscape. As defined in extant literature, culture represents the social heritage of a community (Hall, 2005). In an organizational context, culture encompasses the set of shared beliefs and values among employees (Sun, 2009). Schein (2010) further delineates culture into three levels: artifacts, espoused values, and underlying assumptions.

The contemporary business environment presents organizations with a paradoxical challenge: the need to maintain cultural coherence while simultaneously embracing rapid technological change and organizational adaptation. Digital transformation initiatives frequently fail not due to technological limitations, but rather because of cultural resistance and inadequate leadership approaches to change management (Burke, 2017). Organizations must develop what scholars increasingly term "organizational agility"—the capacity to sense environmental changes, respond rapidly to market shifts, and reconfigure resources and capabilities to seize new opportunities while managing uncertainty.

Leadership becomes the critical fulcrum upon which organizational agility rests. Leaders must simultaneously maintain cultural stability—providing employees with a sense of identity and continuity—while driving the cultural evolution necessary to embrace technological innovation, collaborative practices, and adaptive behaviors. This dual imperative requires leaders to employ sophisticated frameworks such as framing and reframing (Bolman & Deal, 2017) and adaptive leadership (Heifetz et al., 2009) to navigate cultural complexities while championing technology adoption as an enabler of organizational agility.

Problem Statement

Despite widespread recognition that organizational agility is essential for competitive advantage, a critical gap exists in understanding how leaders can effectively integrate cultural transformation with technology adoption to achieve sustained agility. Digital transformation initiatives fail at alarming rates, with cultural resistance cited as the primary barrier (Burke, 2017). While existing literature addresses leadership, culture, and technology separately, insufficient attention has been paid to the dynamic interplay among these three elements and how leaders can orchestrate them synergistically.

The problem is particularly acute because organizations face contradictory pressures. They must preserve cultural identity and continuity while simultaneously disrupting established patterns. They must implement sophisticated technologies while ensuring human-centered adoption. They must break down organizational silos while maintaining functional expertise. These paradoxes create adaptive challenges that cannot be resolved through technical solutions alone, requiring instead fundamental shifts in organizational culture guided by adaptive leadership.

Current research has not adequately addressed how leaders can navigate high-context and low-context cultural dimensions while implementing technology-enabled organizational restructuring. Furthermore, limited empirical investigation exists into how diversity—across demographic, generational, and functional dimensions—interacts with technology adoption and cultural transformation to enhance organizational agility. This chapter addresses these gaps by examining the integrated role of leadership in fostering organizational agility through simultaneous attention to cultural transformation and strategic technology implementation.

Purpose and Significance of the Study

The purpose of this chapter is to examine the critical role of leadership in fostering organizational agility through cultural transformation and strategic technology implementation. This inquiry takes the form of a conceptual analysis grounded in established leadership and organizational theory, supplemented by an illustrative case study of cultural transformation in a Florida government department. The chapter synthesizes multiple theoretical perspectives—including Schein's cultural framework, adaptive leadership theory, and Cameron and Quinn's high-context/low-context cultural dimensions—to develop an integrated understanding of how leaders can simultaneously address culture, technology, and agility.

The significance of this work extends across multiple dimensions. For practitioners, this chapter provides actionable frameworks for navigating the complex interplay between cultural transformation and technology adoption. Leaders will gain insight into how organizational restructuring, diversity integration, and technology enablement can be orchestrated to break down silos and enhance collaborative problem-solving. The chapter demonstrates that cultural transformation and technology adoption must proceed in tandem rather than sequentially, challenging conventional change management approaches that separate these initiatives.

For scholars, this chapter contributes to leadership and organizational theory by bridging previously disconnected literatures. It extends adaptive leadership theory into the domain of technology-enabled organizational change, demonstrating how adaptive challenges manifest when cultural transformation and digital transformation intersect. The integration of high-context and low-context cultural dimensions with technology adoption patterns offers new theoretical insights into why certain leadership approaches succeed or fail in different cultural contexts.

For organizations and their stakeholders, the implications are profound. In an era demanding unprecedented agility, organizations that fail to integrate cultural and technological transformation risk obsolescence. This chapter articulates how purposeful technology integration serves as a catalyst for breaking down organizational silos, enhancing collaboration, accelerating innovation, and ultimately building the adaptive capacity necessary for sustained competitive advantage. The stakes are clear: organizations must learn to cultivate agility through integrated cultural and technological evolution, or face strategic disadvantage in increasingly dynamic competitive environments.

Originality and Rationale

This chapter's originality lies in its integrated theoretical approach to organizational agility. While existing literature often treats leadership, culture, and technology as separate domains, this chapter synthesizes them into a cohesive framework centered on organizational agility as the outcome of interest. The use of Cameron and Quinn's (2011) high-context and low-context cultural dimensions as a lens for understanding technology adoption patterns represents a novel application of cultural theory to digital transformation challenges.

The rationale for this inquiry rests on both theoretical and practical imperatives. Theoretically, the fragmented nature of existing research limits understanding of how leaders can effectively orchestrate multiple change dimensions simultaneously. Practical observation reveals that organizations struggle precisely because they treat cultural transformation and technology adoption as separate initiatives, failing to recognize their interdependence. The Florida government department case study illustrates how leaders successfully integrated these elements, providing empirical grounding for the theoretical synthesis.

Furthermore, the chapter's emphasis on diversity as a mechanism for enhancing organizational agility addresses a critical gap in the literature. While diversity research has established benefits for innovation and problem-solving (Gurin et al., 2002), less attention has been paid to how diversity specifically enhances organizational agility in technology-adoption contexts. The case study demonstrates how demographic, generational, and functional diversity contributed to breaking down silos and fostering the collaborative culture essential for agility, offering both theoretical insight and practical guidance.

Chapter Overview

This chapter explores the critical role of leadership in fostering organizational agility through cultural transformation and strategic technology implementation. Through an analysis of high-context and low-context cultural dimensions (Cameron & Quinn, 2011), combined with examination of established leadership frameworks, this chapter provides insights into the dynamic interplay between leadership strategies, cultural outcomes, and technology-enabled organizational agility. The discussion addresses how purposeful technology integration serves as a catalyst for breaking down organizational silos, enhancing collaboration, accelerating innovation, and ultimately building the adaptive capacity necessary for sustained competitive advantage.

The chapter proceeds through several sections. The literature review examines theoretical foundations across three domains: organizational culture in the digital age, leadership theories relevant to technology-driven transformation, and frameworks for understanding how cultural dimensions influence technology adoption and organizational agility. The case study section presents a detailed examination of leadership-driven cultural transformation in a Florida government department, illustrating how restructuring, diversity integration, and implicit technology enablement combined to enhance organizational agility. The discussion section synthesizes theoretical and empirical insights to articulate how adaptive leadership, diversity, and strategic technology adoption interact to build organizational agility. The chapter concludes with strategic recommendations for leaders and identification of future research directions.

LITERATURE REVIEW

Understanding Organizational Culture in the Digital Age

Organizational culture remains multifaceted, encompassing visible artifacts, shared beliefs, and unconscious assumptions (Schein, 2010). However, the digital age has introduced new dimensions to organizational culture that leaders must navigate. Digital artifacts—from collaboration platforms to data dashboards—now shape employee interactions and decision-making processes. Leaders must navigate these multiple cultural layers to influence behaviors, drive performance, and facilitate technology adoption. The most effective leaders comprehend the cultural underpinnings that guide employee interactions and decision-making processes while understanding how technology can amplify or impede cultural transformation.

The relationship between organizational culture and technology adoption is bidirectional and complex. Culture influences how organizations perceive, evaluate, and integrate new technologies, while technology adoption can fundamentally reshape cultural norms, communication patterns, and work practices. Organizations with cultures characterized by experimentation, learning orientation, and tolerance for ambiguity tend to exhibit greater success in digital transformation initiatives (Weick & Quinn, 1999). Conversely, cultures emphasizing risk aversion, hierarchical decision-making, and resistance to change often struggle with technology adoption, regardless of the technical merits of the systems being implemented.

This bidirectional relationship creates both opportunities and challenges for leaders seeking to enhance organizational agility. Technology can serve as a catalyst for cultural transformation by making new behaviors possible and visible. Collaborative platforms, for example, can break down communication barriers between organizational units, making cross-functional collaboration more feasible and visible. However, technology introduced into resistant cultures may be actively subverted or passively ignored, with employees finding workarounds that preserve existing cultural patterns rather than embracing new possibilities.

Leadership Theories and Organizational Culture in Technology-Driven Environments

Different leadership theories offer varied perspectives on managing organizational culture during periods of technological change. Theory X and Theory Y (McGregor, 1960) contrast authoritarian and participative leadership styles, with particular relevance to technology adoption initiatives. Theory X leaders, who believe employees inherently avoid work and require constant supervision, often struggle to leverage technology as an enabler of employee empowerment. Their control-oriented approach can undermine the collaborative, experimental culture necessary for successful digital transformation.

In contrast, Theory Y leaders, who trust in employees' intrinsic motivation and capacity for self-direction, are better positioned to foster cultures that embrace technological innovation. They view technology not as a surveillance or control mechanism, but as a tool to enhance employee capabilities, facilitate collaboration, and enable more effective decision-making. This fundamental orientation toward employees directly influences how technology is framed, implemented, and ultimately utilized within the organization.

Laissez-Faire leadership, characterized by minimal intervention, often leads to ambiguity and reduced motivation (Northouse, 2017; Skogstad et al., 2007). In the context of technology adoption, this leadership style proves particularly problematic. Technology implementation requires clear vision, consistent support, and active sponsorship from leadership. Laissez-faire leaders who abdicate responsibility for guiding technological change create vacuums that breed confusion, inconsistent adoption, and suboptimal utilization of technological investments. Their lack of involvement in addressing role ambiguity and conflict during technology transitions exacerbates resistance and undermines organizational agility.

Transcendent leadership, as discussed by Avolio and Bass (2002) and Galloway (2016), emphasizes transformational approaches that inspire and develop employees, fostering a culture of innovation and collaboration. Transcendent leaders stimulate their followers' efforts to be innovative and creative by questioning assumptions, reframing problems, and approaching old situations in new ways. In technology-driven transformation, transcendent leaders excel at connecting technological capabilities to organizational mission and employee values. They help employees see technology not as a threat to their roles, but as a means to transcend current limitations, enhance their contributions, and create greater value for the organization and its stakeholders.

Framing and Reframing in Leadership During Technological Change

Bolman and Deal (2017) highlight the importance of framing in leadership, wherein leaders use cognitive models to interpret and address complex situations. The ability to reframe, or view problems from multiple perspectives, is essential for cultural adaptability, particularly during technology adoption initiatives. Leaders who master reframing can synthesize diverse viewpoints regarding technological change, mitigate conflicts between traditional and innovative approaches, and align cultural practices with organizational objectives.

Effective framing of technology initiatives requires leaders to present technological change through multiple lenses simultaneously. From a structural frame, technology can be positioned as a means to streamline processes and improve efficiency. Through a human resource frame, technology becomes a tool for employee development and empowerment. The political frame allows leaders to address power dynamics and resource allocation questions raised by technological change. Finally, the symbolic frame enables leaders to connect technology adoption to organizational identity, values, and aspirational culture.

The process of reframing proves particularly valuable when initial technology implementations encounter resistance or unexpected challenges. Rather than doubling down on a single justification for technological change, adaptive leaders can shift perspectives, finding new ways to connect technology initiatives to employee concerns and organizational goals. This cognitive flexibility, combined with genuine responsiveness to employee feedback, distinguishes leaders who successfully navigate digital transformation from those whose initiatives stall or fail.

High-Context vs. Low-Context Cultures in Technology Adoption

Cameron and Quinn (2011) distinguish between high-context and low-context cultures based on parameters such as association and interaction. In high-context cultures, trust and relationships are paramount, with implicit communication norms. Low-context cultures, on the other hand, prioritize explicit communication and individual autonomy. These cultural dimensions have profound implications for technology adoption and organizational agility.

High-context cultures, characterized by relationship-dependent identity and implicit verbal communication, may initially resist technology that disrupts established social patterns or requires explicit, documented communication. Leaders in high-context cultures must carefully frame technology as a means to strengthen relationships and community rather than replace human interaction. Success requires extended relationship-building, patience with adoption timelines, and careful attention to how technology impacts group dynamics and social capital.

Conversely, low-context cultures, with their individualistic identity and explicit information exchange, may more readily embrace certain technologies that enhance individual productivity or provide clear, measurable benefits. However, these cultures may struggle with collaborative technologies that require interdependence or shared accountability. Leaders must adapt their strategies to these cultural contexts, ensuring alignment between technological capabilities and cultural expectations.

The interaction parameter proves particularly relevant to technology adoption. High-context cultures use communication as a means to interaction between individuals, viewing technology through the lens of how it affects relationships. Technologies perceived as impersonal or isolating face greater resistance. Leaders must emphasize collaboration features, social elements, and relationship-enhancing capabilities when introducing technology in high-context environments. In contrast, low-context cultures focus on direct exchange of information with explicit statements, potentially embracing technologies that improve information access and clarity while resisting those that introduce ambiguity or require implicit understanding.

Digital Maturity and Organizational Agility

The concept of digital maturity has emerged as a critical framework for understanding organizational readiness for technology-driven agility. Digital maturity encompasses not only technological infrastructure and capabilities, but also the cultural attributes, leadership practices, and organizational processes that enable effective technology utilization. Organizations at higher levels of digital maturity demonstrate greater agility, responding more rapidly to market changes and capitalizing on technological innovations to create competitive advantage.

Leadership plays a decisive role in advancing organizational digital maturity. Leaders must address multiple dimensions simultaneously: technology infrastructure, data and analytics capabilities, digital skills and talent, organizational culture and mindset, and governance structures that enable rapid decision-making while managing risk appropriately. Each dimension requires different leadership interventions, yet all must advance in coordinated fashion to build genuine organizational agility.

The relationship between digital maturity and organizational culture is particularly salient. Organizations cannot achieve advanced digital maturity without cultures that embrace experimentation, learning from failure, cross-functional collaboration, and continuous adaptation. Leaders must intentionally cultivate these cultural attributes while simultaneously building technological capabilities, recognizing that cultural transformation and technology adoption must proceed in tandem rather than sequentially.

Technology as a Catalyst for Breaking Down Silos

Organizational silos represent one of the most persistent barriers to agility, innovation, and performance. Silos emerge from various sources: functional specialization, geographic dispersion, cultural differences between units, and systems that reinforce rather than bridge organizational boundaries. Technology, when strategically deployed and culturally supported, offers powerful mechanisms for breaking down these barriers.

Collaborative technologies—including shared platforms, integrated communication tools, and transparent information systems—can fundamentally reshape how organizational units interact and coordinate. However, technology alone cannot eliminate silos. Leaders must actively champion cross-boundary collaboration, model collaborative behavior, and reshape incentive systems that perpetuate siloed thinking. Technology provides the infrastructure for collaboration, but leadership provides the cultural impetus and ongoing support necessary to change entrenched behavioral patterns.

The Florida government department case, examined in detail below, illustrates how leadership leveraged organizational restructuring combined with implicit technological enablement to break down cultural silos. While explicit technology adoption was not the primary intervention, the reorganization created conditions requiring enhanced communication and coordination—needs that technology could address. This suggests that leaders must sometimes reshape organizational structures and cultural expectations before technology can fully realize its potential as a catalyst for agility.

CASE STUDY: Leadership and Cultural Transformation Toward Organizational Agility in a Government Department

Nature of the Study

This case study employs a qualitative, descriptive approach to examine leadership-driven cultural transformation in a Florida local government department. The case study methodology was selected because it allows for in-depth exploration of complex organizational phenomena within their real-world context (Schein, 2010). The case was identified through professional networks and selected based on several criteria: recent organizational restructuring explicitly designed to enhance agility, leadership-driven cultural change addressing diversity and silo reduction, and availability of detailed information about the transformation process and outcomes.

Data for the case study were drawn from multiple sources to ensure comprehensive understanding. Primary sources included detailed interviews with organizational leaders involved in the restructuring, documentation of the organizational structure before and after transformation, and descriptions of implementation processes and strategies employed by leaders. The case analysis employed Schein's (2010) three-level cultural framework to understand how leaders addressed artifacts, espoused values, and underlying assumptions. Cameron and Quinn's (2011) high-context and low-context dimensions provided additional analytical lens for understanding how cultural patterns influenced the transformation process.

The analytical approach involved identifying key leadership interventions, examining how these interventions addressed cultural barriers to agility, and assessing outcomes in terms of diversity integration, silo reduction, and enhanced organizational responsiveness. The case illustrates theoretical principles discussed in the literature review, demonstrating how adaptive leadership, framing and reframing, and attention to cultural dimensions combine to enable organizational transformation. While this single case study does not permit broad generalization, it provides rich illustration of leadership principles and offers insights applicable to other organizations facing similar challenges.

Context and Organizational Challenges

A local government department in Florida serves as an illuminating case study for examining leadership's role in cultural transformation toward greater organizational agility. Faced with the retirement of a key director, the department's leadership team recognized an opportunity to restructure divisions to enhance workflow, foster diversity, break down entrenched silos, and position the organization for greater responsiveness to changing community needs.

The existing organizational structure consisted of one department head overseeing seven divisions. Over time, these divisions had evolved into semi-autonomous units with distinct subcultures, limited cross-functional collaboration, and varying levels of effectiveness. The nature of their work had contributed to homogeneity within teams, creating cultural islands that, while fostering strong internal bonds, limited organizational agility and responsiveness.

For example, the customer service representatives operated under a Hispanic supervisor, and most employees in this unit were Hispanic. While the supervisor justified this composition by noting the need for bilingual staff to address caller needs, the team had become culturally homogeneous. Team members bonded around cultural celebrations and shared language, inadvertently excluding Caucasian team members and limiting cross-cultural learning. This homogeneity, while creating strong internal cohesion, reduced the unit's capacity to understand and respond to the diverse needs of the broader community.

Similarly, the field operations team consisted entirely of men who had developed their own exclusive group dynamics and communication patterns. Their supervisor had made hiring decisions based on stereotypical assumptions rather than competency, preferring candidates who fit the established team profile over more capable individuals who might diversify the group. This pattern exemplified how cultural homogeneity, left unchecked, perpetuates itself and limits organizational adaptability.

The silos extended beyond demographic composition to operational practices. Each division had developed its own processes, norms, and approaches to work. When problems arose, teams defaulted to blaming other divisions rather than collaboratively problem-solving. This finger-pointing culture created inefficiencies, slowed response times, and frustrated both employees and the citizens they served. The organization exhibited low agility, struggling to adapt to changing community needs or leverage the diverse capabilities of its workforce.

Two managers initiated the conversation that ultimately led to transformation by questioning the length of time required to complete certain tasks. Their inquiry revealed that existing organizational boundaries and cultural silos were creating unnecessary delays and inefficiencies. This realization, combined with the impending director retirement, created both urgency and opportunity for transformational change.

Leadership Intervention and Restructuring Strategy

The leadership team, rather than simply filling the retiring director's position and maintaining the status quo, made a bold decision to fundamentally restructure the organization. They split one large division into two new divisions, reorganizing the overall structure around workflow processes rather than historical organizational charts. This decision reflected several leadership principles consistent with adaptive leadership and transformational approaches.

First, the leadership team recognized that the retirement represented a window of opportunity for change. Rather than viewing it as a disruption to be minimized, they reframed it as a catalyst for addressing long-standing organizational challenges. This reframing exemplifies the cognitive flexibility discussed by Bolman and Deal (2017), allowing leaders to see possibilities where others might see only problems.

Second, the restructuring strategy was explicitly designed to break down existing silos and create more diverse teams. The new organizational structure intentionally mixed employees from different backgrounds, skill sets, and former divisions. Jobs typically held by one ethnic or demographic group now included representation from multiple groups. Front-line positions, usually staffed by high school graduates, gained voice and visibility alongside analysts with bachelor's degrees. This generational, educational, and cultural mixing of staff represented a deliberate strategy to enhance organizational agility by leveraging diverse perspectives and capabilities.

Third, the leadership team consciously rejected risk-averse thinking from directors who argued for maintaining the status quo. As Kondra and Hinings (1998) note, organizations often adhere to industry-accepted norms even when those norms no longer serve organizational goals. The leadership team's willingness to challenge conventional wisdom and accepted practices demonstrates the kind of adaptive leadership necessary for building organizational agility.

Implementation Through Adaptive Leadership

The director of one of the newly formed divisions exemplified adaptive leadership principles in implementing the restructuring. Rather than simply announcing changes and expecting compliance, this director employed several key strategies consistent with Heifetz's adaptive leadership framework (Heifetz et al., 2009).

First, the director conducted extensive one-on-one meetings with team members to address concerns, understand existing competencies, and build relationships across former organizational boundaries. These meetings served multiple purposes: they demonstrated genuine concern for employee wellbeing, they surfaced potential obstacles to the transition, and they began building the trust necessary for collaborative work across former silos.

Second, the director focused on placing the right person in the right position, matching individual skillsets with job functions rather than relying on historical assignments or stereotypical assumptions (Chin & Benne, 1969). This meritocratic approach not only improved operational effectiveness but also sent a powerful cultural message about organizational values. Employees recognized that competence and contribution, rather than demographic characteristics or tenure, would determine roles and opportunities under the new structure.

Third, the director maintained open communication about the rationale for changes, addressing the emotional and practical concerns that inevitably arise during organizational transitions. The leadership team emphasized that the restructuring did not result from any team failing to perform their duties correctly—an important framing that reduced defensiveness and blame. Instead, they positioned the change as a proactive strategy to better serve the community and create opportunities for employee growth and development.

Fourth, the director actively managed the political and symbolic dimensions of the transition. Engaging with both formal and informal leaders within the organization, addressing power dynamics that the restructuring disrupted, and creating new symbols of the integrated organizational culture assisted the director in helping employees make sense of the change and see themselves as part of a transformed organization rather than victims of arbitrary reorganization.

Cultural Outcomes and Enhanced Agility

The reorganization produced several significant cultural outcomes that enhanced organizational agility. First, the newly diverse teams exhibited the benefits that Gurin, Dey, Hurtado, and Gurin (2002) associate with racial and ethnic diversity: active thinking skills, intellectual engagement, and enhanced problem-solving capabilities. Employees who had previously worked in homogeneous groups found themselves collaborating with colleagues from different backgrounds, perspectives, and skill sets. This diversity of thought and experience translated into more creative approaches to persistent problems and greater capacity to understand and respond to diverse community needs.

Second, the economic and educational diversity within teams dissolved previously rigid hierarchies and status differences. Front-line code enforcement officers—typically young Hispanic individuals with high school diplomas hired to address lower-income areas—now worked directly with predominantly white, older, and educated building reviewers. This collaboration produced innovative approaches to reducing code violations and penalties for lower-income residents who struggled to afford fines. The front-line officers contributed practical insights about community needs and constraints, while the reviewers provided technical expertise and regulatory knowledge. Together, they developed more effective, equitable, and community-responsive approaches than either group could have generated independently.

Third, the organization shifted from a blame culture to a problem-solving culture. When teams stopped operating in silos, they also stopped blaming each other for stagnations and failures. Instead, employees engaged in constructive conversations about what approaches worked better in which situations and how different capabilities could be combined to improve outcomes. This cultural shift toward collaborative problem-solving represents a fundamental enhancement to organizational agility—the capacity to learn from experience, adapt approaches, and respond effectively to new challenges.

Fourth, the reorganization implicitly created conditions requiring better communication systems and coordination mechanisms. While the case study does not explicitly discuss technology adoption, the new organizational structure necessarily demanded enhanced information sharing, cross-functional visibility, and collaborative work practices. These requirements create natural opportunities for technology to serve as an enabler of the new cultural practices. Leaders could subsequently introduce collaborative platforms, shared information systems, and communication tools not as imposed technologies, but as responses to needs that employees themselves recognized.

Leadership Lessons from the Case Study

Several leadership lessons emerge from this case study with implications for organizations seeking to enhance agility through cultural transformation and technology adoption. First, leaders must recognize and seize windows of opportunity for transformational change. The retirement of a key director, while potentially disruptive, became a catalyst for addressing long-standing organizational challenges. Leaders should remain vigilant for such opportunities—not as problems to be managed, but as occasions for strategic transformation.

Second, structural changes and cultural transformation must proceed in tandem. The Florida department's leadership did not simply preach new values or exhort employees to be more collaborative. They restructured the organization in ways that required collaboration, diversity, and cross-boundary work. This alignment between organizational structure and desired culture reflects systems thinking and whole-systems approaches to change (Brock, 2012).

Third, adaptive leadership requires balancing multiple perspectives and stakeholders during transformation. The directors had to address risk-averse colleagues, concerned employees, skeptical managers, and community stakeholders while maintaining momentum toward the transformation vision. This balancing act requires sophisticated framing and reframing capabilities, emotional intelligence, and genuine commitment to inclusive decision-making.

Fourth, cultural transformation requires sustained leadership attention and support. The director's commitment to one-on-one meetings, ongoing communication, and continuous support during the transition exemplifies the kind of leadership engagement necessary for successful cultural change. Technology implementations, similarly, cannot succeed without sustained leadership sponsorship and support through the inevitable challenges and adjustments that accompany change.

DISCUSSION

Adaptive Leadership in Cultural Contexts During Technology-Driven Transformation

Adaptive leadership is crucial in managing cultural shifts within organizations, particularly during periods of technological transformation. It involves diagnosing challenges, mobilizing resources, and fostering resilience among employees (Heifetz, 2003). Leaders who adopt adaptive strategies can effectively address cultural barriers to technology adoption, ensuring seamless transitions during organizational changes while building the agility necessary for sustained competitiveness.

Adaptive leadership distinguishes between technical problems and adaptive challenges. Technical problems, while perhaps complicated, can be solved with existing knowledge and procedures. Adaptive challenges, in contrast, require learning, experimentation, and often changes to values, beliefs, and behaviors. Technology adoption in organizational contexts almost always presents adaptive challenges rather than merely technical problems. The technology itself—the hardware, software, and systems—represents the technical dimension. The adaptive challenge lies in reshaping organizational culture, work practices, communication patterns, and mindsets to leverage technology effectively.

Leaders employing adaptive leadership during technology transformation must engage in several key activities. First, they must get on the balcony—stepping back from the immediate pressures of implementation to observe patterns, identify sources of resistance, and understand the deeper cultural dynamics at play. This diagnostic work reveals why technology initiatives encounter resistance, which stakeholder groups feel threatened by change, and what cultural values or practices the technology appears to challenge.

Second, adaptive leaders must identify the adaptive challenge clearly and help the organization distinguish it from technical problems. Rather than allowing organizations to treat technology adoption as purely a technical problem (solved by training, support resources, or system refinements), adaptive leaders frame the challenge as one requiring cultural evolution and behavioral change. This framing helps employees understand why technology adoption feels difficult and why leadership support extends beyond technical assistance to encompass cultural transformation.

Third, adaptive leaders regulate distress during technology transformation. Change inevitably creates anxiety, uncertainty, and discomfort. Too little distress results in complacency and insufficient motivation to change. Too much distress overwhelms employees and triggers defensive responses that undermine transformation efforts. Effective leaders carefully calibrate the pace and intensity of technology-driven change, providing enough challenge to motivate adaptation while offering sufficient support to prevent paralysis.

Fourth, adaptive leaders maintain disciplined attention to the adaptive challenge, resisting pressures to declare premature victory or abandon transformation efforts when initial resistance emerges. Technology implementations frequently encounter setbacks, user resistance, and unanticipated complications. Leaders who lack adaptive leadership capabilities often respond by either forcing compliance (which breeds resentment and passive resistance) or retreating from the initiative (which signals that resistance works and undermines future change efforts). Adaptive leaders persist through difficulties, learn from setbacks, and maintain focus on the ultimate goal of enhanced organizational agility.

Fifth, adaptive leaders give the work back to the people. Rather than solving all problems themselves or dictating precisely how technology should be used, adaptive leaders create conditions for employees to experiment, learn, and develop effective practices. This approach builds organizational capacity and ensures that technology utilization evolves in ways that genuinely serve employee needs and organizational goals rather than merely conforming to initial implementation plans.

The Impact of Diversity on Organizational Agility and Technology Adoption

The Florida government department case illustrates how diversity enhances organizational agility by bringing multiple perspectives, knowledge bases, and problem-solving approaches to bear on organizational challenges. Gurin et al. (2002) emphasize that racial and ethnic diversity promotes active thinking and engagement. However, the benefits of diversity extend well beyond racial and ethnic dimensions to encompass generational, educational, functional, and experiential diversity.

Diverse teams demonstrate greater creativity and innovation when addressing complex, ambiguous problems—precisely the kinds of challenges organizations face in rapidly changing technological and market environments. Homogeneous teams often converge quickly on conventional solutions, drawing from shared assumptions and experiences. Diverse teams, while sometimes experiencing more initial conflict and requiring more time to reach consensus, generate more novel approaches and identify a wider range of potential solutions.

In technology adoption contexts, diversity provides several specific benefits. First, diverse teams better represent the range of user needs, preferences, and capabilities within the organization. Technology that serves only highly educated knowledge workers, for example, may fail to support front-line employees who interact directly with customers. Teams that include both populations can identify these gaps and ensure technology serves the full organization.

Second, diverse teams bring different mental models and frames to technology adoption. Some individuals naturally embrace new technology and see opportunities for innovation. Others approach technology cautiously, identifying risks and potential downsides. Both perspectives provide value. Organizations that suppress cautious voices in favor of technology enthusiasts often implement systems with unanticipated negative consequences. Organizations that allow risk-averse voices to dominate never realize the potential benefits of technological innovation. Diverse teams that productively integrate multiple perspectives make better technology decisions.

Third, diversity challenges groupthink and conventional wisdom that often impede organizational agility. Homogeneous groups tend to reinforce existing assumptions and practices, even when these no longer serve organizational goals. Diverse groups naturally question assumptions, surface alternative approaches, and challenge comfortable but outdated practices. This questioning stance proves essential for organizational agility in dynamic environments.

However, diversity alone does not automatically produce these benefits. Leaders must create inclusive environments where diverse voices are heard, valued, and integrated into decision-making. This requires moving beyond surface-level diversity (representation of different groups) to deep-level diversity (genuine inclusion of different perspectives and approaches). Leaders foster this inclusion through several mechanisms: explicitly valuing diverse viewpoints, ensuring psychological safety for dissent and experimentation, designing decision processes that elicit multiple perspectives, and personally modeling openness to unfamiliar ideas and approaches.

Strategies for Cultural Integration During Technology Adoption

To successfully integrate new cultural practices while implementing technology to enhance organizational agility, leaders must employ comprehensive strategies addressing multiple organizational dimensions simultaneously. These strategies synthesize insights from the literature review and case study to provide actionable guidance for leaders navigating cultural transformation and technology adoption.

Communicate the Vision Clearly and Compellingly

Leaders must clearly articulate the rationale for cultural changes and technology adoption, ensuring transparency and buy-in from all stakeholders. However, effective communication extends far beyond simply explaining what will change and why. Leaders must connect the transformation to organizational mission, employee values, and stakeholder needs in ways that make the change personally meaningful rather than abstractly justified.

The communication strategy should address multiple audiences with tailored messages. Executives and senior managers need to understand strategic rationale and competitive imperatives. Middle managers require guidance on how to support their teams through transition. Front-line employees need clarity on how changes will affect their daily work and what support they can expect. Each audience requires different information, different framing, and different channels of communication.

Effective communication about technology-driven transformation also addresses both rational and emotional dimensions of change. Rationally, employees need to understand the business case for change, the problems being solved, and the anticipated benefits. Emotionally, they need acknowledgment of their concerns, reassurance about job security and relevance, and inspiration about possibilities the transformation creates. Leaders who address only rational dimensions leave employees emotionally unprepared for change. Leaders who rely only on emotional appeals without substantive rationale breed cynicism.

The vision communication should be consistent yet flexible. Core messages about why change is necessary and where the organization is heading should remain stable, providing continuity amid change. However, specific implementation details should evolve based on learning and feedback. Leaders who rigidly adhere to initial plans in the face of new information appear out of touch and undermine trust. Leaders who remain anchored to core purpose while adapting approaches demonstrate adaptive leadership and build confidence.

Foster Inclusive Leadership at All Levels

Leaders must adopt inclusive practices that recognize and leverage the strengths of diverse team members. Inclusive leadership involves several specific behaviors and mindsets that directly support both cultural transformation and effective technology adoption.

First, inclusive leaders ensure that all voices are heard in decision-making processes, particularly during technology selection and implementation planning. They recognize that front-line employees often have crucial insights about workflow, customer needs, and practical implementation challenges that executives and technical specialists miss. Creating forums for broad input—through focus groups, pilot programs, feedback mechanisms, and collaborative design sessions—ensures that technology serves the full organization rather than merely satisfying technical specifications or executive preferences.

Second, inclusive leaders address power dynamics and status hierarchies that may silence certain voices or devalue certain perspectives. In many organizations, technical expertise confers status and influence, potentially marginalizing employees without technical backgrounds. Inclusive leaders actively elevate diverse forms of expertise—customer knowledge, process understanding, relationship capabilities—ensuring that technology decisions integrate multiple forms of organizational intelligence.

Third, inclusive leaders recognize and accommodate different learning styles, comfort levels with technology, and paces of adaptation. They resist one-size-fits-all approaches to training and support, instead creating multiple pathways for employees to develop necessary skills and adapt to new ways of working. This might include formal training, peer mentoring, experimentation with low-stakes pilot projects, and extended transition periods where both old and new approaches coexist.

Fourth, inclusive leaders distribute leadership opportunities related to technology adoption. Rather than centralizing all decisions and communications with formal leadership, they identify and empower informal leaders, early adopters, and influential employees who can serve as champions, guides, and support resources for their peers. This distributed leadership approach builds broader capability, reduces dependence on formal authority, and creates more resilient organizational capacity for ongoing technological evolution.

Monitor and Evaluate Progress with Appropriate Metrics

Leaders must implement metrics to assess the impact of cultural initiatives and technology adoption, making adjustments as necessary to achieve desired outcomes. However, metric design requires careful thought to avoid unintended consequences and ensure measures truly reflect organizational agility rather than merely activity or compliance.

Traditional technology adoption metrics—such as system usage rates, training completion, or feature utilization—provide some useful information but fail to capture whether technology is genuinely enhancing organizational agility. More meaningful metrics might include: time required to respond to new market opportunities, employee-initiated innovations using technological capabilities, cross-functional collaboration frequency and effectiveness, speed of decision-making cycles, and customer satisfaction with responsiveness and service quality.

Cultural transformation metrics should similarly focus on behavioral and outcome measures rather than activity counts. Relevant metrics might include: frequency of cross-boundary collaboration, diversity of perspectives included in key decisions, employee perception of psychological safety and inclusion, speed of learning and adaptation when initiatives encounter obstacles, and resilience when facing setbacks or unexpected challenges.

Leaders should employ both quantitative and qualitative assessment methods. Quantitative metrics provide trends, comparisons, and objective benchmarks. Qualitative methods—including interviews, focus groups, observation, and narrative accounts—reveal the deeper dynamics, unintended consequences, and contextual factors that numbers alone cannot capture. The Florida government department case, for example, would show quantitative improvements in process completion times and diversity metrics, but the qualitative shift from blame culture to problem-solving culture represents the more fundamental transformation.

Importantly, leaders must use metrics as learning tools rather than control mechanisms. When metrics reveal shortfalls or unexpected patterns, adaptive leaders respond with curiosity rather than punishment. They investigate root causes, adjust approaches, and involve employees in problem-solving rather than simply demanding improved numbers. This stance toward metrics reinforces the learning orientation and experimental mindset essential for organizational agility.

Build Technology Infrastructure That Enables Rather Than Constrains Agility

Technology can either enhance or impede organizational agility depending on how it is designed, implemented, and governed. Leaders must ensure that technology infrastructure supports the flexible, collaborative, adaptive behaviors that agility requires rather than imposing rigid processes or creating new silos.

Collaborative technologies should be implemented with explicit attention to breaking down organizational boundaries. This requires more than simply providing tools like shared platforms or communication systems. Leaders must examine how information flows (or fails to flow) across organizational boundaries, identify structural and cultural barriers to collaboration, and design both technology and organizational practices to overcome these barriers. The Florida government department case suggests that structural reorganization may precede or accompany technology implementation to create conditions where collaborative technologies can succeed.

Data and analytics capabilities should be designed to accelerate decision-making rather than simply increasing reporting burden. Leaders should focus on providing real-time visibility into organizational performance, customer needs, and market conditions—enabling rapid sensing and response rather than after-the-fact analysis. This requires careful attention to what information is truly decision-relevant, how it can be accessed by those who need it, and how to balance transparency with cognitive overload.

Technology governance structures should enable appropriate risk-taking and experimentation rather than imposing excessive controls that slow adaptation. Leaders must balance legitimate concerns about security, compliance, and risk management with the need for organizational flexibility and speed. Overly restrictive technology policies breed shadow IT, where frustrated employees adopt unsanctioned tools to accomplish their work. More balanced approaches establish clear principles and guardrails while giving employees latitude to experiment with technological approaches that serve organizational goals within those boundaries.

Leaders should also ensure technology infrastructure is itself agile—capable of evolving as organizational needs change, integrating with emerging tools and platforms, and supporting rather than hindering future innovation. This argues for modular, flexible technology architectures rather than monolithic systems that become rigid constraints on organizational evolution.

Cultivate Continuous Learning and Adaptation

Organizational agility requires ongoing learning, experimentation, and adaptation rather than one-time transformation. Leaders must foster cultures where learning is expected, valued, and supported at individual, team, and organizational levels.

This involves creating psychological safety where employees feel comfortable experimenting with new approaches, admitting when things are not working, and seeking help when needed. Leaders model this behavior by acknowledging their own learning journey, discussing mistakes and adjustments openly, and celebrating learning even when initial attempts fall short of goals.

Leaders should also create formal structures and processes supporting organizational learning. This might include regular retrospectives examining what worked and what did not in technology implementation, communities of practice where employees share innovations and effective practices, and systematic capture of lessons learned that inform future initiatives. The goal is to ensure that organizational knowledge accumulates and improves over time rather than being lost when individuals leave or projects conclude.

Continuous learning also requires staying attuned to external environment changes—emerging technologies, evolving customer expectations, competitive innovations, and regulatory developments. Leaders who insulate organizations from external information reduce agility. Leaders who help organizations sense and interpret external changes while maintaining appropriate focus enable proactive rather than reactive adaptation.

ORGANIZATIONAL AGILITY: INTEGRATING CULTURE, LEADERSHIP, AND TECHNOLOGY

The central argument of this chapter is that organizational agility emerges from the integration of cultural transformation, adaptive leadership, and strategic technology adoption. None of these elements alone suffices. Organizations with advanced technology but resistant cultures fail to leverage their technological investments. Organizations with supportive cultures but inadequate technology infrastructure lack the tools to execute on their aspirations. Organizations with both culture and technology but weak leadership struggle to maintain momentum through inevitable challenges and setbacks.

Culture as Foundation for Agility

Organizational culture provides the foundation for agility by shaping how employees perceive change, respond to uncertainty, and collaborate across boundaries. Cultures characterized by learning orientation, experimental mindset, collaborative practices, and tolerance for ambiguity create fertile ground for organizational agility. These cultural attributes allow organizations to sense environmental changes, generate and evaluate response options, and mobilize resources rapidly.

In contrast, cultures emphasizing risk aversion, blame attribution, functional territoriality, and rigid adherence to established practices impede agility. These cultural patterns may have served organizations well in stable environments where consistency and reliability were paramount. However, in dynamic environments requiring rapid adaptation, these same cultural attributes become liabilities.

Leaders cannot directly mandate cultural change, but they can influence culture through multiple mechanisms. They shape culture through their own behavior—what they pay attention to, how they respond to failures and successes, what behaviors they reward and punish, and how they allocate resources. They influence culture through the people they hire, develop, and promote, gradually shifting organizational composition toward individuals who embody desired cultural attributes. They affect culture through organizational structures, systems, and processes that either reinforce or challenge existing cultural patterns.

The Florida government department case illustrates cultural transformation through structural reorganization. By deliberately creating diverse teams working across former functional boundaries, leaders disrupted homogeneous subcultures and created conditions requiring new cultural practices. The reorganization did not eliminate existing cultural attributes overnight, but it made certain behaviors necessary (cross-boundary collaboration) while making others untenable (functional blame and territoriality).

Technology as Enabler and Catalyst

Technology serves multiple roles in building organizational agility. First, it provides infrastructure for the rapid information flow, transparent communication, and collaborative work that agility requires. Shared platforms, real-time data systems, and communication tools allow geographically dispersed or functionally separated teams to coordinate effectively. They make organizational knowledge more accessible, reducing the information asymmetries that slow decision-making and response.

Second, technology can break down organizational silos by creating visibility across boundaries and necessitating coordination across functional areas. When customer relationship management systems integrate sales, service, and product development information, for example, they make functional interdependencies explicit and create natural occasions for cross-functional collaboration. When dashboards provide organization-wide visibility into performance metrics, they discourage functional optimization at the expense of overall organizational effectiveness.

Third, technology can accelerate learning cycles by providing rapid feedback on initiatives, enabling experimentation at scale, and capturing lessons learned for broader application. Analytics capabilities allow organizations to understand what approaches work in which contexts, pilot programs can be quickly evaluated and refined, and successful innovations can be identified and spread.

Fourth, technology can reshape power dynamics and status hierarchies by democratizing access to information and providing platforms for broader participation in decisions. When information about organizational performance, customer needs, and strategic priorities is widely accessible rather than closely held by senior management, it empowers employees throughout the organization to identify opportunities and propose innovations.

However, technology realizes these benefits only when implemented in culturally receptive contexts with strong leadership support. Technology introduced into resistant cultures or without adequate leadership sponsorship often fails to achieve its potential. Employees work around systems that do not fit their work practices, formal adoption metrics mask low substantive utilization, and expensive technology investments yield disappointing returns.

This is why the sequence and integration of cultural transformation and technology adoption matters. Leaders must sometimes prepare organizational culture for technology through preliminary changes that demonstrate commitment to collaboration, inclusion, and adaptation. The Florida case suggests that structural reorganization preceding explicit technology adoption created cultural conditions where technology could subsequently succeed. In other contexts, technology might be introduced first to catalyze cultural conversations about new ways of working, with leaders using technology as a focal point for broader cultural transformation.

Leadership as Integrator and Sustainer

Leadership provides the essential integration and sustained momentum necessary for organizational agility. Leaders connect cultural transformation, technology adoption, and agility imperatives into coherent narratives that make sense to employees. They translate abstract concepts of agility into concrete behaviors and practices. They identify and address obstacles impeding progress. They celebrate successes, learn from failures, and maintain organizational attention on the longer-term transformation even amid short-term pressures.

Adaptive leadership capabilities prove particularly crucial because building organizational agility inevitably presents adaptive challenges rather than merely technical problems. Leaders must help organizations learn new behaviors, question established assumptions, and develop capabilities that do not currently exist. This work requires the diagnostic sensibility, emotional intelligence, and sustained engagement that characterize adaptive leadership.

The different leadership theories examined earlier in this chapter illuminate different aspects of the leadership challenge. Theory X and Theory Y highlight how fundamental assumptions about employee motivation shape leader behavior and organizational culture. Leaders who trust employees and believe in their capacity for self-direction create very different environments than leaders who see employees as inherently lazy and requiring constant supervision. In agility contexts, Theory Y orientations prove essential because agility requires initiative, creativity, and distributed decision-making that Theory X approaches suppress.

Transcendent leadership emphasizes inspiring and developing employees, helping them see how their contributions connect to larger purposes. This inspirational dimension becomes important in sustaining commitment through the difficulties of transformation. When employees understand how cultural transformation and technology adoption serve meaningful purposes—better serving customers, creating more fulfilling work, or enabling organizational survival and success—they demonstrate greater persistence through challenges.

The framing and reframing capabilities discussed by Bolman and Deal (2017) allow leaders to address the multiple dimensions of transformation simultaneously. Cultural transformation has structural dimensions (reorganizing roles and reporting relationships), human resource dimensions (developing new capabilities and addressing employee concerns), political dimensions (managing power and resource allocation), and symbolic dimensions (shaping organizational identity and meaning). Effective leaders move fluidly among these frames, addressing transformation challenges from multiple perspectives rather than relying on a single approach.

STRATEGIC RECOMMENDATIONS FOR LEADERS

Based on the literature review, case analysis, and discussion, several strategic recommendations emerge for leaders seeking to cultivate organizational agility through cultural transformation and technology adoption.

Begin with Honest Organizational Assessment

Leaders should begin by honestly assessing current organizational culture, technological capabilities, and agility levels. This assessment should examine both strengths to build upon and limitations to address. Questions to consider include: How does our culture respond to change and uncertainty? What are the dominant values and assumptions shaping employee behavior? Where do organizational silos impede collaboration and information flow? What is our current digital maturity across multiple dimensions? How rapidly can we sense environmental changes, make decisions, and implement responses?

This assessment should be comprehensive, drawing on multiple data sources and perspectives. Employee surveys, leadership interviews, process analysis, technology audits, and external benchmarking all provide valuable insights. The assessment should surface not only what leaders believe to be true, but also employee perceptions and experiences that may differ from leadership views.

Importantly, the assessment should identify specific agility gaps or opportunities that organizational transformation should address. Rather than pursuing cultural transformation or technology adoption as ends in themselves, leaders should connect these initiatives to concrete organizational needs and strategic goals. This connection makes transformation more meaningful to employees and provides clearer criteria for evaluating progress.

Develop an Integrated Transformation Strategy

Based on assessment findings, leaders should develop integrated transformation strategies addressing culture, leadership practices, and technology adoption in coordinated fashion. The strategy should specify the desired future state across these dimensions, high-level approaches for moving toward that future state, and sequencing considerations governing how different elements of transformation unfold.

The strategy should be comprehensive yet flexible. It should address major cultural shifts required, leadership capability development needed, technology infrastructure to be implemented, and organizational structure or process changes necessary. However, it should also acknowledge uncertainty and the need for adaptation as implementation progresses and the organization learns.

The strategy should identify quick wins that build momentum alongside longer-term initiatives that address fundamental organizational capabilities. Quick wins demonstrate that transformation is actually happening, build confidence and credibility, and generate enthusiasm. Longer-term initiatives address root causes and build sustainable capabilities. Both are necessary.

The strategy should also identify potential obstacles and mitigation approaches. What sources of resistance might emerge? What resource constraints must be addressed? What external factors might help or hinder transformation? Anticipating challenges helps leaders plan responses rather than being caught off-guard when difficulties emerge.

Create a Guiding Coalition

Leaders should assemble a guiding coalition representing diverse organizational constituencies to champion transformation. This coalition should include formal leaders from multiple levels and functions, informal influencers with credibility among peers, technical experts with implementation knowledge, and skeptics who can ensure critical perspectives are considered.

The guiding coalition serves multiple functions. It provides a sounding board for leadership, helping test ideas and identify issues leaders might miss. It extends leadership capacity, distributing transformation work across more individuals. It builds broader ownership, ensuring transformation does not depend solely on a few champions. It provides interpretation and translation, helping communicate transformation rationale in ways that resonate with different audiences.

The coalition should meet regularly throughout transformation, not just during initial planning. Regular engagement maintains momentum, surfaces emerging issues, enables rapid problem-solving, and demonstrates sustained leadership commitment. Coalition members should have real influence, not merely symbolic involvement. Their input should genuinely shape decisions, and they should have authority to champion transformation in their own organizational spheres.

Pilot and Learn Before Scaling

Leaders should employ pilot programs to test approaches, learn from experience, and refine strategies before organization-wide implementation. Pilots allow experimentation with manageable risk, generating learning that informs broader rollout. They provide proof-of-concept that builds confidence and credibility. They identify unanticipated challenges while they are still relatively easy to address.

Effective pilots require several elements. First, they should be genuine tests, not merely symbolic gestures where outcomes are predetermined. Leaders should approach pilots with authentic curiosity about what will work, not merely seeking to validate decisions already made. Second, pilots should be structured to generate learning, with clear hypotheses, defined success metrics, and systematic observation and data collection. Third, pilot learnings should actually influence subsequent decisions. When pilots reveal that initial approaches need modification, leaders should make those modifications rather than ignoring inconvenient findings.

Pilots also provide opportunities to identify and develop champions who can subsequently support broader implementation. Employees who participate in successful pilots often become enthusiastic advocates, helping their peers navigate similar transitions. Leaders should intentionally cultivate these champions, providing them with skills, resources, and platforms to share their experiences and insights.

Invest in Leadership Development

Building organizational agility requires leadership capabilities that many leaders have not previously developed. Organizations should invest in leadership development that builds the adaptive leadership, framing and reframing, and inclusive leadership capabilities necessary for guiding cultural transformation and technology adoption.

This development should combine multiple approaches: formal training in relevant concepts and frameworks, coaching and mentoring relationships providing personalized guidance, action learning projects where leaders apply concepts to real organizational challenges, and peer learning communities where leaders share experiences and support one another.

Leadership development should extend beyond senior executives to middle managers and emerging leaders who will implement transformation on the ground and sustain it over time. Middle managers, in particular, require support because they face unique challenges—translating executive vision into practical reality, supporting employees through change while managing their own transitions, and mediating between organizational imperatives and employee concerns.

Leadership development should be ongoing rather than one-time. As transformation progresses, leaders encounter new challenges requiring new capabilities. Continuous development ensures leaders stay ahead of the evolution they are guiding.

Maintain Disciplined Focus While Remaining Flexible

Leaders must maintain disciplined focus on transformation goals while remaining flexible about specific approaches. This balance—between consistency of purpose and adaptability of method—characterizes effective adaptive leadership.

Disciplined focus means not allowing inevitable short-term pressures, setbacks, or resistance to derail transformation. It means consistently communicating about transformation, allocating resources to support it, making decisions aligned with transformation goals, and holding the organization accountable for progress. Leaders demonstrate this focus through what they pay attention to, what questions they ask, what issues they elevate, and how they allocate their own time and energy.

Flexibility means adjusting specific approaches based on learning and feedback. It means recognizing that initial plans cannot anticipate all challenges and opportunities. It means genuinely listening to employee input and incorporating useful suggestions. It means celebrating experimentation even when initial attempts do not succeed as hoped.

The balance between focus and flexibility can be difficult to strike. Leaders who lean too far toward focus risk rigidity—pursuing approaches that are not working, ignoring valuable feedback, and breeding resentment among employees who feel their perspectives are dismissed. Leaders who lean too far toward flexibility risk being perceived as indecisive or uncommitted—changing direction so frequently that employees become confused or cynical about whether leaders really believe in transformation.

The Florida government department case illustrates this balance. Leaders maintained clear focus on their goal of breaking down silos and creating more diverse, collaborative teams. However, directors implemented this vision flexibly through one-on-one meetings addressing individual concerns, placement decisions matching people with appropriate roles, and adaptation to specific team dynamics and challenges. This combination of clear destination with flexible journey characterizes effective transformation leadership.

IMPLICATIONS FOR THEORY, PRACTICE, AND POLICY

Theoretical Implications

This chapter contributes to organizational theory by demonstrating the interdependence of cultural transformation, adaptive leadership, and technology adoption in building organizational agility. Existing literature often treats these domains separately, limiting understanding of their synergistic effects. The integrated framework presented here extends Schein's (2010) cultural theory by incorporating technology as both a cultural artifact and a catalyst for cultural transformation. It advances adaptive leadership theory (Heifetz et al., 2009) by articulating how adaptive challenges manifest specifically in technology-adoption contexts requiring cultural evolution.

The application of Cameron and Quinn's (2011) high-context and low-context cultural dimensions to technology adoption represents a novel theoretical contribution. This framework illuminates why certain technologies encounter greater resistance in specific cultural contexts and suggests differentiated leadership strategies based on cultural characteristics. Future research can build on this foundation to develop more nuanced understanding of cultural-technological fit and its implications for organizational agility.

The chapter also contributes to diversity and inclusion literature by demonstrating mechanisms through which diversity enhances organizational agility. While Gurin et al. (2002) established cognitive benefits of diversity, this chapter extends that work by showing how diversity specifically enables adaptive responses in technology-driven organizational transformation. The Florida case illustrates how demographic, generational, and functional diversity combined to break down silos and foster collaborative problem-solving essential for agility.

Practical Implications

For practitioners, this chapter offers actionable frameworks for navigating cultural transformation and technology adoption simultaneously. The strategic recommendations provide concrete guidance for leaders at various organizational levels. Senior executives can use the integrated framework to develop comprehensive transformation strategies that address culture, leadership, and technology in coordinated fashion. Middle managers can apply the adaptive leadership principles to support their teams through change while managing their own transitions. Front-line leaders can employ the inclusive leadership practices to ensure diverse voices contribute to technology adoption decisions.

The Florida government department case study provides a template for leveraging organizational restructuring to break down silos and enhance diversity. Leaders facing similar challenges can adapt this approach to their contexts, recognizing that structural interventions often prove more effective than exhortations to change culture. The case demonstrates that leaders need not wait for perfect cultural conditions before restructuring; rather, structural changes can create conditions that necessitate and enable cultural transformation.

The chapter's emphasis on technology as enabler rather than driver of transformation offers important practical insight. Leaders should resist the temptation to view technology implementation as an end in itself, instead positioning technology as infrastructure supporting desired cultural and operational changes. This reframing helps leaders maintain focus on organizational agility as the ultimate goal, with technology serving that goal rather than becoming a distraction from it.

Policy Implications

For policymakers and organizational governance structures, this chapter highlights the importance of policies that enable rather than constrain organizational agility. Technology governance policies, in particular, must balance legitimate concerns about security, compliance, and risk management with the need for experimentation and adaptation. Overly restrictive policies breed shadow IT and undermine transformation efforts, while insufficiently controlled environments create unacceptable risks.

Human resource policies should support diversity not merely as a demographic outcome but as a strategic capability enhancing organizational agility. This requires policies that foster inclusive environments where diverse perspectives are genuinely valued and integrated into decisions. Performance management systems should reward collaborative behavior and cross-boundary problem-solving rather than merely individual or functional achievement.

Investment policies should recognize that building organizational agility requires sustained commitment across multiple dimensions. Organizations cannot achieve agility through technology investments alone, nor through leadership development alone, nor through cultural initiatives alone. Policies should enable coordinated investment across these domains, with appropriate resource allocation and accountability for integrated outcomes rather than separate initiatives.

FUTURE RESEARCH DIRECTIONS

This chapter suggests several promising directions for future research. First, longitudinal studies examining organizational agility over time would provide valuable insight into how cultural transformation, leadership practices, and technology adoption interact dynamically. The Florida case captures a single transformation episode; tracking organizations over multiple years would reveal how agility capabilities are sustained, how they evolve in response to new challenges, and what leadership practices prove most effective for maintaining agility over time.

Second, comparative studies across different organizational contexts would enhance understanding of how industry, size, geographic location, and other contextual factors influence the relationship between culture, leadership, technology, and agility. Does the integrated framework apply similarly in manufacturing and service organizations? Do government agencies face unique challenges compared to private sector firms? How do cultural dimensions vary across national contexts, and what implications do these variations have for technology-adoption strategies?

Third, quantitative research examining relationships among cultural attributes, leadership practices, technology capabilities, and agility outcomes would complement the qualitative and conceptual analysis presented here. Developing valid and reliable measures of organizational agility, cultural characteristics relevant to technology adoption, and adaptive leadership behaviors would enable larger-scale empirical investigation of the theoretical framework proposed in this chapter.

Fourth, research investigating the role of specific technologies in enabling or constraining organizational agility would provide more granular insight. Do collaborative platforms have different effects on organizational culture and agility than analytics systems? How do emerging technologies like artificial intelligence and machine learning influence the cultural transformation required for effective adoption? What technology characteristics best support organizational agility in different contexts?

Fifth, studies examining how generational differences influence technology adoption and cultural transformation would address an increasingly salient organizational challenge. As workforces become more age-diverse, understanding how different generations perceive technology, respond to cultural change, and contribute to organizational agility becomes critical. The Florida case touched on generational diversity, but more focused investigation would deepen understanding.

Finally, action research projects where scholars collaborate with organizations to implement and evaluate agility-building interventions would generate both practical knowledge and theoretical insights. Such research would test the framework proposed here, identify implementation challenges and solutions, and produce evidence about what works in building organizational agility through integrated attention to culture, leadership, and technology.

CONCLUSION

Leadership is a critical determinant of organizational agility in an era demanding rapid adaptation to technological change, market volatility, and competitive intensity. Effective leaders understand that organizational agility emerges from the interaction of supportive culture, strategic technology adoption, and sustained adaptive leadership. They recognize that culture influences how organizations perceive and respond to change, technology provides infrastructure and capabilities enabling rapid sensing and response, and leadership integrates these elements while maintaining organizational momentum through inevitable challenges.

This chapter has examined how leaders can employ established frameworks—including Schein's cultural dimensions, adaptive leadership approaches, and framing/reframing capabilities—to navigate the complexities of building organizational agility. The discussion highlighted how high-context and low-context cultural dimensions shape technology adoption patterns and require differentiated leadership strategies. The Florida government department case study illustrated how leaders can leverage organizational restructuring to break down silos, enhance diversity, and foster the collaborative problem-solving culture essential for agility.

Several key principles emerge from this analysis. First, leaders must address culture and technology in integrated fashion rather than treating them as separate initiatives. Cultural transformation creates conditions for effective technology utilization, while technology adoption can catalyze cultural evolution. Leaders who pursue one without the other limit potential gains.

Second, diversity—across multiple dimensions including race, ethnicity, generation, education, and function—enhances organizational agility by bringing multiple perspectives and capabilities to bear on complex challenges. However, diversity alone does not suffice; leaders must create genuinely inclusive environments where diverse perspectives are elicited, valued, and integrated into decisions.

Third, adaptive leadership capabilities prove essential because building organizational agility presents adaptive challenges requiring learning, experimentation, and often changes to values and behaviors. Leaders who treat agility initiatives as merely technical problems underestimate the change required and typically achieve disappointing results.

Fourth, transformation requires sustained leadership attention and support. Quick wins may build momentum, but fundamental capabilities develop over extended periods. Leaders must persist through setbacks, maintain focus amid competing pressures, and continue supporting transformation even after initial enthusiasm wanes.

Fifth, organizations should learn systematically from experience, capturing insights from both successes and failures to inform ongoing evolution. The most agile organizations are also learning organizations, continuously refining their capabilities based on what they discover through experience.

Finally, leaders should recognize that building organizational agility is not a one-time transformation with a defined endpoint, but rather an ongoing journey of adaptation and development. As environments change and new challenges emerge, organizations must continue evolving their cultures, leadership practices, and technological capabilities.

The contemporary business landscape increasingly rewards organizational agility while punishing rigidity and slowness to adapt. Leaders who can foster cultures supporting change, learning, and collaboration while strategically implementing technologies that break down silos and accelerate decision-making position their organizations for sustained success. This work is difficult, requiring sophisticated leadership capabilities, sustained commitment, and willingness to navigate ambiguity and setbacks. However, the alternative—maintaining rigid cultures and legacy technologies in increasingly dynamic environments—ensures eventual obsolescence and failure.

Leaders should view cultural transformation and technology adoption not as burdens to be borne, but as opportunities to enhance organizational capacity and create competitive advantage. By fostering resilient, inclusive, technologically empowered cultures, leaders enable their organizations to not merely survive but thrive amid uncertainty, seizing new opportunities and delivering increasing value to stakeholders. This chapter provides a roadmap for leaders to enhance cultural alignment, build digital maturity, and achieve organizational agility—creating enterprises capable of sustained success in dynamic, competitive environments.

REFERENCES

Avolio, B. J., & Bass, B. M. (2002). *Developing Potential Across a Full Range of Leadership*. Lawrence Erlbaum Associates.

Bolman, L. G., & Deal, T. E. (2017). *Reframing Organizations: Artistry, Choice, and Leadership*. Jossey-Bass. DOI: 10.1002/9781119281856

Brock, W. (2012). Synthesizing a systems perspective and organizational change: Principles of a whole-systems metrics model. *Organization Development Journal*, *30*(3), 17–28.

Burke, W. W. (2017). *Organization Change: Theory and Practice*. Sage Publications.

Cameron, K. S., & Quinn, R. E. (2011). *Diagnosing and Changing Organizational Culture: Based on the Competing Values Framework*. John Wiley & Sons.

Chin, R., & Benne, K. D. (1969). *General Strategies for Effecting Changes in Human Systems*. Human Relations Center, Boston University.

Galloway, S. M. (2016). What makes a leader transformational? *Leadership Excellence*, *33*(5), 20–21.

Gurin, P., Dey, E. L., Hurtado, S., & Gurin, G. (2002). Diversity and higher education: Theory and impact on educational outcomes. *Harvard Educational Review*, *72*(3), 330–366. DOI: 10.17763/haer.72.3.01151786u134n051

Hall, P. (2005). Interprofessional teamwork: Professional cultures as barriers. *Journal of Interprofessional Care*, 19(sup1), 188-196.

Heifetz, R., Grashow, A., & Linsky, M. (2009). *The Practice of Adaptive Leadership: Tools and Tactics for Changing Your Organization and the World*. Harvard Business Press.

Heifetz, R. A. (2003). Adaptive work. *DEMOS COLLECTION*, 68-78.

Kondra, A. Z., & Hinings, C. R. (1998). Organizational diversity and change in institutional theory. *Organization Studies*, *19*(5), 743–767. DOI: 10.1177/017084069801900502

McGregor, D. (1960). *The Human Side of Enterprise*. McGraw-Hill.

Northouse, P. G. (2017). *Leadership: Theory and Practice* (8th ed.). Sage Publications.

Schein, E. H. (2010). *Organizational Culture and Leadership* (4th ed.). Jossey-Bass.

Skogstad, A., Einarsen, S., Torsheim, T., Aasland, M. S., & Hetland, H. (2007). The destructiveness of Laissez-faire leadership behavior. *Journal of Occupational Health Psychology*, *12*(1), 80–92. DOI: 10.1037/1076-8998.12.1.80 PMID: 17257068

Sun, S. (2009). Organizational culture and its themes. *International Journal of Business and Management*, *3*(12), 137–143. DOI: 10.5539/ijbm.v3n12p137

Weick, K. E., & Quinn, R. E. (1999). Organizational change and development. *Annual Review of Psychology*, *50*(1), 361–386. DOI: 10.1146/annurev.psych.50.1.361 PMID: 15012461

Chapter 12
Exploring the Need to Develop Leadership Skills for Artificial Intelligence (AI) Professionals in Healthcare

Amalisha Sabie Aridi
http://orcid.org/0000-0002-7869-5530
Washington University of Science and Technology, USA

ABSTRACT

As artificial intelligence (AI) becomes integral to healthcare innovation and infrastructure, healthcare organizations face a growing challenge: equipping technically proficient professionals with the leadership competencies necessary to operate effectively at the enterprise level. This qualitative study explores how healthcare organizations either support or impede the leadership development of AI and IT professionals and identifies strategies that best facilitate their transition from technical expertise to strategic leadership. Using three separate focus groups composed of change management consultants, AI technology managers, and leadership development trainers. The findings suggest that most organizations fail to offer effective leadership training programs for AI professionals operating in high-risk, compliance-heavy environments.

INTRODUCTION

AI-powered Clinical Decision Support Systems (CDSS) are transforming diagnostic precision and real-time clinical decision-making in healthcare. These systems harness machine learning algorithms to analyze massive volumes of structured and unstructured clinical data, including electronic health records (EHRs), imaging results, lab tests, and genetic profiles, to generate insights that guide physicians in diagnosis and treatment selection (Burrell, 2023). For instance, an AI model deployed in the emergency department can detect early signs of sepsis six hours before a human clinician might recognize symptoms, triggering alerts that enable life-saving interventions. Such systems have been implemented in hospitals like Johns Hopkins, were real-time predictive models for patient deterioration significantly improved ICU outcomes. By automating routine analyses and identifying high-risk patients, CDSS

DOI: 10.4018/979-8-3373-4027-2.ch012

not only reduces diagnostic error but also empowers clinicians to focus on nuanced care decisions. As healthcare systems continue to embrace AI integration, CDSS will become a cornerstone of precision medicine, offering clinicians cognitive support and enhancing patient safety through timely, data-driven recommendations (Burrell, 2023).

MEDICAL IMAGING AND RADIOLOGY

AI is revolutionizing radiology by enhancing the accuracy, speed, and consistency of medical image interpretation (Burrell, 2023). Deep learning models, especially convolutional neural networks (CNNs), are trained on thousands of annotated images to detect abnormalities such as tumors, fractures, or hemorrhages with high sensitivity (Burrell, 2023). A vivid example is Google Health's AI system, which outperformed radiologists in breast cancer detection during clinical trials, reducing false negatives and false positives. Similarly, Aidoc's triage platform automatically analyzes CT scans to identify urgent cases like intracranial bleeds and prioritizes them for immediate review, dramatically reducing time-to-treatment. These applications allow radiologists to manage higher volumes with greater diagnostic confidence, especially in under-resourced hospitals. AI in radiology represents a paradigm shift, augmenting human expertise with algorithmic precision, ultimately accelerating diagnostic workflows and improving patient outcomes (Burrell, 2023).

Predictive And Preventive Analytics

Predictive analytics powered by AI enables healthcare providers to anticipate health risks and intervene before complications arise (Burrell, 2023). By integrating data from EHRs, wearable devices, socio-demographic variables, and historical patient records, AI models can forecast the onset of chronic conditions like heart disease or diabetes. For example, Mount Sinai Health System uses predictive modeling to identify patients at high risk for heart failure readmission. The system evaluates clinical history and social factors to generate risk scores, prompting early interventions such as remote monitoring or personalized care plans. This proactive approach helps reduce hospital readmissions, minimizes avoidable emergency visits, and improves long-term outcomes. AI-based predictive analytics empowers healthcare systems to shift from reactive treatment to proactive care, ultimately reducing costs and improving population health management (Burrell, 2023).

AI-Powered Virtual Health Assistants and Chatbots

AI-driven virtual assistants are enhancing patient engagement and operational efficiency in healthcare delivery (Burrell, 2023). Using natural language processing (NLP), these assistants can understand and respond to patient inquiries, triage symptoms, schedule appointments, and even deliver behavioral interventions (Burrell, 2023). Babylon Health's AI chatbot, for instance, simulates a conversation with a physician by assessing symptoms and offering guidance or escalation pathways. Similarly, Woebot provides mental health support through conversational AI, using cognitive behavioral techniques to address anxiety and depression in real time. These tools alleviate administrative burdens on staff and provide immediate, 24/7 support to patients who might otherwise lack access to care. As virtual assistants evolve, they will become essential in scaling patient services, especially in underserved or resource-constrained environments.

Genomic Analysis and Precision Medicine

AI is accelerating the field of genomics, enabling precision medicine by identifying individualized treatment strategies based on genetic data. Advanced machine learning models analyze complex genomic datasets to identify patterns and mutations linked to specific diseases, particularly in oncology and rare diseases (Burrell, 2023). One example is Deep Genomics, which uses AI to predict how genetic mutations influence disease development and to identify drug targets for conditions like spinal muscular atrophy. In clinical contexts, AI helps match cancer patients to the most effective immunotherapies based on their tumor's genetic profile. This level of customization allows for treatments that are not only more effective but also carry fewer side effects. By aligning therapies with genetic insights, AI-enabled precision medicine enhances therapeutic efficacy and transforms care from standardized protocols to individualized interventions (Burrell, 2023).

Drug Discovery and Development

AI is dramatically reducing the time and cost required to discover and develop new pharmaceutical compounds (Burrell, 2023). Machine learning algorithms can analyze chemical properties, predict molecular behavior, and simulate clinical outcomes to identify promising drug candidates in weeks rather than years (Burrell, 2023). Atomwise, for example, leverages AI to virtually screen millions of compounds against disease targets, identifying potential treatments for conditions like Ebola and leukemia. Insilico Medicine used its AI platform to design a novel drug molecule in just 46 days, a process that traditionally takes years. These breakthroughs are particularly vital in responding to emerging diseases and unmet therapeutic needs. AI's capacity to optimize drug discovery accelerates innovation in pharmaceutical science and improves the pipeline for life-saving therapies across global health systems.

Robotic Process Automation (RPA) in Administration

AI-enabled robotic process automation (RPA) is transforming the administrative backbone of healthcare organizations (Burrell, 2023). RPA uses rule-based algorithms to automate repetitive, high-volume tasks such as billing, claims processing, and data entry. For example, the Cleveland Clinic implemented RPA bots to manage patient scheduling and insurance verification, reducing administrative workload and freeing up staff for higher-order decision-making. By automating claims adjudication, some providers have cut processing time by over 70%, leading to faster reimbursements and fewer errors. In an industry burdened by paperwork and regulatory demands, AI-powered automation boosts operational efficiency and supports financial sustainability.

AI in Remote Patient Monitoring and Telehealth

AI is revolutionizing remote patient monitoring by transforming wearable devices into intelligent, predictive health management tools (Burrell, 2023). These systems analyze continuous streams of biometric data, such as heart rate, glucose levels, and oxygen saturation, to detect anomalies and prompt clinical interventions (Burrell, 2023). For instance, Fitbit's partnership with Google Cloud allows AI algorithms to monitor atrial fibrillation and notify users of irregular rhythms, prompting early intervention. In chronic care management, platforms like Biofourmis integrate wearable data with AI to personalize treatment plans and anticipate exacerbations in heart failure patients, reducing hospitalization rates. AI-enhanced remote monitoring supports a transition to decentralized, data-driven healthcare that prioritizes early detection and continuous care.

AI IN MENTAL HEALTH

AI is increasingly applied to support mental health diagnosis, monitoring, and intervention delivery. Natural language processing and sentiment analysis allow AI tools to detect mood patterns, identify mental health risks, and deliver therapeutic content via digital platforms (Burrell, 2023). Woebot, an AI-powered mental health chatbot, uses language patterns to detect emotional distress and guide users through structured therapeutic conversations. Additionally, researchers are using AI to analyze voice tone and word choice in teletherapy sessions to detect early signs of depression or psychosis. These technologies offer scalable support, especially in areas facing clinician shortages or stigma around seeking care. By expanding access and personalizing mental health care, AI tools play an increasingly vital role in the early detection and continuous support of emotional well-being (Burrell, 2023).

AI for Health Equity and Population Health Management

AI is being harnessed to reduce health disparities by identifying social determinants of health and targeting population-level interventions (Burrell, 2023). Machine learning models analyze geospatial, demographic, and socioeconomic data to identify patterns that influence community health outcomes. For example, New York City's Department of Health used AI models to predict asthma hotspots based on housing quality, pollution exposure, and income levels, allowing for targeted intervention campaigns. Similarly, health systems are using AI to flag patients experiencing food insecurity or transportation barriers, prompting social service referrals alongside clinical care. AI's ability to integrate clinical and social data makes it a powerful tool for advancing health equity and improving outcomes across diverse populations.

Within the healthcare artificial intelligence (AI) domain, a profound organizational dilemma is unfolding; leaders must reconcile the divergence between technological proficiency and human-centered leadership competencies (McGettrick et al., 2014; Tsado, 2016). This tension manifests in the discord between the skills necessary to oversee AI-driven IT initiatives and those required to nurture and mentor emerging professionals entering the field. As McGettrick et al. (2014) and Tsado (2016) observe, while managing AI healthcare technology demands a mastery of technical systems, mentoring early-career employees, fresh from undergraduate programs in computer science or AI, necessitates emotional intelligence, interpersonal acumen, and leadership fluency. The institutional emphasis has skewed towards recruiting and retaining high-caliber technical personnel, often at the expense of cultivating their capacity for supervisory leadership. Cybersecurity concerns, such as advanced persistent threats and data breaches, exacerbate this imbalance by monopolizing strategic attention and reallocating developmental resources toward technical fortification rather than leadership training (Arbaiza, 2016). This misalignment is further illuminated by research indicating that executive education programs have failed to keep pace with the rapidly shifting dynamics of the AI business environment.

Lester and Parnell (2006) and Burrell (2025) argue that organizations often make the erroneous assumption that exceptional technical performance naturally translates into managerial effectiveness. However, leadership entails a distinct repertoire of capabilities, namely decision-making, team-building, and effective communication, that cannot be acquired through technical proficiency alone (Goldberg, 2006; Rothenberger, 2016; Dzameshie, 2012). This gap becomes particularly acute in healthcare AI, where misaligned role expectations hinder organizational performance and employee development. A vivid illustration lies in the observation that 62% of organizations lack the training necessary to equip technical leaders with situational awareness of business and IT risks (Burrell, 2025). This training deficit signals a broader structural challenge: the inability of organizations to prepare their technical leaders for enterprise-level responsibilities that demand fluency in strategic thinking, risk navigation, and human capital development.

Thus, the transition from technical expert to managerial leader in healthcare AI is neither linear nor guaranteed. It demands deliberate cultivation of soft skills and business acumen, competencies often overlooked amid urgent operational demands (Lester & Parnell, 2006; Dzameshie, 2012). As AI matures into a core business strategy, leaders must transcend the technical sphere to architect organizational vision and mentor the next generation of professionals (Hansib, 2014). Yet task saturation frequently relegates senior healthcare AI leaders to hands-on technical roles, impeding their ability to develop future leadership pipelines. Addressing this imbalance is not merely a talent development issue, it is a strategic imperative for healthcare institutions seeking to align innovation with sustainable leadership practices.

A prevailing challenge in the healthcare artificial intelligence (AI) job roles is the systemic neglect of leadership development for technical professionals, who are often elevated into management roles without the interpersonal and strategic competencies necessary to lead high-performing teams and influence enterprise-level outcomes (Lester & Parnell, 2006; Brokett, 2007). This leadership gap poses significant risks to organizational performance, innovation scalability, and operational resilience within AI-driven healthcare environments.

PROBLEM STATEMENT

In the evolving domain of healthcare artificial intelligence (AI), organizations face a growing leadership deficit among technically proficient professionals who ascend to managerial roles without adequate preparation in strategic, interpersonal, and organizational leadership competencies. While healthcare AI professionals are often hired and promoted for their technical expertise in areas such as machine learning, cybersecurity, and algorithmic development, their roles increasingly require them to engage in tasks that demand emotional intelligence, communication, team-building, and enterprise-level decision-making (Lester & Parnell, 2006; Rothenberger, 2016; Dzameshie, 2012). The absence of structured leadership development pipelines, compounded by organizational overemphasis on technical training and escalating cybersecurity demands, has resulted in a misalignment between leadership expectations and managerial preparedness. This disconnect jeopardizes organizational performance, innovation scalability, and the successful integration of AI into healthcare enterprise strategy (McGettrick et al., 2014; Tsado, 2016; Arbaiza, 2016).

PURPOSE STATEMENT

The purpose of this study is to examine the organizational and developmental barriers that impede healthcare artificial intelligence (AI) professionals from transitioning effectively into leadership roles. This research seeks to identify the competencies most critical to successful leadership in healthcare AI contexts, evaluate the efficacy of current leadership development practices, and explore strategic interventions that align technical expertise with leadership capacity. By understanding these dynamics, the study aims to inform the design of targeted leadership development programs that enhance both individual career trajectories and enterprise-level AI strategy execution.

Significance of the Study

As AI becomes an integral component of healthcare operations, enabling predictive analytics, personalized medicine, and data-driven decision-making, the demand for leaders who can translate technical insights into organizational outcomes has never been more pressing. This study contributes to the existing literature by illuminating the leadership challenges specific to AI professionals within healthcare, a sector characterized by rapid innovation, regulatory complexity, and high-stakes ethical considerations. The findings will be valuable for healthcare administrators, policymakers, and educators seeking to cultivate leadership talent capable of navigating both technical and human dimensions of healthcare transformation. Furthermore, the study responds to a critical need identified by researchers and industry leaders: to equip technical experts with the strategic foresight and people skills necessary to sustain innovation and safeguard organizational integrity in an AI-driven healthcare ecosystem (Klimoski, 2016; Maxwell, 2013; Eich, 2012).

OVERARCHING RESEARCH QUESTION

How do healthcare organizations support or hinder the development of leadership competencies among AI and IT professionals, and what strategies are most effective in enabling the transition from technical expertise to enterprise-level leadership?

Shortcoming in the Healthcare Artificial Intelligence (AI)

A critical organizational shortcoming in the healthcare artificial intelligence (AI) is the persistent underdevelopment of leadership capabilities among technically skilled professionals, who are often promoted based solely on their domain expertise. This oversight undermines the ability of such professionals to lead interdisciplinary teams, drive strategic change, and support the enterprise-wide deployment of AI innovations.

As Lester and Parnell (2006), Burrell (2019), and Brokett (2007) observe, the nature of IT and AI roles, grounded in software engineering, algorithmic modeling, and data systems, typically precludes frequent interaction with diverse teams or exposure to organizational leadership practices. Consequently, when these experts are elevated into management, they often struggle with performance management, cross-functional collaboration, and organizational transformation. Despite the proliferation of sophisticated AI applications in healthcare, such as real-time patient monitoring, predictive analytics for chronic disease management, and AI-assisted diagnostics, most institutions continue to prioritize technical training while overlooking the development of managerial competencies (Dzameshie, 2012; Rothenberger, 2016). Watkins (2013) and Gabarro (2007) argue that effective management transcends technical proficiency, requiring the ability to marshal resources, influence organizational direction, and implement strategic initiatives. Hooving (2007) and Burrell et al., (2018) further reinforce the necessity for leadership skills in communication, delegation, and team development; skills that remain scarce among AI professionals transitioning from solitary technical roles into enterprise leadership positions.

This gap in leadership readiness is particularly detrimental in the healthcare AI context, where innovation must coexist with stringent regulatory oversight, ethical considerations, and dynamic system-level transformation. For instance, an AI specialist may design an advanced predictive algorithm for sepsis detection but fail to secure clinical buy-in or align the innovation with hospital workflow and regulatory constraints. As Maxwell (2013) emphasizes, high-performing leaders must interpret and adapt to complex political, economic, societal, and technological forces to sustain innovation and competitive advantage. Furthermore, in a digital environment where cyber risk is rapidly becoming a cornerstone of enterprise risk management, AI leaders must possess the strategic awareness and interpersonal gravitas to advocate for cybersecurity investments to boards and C-suite executives (Klimoski, 2016). When these leadership traits are absent, organizations face elevated threats of misaligned strategies, compromised data security, and stalled AI integration.

To confront this leadership void, healthcare organizations must embed formal leadership development programs specifically tailored to the evolving demands of AI roles (Hladio & Edwards, 2017; Eich, 2012). These initiatives should cultivate social capital, strategic foresight, and enterprise fluency, equipping AI leaders not just to engineer algorithms, but to inspire teams, communicate vision, and secure stakeholder commitment. As Daft (2015) asserts, digital transformation is catalyzed not by technological capability alone, but by leaders who can synthesize people, process, and innovation into cohesive organizational strategy. In today's AI-powered healthcare ecosystem, the cultivation of such leadership capacity is not a supplemental consideration, it is an organizational imperative.

THE STRATEGIC DEVELOPMENT OF LEADERSHIP COMPETENCIES

In the rapidly evolving landscape of healthcare artificial intelligence (AI), the strategic development of leadership competencies among technical professionals is not a peripheral concern, it is foundational to enterprise security, innovation scalability, and organizational resilience. Leadership, defined as a dynamic relational process grounded in influence and authority (Fiedler, 1972; Burns, 1978), must be deliberately cultivated through structured development initiatives that integrate both technical expertise and human capital strategy (Daft, 2015). Research underscores that leadership development programs serve as powerful mechanisms for cultivating not only leadership traits but also professional growth, strategic capacity, and organizational influence (Daft, 2015; Hladio & Edwards, 2017; Eich, 2012). The Chief Information Security Officer (CISO), often the most senior healthcare AI executive, exemplifies this dual imperative. According to Klimoski (2016), an IBM study emphasized that the CISO should report directly to the Chief Executive Officer, a structural endorsement of the role's strategic value and a recognition of the high-caliber leadership it demands. The CISO is uniquely positioned at the nexus of enterprise-level decision-making, requiring fluency in business strategy, mastery of AI systems, and the interpersonal dexterity to influence across organizational strata. In this context, leadership development becomes indispensable. As Draft (2015) and Burrell (2025) note, organizations that fail to equip leaders with communication proficiency, risk navigation, and team mobilization capabilities risk operational stagnation and security exposure.

Healthcare AI professionals face unparalleled pressure as they steward vast datasets, maintain real-time system integrity, and architect defenses against increasingly sophisticated cyber threats. These responsibilities extend well beyond the bounds of coding and system management, they demand strategic judgment, ethical decision-making, and high-functioning social capital (Klimoski, 2016). Without comprehensive leadership training, technical experts are ill-prepared to anticipate or counterbalance the reputational and financial ramifications of data breaches, ransomware events, and cyber exploitation, the cost of which averages between $4 to $6 million per incident (Burrell, 2019). As organizations digitize and increasingly rely on AI-driven platforms for clinical care, logistics, and diagnostics, the complexity of protecting these digital ecosystems escalates (Burrell, 2025). It is, therefore, untenable for healthcare systems to rely solely on external leadership academies or high-cost corporate seminars, which often lack the depth in critical reasoning, contextual analysis, and sector-specific strategic focus needed to prepare leaders for AI-intensive environments.

Thus, investing in internally curated, academically supported leadership development programs tailored to the healthcare AI context is both a risk mitigation strategy and a value-generation imperative. The dividends, reduced cybersecurity vulnerability, enhanced strategic foresight, and improved organizational cohesion, far outweigh the resource allocation required to establish such initiatives (Hartigan, 1974). In a domain where the failure to lead effectively can result not only in financial catastrophe but also in eroded public trust and shareholder confidence, the return on investment is incalculable. Forward-thinking organizations must not assume that technical leaders inherently possess leadership skills; they must commit to cultivating these capabilities systematically to ensure the sustainability and strategic viability of AI applications in healthcare (Daft, 2015; Hartigan, 1974).

As healthcare organizations increasingly integrate artificial intelligence (AI) technologies into core operations, the imperative to cultivate leadership competencies tailored to this dynamic environment has become strategically indispensable. Leadership development programs must evolve to meet the distinct demands of AI-driven healthcare enterprises, where technical precision must be matched by emotional intelligence, strategic foresight, and cultural alignment. Hladio and Edwards (2017) contend that modern organizations aiming to elevate high-potential talent must implement leadership development strategies that correspond with the hierarchical complexity and cross-functional breadth of today's enterprises. Their findings underscore that cultivating leaders across varying levels requires programs tailored to diverse leadership stages and business units. Jensen (2011) and Eich (2012) emphasize that leadership development initiatives, when designed with activities that foster self-awareness, interpersonal trust, and emotional acuity, can enhance decision-making, strengthen managerial dexterity, and reinforce a resilient organizational culture. Historical leadership scholarship from Burns (1978) and Fiedler (1972) further reinforces that effective leaders must be adept not only at exercising influence but also at forming authentic relationships with subordinates, an ability that is particularly crucial in data-centric healthcare environments where human factors and patient outcomes remain pivotal.

In AI-integrated healthcare systems, the confluence of machine learning, big data analytics, and intelligent automation has transformed leadership from a function of control to one of orchestration. A technically proficient healthcare AI manager might engineer a successful clinical decision support algorithm but falter in aligning that innovation with the broader institutional mission, staff competencies, and regulatory frameworks. Jones (2012) notes that adept leaders align team initiatives with enterprise-wide goals without eroding the integrity of organizational culture or dismantling programmatic benchmarks. Programmatic alignment, anchored in quantitative performance metrics, must coexist with an organizational design that promotes inclusion, low attrition, and workforce engagement (Bass, 1985; Daft, 2015; Jones, 2012). However, as Berson and Stieglitz (2013) observe, the leadership landscape is now shaped by volatility, ambiguity, and accelerating complexity. While AI offers predictive modeling, real-time diagnostics, and operational scalability, its business integration demands leaders capable of navigating ambiguity, leading cross-disciplinary teams, and fostering innovation amidst digital disruption (Kouzes & Posner, 2017; Linden, 2010). Yet, as Sørensen (2017) laments, leadership development programs frequently lag behind technological progress due to a lack of robust evaluative frameworks, inhibiting the adaptation or creation of relevant curricula for next-generation leaders.

Therefore, the modernization of leadership development initiatives is not a discretionary enhancement, it is a strategic requirement for healthcare organizations leveraging AI as a business asset. Institutions must proactively revise or redesign development programs to bridge the widening chasm between legacy leadership models and contemporary demands for adaptability, collaboration, and systems thinking in AI-enabled environments (Hladio & Edwards, 2017; Eich, 2012; Sørensen, 2017). By doing so, healthcare enterprises will not only empower leaders who can manage innovation but also ensure that AI is deployed ethically, strategically, and in harmony with human-centered care delivery.

DEVELOPING LEADERS

As AI technologies become deeply embedded in healthcare operations, cultivating transformational leadership among technical managers and healthcare AI professionals is essential for navigating organizational complexity, enhancing decision-making, and safeguarding institutional resilience. Effective leadership in this domain demands more than operational competence, it requires vision, adaptability, strategic communication, and emotional intelligence to influence dynamic enterprise systems.

Leslie (2009) identifies one of the most pressing organizational imperatives: developing and retaining leaders with the managerial agility to address contemporary challenges in fast-paced, innovation-intensive sectors. These leaders must excel in motivating teams, engaging in visionary planning, and leveraging critical thinking to navigate shifting priorities. However, while many managers grasp the structural "what" of leadership, they often struggle with the relational "how," especially in applying interpersonal influence to shape organizational culture. Berson and Stieglitz (2013) and Eich (2012) argue that this leadership complexity calls for learning and development professionals to transition from static curriculum delivery to facilitating socially constructed leadership experiences that include stakeholders across the organizational hierarchy. To meet this challenge, Jones (2012) proposed a five-level leadership development model focused on strengthening competence at the individual, team, organizational, network, and systems levels, foundational domains that are especially relevant for healthcare AI professionals managing interdependent technologies, regulatory expectations, and interdisciplinary teams.

In an environment where decision-making must be rapid, data-informed, and ethically sound, transformational leadership has emerged as a critical paradigm. As Elkins (2015) reveals, there is a strong correlation between advanced critical thinking and decision-making capacities and effective management of financial, human, and technological resources. This is particularly significant in healthcare AI, where CISOs and AI managers are expected to evaluate emerging cybersecurity threats, allocate technical resources, and articulate complex return-on-investment scenarios to executive stakeholders. Kouzes and Posner (2017) and Lepeley, von Kimakowitz, and Bardy (2016) note that shorter business cycles and rising complexity necessitate leaders who can swiftly align team outputs with overarching strategy. Yet, the constant influx of new technologies often leaves leaders unprepared to update their practices, underscoring the need for bespoke development programs (Assante & Tobey, 2011). Transformational leadership, defined by idealized influence, intellectual stimulation, individualized consideration, and inspirational motivation (Cavazotte et al., 2012; Shadraconis, 2013), is particularly well-suited for AI-driven healthcare, where professionals must communicate urgent regulatory shifts and cybersecurity protocols with clarity and authority, even amid competing organizational demands. The ability to distill complex technical risks into accessible language for non-technical executives is not a soft skill; it is a mission-critical competency (Burrell, 2025).

Organizations that invest in custom leadership development programs for AI and cybersecurity professionals foster not only leadership effectiveness but also long-term institutional sustainability. These initiatives, anchored in coaching, experiential learning, and stakeholder engagement, equip professionals to influence executive decision-making, implement strategic change, and inspire commitment across technical and non-technical domains (Albion & Galiardi, 2011; Khan et al., 2012; Mitchell, 2012). As Thamrin (2012) and Burrell et al. (2018) demonstrate, transformational leadership directly enhances organizational commitment and performance, especially when leaders build cultures of trust and open engagement. Leslie (2009) articulates the competencies most essential for supervisory success, ranging from vision and strategy to innovation and adaptability, underscoring that these traits must be systematically cultivated through structured development, not assumed through role progression. In healthcare AI, where risk is high and the pace of change is relentless, leadership development is not merely a supportive function, it is a strategic asset essential for organizational agility, cybersecurity preparedness, and continuous innovation.

METHODOLOGY AND RESEARCH DESIGN

This study employs a qualitative research design using focus group methodology to explore how healthcare organizations support or impede the development of leadership competencies among artificial intelligence (AI) and information technology (IT) professionals. Qualitative inquiry is appropriate for this research because it facilitates the exploration of perceptions, organizational experiences, and complex social dynamics that quantitative methods may not adequately capture (Creswell & Poth, 2018).

The study is guided by an overarching research question:

How do healthcare organizations support or hinder the development of leadership competencies among AI and IT professionals, and what strategies are most effective in enabling the transition from technical expertise to enterprise-level leadership?

Participants and Sampling

Purposive sampling will be used to recruit a total of 15 participants, organized into three distinct focus groups of five participants each. Each group is selected based on their professional experience and relevance to the topic:

- **Focus Group 1**: Organizational Development Management Consultants certified in change management.
- **Focus Group 2**: AI Technology Managers actively working in healthcare or healthcare-related sectors.
- **Focus Group 3**: Leadership Development Trainers with extensive experience in hiring, onboarding, and training technical professionals in AI and IT fields.

Participants will be recruited through professional networks, LinkedIn communities, and referrals from industry associations. Inclusion criteria require a minimum of five years of relevant professional experience and familiarity with leadership dynamics in technology-driven healthcare environments.

Data Collection

Each focus group session will be conducted via Zoom and will last approximately 60 minutes. Sessions will be audio-recorded with participant consent and transcribed verbatim for thematic analysis. A semi-structured focus group protocol will be used to guide the discussion, allowing for both consistency across groups and the flexibility to explore emerging insights.

The following three open-ended data collection questions were posed during each session:

1. **What leadership competencies do you believe are most critical for AI and IT professionals to successfully transition into enterprise-level leadership roles within healthcare organizations?**

This question elicits expert insight into the specific skillsets and behaviors required for effective leadership beyond technical proficiency.

2. **Based on your experience, what organizational practices or cultural factors support, or hinder, the development of these leadership competencies among technical professionals?**

This question aims to explore environmental, structural, or policy-based enablers and barriers to leadership development in healthcare settings.

3. **What types of leadership development strategies, programs, or interventions have you seen work effectively in preparing technical professionals for executive or strategic roles?**

This question is intended to uncover actionable strategies, best practices, and lessons learned from various organizational contexts.

Ethical Considerations

All participants will be provided with an informed consent form outlining the purpose of the study, procedures, potential risks, and their rights as participants. Anonymity and confidentiality was maintained by assigning pseudonyms and removing identifying details from all transcripts. This study has been designed to comply with institutional review board (IRB) guidelines and ethical standards for human subject research.

DATA RESULTS

Theme 1: Misalignment Between Technical Expertise and Leadership Expectations (14 out of 15 participants mentioned in this perspective as very significant)

Quote (AI Technology Manager):
"Just because someone is brilliant with code or system design doesn't mean they know how to run a team. We often get promoted based on what we can do with technology, but suddenly we're expected to coach people, manage conflict, and explain business outcomes. That's a completely different skillset, and no one really trains us for that jump."
Quote (Leadership Development Trainer):
"We see so many technically gifted professionals struggle when they're asked to lead. They know the systems inside out, but they haven't been taught how to manage people or communicate across departments. It's like asking a surgeon to suddenly run a hospital without any leadership training, it just doesn't work long-term."

Theme 2: Lack of Structured and Role-Specific Leadership Development focused on Technology Professionals (14 out of 15 participants mentioned in this perspective as very significant)

Quote (Organizational Development Consultant):
"Most leadership programs are too generic. They're not built for people leading in high-stakes, tech-heavy environments like healthcare AI. These roles need specialized training that teaches how to balance risk, compliance, innovation, and team dynamics all at once."
Quote (Leadership Development Trainer):
"We have to stop handing technical leads a few PowerPoints on leadership and calling it a day. They need hands-on coaching, real-world simulations, and mentoring that's actually tied to the problems they face, things like cybersecurity strategy, AI ethics, or navigating HIPAA requirements while managing a team."

Theme 3: Organizational Culture and Executive Support as Key Enablers or Barriers (14 out of 15 participants mentioned in this perspective as very significant)

Quote (AI Technology Manager):
"Honestly, whether or not you grow as a leader in healthcare tech depends on your organization. If the executives get AI and see leadership development as an investment, you'll get support. But in many places, leadership training is an afterthought, and you're left to figure it out on your own while putting out fires."
Quote (Organizational Development Consultant):
"Culture is everything. In some healthcare systems, there's a real push to integrate leadership development into their digital strategy. In others, it's all reactionary, training only happens after a security breach or staff turnover. That inconsistency kills momentum for real leadership growth."
(Leadership Development Trainer):

"I have worked on so many organizations where the culture is to only send IT people to IT or technical training. Most of them never invested in leadership training for any employees in IT, cybersecurity, or artificial intelligence."

Theme 4: Critical Role of Communication and Soft Skills in Leading AI Teams. (14 out of 15 participants mentioned in this perspective as very significant)

Quote (Leadership Development Trainer): *"We emphasize soft skills because that's often what's missing. AI leaders have to explain really complex things to non-tech execs, secure buy-in, and sometimes deliver tough news. If they can't communicate well, the best ideas will get buried under confusion or resistance."*

Quote (Organizational Development Consultant):

"I've seen brilliant AI managers fail not because of technical issues but because they couldn't rally their teams or speak the language of business leaders. Leadership is influence, and influence relies on trust, clarity, and human connection more than it does on technical expertise."

Study Limitations

While this study offers valuable insights into how healthcare organizations support or hinder leadership development among AI and IT professionals, it is not without limitations. The study's qualitative design, though appropriate for exploring perceptions and experiences, inherently limits generalizability. The sample size, comprised of 15 professionals across three focus groups, provides a deep but narrow view of the topic. Although purposive sampling ensured participants had relevant expertise, their perspectives may not fully represent the diversity of experiences across all healthcare organizations, particularly those outside the U.S. or in smaller, less digitally mature institutions.

Additionally, the exclusive use of virtual Zoom sessions may have constrained the richness of interpersonal dynamics typically observed in in-person focus groups. Nonverbal cues, informal exchanges, and the broader contextual awareness available in physical settings were necessarily limited. Another limitation lies in the composition of the focus groups themselves. Group 1 consisted of change management consultants, Group 2 included AI technology managers, and Group 3 was composed of leadership trainers. While this triad of perspectives is strategically valuable, it omits the voices of C-suite executives, frontline clinicians interacting with AI systems, and end-users of leadership programs, stakeholders whose input might have provided greater contextual nuance.

Furthermore, the data reflects perceived needs and observed barriers rather than measured outcomes. Participants shared experiential insights rather than empirical evidence on leadership program effectiveness or longitudinal success in transforming technical talent into enterprise leaders. This gap highlights the need for future studies that incorporate longitudinal data and mixed methods to validate and expand upon these initial findings.

FINAL RECOMMENDATIONS

Implement Role-Specific Leadership Development Programs

To meet the demands of AI-driven innovation in healthcare, organizations must abandon generic leadership workshops in favor of customized programs that address the nuanced realities of AI and IT professionals. These leaders are not simply overseeing project timelines, they are managing complex, high-stakes systems that influence patient care outcomes, cybersecurity integrity, and institutional credibility. For instance, a Chief Information Security Officer (CISO) must make strategic decisions about enterprise vulnerability while translating those risks to non-technical executives. Leadership development must therefore reflect scenarios like navigating HIPAA compliance during an AI model deployment or resolving ethical dilemmas involving data bias in diagnostic tools. Real-world simulations, executive coaching, and mentorship by seasoned leaders in digital health can dramatically increase the readiness of these professionals for executive responsibilities.

Redefine Promotion Criteria for Technical Talent

One of the most glaring insights from this study is the persistent gap between technical expertise and leadership readiness. Promotions within healthcare IT are too often based on algorithmic proficiency or systems integration skills alone, rather than a candidate's ability to lead people, manage ambiguity, or communicate vision. For example, a machine learning engineer who designs a successful predictive model for readmission risk might be promoted to a leadership role without any preparation to handle team dynamics, cross-functional negotiation, or enterprise resource planning. Organizations must adopt more robust promotion frameworks that incorporate leadership assessments, peer evaluations, and behavioral interview processes to ensure technical professionals are truly ready for the multidimensional nature of leadership.

Embed Leadership Development into Organizational Culture

Leadership development should not exist on the fringes of organizational activity or be limited to high-profile retreats once a year. Instead, it should be woven into the fabric of healthcare organizations as a strategic imperative. This means having CEOs and department heads not only endorse but model and participate in leadership growth initiatives. Consider a scenario where a hospital system integrates leadership coaching into its digital transformation agenda, making it a requirement for department heads who manage AI systems tied to patient diagnostics. This proactive integration signals to the entire enterprise that leadership development is valued, resourced, and non-negotiable. Conversely, when development is reactionary, only offered after a data breach or leadership turnover, the opportunity for sustained growth and strategic alignment is lost.

Prioritize Soft Skills and Communication Training

Healthcare AI professionals often face the daunting challenge of communicating complex, technical concepts, such as encryption protocols or anomaly detection algorithms, to executive teams, compliance officers, or even frontline clinicians. The research reveals that failure to communicate effectively is a more common cause of project delays and leadership breakdown than technological barriers. For example, an AI lead might develop a breakthrough in early cancer detection but fail to gain buy-in from clinical teams due to poor articulation of the tool's function and ethical safeguards. To avoid such breakdowns, leadership development must emphasize communication strategies, stakeholder engagement, and influence without authority. This training should include role-playing with difficult conversations, practice in executive briefings, and guidance on how to "translate" technology for diverse audiences.

IMPLICATIONS OF THE STUDY

Practical Implications

The findings from this study highlight the critical need for healthcare organizations to prepare their AI and IT professionals not only as technologists but as future enterprise leaders. When equipped with the right leadership tools, these professionals are better positioned to oversee secure, effective, and scalable innovation. For instance, a trained AI leader is more likely to foresee system vulnerabilities during an EHR integration, plan stakeholder engagement proactively, and make ethical decisions that reduce litigation risk. These skills translate into improved project outcomes, fewer regulatory missteps, and better overall alignment with strategic health objectives.

Social Implications

From a societal perspective, investing in the leadership development of AI professionals promotes greater equity and inclusivity in healthcare leadership pipelines. Often, technically trained individuals, particularly those from underrepresented groups, lack access to mentorship and leadership training that could propel them into executive roles. By institutionalizing leadership development, healthcare organizations can level the playing field and ensure that innovation leadership is as diverse and inclusive as the populations they serve. Furthermore, as healthcare AI becomes increasingly involved in patient-facing decisions, leaders with strong ethical grounding and soft skills will play a pivotal role in ensuring that technologies are deployed humanely and responsibly.

Organizational Implications

The long-term health and strategic agility of healthcare organizations are directly tied to their ability to cultivate leadership in technical domains. Organizations that integrate leadership development into their digital transformation strategy are far more likely to succeed in executing large-scale AI deployments, defending against cybersecurity threats, and maintaining stakeholder trust. For example, a healthcare system that proactively trains its IT and AI managers in enterprise risk management, ethical governance, and organizational communication is far better equipped to handle sudden regulatory changes or public scrutiny. In contrast, organizations that neglect these areas often experience costly project failures, internal talent attrition, and reduced market competitiveness.

Leadership complexities and challenges

In the evolving realm of healthcare artificial intelligence (AI), leadership demands are becoming increasingly complex, necessitating deliberate and strategic investments in leadership development. The Burrell Leadership Intricacy Model (Burrell, 2019) identifies the multifaceted nature of these challenges, arguing that cultivating leadership competencies among technical managers and AI supervisors is no longer optional but essential to sustaining enterprise performance and innovation.

Developed through a series of focus group interviews with technical managers at the 2017 International Studying Leadership Conference hosted by the University of Richmond, the Burrell Leadership Intricacy Model articulates eleven thematic complexities that confront today's leaders in technologically intensive environments (Burrell, 2019). These themes reflect the nuanced pressures that arise from managing rapid technological transformation, cross-disciplinary coordination, cybersecurity threats, and the ethical governance of AI systems in healthcare contexts. For example, participants described how managing machine learning teams involved not only overseeing algorithmic performance but also addressing data privacy concerns, regulatory compliance, and the emotional labor of leading diverse technical teams under high-stakes clinical conditions.

What the Burrell Model reveals is that leadership in healthcare AI is not merely about guiding projects, it is about navigating interconnected systems where the technical, human, and organizational dimensions collide. Technical managers, particularly those overseeing AI applications like diagnostic support tools or predictive analytics engines, face elevated expectations to serve as both architects of innovation and stewards of strategic alignment. In such an environment, traditional leadership paradigms, rooted in linear hierarchies or task delegation, prove inadequate. Instead, leaders must cultivate adaptive thinking, ethical decision-making, and cross-functional fluency to meet the demands of data-intensive, high-risk healthcare ecosystems. These expectations underscore the model's central argument: leadership development is not a discretionary initiative, but a mission-critical organizational imperative.

Table 1.

Intricacy variables	Burrell Leadership Intricacy Model (2019)
Theme 1	Managerial retrospection does not lead to foresight since the variables and conditions of internal and external environment can be in unremitting instability, which makes adaptability and change management skills precious.
Theme 2	Exchanges and engagements between system elements are nonlinear and interconnected in such a way that small alterations can manufacture inexplicably sizeable impacts and consequences.
Theme 3	Information in both the international and external environment is often exceedingly overloaded, uncertain, incomplete, or indecipherable.
Theme 4	Innovations, breakthroughs, and solutions can be developed from the congruent dynamics within the organizational system and cannot be imposed from external forces with inevitable and predictable outcomes.
Theme 5	New technologies are disrupting mature work practices, shifting the nature of old communication approaches, and taxing elderly collaboration approaches.
Theme 6	Expertly comprehending the most effective and efficient ways to leverage organizational strengths and industry best practices is one of the most critical duties of leadership.
Theme 7	Traditional organizational boundaries are dissolving in ways that necessitate unlocked transparency, flexible hierarchies, dispersed resources, distributed decision-making, loosening of centralized controls to foster the development of an organizational learning culture at every level of the organization.
Theme 8	Increased globalization and enlarged employee diversity will require fresh levels of cooperation, pioneering ways of thinking, modern ways of comprehension that require respect, learning-centered curiosity, sympathy, and empathy.

continued on following page

Table 1. Continued

Intricacy variables	Burrell Leadership Intricacy Model (2019)
Theme 9	The ability to tap into the organization's expertise talent and collective intelligence are the most valuable organizational asset.
Theme 10	Social capital and the ability to tap into expertise and knowledge networks are very critical because they provide access to data and information that is essential to complex problem solving and effectual decision-making,
Theme 11	The need to create and support cultures in which it is safe to take calculated risks and still have tolerance and appreciation for what can be learned from failure to improve both business process and organizational strategy.

CONCLUSION

This study reveals a fundamental structural weakness in how healthcare organizations approach artificial intelligence (AI) leadership: technical capability is advancing faster than the organizational capacity to lead, govern, and sustain it. The findings suggest that the challenge is not a simple skills deficit among AI and IT professionals, but a systemic misalignment embedded in promotion practices, leadership development frameworks, and cultural priorities. As healthcare systems increasingly rely on AI to support clinical decision-making, cybersecurity, and operational efficiency, this leadership gap represents a strategic vulnerability rather than a peripheral human capital concern.

Participants consistently described environments in which technical expertise is rewarded and rapidly elevated into management roles without sufficient preparation for the relational, strategic, and ethical responsibilities that accompany enterprise leadership. This creates a predictable pattern of role strain: newly promoted leaders are expected to influence clinicians, executives, and regulators, yet lack structured opportunities to develop communication fluency, political awareness, and systems-level thinking. In high-risk healthcare settings, this misalignment does not merely slow innovation; it undermines trust, weakens cross-functional coordination, and increases exposure to regulatory and cybersecurity failures.

The four dominant themes identified in this study function together as an interconnected system rather than isolated problems. Misalignment between technical expertise and leadership expectations initiates the leadership deficit. The absence of role-specific leadership development removes the corrective mechanism that could address this misalignment. Organizational culture and executive sponsorship determine whether leadership development is reinforced or neglected, while communication and soft skills serve as the primary mechanism through which AI leaders translate technical capability into organizational action. When any of these elements are weak, AI initiatives become fragile, highly dependent on individual effort rather than institutional support, and vulnerable to breakdown under pressure.

Critically, the findings challenge the long-standing organizational assumption that high technical performance naturally predicts leadership effectiveness. In healthcare AI, this assumption is particularly hazardous because leadership failures rarely remain contained within a single team or project. An AI leader who cannot articulate risk, negotiate workflow change, or address ethical concerns can inadvertently compromise patient safety, erode clinician confidence, or expose the organization to legal and reputational harm. The study therefore reframes leadership development as an enterprise risk management function; one that directly affects the integrity, scalability, and sustainability of AI deployment.

The analysis further suggests that leadership development must move beyond generic training models toward intentionally designed, context-sensitive pathways. Effective development requires alignment with the specific demands of healthcare AI roles, including regulatory navigation, ethical stewardship of data, cross-disciplinary collaboration, and executive-level communication. Leadership capability must be assessed, reinforced, and rewarded throughout the career lifecycle, not assumed at the point of promotion. Without these structures, organizations inadvertently reinforce a cycle in which technical experts are set up to fail in leadership roles, leading to burnout, attrition, and stalled innovation.

Ultimately, this study argues that the success of AI in healthcare will be determined less by algorithmic sophistication than by leadership capacity. Organizations that fail to integrate leadership development into their digital transformation strategies risk creating technically advanced systems that lack organizational coherence and human alignment. Conversely, those that intentionally cultivate leaders who can integrate technical insight with strategic judgment, ethical reasoning, and human-centered influence are far more likely to realize AI's full potential as a sustainable enterprise capability. Addressing the leadership gap identified in this research is therefore not optional; it is essential to the future viability, credibility, and effectiveness of AI-driven healthcare systems.

RECOMMENDATIONS FOR FUTURE RESEARCH

Given the compelling themes that emerged from this study, particularly the critical gaps in leadership preparedness, the need for role-specific development, and the influence of organizational culture, future research should move beyond perception-based analysis to applied, context-sensitive exploration. Two promising methodological approaches stand out: action research and implementation science.

Action research is especially well-suited for exploring how leadership development initiatives can be designed, tested, and refined in real-world healthcare settings. Future studies should collaborate with hospitals, health tech startups, or academic medical centers to co-create leadership interventions tailored to AI and IT professionals. These interventions could include modular training on soft skills, scenario-based simulations for AI ethics and cybersecurity decision-making, or mentorship programs that pair rising technical leaders with experienced executives. Through iterative cycles of implementation, feedback, and adaptation, action research would allow scholars and practitioners to observe the direct impact of these programs on performance, engagement, and organizational alignment.

Implementation science offers a complementary lens for examining how evidence-based leadership strategies can be effectively adopted, scaled, and sustained in complex healthcare environments. Leadership development does not fail due to poor ideas, but often due to poor execution, misaligned incentives, or cultural resistance. Implementation research could investigate which organizational conditions, such as executive sponsorship, digital maturity, or interdepartmental collaboration, facilitate the successful integration of leadership training into AI departments. For example, researchers might study how embedding leadership coaching into onboarding for technical staff affects retention, psychological safety, or innovation productivity.

Both action research and implementation science can provide the critical next step in building an empirical foundation for leadership development in AI healthcare settings. By moving from diagnosis to applied experimentation, future research can help, organizations not only understand the leadership gap, but bridge it in real time, with measurable results.

REFERENCES

Albion, M. J., & Gagliardi, R. (2011). A study of transformational leadership, organizational change and job satisfaction. *Journal of Organizational Change Management*, *2*(1), 23–32. https://research.usq.edu.au/item/9y5v9/a-study-of-transformational-leadership-organisational-change-and-job-satisfaction

Arbaiza, L. (2016). A Human Centered Approach in Executive Education at ESAN Graduate School of Business in Peru. In *Human Centered Management in Executive Education* (pp. 82-95). Palgrave Macmillan UK. https://link.springer.com/chapter/10.1057/9781137555410_5

Assante, M. J., & Tobey, D. H. (2011). Enhancing the healthcare artificial intelligence workforce. *IT Professional*, *13*(1), 12–15. https://ieeexplore.ieee.org/abstract/document/5708280?casa_token=yxPpApYJEIsAAAAA:Vzm7QYPYm-3qn8bzBT0whOlsDDnJTKe9pgzEAVZ8wxvVE4z1QGx1HMT3Gzd92vo_VC6tXW5bMzE. DOI: 10.1109/MITP.2011.6

Bass, B. M. (1985). *Leadership and Performance beyond Expectations*. Free Press.

Berson, A., & Stieglitz, R. (2013). *Leadership Conversations: Challenging High Potential Managers to Become Great Leaders*. Jossey-Bass Publishing.

Burns, J. M. (1978). *Leadership*. Harper & Row.

Burrell, D. N. (2019). An exploration of the critical need for formal training in leadership for cybersecurity and technology management professionals. In *Human Performance Technology: Concepts, Methodologies, Tools, and Applications* (pp. 1420-1432). IGI Global. https://www.igi-global.com/chapter/an-exploration-of-the-critical-need-for-formal-training-in-leadership-for-cybersecurity-and-technology-management-professionals/226624

Burrell, D. N. (2023). Dynamic evaluation approaches to telehealth technologies and artificial intelligence (AI) telemedicine applications in healthcare and biotechnology organizations. *Merits*, *3*(4), 700–721. https://www.mdpi.com/2673-8104/3/4/42. DOI: 10.3390/merits3040042

Burrell, D. N. (2025). Cyber-Psychological System Failures that Translate Deep-Fake and other Social Engineering Attacks in Ways that Hamper Organizational Resilience. *Bulletin of the Transilvania University of Braşov. Series VII: Social Sciences• Law*, 409-422.

Burrell, D. N., Aridi, A. S., & Nobles, C. (2018). The critical need for formal leadership development programs for cybersecurity and information technology professionals. In *International Conference on Cyber Warfare and Security* (pp. 82–91). Academic Conferences International Limited., https://books.google.com/books?hl=en&lr=&id=eHpTDwAAQBAJ&oi=fnd&pg=PA82&dq=+Leadership+training+and+darrell+norman+Burrell&ots=9VOX4c0qw0&sig=Imkq77BTHWaCkNlmn-jeO8xJ6g4#v=onepage&q=Leadership%20training%20and%20darrell%20norman%20Burrell&f=false

Cavazotte, F., Moreno, V., & Hickmann, M. (2012). Effects of leader intelligence, personality and emotional intelligence on transformational leadership and managerial performance. *The Leadership Quarterly*, *23*(3), 443–455. https://www.sciencedirect.com/science/article/abs/pii/S1048984311001615?casa_token=AK7Eh88E1u0AAAAA:9RUv4pWWEAlfrtLC7Tna7n6Cj82goWBd7lFuzIS5GxPzp2aKO11YLm4mYcNUHfaBmKsLCdhywx8. DOI: 10.1016/j.leaqua.2011.10.003

Creswell, J. W., & Poth, C. N. (2018). *Qualitative inquiry and research design: Choosing among five approaches* (4th ed.). SAGE Publications.

Daft, R. (2015). *Management.* South-Western College Publishing.

Dzameshie, D. O. (2012). Leadership in project management: The behaviors of successful male project managers in information technology (Order No. 3499910). Available from ProQuest Dissertations & Theses Global. (962412637). https://www.proquest.com/openview/fb508641a440199ee731c3179ef0def9/1?pq-origsite=gscholar&cbl=18750

Eich, D. (2012). *Root Down and Branch Out: Best Practices for Leadership Development Programs.* CreateSpace Independent Publishing., https://www.amazon.com/Root-Down-Branch-Out-Development/dp/1468034782

Elkins, R. (2015). *Business: Golden Nugget Methods for High Effectiveness - Leadership, Management & Communication.* CreateSpace Independent Publishing Platform., https://www.amazon.com/Management-Effectively-Personnel-Conflict-Resolution/dp/1515041441

Fiedler, F. E. (1972). How Do You Make Leaders More Effective? *Organizational Dynamics, 1*(2), 2–18. https://www.sciencedirect.com/science/article/abs/pii/0090261672900083. DOI: 10.1016/0090-2616(72)90008-3

Gabarro, J. (2007). When a New Manager Takes Charge. *Harvard Business Review, 85*(1), 104–117. https://hbr.org/2007/01/when-a-new-manager-takes-charge

Goldberg, J. R. (2006). Making the transition from technologist to manager. *Biomedical Instrumentation & Technology, 40*(6), 465–468. https://array.aami.org/doi/full/10.2345/i0899-8205-40-6-465.1. DOI: 10.2345/i0899-8205-40-6-465.1 PMID: 17190088

Hartigan, R. (1974). Training and development toward leadership. *Occupational Health Nursing, 22*(9), 12–16. https://journals.sagepub.com/doi/abs/10.1177/216507997402200903. DOI: 10.1177/216507997402200903 PMID: 4859571

Hladio, M., & Edwards, R. (2017). *Developing Leaders: Why Traditional Leadership Training Misses the Mark.* Morgan James Publishing.

Jensen, M. L. (2011). Nurturing self-knowledge: The impact of a leadership development program. *OD Practitioner, 43*(3), 30–35. https://openurl.ebsco.com/EPDB%3Agcd%3A9%3A954665/detailv2?sid=ebsco%3Aocu%3Arecord&id=ebsco%3Agcd%3A63991047&bquery=IS%201086-2609%20AND%20VI%2043%20AND%20IP%203%20AND%20DT%202011&page=1&link_origin=scholar.google.com&searchDescription=OD%20Practitioner%2C%202011%2C%20Vol%2043%2C%20Issue%203&crl=f

Jones, G. (2012). *Organizational Theory, Design, and Change.* Pearson Publishing.

Khan, M., Khan, N., Ahmed, S., & Mahfooz, A. (2012). Connotation of organizational effectiveness and factors affecting it. *International Journal of Business and Behavioral Sciences*, *2*(9), 21–30. https://d1wqtxts1xzle7.cloudfront.net/54315801/20-libre.PDF?1504327628=&response-content-disposition=inline%3B+filename%3D20_PDF.pdf&Expires=1770159723&Signature=EKcfp1JMA9DNucDH6pma3d0-WpEcBzcqoC8lxsE-iPclP~UE5o9MM7aGtT4jK7fds6xQnuXgH7ntNIZKMTb23DPVLBhySuQDTMfGToronWxpu-JWs7Fn82zpJHkHfvpehNUHflMj0ugMRJODo9DAYTQ1a7EAAEZ9F~NMJV2vP3wdJpGuO~AGbfqKiQBU9Y9waTDEU6FahOsP9T9sNfF2kxpo4UGej0NXN7aRldfbY~DgzbGGgk2wtnBZgA~KF6hxfu-MVIiB3Io9aQaWbSOFdRf6rZ87arhTCdEMdk3hPhgfmzjS6qZHjSTB9phWsBp2-IBjpYKfiuY92pEFMh2dUA__&Key-Pair-Id=APKAJLOHF5GGSLRBV4ZA

Klimoski, R. (2016). Critical success factors for healthcare artificial intelligence leaders: Not just technical competence. *People and Strategy, 39*(1), 14-18. Retrieved from https://www.researchgate.net/profile/Richard-Klimoski/publication/325347163_Critical_Success_Factors_for_Cyber_Security_Leaders_Not_Just_Technical_Competence/links/5b0716d4aca2725783deaa2f/Critical-Success-Factors-for-Cyber-Security-Leaders-Not-Just-Technical-Competence.pdf

Kouzes, J., & Posner, B. (2017). *The Leadership Challenge: How to Make Extraordinary Things Happen in Organizations.* Harvard Business Review Publishing.

Lepeley, M. T., von Kimakowitz, E., & Bardy, R. (Eds.). (2016). *Human Centered Management in Executive Education: Global Imperatives, Innovation and New Directions.* Springer., https://link.springer.com/content/pdf/10.1057/9781137555410.pdf DOI: 10.1057/9781137555410

Leslie, J. (2009). What you need, and don't have, when it comes to leadership talent. Center for Creative Leadership. Retrieved from https://www.ccl.org/wp-content/uploads/2015/05/leadership-gap-what-you-need-research-paper-center-for-creative-lea

Lester, D. L., & Parnell, J. A. (2006). The Desktop Manager. S.A.M. *Advanced Management Journal*, 71(4), 43-49,3. https://libres.uncg.edu/ir/uncp/f/The%20Desktop%20Manager.pdf

Linden, R. (2010). *Leading Across Boundaries: Creating Collaborative Agencies in a Networked World.* Jossey-Bass Publishing.

Maxwell, J. (2013). *The 5 levels of leadership: Proven steps to maximize your potential.* Center Street Publishing.

McGettrick, A., Cassel, L. N., Dark, M., Hawthorne, E. K., & Impagliazzo, J. (2014, March). Toward curricular guidelines for cybersecurity. In *Proceedings of the 45th ACM technical symposium on Computer science education* (pp. 81–82). ACM., https://dl.acm.org/doi/abs/10.1145/2538862.2538990 DOI: 10.1145/2538862.2538990

Mitchell, G. (2012). The construct of organizational effectiveness: Perspectives from leaders of international nonprofits in the United States. *Nonprofit and Voluntary Sector Quarterly*, *42*(2), 324–345. https://journals.sagepub.com/doi/full/10.1177/0899764011434589?casa_token=uc8mXBA3TBMAAAAA%3AfpXBbFtfdxJZNbZE4dcawl9l7uzWstMslGC47qsLJFAkaBECMf53n8DeEz9gfxTxFN2rrQAtbzs_yw. DOI: 10.1177/0899764011434589

Rothenberger, K. E. (2016). A quantitative study of perceptions about leadership competencies of IT project managers (Order No. 10132045). Available from ProQuest Dissertations & Theses Global. (1810428469). https://www.proquest.com/openview/3ebc148fa5e7ce38741c0a1462cfefc8/1?pq-origsite =gscholar&cbl=18750

Shadraconis, S. (2013). Organizational leadership in time of uncertainty: Is transformational leadership the answer. LUX: *A Journal of Transdisciplinary Writing and Research,* 2(1), 1-15. https://scholarship .claremont.edu/lux/vol2/iss1/28/

Sørensen, P. (2017). What research on learning transfer can teach about improving the impact of leadership-development initiatives? *Consulting Psychology Journal, 69*(1), 47–62. https://psycnet.apa .org/buy/2016-55619-001. DOI: 10.1037/cpb0000072

Thamrin, H. M. (2012). The influence of transformational leadership and organizational commitment on job satisfaction and employee performance. *International Journal of Innovation, Management and Technology, 3*(5), 566–572. https://www.ijimt.org/show-39-520-1.html

Tsado, L. K. (2016). *Analysis of healthcare artificial intelligence threats and vulnerabilities: Skills gap challenges and professional development* (Doctoral dissertation, Texas Southern University). https://www .proquest.com/openview/815feaa0609c2434c71526139576fc7e/1?pq-origsite=gscholar&cbl=18750

Watkins, M. D. (2013). *The First 90 Days: Proven Strategies for Getting Up to Speed Faster and Smarter*. Harvard Business Review Publishing., https://d1wqtxts1xzle7.cloudfront.net/63499530/ The-First-90-Days-Proven-Strategies-For-Getting-Up-To-Speed-Faster-And-Smarter-Updated-And -Expande20200601-70801-hsk65w-libre.pdf?1591079475=&response-content-disposition=inline %3B+filename%3DThe_First_90_Days_Proven_Strategies_for.pdf&Expires=1770162233&Signature =XMjEd1kPmeF8x-WkKnyhWFpvkdEhVcW4XBgaS0-Q18VaaTIceUCQMZX01Qwrtvermcef FdLG7eZzPFAYRwK0wGNnebrJUMzvYJMe1EZmUMFtjr53ej6lnF-0kO64KzvbkXaw7VwH 51QSVS1XrxiLfoOhMQiCiYOIAZg6Ek~EjmtCxcxKtuo4FNSsBXG67qYaRRrM4q4JO6r73Ne0 2ZtsrhDBEUQxv9mMnyYsuo8nJfe25j0ZsSB99sqaRHsTvoth6dEdL7IMETXLIoAwcqbACB xuxTXzaRgtUvS0MDMVcUET49XJudKJOojZMfseq9~H0zmV645ORuZgTAsuKPcA6g__&Key-Pair -Id=APKAJLOHF5GGSLRBV4ZA

Chapter 13
The Influence of Military Leader Communication on Motivation in Portugal

Felipa Lopes dos Reis
http://orcid.org/0000-0001-8462-0810
Lusofona University, Portugal

Diogo Lisboa Esteves
Lusofona University, Portugal

ABSTRACT

The regular functioning of the Armed Forces of a state depends on the ability to obtain and retain human resources in the ranks, this work falls within the scope of the difficulties experienced in recruitment and retention that exist in the Portuguese Armed Forces (FFAA) having as one of the factors is lack of motivation and their general objective is to contribute to studying the forms of communication and leadership that military leaders exercise towards their subordinates and how this influences their motivation and consequently its performance. To this end, the following question underlying the investigation was outlined: "Does communication from leaders influence the performance of the Portuguese military through their strength?". This is a descriptive study of a quantitative nature, and the data were collected through a questionnaire survey, applied to the active population, reserves and the availability of military organizations dependent on the General Staff of the Armed Forces,

1. INTRODUCTION

This work aims to contribute to research on leadership, communication, motivation and organizational performance, based on the understanding of the mechanisms that generate motivation and the analysis of how communication serves as a fundamental link to exercise leadership that can influence the performance of those led. According to Ceitil (2023), individuals' skills are essential for the organization's collective performance. The organizational climate, which is directly related to the motivation

DOI: 10.4018/979-8-3373-4027-2.ch013

of members, depends on how leaders communicate, as disagreements can reduce motivation and affect organizational success.

The case study is applied to the Portuguese Armed Forces, and the aim is to analyze the communication of military superiors and their way of leading their subordinates, so that it is possible to verify the influences on their motivation, and consequently, organizational performance, and to identify specific factors that contribute to the lack of motivation of Portuguese military personnel.

We are currently experiencing a turbulent phase regarding the lack of human resources in Portuguese military organizations, and due to this, this study aims to find ways to solve the problem related to attracting and retaining military personnel in these organizations. Studying the forms of communication and leadership of their leaders can be fundamental to understanding whether these factors are directly related to the motivation of military personnel and whether this constitutes a relevant factor causing low adherence to the ranks and the option for other public or private sectors of activity by military personnel.

Within the above, the theme chosen for this dissertation consists of the influence that leaders exert on organizational motivation, the institution chosen was the military institutions, members of the Portuguese Armed Forces, constituted by the Portuguese Air Force (FAP), Portuguese Army (EP) and Portuguese Navy (Armada). To investigate this topic, a starting question was established that will serve as a basis for the methodological study, the starting question is "Does the communication of leaders influence the performance of Portuguese military personnel through their motivation?" The type of research developed also falls within the scope of correlational research, as the objective is to establish a relationship between several variables.

2. LITERATURE REVIEW

2.1 Communication

Communication is an interactive and participatory process that involves the exchange of messages and the acquisition of information, being essential for building a relationship (Molena, 2009, cited by Costa & Oliveira, 2020). According to Félix (2020), communication occurs at all levels, both internally and externally. Costa (2021) emphasizes that, in addition to transmitting information, communication involves the sharing of opinions, feelings, and attitudes, and it is important for the sender to consider how the receiver will interpret the message.

Communication can be formal when following the organization's official channels or informal when it does not follow the official route and circulates among employees. It can occur in three directions: horizontal (between colleagues at the same hierarchical level), vertical upward (from employees to superiors), and vertical downward (from superiors to employees). Vertical upward communication is less common, as employees may feel uncomfortable sharing negative information due to the fear of reprisals.

2.2 Leadership

Organizations have increasingly invested in structures that foster effective behaviors among employees, with leadership emerging as a key element in this process (Neves, 2022). Leadership is understood as a process of social influence aimed at achieving common goals, playing a vital role in motivating teams, particularly during crisis situations. Da Silva et al. (2020) define leadership as the ability to influence others through dialogue, example, and attitude, guiding the team toward the achievement of established objectives.

This process involves interpersonal relationships and the exercise of power through multiple sources of authority, such as knowledge, formal position, and seniority. In the context of Military Organizations within the public sector, the leader is responsible for fostering cooperation and mobilizing resources. According to da Costa (2021), leadership is a relational skill grounded in the establishment of trust and leader credibility, which are essential for driving change and enhancing organizational competitiveness.

Communication is also highlighted as a critical factor. When appointing individuals to leadership positions, organizations must ensure that communication is strategically planned, as effective communication contributes to positive relationships with subordinates and, consequently, to improved employee performance and overall organizational productivity.

2.2.1 Leadership Theories

Transactional vs transformational leadership

Transactional leadership is leadership that emphasizes the relationship between performance and rewards and is oriented towards defining goals and achieving results, that is, the employee upon achieving a certain performance obtains the corresponding compensation, whereas in Transformational leadership there is a way of leadership aimed at raising team members' awareness of the objectives to be achieved, that is, in this situation the leader serves as a transformer of the organizational reality and of the people in the group, he will mobilize people's efforts so that they can achieve the established objectives. Amaral (2022) states that the transformational leader, through her experiences and visions, motivates the team to be able to have a positive impact on the organization.

2.2.2 Leaders' behavioural Styles

Leadership style refers to the way in which a leader manages their team. There is no single ideal style; rather, it is essential for leaders to adapt their approach according to the situation and the characteristics of their subordinates, as proposed by situational leadership theory. The use of different leadership styles fosters the development of employee competencies and contributes to enhanced organizational performance (Amaral, 2022). Behavioral styles describe the various ways in which a leader exercises their role.

Authoritarian Style

The authoritarian style consists of the use of power to control the actions and reactions of those led when performing their duties. Leadership is carried out through threats and pressure on employees. One of the positive sides of this leadership, when new employees enter the organization, they are disciplined within the organization's rules. However, it is a leadership has many negative points because leadership imposes decisions in an authoritarian way, which makes the work environment tense and with little initiative and ends up generating demotivation. It is a very common behaviour of leaders in military organizations (Amaral, 2022).

Democratic Style

Unlike the autocratic style, the democratic leadership style does not exercise control over its leaders, on the contrary, in this case the followers are close to the leaders, the leader asks the followers for advice and passes responsibilities to them, it is a style that promotes trust and motivation (Amaral, 2022). Da Costa (2021) agrees, noting that democratic leadership portrays participatory leadership, where there is an opportunity for each member of the group to be encouraged to think about options for decision-making, which will be taken to debate and, subsequently, approved by the group.

Liberal or laissez-faire style

The liberal leadership style, opposite to the authoritarian style, allows employees to define their own tasks, requiring maturity and responsibility. When properly applied, it increases employee motivation and self-confidence (Amaral, 2022). This style enhances trust by delegating decisions and granting freedom, being effective for assessing maturity and interpersonal relationships. The liberal leader believes that their subordinates do not require constant monitoring (Da Costa, 2021).

2.2.3 Leadership in a Military Context

Leadership within military organizations differs from that in civilian organizations due to the inherent obligation of obedience among subordinates, which facilitates the exercise of leadership power but also presents disadvantages such as stress and risk, negatively impacting performance (Neves, 2022). Although slower to adapt, military organizations are striving to adopt more contemporary leadership models, such as competency-based management, within an organizational culture grounded in solid values and formal duties established by the Armed Forces Military Statute (Neves, 2022).

In the military, personnel are seen as the driving force behind the mission, and leadership often stems from hierarchical position rather than individual leadership capabilities, which can present challenges (Contreras, 2023). Military leadership should be understood as a process of influencing individuals by providing purpose, direction, and motivation. Furthermore, it must include an ethical dimension, focusing on the well-being of subordinates, motivation, and troop morale. The ability to inspire in peacetime is considered an indicator of effectiveness in wartime.

2.3 Motivation

Motivational theories

Motivational theories in an organizational context are ways of thinking that explain how the processes lead to increased performance work. In the literature there are several theories that attempt to demonstrate how this increase in performance through motivation occurs, among them, we can highlight the following:

Expectancy Theory

The theory developed by Victor Vroom around 1964 proposes that people strive to achieve results and rewards that are important to them while avoiding results that are not desirable. In this theory, each person decides the effort required for each work situation and thus obtains the desired rewards. What this theory then refers to is that the tendency to act in a certain way depends on the strength of the expectation of the result of the action (da Costa, 2021).

Hierarchy of Needs Theory

The Hierarchy of Needs theory is a theory developed by Abraham Maslow in 1954 and has the premise that the human being has a hierarchy of needs being demonstrated in a pyramid which contains 5 categories of needs and are organized according to their degree of importance. The base, as you can see in the following figure, corresponds to physiological needs, when this level is satisfied, safety needs follow and so on until reaching the top of the pyramid (da Costa, 2021).

Two-Factor Theory

Theory developed by Herzberg in 1974 argues that there are two factors that cause satisfaction or dissatisfaction. According to Herzberg they are:

- Intrinsic factors (also called motivational factors): these are the factors that lead to increased motivation at work.
- Extrinsic factors: these are factors that contribute to job satisfaction, such as working conditions.

Figure 1. Source: Authors

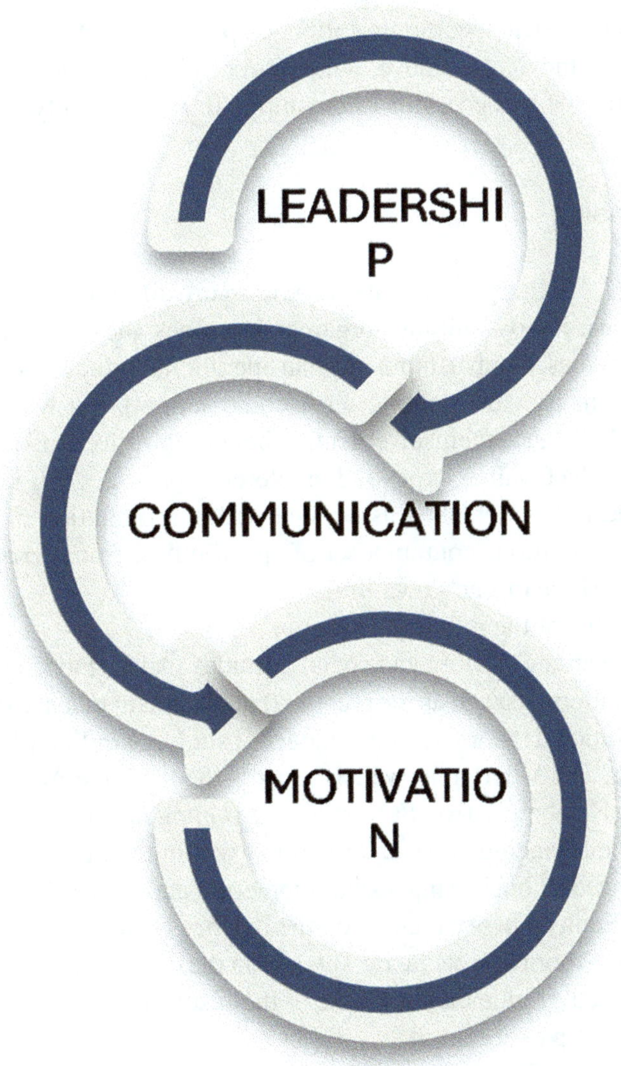

The following figure demonstrates the process that leads to increased performance.

According to the theories analyzed, motivation is intrinsic to human beings. Individuals need to set goals, achieve rewards, and satisfy both personal and professional needs. For an organizational environment to foster such motivational conditions, certain structural and behavioral factors must be in place.

In this context, the role of the leader is essential. It is the leader's responsibility to create a conducive environment in which team members can accomplish their goals, obtain rewards, and fulfill their needs. However, for leadership to be truly effective, all aspects related to organizational communication must be aligned and operate in an integrated manner.

Leadership effectiveness is directly linked to the quality of internal communication. Communication channels and information transmission systems within the organization must be properly implemented and optimized. Furthermore, the leader must possess advanced communication skills. Being an effective communicator is not merely a desirable trait—it is an essential requirement for ensuring that information is accurately conveyed and understood by team members.

Without clear, objective, and efficient communication, employees may fail to understand their goals, responsibilities, or the benefits they can achieve, which directly impacts their motivation. Therefore, communication is a key element for successful leadership and, consequently, for the motivation and performance of the team.

2.3.1 The Military Profession

According to Santos (2021), military organizations have many differences when compared to other public or private organizations. Firstly, military organizations seek the security of communities and achieve this through peace activities, combat, humanitarian operations and actions to support populations, while other public organizations provide a public service and support, but which in no way interfere with responsibility. The FFAA distance themselves from other organizations also due to the existence of various codes of honor and conduct, values expressed in reference practices substantiated in the concept of "military status" enshrined in law, which is associated with the limitation of the exercise of some "citizenship rights". Military conditions contain a set of specificities, from permanent availability for service (if necessary at the sacrifice of one's own life).

Complexities and motivations of the military condition

The text analyzes the motivational factors and social attitudes that influence individuals' entry into and retention in military institutions, as well as the reasons that lead them to leave quickly. Santos (2021) highlights that there are motivational theories more suitable for studying military life, such as the content theories of Maslow, Herzberg, and Alderfer, as well as process theories like Adams' Equity Theory and Vroom's Expectancy Theory. Herzberg's Two-Factor Theory is applied because it addresses both motivational and hygiene factors, influencing entry and retention within the ranks. Alderfer's ERG Theory helps identify and prioritize needs, considering social interaction and professional development within the military context. Adams' Equity Theory focuses on the balance between effort and rewards, such as remuneration and recognition. Vroom's Expectancy Theory, on the other hand, relates to soldiers' expectations regarding outcomes and the value they attribute to the institution, influencing their motivation.

Military Culture and leadership expectation

In the case of the Armed Forces (FFAA), the existence of a common communication strategy enables the dissemination of unified messages across the Navy, Army, and Air Force. Its absence hinders the transmission of messages, fails to enhance synergies between branches, and reduces the overall coherence of the FFAA's communication with its various audiences. In general, the FFAA are culturally highly hierarchical organizations, where communication processes stem from a solid hierarchical structure. Personnel are trained from an early stage to adapt to this form of communication.

Communication across different processes is conducted in a formal manner. However, this does not preclude certain senior officers from interacting informally with many of their subordinates. Communication typically follows a top-down vertical flow, and a superior officer is considered a good communicator when he or she communicates clearly, rationally, and with emotional awareness—although, in many cases, the emotional component is deliberately subordinated to rationality.

Leadership in Portuguese military organizations differs from that in civilian organizations, largely due to the duty of obedience imposed on subordinates (Neves, 2022). While this structure reinforces formal authority, it also contributes to high stress levels. The FFAA have been gradually adopting competency-based leadership models, albeit more slowly than civilian institutions. Whereas civilian employees are regarded as human capital, in the FFAA, military personnel are viewed as an integral part of the mission itself (Neves, 2022). Leadership is derived from rank rather than from individual capability, though military training is designed to foster leadership development.

Studies highlight essential leadership competencies such as conscientiousness, discipline, self-control, decision-making, and interpersonal skills (Neves, 2022). According to Contreras (2023), a military leader must influence, motivate, and integrate individuals, embodying attributes such as integrity, loyalty, and determination.

In wartime contexts, transformational leadership becomes particularly relevant, as it fosters mutual trust between leader and subordinate (Gonzales, 2016, cited in Contreras, 2023).

3. RESEARCH METHODOLOGY

3.1 Type of Study

The study uses the hypothetical-deductive method and descriptive research, which aims to study and explain the situation of the research object, according to Reis (2022). The research is quantitative, analyzed through SPSS, and an inductive analysis of unquantified responses was also conducted. The methodology followed is the case study, focused on a company where communication and leadership are essential for organizational success.

Study variables

Considering the objectives of the study, in the analysis of the questionnaire, 16 nominal and ordinal qualitative variables were quantified with the aim of being correlated and from this correlation drawing conclusions that allow responding to the proposed objectives. When the variables were tested in SPSS it was found that only some of them were captured by the model to carry out the correlations, therefore the variables used are as follows:

Chosen variables:

V01 “Gender” - Nominal variable V02 “Category” - Nominal variable V03 “Age” - Ordinal variable

V04 “Time at the institution” - Ordinal variable

V05 “Degree of satisfaction with boss” - Ordinal variable

V06 “What is the communication network at your workplace” - Nominal variable

V07 “Your performance is directly related to your level of motivation” - Ordinal variable

V08 “Which of the following contributes to achieving better performance” - Nominal variable

V09 “How much do you attribute to the level of motivation they have in their workplace” - Ordinal variable V10 “Performance is affected by the way managers communicate” - Ordinal variable

V11 “Motivation is the factor in military personnel leaving” - Ordinal variable

V12 “Bosses adopt different leadership positions depending on the situation”: Ordinal variable V13 “Your institution can keep employees motivated through communication”: Ordinal variable V14 “What is the communication flow”: Nominal variable

V15 “Do you feel safe saying what you think?”: Ordinal variable

V16 “How much do you attribute to the influence of your boss’s communication on your motivation”: Ordinal variable V17 “I feel proud to work here”: Ordinal variable

Variables used:

Dependent variable: V09 – Level of motivation in the workplace;

Independent variable: V12 – Bosses adopt different leadership positions depending on the situation; V13 – The institution manages to keep employees motivated through communication; V16 - influence of the boss's communication on motivation; V17 – Proud to work at the institution.

3.2 Research Population

The accidental non-probabilistic sample used for this investigation was taken from the target population which cannot be measured accurately, however the AAFF in 2021 contained around 27,741 employees (according to the website www.portugal.gov.pt), however In more recent news, CNN reports on October 31, 2023, a much smaller number of personnel than this, stating that the AAFF contained 23,425 soldiers, the source was the CEMGFA. The questionnaire carried out was sent to military personnel and civilians who are in very different professional situations, such as active or reserve status, and it was possible to obtain 105 responses. The respondents among men and women are enlisted men, sergeants, officers and civilian workers who are between 19 and 65 years old.

3.3 Survey Instruments

To enrich this work, the quantitative method will be used, through correlational research and comparative research, and the qualitative method will also be used through bibliography analysis and a questionnaire. This data collection process (questionnaire) consists of an ordered series of questions to be asked, in writing, to respondents to obtain information about the questions and objectives of the investigation. The questionnaire was created and made available on the “Google Forms” platform and was simple to carry out and access. It was then distributed via email and “WhatsApp” which allowed many responses to be obtained in a short space of time, guaranteeing the anonymity of respondents who This way, they responded more honestly to the questions asked. I used my personal “WhatsApp” to send the questionnaire to personal contacts and to groups containing soldiers from the three branches of the Armed Forces, in which they were asked to disseminate the questionnaire to their comrades and friends who were interested in responding. The questions addressed were constructed using various scales, such as the “Thurstone”, numerical or “Likert” scale, direct questions or bivariate answers were also asked. The first section concerns the data that characterize the participants, such as their age, gender, level of education or seniority. The second section addresses the topic of communication, and some multiple-choice questions were available, questions in which the respondent answers depending on their agreement on a "Likert" scale, being positioned on 5 levels, with 1 meaning Totally Satisfied, and 5 Not Satisfied and questions with varied answers. In the third section, the respondent is challenged to answer questions about Leadership in their work context, such as the type of Leadership used by management, ways of leading, acting, levels of satisfaction with leadership, subordinate integration, among others. In the fourth section, the respondent answers questions that allow them to assess their level of motivation and what affects their motivation in their performance. Finally, in the fifth section, you are asked to answer questions that interconnect the three themes, for example, specific questions were asked depending on the position of the respondent.

The questionnaire was designed solely for this purpose, having previously been tested by eight people working in the FAP branch and two more from the Army. The questionnaire, after undergoing many changes and corrections, was made available and sent to respondents between 10/20/2023 and 12/08/2023, with 105 valid responses being collected.

Considering the population, more responses could have been obtained, however there was some difficulty in getting the questionnaire formally reached to the 3 branches. Many of the responses were obtained informally, sent to known military personnel from all branches with the request that they share it among themselves, the FFAA are very closed organizations and considering the content of the dissertation (sensitive topic) it would be difficult for it to be accepted by formal institutional pathways. The questionnaire was based on a literature review, to respond to the proposed research objectives.

Regarding the data processing method, a qualitative analysis of the responses obtained was carried out. Multivariate analysis was also used, using the SPSS software, as previously mentioned in this dissertation, and various relationships between variables were explored with the aim of achieving and proving the hypotheses considered. The descriptive statistics technique was used, in which correlation coefficients were used. "Pearson", as this method was not sufficient for the analysis, the "Stepwise" method, "Ridge" regression and "lasso" regression were also used.

4. RESULTS AND DISCUSSIONS

This section interprets the data and draws conclusions from the study, analyzing the results based on the verified hypotheses. The sample is predominantly made up of males (83.8%) and individuals over 50 years old (47.1%). Regarding professional categories, most participants are sergeants (79%), followed by enlisted personnel (16.2%). The analysis focuses on the categories with the largest number of respondents, as responses from officers and civilians are insufficient for inclusion. Age and gender diversity may influence perceptions of leadership and communication

The length of time in the role gives us good perspectives and good visibility into what turnover is in the military, as respondents, when asked about their time in the role, 37.1% said they had been in the role for less than 2 years and 42.9% were between 2 to 5 years in the role, which shows that there is turnover. Regarding branches, among the 105 respondents, 41.9% are from the FAP, 38.1% from the army, 13.3 from the navy and 6.7% are outside the branch.

Hypothesis 1 – The form of communication of hierarchical superiors in the AAFF influences the motivation of subordinates.

The analysis reveals that the FFAA do not view communication as a strategic tool within the organization. The majority of respondents (67.6%) indicate that vertical communication flow predominates in their work, and opinions regarding satisfaction with how superiors communicate are balanced. Regarding communication networks, 58.1% consider the formal network the most predominant, while 41.9% point to the informal network as significant, highlighting that both forms are necessary. Formal communication is effective in work processes, while informal communication fosters more positive climates and stable interpersonal relationships, thereby increasing motivation levels. In terms of organizational climate, there is a positive trend, and information distortion is generally nonexistent. Finally, most respondents agree that communication impacts performance.

Most conflicts within the FFAA are caused by communication, demonstrating its influence in this regard. Although the communication climate is positive, communication is not open, which is characteristic of hierarchical structures. The factors that most affect communication in the workplace are individuals' behavior. The way leaders communicate was identified as the third most influential factor on motivation and performance. The majority of respondents consider communication with management to be good, especially among enlisted personnel and sergeants, indicating that, despite some limitations, communication within the FFAA is generally positive and impacts organizational motivation

From the analysis carried out on the results obtained by SPSS, about regarding the influence of communication on motivation, respondents prefer informal to formal communication. Through the various correlations carried out, it appears that there is a significant correlation between variable 9 with variable 13, which means that V13 positively influences motivation. This result supports the veracity of this hypothesis. V9 was also correlated with V16 "influence of boss communication on motivation", which means that V16 positively influences motivation.

Hypothesis 2 – Intrinsic factors are those that most affect motivation at work

The results show that lack of appreciation is the main factor negatively influencing performance, highlighting it as an intrinsic factor. Most of the options affecting motivation and performance are related to intrinsic factors, such as the subordinate/leader relationship, the leader's communication style, work environment, and leadership approach. These choices reflect feelings of esteem and belonging, which are at the top of Maslow's hierarchy of needs. Motivation theories, such as Maslow's, ERG, and Herzberg's, indicate that intrinsic factors are the most motivating. Regarding dissatisfaction factors, salary, lack of recognition, and career progression stand out as extrinsic factors. However, perceptions vary by professional category, with enlisted personnel prioritizing the work environment and career progression, while sergeants emphasize salary as the main motivator.

In the case of the data obtained in SPSS regarding this hypothesis, we can be concluded it is demonstrated here that this intrinsic factor influences motivation, that is, those who have less pride in working in the organization have less motivation, however it is important to highlight that during the correlation of these two variables, those who chose to disagree about "being proud" have greater impact of those who agreed to "be proud", which is evident here that negative emotions tend to have greater expressiveness than positive ones. We also see from the "Ridge" regression that the "age" factor also influences motivation, it appears that the older people are, the more motivated they are, we saw that this regression also identified that V05 "degree of satisfaction with the boss" influence positively the motivation (V09), that is, another intrinsic aspect. Following the analysis of the "Elastic net" regression method, we saw that V08 "which form of communication contributes to better performance" in the case of formal, negatively influences V9, that is, the more formal the communication is, the less motivated people are, and the communication that contributes most to intrinsic factors is formal communication, so this translates into another factor in favor of intrinsic factors.

It is therefore concluded that the intrinsic factors are those that effectively influence organizational motivation the most, however, the extrinsic factors cannot be removed from this equation. Taking these results into account, it can be confirmed that the hypothesis is true.

Hypothesis 3 - The leadership practices used contribute to a good motivational environment

The hypothesis aims to verify the influence of leadership on motivation and performance, as well as its impact on the early abandonment of soldiers in the FFAA. The analysis reveals that the most prominent characteristics in military leaders are assertiveness, motivation, communication, empathy, and democratic qualities, although there is a lack of traits such as vision, charisma, and creativity. There is no single leadership style that is most appropriate; rather, a combination of characteristics is required depending on the context. Leadership was identified as an important factor influencing motivation and performance, but empathy and the leader's objectives were not considered significant motivators for subordinates. While leadership does influence motivation, military personnel prefer a positive work environment and feel more motivated when they have the freedom to express their opinions.

Regarding the result in SPSS, in relation to this hypothesis, variable 9 "level of motivation at work" was correlated with variable 12 "bosses adopt different leadership postures" and it was found that the adoption of different leadership postures influences negatively on motivation levels, this result is unexpected, it would be expected that bosses with different and more adaptive attitudes would increase motivation.

Therefore, it can be concluded that there is an influence of leadership on organizational motivation, however, despite leaders meeting the standards of good leadership, they are not efficient in relation to motivation, leading us to think that employees have preferences for a type of neutral leadership, which creates a good work environment, but does not actively involve them in what the leadership objectives are, yet in general the characteristics presented are positive and demonstrate that these leaders are capable of creating good organizational environments, therefore the veracity of the hypothesis is confirmed.

CONCLUSION

The conclusion of the dissertation allows for a set of conclusions to be drawn based on the presentation and interpretation of the results. A table was created showing the positive and negative aspects of the three topics addressed.

Table 1. Summary of study results

Motivation Leadership Communication					
+	-	+	-	+	-
The greater the	Civilians and soldiers	Leaders are	Generates	creates a	Distorted
satisfaction	are those with the	assertiveness	some doubts	pleasant	information is
with bosses,	lowest levels of		in the eyes	atmosphere	what most
the greater the	motivation		of those led		contributes to
motivation					conflicts
People over the	Those who think that	Leaders can	Different	Participatory	Very closed
age of 25 are	motivation contributes	motivate	leadership	and interactive	communication

continued on following page

Table 1. Continued

Motivation Leadership Communication					
+	-	+	-	+	-
more	to the military leaving		postures		
motivated	are more unmotivated		generate		
			demotivation		
There is	Lack of personal	Leaders have	There is a	It is satisfying	People's
general	appreciation/recognition	the ability to	lack of	and positive	behaviour is
satisfaction	leads to demotivation	mobilize	vision		what most
among bosses					affects
					communication
Most strive to always do more	Inappropriate work environments reduce motivation	The leaders are democratic	Lack if charisma	Safety in expressing opinions	Lack of communicative guidance
Feeling of	The form of leadership	Empathetic	Lack of	Formal	Closed
pride	contributes to	Leaders	creativity	network is	communication
	demotivation			better suited to	with some
				performance	barriers
Role Content	Salary is one of the	Leaders are	Unliberal	Influences	Bosses
contributes to	factors that causes	communicators	Leaders	motivation and	influence
more	demotivation			performance	motivation
motivation					thought
					communication
Bosses with	Lack of career	Leaders		Good Levels of	
good	progression contributes	convey		communication	
communication	to higher levels of	confidence		are related to	
skills are	demotivation			higher levels of	
positively				communication	
related to					
motivation					
I like military	Lack of motivation is			Formal and	
life	the cause of leaving			informal	
	organizations			communication	
				are present	

Using these tables, we were able to analyse the main results obtained in relation to the various components of the three themes covered, and it was evident that, in general, there is motivation within the FFAA, although it is not perfect. Communication and leadership have a huge contribution to motivation. At class level, it was clear that enlisted personnel are the category that most lack motivation, which is mostly due to aspects such as lack of personal appreciation, lack of career progression and low salaries. Leaders possess many of the characteristics that, according to the theoretical framework, are suitable for good leadership. However, an unexpected result demonstrates that the military does not react well to leaders who adopt various forms of leadership, as it is assumed that in the FFAA there is a greater level of comfort when a subordinate knows what stance his hierarchical superior normally adopts in his usual day-to-day. Although communication is quite formal, in these cases it proves to be positive in relation to motivation. Perhaps this is due to the natural desire, originating from the time of initial training, for forms of communication, in general, to be quite formal in nature, which does not make it a negative factor.

The first hypothesis of the investigation, which states that the communication of hierarchical superiors influences motivation, was confirmed as valid. The results showed that good communication is associated with higher motivation levels. Both formal and informal communication networks contribute to this increase, with respondents' perceptions of the influence of communication on motivation being predominantly positive. However, communication can also generate conflicts, leading to greater demotivation. The way superiors communicate was identified as one of the main factors affecting motivation, and there is insecurity in expressing opinions, which also contributes to demotivation.

The research revealed that intrinsic factors have a greater impact on work motivation, with emphasis on recognition, career progression, and pride in working for the military institution. Although salary is also relevant, especially among sergeants, the second hypothesis was confirmed, as intrinsic factors prevail over extrinsic ones in motivation.

The research confirmed that leaders possess positive characteristics, although traits like charisma and creativity are lacking. The variation in leadership styles was poorly received, despite the presence of a good environment of trust and communication.

The investigation concludes that communication and leadership within military institutions have a direct impact on the motivation of military personnel, which is essential for their performance. The main demotivating factors identified are lack of career progression, insufficient professional recognition, and salary-related issues.

Limitations of the Study

Some of the limitations of the investigation are related to the size of the sample, an organization with a population of around 23 thousand people (approximate value), containing only a sample of 105 people is below expectations, therefore it was not possible for the study to be representative of the population. People's low adherence to the questionnaire was due to the difficulties in disseminating it, the three branches of the AAFF were unavailable to disseminate the questionnaire internally, the request was requested, but was not accepted. This situation is (probably) due to the AAFF being very closed organizations, and the topic being sensitive nowadays. There was also an attempt to promote internal information in the various units of each branch, especially in the Air Force via email, but once again the requests were denied. The content of the questions in the applied questionnaire also proves to be a limitation in relation to the answers to the objectives, the questions could have been formulated in a quantitative way, as this would facilitate the application in SPSS, due to this a division had to be made, some answers were explained theoretically, and others were applied in SPSS. This situation was because the application of SPSS was not initially planned. Another limitation of the investigation was the fact that the investigation did not reach the officers and civilians in the same way that it reached the sergeants and enlisted men, so the study focuses only on the opinion of these two classes, if it had reached all the classes, we could draw generic conclusions about the AAFF.

Direction of Future Investigations

At the level of the future suggestions, I leave the challenge here to perform this study in an individual manner in each of the FFAA branches, and the topic could also be applied to other public organizations to thus be made a comparison between military organizations and the others. Considering the importance of the study would be important to conduct more studies that would allow to identify ways to motivate the military and civilians to which they allow their attraction and retention in the military world. In the case of motivations, the financial incentive does not currently exist in FFAA, so it will be necessary for forward to equate this financial compensation related to role performance. The theme of communication, motivation and leadership is a topic already much covered in science, so the directions of future investigations should also focus on their consolidation over time as, ways to communicate, motivate and lead are constantly changing, and it is always necessary to find new ways that bring benefits to organizations and employees. Further studies focused on the relationship between the three subjects should be developed, through investigations to all kinds of firms. Performing the same type of study to the private sector will bring many advantages, it could be possible to carry out a paradox between the two realities.

REFERENCES

Amaral, A. M. D. S. (2022). O papel dos líderes na comunicação interna dos processos de gestão de mudança: o caso da implementação do SIGDN na Marinha Portuguesa (Dissertação de Doutoramento). Instituto Politécnico de Lisboa, Escola Superior de Comunicação Social, Lisboa.

Ceitil, M. (2023). *Gestão e desenvolvimento de competências, (2º Edição)*. Edições Sílabo.

Costa, E., & da Silva Oliveira, T. (2020). Comunicação organizacional: Uma ferramenta estratégica de compatibilização de interesses. *Revista Alterjor, 22*(2), 397–409. DOI: 10.11606/issn.2176-1507.v22i2p397-409

Costa, M. B. S. D. (2021). *Especificidades da Comunicação em Organizações da Administração Pública–o caso da Câmara Municipal de Penacova (Tese de Mestrado)*. Faculdade de Letras da Universidade de Coimbra.

da Costa, H. C. M. (2021). Liderança e Motivação no Contexto Organizacional (Dissertação de Doutoramento). Instituto Politécnico do Porto, Porto.

Da Silva, C. P., Paschoalotto, M. A. C., & Endo, G. Y. (2020). Liderança organizacional: Uma revisão integrativa brasileira. *Revista Pensamento Contemporâneo em Administração, 14*(1), 146–159. DOI: 10.12712/rpca.v14i1.36370

da Silva Duque, J. I. (2020). A Influência da Motivação Para O Serviço Militar No Comprometimento Organizacional: O Efeito Moderador do Vínculo Contratual dos Militares da Força Aérea Portuguesa (Dissertação de Doutoramento). Universidade de Lisboa, Lisboa.

Félix, F. J. D. (2020). *Comunicação Estratégica e Integrada: A visão de 23 renomados autores de 5 países*. Editora Rede Integrada.

Neves, S. C. L. D. (2022). O modelo de competências de liderança nas Forças Armadas (Dissertação de Mestrado em Ciências Empresariais), Instituto Superior de Economia e Gestão, Lisboa Santos, A. F. C. D. (2021). A Gestão Estratégica de Recursos Humanos no Setor Público e os Sistemas de Avaliação de Desempenho. O Sistema Integrado de Gestão e Avaliação do Desempenho na Administração Pública (SIADAP). Relatório de Estágio em Administração Público-privada, Coimbra.

Santos, L. A. B. D. (2021). As Forças Armadas Portuguesas no mercado de trabalho: análise crítica do atual modelo de prestação de serviços militar em regime de contrato. http://hdl.handle.net/11067/6054

REFERENCES

Chapter 14
Financial Cybersecurity:
How Cyber Disclosures Shape Retail Investment Decisions

Lawrence Ejime Iweriebor
http://orcid.org/0009-0004-4812-3787
Capitol Technology University, USA

Eugene Lewis
http://orcid.org/0000-0002-2956-0760
Capitol Technology University, USA

ABSTRACT

This study investigates how cybersecurity risks influence retail investors' financial decisions through mixed-methods research. Data from 21 investors reveal that cybersecurity is viewed as a core financial risk comparable to traditional metrics. Investors trust formal filings over social media and value transparent, specific disclosures. Board-level oversight significantly enhances confidence, with 40% requiring 5%+ risk premiums for elevated cyber risk. Findings extend Signaling Theory and provide actionable guidance for corporate disclosure and regulatory policy.

INTRODUCTION

The increasing number of cyber threats has shown how vital good cybersecurity management is, especially in the finance industry. Investors are more worried about how companies handle cyber risks since these risks can directly affect financial results and influence their investment choices. Cyberattacks on the financial sector have increased significantly, with estimated annual losses from cybercrime reaching $97 billion, accounting for approximately 9% of global banking net profits in 2016 (Bouveret, 2018). Prior research has emphasized the role of cybersecurity transparency and how incidents impact investor confidence (Yang et al., 2020; Cheng et al., 2022). Yang et al. (2020) found that when companies share information about cybersecurity risks, it builds investor confidence and shows the importance of being

DOI: 10.4018/979-8-3373-4027-2.ch014

transparent about cybersecurity efforts. Cyber incidents also affect financial outcomes, like stock prices, with investors often seeking higher returns to justify the risks of cyber threats (Celeny & Maréchal, 2024).

The direct financial repercussions of cybersecurity breaches are staggering. According to the IMF, global financial institutions face persistent cyber threats, forcing banks to allocate an increasing portion of their budget to cybersecurity. The technology overhead for banks has risen to 7.16% of gross revenue, the highest among all industries (Kark, 2018). Beyond the immediate financial loss, firms that suffer data breaches experience a decline in stock market performance, operational disruptions, and reputational damage (Liu & Babar, 2024). A single security breach can lower a firm's market value by 3% to 5% in the days following an incident.

Studies by Shaker et al. (2023) and Shaikh & Siponen (2023) show that good IT management and learning from past mistakes are key to making smart cybersecurity investments. These investments help lower risks and keep investors' trust as cyber threats continue to grow. For investors, cybersecurity risk is no longer an IT issue—it is a core financial risk. Investors must now evaluate a company's cyber resilience before making financial decisions, as firms with poor cybersecurity governance face higher equity costs, increased systematic risk, and lower investor confidence (Al-Mohareb, 2025). Furthermore, companies struggling with cyber risks often reduce dividend payouts to preserve liquidity, affecting shareholder returns. The challenge for financial decision-makers is balancing cybersecurity investment with profitability, ensuring robust defenses without negatively impacting shareholder value.

This research investigates how retail investors respond to cybersecurity risks when making investment decisions by examining how concerns about data breaches, and other cybersecurity threats shape investors' trust in companies, influence their stock selections, and affect their overall approach to investing. By focusing on retail investors rather than institutional investors, this research aims to uncover what aspects of cybersecurity risk matter most to individuals managing their portfolios and how these perceptions translate into concrete investment choices.

BACKGROUND OF STUDY

The intersection of cybersecurity and financial investment represents a relatively recent but rapidly evolving area of concern. Historically, corporate security was viewed primarily as an operational IT issue with minimal investor visibility. This perspective shifted dramatically following several high-profile incidents that demonstrated the material financial consequences of cybersecurity failures (Cavusoglu et al., 2004).

Empirical research has documented substantial market impacts. Cavusoglu et al. (2004) documented negative abnormal returns averaging -2.1% surrounding breach disclosures. Hammouchi et al. (2019) analyzed over 9,000 breaches from 2005 to 2018, finding that hacking breaches have become dominant since 2013, with seven of the ten largest breaches by record volume being hacking incidents. The 2013 Target breach compromised 40 million payment cards, resulting in over $290 million in direct costs and CEO resignation (Plachkinova & Maurer, 2018). The 2017 Equifax breach exposed 147 million individuals' information, costing over $1.4 billion, with delayed disclosure intensifying investor backlash (Rickett & Smith, 2026). The 2019 Capital One breach affecting 100 million customers resulted from misconfigured cloud infrastructure (Khan et al., 2022).

These incidents illuminate persistent challenges. Information asymmetry exists between companies that possess detailed vulnerability knowledge and investors who rely on limited disclosures, creating adverse selection (Akerlof, 1970). Companies face conflicting pressures where transparency builds trust but risks revealing vulnerabilities. Cybersecurity threats evolve rapidly, with hacking breaches increasing dramatically from 2009 to 2013 (Hammouchi et al., 2019). Cyber risks resist precise quantification because the attack probability is uncertain, and potential losses range from negligible to catastrophic, with an average cost per lost record estimated at $148 (Hammouchi et al., 2019).

These challenges particularly affect retail investors who lack institutional resources for independent assessments and rely primarily on public disclosures and personal judgment (Barber & Odean, 2001). These information constraints make the effective incorporation of cybersecurity risk especially difficult for retail investors, creating a need for research examining how this segment perceives, processes, and responds to cybersecurity information in practice.

PROBLEM STATEMENT

In an ideal investment environment, cybersecurity risk would be transparent, quantifiable, and systematically integrated into financial analysis frameworks. Investors would access standardized metrics describing companies' security posture and incident history, while companies would disclose material information promptly. However, the actual state diverges significantly from this ideal. Research presents conflicting findings about how cybersecurity events affect market valuation. While Liu and Babar (2024) documented that stock price declines increased from approximately 1% in the early 2010s to 3-5% by 2020-2023, many market reactions prove temporary as media attention fades, suggesting investors exhibit bounded rationality and limited attention spans.

Empirical evidence on disclosure effectiveness remains inconclusive. Yang et al. (2020) found that structured cybersecurity disclosures following recognized frameworks enhance investor confidence by facilitating cross-company comparison. However, Cheng et al. (2022) identified a critical paradox where excessive technical detail paradoxically reduces confidence by overwhelming non-expert audiences, suggesting an inverted-U relationship where moderate disclosure optimizes trust while excessive disclosure overwhelms investors. These conflicting findings leave companies without clear guidance on optimal communication strategies.

Existing theoretical frameworks inadequately explain retail investor behavior regarding cybersecurity risk. Signaling Theory (Spence, 1973) predicts credible signals of strong security should attract investment, but does not specify which signals retail investors consider credible or how they distinguish authentic security from "security theater." Prospect Theory (Kahneman & Tversky, 1979) predicts loss aversion should make investors sensitive to breach risks, but does not explain why market reactions are often temporary despite predictions that potential losses should persistently reduce valuations.

Critical knowledge gaps persist regarding how retail investors actually process cybersecurity information. Which sources do they trust—technical disclosures, news summaries, or social media? Which risk dimensions matter most—prevention capabilities or response effectiveness? How does trust in governance develop and erode? Do considerations differ across investor types based on experience or technical background? Most research examines institutional investors with dedicated analysts and proprietary models, leaving retail investor perspectives substantially underrepresented despite retail investors accounting for approximately 25-30% of U.S. equity market trading volume.

Retail investors face several barriers to incorporating cybersecurity risk into investment analysis. First, evaluating cybersecurity requires technical expertise most retail investors lack, forcing reliance on simplified proxies. Second, companies produce voluminous disclosures where cybersecurity information may be scattered or buried in technical jargon. Third, investors receive information from multiple sources of varying reliability, making credible information difficult to distinguish from speculation. Fourth, cybersecurity investments yield benefits over extended timeframes while investors often have shorter horizons, potentially leading to undervaluation of long-term security investments. Fifth, unlike standardized financial metrics, cybersecurity disclosures lack comprehensive standardization, preventing systematic cross-company comparison (Shaikh & Siponen, 2023; Shaker et al., 2023).

This research directly addresses these gaps by empirically investigating retail investor perceptions through primary data collection combining quantitative and qualitative methods. Unlike studies inferring behavior from market data, this research directly asks retail investors how they perceive risks, which sources they trust and why, what disclosure characteristics they find credible, and how cybersecurity influences actual decisions. By exploring information source hierarchies, this study illuminates pathways through which information actually influences decisions. Through qualitative inquiry, it identifies specific attributes including transparency, specificity, and action-orientation that build trust, providing actionable guidance for corporate communications (Yang et al., 2020; Cheng et al., 2022). By examining how investors make decisions when technical evaluation exceeds expertise, this study reveals heuristics and simplifying rules, potentially explaining why market reactions sometimes diverge from theoretical predictions (Kahneman & Tversky, 1979). By grounding findings in Signaling Theory and Prospect Theory while remaining open to unexpected patterns, this research tests whether existing theories adequately explain retail investor responses.

Findings will inform regulatory policy by revealing whether retail investors can effectively interpret current disclosures or whether standardized frameworks are needed. Understanding which disclosure attributes build trust guides corporate communications in developing more effective investor communications balancing legal defensibility, security considerations, and accessibility (Al-Mohareb, 2025). Identifying gaps between theoretical predictions and behavior highlights areas requiring additional development. Revealing how investors process information, what sources they trust, and what heuristics they employ informs educational initiatives to improve financial literacy in this emerging domain (Kafi & Akter, 2023; Uddin et al., 2020).

THEORETICAL FRAMEWORK

This study employs three complementary theoretical perspectives to explain how retail investors perceive and respond to cybersecurity risks, with Signaling Theory serving as the primary lens.

Signaling Theory, originating in Spence's (1973) work on job market dynamics, explains how parties communicate unobservable qualities through observable indicators when information asymmetry exists. In investment contexts, companies possess superior information about their cybersecurity posture while investors rely on limited public information. Companies signal cybersecurity strength through formal disclosures in SEC filings, third-party certifications such as ISO 27001 or SOC 2, board-level oversight, transparent breach disclosure, and visible security investments. Signaling Theory predicts investors place greater weight on signals that are costly to mimic, consistent across channels, independently verifiable, and specific rather than vague (Spence, 1973).

Kahneman and Tversky's (1979) Prospect Theory demonstrates that individuals weight losses more heavily than equivalent gains (loss aversion), evaluate outcomes relative to reference points, and overweight low-probability catastrophic risks. Applied to cybersecurity, this predicts investors will avoid companies with perceived vulnerabilities even when expected returns are higher, respond more strongly to negative breach information than positive security improvements, and may overweight rare but catastrophic breach risks.

Building on Akerlof's (1970) "Market for Lemons" analysis, Information Asymmetry Theory explains how information disparities create market inefficiencies. Companies possess detailed vulnerability knowledge that investors cannot observe directly, creating adverse selection where investors may penalize all firms equally. This theory explains why investors seek independent verification through third-party audits and why they may distrust company communications (Akerlof, 1970).

These three theories create a comprehensive framework where Signaling Theory explains how disclosures convey information, Prospect Theory explains heightened sensitivity and loss aversion, and Information Asymmetry Theory explains why disclosure quality matters. This multi-theoretical approach captures real-world retail investor behavior complexity.

LITERATURE REVIEW

Empirical research on cybersecurity and investment addresses three key areas: financial impacts of breaches, disclosure effectiveness, and governance responses.

Liu and Babar (2024) conducted a systematic review documenting that average stock price declines following breach disclosure increased from approximately 1% in the early 2010s to 3-5% by 2020-2023, with financial services firms experiencing particularly severe reactions averaging 5.8%. They attributed this escalation to growing breach sophistication, increased regulatory penalties, and heightened investor awareness. Bouveret (2018) quantified aggregate costs at $97 billion globally, representing approximately 9% of banking sector net profits, illustrating cybersecurity as a systemic concern affecting industry profitability.

Yang et al. (2020) found that structured disclosures following standardized frameworks such as NIST or ISO 27001 enhanced investor confidence by implying adherence to best practices and facilitating cross-company comparison. However, Cheng et al. (2022) identified a critical paradox where highly detailed disclosures spanning five or more pages reduced investor confidence relative to concise summaries, attributing this to information overload and perceived obfuscation. This suggests an inverted-U relationship where moderate disclosure optimizes confidence while excessive disclosure overwhelms audiences. Celeny et al. (2024) found that firms disclosing within 72 hours of breach discovery experienced smaller negative returns than those delaying beyond 30 days, with delayed disclosure triggering heightened regulatory scrutiny and litigation, underscoring that prompt transparency mitigates long-term damage.

Shaker et al. (2023) found that IT governance quality, incorporating board-level oversight and dedicated cybersecurity committees, positively predicted investor confidence, though the effect was mediated by actual outcomes, where strong governance only enhanced confidence when accompanied by low breach frequency. This suggests investors value structures that demonstrably reduce risk rather than governance theater. Shaikh and Siponen (2023) documented that firms where breaches were externally discovered increased cybersecurity spending by 47% compared to 18% when internally detected, suggesting managerial complacency and that governance structures ensuring continuous improvement may be more reliable indicators than historical incident rates. Al-Mohareb (2025) found that firms with weak cyber governance were significantly more likely to cut dividends following incidents, suggesting that proactive cybersecurity investment functions as financial insurance.

Kafi and Akter (2023) identified heuristics retail investors employ when technical evaluation exceeds expertise, including favoring large-cap firms, avoiding high-risk sectors regardless of specific firm security, and relying on the absence of negative news as a proxy for adequate security. These heuristics could lead to suboptimal decisions as large firms may be frequent targets, and the absence of breaches may reflect luck rather than strong security. Uddin et al. (2020) found that investors who personally experienced identity theft expressed significantly lower trust in corporate disclosures and demanded higher risk premiums, suggesting personal experiences shape investment behavior.

Literature establishes that breaches generate negative stock reactions of 2-5%, while structured, timely disclosures mitigate damage; excessive detail, however, can overwhelm. Strong governance enhances confidence when accompanied by demonstrable improvements. However, most research infers behavior from market data rather than investigating individual decision-making. The specific information sources retail investors use, cognitive processes for evaluating risk, and psychological factors, including fear and trust, shaping responses, remain underexplored. This study addresses these gaps by directly examining retail investor perceptions, information processing, and decision-making through mixed-methods inquiry.

CONCEPTUAL FRAMEWORK

This study's conceptual framework illustrates relationships among cybersecurity events, disclosure practices, investor perceptions, and investment decisions. Independent variables include cybersecurity events (data breaches, ransomware attacks, system intrusions) and disclosure characteristics (timing, content quality, channel, and tone). These shape the mediating variable of investor risk perception, encompassing probability assessment, impact assessment, resilience assessment, and trust in management, which are influenced by information source credibility, investor characteristics, and contextual factors. Risk perceptions translate into dependent variables in investment decision-making, including entry and exit decisions, portfolio allocation, and adjustments to required returns. Moderating factors include investor sophistication, disclosure quality, company reputation, and sector context.

METHODOLOGY

This study employs a mixed-methods approach combining quantitative survey data with qualitative open-ended responses. The research focuses exclusively on retail investors—individuals participating in the stock market without professional financial intermediaries. Purposive sampling targeted investors with experience evaluating investment opportunities and familiarity with corporate cybersecurity disclosures. Thematic analysis following Braun and Clarke (2006) examined qualitative data. To enhance credibility, the study employed triangulation across investor segments, reflexivity to acknowledge researcher biases, and member checking to validate findings.

The survey instrument captured quantitative and qualitative insights through an online questionnaire distributed via Google Forms, requiring approximately 7-10 minutes. The questionnaire consisted of nine sections: consent and screening, investment profile, cybersecurity risk perception using Likert scales, information sources and trust, disclosure credibility, risk tolerance and behavioral responses, breach response evaluation, resilience demonstration, and demographics.

The questionnaire was developed iteratively. First, 35 candidate items were generated based on Signaling Theory (Spence, 1973), Prospect Theory (Kahneman & Tversky, 1979), and the conceptual framework. Second, three subject matter experts reviewed items for clarity and validity. Third, it was piloted with 5 retail investors. Fourth, based on feedback, three items were removed due to redundancy, wording was simplified in four items, two questions were reframed, and a screening question was added.

Recruitment employed online investment communities (Reddit r/investing and r/stocks, Bogleheads forum), investment platforms (Seeking Alpha, Motley Fool), LinkedIn networks, and snowball sampling over six weeks. Inclusion criteria required self-identified retail investors with at least one trade in the past 12 months, investment in publicly traded equities, age 18 or older, and English proficiency. Exclusion criteria eliminated professional advisors, institutional managers, inactive investors, and cybersecurity firm employees. The target of 20-30 participants aligns with exploratory mixed-methods research guidelines (Braun & Clarke, 2006). Purposive sampling targeted variation across investment experience, technical familiarity, portfolio size, investment style, and sector focus.

Retail investors represent the ideal population because they rely on publicly available disclosures, are susceptible to cognitive biases identified in Prospect Theory (Kahneman & Tversky, 1979), collectively hold 25-30% of U.S. equity trading volume, and remain underrepresented in literature despite their market significance.

The survey yielded 21 consenting participants who began the questionnaire, of whom 10 (47.6%) met inclusion criteria as active retail investors and completed the full survey. Among respondents, 60% hold investments for multiple years, investment styles included 60% growth and 50% buy-and-hold, 50% trade infrequently (less than monthly), cybersecurity familiarity included 40% beginner and 40% intermediate, 50% aged 45-54, and education included 40% master's and 30% bachelor's degrees.

ETHICAL CONSIDERATIONS

This study was determined to be exempt from Institutional Review Board (IRB) review as it involved adult participants completing a voluntary, anonymous survey with no more than minimal risk, consistent with federal regulations 45 CFR 46.104(d)(2). All participants in this research provided informed consent electronically, which included a statement of the research purpose, their voluntary participation, the right to withdraw without penalty, data usage protocols, the estimated 7–10-minute commitment, and their contact information. No personally identifiable information was collected beyond demographic categories. Survey responses were submitted using anonymous links that did not record IP addresses. Data files were stored on password-protected, encrypted devices accessible only to the research team. All reported findings use aggregate data or anonymized quotes with pseudonyms. The research posed minimal risk with no deceptive practices or requests for sensitive financial details. Participants could skip questions and were informed of withdrawal rights.

DATA ANALYSIS

Likert-scale responses were analyzed using descriptive statistics, including frequency distributions, mean scores, and standard deviations, cross-tabulation by demographic variables, and correlation analysis examining relationships between trust and risk perception. Given the exploratory nature and sample size, inferential statistics were not employed; descriptive patterns contextualized qualitative findings.

Open-ended responses were analyzed following Braun and Clarke's (2006) six-phase thematic analysis framework. Phase 1: familiarization through multiple readings with observations noted in research memos. Phase 2: generating initial codes using NVivo 14 with deductive codes derived from Signaling Theory, Prospect Theory, and Information Asymmetry Theory, supplemented by inductive codes emerging from the data; two researchers independently coded 30% establishing inter-coder reliability (Cohen's kappa = 0.82). Phase 3: searching for themes by grouping codes examining patterns and organizing hierarchically. Phase 4: reviewing themes checking coherence and dataset representation, refining as necessary. Phase 5: defining and naming themes precisely with concise descriptive names. Phase 6: producing the report integrating themes with representative quotes selected for clarity and typicality.

Triangulation enhanced credibility through data triangulation combining quantitative and qualitative responses, investigator triangulation with multiple researchers comparing interpretations, and method triangulation examining convergence between scaled and open-ended responses. Member checking involved sharing preliminary analysis with 8 participants (80% response rate) who confirmed theme accuracy and provided clarifying comments incorporated into final analysis. Comprehensive audit trail documentation included research memos, codebook, theme development documents, and meeting notes allowing independent review. Researchers maintained reflexive journals documenting assumptions and biases with regular team meetings questioning interpretations. Data saturation was assessed by monitoring when new responses ceased generating new themes, occurring by participant 21. Quantitative and qualitative results were integrated through convergent design, with convergence strengthening confidence while divergence prompted investigation into contextual factors.

FINDINGS AND RESULTS

As described in the methodology, 10 active retail investors completed the full questionnaire. Quantitative responses confirmed retail investors view cybersecurity as a material financial concern, assigning the highest importance to regulatory/legal exposure from incidents, ransomware risk, and data breach/exfiltration risks. Clear trust hierarchies emerged, with news outlets and company filings being the most trusted sources, while social media was the least trusted (30% explicitly cited it). Usage patterns revealed a pragmatic approach: 80% use company incident notices and news outlets, 70% use social media despite low trust as an early warning, then verify through authoritative channels before acting.

Thematic analysis revealed four credibility dimensions: authenticity and transparency, focus on incident and clients rather than company emphasis, independence from company control, and incident disclosure specificity. Independent penetration-test summaries received highest credibility scores, followed by ISO 27001 certification and dedicated board committees. A strong consensus emerged that board-level oversight increases confidence, aligning with Signaling Theory's (Spence, 1973) prediction that costly, verifiable governance structures signal management commitment.

Consistent with Prospect Theory (Kahneman & Tversky, 1979), respondents demonstrated heightened sensitivity to cybersecurity risk. When asked whether they would demand higher returns for firms with elevated cyber risk, 40% indicated requiring returns at least 5% higher, supporting the existence of a cyber risk premium. Fear of losses statement received predominantly high agreement (modal rating: 5), indicating loss aversion influences position sizing. Responses to accepting lower returns for resilience were mixed (modal rating: 3), suggesting investors penalize weakness more than reward strength, consistent with loss aversion.

Regarding position changes due to cyber news, 40% reported changes in the past 12 months, while 60% reported none. Most common breach response was "wait for the company's disclosure/remediation details" (modal rating: 5), suggesting "watch and assess" posture. Factors most influencing breach reactions included severity (80%), regulatory/legal exposure (60%), and leadership/accountability changes (60%). Actions restoring confidence included leadership changes (80%), increased security investment with specifics (70%), and clear timelines and updates (50%).

Thematic analysis revealed companies should demonstrate resilience through a proactive approach and awareness, transparent reporting and governance, treating cyber as a core business issue, continuous security investment and compliance programs, and continuous client updates. Additional insights revealed cybersecurity as a core value driver where "strong practices signal resilience and disciplined risk management while weaknesses risk fines, reputational damage, and unstable earnings," investor reliance on intuition and heuristics, and data protection criticality.

These findings support that cybersecurity risk has become a core financial consideration for retail investors, integrated into decisions through trust assessment, loss aversion mechanisms, and governance signal evaluation. Investors demonstrate sophistication, distinguishing credible from non-credible disclosures, value transparency and accountability, and demand risk premiums or adjust positions based on perceived cyber risk exposure.

NATURE AND SIGNIFICANCE OF THE STUDY

Cybersecurity risks have become a fundamental factor in financial decision-making, influencing how investors evaluate companies. The increasing number of data breaches, ransomware attacks, and insider threats has made strong cybersecurity measures more critical than ever to protect sensitive information. Understanding how retail investors perceive cybersecurity risks can help organizations develop strategies to mitigate concerns and improve investor confidence. This study seeks to explore how investors recognize and incorporate cybersecurity risks into their investment decisions and what cybersecurity-related information they find most relevant.

AN OVERVIEW OF CYBERSECURITY RISK

Cybersecurity risk refers to the potential danger of loss or harm when information systems and data are not adequately protected from cyber threats (Strupczewski, 2021). It includes the weaknesses within an organization's technology setup that could be targeted by hackers (Shaker et al., 2023). With the fast pace of digital change, cybersecurity risk has become a significant concern across all industries. The financial sector is vulnerable to these risks due to the sensitive information it handles and the growing complexity of cyberattacks (Celeny & Maréchal, 2024).

Effectively managing cybersecurity risk requires organizations to take strong preventive measures, detect threats early, and reduce their potential impact using technical, procedural, and administrative safeguards (Shaikh & Siponen, 2023). Managing cybersecurity risks is crucial because it directly affects a company's reputation and investor trust. When these risks are not managed well, they can result in a significant financial loss to the organization and cause reputational harm to the organization (Yang et al., 2020).

UNDERSTANDING FINANCIAL INVESTMENT IN THE DIGITAL AGE

Financial investment today is heavily influenced by technology advancements and the cybersecurity risks that come with them. Investors now factor in the potential risks cyber threats pose when deciding whether a company is a good investment. As financial transactions and investments shift to digital platforms, investors increasingly focus on how well companies handle these cybersecurity risks (Cheng et al., 2022). The increasing number of data breaches, ransomware attacks, and insider threats has made strong cybersecurity measures more critical than ever to protect sensitive information (Kafi & Akter, 2023).

Effective cybersecurity is increasingly recognized as a tool for risk mitigation and a way to build investor trust. An important concept emerging in this context is the cyber risk premium—the idea that investors expect higher returns from organizations facing more significant cyber risks (Celeny & Maréchal, 2024). This shows that investors are becoming more aware of how cybersecurity issues can affect a company's stability, profits, and long-term success. Proactive steps to strengthen an organization's cybersecurity systems are needed to ease the concerns of investors and reduce the cyber risk premiums to an organization. Kafi and Akter (2023) in their research highlight the importance of measures like network segmentation, encryption, and robust access controls to safeguard financial data and reduce perceived risks.

Retail investors are quite sensitive to perceived cybersecurity risks, which can directly impact their trust and willingness to invest (Yang et al., 2020). In this digital age, companies must adopt proactive cybersecurity measures to reassure investors that their assets are secure against emerging threats.

AWARENESS OF CYBERSECURITY AND INVESTOR KNOWLEDGE

Investors' growing awareness of cyber threats is becoming a key factor when making investment decisions. Investors are more focused on how an organization's cybersecurity systems affect its financial health and reputation. The growing number of cyber incidents has made investors to be more critical of how organizations protect their assets. High-profile data breaches and their effects on stock prices further highlight this issue, acting as strong reminders of the risks linked to weak cybersecurity (Shaikh & Siponen, 2023).

Research shows that informed investors are more likely to consider an organization's cybersecurity practices and track record when making investment decisions (Yang et al., 2020), however, some investors lack the technical knowledge on how to evaluate an organization's cybersecurity practices, which highlights the importance of clear cybersecurity disclosures to help investors make well-informed decisions (Shaker et al., 2023).

FINANCIAL INVESTMENT AND CYBERSECURITY RISK

The connection between an organization's cybersecurity risks and financial investments is closely linked because these risks affect how investors see a firm's stability and capacity to generate future profits. As Celeny and Maréchal (2024) pointed out, investors demand a risk premium to make up for the uncertainty that comes with potential cyber threats, which can impact stock prices and market performance. Yang et al. (2020) also found that structured cybersecurity disclosures can help reduce these risks by giving investors' confidence in a company's ability to handle cyber threats. Cheng et al. (2022) found that poorly handled cybersecurity disclosures, especially after breaches, can cause negative investor sentiment and a decline in market value.

To address this, organizations should proactively share their risk management strategies to reassure investors and maintain financial stability (Shaikh & Siponen, 2023). The link between cybersecurity risks and financial investments is complex, involving both the real and perceived impacts of cyber incidents on investor decisions and financial outcomes. Cyber breaches have been found to cause significant financial costs, including direct losses like legal fees and indirect costs such as damage to reputation and loss of customer trust (Shaikh & Siponen, 2023). As a result, companies that experience breaches may suffer a negative impact on market value, as investors often see these incidents as signs of poor risk management (Celeny et al., 2024).

Celeny and Maréchal (2024) in their research found that investors demand higher returns when dealing with companies that face more significant cyber threats, indicating that some investors know that cyber risks can affect a company's finances and expect compensation for any potential losses. A company's financial health relies on how well it manages cybersecurity risks; poor handling can cause stock prices to drop and reduce investor trust. Yang et al. (2020) found that clear cybersecurity risk disclosures can improve investors' confidence in an organization, encouraging more investment. Being transparent reassures investors that the organization is actively managing cyber threats. However, a poorly timed and managed disclosure after breaches can damage investor confidence (Cheng et al., 2022), emphasizing the need for both high-quality and well-timed communication to build and maintain investor trust.

Organizational learning is crucial for guiding cybersecurity investments. Shaikh & Siponen (2023) emphasized the importance of learning from previous breaches. Shaikh & Siponen (2023) found that organizations that learn from past breaches and make efforts to strengthen their cybersecurity systems are more likely to rebuild investor trust. Their study also found that organizations often increase cybersecurity spending when breaches are uncovered by third parties, underscoring the importance of ongoing improvement and proactive risk management. Information Technology (IT) governance plays a key role in building investor confidence. Shaker et al. (2023) found that strong IT governance improves cybersecurity, which can have a positive impact on how investors perceive the organization. However, they noted that IT governance alone has a limited effect on investor perceptions; integrating IT governance with broader cybersecurity strategies is key to maximizing its impact on investment decisions.

The relationship between cybersecurity risk and financial investment is influenced by transparency, proactive risk management, organizational learning, and effective governance. Investors are paying more attention to how well a company manages cyber risks, making strong cybersecurity practices essential for financial stability and earning investor trust.

THEORETICAL BACKGROUND EXPLAINED

This study draws on two key theories to understand how investors react to cybersecurity risks. One of these is Signaling Theory, introduced by Spence (1973), which suggests that companies share cybersecurity disclosures to show investors that they are trustworthy and prepared to manage risks. According to this theory, investors interpret these signals to assess whether a company has strong cybersecurity governance, the likelihood of experiencing future breaches, and the extent to which cybersecurity vulnerabilities could impact financial performance. Signaling Theory provides a valuable lens through which to examine how different levels of cybersecurity transparency affect investor confidence and decision-making.

In addition to Signaling Theory, Prospect Theory, as proposed by Kahneman and Tversky (1979), offers further insight into how retail investors respond to cybersecurity risk. The Prospect Theory suggests that investors are more sensitive to potential losses than gains, leading them to avoid investments in companies perceived to be at high risk of cybersecurity breaches. With cybersecurity threats being so unpredictable, investors tend to play it safe by favoring companies that are transparent about their cybersecurity measures and have a history of actively managing risks. This hesitation to take risks shows how emotions and psychology play a big role in investment decisions, especially when it comes to how retail investors react to cybersecurity issues.

CYBERSECURITY RISK AND RETAIL INVESTMENT

The conceptual model for this research investigates how cybersecurity disclosures, retail investor perceptions, and investment decisions are connected. When companies share cybersecurity information or experience a breach, it can influence how investors feel about the company. Their perception of risk plays a key role in shaping trust—whether they believe the company can effectively manage cyber threats. These perceptions then impact investment choices, such as whether investors are willing to invest, how much risk they are comfortable taking, and whether they decide to buy or sell stocks.

The connection between these variables can be illustrated as follows.:

Cybersecurity Events and Disclosures → Investor Perception of Risk → Investment Decision-Making.

Investors who perceive cybersecurity disclosures as a positive signal of strong governance and risk management are more likely to invest confidently. Conversely, those who interpret cybersecurity risks as an indicator of financial instability may demand higher risk premiums or avoid investment altogether.

DATA COLLECTION

This study uses a survey to understand how retail investors perceive and respond to cybersecurity risk. A structured questionnaire was distributed online to investors with different levels of market experience. It captured three areas: (i) perceptions of cybersecurity risk, (ii) trust in and credibility of different disclosure sources (e.g., news, company filings or incident notices, third-party certifications, social media), and (iii) self-reported actions taken in response to cyber threats (e.g., reallocating funds, raising required returns, or avoiding a stock). Most items used 5-or 7-point Likert scales, with a few open-ended questions for brief explanations.

The questionnaire was refined, and eligible participants were self-identified retail investors who had made at least one trade or allocation decision in the past 12 months. Purposive sampling was used to ensure variation in investment experience, sector focus, and technical familiarity, and recruitment drew on broad outreach channels to widen representation.

FINDINGS AND RESULTS

Findings from this study reveal that retail investors treat cybersecurity as a core financial risk, not just a technical issue. When they perceive weak cybersecurity, they expect higher returns to compensate, or they avoid the issuer altogether. This pattern aligns with the study's framing that cyber events and disclosures shape risk perceptions, which then influence investment choices. Respondents place the most trust in reputable news outlets and formal company disclosures such as filings or incident notices. They use third-party certifications mainly to corroborate other sources. Social media is the least trusted channel, largely due to the prevalence of unverified information.

Participants distinguish credible disclosures from "marketing" by their authenticity, transparency, and specificity. Communications that present the facts of the incident, explain the client impact, and detail concrete corrective actions are viewed as useful; messaging that feels promotional or vague erodes credibility. Investors say companies demonstrate resilience by showing proactive readiness, reporting transparently, stress-testing response plans (including tabletop exercises), and maintaining visible governance that treats cyber as a core business issue. Ongoing client updates, established security programs, compliance efforts, and formal oversight structures further strengthen credibility.

A smaller subset of respondents relies on personal intuition or "reasonable risk" rules when signals are noisy, highlighting the role of heuristics and loss aversion in decision-making.

CONCLUSION

This mixed-methods study investigated how cybersecurity risks influence retail investors' financial decision-making through examination of 21 participants' perceptions, information sources, and behavioral responses. The research addressed a critical gap in understanding how individual investors, representing 25-30% of U.S. equity trading volume, evaluate and respond to cybersecurity threats that have cost companies billions in market value, from Target's $290 million losses to Equifax's $1.4 billion settlement.

Findings reveal that retail investors treat cybersecurity as a core financial risk comparable to traditional metrics, with 40% requiring risk premiums of 5% or higher for companies with elevated cyber exposure. Board-level oversight emerged as the most powerful governance signal, while credible disclosures required four key attributes: authenticity, impact focus, independence, and specificity. Participants demonstrated clear information hierarchies, trusting formal filings and reputable news while remaining skeptical of social media despite using it for early warnings. Consistent with Prospect Theory, participants exhibited pronounced loss aversion regarding cybersecurity weaknesses, responding more strongly to perceived vulnerabilities than to security strengths.

The study extends Signaling Theory by demonstrating that signal effectiveness depends critically on audience sophistication and accessibility, with complex technical disclosures failing to build trust among non-expert investors. This finding challenges assumptions underlying current disclosure practices and suggests that companies may inadvertently undermine credibility through excessive technical detail. The research also reveals that retail investors have developed sophisticated heuristics for evaluating cybersecurity risks despite lacking formal technical expertise, using governance structures and disclosure characteristics as proxies for unobservable security quality.

While this exploratory study's sample size (n=10) and U.S. focus limit statistical generalizability, the rich qualitative insights, theoretical grounding, and mixed-methods triangulation provide robust foundation for future large-scale investigations across diverse investor populations and international market contexts. The high inter-coder reliability (Cohen's kappa = 0.82) and member checking with 80% participant response rate enhance confidence in thematic findings.

These findings have important implications for market efficiency and capital allocation. Misaligned cybersecurity disclosures may lead to suboptimal investment decisions that neither adequately protect investors nor effectively incentivize corporate security improvements. By revealing the specific disclosure attributes that build or erode investor trust, this research provides actionable guidance for corporate communications seeking to balance legal requirements, security considerations, and investor accessibility. The documented cyber risk premium demonstrates that cybersecurity weaknesses directly affect cost of capital, creating financial incentives for proactive security investments beyond mere regulatory compliance.

Future research should explore how these findings generalize across cultural contexts, test disclosure format effects experimentally through randomized designs, examine differences in evaluation criteria between institutional and retail investors, and investigate whether targeted educational interventions can reduce reliance on potentially misleading heuristics while preserving investors' ability to identify genuine security signals.

As cyber threats continue escalating and breach costs mount, bridging the communication gap between corporate security practices and investor understanding becomes increasingly critical for maintaining efficient capital markets. By revealing how retail investors actually process cybersecurity information—rather than how they theoretically should—this research provides foundational understanding that can inform more effective disclosure standards, enhance investor decision quality, and ultimately strengthen the link between corporate cybersecurity investments and appropriate capital allocation. In an era where digital security failures can erase billions in market value within hours, understanding and improving cybersecurity risk communication represents not merely an academic exercise but an urgent practical imperative for market stability and investor protection.

Information Source Hierarchies and Credibility

Participants demonstrated clear trust hierarchies with formal company filings and reputable news outlets receiving highest trust while social media received lowest. Participants valued formal filings because they are "legally binding and audited," aligning with Signaling Theory's prediction that costly signals imposing penalties for misrepresentation are more credible. Third-party certifications occupied middle position, with participants expressing uncertainty about what certifications verify, suggesting their potential as credibility signals is undermined by limited investor literacy. Participants distinguished credible disclosures from "security theater" through specificity and action-orientation, consistently emphasizing concrete details rather than vague assurances. This strongly supports Signaling Theory's prediction that credible signals must be costly or difficult to fake. Participants valued disclosures emphasizing concrete actions rather than solely describing incidents, reflecting Prospect Theory's (Kahneman & Tversky, 1979) loss aversion principle. However, excessive technical detail could backfire, echoing Cheng et al.'s (2022) evidence of inverted-U relationship between disclosure length and credibility.

Demonstrated Resilience and Heuristics

Board-level oversight emerged as particularly important, with visible governance structures increasing confidence. Proactive security investments signaled resilience while reactive investments only after breaches were viewed skeptically. Evidence of organizational learning from incidents provided another resilience signal, aligning with Shaikh and Siponen's (2023) research, though learning must be visible and demonstrable. While many participants demonstrated sophisticated understanding, a subset relied on heuristics including size-based assumptions, sector-based blanket assessments, and absence-of-news assumptions. These heuristics reflect bounded rationality consistent with Kahneman and Tversky's (1979) Prospect Theory, suggesting investor education initiatives should address common biases.

The Cyber Risk Premium and Integrated Model

Consistent with Prospect Theory's loss aversion prediction, participants demonstrated heightened sensitivity to potential cybersecurity losses, with many requiring substantial risk premiums (≥5% higher returns) for companies with elevated cyber risk. This has important valuation implications where companies with perceived cybersecurity weaknesses may face higher costs of capital, creating direct financial incentives for strong cybersecurity as value preservation mechanism. Integrating findings, an integrated model emerges: initial attention triggered by cybersecurity events, information gathering with hierarchical trust structures, credibility assessment using specificity and action-orientation, resilience evaluation of governance and investments, risk perception formation based on information quality and signals, decision translation through loss aversion mechanisms, and monitoring and updating perceptions. This model provides comprehensive framework integrating psychological, informational, and rational economic factors.

Managerial Implications

This study provides actionable insights for corporate managers, investor relations professionals, and chief information security officers seeking to communicate effectively with retail investors about cybersecurity risks.

For Corporate Managers and Investor Relations

Prioritize Disclosure Specificity: Investors dismiss generic assurances like "robust controls" or "industry-standard practices" as marketing rhetoric. Instead, provide verifiable details: cybersecurity budget percentages, team size and qualifications, testing frequency, and specific certifications (ISO 27001, SOC 2 Type II). Rather than "world-class security," state "ISO 27001 certified, SOC 2 Type II attested, quarterly third-party penetration testing." Specificity signals credibility and enables meaningful assessment.

Elevate Cybersecurity Governance: Board-level oversight significantly enhances investor confidence. Establish dedicated cybersecurity board committees, appoint directors with relevant expertise, ensure CISO reports to CEO or board, and document this governance in proxy statements and annual reports. Visible board involvement signals strategic prioritization and executive accountability, building trust even without detailed technical disclosures.

Emphasize Proactive Investment. Communicate ongoing security enhancements before incidents occur. Investors view proactive investment as prudent risk management but question reactive spending after breaches. When incidents happen, frame response as accelerating existing roadmaps rather than implying previous inadequacy. Frame security improvements as continuous enhancement programs rather than incident-driven reactions.

Leverage Third-Party Validation with Context. While certifications provide independent verification, explain their meaning in plain language. Rather than merely citing "ISO 27001 certification," explain what independent audits verify and why it matters. Name respected assessment firms (e.g., Mandiant) to enable verification. However, recognize certifications supplement rather than substitute for substantive security practices.

Master Crisis Communication. When breaches occur, prioritize speed, transparency, specificity, and action-orientation. Disclose promptly with initial assessments rather than waiting for complete investigations. Provide specific incident details: affected systems, data compromised, timeline, root causes, and remediation actions. Structure communications around: (1) what happened, (2) what we're doing, (3) how we're preventing recurrence, and (4) how we're protecting stakeholders. Consider leadership accountability signals when breaches reveal fundamental governance failures.

Maintain Ongoing Communication. Include cybersecurity updates in annual reports describing program enhancements, governance evolution, and technology investments. Consider separate annual cybersecurity reports for security-focused investors. Develop accessible metrics showing security posture trends over time, enabling investors to assess whether risk profiles are improving or deteriorating.

For Regulators and Policymakers

Balance Standardization with Flexibility: Establish minimum disclosure standards covering governance structures, investment trends, incident histories, and third-party validations while allowing companies to provide additional detail matching their risk profiles. Standardized disclosures enable comparison while accommodating industry differences.

Adopt Two-Tier Disclosure Frameworks: Require summary disclosures accessible to general investors alongside detailed technical appendices for expert evaluation, similar to financial statement presentation combining numbers with management discussion and analysis.

Enhance Investor Education: Develop educational materials explaining how to evaluate governance signals, certification meanings, and red flags (delayed disclosure, vague communications, reactive investment) versus green flags (prompt transparency, specific claims, visible governance, proactive investment).

Consider Mandatory Third-Party Ratings: Explore security rating requirements analogous to credit ratings, enabling systematic comparison through expert assessments supplementing company self-disclosures. Pilot programs or voluntary safe harbor provisions could precede universal mandates.

For Security Practitioners

Frame Security as Business Enabler: Communicate investments as enabling digital transformation, customer trust, and competitive differentiation rather than merely defensive expenses. Quantify returns through avoided breach costs, reduced insurance premiums, and customer retention benefits. This value-oriented framing facilitates executive buy-in and strategic prioritization.

Prioritize Visible Governance. Establish board-level reporting mechanisms, clear accountability structures, and regular executive attention documented in governance materials. When communicating with non-technical audiences, emphasize governance, accountability, and strategic alignment rather than technical implementation details. Translate security achievements into business terms (protecting customer data, ensuring operational continuity, maintaining compliance) rather than technical jargon.

Future Research Directions

Future research should quantify how disclosure credibility, governance visibility, and source trust affect investment intent and required returns among retail investors. Experimental or conjoint designs grounded in this study's model (disclosures → risk perception → investment choices) would enable causal inference.

Randomized tests of disclosure formats could identify effects of incident-first action-oriented updates versus promotional releases or third-party-validated summaries on trust and investment willingness. Process-tracing studies should examine how investors sequence and weight multiple sources—news, filings, incident notices, certifications—when verifying cybersecurity claims under time pressure.

Segmented analyses comparing novice and experienced investors, or those with differing technical familiarity, can reveal where sensitivities to cyber signals diverge and which governance artifacts (oversight committees, compliance programs, tested incident response plans) most effectively reduce perceived risk and enhance investment confidence.

Theoretical Implications

This study extends Signaling Theory (Spence, 1973) by revealing that signal effectiveness depends on audience sophistication. Retail investors rely heavily on independently verifiable signals like third-party certifications and regulatory filings, while the same disclosure may appear as jargon to non-experts. This highlights the importance of signal translation and accessibility in information asymmetry contexts.

The findings confirm Prospect Theory (Kahneman & Tversky, 1979) in cybersecurity contexts while revealing boundary conditions. Loss aversion significantly influences investor responses, but framing effects can moderate this impact. Action-oriented disclosures emphasizing response and learning reduce negative reactions compared to incident-focused communications, demonstrating that framing can shift reference points and alter loss-gain asymmetry.

The research contributes to Information Asymmetry Theory (Akerlof, 1970) by identifying systematic heuristics investors employ: favoring board-level governance visibility, relying on third-party certifications, and using prompt disclosure as a management competence proxy. However, these strategies carry risks as investors may conflate governance theater with actual capability.

Finally, this study demonstrates that investment decisions reflect simultaneously rational information processing (Signaling Theory), psychological biases (Prospect Theory), information constraints

(Information Asymmetry Theory), relational considerations (Stakeholder Theory), and trust dynamics (Trust and Credibility Theory). Multi-theoretical frameworks provide more complete understanding than single perspectives alone.

Practical Implications

For retail investors, prioritize companies with visible board-level cybersecurity governance rather than evaluating technical measures directly. Seek prompt transparent disclosure, focus on response quality after incidents, use third-party certifications as supplementary verification, and diversify information sources while treating social media skeptically.

For financial advisors, integrate cybersecurity into standard analysis frameworks and educate clients about cyber as financial risk. Develop simplified frameworks for evaluating governance signals and help clients distinguish legitimate concerns from market overreactions. Monitor disclosure quality across portfolios as it predicts future governance effectiveness.

For educational institutions, incorporate cybersecurity risk assessment into investment courses and teach recognition of credible versus non-credible signals. Address psychological aspects including loss aversion and recency bias. Given that personal identity theft experiences affect investor trust (Uddin et al., 2020), help investors separate personal experiences from systematic evaluation.

For investment platforms, integrate cybersecurity indicators into company profiles with standardized metrics on disclosure timeliness, governance structure, and incident history. Develop simplified risk dashboards and implement alert systems for portfolio-affecting events. Facilitate peer learning communities where investors share evaluation experiences.

Recommendations

Companies should establish dedicated cybersecurity disclosure strategies as strategic priorities. Develop annual cybersecurity reports with specific metrics including budget percentages, personnel qualifications, assessment frequency, and security posture trends. Implement proactive communication rhythms and prioritize immediate transparent disclosure when incidents occur. Appoint board members with cybersecurity expertise visible in proxy materials.

Regulators should develop standardized disclosure frameworks specifying minimum requirements for governance, investments, incidents, and validations while allowing industry flexibility. Mandate prompt breach disclosure and adopt two-tier approaches with executive summaries for general investors and technical appendices for experts. Invest in investor education explaining evaluation methods and certification meanings.

Academic researchers should investigate perceptions across different market conditions and contexts to assess generalizability. Conduct experimental studies testing disclosure formats, timing, and content effects on trust and decisions. Develop validated instruments for measuring cybersecurity risk perception and examine how perceptions evolve over time. Comparative international research could reveal cultural factors affecting risk perception.

Investment platforms should display governance indicators alongside financial metrics and develop customizable alert systems. Create educational content in investment terms using concrete examples. Partner with cybersecurity rating agencies to provide expert assessments previously available only to institutional investors, improving retail investor capability.

REFERENCES

Akerlof, G. A. (1970). The market for "Lemons": Quality uncertainty and the market mechanism. *The Quarterly Journal of Economics*, *84*(3), 488–500. DOI: 10.2307/1879431

Al-Mohareb, M. (2025). The impact of cyber governance quality on dividend policy in mitigating cybersecurity breaches. *Risks*, *13*(2), 34. DOI: 10.3390/risks13020034

Barber, B. M., & Odean, T. (2001). Boys will be boys: Gender, overconfidence, and common stock investment. *The Quarterly Journal of Economics*, *116*(1), 261–292. DOI: 10.1162/003355301556400

Bouveret, A. (2018). Cyber risk for the financial sector: A framework for quantitative assessment. *IMF Working Paper*, *18*(143), 1–37. DOI: 10.5089/9781484360750.001

Braun, V., & Clarke, V. (2006). Using thematic analysis in psychology. *Qualitative Research in Psychology*, *3*(2), 77–101. DOI: 10.1191/1478088706qp063oa

Cavusoglu, H., Mishra, B., & Raghunathan, S. (2004). The effect of internet security breach announcements on market value: Capital market reactions for breached firms and internet security developers. *International Journal of Electronic Commerce*, *9*(1), 70–104. DOI: 10.1080/10864415.2004.11044320

Celeny, D., Maréchal, L., Rousselot, E., Mermoud, A., & Humbert, M. (2024). Prioritizing investments in cybersecurity: Empirical evidence from an event study on the determinants of cyberattack costs. SSRN Electronic Journal. DOI: 10.2139/ssrn.4717020

Cheng, X., Hsu, C., & Wang, T. (2022). Talk too much? The impact of cybersecurity disclosures on investment decisions. *Communications of the Association for Information Systems*, *50*(1), 481–485. DOI: 10.17705/1CAIS.05022

Hammouchi, H., Cherqi, O., Mezzour, G., Ghogho, M., & El Koutbi, M. (2019). Digging deeper into data breaches: An exploratory data analysis of hacking breaches over time. *Procedia Computer Science*, *151*, 1008–1015. DOI: 10.1016/j.procs.2019.04.141

Kafi, M. A., & Akter, N. (2023). Securing financial information in the digital realm: Case studies in cybersecurity for accounting data protection. *American Journal of Trade and Policy*, *10*(1), 15–26. DOI: 10.18034/ajtp.v10i1.659

Kahneman, D., & Tversky, A. (1979). Prospect theory: An analysis of decision under risk. *Econometrica*, *47*(2), 263–291. DOI: 10.2307/1914185

Kark, K. (2018, March 11). IT spending: From value preservation to value creation. WSJ CIO. https://deloitte.wsj.com/cio/it-spending-from-value-preservation-to-value-creation-1520830927

Khan, S., Kabanov, I., Hua, Y., & Madnick, S. (2022). A systematic analysis of the Capital One data breach: Critical lessons learned. *ACM Transactions on Privacy and Security*, *26*(1), 3. Advance online publication. DOI: 10.1145/3546068

Liu, C., & Babar, M. A. (2024). Corporate cybersecurity risk and data breaches: A systematic review of empirical research. *Australian Journal of Management*, *49*(1), 31–62. DOI: 10.1177/03128962241293658

Plachkinova, M., & Maurer, C. (2018). Teaching case: Security breach at Target. *Journal of Information Systems Education*, *29*(1), 11–20.

Rickett, L. K., & Smith, D. (2026). Major cybersecurity breaches: Shaping corporate cybersecurity policies and closing the gaps. *Journal of Corporate Accounting & Finance*, jcaf.70032. Advance online publication. DOI: 10.1002/jcaf.70032

Shaikh, F. A., & Siponen, M. (2023). Organizational learning from cybersecurity performance: Effects on cybersecurity investment decisions. *Information Systems Frontiers*, *26*(3), 1109–1120. DOI: 10.1007/s10796-023-10404-7

Shaker, A. S., Al-Shiblawi, G. A., Union, A. H., & Hameed, S. (2023). The role of information technology governance on enhancing cybersecurity and its reflection on investor confidence. *International Journal of Professional Business Review*, *8*(6), e01605. DOI: 10.26668/businessreview/2023.v8i6.1605

Spence, M. (1973). Job market signaling. *The Quarterly Journal of Economics*, *87*(3), 355–374. DOI: 10.2307/1882010

Strupczewski, G. (2021). Defining cyber risk. *Safety Science*, *135*, 105143. DOI: 10.1016/j.ssci.2020.105143

Uddin, M. H., Ali, M. H., & Hassan, M. K. (2020). Cybersecurity hazards and financial system vulnerability: A synthesis of literature. *Risk Management*, *22*(3), 239–309. DOI: 10.1057/s41283-020-00063-2

Yang, L., Lau, L., & Gan, H. (2020). Investors' perceptions of the cybersecurity risk management reporting framework. *International Journal of Accounting & Information Management*, *28*(1), 167–183. DOI: 10.1108/IJAIM-02-2019-0022

KEY TERMS AND DEFINITIONS

Cybersecurity Risk: The potential for loss or harm from unauthorized access, use, disclosure, disruption, modification, or destruction of information systems and data (Strupczewski, 2021). Encompasses technical vulnerabilities, human factors, organizational weaknesses, and external threats. In investment contexts, represents the possibility that cyber incidents will cause financial losses, reputational damage, operational disruptions, regulatory penalties, or litigation affecting valuation and returns.

Disclosure Credibility: The degree to which disclosed information is perceived as truthful, accurate, complete, and reliable. Depends on specificity, timeliness, transparency, consistency, and independence. Investors distinguish credible disclosures from marketing rhetoric based on these attributes. Mediates the relationship between cybersecurity events and investor responses.

Governance Visibility: The extent to which governance structures, oversight mechanisms, and accountability systems for cybersecurity risk management are apparent to external stakeholders. Includes board-level committees, director expertise in proxy materials, CISO reporting structure, and documented board reporting. Significantly enhances investor confidence as it signals management commitment and strategic prioritization.

Information Asymmetry: A situation where one party possesses superior information compared to another, creating market inefficiencies, adverse selection, and moral hazard (Akerlof, 1970). Companies have detailed knowledge of vulnerabilities and risk management that investors cannot observe. Explains why investors demand independent verification and why disclosure quality matters for market efficiency.

Prospect Theory: A behavioral economics theory describing decision-making under risk and uncertainty (Kahneman & Tversky, 1979). Demonstrates systematic deviations from rationality including loss aversion, reference dependence, and probability weighting. Predicts investors are more sensitive to breach losses than security improvement gains and evaluate companies relative to peers rather than absolute levels.

Retail Investor: An individual investing in securities for personal accounts without professional intermediaries managing portfolios. Unlike institutional investors with proprietary research and sophisticated models, retail investors rely on publicly available information and personal judgment. Collectively hold approximately 25-30% of U.S. equity trading volume (Kafi & Akter, 2023).

Signaling Theory: A framework explaining how parties communicate unobservable qualities through observable indicators when information asymmetry exists (Spence, 1973). Companies convey information about management quality, financial health, or security posture through costly signals including disclosures, certifications, and governance structures. Credible signals are those poor-quality firms cannot easily replicate.

APPENDIX A: SURVEY QUESTIONNAIRE

Retail Investor Cybersecurity Perceptions Survey

Purpose: This survey investigates how retail investors perceive and respond to cybersecurity risks when making investment decisions.
Estimated Time: 7-10 minutes
Confidentiality: All responses are anonymous and will be used for research purposes only.

Section 1: Consent And Screening

Q1. Consent: I am 18+ and agree to take part.

- Yes
- No

(If "No," survey ends)
Q2. Do you currently invest in publicly listed companies (through a broker or app)?

- Yes
- No

(If "No," survey ends)

Section 2: Investment Profile

Q3. Your usual holding period (pick closest):

- Days
- Weeks
- Months
- Years

Q4. Your investing style (select all that apply):

- Buy-and-hold
- Swing/position
- Day trading
- Value
- Growth
- Momentum
- Income/dividend

Q5. Trading frequency:

- <1 trade/month
- 1-3 trades/month
- 1-2 trades/week
- 3+ trades/week

Q6. Cybersecurity familiarity:

- Beginner
- Intermediate
- Advanced
- Work in cybersecurity

Section 3: Cybersecurity Risk Perception

Table 1. **Q7. How important are the items below?** *(1 = Not important, 5 = Extremely important)*

Risk Dimension	**1**	**2**	**3**	**4**	**5**
Overall cybersecurity risk management					
Risk of ransomware (malware that locks systems for payment)					
Third-party/vendor risk (suppliers/partners causing risk)					
Data breach / data exfiltration (customer data taken)					
Operational downtime (outage interrupts business)					
Regulatory/legal exposure (fines/lawsuits after incidents)					

Q8. Have you ever avoided buying or sold a stock mainly due to cybersecurity concerns?

- Yes
- No

Q9. If yes, briefly why? (optional)
[Open text response field]

Section 4: Information Sources And Trust

Q10. Which sources do you use for cyber information? (select all that apply)

- Company filings (10-K/20-F risk factors)
- Company incident notices / press releases
- Earnings calls / investor days

- Third-party certifications (e.g., SOC 2, ISO 27001)
- News outlets / analyst reports
- Social media / forums

Q11. Which do you trust most? (pick up to 2)
[Open text response field]
Q12. Which do you trust least? (pick up to 2)
[Open text response field]

Section 5: Disclosure Credibility

Table 2. **Q13. Please indicate your agreement** *(1 = Strongly disagree, 5 = Strongly agree)*

Statement	1	2	3	4	5
I look at cybersecurity info in 10-K/20-F or similar filings.					
I trust companies more when they openly disclose cyber incidents.					
The quality and timing of breach disclosures affect my decisions.					
Board-level oversight of cybersecurity increases my confidence.					

Table 3. **Q14. How credible are the following signals?** *(1 = Not credible, 5 = Highly credible)*

Signal	1	2	3	4	5
SOC 2 Type II report (external audit of controls over time)					
ISO 27001 certification (meets a security standard)					
A dedicated board risk/cyber committee					
Clear, regular breach notifications					
Independent penetration-test summaries					

Q15. In a few words: What makes a disclosure feel like marketing vs a credible signal?
[Open text response field]

Section 6: Risk Tolerance And Behavioral Responses

Table 4. **Q16. Please indicate your agreement** *(1 = Strongly disagree, 5 = Strongly agree)*

Statement	1	2	3	4	5
I would accept lower expected returns for a company I judge to be more cyber-resilient.					
I require higher expected returns to hold companies with higher cyber risk.					
Fear of losses from cyber incidents affects my position size.					

Q17. Imagine two similar firms, but one has higher cyber risk. Would you demand a higher expected return to hold it?

- No
- Yes, by ~1-2%
- Yes, by ~3-4%
- Yes, by ≥5%
- Not sure

Q18. In the past 12 months, did cyber news make you change an investment position?

- Yes
- No

Q19. If yes, what did you do?

- Bought
- Sold/Reduced
- Held/No change

Section 7: Breach Response Evaluation

Table 5. **Q20. When a company you follow reports a breach, how likely are you to...** *(1 = Very unlikely, 5 = Very likely)*

Action	1	2	3	4	5
Reduce or exit the position immediately					
Wait for the company's disclosure/remediation details					
Add on weakness if response seems strong					

Q21. Which 3 factors most influence your reaction? (pick up to 3)

- Severity of the incident
- Type of data affected
- Operational downtime/business impact
- Regulatory/legal exposure
- Speed & quality of disclosure
- Leadership/accountability changes
- Independent audit/attestation outcome

Q22. After a breach, which actions would restore your confidence? (select all that apply)

- Leadership/accountability changes
- Increased security investment with specifics
- Third-party assessments (e.g., SOC 2 Type II)
- Clear timelines and progress updates
- Customer protection (credits, monitoring)

Q23. Rank these by importance *(drag to rank: 1 = most, 6 = least)*

- Ransomware exposure
- Third-party/vendor risk
- Data breach / data exfiltration
- Operational downtime risk
- Regulatory/legal exposure
- Business email compromise / fraud risk

Section 8: Resilience Demonstration (Qualitative)

Q24. In your own words: How should companies demonstrate cyber resilience to investors?
[Open text response field]
Q25. Anything else to share about cybersecurity and investing?
[Open text response field]

Section 9: Demographics

Q26. Age:

- 18-24
- 25-34
- 35-44
- 45-54
- 55-64
- 65+
- Prefer not to say

Q27. Country/State:
[Open text response field]
Q28. Education:

- High school
- Some college
- Bachelor's
- Master's
- Doctorate
- Other/Prefer not to say

End Of Survey

Thank you for participating in this research!

Your responses will help improve understanding of how retail investors evaluate cybersecurity risks and inform better corporate disclosure practices.

If you have questions about this research, please contact Lawrence Iweriebor at leiweriebor@yahoo.com

Chapter 15
Artificial Intelligence and ISO 9001-2026:
Transforming Quality Management Systems - Challenges, Opportunities, and Future Directions

Omar A. Guirette-Barbosa
http://orcid.org/0000-0003-1336-9475
Universidad Politécnica de Zacatecas, Mexico & Broward International University, Mexico

Gabriela R. Romo-Flores
http://orcid.org/0009-0008-5875-2770
Universidad Autónoma de Zacatecas, Mexico

José de Jesús Reyes-Sánchez
http://orcid.org/0000-0002-3866-2363
Instituto Tecnológico de Fresnillo, Mexico

Martha Angélica Ramírez-Salazar
http://orcid.org/0000-0001-6536-4161
Universidad Politécnica de Zacatecas, Mexico

ABSTRACT

The ISO 9001 standard is the most widely used quality management standard globally, offering a framework for continuous improvement and customer satisfaction. The upcoming update, ISO 9001:2026, incorporates a renewed emphasis on digital transformation, where Artificial Intelligence (AI) is presented as a strategic enabler capable of redefining process, risk and stakeholder relationship management. However, there is a considerable gap in literature and practice regarding the effective integration of AI into certified quality management systems. The purpose of this chapter is to examine the interaction between ISO 9001:2026 and Artificial Intelligence, identifying the main challenges and opportunities arising from this convergence. Likewise, conceptual and practical guidelines are proposed to guide its

DOI: 10.4018/979-8-3373-4027-2.ch015

implementation in different aspects of a quality management system. The discussion is supported by a documentary review of the evolution of the standard and current applications of AI, complemented by a prospective analysis of the requirements of the 2026 version.

1. INTRODUCTION

ISO 9001 has been recognized for more than three decades as the international reference standard for quality management systems. According to the International Organization for Standardization (ISO, 2022), it has been adopted by more than 1.2 million organizations in 178 countries. The primary objective of the standard has been to ensure process consistency, increase stakeholder trust, and establish a common framework for continuous improvement (Bravim et al., 2020; Bravi & Murmura, 2021). However, the rapid changes occurring in the digital economy, the globalization of markets, and the incorporation of disruptive technologies are radically transforming the concept of quality in the third decade of the twenty-first century. These dynamics generate new demands for the planned revision of the standard in 2026 (Lazibat & Damić, 2022; Avruscio et al., 2022; Pylypchuk & Holitsyn, 2025).

Digitalization and the adoption of emerging technologies are decisive factors in this scenario. Among them, Artificial Intelligence (AI) has established itself as a cross-cutting driver of innovation. Recent reports estimate that more than 50% of global organizations are experimenting with AI in critical processes (Gartner, 2023), while consulting firms such as McKinsey (2022) indicate that its adoption could add up to $13 trillion to global GDP by 2030. These figures highlight both the magnitude of the phenomenon and the urgency of analyzing how AI will be integrated into regulatory frameworks such as ISO 9001:2026 (Pereira et al., 2021; Ahmed & Ruth, 2024).

The incorporation of AI into quality management systems, like any innovation, presents both opportunities and risks. On the one hand, the ability to process large volumes of data in real time strengthens evidence-based decision-making, aligning with one of the guiding principles of the standard (Tahrir & Barus, 2023). On the other hand, concerns arise regarding algorithmic transparency, data reliability, inherent biases, and the ethical implications of delegating critical decisions to intelligent systems (Anttila & Jussila, 2021; Bravi & Murmura, 2021). This regulatory gap constitutes a research gap: the absence of clear guidelines for the responsible integration of AI in certified QMS.

This analysis must also be framed within broader dynamics. The COVID-19 pandemic accelerated organizational digitalization, exposing vulnerabilities in the resilience of quality systems (Ikram et al., 2021; Zineb et al., 2022). At the same time, international regulations are advancing around the ethical use of AI, with initiatives such as the European Union's Artificial Intelligence Act (2023), which establishes regulatory precedents that organizations cannot ignore (Kılıç, 2021). These trends reinforce the urgency of anticipating how ISO 9001:2026 will incorporate clear guidelines for the use of AI (Ferouali, 2021).

To better understand this convergence, it is useful to examine specific sectors where AI is already generating measurable impacts. In manufacturing, computer vision applied to quality control has reduced defects by up to 30% in the automotive industry (Sarfraz et al., 2022). In healthcare, deep learning algorithms have optimized diagnostic processes with accuracy levels comparable to clinical experts (Ahmad et al., 2022). In financial services, AI is used for automated audits and fraud detection, thereby strengthening transparency and reducing operational risks (Herath & Gamlath, 2025). These examples illustrate AI's transformative potential and the need to align this potential with standardized regulatory frameworks such as ISO 9001.

In academia, recent literature highlights a growing consensus on the need to integrate ethical governance guidelines into the application of AI for quality management (Lopez & Alcaide, 2020; Moghaddasi, 2021). However, few studies have directly examined the intersection between AI and ISO 9001, confirming a theoretical and practical gap in this field (Yakushova et al., 2022). This lack, however, represents a strategic opportunity for this chapter, as it provides an interpretative framework that connects technological advances with the demands of management systems.

The purpose of this introduction is to situate the reader in the context of change that gives rise to ISO 9001:2026, explicitly emphasizing its convergence with Artificial Intelligence as one of the most significant challenges for quality management in the coming decades. By relying on recent literature and verifiable trends, the conceptual bases for subsequent analysis are established. This chapter not only identifies the academic and practical gap but also offers a framework to guide researchers, academics, and practitioners in anticipating the challenges and opportunities arising from the incorporation of AI into quality management systems. In this way, the scientific, practical, and social relevance of addressing this convergence at this historical moment is underlined.

2. STATEMENT OF THE PROBLEM

The rapid advancement of Artificial Intelligence (AI) has transformed multiple productive sectors; however, its integration into quality management systems under the ISO 9001 standard remains incipient and lacks clear guidelines. Although the current version of ISO 9001 promotes evidence-based decision-making and risk management, it does not explicitly consider the role of intelligent technologies in these processes. This omission creates a regulatory gap that becomes critical in view of the imminent publication of ISO 9001:2026, which must respond to the challenges of digitalization and the growing expectations of transparency, traceability, and trust.

Recent studies indicate that 45% of manufacturing companies implementing AI solutions in quality control reported initial failures due to the absence of standardized protocols (Minglana et al., 2021). Similarly, an Accenture (2022) report shows that 37% of managers in ISO 9001-certified organizations acknowledge difficulties aligning their management systems with emerging AI applications. These challenges generate uncertainty in audit and recertification processes (Reyes & Barillo, 2024; Jeremić & Luka, 2024). Such data demonstrate that the problem is not only theoretical but also has practical and measurable consequences (Li & Goel, 2025; Ivakhnenkov, 2023).

Academic literature highlights potential benefits of AI in automated internal audits, real-time process control, and predictive risk analytics (Onwubuariri et al., 2024; Adelakun, 2022). However, significant doubts remain regarding how to ensure data reliability, avoid algorithmic bias, and justify automated decisions (Murikah et al., 2024; Li & Goel, 2025). Empirical studies on the adoption of AI in quality management systems are still limited, and no consensus exists on integrative models that connect these technologies with the regulatory principles of ISO 9001 (Minglana et al., 2021). This lack of clarity represents a critical problem for both academic and professional communities.

In practical terms, the problem translates into significant risks. Organizations implementing AI without a regulatory framework may face inconsistent audits, loss of customer and supplier trust, and failures in the traceability of critical information. Documented cases of algorithmic bias in procurement systems (Raghavan et al., 2020) or failures in automated control systems in the manufacturing industry (Zhang, 2024) demonstrate that these risks are tangible rather than hypothetical. In fact, the International Labour

Organization (ILO, 2021) warns that the lack of clear guidelines on AI in industrial processes could increase regulatory non-compliance incidents in highly digitized environments by up to 20%.

From an academic perspective, the lack of systematic research on the convergence between AI and ISO 9001 creates a theoretical gap that limits knowledge advancement (Sankaran, 2025). Although studies exist on AI applied to operations management, research has not yet analyzed how these advances directly impact quality regulatory requirements. This mismatch between technological practice and international standards lies at the core of the problem addressed in this chapter.

In summary, the central issue is the lack of clarity, guidelines, and concrete proposals for the responsible incorporation of AI into QMS under ISO 9001:2026. Addressing this gap has theoretical, practical, and social implications: it affects the credibility of quality systems, organizational competitiveness, and consumer confidence in an increasingly digitized global environment. Defining this problem is therefore the essential starting point for formulating research questions and methodological proposals aimed at bridging this gap in both knowledge and practice.

3. PURPOSE/IMPORTANCE

The purpose of this study is to clarify and substantiate the importance of analyzing the convergence between Artificial Intelligence (AI) and the upcoming ISO 9001:2026 standard. The academic, professional, and practical relevance of this work derives from three main factors: the growing penetration of AI in strategic sectors, the absence of specific regulatory guidelines for its application in quality management systems (QMS), and the imminent revision of a standard that affects more than one million organizations worldwide.

First, from an academic perspective, this chapter seeks to fill a clear gap in the literature. Although extensive research exists on AI applications in operations, manufacturing, and service management, few studies focus directly on the relationship between AI and quality management standards (Minglana et al., 2021). The importance of this analysis lies in the fact that ISO 9001 is not only a technical framework but also a global common language for quality management. Understanding how AI is integrated into this standard expands the frontier of knowledge on QMS digitalization and provides valuable inputs for future research (Johannesen et al., 2020).

Second, professional relevance is linked to the immediate challenges organizations face in certification, auditing, and continuous improvement processes. According to Gartner (2023), more than half of global companies are experimenting with AI yet lack clear guidelines for demonstrating compliance in ISO audit contexts. A Deloitte (2022) study further indicates that 40% of surveyed firms in regulated sectors have postponed AI integration in key processes for fear of failing to meet quality requirements. Therefore, this study aims to provide conceptual and practical clarity to support decision-making by managers, quality leaders, and internal auditors, offering frameworks that reduce uncertainty in AI integration (Rustam & Widiastutik, 2024; Luna-Pérez et al., 2023).

Third, the social and economic importance of this issue is undeniable. AI has the potential to transform supply chains, healthcare services, transportation, and education, but it can also exacerbate inequalities and risks if applied without proper controls. In healthcare, for example, implementation in clinical diagnosis has reduced patient care time by up to 25%, yet controversies have arisen when algorithms exhibit racial or gender bias (Esteva et al., 2019). In manufacturing, automotive companies report productivity increases of up to 15% thanks to computer vision systems (Zhang et al., 2021), highlighting not only the potential but also the need for clear regulation (Wolniak, 2021).

This chapter also emphasizes the urgency of establishing clear governance frameworks. Regulatory initiatives such as the European Union's Artificial Intelligence Act show that the discussion has transcended the technical domain and has become a public policy issue. Ignoring the importance of integrating these debates into ISO 9001 could place organizations at a disadvantage considering emerging international regulations. The World Bank (2022) warns that the absence of AI governance standards could result in global efficiency losses of up to $3 trillion over the next decade, adding further pressure to the demand for clear guidelines (Benraouane, 2024).

In conclusion, the importance of this study lies in its ability to serve as a bridge between academia and professional practice. By providing an analysis grounded in recent literature and practical examples, it aims to become a reference point for researchers, practitioners, and policymakers interested in anticipating the changes that the convergence of AI and ISO 9001:2026 will bring. Thus, the study not only justifies its relevance but also underscores its added value to the field of quality management in the digital age.

4. METHODOLOGY

4.1 Methodology and nature of the study

This research adopts a qualitative approach with exploratory and comparative components, complemented by elements of systematic review and case studies. The choice of a qualitative design is justified by the emerging nature of the phenomenon, as the interaction between Artificial Intelligence (AI) and ISO 9001:2026 still lacks robust and standardized empirical frameworks. A strictly quantitative approach would be insufficient, since consolidated statistical series do not yet exist to numerically model the impact of these regulatory transformations.

The methodological approach is further justified from an interpretive epistemological perspective, which seeks to understand meanings, practices, and perceptions regarding the integration of AI into quality management systems. Qualitative orientation is combined with documentary and comparative analysis techniques to ensure a balance between academic rigor and practical relevance.

For data collection, three main strategies are used:

- Systematic literature review: Articles from indexed journals, technical documents, and institutional reports from organizations such as ISO, IEEE, and OECD are analyzed, prioritizing publications from the last five years.
- Normative-comparative analysis: ISO 9001:2015 guidelines are compared with drafts and technical discussions anticipating the changes in ISO 9001:2026, identifying areas where AI plays a significant role.
- Case studies: Organizations pioneering AI in quality assurance processes are selected to observe patterns, best practices, and challenges.

Information analysis is conducted through source triangulation to strengthen the validity of findings. This approach combines empirical evidence, regulatory frameworks, and perceptions collected from case studies.

4.2 Scope of the study

The scope of this research is defined across three dimensions: population, temporal, and thematic.

- Population: The study focuses on industrial and service organizations that have begun integrating AI into quality management, without restricting the analysis to a specific sector. This allows for the identification of cross-cutting patterns beyond individual industries.
- Temporal: The analysis covers the period 2020–2025, emphasizing the transition toward the publication of ISO 9001:2026. This time frame captures both immediate background and normative projections.
- Thematic: The research examines the relationship between ISO 9001 and AI, excluding other standards (e.g., ISO 14001 or ISO 45001) and avoiding technical discussions on specific AI algorithms.

Among the methodological limitations are the lack of global quantitative databases on AI implementation in quality management, reliance on documentary information in some cases, and the inability to generalize findings uniformly across all sectors. Ethical and logistical constraints are also acknowledged, as some organizations may restrict access to sensitive AI-related information. Despite these restrictions, the study is designed to provide an analytical and strategic perspective, useful for both academics and quality management professionals preparing their organizations for upcoming regulatory challenges

5. THEORETICAL FRAMEWORK

5.1 Conceptual foundations of quality

The concept of quality has evolved over recent decades, shifting from a notion associated merely with compliance with technical specifications to a comprehensive approach to organizational management. Traditionally, quality was understood as the absence of defects or conformity with established standards. However, with the development of management theories and the contributions of specialists such as Deming, Juran, and Crosby, quality began to be conceived as a continuous improvement process involving the entire organization, from top management to the operational level.

In this sense, quality ceased to be a static attribute, becoming a dynamic system of value generation. Customer orientation, process efficiency and continuous improvement have been consolidated as central axes of contemporary quality models. These transformations have been driven by globalization, the opening of markets, digitalization, and the growing demand of consumers, who no longer agree with compliant products, but expect innovative and safe experiences and solutions (Kiarie, 2020).

5.2 ISO 9001 as a global benchmark

ISO 9001 represents one of the most influential frameworks in quality management. Since its first edition in 1987, it has become an international standard that defines the requirements for establishing, implementing, maintaining, and improving a quality management system (QMS). Its flexible nature, applicable to any type of organization regardless of size, sector, or geographical location, has enabled millions of companies worldwide to adopt it (Ćwiklicki et al., 2020).

The essence of ISO 9001 lies in the Plan-Do-Check-Act (PDCA) cycle, which structures management around continuous improvement. It also incorporates fundamental principles such as customer orientation, organizational leadership, employee engagement, process-based management, evidence-based decision-making, and stakeholder relationship management.

The impact of the standard has been significant: it not only establishes a technical framework but also builds confidence in international markets, enhances organizational competitiveness, and promotes a corporate culture oriented toward excellence (Gamit et al., 2024). However, the current challenge lies in its ability to adapt to disruptive environments, where rapid technological change and global uncertainty demand new responses (Maqbool, 2023).

5.3 Artificial Intelligence: fundamentals and application in management

Artificial Intelligence (AI) is one of the most innovative technologies of the 21st century, and its influence on organizational management is increasingly evident. Broadly defined, AI refers to the ability of computer systems to perform tasks that typically require human intelligence, such as pattern recognition, learning, prediction, and decision-making.

In quality management, AI has become a strategic tool for optimizing processes, anticipating failures, improving traceability, and ensuring efficiency. Machine learning algorithms, neural networks, and predictive models allow managers to analyze large volumes of data in real time, identify hidden trends, and generate actionable insights that would otherwise be inaccessible (Chiarini & Cherrafi, 2023).

Examples include the use of AI in automated product inspection through computer vision, early detection of deviations in manufacturing processes, demand forecasting with advanced statistical models, and the personalization of services in digital environments. These applications not only reduce costs and cycle times but also strengthen customer confidence in products and services (Muruganandham et al., 2022).

5.4 Integration of ISO 9001 and Artificial Intelligence

The convergence of ISO 9001 and AI marks a new horizon for quality management. While the standard provides a structured and widely recognized regulatory framework, AI delivers the technical capabilities required to transform data into knowledge and knowledge into strategic decisions.

AI is also integrated into each stage of the continuous improvement cycle (PDCA), a pillar of quality management. In the Planning (P) phase, algorithms can analyze data to identify opportunities for improvement. In the Do (D) phase, automate tasks, which reduces errors and increases efficiency. In the Verify phase (C), it allows continuous monitoring of processes. Finally, in the Act phase (A), it facilitates the analysis of the root cause of non-conformities (Gueorguiev, 2025).

Beyond technical aspects, this integration also implies a cultural shift within organizations. Employees must develop new digital skills, and organizational structures must adapt to fully exploit AI's potential (Matos et al., 2022). Thus, quality evolves from a reactive process to a proactive and intelligent system.

5.5 Systems theory as an integrative foundation

Systems theory, first proposed by Ludwig von Bertalanffy in the 1950s, argues that phenomena should be analyzed as interrelated wholes rather than the sum of their parts. This perspective is essential to understanding both quality and the role of AI in organizational processes.

In quality management, systems theory highlights that each process, department, or activity is interconnected, and changes in one component inevitably affect the others. ISO 9001 reflects this perspective by promoting a vision of organizations as a set of interrelated processes that must be managed in a coordinated manner to achieve consistent and sustainable outcomes (Anttila & Jussila, 2021).

AI also aligns naturally with systems theory, since it processes large volumes of data from multiple sources. By integrating dispersed information, AI identifies global patterns, detects bottlenecks, and optimizes entire value chains (Minglana et al., 2021). Rather than analyzing isolated elements, AI reveals systemic dynamics that may go unnoticed in partial evaluations (Somasundaram et al., 2020).

The convergence of ISO 9001, AI, and systems theory offers a robust framework that overcomes fragmented management views. For example, in a manufacturing system, a calibration failure in one machine not only disrupts production but also affects inventories, logistics, customer satisfaction, and organizational competitiveness. Under this logic, quality is best understood as the emerging result of a system in dynamic equilibrium, with AI acting as a catalyst for stability and adaptability (Muruganandham et al., 2022; Kowalczyk, 2024).

Finally, systems theory provides a holistic and ethical vision, emphasizing that organizations are part of broader social, economic, and environmental systems. Thus, the theoretical framework of this study is not limited to technical efficiency but also recognizes the interdependence between quality decisions, AI use, and their societal impact (Anttila & Jussila, 2021; Pylypchuk & Holitsyn, 2025).

5.6 Challenges and theoretical perspectives

From a theoretical standpoint, it is necessary to rethink the classic foundations of quality by incorporating emerging dimensions such as algorithmic ethics, digital governance, and technological sustainability. Academic research also faces the challenge of building models that integrate ISO 9001 requirements with the adaptive capabilities of AI, without losing sight of the human and social dimensions of organizations (Shoira Azimovna, 2024).

Within this framework, the analysis highlights the need to generate knowledge that bridges regulatory and technological perspectives. It explores how AI not only strengthens quality under ISO 9001 but also redefines management paradigms in the 21st century (Sadikin et al., 2022).

6. LITERATURE ANALYSIS / REVIEW

6.1. The New Quality Paradigm: ISO 9001:2026 and the Age of AI

The upcoming revision of ISO 9001 has generated great excitement in the quality management community. Although the publication was initially scheduled for the end of 2025, the date has been postponed and is now expected to be September 2026 (Majstorović & Babić, 2025). Work on such an update is underway with experts from more than 40 nations who have come together to address feedback on key issues. The decision to undertake an "early" review stems from the need for the standard to remain aligned with the "*evolving needs of organizations*" and address the "*current challenges*" of the business environment (Glogovac & Ruso, 2022).

It is expected to maintain the high-level structure (HLS), which will be updated to the Harmonized Structure (HS), which will ensure better alignment and a smoother transition for organizations that already have other management systems such as ISO 14001 and ISO 45001 in place. The key topics that are expected to be included or given greater emphasis are: resilience, supply chain management, change management, sustainability, ethics and integrity, as well as organizational knowledge (Glogovac & Ruso, 2020). A central theme in this revision is the integration of digital transformation and Industry 4.0, for which it is planned that the standard will include guidelines on the use of technologies such as AI, big data and advanced analytics (Chiarini & Cherrafi, 2023).

Although ISO 9001:2026 will not contain an explicit clause with the name "Artificial Intelligence" (as high-level ISO standards avoid prescribing specific technologies), it follows that it will act as a vehicle and an indispensable catalyst to meet the projected new requirements. For example, the standard will place a reinforced emphasis on risk management and resilience, concepts that in the modern environment are based on the ability to identify emerging threats and their potential impacts. This task is carried out more effectively and proactively with the support of AI-powered predictive analytics (Glogovac et al., 2022). The demand for greater attention to "organizational knowledge" is also directly related to AI's ability to process large volumes of unstructured data and extract valuable insights (Majstorović & Babić, 2025). Therefore, although it is not explicitly mentioned, it is presented as a functional requirement for organizations seeking to achieve the highest levels of compliance and excellence under the new standard.

6.2. AI as the Axis of the Transformation of QMS

The focus of ISO 9001 has been on data-driven quality and informed decision-making. The current standard, ISO 9001:2015, already requires the "analysis and evaluation" of data for fact-based decision-making, according to clause 9.1.3. The 2026 revision is expected to raise this requirement, requiring decisions to be increasingly based on "advanced evidence and analytics" (Georgyev, 2025). AI is critical to processing the vast amount of information, including the "petabytes of data" that organizations currently manage. AI technologies can identify hidden trends, correlations, and patterns in large data sets, something that traditional analytical methods cannot achieve (Andrianandrianina Johanesa et al., 2024).

Table 1. The PDCA Cycle

PDCA Phase	Traditional QMS Focus	AI-enabled Enhancement	Expected Benefit
Plan	Define quality objectives, risk assessment, process design	Predictive analytics for demand and defect forecasting; NLP for customer feedback analysis; simulation models for planning	Improved accuracy of risk-based thinking; proactive decision-making
Do	Execute processes, implement controls	Robotic Process Automation (RPA) for repetitive quality tasks; AI for supplier monitoring; computer vision for defect detection	Reduced manual workload; faster detection of nonconformities; supply chain resilience
Check	Monitor, measure, and audit performance	AI-driven anomaly detection; automated internal audits; LLM-assisted compliance documentation	Increased audit efficiency; reduced error rates; enhanced data-driven oversight
Act	Implement corrective actions and continuous improvement	Reinforcement learning to optimize corrective actions; AI dashboards for trend analysis; digital twins for process improvement	Accelerated continuous improvement; better resource allocation; measurable ROI

The goal of any QMS is to improve customer satisfaction. AI contributes to this goal indirectly and directly. Indirectly, it improves product quality through proactive fault detection and process optimization, resulting in fewer defects. Directly, you can analyze "social media and CRM sentiment" to measure "actual perception of the service" (Gaidhani et al., 2025). This offers a deeper, real-time understanding of customer satisfaction, going beyond the traditional survey methods used at the time of ISO 9001:2015. This is a clear example of how technology not only helps meet existing requirements but also redefines the way the goals of the standard are measured and achieved.

The table below (Table 2) details the strategic intersection points between the anticipated changes in ISO 9001:2026 and the capabilities of artificial intelligence.

Table 2.

New Approach or Advance Clause	ISO 9001:2015 Principle Underpinning It	AI Enabler	Benefits for the QMS
Increased Emphasis on Risk Management	Clause 6.1 Actions to Address Risks and Opportunities	Predictive Analytics and Emerging Threat Detection	Improving Operational Resilience and Strategic Decision-Making
Organizational Knowledge Management	Clause 7.1.6 Organizational Knowledge	Natural Language Processing (NLP) and Data Mining	Centralization and accessibility of corporate knowledge, facilitating business continuity
Data-driven Quality	Regulation 9.1.3 Analysis and Evaluation	*Big Data* and Advanced Analytics	More accurate decisions, identification of non-conformity patterns and process optimization
Quality Control in Production	Clause 8.5 Production and Provision of the Service	Machine Vision and *Machine Learning*	Real-time defect detection and reduced human error
Proactive Approach to Continuous Improvement	Clause 10.3 Continuous Improvement	Predictive Models for Fault Detection	Preventative intervention before problems occur, reducing costs and downtime

6.3 Strategic Applications of AI in Quality Management Systems

6.3.1 Document and Knowledge Management

ISO 9001:2015 requires organizations to maintain adequate and up to date "documented information" for their management system. The 2026 version is expected to delve into this aspect, with a "greater demand for capturing and managing organizational knowledge" (Majstorović & Babić, 2025). AI offers solutions to transform document management, which has traditionally been a time-consuming manual task.

By using technologies such as natural language processing (NLP) and chatbots, organizations can allow employees to "converse with documents" and conduct automated searches for specific procedures, policies, or records (Pereira et al., 2021). In addition, AI tools can extract data from unstructured documents, such as emails, contracts, and forms, ensuring consistency and accuracy in quality records (Vazirizade et al., 2020). Practical examples of this application include systems that analyze the content of emails to automatically route them, or classify and label documents based on their text, structure, and context, automating tasks that would otherwise require considerable manual effort (Almeida et al., 2021).

6.3.2 Quality Control and Non-Conformity Detection

ISO 9001 sets out requirements for the "monitoring and measurement" of processes to ensure their effectiveness (clause 9.1) and the "identification of root causes" of non-conformities (clause 10.2). AI offers a powerful set of tools to significantly improve these processes. One of the most prominent applications is computer vision, which is used to carry out in-line quality inspections (Parmar, 2022; Al-Salah et al., 2025). These systems, powered by deep learning algorithms, can accurately detect surface defects such as "scratches, cracks, or irregularities" in components, as well as verify the correct assembly and alignment of products. Examples in the automotive and food industry show how machine vision is used to inspect vehicle doors or sort fruits by size and color (Minglana-Tobias et al., 2021).

On the other hand, predictive models based on machine learning are critical to shift from a reactive to a proactive quality approach. These algorithms could analyze "historical and current data to predict future failures before they occur," allowing organizations to take preventative measures, reduce downtime, and decrease maintenance costs (Senanayake & Naveen, 2021; Al-Salah et al., 2025).

6.3.3 Intelligent and Predictive Internal Audits

Internal audits are a fundamental pillar of the QMS to assess compliance and effectiveness. With the increased emphasis on risk management and resilience in ISO 9001:2026, AI will transform audits from a manual process to an "advanced and strategic approach" (Wolniak, 2021; Levytska, 2024).

AI enables real-time monitoring of activities and transactions, making it easier to detect anomalies or non-compliant behaviors before the audit is conducted. In addition, by analyzing historical data, you can "determine critical areas" or high-risk areas for auditors to focus their efforts more efficiently (Kahyaoglu & Aksoy, 2021; Arinola & Olalekan, 2023). This predictive capability allows for a more proactive, risk-based approach, rather than a simple periodic compliance review.

AI can also automate repetitive tasks in the audit process, such as generating detailed reports, extracting data from scattered sources, and creating checklists. This frees up auditors to focus on higher-value tasks, such as evaluating complex findings and communicating strategic insights to senior management. The role of the auditor evolves from a simple compliance verifier to an expert in professional judgment who validates AI results, focusing on "human oversight" and continuous improvement of the QMS (Lenning & Gremyr, 2021; Walawalkar et al., 2024).

The table below (Table 3) details how AI can transform key quality processes.

Table 3.

QMS Process	Application of AI	Detailed Description of the Use Case	Benefit to the Organization	Reference to the Rule Clause
Quality Control	Machine Vision	AI camera systems that inspect products in real-time to detect surface defects, assembly errors, or mislabeling.	Increased efficiency in quality control, reduction of costs associated with reprocesses and reduction of defective products.	Regulation 8.6 Release of products and services
Internal Audit	Predictive Analytics	AI algorithms that analyze historical audit and non-conformance data to identify patterns and predict areas of greatest risk in the QMS.	Prioritization of audit efforts, focus on critical areas, and transition to a more proactive and risk-based approach.	Regulation 9.2 Internal audit
Document Management	Natural Language Processing (NLP)	*Chatbots* and virtual assistants that allow employees to search for and access specific procedures and records through natural language.	Reduction of search times, improvement in knowledge management and increase in operational efficiency.	Regulation 7.5 Documented information
Management of non-conformities	AI Root Cause Analysis	Models that analyze large volumes of incident data to identify the root causes of nonconformities with greater accuracy than manual methods.	Accurate and rapid diagnosis of problems, facilitating the implementation of effective and targeted corrective actions.	Regulation 10.2 non-conformity and corrective action

6.4 Challenges and Strategies for Successful AI Integration

6.4.1 Data Quality

The adoption of AI in quality management presents significant challenges, and data reliability is one of the most critical. The accuracy of any AI solution depends "largely on the quality of the data." AI models can produce erroneous results if they are trained or fed with inconsistent, incomplete, or biased data. This challenge is particularly relevant, as 45% of CEOs see "data protection" as an obstacle to AI adoption (Hakimi et al., 2024).

To mitigate such risk, organizations must establish a data governance strategy. This involves creating a "data governance framework" with clearly defined roles and responsibilities. Organizations must implement automated "data profiling and cleansing" tools to correct inaccuracies and resolve inconsistencies, ensuring data is ready for advanced analysis. In addition, the use of "real-time monitoring" tools and machine learning algorithms can help detect anomalies in data on an ongoing basis (Li, 2025). If the future ISO 9001:2026 calls for data-driven quality, then data governance becomes a prerequisite for ensuring that data is trusted by AI.

6.4.2 Training and Development of Digital Skills

A lack of technical expertise and the need for "digitally skilled personnel" are significant barriers to AI integration. To close this "skills gap", it is necessary for companies to adopt proactive strategies (Singh, 2024).

An effective approach is to develop comprehensive and flexible training programs that are tailored to the different levels of knowledge of the staff. They will have to teach technical skills in areas such as machine learning, data analysis and programming languages such as Python and R. But AI itself can be used for training, creating personalized training content and assessments for employees. Strategic alliances with external consultancies and experts can also accelerate the implementation of AI and the development of internal skills (Sharma & Haralayya, 2025).

6.4.3 Ethics, Transparency and Regulatory Compliance

The use of AI introduces "real risks" into the QMS, such as "bias and discrimination in algorithms", "lack of transparency" in decision-making and "security vulnerabilities". The future ISO 9001:2026 will emphasize "customer trust", so the use of AI must be "explainable, traceable and secure" (Hooper & Lunn, 2024; Engelmann, 2023).

To address these challenges, organizations can turn to ISO/IEC 42001:2023, the "first certifiable framework for an AI management system (AIMS)" (Benraouane, 2024). It is presented as the ideal complementary standard to ISO 9001:2026, as it addresses the management of AI risks (including bias and privacy), establishes accountability and oversight, and promotes "trust, transparency and ethics" (Suredranath, 2025).

The synergy between ISO standards is decisive. ISO 9001:2026 will call for excellence in quality, while ISO/IEC 42001:2023 will provide the framework for the implementation of AI in an ethical and safe manner. Organizations that are already ISO 9001 certified have a solid foundation for integrating the ISO 42001 framework, as both are designed with similar structures and principles (Sankaran, 2025).

6.4.4 Cultural Transformation: From Reactive to Proactive Approach

The shift from a culture of quality that focuses on "reacting to problems" to one that "predicts and prevents them" is a profound cultural challenge. Employee "lack of engagement" is a common obstacle in implementing new systems (Larsson & Heintz, 2020).

An effective strategy to overcome this obstacle is to secure the commitment of senior management, as their support is critical to driving the vision and allocating the necessary resources. It is advisable to start with "pilot projects" in specific areas to assess the impact of AI. This approach helps mitigate risks, demonstrate the benefits of technology on a smaller scale, and allow the organization to adapt before a large-scale deployment. In addition, it is crucial to foster a culture where learning and innovation are an integral part of the corporate culture, so that the team stays up to date with the latest AI trends (Sharma & Haralayya, 2025).

Table 4.

Challenge	Impact on QMS and Compliance	Recommended Strategies	Support Reference
Data Reliability	Risk of erroneous decision-making, biased results, and unexpected non-conformities.	Implement a data governance framework and automated cleansing and normalization tools.	Clause 9.1.3 Analysis and Evaluation, ISO/IEC 42001
Staff Training	Delayed implementation, inefficient use of tools, and low adoption of technology.	Develop flexible training programs, invest in digital staff training, and collaborate with external experts.	Clause 7.2 Jurisdiction
Ethics and Transparency	Risks of bias in algorithms, loss of customer trust, and regulatory penalties.	Align the QMS with ISO/IEC 42001, implement bias testing, and establish clear oversight and accountability.	Clause 5.1 Leadership and Commitment, ISO/IEC 42001
Cultural Transformation	Resistance to change, lack of commitment from senior management, and failure to implement.	Promote pilot projects, ensure leadership commitment and foster a culture of innovation and continuous learning.	Clause 5.1 Leadership and Commitment

6.5. The Future of Quality Management

The revision of ISO 9001:2026 represents a turning point in the history of quality management. Beyond being a simple update, this standard acts as a catalyst for the digital transformation of QMS. The analysis indicates that artificial intelligence is not an accessory tool, but a fundamental driver to meet the new requirements of the standard, particularly those related to data-driven quality, risk management, and continuous improvement (Chiarini & Cherrafi, 2023; Minglana-Tobias et al., 2021).

The future of quality management will focus less on reactive compliance and more on proactive operational excellence and resilience (Al Balushi, 2024; Yazo-Cabuya et al., 2025). Success will no longer depend solely on compliance, but also on an organization's ability to balance innovation with accountability and ethics. The strategic integration of technologies such as AI will not only ensure compliance with the revised standard but will also offer a sustainable competitive advantage by increasing efficiency, reducing costs, and significantly improving customer satisfaction (Hassan et al., 2024). Therefore, organizations that address this transition proactively, investing in data governance, training, and a culture of innovation, will be better positioned to thrive in the new era of quality (Muruganandham et al., 2022).

6.6 Cybersecurity and Resilience for AI-Powered QMS

Why it matters. When AI parts are added to a Quality Management System (QMS), new ways for hackers to get in appear at every stage of the AI lifecycle, including data collection, model training, deployment, human-AI interaction, and supply chains. Cybersecurity for AI in a QMS must therefore extend beyond traditional IT controls to cover AI-specific risks such as data poisoning, adversarial examples, model theft, prompt/response manipulation (for LLM-assisted documentation or audits), and insecure output handling. A defensible approach to AI governance is in line with existing security standards (like ISO/IEC 27001), AI-specific management systems (ISO/IEC 42001), and risk frameworks (ISO/IEC 23894; NIST AI RMF).

6.6.1. AI threat model for QMS

Things that you own. Training and validation datasets; feature stores; model artifacts and registries; prompts, retrieval indexes, and output logs; MLOps/CI-CD pipelines; third-party models/APIs; and QMS records made by AI, like nonconformity triage and CAPA suggestions.

Enemies and strategies. Data poisoning or contamination; model evasion and extraction; membership inference; prompt injection and insecure output handling for LLM tools; supply-chain tampering in datasets, libraries, or model weights. Use reference taxonomies like MITRE ATLAS (for adversarial ML) and OWASP Top 10 for LLM Applications to list techniques and protections.

When to use it. (a) AI helps with document control and internal audits; (b) AI finds problems in manufacturing or service processes; (c) AI keeps an eye on the quality of suppliers; and (d) AI analyzes customer feedback to find risks and opportunities.

6.6.2. Standard mapping and control framework

Use a layered control set that connects AI risks to security and quality clauses. Data poisoning or loss of integrity → Data lineage, versioning, and immutable logs; dataset acceptance criteria; dual control for label changes → Dataset inventory, lineage graphs, change logs, and hash/signature proofs → ISO 9001 (7.5, 8.x documented info & operations), ISO/IEC 27001 (ISMS controls for integrity, logging, supplier), ISO/IEC 23894 (AI risk), and NIST AI RMF (Map/Measure).

Adversarial evasion/drift → Robustness testing, OOD detection, shadow models, canary deployments; rollback playbooks → Test reports, drift alarms, rollback records → ISO/IEC 42001 (controlling how AI systems work), ISO/IEC 27001 (monitoring and managing changes).

Prompt injection and insecure output handling (LLM) can be fixed by validating input and output, using policy-based post-processing, sandboxing tools, and least-privilege connectors. OWASP LLM Top 10 controls include guardrails configs, red-team findings, and blocked-prompt logs. Under ISO 9001 documented info and ISO/IEC 27001 monitoring, log evidence is required.

Model/API supply-chain risk → Component inventory (models, datasets, libs), provenance, licensing checks; vulnerability monitoring → "AI asset register", SBOM/"model card" bundle, supplier SLAs → ISO/IEC 27001 (supplier relationships), ISO/IEC 42001 (AI governance of suppliers).

Privacy and confidentiality → Data minimization, masking, access control, encryption (in transit and at rest), and secure enclaves → Access reviews, records of key management, and DLP events ISO/IEC 27001 controls; fit with "Govern/Manage" from NIST AI RMF.

Note. Use ISO/IEC 42001 to set roles, goals, and AI controls at the management-system level; use ISO/IEC 27001 to set security baselines; and use ISO/IEC 23894 + NIST AI RMF to put AI risk identification, analysis, mitigation, and monitoring into action.

6.6.3. AI-aware incident response (IR) playbook

Add AI-specific triggers and containment to the ISO 9001 loop for nonconformity and corrective action.

Find and sort. Drift and OOD detectors send out alerts; there are spikes in false nonconformities; prompts and outputs that don't make sense; and changes to the model registry. (Use ATLAS techniques as examples for red-team scenarios, atlas.mitre.org.) Contain. Quarantine model version; turn off risky tools and connectors; go back to the last known good model; make sure that manual review gates are in place.

Get rid of and get back. Remove bad data, retrain with clean sets, change passwords, reissue signed artifacts, and release canaries in stages. What we learned. Add to the risk register, make the guardrails stronger, and add more tests. Give CAPA the root cause (data, pipeline, supplier).

Trail of audits. Keep prompts, training lineage, model cards, and the IR timeline as written records.

6.6.4. Audit evidence and key performance indicators (KPIs)

Suggested metrics to find a balance between quality, security, and dependability:

- Time to find model drift (TTD) and time to go back (TTR).
- Adversarial detection rate in red-team exercises (ATLAS-mapped scenarios). atlas.mitre.org
- % datasets with verified lineage and acceptance criteria before training.
- % AI changes with a review by two people (data and model).
- Escaped defect rate caused by AI decisions (trend ↓).
- % LLM outputs that pass validation and post-processing gates (trend ↑).
- Supplier risk coverage: % of third-party models/libs checked for vulnerabilities.

Model cards, dataset datasheets, change-control records, red-team and robustness test reports, access reviews, monitoring dashboards, and IR logs are all examples of evidence. Make sure they match up with ISO/IEC 27001 (monitoring, logging, suppliers) and ISO 9001 (documented information; monitoring & measurement; improvement).

6.6.5. Minimum viable controls for SMEs (based on risk)

If your organization doesn't have a lot of resources, start with a starter set:

- Keep a list of your AI assets, including models, datasets, APIs, owners, and versions.
- Set rules for what data can be accepted and where it came from (no "mystery data").
- For AI tools, use role-based access control and key rotation.
- Add guardrails and input/output validation to any LLM (owasp.org).
- Use 3 to 5 ATLAS techniques to run AI red-team drills every three months.
- Monitor drift and OOD with the ability to roll back.
- Keep logs of datasets, model versions, prompts, and outputs that can't be changed.
- Add AI scenarios to your IR playbooks and CAPA.
- Ask suppliers to sign off on their security practices and how often they update them.
- Keep an eye on the KPIs above and talk about them in management review.

7. CASE STUDY

To gain a clearer understanding of the impact that the new version of ISO 9001 will have in combination with artificial intelligence (AI), it is essential to analyze use cases across different industries. The transition to ISO 9001:2026 will not only represent a change in regulatory compliance but will also drive a transformation in the way organizations conceive and manage quality. These case studies provide insight into the dynamics, challenges, and solutions implemented in key sectors such as manufacturing, financial services, healthcare, and technology.

Manufacturing Sector. In the manufacturing sector, organizations are already developing AI integration pilots to strengthen supply chain resilience, optimize material traceability, and ensure more accurate quality control through artificial vision (Sanchez Lizarraga et al., 2020; Ikram et al., 2020). In such an environment, expected impacts include a significant reduction in non-conformance costs, increased responsiveness to global disruptions, and the consolidation of predictive monitoring systems that anticipate failures in critical machinery (Chowdhary & Kumar, 2023). In the next three years of transition, companies will need to invest in digital platforms and in the training of internal auditors to interpret AI-generated data, thus ensuring the correct validation and verification of the results (Omisola-Shiyanbola, 2024).

Impact on the Financial Services Sector. Financial institutions are among the industries that rely the most on real-time data. The incorporation of ISO 9001:2026, with a focus on advanced analytics, will allow for the establishment of more robust mechanisms for risk control, fraud prevention, and customer satisfaction (Paoletti, 2024). Banks and insurers are expected to integrate AI systems to monitor operations, detect anomalous behavior patterns, and meet predictive audit requirements (Başaran, 2021).

During the transition period, auditors will play a crucial role in validating the reliability of AI models, ensuring that the results are interpretable and transparent. The biggest challenge will be the creation of ethics and transparency protocols, considering that automated decision-making in financial services has a direct impact on user trust (Benraouane, 2024). In this scenario, the standard will contribute to a more robust and resilient financial system, in which quality management not only implies efficiency, but also security and credibility.

Impact on the Health Sector. Health is one of the areas where quality has a direct impact on people's lives. The application of ISO 9001:2026 in hospitals and clinics will focus on improving the management of critical processes such as diagnosis, patient care, and clinical data management (Ramese et al., 2024). In this context, AI will be applied in the interpretation of medical images, in the prediction of epidemiological outbreaks and in the optimization of hospital resources.

The expected impacts include a reduction in diagnostic errors, better distribution of medical supplies, and a reinforced response capacity to health emergencies. During the three-year transition, healthcare institutions are expected to work closely with specialized auditors to oversee the traceability of clinical information, the confidentiality of data, and the effectiveness of predictive models applied in healthcare (Rakić et al., 2024). The main challenge will be to balance technological innovation with medical ethics and the protection of patient rights.

Impact on the Technology and Innovation Sector. Technology companies will be pioneers in the adoption of ISO 9001:2026, as much of their operations are already supported by AI. In these organizations, the standard will represent a strategic framework to ensure the transparency of algorithms, the reliability of automated systems, and the continuous improvement of digital products (Ahmed & Ruth, 2024). Technology companies will not only have to comply with the requirements but also serve as a reference for good practices for other sectors (Carvalho-Ishikura, 2024).

In the transition period, technology auditors will take on a role of strategic advisors, assessing both the technical robustness of AI models and their impact on the customer experience. Companies that integrate the standard with an ethical and responsible approach will gain competitive advantages by demonstrating the quality, reliability, and safety of their technological solutions (Benraouane, 2024).

7.1 Success Stories

Below are three examples of success stories in the integration of quality management systems with AI, which serve as an application reference for ISO 9001:2026.

Case 1: Siemens (Manufacturing sector).

Context: Siemens faced challenges related to component traceability and failure prevention in large-scale industrial equipment.

Implementation: Implemented artificial vision systems and predictive algorithms that made it possible to anticipate failures in critical machinery. In addition, it integrated internal chatbots to manage QMS documentation (Erdal et al., 2023).

Results: Product inspection time was reduced, operational reliability was increased, and customer satisfaction was improved by reducing returns (ENISA, 2023).

Case 2: Banco Santander (Financial Services).

Context: The bank needed to strengthen its risk control system in the face of the increase in digital fraud and suspicious transactions.

Implementation: An AI model based on advanced analytics was developed to detect anomalous transactions in real time, aligned with the risk and transparency clauses required by ISO 9001.

Results: Fraud incidents were reduced by 40% and customer confidence increased, thus improving satisfaction rates by 20% during the first year of implementation (Paoletti, 2024).

Case 3: Mayo Clinic (Health Sector).

Context: The institution sought to reduce diagnostic errors and optimize the management of hospital resources.

Implementation: Machine learning algorithms were applied in the interpretation of medical images and in the prediction of epidemiological outbreaks. In addition, a traceability system was created to ensure the integrity of clinical data (Loufek et al., 2024).

Results: A 35% reduction in diagnostic errors was achieved, efficiency in the use of medical supplies was improved by 40%, and patient confidence was strengthened thanks to the transparency of the processes (Yu et al., 2025).

Balancing Successes and Challenges in AI-enabled QMS

While Siemens, Banco Santander, and the Mayo Clinic represent flagship examples of AI-driven quality management, they do not capture the full range of outcomes. Many organizations, particularly small and medium-sized enterprises (SMEs), have faced difficulties that highlight the risks of uncritical adoption. Presenting both successes and failures provides a balanced and realistic perspective for practitioners.

7.2 Reported failures and partial implementations

Automotive supplier (Europe, 2022)

A Tier-2 supplier piloted an AI anomaly detection tool to monitor welding defects. Although accuracy improved during testing, in production the model generated false positives exceeding 25%, leading to inspection bottlenecks. The project was suspended, and the firm reverted to traditional sampling until retraining strategies were developed. Lesson learned: Robustness testing and phased deployment are essential before scaling.

SME electronics manufacturer (Latin America, 2021)

A mid-sized manufacturer attempted to adopt AI-supported audit documentation. Limited IT infrastructure and reliance on cloud services resulted in unexpected costs (30% over budget) and delays in certification renewal. Lesson learned: SMEs must perform cost–benefit analysis and carefully plan investments before embarking on AI integration.

Healthcare provider (Asia, 2020) A hospital integrated an AI tool for analyzing patient feedback to identify nonconformities in service quality. However, linguistic bias in natural language models misclassified culturally specific complaints, reducing the system's credibility among auditors and patients.

Lesson learned: Cultural and linguistic context must be considered when deploying NLP tools in QMS.

Food industry SME (North America, 2023) An SME attempted to implement an AI-based supplier risk evaluation system. Due to limited in-house expertise, the firm became dependent on external consultants. When the contract ended, knowledge transfer was insufficient, and the system was abandoned.

Lesson learned: Knowledge retention and internal capacity building are crucial for long-term success.

Comparative perspective

- A comparative analysis of success stories vs. failures shows that:
- Large enterprises benefit from resources, robust IT infrastructures, and dedicated AI teams.
- SMEs often face financial constraints, skills shortages, and cultural resistance.
- Failures typically stem from inadequate risk assessment, underestimating costs, or overlooking human/organizational factors (e.g., staff training, acceptance).

Managerial implications

- Managers should approach AI adoption in QMS with measured expectations, understanding that not all implementations lead to immediate gains.
- A phased approach with pilots is recommended to minimize disruption.
- Including cost–benefit analysis, resilience planning, and stakeholder training is critical to reduce the likelihood of project abandonment.
- Organizations should learn equally from failures and successes, adapting strategies accordingly.

Global impact

The global impact of ISO 9001:2026 is projected as a catalyst for digital transformation in quality management. The standard is expected to drive the adoption of sustainability, resilience, and ethics practices across sectors, while strengthening international competitiveness (Kartha, 2022; Başaran, 2021). During the transition, global discussion forums, collaborative networks and complementary certification schemes will emerge that will facilitate the interpretation of the new requirements.

In terms of the future, it is anticipated that ISO 9001 will evolve into a standard that not only measures the effectiveness of management systems, but also their ability to generate sustainable value, ensure customer trust and respond proactively to emerging challenges. The conjunction between AI and quality management will mark a new era, in which innovation and integrity will be the fundamental pillars of organizational success (Montenegro Gutierrez & Aragon Casas, 2023).

8. RECOMMENDATIONS / IMPLICATIONS

8.1. Strategic Recommendations for the Implementation of ISO 9001:2026

The transition to ISO 9001:2026, framed by the incorporation of artificial intelligence (AI), demands a strategic approach from organizations. One of the main recommendations is for companies to progressively integrate AI systems into their quality management processes, prioritizing those areas with the greatest impact on traceability, continuous improvement and customer satisfaction (Rahman et al., 2025). Similarly, the creation of interdisciplinary teams that include quality specialists, data scientists, and internal auditors is recommended, with the aim of ensuring the correct interpretation of the information generated by algorithms (Fonseca et al., 2021).

In the same way, it is advisable for managers to promote continuous training programs, not only in the technical aspects of AI, but also in ethics, transparency and data governance. This will allow compliance with the standard to become a differentiating factor in the global market, strengthening the trust of customers and stakeholders (Chen et al., 2024).

8.2. Organizational Implications

8.2.1. Change management as an enabler of AI adoption

Adopting AI within ISO 9001:2026 requires more than technical integration; it demands organizational transformation. Structured change management frameworks can bridge the gap between strategic intent and operational reality.

Kotter's 8-Step Model: Provides a stepwise path from creating urgency to anchoring change in culture. For AI-enabled QMS, urgency is established by linking digital transformation to competitiveness; the guiding coalition should include both quality and IT leaders; quick wins can be achieved through pilot projects demonstrating measurable benefits.

ADKAR model (Awareness, Desire, Knowledge, Ability, Reinforcement): Focuses on the human dimension. Employees must first understand why AI is needed (Awareness), develop motivation to engage (Desire), receive training (Knowledge), practice new skills (Ability), and receive continuous support (Reinforcement).

Practical tools: Internal communication campaigns, workshops, and cross-functional task forces can reduce resistance. Periodic feedback loops and townhall-style meetings help align employees' expectations with organizational goals.

8.2.2. Leadership and organizational agility

The role of leadership is decisive in ensuring that AI strengthens, rather than disrupts, quality systems. Historically, updates to ISO 9001 have elevated leadership responsibility (e.g., ISO 9001:2015 introduced the concept of "leadership and commitment"). In ISO 9001:2026, the integration of AI raises new demands.

Senior management's role: Executives must act as sponsors of AI adoption, allocating resources and embedding AI considerations into strategic planning.

Adaptive leadership: Leaders should foster a culture of experimentation, tolerating pilot failures while learning from them. This mindset promotes agility by enabling rapid adaptation to market, regulatory, and technological changes.

Agility enablers:

- Decentralized decision-making: Empower frontline teams to make real-time quality adjustments supported by AI insights.
- Dynamic resource allocation: Invest flexibly in skills, infrastructure, and partnerships.
- Continuous learning: Encourage training programs combining digital literacy with ethical and regulatory awareness.
- Managerial example: In firms like Siemens or Santander, leadership created steering committees dedicated to AI in quality management. By contrast, in SMEs, leadership commitment often defines whether adoption progresses or stalls due to resource constraints.

8.2.3. Key takeaway

The adoption of ISO 9001:2026 with a focus on artificial intelligence will imply a significant cultural transformation in organizations. Management systems will cease to be mere control instruments and will become dynamic platforms for analysis, prediction and improvement (Matos et al., 2022). All of which will impact the way decisions are made, which will go from being reactive to proactive, based on predictive models that anticipate risks and opportunities (Rahman et al., 2025).

In terms of resources, companies will need to invest heavily in technology infrastructure, software licensing and staff training. In the medium term, these investments will translate into a reduction in costs for non-conformities, greater resilience to global crises and an increase in competitiveness. The standard will also imply a more complex role for auditors, who will have to strengthen their competencies in advanced analytics, digital ethics, and evaluation of intelligent systems (Fonseca et al., 2021).

8.3. Ethical and Social Implications

The incorporation of AI into quality management systems not only has technical and economic consequences, but also ethical and social ones. It will be essential for organizations to ensure the transparency of the algorithms used, avoiding biases that may affect equity and inclusion (Chen et al., 2024). In addition, they will have to strengthen data protection mechanisms and user privacy, which are increasingly relevant in a digitalised global environment (Mujtaba, 2024).

From a social perspective, the correct implementation of the standard can contribute to generating greater confidence in products and services, as well as in health, financial and technological systems that have a direct impact on daily life. Responsible compliance with the requirements will strengthen institutional reputation and foster stronger relationships with customers, suppliers, and regulators (Rahman et al., 2025).

8.4. Implications for Global Competitiveness

Compliance with ISO 9001:2026 will position organizations at a higher level of competitiveness. Those companies that effectively integrate the standard will demonstrate not only compliance capacity, but also leadership in innovation and sustainability (Ejjami, 2024). In this sense, the recommendation is that organizations do not limit implementation to a certification requirement but rather use it as a strategic differentiation framework in increasingly demanding markets (Fonseca et al., 2021).

Multinational organizations will be able to align their global operations under the same standard that incorporates intelligent technologies, ensuring consistency in quality and consistency in risk management. Thus, ISO 9001:2026 is projected as a key instrument to respond to the growing demand for transparency, resilience and sustainability in the global economy (Rahman et al., 2025).

8.5. Academic Implications

From an academic perspective, the incorporation of artificial intelligence into ISO 9001:2026 opens new lines of research in the fields of quality management, industrial engineering, digital ethics, and data science (Mujtaba, 2024). The standard not only redefines business practice, but also poses challenges to existing theory, forcing a rethinking of concepts such as continuous improvement, statistical process control, and knowledge management (Matos et al., 2022).

Universities and research centers will have the opportunity to generate empirical studies that measure the impact of AI on the effectiveness of quality management systems, comparing organizations that have adopted these technologies early against those that still operate under traditional models. In addition, the integration of topics such as algorithmic governance, intelligent audits, and transparency in automated decision-making will enrich the curricula of careers related to management, engineering, and computer science (Chen et al., 2024).

On the other hand, the regulation also calls for strengthening collaboration between academia and industry. The development of joint projects will allow the validation of conceptual frameworks and the construction of predictive models applicable to different sectors. Thus, ISO 9001:2026 will become a catalyst for academic innovation, which will give impetus to interdisciplinary research and the creation of new teaching methodologies aimed at analyzing risks and opportunities arising from AI (Rahman et al., 2025).

8.6. A Workable Roadmap for Using AI to Implement ISO 9001:2026

Why a roadmap matters. Organizations frequently struggle with the "how" of implementing AI in quality management systems (QMS), even though strategic perspectives explain the "why." Organizations of all sizes, but particularly SMEs, can benefit from the staged roadmap, checklists, and maturity levels in this section as they implement ISO 9001:2026 in an AI-enabled environment.

8.6.1. A roadmap in phases

Assessment of awareness and preparedness (0–3 months)

1. Assess the infrastructure, culture, and skill levels of AI readiness.
2. Determine which business processes—such as audits, document control, and defect detection—may benefit from AI augmentation.
3. Analyze the gaps by contrasting the current QMS with the requirements of ISO 9001:2026 and AI.

Three to six months for planning and pilot design

1. Describe the extent of the AI integration (limited pilot vs. organization-wide).
2. Create governance positions (data steward, QMS lead, and AI product owner).
3. NIST AI RMF and ISO/IEC 23894 are used for risk assessment.
4. Choose a pilot process (such as audit sampling or supplier evaluation).

Implementation and assessment of the pilot (6–12 months)

1. Implement AI solutions in a regulated environment under human supervision.
2. Record KPIs (accuracy, audit time saved) and document controls in accordance with ISO 9001:2026.
3. Conduct internal audits and collect input from stakeholders and employees.
4. Refinement is fueled by lessons learned and corrective actions.

Integration and scaling (12–24 months)

1. Expand the use of AI to other procedures (risk analysis, training records, and customer complaints).
2. Assure compatibility with other management systems, such as ISO 45001 and ISO 27001.
3. Implement automated data integrity and model drift monitoring.
4. To institutionalize AI practices, update the QMS manual and procedures.

Constant improvement for more than 24 months

1. Review KPIs on a regular basis during management review sessions.
2. Compare yourself to peers in the same sector.
3. Extend governance to cover the social, ethical, and environmental effects of AI in QMS.
4. Use feedback loops from audits and AI performance to iteratively improve procedures.

8.6.2. AI maturity model in QMS

- Level 1-Ad hoc: informal use of AI tools without QMS integration.
- Level 2-Emerging: Pilot projects with minimal governance and documented procedures.
- Level 3-Managed: AI integrated into specific QMS procedures; distinct roles and oversight.
- Level 4-Integrated: cross-functional integration; AI completely compliant with ISO 9001:2026.
- Level 5-Optimized: AI-enabled QMS for the entire organization; benchmarking and ongoing improvement.

8.6.3. Checklist for practitioners

Assessment of AI readiness (skills, infrastructure, governance) is finished.
Processes and scope of the pilot are established.
Roles and responsibilities in governance are documented.
A risk assessment was conducted (ISO/IEC 23894, NIST AI RMF).
KPIs (accuracy, defect reduction, ROI) were identified and monitored.
Documented human-in-the-loop mechanisms.
Implementation of lineage and data integrity controls.
Drift detection and AI monitoring are in place.
Internal audits of AI-related procedures are carried out.
Lessons learned and corrective measures are incorporated into the QMS.

8.6.4. A visual roadmap

Figure 1.

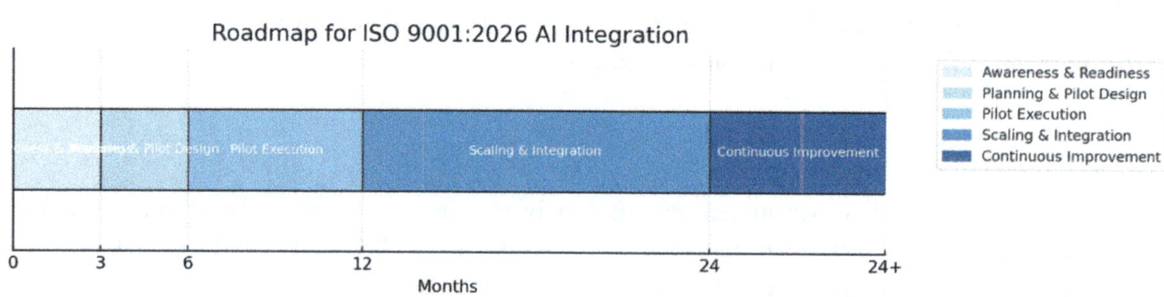

8.6.5. Crucial elements for success

- Leadership commitment: Senior management is responsible for communicating the vision and allocating resources.
- Stakeholder engagement: Active participation is encouraged from suppliers, auditors, and employees.

- Ambition in balance: Begin small, verify outcomes, and then grow.
- Integration with other standards: Use ISO/IEC 42001 for AI governance, ISO 14001 for sustainability, and ISO 27001 for security.
- Ongoing education: Encourage training initiatives to build ethical and digital skills.

8.7. Cost–Benefit Analysis and Return on Investment (ROI) for AI in QMS

Integrating AI into ISO 9001:2026 offers tangible benefits, but managers require evidence-based justification to support investment decisions. A structured cost–benefit analysis clarifies trade-offs and helps organizations, particularly SMEs, make informed choices.

8.7.1. Categories of investment (costs)

- Technology acquisition: AI software licenses, cloud computing services, model training infrastructure.
- Training and skills development: Upskilling employees on data literacy, AI auditing, and digital quality tools.
- Consulting and external support: Advisory services, implementation partners, certification audits.
- Operational overhead: Ongoing monitoring, model retraining, and cybersecurity controls.

8.7.2. Categories of measurable benefits

- Process efficiency: Reduction in audit cycle times, fewer non-value-adding activities.
- Quality improvement: Lower defect rates, improved root-cause analysis, enhanced corrective actions.
- Customer satisfaction: Fewer complaints and product returns, improved service quality.
- Financial resilience: Cost savings, faster decision-making, avoidance of compliance penalties.

8.7.3. Comparative table of costs and benefits

Table 5.

Dimension	Investment (Cost)	Expected Benefit (ROI)
Technology	AI licenses, cloud services, integration (50k–200k)	10–30% reduction in audit/documentation time; 15–25% lower inspection costs
Training & Skills	Employee training programs, workshops (5k–50k)	20–40% faster adoption curve; reduced resistance; fewer external consulting hours needed
Consulting & Support	External advisors, certification audits (20k–100k)	Shorter certification timelines; improved compliance; 10–15% reduction in re-audit costs
Cybersecurity & Risk	Robustness testing, monitoring tools (10k–70k)	Avoidance of costly breaches; reduction of nonconformities caused by AI errors (5–10%)
Operational Efficiency	Ongoing monitoring, retraining (15k–80k per year)	10–20% increase in defect detection accuracy; improved predictive maintenance (esp. industry)
Customer Impact	Communication, surveys, feedback platforms (5k–30k)	5–15% increase in customer satisfaction scores; reduced product returns (up to 20%)

8.7.4. ROI estimation formula

A simplified formula for practitioners:

$$ROI = \frac{\text{Total Benefits (quantified savings + revenue gains)}}{\text{Total Costs (initial + operational)}} x100$$

Example:
Total annual costs: 200,000 (technology, training, consulting, operations).
Total annual benefits: 350,000 (audit efficiency, defect reduction, reduced complaints).
ROI = (350,000 ÷ 200,000) × 100 = 175% within the first year.

8.7.5. Managerial takeaway

- Large enterprises can justify investment through measurable efficiency and risk reduction.
- SMEs should start small with pilots, focusing on processes where ROI is fastest (e.g., defect detection, supplier audits).
- ROI should be tracked continuously through KPIs (audit cycle time, defect rate, customer satisfaction).
- A cost–benefit lens ensures that AI adoption in ISO 9001:2026 is strategic, sustainable, and financially viable.

9. SCOPE AND LIMITATIONS

The scope of this research focuses on the analysis of ISO 9001:2026 in combination with artificial intelligence, assessing its potential impacts on key sectors such as manufacturing, financial services, healthcare, and technology. The study covers both the technical aspects of the implementation of AI systems in quality management and the ethical, social and organizational implications that arise from this integration. Likewise, success stories and transition scenarios are included that illustrate how different industries can adopt the standard strategically.

However, the study has limitations that must be recognized. First, the prospective nature of the analysis implies that many of the findings are based on projections and simulations, which could differ from the results observed in practice once the standard is fully implemented. Second, although representative sectors were examined, it was not possible to cover all industries that may be impacted by the new version of ISO 9001, which restricts the generalization of the results.

Another limitation lies in the availability and transparency of data related to the early implementation of the standard, given that many organizations keep their adaptation strategies in reserve. This restricts the possibility of carrying out more in-depth empirical comparisons, in addition to limiting the statistical validation of certain assumptions.

Finally, it should be noted that the research does not delve into the legal analysis or regional regulatory differences that could influence the interpretation and application of ISO 9001:2026. In this sense, future research could address in greater detail how the legal and cultural particularities of each country or region affect the adoption of international quality standards supported by artificial intelligence.

10. CONCLUSION

The present study has shown that the evolution of the ISO 9001:2026 standard, together with artificial intelligence (AI) tools, is not only a regulatory update, but a true epistemological and practical transformation of quality management. Throughout this analysis, it has been possible to show that the standard, beyond guaranteeing standardized processes, is consolidated as a dynamic framework for adaptation to complex, globalized and profoundly technological environments.

One of the most relevant findings is that the incorporation of AI in quality management systems is not limited to the operational sphere but also reaches a strategic dimension. The possibility of carrying out predictive analysis, advanced traceability, automated decision-making and real-time monitoring represents a break with the traditional conception of quality as post-control. The new vision proposed by ISO 9001:2026 will redefine quality as an anticipatory system, capable of preventing failures, optimizing resources and strengthening organizational resilience.

Likewise, this analysis reveals that the transition to ISO 9001:2026 will involve not only technological investments, but also a profound cultural and organizational reconfiguration. The figure of the auditor evolves towards a hybrid profile, with competencies in ethics, data analysis and computational intelligence, which anticipates the emergence of a new professional paradigm in the field of quality management. This transformation will have a transversal impact on academic training, job training and the construction of public policies aimed at certification and social trust.

In academic terms, it contributes to consolidating a bridge between systems theory, quality management and artificial intelligence, showing that the integration of these approaches is not only possible, but necessary to face the challenges of the fourth industrial revolution. On a practical level, it has been evidenced through case studies that the application of ISO 9001:2026 with the support of AI is already generating positive results in key sectors such as manufacturing, financial services, health and technology, thus confirming its global viability and relevance.

Finally, the research concludes that ISO 9001:2026, by aligning with advances in artificial intelligence, opens a new stage where quality will not be understood as a static goal, but as a living process of continuous, ethical and technologically assisted improvement. Such a paradigmatic shift is both a challenge and a historic opportunity: a challenge, because it forces organizations to reinvent themselves in a critical transition period; and opportunity, because it offers the tools to build more transparent, reliable and sustainable management systems.

In short, the quality management of the future will not only be a regulatory practice, but also a strategic, interdisciplinary and transformative discipline, called to guarantee not only the efficiency of organizations, but also their ability to generate sustainable value and social trust in an increasingly complex and digitalized world.

Ultimately, the convergence between ISO 9001:2026 and artificial intelligence transcends the merely technical and is inscribed in an ethical and civilizational horizon. If quality in the twentieth century was conceived as a guarantee of uniformity and reliability, in the twenty-first century it stands as a search for meaning during complexity, where each organizational decision has an impact on global production chains, on the sustainability of the planet and on the trust of society. Thus, quality can no longer be understood only as a standard of compliance, but as a collective responsibility that challenges humanity to build fairer, more transparent and resilient systems.

11. FUTURE RESEARCH

The integration of ISO 9001:2026 with artificial intelligence opens a wide field, still unexplored, that requires further analysis in future studies. Although this work provides a conceptual and practical basis for the transition to a quality management model enhanced by AI, there are still multiple aspects that deserve academic and applied attention.

In the academic field, it will be necessary to carry out longitudinal research that evaluates how the implementation of the standard has a sustained impact on organizational culture, on the formation of professional competencies and on the generation of new ethical frameworks associated with the supervision of algorithms. In addition, comparative studies are required between sectors, regions and company sizes, to determine whether the benefits of ISO 9001:2026 are homogeneous or present significant differences depending on the context.

From a practical perspective, future research should focus on the creation of specific metrics to audit intelligent systems under the guidelines of the standard. This implies developing evaluation tools that not only measure document conformity, but also the transparency, reliability, and robustness of AI models applied to critical processes. Similarly, it will be relevant to inquire about the costs of adoption and about the continuous training models that allow auditors and quality professionals to maintain the validity of their competencies in a changing technological environment.

On the technological front, future research should explore the intersection of ISO 9001 with other emerging trends, such as blockchain for data traceability, the Internet of Things (IoT) for real-time monitoring, and digital sustainability as a pillar of quality in the 21st century. Likewise, it will be essential to examine how advances in Artificial Intelligence can become a standard of transparency within management systems.

In short, the future of research on ISO 9001:2026 and artificial intelligence is projected as fertile ground for interdisciplinary innovations. By integrating technical, organizational and ethical perspectives, the coming studies will not only expand knowledge but will also help in the construction of more resilient, reliable organizations oriented to generate sustainable value in an increasingly digitized world.

REFERENCES

Adelakun, B. O.Beatrice Oyinkansola Adelakun. (2022). The impact of AI on internal auditing: Transforming practices and ensuring compliance. *Finance & Accounting Research Journal, 4*(6), 350–370. Advance online publication. DOI: 10.51594/farj.v4i6.1316

Ahmad, M., Ahmed, I., & Jeon, G. (2022). A sustainable advanced artificial intelligence-based framework for analysis of COVID-19 spread. *Environment, Development and Sustainability, 24*(10), 1–16. DOI: 10.1007/s10668-022-02584-0

Ahmed, S. A., & Ruth, D. (2024). *The benefits of ISO 9001 certification for small to medium-sized engineering firms*. Performance Improvement Journal., DOI: 10.56811/PFI-24-0010

Al Balushi, M. (2024). The impact of quality management systems on organizational resilience. *International Journal of Quality & Reliability Management*. Advance online publication. DOI: 10.1108/IJQRM-05-2023-0169

Al-Salah, A., Al-Harbi, F., & Al-Mutairi, S. (2025). Revolutionizing industrial management: A review of artificial intelligence applications in manufacturing operations. *Al-Noor Journal of Engineering Management and Computer Science, 1*(2), 19–28. DOI: 10.71229/njemcs.v1i2.3

Almeida, F., Silva, M., & Pinto, M. (2021). Chatbot application in document management: A natural language processing approach. *Computer Science Proceeded, 181*, 1080–1087. DOI: 10.1016/j.procs.2021.01.291

Andrianandrianina Johanesa, T. V., Equeter, L., & Mahmoudi, S. A. (2024). Survey on AI applications for product quality control and predictive maintenance in Industry 4.0. *Electronics (Basel), 13*(5), 976. DOI: 10.3390/electronics13050976

Anttila, J., & Jussila, K. (2021). ISO 9004 - A stimulating quality management standard for the creative leaders of contemporary sustainable organizations. *Production Engineering Archives, 27*(2), 148–155. DOI: 10.30657/pea.2021.27.19

Arinola, A. F., & Olalekan, A. (2023). Artificial intelligence & internal audit quality of commercial banks in Nigeria. *International Journal of Management and Economics Invention, 9*(4), 123–134. DOI: 10.47191/ijmei/v9i4.05

Avruscio, G., Ragazzo, S., Ceccato, D., Adamo, A., Napoli, C., Cacco, L., Scalzotto, F., Canciani, M., Cognolato, M., Fedele, A., Scipioni, A., & Tocco Tussardi, I. (2022). Implementation of a quality management system according to ISO 9001:2015 standards in an Angiology Unit: an Italian experience. *Annali di igiene : medicina preventiva e di comunità*. Advance online publication. DOI: 10.7416/ai.2022.2501

Başaran, B. (2021). The past, present and future ISO 9001 quality management system standard. Business and Management Studies. *International Journal (Toronto, Ont.), 9*(1), 227–247. DOI: 10.15295/bmij.v9i1.1756

Benraouane, S. (2024). *AI management system certification according to the ISO/IEC 42001 standard*. Routledge., DOI: 10.4324/9781003463979

Bravi, L., & Murmura, F. (2021). Evidence about ISO 9001:2015 and ISO 9004:2018 implementation in different-size organisations. *Total Quality Management & Business Excellence*, *33*(11–12), 1366–1386. DOI: 10.1080/14783363.2021.1954900

Bravim, M., Lira, T., De Freitas, R., & Xavier, T. (2020). A evolução nos estudos da gestão da qualidade baseado na norma iso 9001:2015: um estudo bibliométrico: the evolution in quality management studies based on iso 9001: 2015 standard: a bibliometric study. *Brazilian Journal of Production Engineering* - BJPE, 88-106. https://digitalcommons.unl.edu/cgi/viewcontent.cgi?article=10411&context=libphilprac &utm_source=chatgpt.com

Carvalho-Ishikura, R. (2024). *Impact of ISO 9001 implementation on financial results: A case study on publicly traded companies*. Scientific Journal of Applied Social and Clinical Science., DOI: 10.22533/at.ed.216432431014

Chen, R., Ren, X., He, L., & Huang, J. (2024). Editorial: AI as intelligent technology and agent to understand and be understood by human minds. *Frontiers in Psychology*, *15*, 1461881. DOI: 10.3389/fpsyg.2024.1461881

Chiarini, A., & Cherrafi, A. (2023). Artificial intelligence and quality management: A systematic literature review and research agenda. *The TQM Journal*, *35*(5), 1050–1071. DOI: 10.1108/TQM-08-2022-0259

Chiarini, A., & Cherrafi, A. (2023). Integrating ISO 9001 and Industry 4.0: An implementation guideline and PDCA model for manufacturing sector. *Total Quality Management & Business Excellence*, *34*(15–16), 1629–1654. DOI: 10.1080/14783363.2023.2192916

Chowdhary, Y., & Kumar, B. (2023). Advancement and benefits associated with ISO 9000 series. *Asian Journal of Pharmaceutical Research*. DOI: 10.52711/2231-5691.2023.00008

Ćwiklicki, M., Wojnarowska, M., & Pilch, K. (2020). Diffusion of ISO 9001 quality management system in service and manufacturing organizations. *The TQM Journal*, *32*(6), 1059–1077. DOI: 10.1108/TQM-10-2019-0252

Deloitte. (2022). State of AI in the Enterprise, 5th Edition: Thriving in the era of pervasive AI. Retrieved from: https://www2.deloitte.com/us/en/insights/focus/cognitive-technologies/state-of-ai-and-intelligent-automation-in-business-survey.html

Ejjami, R. (2024). Leveraging AI to enhance marketing and customer engagement strategies in the French market. *International Journal for Multidisciplinary Research*, *6*(3), 120–131. DOI: 10.36948/ijfmr.2024.v06i03.23147

Engelmann, A. (2023). Algorithmic transparency as a fundamental right in the democratic rule of law. *Brazilian Journal of Law. Technology and Innovation*, *1*(2), 169–188. DOI: 10.59224/bjlti.v1i2.169-188

Erdal, B. S., Laugerette, A., Fair, K. H., Zimmermann, M., Demirer, M., Gupta, V., O'Donnell, T., & White, R. D. (2023). AI algorithm deployment and utilization: Strategies to facilitate clinical workflow implementation and integration. *medRxiv*. DOI: 10.1101/2023.09.19.23295729

Esteva, A., Robicquet, A., Ramsundar, B., Kuleshov, V., DePristo, M., Chou, K., Cui, C., Corrado, G., Thrun, S., & Dean, J. (2019). A guide to deep learning in healthcare. *Nature Medicine*, *25*(1), 24–29. DOI: 10.1038/s41591-018-0316-z

Ferouali, S. E. (2021). Governance of the digital transformation in Moroccan universities: Case study of Cadi Ayyad University-Marrakech. *Journal of Economics. Finance and Management Studies*, *4*(9). Advance online publication. DOI: 10.47191/jefms/v4-i9-22

Fonseca, L., Cardoso, M. C., & Nóvoa, M. H. (2021). Motivations for ISO 9001 quality management system implementation and certification mapping the territory with a novel classification proposal. *International Journal of Quality and Service Sciences*, *13*(4), 585–603. DOI: 10.1108/IJQSS-02-2021-0031

Gaidhani, Y., Ramesh, J. V. N., Singh, S., Dagar, R., Rao, T. S. M., Godla, S. R., & El-Ebiary, Y. A. B. (2025). AI-driven predictive analytics for CRM to enhance retention, personalization and decision making. *International Journal of Advanced Computer Science and Applications*, *16*(4). Advance online publication. DOI: 10.14569/IJACSA.2025.0160456

Gamit, R., Prajapati, R., & Gohil, A. (2024). ISO 9001 and competitiveness: Empirical evidence from Indian manufacturing firms. *Journal of Business Excellence*, *18*(1), 42–56. DOI: 10.1504/IJBEX.2024.100602

Gartner. (2023). Gartner Survey Finds More Than Half of Organizations Have AI in Production. Retrieved from: https://www.gartner.com/en/newsroom/press-releases/2023-08-22-gartner-survey-finds-more-than-half-of-organizations-have-ai-in-production

Glogovac, M., & Ruso, J. (2020). ISO 9004 maturity model for quality in Industry 4.0. *International Journal of Quality & Reliability Management*, *37*(8), 1101–1117. DOI: 10.1080/14783363.2020.1865793

Glogovac, M., Ruso, J., & Anđelković, A. (2022). Leadership for Quality 4.0: Improvement, learning and innovation. *Total Quality Management & Business Excellence*, *33*(11–12), 1197–1214. DOI: 10.1080/10429247.2022.2108668

Gueorguiev, T. (2025). An approach to integrate Artificial Intelligence in ISO 9001-based quality management systems. *Measurement. Sensors*, *38*, 101787. DOI: 10.1016/j.measen.2024.101787

Hakimi, M., Zarinkhail, M. S., & Musawi, S. Z. (2024). Exploring the fusion of enterprise architecture, blockchain, and AI in digital governance: A systematic review. *International Journal Software Engineering and Computer Science*, *4*(2), 45–61. DOI: 10.35870/ijsecs.v4i2.2832

Hassan, R. R., Talib, M. A., Dweiri, F., & Roman, J. (2024). An artificial intelligence (AI) framework to predict operational excellence: UAE case study. *Applied Sciences (Basel, Switzerland)*, *14*(6), 2569. DOI: 10.3390/app14062569

Herath, H. M. D. K., & Gamlath, M. (2025). Impact of digital transformation on financial performance of licensed commercial banks in Sri Lanka pre and post COVID-19 pandemic. *Sri Lanka Journal of Social Sciences*, *47*(2), 145–163. Advance online publication. DOI: 10.4038/sljss.v47i02.9019

Hooper, K., & Lunn, S. (2024). A scoping review of transparency and explainability in AI ethics guidelines. *The International FLAIRS Conference Proceedings*, 37(1), 135–143. DOI: 10.32473/flairs.37.1.135594

Ikram, M., Shen, Y., Ferasso, M., & D'Adamo, I. (2021). Intensifying effects of COVID-19 on economic growth, logistics performance, environmental sustainability and quality management: Evidence from Asian countries. *Journal of Asia Business Studies, 15*(5). Advance online publication. DOI: 10.1108/JABS-07-2021-0316

Ikram, M., Zhang, Q., & Sroufe, R. (2020). Future of quality management system (ISO 9001) certification: Novel grey forecasting approach. *Total Quality Management & Business Excellence, 32*(16–17), 1666–1693. DOI: 10.1080/14783363.2020.1768062

International Labor Organization. (2021). The impact of artificial intelligence at work: risks and opportunities in industrialized environments. Geneva: ILO. Retrieved from: https://www.ilo.org/global/publications/WCMS_823260/lang--es/index.htm

International Organization for Standardization. (2022*). The ISO Survey of Management System Standard Certifications* – 2021. https://www.iso.org/the-iso-survey.html

International Organization for Standardization. (2022). ISO/IEC 27001:2022, *Information security management systems*. ISO. https://www.iso.org/standard/82875.html (Accessed September 2, 2025)

Ivakhnenkov, S. (2023). Artificial intelligence application in auditing. *Scientific Papers NaUKMA. Economics*, 8(1), 54–60. DOI: 10.18523/2519-4739.2023.8.1.54-60

Jeremić, N., & Luka, S. (2024). *Artificial intelligence – challenges of use in auditing*. Revizor., DOI: 10.56362/Rev24107043J

Johannesen, D. T. S., Lindøe, P. H., & Wiig, S. (2020). Certification as support for resilience? Behind the curtains of a certification body—A qualitative study. *BMC Health Services Research, 20*(1), 1–13. DOI: 10.1186/s12913-020-05608-5

Kahyaoglu, S., & Aksoy, T. (2021). Artificial intelligence in internal audit and risk assessment. In Kahyaoglu, S. (Ed.), *Digital Business Strategies in Blockchain Ecosystems* (pp. 179–192). Springer., DOI: 10.1007/978-3-030-72624-9_8

Kartha, C. P. (2022). An empirical investigation of the impact of ISO 9001 certification: A comparative study. *International Journal of Business Excellence, 26*(3), 362–378. DOI: 10.1504/IJBEX.2022.124457

Kiarie, D. (2020). The evolution of quality management and customer-centric approaches. *International Journal of Qualitative Research, 14*(4), 957–972. DOI: 10.24874/IJQR14.04-17

Kılıç, M. (2021). Ethico-juridical dimension of artificial intelligence application in the combat to COVID-19 pandemics. In *Artificial Intelligence and Ethics in the Pandemic Era* (pp. 299–317). Springer., DOI: 10.1007/978-981-33-6811-8_16

Kowalczyk, A. (2024). *Quality management system according to standard ISO 9001:2015*. Problemy Techniki Uzbrojenia., DOI: 10.5604/01.3001.0054.7510

Larsson, S., & Heintz, F. (2020). Transparency in artificial intelligence. *Internet Policy Review, 9*(2). Advance online publication. DOI: 10.14763/2020.2.1469

Lazibat, T., & Damić, M. (2022). Determinants, barriers and outcomes of ISO 9001 implementation in SMEs. *Poslovna izvrsnost - Business excellence*, 16(1), 93–115. DOI: 10.22598/pi-be/2022.16.1.93

Lenning, J., & Gremyr, I. (2021). Unleashing the potential of internal audits: A review and research agenda. *Total Quality Management & Business Excellence, 33*(9–10), 994–1010. DOI: 10.1080/14783363.2021.1911635

Levytska, S. (2024). Risks of the auditing services quality. *Fìnansi Ukraïni*, 2(2), 101–118. DOI: 10.33763/finukr2024.02.101

Li, Y., & Goel, S. (2025). Artificial intelligence auditability and auditor readiness for auditing artificial intelligence systems. *International Journal of Accounting Information Systems, 56*, 100739. DOI: 10.1016/j.accinf.2025.100739

Loufek, B., Vidal, D., McClintock, D. S., Lifson, M., Williamson, E., Overgaard, S., McNaughton, K., Lipford, M. C., & Pardi, D. S. (2024). Embedding internal accountability into health care institutions for safe, effective, and ethical implementation of artificial intelligence into medical practice: A Mayo Clinic case study. *Mayo Clinic Proceedings. Digital Health*, 2(4), 574–583. Advance online publication. DOI: 10.1016/j.mcpdig.2024.08.008

Luna-Pérez, A., Martínez-Mendoza, S. M., Hernández-Acevedo, R. E., Santos-Pineda, L. Á., Vasquez-Martinez, M., Bartolo-Alemán, M. H., Martínez-López, M., Silva-Montes, G., Morales-Castillo, V., & Cordova-Mireles, D. A. (2023). The internal audit process as a tool for the certification of management systems. *Asian Journal of Current Research*. DOI: 10.56557/ajocr/2023/v8i18218

Majstorović, V. D., & Babić, V. (2025). Development of business standardization and the new ISO 9001:2026 model. *Advances in Production Engineering & Management, 20*(1), 45–56. DOI: 10.14743/apem2025.1.456

Maqbool, S. (2023). Digital transformation, ISO 9001 and dynamic capabilities: A systematic review. *Total Quality Management & Business Excellence, 34*(3–4), 267–285. DOI: 10.1080/14783363.2021.2012117

Matos, F., Vairinhos, V., Anes, A., Matos, M., & Vale, J. (2022). Relating organizational knowledge with ISO 9001:2015: An empirical approach. *European Conference on Knowledge Management*, 23(2), 812–821. DOI: 10.34190/eckm.23.2.812

Matos, F., Vairinhos, V., & Velez, P. (2022). Competence development in the age of AI: Implications for ISO 9001 organizations. *Journal of Intellectual Capital, 23*(5), 1068–1085. DOI: 10.1108/JIC-09-2021-0241

McKinsey & Company. (2022). The State of AI in 2022—and a Half Decade in Review. Retrieved from: https://www.mckinsey.com/capabilities/quantumblack/our-insights/the-state-of-ai-in-2022-and-a-half-decade-in-review

Minglana, J., Tobias, R. R., & Roxas, R. (2021). Artificial intelligence applications in quality management system: A bibliometric study. *TENCON 2021 - IEEE Region 10 Conference (TENCON),* 947–952. DOI: 10.1109/TENCON54134.2021.9707340

MITRE Corporation. (n.d.). MITRE ATLAS: Adversarial Threat Landscape for Artificial-Intelligence Systems. MITRE. https://atlas.mitre.org/ (Accessed September 2, 2025)

Moghaddasi, H. (2021). The role of information management in the process of digital health confrontation with COVID-19. *Biomedical Journal of Scientific & Technical Research, 38*(2), 6123–6132. DOI: 10.26717/BJSTR.2021.38.006123

Montenegro Gutiérrez, E., & Aragón Casas, L. G. (2023). Improving customer satisfaction through the ISO 9001 quality management system and quality control design: A case study. Proceedings of the 21st *LACCEI International Multi-Conference for Engineering, Education and Technology.* DOI: 10.18687/LACCEI2023.1.1.692

Mujtaba, B. (2024). Clarifying ethical dilemmas in sharpening students' artificial intelligence proficiency: Dispelling myths about using AI tools in higher education. *Business Ethics and Leadership, 8*(2), 107–127. DOI: 10.61093/bel.8(2).107-127.2024

Murikah, W., Nthenge, J. K., & Musyoka, F. (2024). Bias and ethics of AI systems applied in auditing – A systematic review. *Scientific African, 23*, e02281. DOI: 10.1016/j.sciaf.2024.e02281

Muruganandham, R., Venkatesh, K., Devadasan, S., & Harish, V. (2022). TQM through the integration of blockchain with ISO 9001:2015 standard-based quality management system. *Total Quality Management & Business Excellence, 34*(3–4), 291–311. DOI: 10.1080/14783363.2022.2054318

Muruganandham, S., Kumar, S., & Singh, A. (2022). Application of artificial intelligence in quality management and predictive maintenance. *Journal of Manufacturing Technology Management, 33*(8), 1352–1371. DOI: 10.1108/JMTM-02-2021-0065

National Institute of Standards and Technology. (2023). Artificial Intelligence Risk Management Framework (AI RMF 1.0). NIST., Retrieved September 2, 2025, from, DOI: 10.6028/NIST.AI.100-1

Omisola-Shiyanbola, A. (2024). A systems-based framework for ISO 9000 compliance: Applying statistical quality control and continuous improvement tools in U.S. manufacturing. *International Journal of Advanced Multidisciplinary Research and Studies, 4*(6), 4052. DOI: 10.62225/2583049X.2024.4.6.4052

Onwubuariri, E. R., Adelakun, B. O., Olaiya, O. P., & Ziorklui, J. E. K.Ebere Ruth OnwubuaririBeatrice Oyinkansola AdelakunOmolara Patricia OlaiyaJoseph Elikem Kofi Ziorklui. (2024). AI-driven risk assessment: Revolutionizing audit planning and execution. *Finance & Accounting Research Journal, 6*(6), 1069–1090. Advance online publication. DOI: 10.51594/farj.v6i6.1236

Open Worldwide Application Security Project. (2024). OWASP top 10 for large language model applications v1.1. OWASP. https://owasp.org/www-project-top-10-for-large-language-model-applications/ (Accessed September 2, 2025)

Paoletti, M. (2024). ISO/IEC standards and design of an artificial intelligence system. *2024 IEEE 13th International Conference on Artificial Intelligence Systems (ICAIS),* 39–43. DOI: 10.1109/ICAIS59948.2024.10472957

Parmar, J. (2022). Artificial intelligence in high-tech manufacturing: A review of applications in quality control and process optimization. *International Journal of Innovative Research in Engineering & Multidisciplinary Physical Sciences, 10*(6), 55–61. DOI: 10.37082/IJIRMPS.v10.i6.231961

Pereira, A., Henriques, R., & Barata, J. (2021). An ArchiMate-based approach to ISO 9001:2015 quality management: Shifting to IT-enabled documented information. *2021 IEEE 23rd Conference on Business Informatics (CBI),* 2, 125–133. DOI: 10.1109/CBI52690.2021.10063

Pereira, A., Monteiro, A., & Silva, T. (2021). Conversational agents for document retrieval: Enhancing organizational knowledge access. *Information Systems Frontiers, 23*(3), 743–756. DOI: 10.3390/app15010223

Pylypchuk, O., Holitsyn, O., & Vasilkova, N. (2025). International standards of the ISO 9000-9004 series in the system of marketing management. *Marketing and Digital Technologies, 9*(1), 130–139. Advance online publication. DOI: 10.15276/mdt.9.1.2025.7

Raghavan, M., Barocas, S., Kleinberg, J., & Levy, K. (2020). Mitigating bias in algorithmic hiring: Evaluating claims and practices. *Proceedings of the 2020 Conference on Fairness, Accountability, and Transparency,* 469–481. DOI: 10.1145/3351095.3372828

Rahman, H., Hossain, M., Mintoo, A. A., & Islam, S. (2025). A systematic review of intelligent support systems for strategic decision-making using human-AI interaction in enterprise platforms. *American Journal of Advanced Technology and Engineering Solutions, 4*(2), 33–47. DOI: 10.63125/a5yh1293

Rakić, B., Ubavić, V., Živanović, V., & Babić, D. (2024). *Implementation of integrated ISO standards (ISO 9001, ISO/IEC 27001 and ISO/IEC 27701): Proof of quality and safe business processes and services.* Urbanism and Sustainable Development., DOI: 10.46793/Urbanizam24.277R

Ramese, W. K. D., Jayasooriya, S. D., & Lakmal, A. H. (2024). Adopting ISO 9001:2015 & ISO 21001:2018 EOMS to the Sri Lankan higher educational institutions: A review of literature. *KDU Journal of Multidisciplinary Studies, 6*(1), 145–157. Advance online publication. DOI: 10.4038/kjms.v6i1.118

Reyes, I. O., & Barillo, E. A.IMELDA O. REYESEFREN A. BARILLO. (2024). Challenges encountered in the implementation of ISO 9001:2015 risk management system DNV-GL. *International Journal For Multidisciplinary Research, 6*(2), 16380. Advance online publication. DOI: 10.36948/ijfmr.2024.v06i02.16380

Rustam, A. R., & Widiastutik, R. N. (2024). Pendampingan audit mutu perusahaan (ISO 9001). *Jurnal ABM Mengabdi, 11*(1), 46. Advance online publication. DOI: 10.31966/jam.v11i1.1407

Sadikin, A., Wibowo, H., & Rahman, R. (2022). Artificial intelligence and ISO 9001: Theoretical perspectives and future challenges. *Computer Science, 197*, 601–610. DOI: 10.1016/j.procs.2021.12.178

Sánchez Lizárraga, M. A., Limón Romero, J., Tlapa Mendoza, D., & Báez López, Y. (2020). ISO 9001 standard: Exploratory analysis in the manufacturing sector in Mexico. *Dyna, 87*(213), 202–211. DOI: 10.15446/dyna.v87n213.83230

Sankaran, S. (2025). Enhancing Trust Through Standards: A Comparative Risk-Impact Framework for Aligning ISO AI Standards with Global Ethical and Regulatory Contexts. *ArXiv, abs/2504*.16139. *l* arXiv.2504.16139.DOI: 10.1109/ACDSA65407.2025.11166403

Sarfraz, A., Sarfraz, Z., Sarfraz, M., Abdul Razzack, A., Bano, S., Makkar, S. S., Thevuthasan, S., Paul, T., Sana, M. K., Azeem, N., Félix, M., & Chérrez-Ojeda, I. (2022). Industry 4.0 technologies for the manufacturing and distribution of COVID-19 vaccines. *Journal of Primary Care & Community Health, 13*, 21501319211068638. Advance online publication. DOI: 10.1177/21501319211068638

Senanayake, N., & Naveen, R. (2021). Process performance evaluation in mechanical engineering industries in accordance with ISO 9001. *IOP Conference Series. Materials Science and Engineering, 1057*(1), 012067. DOI: 10.1088/1757-899X/1057/1/012067

Sharma, R., & Haralayya, B. (2025). Corporate governance and AI ethics: A strategic framework for ethical decision-making in business. *Journal of Information Systems Engineering & Management, 10*(30s), 233–247. DOI: 10.52783/jisem.v10i30s.4775

Shoira Azimovna, K. (2024). Ethical governance of artificial intelligence in quality management systems. *International Journal of Ethics and Systems, 40*(1), 19–35. DOI: 10.1108/IJOES-06-2023-0112

Singh, C. L. (2024). Implications of AI and metaverse in media and communication spaces. *SN Computer Science, 5*(1098), 1–15. DOI: 10.1007/s42979-024-03415-x

Somasundaram, M., Junaid, K., & Mangadu, S. (2020). Artificial intelligence (AI) enabled intelligent quality management system (IQMS) for personalized learning path. *Procedia Computer Science, 172*, 438–442. DOI: 10.1016/j.procs.2020.05.096

Suredranath, R. (2025). A systematic approach to AI security governance: Leveraging ISO 42001. *International Journal of Innovative Science and Research Technology, 10*(4), 394–401. DOI: 10.38124/ijisrt/25apr394

Tahrir, M., & Barus, M. D. B. (2023). The effectiveness of implementing the quality management system ISO 9001:2015 in supervising road and bridge projects in South Sulawesi Province. *International Journal of Economic. Technology and Social Sciences (Injects), 3*(2), 375–380. Advance online publication. DOI: 10.53695/injects.v3i2.857

Vazirizade, S. M., Alikhani, M., & Shams, M. (2020). Using NLP and machine learning for document classification and knowledge management in organizations. *Journal of Information Science, 46*(5), 635–650. DOI: 10.1177/0165551519893281

Walawalkar, A., Swamy, R. M., & Kuttimarks, M. S. (2024). Improving organizational performance with ISO 9001 QMS audits. *International Journal for Research in Applied Science and Engineering Technology, 12*(6), 456–465. DOI: 10.22214/ijraset.2024.65667

Wolniak, R. (2021). *Internal audit and management review in ISO 9001:2015. Silesian University of Technology Scientific Papers, Organization and Management*. Series., DOI: 10.29119/1641-3466.2021.151.49

Yakushova, E., Cherepovskaya, N., Litvin, I., Chemodanova, O. N., & Gainochenko, T. M. (2022). Transformation of hospitality industry under the COVID-19 crisis. In *Strategies and Trends in Organizational and Project Management* (pp. 145–157). Springer., DOI: 10.1007/978-3-030-94245-8_11

Yazo-Cabuya, E. J., Ibeas, A., & Rey-Caballero, R. (2025). Multi-criteria decision making for risk management in quality management systems. *Sustainability (Basel)*, *17*(3), 1092. DOI: 10.3390/su17031092

Yu, Y., Hu, X., Rajaganapathy, S., Feng, J., Abdelhameed, A., Li, X., Li, J., Liu, K., Yang, L., Taner, N., Fiero, P., Boroumand, S., Larsen, R., Goyal, M., Otley, C., Zong, N., Halamka, J., & Tao, C. (2025). Launching Insights: A Pilot Study on Leveraging Real-World Observational Data from the Mayo Clinic Platform to Advance Clinical Research. *ArXiv, abs/2504.16090*. /arXiv.2504.16090.DOI: 10.48550

Zhang, S. (2024). Research on the application of AI technology in auditing. *Economic Management & Global Business Studies*, *3*(2), 41–50. DOI: 10.69610/j.emgbs.20240831

Zhang, Z., Zhao, Y., & Xu, W. (2021). AI-based visual inspection in automotive manufacturing. *Journal of Manufacturing Systems*, *60*, 555–564. DOI: 10.1016/j.jmsy.2021.03.009

Zineb, A., Zineb, F., Ismael, E. O., & Ikram, M. (2022). Effects of COVID-19 on population, economic growth, logistics performance, and quality management in Africa: Grey relational analysis. *International Journal of Grey Systems*, *2*(3), 18–33. Advance online publication. DOI: 10.52812/ijgs.56

Chapter 16
ISO 9001:2026:
Facing the Future, Smart Quality and Digital Ecosystems in Industry 4.0

Omar A. Guirette-Barbosa
http://orcid.org/0000-0003-1336-9475
Universidad Politécnica de Zacatecas, Mexico & Broward International University, Mexico

Selene Castañeda-Burciaga
http://orcid.org/0000-0002-2436-308X
Universidad Politécnica de Zacatecas, Mexico & Broward International University, Mexico

Oscar Cruz-Domínguez
http://orcid.org/0000-0003-1320-4371
Universidad Politécnica de Zacatecas, Mexico

Héctor A. Durán-Muñoz
Universidad Politécnica de Zacatecas, Mexico

Martha Angélica Ramírez-Salazar
http://orcid.org/0000-0001-6536-4161
Universidad Autónoma de Fresnillo, Mexico & Universidad Politécnica de Zacatecas, Mexico

ABSTRACT

This chapter explores how Manufacturing 4.0 and emerging technologies, such as Artificial Intelligence (AI), Blockchain, and the Internet of Things (IoT), are transforming quality management systems in anticipation of the upcoming revision of the ISO 9001:2026 standard. These digital tools are enabling the development of intelligent processes, connected supply chains, and organizational structures that are more resilient, agile, and sustainable. AI is portrayed as the driving force behind "Smart Quality", capable of predicting failures, enhancing decision-making, and enriching the customer experience. Blockchain is highlighted as a foundation for traceability and decentralized trust, while IoT facilitates large-scale, real-time data collection to support continuous improvement initiatives. Importantly, the chapter emphasizes that these technologies do not replace human involvement; rather, they enhance and empower human roles within the digital production ecosystem.

DOI: 10.4018/979-8-3373-4027-2.ch016

1. INTRODUCTION

In the current era, characterized by profound global interconnectedness and the accelerated flow of digital information, organizations are confronted with the imperative of maintaining competitiveness while upholding elevated standards of quality, sustainability, and resilience (Kovtunenko et al., 2024; Chepeliuk, 2024). Within this scenario, the ISO 9001 framework has emerged as a pivotal instrument in fostering the ongoing enhancement of processes, products, and services, relying on a risk-based orientation and a deliberate focus on fulfilling the expectations and needs of both customers and stakeholders (Stravinskienė & Serafinas, 2020; Alhamad et al., 2022). Nevertheless, the volatile and fast-evolving nature of contemporary industry demands a paradigm shift in quality management systems (QMS), particularly regarding the deliberate and strategic adoption of disruptive technologies, including Artificial Intelligence (AI), the Internet of Things (IoT), Blockchain, and advanced analytics (Balabanova et al., 2024; Tzempelikos, 2021).

These technological innovations extend beyond enhancing efficiency and traceability; they facilitate a predictive and preventive approach to quality management, coupled with more accurate decision-making supported by real-time data streams. The forthcoming ISO 9001:2026 standard offers a strategic avenue to reshape quality management in alignment with the principles of digital transformation, Industry 4.0, and sustainability (Anttila & Jussila, 2021). In this context, quality, sustainability, and resilience are conceptualized as mutually reinforcing pillars, each contributing to the long-term competitiveness and operational excellence of organizations. Integrating such digital tools fosters the evolution from a traditional compliance-based model toward an intelligent, predictive, and verifiable framework for quality assurance.

The deployment of ISO 9001:2026 is expected to play a decisive role in not only improving operational performance but also ensuring transparency throughout the value chain, strengthening stakeholder confidence, and advancing adherence to environmental, social, and governance (ESG) standards. Given the increasing complexity of the global environment, organizations are called to embrace innovation while simultaneously ensuring that their processes remain resilient, adaptive, and environmentally responsible (Asachi, 2021). Consequently, the future of quality management demands a systemic perspective supported by digital ecosystems capable of responding to the challenges of the present and anticipating the demands of the future. Within this framework, ISO 9001:2026 will play a critical role in guiding organizations towards a model of excellence that integrates technological tools, transparency, and intelligent decision-making as key enablers of sustainability, continuous improvement, and customer satisfaction.

This chapter examines the far-reaching implications of the current transformation in quality management, emphasizing the interplay between quality systems, emerging technologies, and sustainability as core pillars in building resilient, future-oriented organizations. In contemporary scenarios defined by competitiveness and sustainability imperatives, quality management has proven to be indispensable, given that economic, social, environmental, and governance considerations have become central to strategic planning and decision-making (Solodkovska & Avksientiev, 2024).

Historically, during the initial phases of industrial expansion, productivity gains and cost efficiency were largely attained through manual oversight and fragmented optimization efforts. In contrast, the integration of data-driven and digital solutions has fundamentally reshaped quality assurance, positioning it as a strategic cornerstone in present-day organizations. Within today's environment of rapid digital transformation and interconnected value chains, quality management should transcend reactive detection and correction functions, evolving instead toward anticipating deviations, adapting dynamically to changes, and ensuring transparency across the full lifecycle of products and services (Silverio & Pestana, 2022). ISO 9001 has traditionally provided a structured path toward superior process management and continuous improvement, embedding principles such as leadership, risk-oriented thinking, evidence-based decision-making, and stakeholder engagement. The forthcoming 2026 revision is expected to heighten the emphasis on transparency, traceability, and intelligent oversight, thereby safeguarding data integrity, enhancing information reliability, and reinforcing operational sustainability (Ross Gray et al., 2022). This progress will be reinforced by advanced technologies—such as AI, blockchain, and IoT—that facilitate the seamless integration of quality objectives with strategic risk governance, operational resilience, and ESG compliance.

Aligned with contemporary and anticipated challenges, the ISO 9001:2026 framework seeks to establish a comprehensive approach to quality management that nurtures innovation, sustains continuous improvement, and ensures long-term organizational sustainability (Osorio et al., 2021). Fundamentally, the shift toward Smart Quality represents a move away from compliance-centered paradigms toward proactive, data-enabled, and interconnected systems that generate value, foster trust, and secure sustainable growth. Despite the transformations it has undergone, the essence of quality management remains anchored in its capacity to meet needs, deliver value, and cultivate stakeholder confidence—elements that, in turn, contribute to enduring organizational benefits, a supportive internal culture, and a consistent customer-centric orientation (Karan et al., 2022).

2. PROBLEM STATEMENT

Although ISO 9001:2015 has achieved broad adoption, a persistent disparity remains between documented process control and the actual, real-time, end-to-end quality performance observed across multi-tier supply chains. In many cases, quality-critical information is dispersed among ERP, MES, LIMS, PLM systems, and external partner platforms, which limits the capacity for early risk detection, root-cause analysis, and auditable traceability beyond the immediate supply tier. This fragmentation results in delayed warning signals, inconsistent defect rates, increased cost of poor quality (CoPQ), and credibility challenges in ESG-related disclosures. The anticipated ISO 9001:2026 revision aims to intensify requirements for predictive, data-driven, and auditable quality management, thereby underscoring the need to implement Smart Quality principles throughout the entire value chain.

Key operational indicators such as CoPQ, Mean Time to Detect (MTTD), and Mean Time to Repair (MTTR) are pivotal in determining manufacturing efficiency, profitability, and customer satisfaction. Elevated CoPQ values—sometimes amounting to as much as 40% of operating expenses—represent significant resource depletion arising from defects, rework, and inefficiencies. Likewise, extended MTTR intervals and high MTTD figures exacerbate downtime costs, diminish equipment reliability, and delay production schedules. Targeting these metrics through structured continuous improvement frameworks, including Six Sigma, predictive maintenance, and process optimization, can substantially mitigate waste while enhancing sustainable competitiveness. Empirical evidence indicates that systematic quality initiatives have the potential to markedly reduce CoPQ and MTTR, thereby restoring lost productivity and improving financial outcomes (Kumar & Khanduja, 2021; Faciane et al., 2021; Fatma et al., 2020).

Despite ISO 9001's wide recognition, progress toward digital maturity remains uneven; surveys reveal that approximately 30% of manufacturing firms still depend on manual or semi-manual evidence collection during audits (Naveen et al., 2021). Industry analyses estimate that CoPQ can reach 20% of sales or operating expenditures, with losses magnified during supply chain disruptions (Chumba et al., 2019). Conversely, facilities that have deployed predictive analytics and IoT solutions report measurable gains, including reduced unplanned downtime and improvements of up to 20% in MTTD and MTTR, which translate into higher right-first-time rates and enhanced service levels for customers (Deloitte, 2017).

In operational practice, these gaps are aggravated by disparate data structures, insufficient interoperability between internal information systems and supplier platforms, reliance on manual evidence collection during audits, and varying levels of digital capability among supply chain tiers. Such limitations hinder timely detection and recovery (MTTD/MTTR), weaken preventive measures, and complicate the validation of product histories and sustainability claims. Effectively addressing these challenges necessitates a socio-technical strategy that integrates robust governance mechanisms (roles, policies, and controls), advanced technology deployment (AI, blockchain, IoT), and capacity-building initiatives for supply chain partners.

3. PURPOSE OF THE STUDY

This chapter presents a pragmatic Smart Quality framework that aligns with the forthcoming ISO 9001:2026 standard, demonstrating how Artificial Intelligence (AI), blockchain, and the Internet of Things (IoT) can be embedded within quality management systems (QMS) to address existing deficiencies in visibility, predictability, and traceability. The approach follows three main steps: (1) establishing explicit linkages between ISO principles and clauses and corresponding digital capabilities such as monitoring, predictive analysis, and verifiable record-keeping; (2) outlining integration pathways across key QMS domains, including planning, operational execution, performance evaluation, continuous improvement, and supplier relationship management; and (3) illustrating the proposed framework through a practice-based case study. The scope is centered on manufacturing and logistics within multi-tier supply chains, targeting an audience composed of quality leaders, supply chain managers, and auditors preparing for compliance and readiness by 2026.

The proposed outputs encompass a comprehensive mapping of ISO clauses to digital capabilities, a structured adoption roadmap incorporating interoperability checkpoints, and a succinct maturity checklist designed for both audits and self-assessment exercises. This work intentionally excludes highly detailed, sector-specific regulatory discussions and the execution of primary field experiments. Instead, it synthesizes insights from recent academic research and industry practice to produce actionable guidance that remains independent of specific sectoral constraints while maintaining compatibility with the ISO 9001:2026 framework.

4. IMPORTANCE AND JUSTIFICATION

The importance of iso 9001:2026 a standard that promotes operational excellence.

The ISO 9001 standard, dedicated to the development of Quality Management Systems (QMS), has established itself as a global reference for best business practices. In an economic environment defined by rapid technological progress, heightened market competition, and the gradual elimination of trade barriers, organizations require management models capable of delivering agile and precise responses to emerging challenges (Kurniawati et al., 2022).

Within this framework, the process-based management approach promoted by ISO 9001 offers a robust platform for transforming environmental complexity into a source of strategic advantage (Kowalczyk, 2024). This methodology strengthens operational efficiency, reduces process variability, and enhances the capacity to adjust to evolving customer expectations (Gutiérrez & Aragón Casas, 2023).

The pursuit of excellence described in this context should be understood not as a static objective but as a continuous and adaptive process. Such a perspective requires organizations to cultivate a strong culture of ongoing improvement, enabling them to proactively identify vulnerabilities and implement timely corrective or developmental actions to capitalize on opportunities (Egbumokei et al., 2024). Strategic decision-making grounded in accurate data and the enhancement of critical processes fosters more resilient management structures that optimize resources, generate sustained value, and anticipate environmental risks (Rezki & Mansouri, 2023).

Sector leadership is determined not only by the quality of the products or services offered but also by the customer experience, which is shaped by efficient, consistent, and innovative internal operations. In many cases, customer satisfaction directly reflects the operational quality embedded in these processes (Majumdar, 2024). Consequently, continuous improvement, innovation capacity, and a commitment to excellence have become indispensable components for maintaining competitiveness, ensuring sustainability, and securing long-term growth (Chandran, 2024).

In light of these considerations, ISO 9001 serves as an integrated methodological instrument, delivering a versatile framework adaptable to organizations of various sectors and scales for the creation of resilient, results-oriented management systems. Its significance extends beyond process standardization to include the strengthening of organizational culture, the stimulation of innovation, and the consolidation of a strategic vision that enables firms to prosper in complex and evolving contexts (Kowalczyk, 2024).

Sustainability as a Central Pillar in ISO 9001:2026

Sustainability, conceived as the equilibrium between economic, social, and environmental spheres, has emerged as a critical prerequisite for organizations aiming to secure long-term viability and institutional legitimacy. Within the framework of ISO 9001:2026, sustainability is anticipated to function as a cross-cutting dimension of quality management systems, embedding practices such as life cycle assessment, ethical supplier selection, and transparent performance disclosure. The integration of sustainability considerations into quality management responds to the increasing expectations of stakeholders, regulatory authorities, and markets, all of which demand tangible evidence of ethical behavior, environmental stewardship, and positive social impact.

This evolution also aligns with the progression toward circular economy paradigms, where strategies of waste minimization, product reuse, and material recycling are prioritized to enhance efficiency and deliver value across the entire product lifecycle. Consequently, sustainability becomes a foundational pillar that elevates the strategic significance of quality management, reinforcing its role in shaping organizations that are resilient, credible, and prepared to navigate future challenges.

5. METHODOLOGY

This study employs a qualitative, descriptive, and analytical methodology grounded in documentary research and a systematic review of specialized literature. Such a design enables a thorough examination of the transition toward ISO 9001:2026 within the broader framework of Industry 4.0, allowing for the identification of regulatory, technological, and strategic factors that define the concept of Smart Quality and its integration within industrial digital ecosystems. The overarching methodological objective is to map the convergence between regulatory developments and technological advancements, thereby constructing a conceptual model that can serve as a foundation for practical implementation in organizations aiming to align with the updated standard.

The research was structured into four interconnected phases:

- Phase 1: Study design. Definition of the research problem and formulation of the main objectives. Delimitation of the thematic scope to ISO 9001:2015 and anticipated provisions of ISO 9001:2026, incorporating Industry 4.0 perspectives. Identification of critical conceptual variables, including Smart Quality, digitization, traceability, automation, and organizational resilience.
- Phase 2: Systematic document review. Selection of primary and secondary sources published between 2020 and 2025, emphasizing peer-reviewed academic studies, technical reports from recognized bodies (ISO, ISO/TC 176, IEC), and specialized literature. Inclusion criteria included thematic relevance, recency, and empirical evidence related to the application of quality management systems in digital environments. Studies lacking empirical grounding or unrelated to technological integration in quality management were excluded.
- Phase 3: Comparative analysis and thematic coding. Structural comparison between ISO 9001:2015 and preliminary drafts or discussions of ISO 9001:2026. Coding of findings under categories such as regulatory requirements, digital tools, process impacts, and organizational cultural shifts. Integration of documented implementation cases from sectors including advanced manufacturing, logistics, and energy.
- Phase 4: Interpretive synthesis and conceptual model development. Formulation of the Intelligent Quality conceptual framework as the central axis. Proposal of actionable strategies and recommendations to support adoption of the revised standard. Theoretical validation was conducted through cross-referencing with global trends in quality management and digital transformation.

The selection of a qualitative methodology is justified by the study's primary goal: not to quantify the impact of the revised standard, but to gain an in-depth understanding of how and why organizations will be required to adapt their management systems. This approach facilitates the capture of the complexity inherent in technological integration, the exploration of interactions between regulatory, cultural, and technological factors, and the provision of a framework adaptable to multiple sectoral contexts. By employing this methodological design, the research ensures both the theoretical robustness and practical relevance of its findings, thereby bridging the gap between academic discourse and organizational practice.

6. THEORETICAL FRAMEWORK

6.1 Smart Quality and Resilience

The convergence of quality management, digital transformation, and sustainability is not a random occurrence but the result of three interdependent global trends.

Regulatory evolution: ISO 9001 has progressed from an initial focus on documentary compliance in its earliest versions to a process-based model (ISO 9001:2000), later integrating risk management principles (ISO 9001:2015), and, in its forthcoming 2026 revision, incorporating components explicitly related to digitalization and sustainability.

Industry 4.0: The integration of technologies such as the Internet of Things (IoT), Artificial Intelligence (AI), Blockchain, and Collaborative Robotics is reshaping quality management systems into predictive, interconnected, and data-driven platforms.

Agenda 2030 and ESG criteria: Management systems are increasingly required to demonstrate not only technical compliance but also tangible contributions to social well-being and environmental protection.

Main related theories

6.1.1 Systems Theory

From this perspective, quality management is conceptualized as an open system composed of interdependent processes that receive inputs, generate outputs, and incorporate feedback mechanisms. Within the ISO 9001:2026 framework, this theory is expanded to include real-time data flows, AI-driven feedback, and integration with external platforms such as blockchain-based traceability systems (Madhani, 2020).

6.1.2 Theory of Continuous Improvement (Kaizen)

The Kaizen philosophy asserts that improvement should be incremental, ongoing, and participatory. In the updated ISO standard, this principle is reinforced by digital technologies that facilitate the continuous monitoring of key quality indicators (KQIs), enable real-time adjustments through predictive analytics, and enhance workforce engagement via collaborative digital interfaces (Mahdikhani, 2023).

6.1.3 Theory of Creating Shared Value

This theory proposes that businesses can generate economic value while addressing societal and environmental challenges. In the context of ISO 9001:2026, it manifests through processes designed to reduce waste and carbon emissions, the development of products and services with measurable social benefits, and the integration of ESG metrics into the quality management framework (Porter & Kramer, 2011).

6.1.4 Theory of Disruptive Technological Change

This theoretical approach explains how emerging technologies can fundamentally reshape established processes. Practical applications within ISO 9001:2026 include the substitution of traditional audits with remote, automated assessments, and the adoption of digital twins to simulate and optimize processes before full-scale implementation (Bankoff et al., 2022).

6.2 Smart Quality and Resilience in the Supply Chain

The ISO 9001 standard has demonstrated its value as a fundamental instrument for reinforcing organizational resilience. Although it does not prescribe specific metrics for its direct measurement, it establishes the foundations for developing systems capable of responding effectively to adverse events. Among the relevant metrics, one of the most indicative of resilience is the recovery time required to reestablish normal operations. This includes the restoration of production processes, the reactivation of communication channels, the procurement of critical inputs, and the resumption of commercial and financial activities, along with assessing the repercussions across the entire logistics network (Wallace, 2021).

The forthcoming ISO 9001:2026 revision is expected to incorporate a significant innovation: the concept of Smart Quality. This paradigm promotes the integration of self-monitoring functionalities into products and services through the use of advanced technological systems. It moves beyond the scope of regulatory compliance by embedding predictive and adaptive mechanisms, linked to performance indicators such as resource utilization efficiency, defect rates, and comprehensive risk management (Henrichs & Krupitzer, 2024). In this way, Smart Quality emerges as a proactive, optimized, and perpetually evolving management model.

6.3 Fundamentals of Smart Quality

Smart Quality is founded on the capacity to convert intangible assets—such as corporate reputation, customer loyalty, and innovation—into measurable and controllable variables directly associated with organizational performance. This perspective demands that all organizational units possess a thorough understanding of the business model and align their activities with the company's overarching strategic objectives (Trequattrini et al., 2022).

Achieving this transformation requires the establishment of mechanisms for the evaluation and processing of information, enabling the translation of abstract aspirations into tangible, quantifiable, and strategically aligned actions. The higher the degree of intangibility of an asset, the greater the value derived from its effective management (Chaikovskaya, 2021). The core purpose of Smart Quality is precisely to structure this conversion, ensuring that intangible factors are objectively incorporated into systems for assessment and continuous improvement.

The ISO 9000 family of standards provides the foundational framework for this approach, offering guidance for the creation of products and services that satisfy evolving market expectations. Nonetheless, certification practices are expected to evolve, placing greater emphasis on the individual performance of process operators (Semenova et al., 2024). In this context, continuous monitoring of non-conformities, organizational learning capacity, adaptability, and the active contribution of each participant within the Quality Management System (QMS) will acquire heightened relevance in driving organizational transformation.

Advanced technologies such as artificial intelligence, machine learning, and big data analytics will enable the conversion of even the most basic data into critical insights for ongoing improvement. Anticipated developments include the deployment of systems capable of self-regulation, predictive analysis, and autonomous decision-making, thereby fostering the continuous enhancement of overall organizational performance (Trequattrini et al., 2022).

6.4 Supply Chain Resilience

Resilience should not be understood solely as the ability to recover after a disruption, but as an active strategy that prepares the organization to respond, adapt, and evolve in the face of uncertain scenarios. This approach involves developing competencies that allow for anticipating changes, reducing their impact, and strengthening operational continuity.

To build truly resilient supply chains, the following are required: Proactive Process Management Focused on People and Resources: It's essential to map critical processes, identify points of vulnerability, and define robust contingency plans. Added to this is the importance of effective human talent management, the efficient use of resources, and the implementation of dashboards that offer real-time information (Xue, 2024).

Diversification and sustainability of sources: Relying on a limited number of suppliers creates significant risks. It is recommended to secure at least one alternative source for each critical flow, taking into account aspects like raw material availability, regulatory stability, quality variability, and sustainability of operations. A resilient supplier will be one that demonstrates adaptability, regulatory compliance, and environmental and social commitment (Zhang, 2024).

In this framework, ISO 9001:2026 will consolidate its role as a catalyst for resilience through the following mechanisms:

- Systematic vulnerability analysis: The identification of Single Points of Failure (SPOFs) and systemic risks that could compromise business continuity will be promoted (The 2024 CD2 draft of ISO 9001:2026 includes a new explicit section on evaluating "Single Points of Failure" (SPOFs) and systemic risks, reinforcing the proactive identification of vulnerabilities in critical processes).
- Business Continuity Planning (BCP): The standard will include explicit requirements to integrate contingency and recovery plans into quality management systems (According to the already circulated draft (Committee Draft 2, early 2025), the standard will incorporate direct requirements to integrate business continuity plans as a structural part of the quality management system).
- Strategic application of emerging technologies: Tools such as AI, blockchain, and IoT will help to anticipate risks, improve traceability, and increase the capacity to react to abrupt changes (Both CD1 and CD2 drafts, revised between April and September 2024, explicitly incorporate the adoption of AI, blockchain, and IoT as key tools for anticipating risks, ensuring traceability, and enhancing responsiveness to disruptions).

In conclusion, the ISO 9001:2026 standard will not only propose mechanisms for recovering operations after a crisis but will also foster the creation of adaptive, intelligent, and sustainable business ecosystems capable of thriving in complex environments, thereby ensuring long-term continuity and operational excellence.

7. LITERATURE REVIEW

7.1 The evolution of iso 9001, from conformity to strategic management and sustainability

Since its establishment in 1947, the International Organization for Standardization (ISO) has consolidated its role as a central authority in the harmonization of global standards. Within its extensive portfolio, ISO 9001 has emerged as the most widely adopted standard, serving as a strategic reference for organizations seeking to develop resilient and effective quality management systems (Wella & Chia, 2020). Since its debut in 1987, ISO 9001 has undergone successive revisions—in 1994, 2000, 2008, and 2015—that attest to its capacity to adapt to technological, economic, and social shifts, as well as evolving stakeholder demands (Simão et al., 2020).

The 2015 revision represented a pivotal transformation, crafted to address the challenges of a global environment increasingly characterized by volatility, uncertainty, complexity, and ambiguity—commonly framed by the acronym VUCA (Martins et al., 2021). This edition promoted a strategic orientation centered on risk-based thinking, the anticipation of scenarios, and compatibility with other management frameworks through the adoption of Annex SL's high-level structure. It also incorporated explicit requirements for defining the organizational context and identifying relevant stakeholders, thereby embedding strategic alignment into the very core of quality management (Simão et al., 2020).

These changes did more than modernize the technical language of the standard; they redefined the operational mindset expected from organizations. By emphasizing prevention over reaction, the 2015 edition shifted quality management from a corrective paradigm toward one that actively anticipates and mitigates risks in critical processes (Gamit et al., 2024). This strategic repositioning has not only strengthened operational resilience but also enhanced the capacity of organizations to integrate quality objectives with broader governance, sustainability, and innovation agendas.

The historical evolution of ISO 9001 illustrates its ability to remain relevant across decades of disruptive change. Its adaptability, evidenced through progressive revisions, sets the stage for the forthcoming ISO 9001:2026 update, in which digital transformation, sustainability, and "Smart Quality" will converge. By tracing this trajectory, it becomes clear that the standard is not merely a compliance tool but a dynamic framework capable of guiding organizations toward sustained competitiveness and value creation in a rapidly evolving global landscape.

7.2 Historical Evolution of ISO 9001: From Rigid Conformity to Strategic Agility

he ISO 9000 family of standards was created to address the global demand for a unified quality management language, enabling organizations from diverse sectors and geographies to communicate and operate under shared principles (Bravi & Murmura, 2021). The 1994 revision placed significant emphasis on documentation and procedural control, a stance that, while improving formal consistency, attracted criticism for generating excessive bureaucratic load (Bravim et al., 2020). This initial phase, though well-intentioned, revealed that rigid documentation could hinder adaptability and responsiveness—two qualities essential in dynamic business environments. The transformative 2000 revision addressed this by introducing a process-based approach, which fostered the connection between activities, emphasized reviewing process interactions, and institutionalized continuous improvement via the PDCA cycle (Plan, Do, Check, Act), also known as the Deming Circle (Wella & Chia, 2020). By reframing quality management as an integrated system across the entire value chain, the standard transitioned from administrative compliance to strategic process orchestration. This shift laid the groundwork for later versions, proving that ISO standards could evolve beyond prescriptive control toward a model that promotes systemic thinking and sustainable operational excellence.

The 2015 revision of ISO 9001 strengthened the strategic orientation of the standard, reflecting the realities of globalization, increasingly complex supply chains, and customers who demand tailored, high-value experiences. This version advanced beyond compliance, embedding proactive leadership, risk-based planning, and enhanced channels for both internal and external strategic communication (Reyes & Barillo, 2024). By integrating leadership responsibility and risk management into the core of quality management, the standard positioned itself as a driver of organizational agility and resilience. It recognized that quality outcomes are not only the product of controlled processes but also of strategic alignment, stakeholder engagement, and the capacity to anticipate market shifts. This evolution also bridged operational execution with corporate vision, ensuring that quality became a competitive differentiator rather than merely a regulatory requirement. The 2015 edition thus served as a critical bridge toward the forthcoming ISO 9001:2026, setting the stage for deeper integration with digital transformation, sustainability goals, and the emerging Smart Quality paradigm.

7.3 Key Advances in ISO 9001:2015 and Projections for ISO 9001:2026

The 2015 revision of ISO 9001 introduced substantial innovations, among which the emphasis on understanding both the internal and external operating context was particularly transformative. This focus enabled organizations to adapt their management approaches to shifting market conditions with greater agility. Additionally, the formalization of stakeholder identification including employees, suppliers, regulators, local communities, and civil society expanded the scope of quality management beyond the organization's immediate boundaries (Gamit et al., 2024). This holistic perspective fostered stronger alignment between corporate objectives and environmental expectations, reinforcing the strategic relevance of proactive leadership, data-driven decision-making, and forward-looking strategies. In doing so, the standard encouraged organizations to view quality not merely as an internal metric, but as an interconnected element influenced by and influencing—a wider ecosystem.

Looking toward 2026, the upcoming revision of ISO 9001 is expected to build upon these advances while introducing a sharper focus on two central pillars: strategic supply chain management and organizational sustainability (Chowdhury, 2025). These pillars respond to global imperatives that demand resilient, transparent, and sustainable value chains, as well as governance models capable of integrating environmental and social priorities into operational performance. The following sections will provide a detailed exploration of these pillars, outlining the anticipated developments in the ISO 9001:2026 edition and their implications for organizations seeking to remain competitive and future-ready in a rapidly evolving global landscape.

7.3.1. Strengthening the Focus on the Supply Chain:

Supplier evaluation and risk management: The standard is expected to reinforce the need for continuous analysis of suppliers, prioritizing their responsiveness to disruptions and operational resilience (Walters, 2020), rather than just the traditional supplier evaluation approach.

Transparency and traceability: Technologies like blockchain will be encouraged to improve visibility over the origin and quality of products and components (Drankova & Denisova, 2023).

Collaboration between links: Fluid communication and greater cooperation between key supply chain actors will be promoted, fostering real-time decision-making (Vanichchinchai, 2021).

Digitalization: The adoption of tools such as IoT, artificial intelligence, and big data analytics will be fundamental for optimizing efficiency, reducing errors, and anticipating needs (Rojo-Gallego-Burín et al., 2020).

7.3.2. Advanced Integration of Sustainability Principles:

The forthcoming ISO 9001:2026 revision is expected to embed sustainability at the core of quality management through mechanisms such as the life cycle approach, requiring organizations to systematically evaluate social and environmental impacts from product conception to final disposal (Topuz, 2022; Nikolakis et al., 2024). This orientation extends to the supply chain, where environmental, social, and governance (ESG) criteria will play a decisive role in supplier selection and evaluation processes (Honorato & Peroni, 2024; Zamlynskyi et al., 2023). By aligning procurement decisions with ESG principles, organizations will not only ensure compliance with stakeholder expectations but also mitigate reputational and operational risks associated with unsustainable practices. This integration reinforces the notion that quality performance is inseparable from responsible value chain management.

Corporate Social Responsibility (CSR) principles will become a structural element within the ISO 9001:2026 framework, directly influencing the quality management philosophy (Niyommaneerat et al., 2023). Alongside CSR, the circular economy will gain prominence through incentives for practices that minimize waste, promote material reuse, and encourage systematic recycling (Valdivia et al., 2024; Attanayake & Ratnayake, 2024). These initiatives go beyond environmental stewardship—they generate operational efficiencies, open new market opportunities, and enhance long-term competitiveness. The incorporation of CSR and circular economy principles into quality systems underscores the shift toward a model where operational excellence is measured not only by output quality but also by societal and environmental contributions.

Far from representing a routine or minor update, ISO 9001:2026 is projected to deliver a substantive transformation in the role of quality management. The new edition will be designed to equip organizations with the capacity to operate with excellence, responsibility, and adaptability in a global context shaped by uncertainty, rapid digitalization, and pressing climate challenges (Balabanova et al., 2024). In this sense, the standard will act as a strategic compass, guiding companies toward becoming smarter, more resilient, and more sustainable entities (Orwa & Ragui, 2024). This evolution signifies not just a compliance requirement but a pathway to future-proof organizational performance against the intertwined demands of markets, technology, and the planet.

7.4. Digital Supply Chains: The Union of Quality, Sustainability, and Technology

Digital transformation has profoundly reshaped how companies operate, giving rise to concepts like Industry 4.0 and Logistics 4.0. Both are closely linked to the emergence of Digital Supply Chains (DSCs), which represent a significant evolution from traditional models (Lyandau & Biryukov, 2022). This transformation is based on the digitalization and connection of every link in the chain, from production to consumption, leading to more agile, efficient, adaptable, and personalized networks (Zhang & Huo, 2022). The level of digital maturity of both suppliers and customers determines the pace and scope of this evolution (Tiss & Orellano, 2023).

Ideally, a DSC should operate under a collaborative business model with full interconnection. However, resistance to sharing critical data, driven by security, privacy, and competitive concerns, represents a considerable obstacle to total integration (Kandil et al., 2024). Despite this, the benefits offered by digitalization far outweigh these barriers, solidifying it as an indispensable tool (Zhang & Gong, 2021).

At each phase of a product's journey to the final consumer, various intermediary services, such as increasingly common ERP systems or inventory management, generate and process large amounts of data. DSCs make it possible to capture, analyze, and use this information in real time, something that traditional, fragmented, and static systems cannot do with equal effectiveness (Mohammed et al., 2024).

7.4.1 Definition and Characterization of Digital Supply Chains (DSCs)

Digital Supply Chains (DSCs) are conceptualized as collaborative, adaptive, and highly interconnected structures that bring together diverse stakeholders with the shared objective of meeting end-customer demands whether through goods or services (Thakur, 2024; Mullapudi, 2025; Famoti et al., 2025). Their effectiveness relies on the strategic deployment of digital technologies to collect, process, and analyze data, enabling decision-making that is both efficient and timely (Kumari & Lele, 2023; Enyejo et al., 2024). This capability not only enhances operational responsiveness but also fosters resilience, transparency, and the capacity to anticipate market fluctuations, thereby positioning DSCs as a critical enabler of competitive advantage in the context of Industry 4.0. The fundamental attributes that distinguish a DSC include:

- Comprehensive digital connectivity: The entire network, from manufacturing (and even suppliers) to the consumer, is interconnected through constant digital information flows, enabling real-time monitoring of processes and decisions (Bendhi, 2025).
- End-to-end visibility: Each participant has updated access to the status of processes, inventories, and deliveries, allowing for proactive and strategic action in the face of potential bottlenecks or disruptions (Osho et al., 2024).
- Data-driven management: The use of tools such as artificial intelligence (AI), machine learning, and predictive analytics allows DSCs to detect patterns, anticipate consumer behavior, and continuously optimize their operations (Owusu-Berko, 2025).
- Structural agility and resilience: Technological interconnection and immediate access to critical information strengthen the ability to adapt to sudden changes and improve resistance to disruptive events (Maghroor et al., 2024).

- Intelligent automation: Beyond automating routine tasks, DSCs integrate systems capable of learning, making autonomous decisions, and prioritizing and freeing up human resources for strategic functions (Guduru, 2025).
- Enhanced collaboration: The availability of shared data in real time fosters stronger and more efficient relationships among all actors in the chain: suppliers, manufacturers, distributors, and customers (Hugo, 2024).
- Mass personalization: The ability to deeply analyze consumer preferences makes it possible to offer products and services tailored to their specific needs, thereby enhancing the customer experience (Guduru, 2025).

7.4.2 Digitalization as a Strategy for Business Competitiveness and Sustainability

In the current context of economic slowdowns and intensifying competition, digitalization has shifted from an option to an essential requirement for business survival and growth (Jain, 2024). An organization's ability to reinvent itself, innovate, and remain relevant is directly linked to its level of digitalization. Technologies such as digital twins allow processes to be simulated in virtual environments before implementation, representing a qualitative leap in operational planning (Fantozzi et al., 2025), (Hänel et al., 2021).

Digitalization involves a deep reconfiguration of organizational structures, transforming not only internal processes but also external relationships and business models. Unlike conventional automation (which stays within a company's walls), this transformation focuses on redesigning workflows to achieve higher levels of scalability, efficiency, and value generation (Veroba & Azmi, 2021).

The key benefits of this digital evolution include:

- Increased operational efficiency: Intelligent automation and the efficient use of resources reduce human errors and significantly boost organizational performance (Adama et al., 2024), (Adeyinka et al., 2022), (Olutimehin et al., 2021).
- Data-driven decisions: Access to real-time information allows for more accurate, faster decision-making that is aligned with the company's strategic objectives (Tazvivinga & Samuels, 2024), (Gupta et al., 2024).
- Greater organizational agility: Digitally mature companies can respond more quickly and flexibly to technological, economic, or political disruptions (Eyieyien et al., 2024), (Joel et al., 2024).
- Improved customer experiences: Digitalization enables a deeper understanding of individual consumer expectations, facilitating the delivery of highly personalized products and services (Olutimehin et al., 2021), (Bhuiyan et al., 2024).
- Constant innovation: The digital environment enables the creation of disruptive business models and the strategic monetization of data, generating new revenue streams (Shostak & Pavlova, 2024).
- Supply chain optimization: Digital technologies allow for advanced traceability and visibility, which increases the ability to anticipate risks and respond effectively to incidents (Adeyinka et al., 2022).
- Commitment to sustainability: Digitalization actively contributes to environmental and social objectives by reducing energy consumption, minimizing waste, and rigorously monitoring the carbon footprint (Liu & Liu, 2025), (Ejiga et al., 2024).

Ultimately, digitalization not only strengthens competitiveness but also paves the way for a more responsible, resilient, and customer-centric business management. By explicitly integrating these principles into its structure, the upcoming ISO 9001:2026 standard will become an essential resource for organizations to not only respond to change but to lead it (Holitsyn et al., 2025), thereby compelling all certified companies toward this evolutionary transition.

7.5. Sustainability as a Central Pillar in ISO 9001:2026

The forthcoming ISO 9001:2026 standard is expected to deliver a profound transformation by explicitly embedding sustainability principles across its requirements (Ceko, 2023). This expanded scope will transcend the environmental dimension to incorporate social and ethical considerations, fundamentally redefining the responsibilities of quality managers (Aktürk, 2024). Under this paradigm, these professionals will transition from being compliance-focused specialists to becoming strategic facilitators of both corporate and societal sustainability. Their mandate will include aligning internal operational practices with the expectations of a diverse range of stakeholders, customers, employees, suppliers, regulators, local communities, and society at large (Melnyk & Gallagher, 2024). Such alignment will not only strengthen corporate legitimacy but also enhance organizational resilience and value creation in complex and dynamic environments.

Despite these advancements, certain recent standards have revealed shortcomings by overlooking the intrinsic link between quality and sustainability (Dreković et al., 2021). For instance, the analysis of "Context of the Organization" requirements could be strengthened by incorporating disruptive trends associated with the Fourth Industrial Revolution—such as Digital Supply Chains and Digital Threads—that leverage IoT, Big Data, artificial intelligence, and cyber-physical systems (Hall & Taylor, 2024). Achieving genuine transformation under ISO 9001:2026 will therefore require adopting a culture of comprehensive change, one that extends beyond internal processes to encompass the entire value ecosystem (Ceko, 2023). This holistic shift will ensure that quality management becomes a catalyst for innovation, sustainability, and competitive advantage in the digital era.

7.5.1 The Fundamentals of Sustainability in ISO 9001:2026

Sustainable development, as popularized by the Brundtland Report (1987), is founded on the principle of meeting present needs without compromising the capacity of future generations to meet their own (Hoffmann, 2007). This paradigm underscores the interconnectedness of human well-being, productive systems, and environmental balance, promoting objectives such as the satisfaction of basic needs, the advancement of social equity, the eradication of poverty, and the enhancement of quality of life (Montoya, 2024). By integrating these dimensions, sustainable development functions as both a guiding framework for policy and a strategic imperative for organizations seeking to align long-term viability with societal and ecological responsibility.

For companies to actively contribute to this paradigm, they must redesign their corporate behavior from a holistic perspective, which includes:

a) Relationships with sustainable suppliers: Establishing alliances with actors who demonstrate responsible practices in both environmental and social aspects (Garza-Reyes et al., 2017). b) Offering sustainable products and services: Integrating sustainability criteria from design to post-sale, prioritizing resource efficiency, durability, and recyclability (Orlov et al., 2024). c) Sustainable internal organization:

Promoting a culture that internalizes sustainability at all hierarchical levels and functional departments (Kaswan & Rathi, 2020).

As described earlier, many quality management methodologies like Lean Manufacturing, 5S, Six Sigma, Zero Defects, or Just in Time, which traditionally focused on continuous improvement, efficiency, and waste reduction, also generate positive impacts in terms of sustainability. These are complemented by specific tools such as calculating the carbon footprint, water footprint, energy efficiency, Green Supply Chains, and Green Logistics (Ahmad et al., 2025).

Furthermore, Corporate Social Responsibility (CSR) broadens the corporate vision by considering both resource use and interaction with the environment. In this new framework, the ISO 9001:2026 standard seeks to position itself as a guide for creating companies that are not only competitive but also socially responsible and committed to sustainable development (Nagy & Szentesi, 2024).

7.5.2 Sustainability Integrated into Quality Management and the Supply Chain

For sustainability to be an operational reality rather than an isolated concept, it must be present at all levels of business management. The adoption of a product life cycle approach, from its conception to final disposal, in conjunction with a structured quality system, is key to achieving large-scale sustainable transformation (Nunhes et al., 2021).

Both the ISO 9000 and ISO 14000 families of standards include elements that promote continuous improvement (through the PDCA cycle), as well as the evaluation of risks associated with the environment (Stefanova-Stoyanova & Danov, 2022). However, in the new ISO 9001:2026, a further step is expected by making the relationship between quality and sustainability explicit in the following aspects:

- Life cycle assessment of products and services: The standard will promote a comprehensive evaluation of social and environmental impact at each stage of the life cycle (Valdivia et al., 2021).
- Sustainable supply chain management: A more complete analysis of the sustainable performance of suppliers will be required, going beyond traditional criteria like cost and quality (Bastas & Liyanage, 2018).
- Key sustainability indicators (KPIs): The standard will encourage the incorporation of metrics such as water footprint, carbon footprint, and the amount of waste generated as part of the quality management system (Brankley et al., 2017).
- Sustainability-aligned resilience: The ability to recover from a crisis must not only be rapid but also reinforce ethical and environmental commitments (Prazian, 2023).
- Transparency in communicating sustainable performance: Clear and verifiable dissemination of sustainable progress, both internally and externally, will be encouraged (Pyun et al., 2023).

In summary, ISO 9001:2026 will consolidate the idea that the quality of a product or service cannot be evaluated in isolation. It is intrinsically linked to how it was produced and the impact its creation, distribution, and consumption generate. Sustainability will cease to be a secondary aspiration and will become a guiding principle of organizational management (Kondratieva, 2025).

7.6 Emerging Technologies: Enabling Pillars of ISO 9001:2026 in Quality Management, the Supply Chain, and Manufacturing 4.0

In the 21st century, the capacity to innovate and adapt has become a decisive factor for organizational survival, particularly in environments shaped by rapid technological evolution. Emerging technologies are redefining both quality management and supply chains, elevating them to unprecedented levels of efficiency, visibility, and predictive capability. These advancements not only enable internal process optimization but also strengthen relationships with diverse stakeholder groups, especially as sustainability emerges as a determining factor in competitive positioning. Reflecting this reality, the forthcoming ISO 9001:2026 will explicitly recognize and promote the strategic integration of Artificial Intelligence (AI), Blockchain, and the Internet of Things (IoT) as foundational components of modern quality management systems (Muruganandham et al., 2022). By institutionalizing these technologies within the standard, organizations will be better positioned to anticipate risks, enhance operational transparency, and create sustainable value across their entire value chain.

7.6.1. Artificial Intelligence (AI): The Core of Smart Quality

Artificial Intelligence (AI) has evolved from being a mere technological tool to a disruptive force that is redefining how organizations conceptualize and manage quality. It refers to systems capable of executing tasks that traditionally required human intelligence, leveraging advanced algorithms and continuous learning from extensive datasets—commonly referred to as Big Data—to perform actions without direct human intervention (Morandín-Ahuerma, 2022). This ability to learn and refine performance through iterative interactions positions AI as a transformative element in modern quality management systems.

A distinctive strength of AI lies in its capacity to process multiple tasks simultaneously with exceptional accuracy while detecting intricate patterns concealed within vast repositories of data. Its inherently objective analyses generate real-time insights, significantly accelerating decision-making processes. One particularly revolutionary capability is "comparative qualitative diagnosis," through which AI can extract deep customer perceptions from unstructured feedback, surpassing the scope of conventional surveys and providing nuanced perspectives on needs and expectations (González M., 2024).

Recognizing this potential, the ISO Central Secretariat (2022–2025) has announced its intention to revise ISO 9001:2015 to explicitly integrate and promote the use of AI. The forthcoming ISO 9001:2026 is expected to introduce more detailed requirements for documenting AI applications, defining their operational scope, and ensuring their alignment with organizational objectives. This inclusion will enable quality management systems to intelligently optimize processes, anticipate potential defects before they occur, and adopt a more proactive approach to risk management.

In the context of supply chain and quality management, AI offers a spectrum of transformative applications. These include accurate demand forecasting—leveraging historical data, market trends, and external variables to optimize inventory and minimize waste (Ullah, 2025); smart predictive maintenance—combining IoT sensors with AI algorithms to anticipate equipment failures and reduce downtime (Profesor., 2025); and automated quality control—using computer vision and machine learning to detect defects on production lines with precision exceeding human capabilities (Ozek et al., 2025). Each of these applications enhances operational efficiency, reduces costs, and strengthens product reliability.

Additional high-impact implementations involve real-time logistics route optimization, where AI analyzes factors such as traffic, weather, and delivery schedules to reduce fuel consumption, delivery times, and carbon footprint (Ozek et al., 2025); predictive risk management, which identifies patterns signaling potential supply chain disruptions like supplier insolvency or extreme weather events (Ramaswany, 2018); and customer feedback analysis using Natural Language Processing (NLP) to process large volumes of unstructured comments from social media or surveys to pinpoint quality issues (Profesor., 2025). Furthermore, robotics and intelligent automation powered by AI are streamlining warehouse and production line operations, improving safety, and minimizing operational errors (Ullah, 2025). Collectively, these applications demonstrate AI's potential to reshape both the scope and the strategic impact of quality management under ISO 9001:2026.

7.6.2. Blockchain: A Pillar of Decentralized Trust for the Supply Chain

Blockchain technology has made a strong entry, driving unprecedented levels of trust, security, and transparency in transaction and data management. Although its origin is linked to cryptocurrencies, its potential has rapidly expanded to corporate data sharing. As a distributed and immutable digital ledger, Blockchain ensures the veracity of information, with applications ranging from unique asset identification to comprehensive information traceability throughout the entire value chain (Rahman et al., 2025).

The ability to uniquely identify items and services via Blockchain has revolutionary applications in quality management systems and the supply chain. It allows for complete traceability, for example, of a product's carbon footprint, the origin of food, or the authenticity of medicines. Furthermore, it can verify manufacturing and transport conditions, adding a previously unthinkable layer of trust (Sahoo, 2024).

Blockchain's versatility allows for the implementation of different algorithms, and its open-source nature facilitates the development of innovative solutions. "Smart contracts" pieces of code that automatically execute when certain predefined conditions are met add a layer of automation and trust. The integration of Blockchain with IoT can, for instance, ensure that data generated by sensitive devices is immutable, sealing information such as the temperature of perishable product shipments (Shivale et al., 2025). Although its use in logistics can be complex due to the need to design interconnected and interoperable systems, ISO 9001:2026 will undoubtedly promote the exploration of Blockchain to enhance traceability, transparency, and trust throughout the supply chain.

Potential Strategic Applications of Blockchain in the Supply Chain and Quality Management (ISO 9001:2026):

- Product Traceability: Offers an inviolable record of the origin, movement, and status of products along the chain, guaranteeing their authenticity and safety.
- Certified Quality and Conformity Management: Allows for the immutable recording of quality test results, certifications, and audits, creating a verified and accessible history.
- Transparent Supplier Management: A verifiable record of suppliers' certifications, ESG (Environmental, Social, and Governance) performance, and standard compliance.
- Smart Contracts for Automation: Automates critical processes, such as automatic payments once delivery and quality conditions are met, or automatic alerts for standard non-compliance.
- Intellectual Property Protection: Serves as a secure record for designs, patents, and other intellectual property assets throughout the value chain.
- Optimized Supply Chain Finance: Facilitates access to financing and the execution of secure and efficient payments among supply chain partners.

- Driving the Circular Economy and Sustainability: Allows for the recording of the life cycle of materials and products, supporting circularity models and carbon footprint transparency.

7.7. IoT (Internet of Things): Real-Time Data Collection for Quality

The Internet of Things (IoT) refers to an extensive network of physical devices equipped with sensors, software, and other technologies that enable seamless connectivity and data exchange over the Internet. This increasingly pervasive digital infrastructure has the fundamental capability to collect real-time data from an almost limitless number of sources, encompassing parameters such as humidity, noise, gas concentrations, and the structural integrity of components (Bedi et al., 2024). In the context of digital supply chains, the quantity and diversity of information generated by IoT is virtually boundless, providing a transformative foundation for operational improvement and quality enhancement.

By leveraging a continuous and real-time flow of data, organizations can achieve unprecedented gains in process efficiency and product quality. IoT integration enables functionalities that previously demanded significant manual intervention, thereby allowing companies to respond more effectively to competitive pressures. The strategic advantage lies in the capacity to convert raw, dispersed data into actionable insights, facilitating rapid, evidence-based decision-making that aligns with both operational and strategic goals.

Within the production environment, embedding IoT sensors into product design offers dual benefits: it allows for direct control over the device's internal functions and provides precise, context-specific data on its actual performance in the customer's environment. This evidence-based feedback is essential for informed decision-making regarding future improvements, the development of upgraded versions, and the optimization of manufacturing processes. Additionally, IoT can refine service delivery through personalization, streamline procurement and sales automation, and enable proactive interventions by suppliers and distributors (Bedi et al., 2024). Such capabilities significantly enhance the adaptability and competitiveness of organizations operating in dynamic markets.

The potential of IoT extends across the entire value chain, from factories and warehouses to transportation units, creating an uninterrupted flow of information that serves as a decisive competitive differentiator. This interconnected system enhances strategic decision-making by offering superior control, deep integration across operational stages, and unparalleled access to detailed analytics. These capabilities not only bolster an organization's responsiveness but also its resilience in the face of market volatility. As a result, ISO 9001:2026 is expected to actively promote the adoption of IoT as a core enabler for advancing operational quality, efficiency, and long-term organizational sustainability.Strategic Applications of IoT in the Supply Chain and Quality Management (ISO 9001:2026):

- Real Time Monitoring of Storage and Transport Conditions: Temperature, humidity, light, and vibration sensors ensure the quality and safety of sensitive products, such as food or medicine, throughout their chain of custody.
- Real Time Inventory Management: Sensors and smart tags automatically update inventory levels, reducing costly stockouts and excess stock.
- Predictive Asset Maintenance: Constant monitoring of machinery and vehicle fleets allows for predicting failures before they occur, optimizing maintenance schedules and minimizing downtime.
- Dynamic Optimization of Production Processes: The collection of data from the production line allows for identifying bottlenecks, optimizing workflows, and improving overall efficiency.

- Enhanced Traceability and Visibility: Real-time tracking of shipment location and status offers unprecedented visibility, improving security and response to incidents.
- In-Line and Automated Quality Control: Integrated sensors detect defects in real time during the manufacturing process, allowing for immediate corrective actions.
- Fleet Management and Fuel Efficiency: Monitoring vehicle performance in real time allows for optimizing fuel consumption and fleet efficiency.

Artificial Intelligence, Blockchain, and the Internet of Things are not merely isolated tools but interconnected pillars of digital transformation. Together, they will allow organizations to not only meet the requirements of ISO 9001:2026 but to exceed its expectations, building supply chains that are inherently intelligent, resilient, and deeply sustainable.

8. CASE STUDIES: ISO 9001 IN PRACTICE FOR RESILIENT AND SUSTAINABLE SUPPLY CHAINS

The global expansion of multinational corporations has led to supply chains of unprecedented complexity vast and intrinsically interdependent. While this reality creates new business opportunities, it also magnifies the potential for devastating domino effects from any disruption, whether due to extreme weather events, political instability, or technological breakdowns. Such disruptions not only damage a company's reputation but can also quickly reverse growth expectations.

The case studies presented below aim to illustrate how various multinational companies have capitalized on the implementation of the ISO 9001 standard in their supply chains, contributing to the creation of more sustainable and resilient logistics systems. The methodology used for selecting and analyzing these cases included a systematic review of academic literature and case studies published after 2020, focusing on disclosure, supply chains, and sustainability, supplemented with data from relevant governmental and non-governmental organizations. For this analysis, the examples of Jacobs Douwe Egberts (JDE Peet's) (Solace, n.d.) has been considered.

The findings from these case studies, particularly significant for supply chains, reveal that the implementation of an independent quality management evaluation system, formalized through ISO 9001 certification for suppliers, has generated notably positive effects:

- Constraint on Supply Chain Member Actions: The standard imposes a discipline and level of compliance that helps standardize processes and expectations.
- Clear Imposition of Responsibility: It unequivocally defines the responsibilities of each actor within the chain, fostering accountability.
- Reduction of Malicious Bargaining Power: By standardizing quality and performance requirements, information asymmetries and the potential for abusive negotiation power are mitigated.
- Strengthening of Supplier Evaluations: It encourages systematic internal audits and rigorous documentation, which raises the level of scrutiny on supplier performance.

In summary, the adoption of ISO 9001 has driven organizations to develop robust business continuity systems in their supply chains. These systems not only allow for the effective management of exogenous disruptions but also for the strategic reallocation of resources, prioritizing operational recovery and business continuity. This denotes a fundamental shift: from a reactive mindset to a proactive and deeply resilient one.

8.1. Industry Success Story: Jacobs Douwe Egberts

A Sustainable Digital Supply Chain (SDSC), by being interconnected, provides real-time information that is fundamental for making correct and effective decisions. This translates into a significant improvement in profitability and operational efficiency, minimizing the use of environmental resources, reducing response times, and optimizing procurement processes. However, if not properly managed, an SDSC can also introduce errors or inefficiencies that generate a negative global impact (Solace, n.d.).

Jacobs Douwe Egberts, one of the largest corporations in the coffee and tea industry with a vast and complex global supply chain, had implemented ISO 9001 to ensure the quality of its products. With the accelerated digitalization of its operations, the Group faced a considerable challenge: verifying that its Integrated Management System (which included quality, environment, and sustainability) worked optimally in conjunction with the new digital systems implemented.

Following an exhaustive analysis, JDE Peet's decided to conduct a deep evaluation of its supply chain through simulation, using advanced modeling software (such as the creation of digital twins of its operations). The results of this simulation were revealing: although the individual components of its chain operated with commendable efficiency, the overall system performance was below expectations. Critical inefficiencies were identified that were directly attributed to a lack of synchronization and integration in decision-making, as the holistic constraints of the entire set of components were not being considered.

This case of JDE Peet's clearly underscores the imperative to not only digitize processes but to integrate that digitalization with systemic quality management and a sustainability approach that encompasses the supply chain as a holistic and interconnected entity. ISO 9001:2026, by placing a strong emphasis on integration, risk management, and sustainability throughout the entire value chain, will provide the conceptual and practical framework for companies like JDE Peet's to address these challenges head-on. Its implementation will ensure that local optimizations do not compromise global efficiency and sustainability but rather contribute to superior performance across the entire chain.

ISO 9001:2026, by integrating sustainability into its deepest core, will force organizations to consider it as an intrinsic part of their quality management. This will transform sustainability from a "requirement" into a decisive competitive advantage and a driver of long-term value.

9. RECOMMENDATIONS

Overview. Recommendations focus on operationalizing Smart Quality in alignment with ISO 9001:2026, without changing your original narrative. They are structured for direct use in implementation roadmaps and management reviews:

- Strategic alignment: Declare Smart Quality as a strategic objective linked to customer, resilience and ESG outcomes; cascade targets to sites and suppliers via management review (Clause 9). Update the Quality Policy to include data governance, digital traceability and predictive control as commitments (Clauses 5 & 7).

- Clause-driven actions: Clause 4 (Context): maintain a living risk & stakeholder map; add supplier-market sensing dashboards. Clause 6 (Planning): adopt digital FMEA and scenario analysis; tie objectives to leading indicators (FPY, MTTD/MTTR, % provenance-complete lots). Clause 7 (Support): formalize data/model governance, skills matrix for AI/IoT, and auditable records (append-only logs/ledger) for critical processes. Clause 8 (Operation): instrument critical quality points with IoT; automate SPC; enforce recipe/parameter control; extend supplier portal for evidence exchange. Clause 9 (Performance evaluation): real-time KPI panels; model monitoring; supplier scorecards with digital evidence coverage. Clause 10 (Improvement): analytics-driven RCA, CAPA orchestration with effectiveness checks and lessons-learned reuse.
- Data & technology foundations: Establish a data fabric connecting ERP/MES/LIMS/PLM and supplier feeds; define event semantics (NC, deviation, change request). Master data stewardship (materials/specs/suppliers), API contracts and security (identity, access, tamper-evidence). Treat AI models as controlled items with validation, versioning, and rollback.
- Adoption patterns by technology: AI/ML: start with high-signal use cases (scrap prediction, anomaly detection); validate with blind-holdout; monitor drift; gate actions with human-in-the-loop. Blockchain/ledger: apply to batch/lot genealogy, certificate custody, and supplier attestations; integrate with existing DMS to avoid double entry. IoT: prioritize CTQs and constraints (temp/vibration/torque); ensure calibration and data provenance; enable edge alerts for containment.
- Metrics & targets: Leading: prediction alert precision/recall, time-to-containment, % digitally evidenced process steps. Lagging: FPY/Right-First-Time, DPPM, CoPQ breakdown, audit findings closure time, % lots with end-to-end provenance.

10. CONCLUSION

The 2026 version of the ISO 9001 standard not only represents an update but also embodies a methodological guide of advanced requirements aimed at transforming management systems in companies. This new approach will emphasize structured processes, operational efficiency, and the full satisfaction of key stakeholders in each organization. Its application seeks to harmonize operations, optimize resource use, systematically reduce waste (productivity), and continuously improve performance. Companies that lead this change will integrate emerging technologies that will enable them to strengthen their supply chains and achieve higher levels of productivity, agility, and integral sustainability. Manufacturing 4.0 is expected to become an explicit expectation for companies certified under this standard.

Recent global disruptions, from the COVID-19 health emergency to geopolitical tensions and economic imbalances, have starkly revealed the systemic vulnerabilities of many organizations (VUCA). These experiences will accelerate the need for strategies that contemplate a wider range of threats: from technological and climate risks to health and social ones. In response, there will be a prioritization of diversifying sourcing, decentralizing critical processes, and strategically expanding the supplier base. Simultaneously, investments in technological tools will grow to maximize traceability, reinforce transparency, and elevate the capacity for anticipation at every link of the logistics chain. The security of physical and digital environments will also be strengthened, with greater attention to remote work and cyber protection.

This new technological paradigm does not imply displacing humans; quite the opposite: it places them at the center of organizational development. Solutions like artificial intelligence (AI), the internet of things (IoT), and blockchain technologies will be implemented to complement human talent, improve working conditions, and consolidate a model where people are recognized as pillars of strategic value. Far from replacing human teams, these tools will be at the service of their empowerment, enhancing their creativity, well-being, and contribution to achieving institutional objectives.

In this context, ISO 9001:2026 will assume a central role as a compass for building digital, sustainable, and resilient supply chains. The 2026 version of the standard will clearly integrate principles focused on human well-being, organizational adaptability, and long-term sustainability. Furthermore, it aligns with the vision of making the ISO 9000 family the normative axis around which future revisions (and other associated standards) are structured, consolidating a common framework to promote collaborative relationships, rational resource use, and continuous improvement. This will include a renewed commitment to the environment, supported by green technologies and good practices aimed at caring for the planet. Thus, the standard will become an essential instrument for organizations to successfully navigate environments of high uncertainty.

Finally, the experiences gained during recent global crises should not be seen solely as challenges overcome but as catalysts for profound transformation. Organizations that bet on collaborative models, adopt disruptive technologies, and embrace sustainability as a guiding principle will not only survive but will set the course for 21st-century business development. ISO 9001:2026 will offer the normative structure and strategic vision necessary to lead this transformative process in a solid, coherent, and sustainable way.

11. SCOPE AND LIMITATIONS

Scope. The analysis targets manufacturing and logistics contexts operating in multi-tier supply chains, with an emphasis on integrating AI/ML, blockchain-style provenance, and IoT sensing into ISO 9001 processes. Evidence sources include peer-reviewed literature (2020–2025) and practice-based public materials (e.g., sustainability reports, technical white papers). Outcomes considered include right-first-time quality, cost-of-poor-quality, resilience, and traceability/ integrity.

Limitations. Findings rely on secondary evidence and a practice-based case, which constrain causal inference. Generalizability may be limited for sectors with highly specific regulations or unique data architectures. The exact text of ISO 9001:2026 may evolve; mappings are conceptual and may require tailoring. Implementation impact depends on data quality, partner connectivity, and organizational change capacity. Security, privacy, and IP restrictions can limit cross-organizational data sharing.

Delimitations. We intentionally focus on core ISO 9001 processes (planning, support, operation, performance evaluation, improvement) rather than sector-specific regulatory overlays. Technology coverage centers on AI/ML, blockchain-like audit trails, and IoT; other tools (digital twins, AR/VR, RPA) are referenced only where they directly support Smart Quality.

REFERENCES

Adama, H., Popoola, O., Okeke, C., & Akinoso, A. (2024). Economic theory and practical impacts of digital transformation in supply chain optimization. *International Journal of Advanced Economics*. .DOI: 10.51594/ijae.v6i4.1072

Ahmad, H., Habidin, F., & Mustapha, I. (2025). The role of lean six sigma and discrete event simulations in achieving sustainability goals in logistics: reduce carbon emissions and minimizing waste. *International Journal of Innovation and Industrial Revolution*. .DOI: 10.35631/IJIREV.720005

Aktürk, E. B. (2024). The role of social quality in enhancing total quality management: An assessment through corporate social responsibility and business ethics. *Business & Management Studies: An International Journal, 12*(4), 1106–1122. DOI: 10.15295/bmij.v12i4.2477

AlHamad, A., Kurdi, A., Alshurideh, M., & Alrawabdeh, W. (2022). Impact of business process management and lean operations on cost of quality. [IJBAS]. *International Journal of Business Analytics and Security, 1*(1), 173–192. DOI: 10.54489/ijbas.v1i1.141

Amazon Web Services. (2023). Nestlé centralizes its IoT data on AWS IoT Core to improve customer experiences. *AWS Case Studies*. https://aws.amazon.com/solutions/case-studies/nestle-aws-iot-case-study/

Anttila, J., & Jussila, K. (2021). ISO 9004 – A stimulating quality management standard for the creative leaders of contemporary sustainable organizations. *Production Engineering Archives, 27*(2), 148–155. DOI: 10.30657/pea.2021.27.19

Asachi, G. (2021). Total Quality Management vs. Six Sigma. *IOSR Journal of Engineering (IOSRJEN), 11(07)*, pp. 05–15

Attanayake, A., & Ratnayake, R. (2024). Transitioning to Circular Economy in Power Distribution Utilities: A Framework Integrating ISO 9001 Quality Management Standards. *2024 IEEE International Conference on Industrial Engineering and Engineering Managemen*t, 760-764. DOI: 10.1109/IEEM62345.2024.10857066

Balabanova, Y., Lukyanova, A., & Shatskaya, E. (2024). Digital transformation in human resources management and its impact on the performance of enterprises. Вестник Северо-Кавказского федерального университета, 0(2), 24–30. DOI: 10.37493/2307-907X.2024.2.3

Bankoff, K. P., Muñoz, R., Pasini, A., & Pesado, P. (2022). Quality Management Systems and Blockchain in the 4.0 Era: A Literature Review. DOI: 10.1007/978-3-031-34147-2_10

Bastas, A., & Liyanage, K. (2018). ISO 9001 and Supply Chain Integration Principles Based Sustainable Development: A Delphi Study. *Sustainability (Basel), 10*(12), 4569. DOI: 10.3390/su10124569

Bedi, K., Singh, P., Kohli, N., Kaur, H., Angra, P., & Cheema, G. (2024). Effectiveness of IoT (Internet of Things) in Real Time Supply Chain Monitoring and Management. *2024 Second International Conference Computational and Characterization Techniques in Engineering & Sciences*, 1-5. DOI: 10.1109/IC3TES62412.2024.10877555

Bendhi, M. (2025). Supply Chain Transparency: Real Time Analytics for Product Tracking, Bottleneck Detection, and Logistics Optimization. *International Journal of Scientific Research and Management*. .DOI: 10.18535/ijsrm/v13i04.ec02

Bhuiyan, M., Faraji, M., Rashid, M., Bhuyan, M., Hossain, R., & Ghose, P. (2024). Digital Transformation in SMEs Emerging Technological Tools and Technologies for Enhancing the SME's Strategies and Outcomes. *Journal of Ecohumanism*. DOI: 10.62754/joe.v3i4.3594

Brankley, L., Tuğrul, A., Anderson, J., & Knight, D. (2017). *A manufacturing sector's experience of integrating EPD alongside product, management system and responsible sourcing certification for public procurement*. En *LCM 2017 Conference* – Lifecycle Management, Luxemburgo.

Bravi, L., & Murmura, F. (2021). Evidences about ISO 9001:2015 and ISO 9004:2018 implementation in different-size organizations. *Total Quality Management & Business Excellence, 33*(11–12), 1366–1386. DOI: 10.1080/14783363.2021.1954900

Bravim, M., Lira, T., De Freitas, R., & Xavier, T. (2020). A evolução nos estudos da gestão da qualidade baseado na norma iso 9001:2015: um estudo bibliométrico: the evolution in quality management studies based on iso 9001: 2015 standard: a bibliometric study. *Brazilian Journal of Production Engineering*, 88-106. http://DOI: 10.17632/4d3m89f2s8.1

Ceko, E. (2023). On the Relationship Between ISO Standards and Sustainable Development. *Problemy Ekorozwoju / Problems of Sustainable Development*, 18(2), 148–158. DOI: 10.35784/preko.3953

Chaikovskaya. L. (2021). Accounting of Intangible Assets and Their Reflection in Corporate Reporting in Conditions of Digital Transformation. *Intellectual property law* .DOI: 10.18572/2072-4322-2021-2-19-22

Chandran, V. (2024). Operational Excellence: Process optimization for competitive edge. *International Journal for Multidimensional Research Perspectives*. .DOI: 10.61877/ijmrp.v2i10.203

Chepeliuk, M. (2024). Transformation of Ukrainian business in the face of global challenges. *Ukrainian Journal of Applied Economics and Technology, 2024*(4), 187–191. DOI: 10.36887/2415-8453-2024-4-28

Chowdhury, A. (2025). A systematic review of risk-based procurement strategies in retail supply chains: sourcing flexibility and vendor disruption management. *American Journal of Advanced Technology and Engineering Solutions*. DOI: 10.63125/jr03rv07

Chumba, P., Sang, H., Kibett, J., & Kirui, J. (2019). Relationship between ISO 9001 Certification and the Number of Non Conformities Identified during System Audits in Selected Public Universities in Kenya. *EngRN: Operations Research*. DOI: 10.2139/ssrn.3517114

Deloitte. (2017). Predictive maintenance and the smart factory. Deloitte Insights. https://www2.deloitte.com/us/en/insights/focus/industry-4-0/using-predictive-technologies-for-asset-maintenance.htm

Drankova, N. A., & Denisova, Y. V. (2023). Successful supplier audit practices taking into account the risk-based approach. *Izvestiia Samarskogo Nauchnogo Tsentra Rossiiskoi Akademii Nauk, 25*(4), 13–22. DOI: 10.37313/1990-5378-2023-25-4-13-22

Dreković, E., Radosavljević, M., & Bejtović, M. (2021). Analysis of limitations of ISO standards implementation from the external stakeholders' point of view. *Facta Universitatis, Series: Economics and Organization*. .DOI: 10.22190/FUEO210402010D

Egbumokei, P. I., Dienagha, I. N., Digitemie, W. N., Onukwulu, E. C., & Oladipo, O. T. (2024). Driving operational excellence in the LNG industry: Leveraging Six Sigma principles for continuous improvement. *International Journal of Multidisciplinary Research and Growth Evaluation*, *5*(4), 1298–1310. DOI: 10.54660/.IJMRGE.2024.5.4.1298-1310

Enyejo, J. O., Fajana, O. P., Jok, I. S., Ihejirika, C. J., Awotiwon, B. O., & Olola, T. M. (2024, November). Digital Twin Technology, Predictive Analytics, and Sustainable Project Management in Global Supply Chains for Risk Mitigation, Optimization, and Carbon Footprint Reduction through Green Initiatives. *International Journal of Innovative Science and Research Technology*, *9*(11), 609–630. Advance online publication. DOI: 10.38124/ijisrt/IJISRT24NOV1344

Eyieyien, O., Paul, P., & Ijomah, T. (2024). *Strategic approaches for successful digital transformation in project management across industries*. International Journal of Frontiers in Engineering and Technology Research., DOI: 10.53294/ijfetr.2024.7.1.0037

Faciane, M., Fan, S., & Dwyer, R. (2021). *Returning to Solvency Through Quality Improvement*. International Journal of Applied Management and Technology., DOI: 10.5590/IJAMT.2021.20.1.01

Famoti, O., Omowole, B., Nzeako, G., Shittu, R., Ezechi, O., Ewim, C., & Omokhoa, H. (2025). A Digital Transformation Framework for U.S. E Commerce Supply Chains. International Journal of Scientific Research in Computer Science, *Engineering and Information Technology*. .DOI: 10.32628/CSEIT251112202

Fantozzi, I., Santolamazza, A., Loy, G., & Schiraldi, M. (2025). Digital Twins: Strategic Guide to Utilize Digital Twins to Improve Operational Efficiency in Industry 4.0. *Future Internet*, *17*(1), 41. DOI: 10.3390/fi17010041

Fatma, N., Ponda, H., & Kuswara, R. (2020). Analisis preventive maintenance dengan metode menghitung mean time between failure (MTBF) dan mean time to repair (MTTR) (*studi kasus pt. Gajah tunggal tbk).*17, 87-94. DOI: 10.30996/heuristic.v17i2.4648

Gamit, A. M., Santos, A. R., Armas, K. L., & Villegas, M. N. (2024). Implementation of ISO 9001:2015 in state universities and colleges: A quality management, organizational performance, and legal framework. *Corporate Law & Governance Review*, *6*(4), 94–102. DOI: 10.22495/clgrv6i4p9

Garza-Reyes, J. A., Kumar, P., Chen, F., & Wang, Y. (2017). Editorial: Seeing green: Achieving environmental sustainability through Lean and Six Sigma. *International Journal of Lean Six Sigma*, *8*(1), 2–11. DOI: 10.1108/IJLSS-01-2017-0005

González, M. (2024). *Integración de Inteligencia Artificial en la Inteligencia de Negocio: potencial de los datos no estructurados para la toma de decisiones estratégicas*. UCV-Scientia., DOI: 10.18050/revucv-scientia.v16n2a5

Gray, J., Ross, J., & Badrick, T. (2022). The path to continual improvement and business excellence: Compliance to ISO standards versus a business excellence approach. *Accreditation and Quality Assurance*, *27*(4), 195–203. DOI: 10.1007/s00769-022-01503-0

Guduru, A. (2025). Reinventing supply chain dynamics: The rise of intelligent AI Agents. *World Journal of Advanced Engineering Technology and Sciences, 15*(2), 721–729. DOI: 10.30574/wjaets.2025.15.2.0581

Gupta, R., Biswas, D., Ronty, A., Kapali, S., & Khan, M. (2024). Empowering Digital Transformation: The Strategic Role of Artificial Intelligence in Enterprise Innovation. *European Journal of Theoretical and Applied Sciences*. .DOI: 10.59324/ejtas.2024.2(6).16

Hall, K., & Taylor, J. (2024). Standardizing technical understanding to support a robust, archivable and accessible digital thread Supported by ISO 10303 STEP and IEC/ISO 81346 standards. AIAA SCITECH 2024 Forum. DOI: 10.2514/6.2024-0480

Hänel, A., Seidel, A., Frieß, U., Teicher, U., Wiemer, H., Wang, D., Wenkler, E., Penter, L., Hellmich, A., & Ihlenfeldt, S. (2021). Digital Twins for High-Tech Machining Applications—A Model-Based Analytics-Ready Approach. *Journal of Manufacturing and Materials Processing*, *5*(3), 80. Advance online publication. DOI: 10.3390/jmmp5030080

Henrichs, E., & Krupitzer, C. Towards a Self Adaptive, Real-Time Monitoring System for Food Quality Assessment. 2024 IEEE International Conference on Autonomic Computing and Self-Organizing Systems Companion (ACSOS-C) (2024): 178-179. DOI: 10.1109/ACSOS-C63493.2024.00056

Hoffmann, E. (2007). Consumer integration in sustainable product development. *Strategic Direction*, *24*(1), sd.2008.05624aad.005. Advance online publication. DOI: 10.1108/sd.2008.05624aad.005

Holitsyn, A., Pylypchuk, V., & Vasilkova, N. (2025). *International standards of the ISO 9000-9004 series in the system of marketing management*. Marketing and Digital Technologies., DOI: 10.15276/mdt.9.1.2025.7

Honorato, G., & Peroni, R. (2024). *Convergences between ESG and circular economy: A comparative analysis of implementation practices in Brazil*. Revista Gestão da Produção, Operações e Sistemas., DOI: 10.15675/gepros.3039

Hugo, A. (2024). Impact of Digital Technologies on Enhancing Supplier Collaboration and Performance in Sweden. *Global Journal of Purchasing and Procurement Management*, *3*(2), 1–12. DOI: 10.47604/gjppm.2752

Jain, V. (2024). Creating a Roadmap for Digital Transformation. *Journal of Artificial Intelligence & Cloud Computing*, *3*(6), E255. Advance online publication. DOI: 10.47363/JAICC/2024(3)E255

Joel, O., Oyewole, A., Odunaiya, O., & Soyombo, O. (2024). *Navigating the digital transformation journey: strategies for startup growth and innovation in the digital era*. International Journal of Management & Entrepreneurship Research., DOI: 10.51594/ijmer.v6i3.881

Kandil, S., Marzbani, F., & Shamayleh, A. (2024). Beyond Blockchain: Enhancing Data Sharing in Supply Chains through Horizontal Federated Learning in IoT Enabled VMI Systems. 2024 Advances in Science and Engineering Technology International Conferences (ASET), 01-07. DOI: 10.1109/ASET60340.2024.10708671

Karan, A., Jayaprakash, V., & Ghosh, M. (2022). Review on statistical methods applied in pharmaceutical quality control and quality assurance. *Journal of Pharmaceutical Chemistry*, *8*, 1–4. DOI: 10.14805/jphchem.2022.art122

Kaswan, M. S., & Rathi, R. (2020). Green Lean Six Sigma for sustainable development: Integration and framework. *Environmental Impact Assessment Review*, *83*, 106396. DOI: 10.1016/j.eiar.2020.106396

Kondratieva, H. (2025). Formation of organizational sustainability in organizations in the context of sustainable development goals. *Economic scope*. DOI: 10.30838/EP.196.244-248

Kovtunenko, Y., Kovtunenko, D., Hryhoriuk, H., & Kucherenko, Y. (2024). Global transformations as the background of the emergence of threats and opportunities for management. *Economics. Finances. Law.*, *3/2024*(3), 22–24. DOI: 10.37634/efp.2024.3.4

Kowalczyk, A. (2024). Quality management system according with standard ISO 9001:2015. *Problemy techniki uzbrojen*. DOI: 10.5604/01.3001.0054.7510

Kumar, S., & Khanduja, D. (2021). *Cost of poor-quality reduction in auto sector: an exploration with Six-Sigma*. International Journal of Six Sigma and Competitive Advantage., DOI: 10.1504/IJSSCA.2021.120249

Kumari, S., & Lele, V. (2023). Synergy of CRM and Industry 4.0: Advancing Supply Chain Management and Customer Experience via Digital Innovations. *International Journal of Industrial Engineering*, *10*(1), 20–25. Advance online publication. DOI: 10.14445/23499362/IJIE-V10I1P104

Kurniawati, P., Nursalam, N., & Neolaka, M. (2022). Analysis of the Implementation of ISO 9001:2015 Quality Management System to Improve Organizational Performance (Study in the Regional Human Resource Development Agency in NTT Province). *Journal of Governance, Taxation and Auditing*. DOI: 10.38142/jogta.v1i2.445

Liu, S., & Liu, C. (2025). Mapping the Digitalization Across Fashion Value Chain: A Meta analysis of Applications, Challenges, and Opportunities. *Making Waves Toward a Sustainable and Equitable Future*. DOI: 10.31274/itaa.18752

Lyandau, Y., & Biryukov, E. (2022). Digital Transformation of Organization as Way to Raise the Level of Digital Maturity of Industry 4.0. *Vestnik of the Plekhanov Russian University of Economics*. DOI: 10.21686/2413-2829-2022-6-11-16

Madhani, P. M. (2020). Enhancing supply chain efficiency and effectiveness with Lean Six Sigma approach. *International Journal of Project Management and Productivity Assessment*, *8*(1), 40–65. DOI: 10.4018/IJPMPA.2020010103

Maghroor, H., Madanchi, F., & O'Neal, T. (2024). The Role of Generative AI in Supply Chain Resilience: A Fuzzy AHP Approach. *Proceedings of the International Conference on Industrial Engineering and Operations Management*. DOI: 10.46254/NA09.20240049

Mahdikhani, M. (2023). Total quality management and Lean Six Sigma impact on supply chain research field: Systematic analysis. *Total Quality Management & Business Excellence*, *34*(15–16), 1921–1939. DOI: 10.1080/14783363.2023.2214506

Majumdar, S. M. (2024). Quality Management System implementation at construction projects. *International Journal of Scientific Research in Engineering and Management*, *8*(12), 1–7. DOI: 10.55041/IJSREM39978

Martins, Y., Da Silva, C., Sampaio, P., & Gabriel, L. (2021). ISO 9001:2015 and risk-based thinking: scientific research insights. *Total Quality Management & Business Excellence*, *33*(11-12), 1326–1343. DOI: 10.1080/14783363.2021.1954898

Mohammed, A., Mustapha, R., & Haruna, K. (2024). An Improved Collaborative Supply Chain Framework. *Kasu Journal of Computer Science*, *1*(1), 28–40. DOI: 10.47514/kjcs/2024.1.1.003

Montoya, A. (2024). Troubling environmental governance: Citizen legal experiments with transboundary commons. *Oxford Development Studies*, *52*(4), 396–412. DOI: 10.1080/13600818.2024.2395008

Morandín-Ahuerma, F. (2022). What is Artificial Intelligence? *International Journal of Research Publication and Reviews*. DOI: 10.55248/gengpi.2022.31261

Mullapudi, L. B. (2025). Optimizing supply chain management with real-time data integration platform. *International Journal on Computer Science and Engineering*, *13*(5), 40–48.

Muruganandham, R., Venkatesh, K., Devadasan, S., & Harish, V. (2022). TQM through the integration of blockchain with ISO 9001:2015 standard based quality management system. *Total Quality Management & Business Excellence*, *34*(3-4), 291–311. DOI: 10.1080/14783363.2022.2054318

Nagy, G., & Szentesi, S. (2024). Green logistics: Transforming supply chains for a sustainable future. *Advanced Logistic Systems –. Theory into Practice*, *18*(3), 29–42. DOI: 10.32971/als.2024.026

Naveen, K., Senanayake, R., & Selvan, C. (2021). Process performance evaluation in mechanical engineering industries in accordance with ISO 9001. *IOP Conference Series. Materials Science and Engineering*, *1057*(1), 012067. Advance online publication. DOI: 10.1088/1757-899X/1057/1/012067

Nikolakis, N., Catti, P., Chaloulos, A., Van De Kamp, W., Coy, M., & Alexopoulos, K. (2024). A methodology to assess circular economy strategies for sustainable manufacturing using process eco-efficiency. *Journal of Cleaner Production*, *141289*, 141289. Advance online publication. DOI: 10.1016/j.jclepro.2024.141289

Niyommaneerat, W., Suwanteep, K., & Chavalparit, O. (2023). Sustainability indicators to achieve a circular economy: A case study of renewable energy and plastic waste recycling corporate social responsibility (CSR) projects in Thailand. *Journal of Cleaner Production*, *391*, 136203. Advance online publication. DOI: 10.1016/j.jclepro.2023.136203

Nunhes, T., Campos, T., Francisco, F., & Oliveira, O. (2021). Contributions of Annex SL to Corporate Sustainability. DOI: 10.3389/frsus.2021.745350

Olutimehin, D. O., Falaiye, T. O., Ewim, C. P.-M., & Ibeh, A. I. (2021). Developing a framework for digital transformation in retail banking operations. *International Journal of Multidisciplinary Research and Growth Evaluation*, *2*(1), 608–622. DOI: 10.54660/.IJMRGE.2021.2.1.608-622

Orlov, A., Riad, R., Subbarayudu, Y., Kapoor, T., Kumar, P., Kansal, L., Bhardwaj, N., Kumar, Y., & Lakshmi, P. (2024). Circular Economy in Manufacturing: Optimization using Lean Six Sigma. *E3S Web of Conferences*. DOI: 10.1051/e3sconf/202458101016

Orwa, O., & Ragui, M. (2024). *International Quality Standard 9001: 2015 And Sustainability of Iso Certified Deposit Taking Saccos in Nairobi City County*. International Journal of Business Management, Entrepreneurship and Innovation., DOI: 10.35942/ytd95805

Osho, G., Omisola, J., & Shiyanbola, J. (2024). An Integrated AI-Power BI Model for Real-Time Supply Chain Visibility and Forecasting: A Data Intelligence Approach to Operational Excellence. *International Journal of Advanced Multidisciplinary Research and Studies*. https://www.multiresearchjournal.com/admin/uploads/archives/archive-1744730594.pdf?utm_source=chatgpt.com

Osório, A. L., Camarinha-Matos, L. M., Dias, T., Gonçalves, C., & Tavares, J. (2021). Open and collaborative micro services in digital transformation. En *PRO-VE 2021: Smart and Sustainable Collaborative Networks 4.0* (pp. 393–402). Springer. DOI: 10.1007/978-3-030-85969-5_36

Owusu-Berko, L. (2025). Advanced supply chain analytics: Leveraging digital twins, IoT and blockchain for resilient, data-driven business operations. *World Journal of Advanced Research and Reviews, 25*(2), 1777–1799. DOI: 10.30574/wjarr.2025.25.2.0572

Ozek, A., Seçkin, M., Demircioğlu, P., & Bogrekci, I. (2025). Artificial Intelligence Driving Innovation in Textile Defect Detection. *Textiles, 5*(2), 12. Advance online publication. DOI: 10.3390/textiles5020012

Porter, M. E., & Kramer, M. R. (2011). Creating shared value: How to reinvent capitalism—and unleash a wave of innovation and growth. *Harvard Business Review, 89*(1/2), 62–77.

Prazian, M. (2023). Resilience for Better Sustainability. ISO 28000: 2022 vs 2007. *Comparative Analysis. Nuclear and Radiation Safety, 1*(97), 67–70. DOI: 10.32918/nrs.2023.1(97).08

Pyun, J., Kim, D., & Rha, J. (2023). *Understanding the EU Directive on Corporate Sustainability Due Diligence and Examining Strategic Responses*. Korean Production and Operations Management Society., DOI: 10.32956/kopoms.2023.34.4.495

Rahman, M., Honey, U., Rangari, S., & Wu, F. (2025). Blockchain-Based Supply Chain Management for Ensuring the Quality and Traceability of Fresh Produce: *An Illustrative Analysis. 2025 IEEE 15th Annual Computing and Communication Workshop and Conference (CCWC),* 00038-00044. DOI: 10.1109/CCWC62904.2025.10903802

Reyes, I., & Barillo, E. (2024). Challenges Encountered in the Implementation of ISO 9001:2015 Risk Management Systems. *International Journal for Multidisciplinary Research*. DOI: 10.36948/ijfmr.2024.v06i02.16380

Rezki, N., & Mansouri, M. (2023). Improving supply chain risk assessment with artificial neural network predictions. *Acta logistica*. DOI: 10.22306/al.v10i4.444

Rojo-Gallego-Burin, A., Montes, F., Perez-Arostegui, M., & Stevenson, M. (2020). Ambidextrous supply chain strategy and supply chain flexibility: The contingent effect of ISO 9001. *Industrial Management & Data Systems, 120*(9), 1691–1714. DOI: 10.1108/IMDS-01-2020-0038

Sahoo, S. (2024). Blockchain-enabled traceability systems for supply chain quality management: Empirical insights from pharmaceutical manufacturers. *International Journal of Quality & Reliability Management*. Advance online publication. DOI: 10.1108/IJQRM-03-2024-0091

Semenova, S., Shpyrko, O., Androsenko, O., Afanasieva, I., Kolumbet, O., & Vorchakova, I. (2024). The essence of goodwill in disclosing the intangible value of business in the context of digital transformation. *Financial and credit activity problems of theory and practice*. DOI: 10.55643/fcaptp.4.57.2024.4449

Shivale, N., Patwal, P., & Mahalle, D. (2025). Enhanced Traceability and Transparency in Medical Supply Chain Management Using Blockchain-Based Customized Smart Contracts. *Journal of Information Systems Engineering & Management*, *10*(10s), 478–489. Advance online publication. DOI: 10.52783/jisem.v10i10s.1410

Shostak, L., & Pavlova, S. (2024). Formation of the potential of a business model in the context of digitalization. *Intellect*, *XXI*(3, 2024). Advance online publication. DOI: 10.32782/2415-8801/2024-3.15

Silvério, J., & Pestana, G. F. (2022). Integrated Risk Monitoring in the Quality Management System. *En A. Rocha, H. Adeli, G. Dzemyda, & F. Moreira (Eds.), Information Systems and Technologies – WorldCIST 2022* (*Vo*l. 470, pp. 3–12). Lecture Notes in Networks and Systems. Springer. DOI: 10.1007/978-3-031-04829-6_1

Simão, V., Bonina, N., Lima, G., & Gonçalves, O. (2020). Comparative analysis between ABNT NBR ISO 9001:2015 and ABNT NBR ISO 31000:2009: The risk mindset in quality management systems. *Sistemas & Gestão*, 14(3), 310–322. https://link.springer.com/chapter/10.1007/978-3-030-14969-7_22

Solace. (n.d.). Customer Success Story: JDE. Solace. Retrieved August 13, 2025, from https://solace.com/resources/case-studies/customer-success-story-jde--casestudy

Solodkovska, G., & Avksientiev, Y. (2024). *Digital transformation of the global service market: trends, challenges, and prospeCTS*. Business Navigator., DOI: 10.32782/business-navigator.77-61

Stefanova-Stoyanova, V., & Danov, P. (2022). Comparative Analysis of Specialized Standards and Methods on Increasing the Effectiveness and Role of PDCA for Risk Control in Management Systems. *2022 10th International Scientific Conference on Computer Science (COMSCI*), 1-4. DOI: 10.1109/COMSCI55378.2022.9912583

Stravinskienė, I., & Serafinas, D. (2020). The Link between Business Process Management and Quality Management. *Journal of Risk and Financial Management*, *13*(10), 225. Advance online publication. DOI: 10.3390/jrfm13100225

Tazvivinga, K., & Samuels, A. (2024). Digital transformation and its role in FMCG supply chain resilience. *International Journal of Business Ecosystem & Strategy* (2687-2293). DOI: 10.36096/ijbes.v6i5.606

Thakur, V. (2024). Collaborative supply chain network: Confusion or way ahead. *International Journal of Multidisciplinary Research and Growth Evaluation*. DOI: 10.54660/.IJMRGE.2024.5.4.688-694

Tiss, S., & Orellano, M. (2023). A Maturity Model of Digital Transformation in Supply Chains: A Multidimensional Approach. *2023 27th International Conference on Information Technology (IT)*, 1-7. DOI: 10.1109/IT57431.2023.10078510

Topuz, E. (2022). Integration of ecotoxicity assessment with product design for circularity management. *Integrated Environmental Assessment and Management, 18*(2), 305–307. DOI: 10.1002/ieam.4580 PMID: 35262254

Trequattrini, A. L., Cuozzo, B., & Manfredi, S. (2022). *Intangible assets management and digital transformation: evidence from intellectual property rights-intensive industries.* Meditari Accountancy Research., DOI: 10.1108/MEDAR-03-2021-1216

Tzempelikos, N. (2021). Business-to-Business Marketing in the Light of the Evolution of the Business Environment. *Journal of Business-To-Business Marketing, 28*(2), 101–104. DOI: 10.1080/1051712X.2021.1920696

Ullah, A. (2025). The Effect of Artificial Intelligence (AI) on Customer Satisfaction: A Review of Bangladesh Perspective. *International Journal of Science. Technology in Society, 13*(2), 54–60. Advance online publication. DOI: 10.11648/j.ijsts.20251302.13

Valdivia, S., Backes, J., Traverso, M., Sonnemann, G., Cucurachi, S., Guinée, J., Schaubroeck, T., Finkbeiner, M., Leroy-Parmentier, N., Ugaya, C., Peña, C., Zamagni, A., Inaba, A., Amaral, M., Berger, M., Dvarionienė, J., Vakhitova, T., Benoît-Norris, C., Prox, M., & Goedkoop, M. (2021). Principles for the application of life cycle sustainability assessment. *The International Journal of Life Cycle Assessment, 26*(9), 1900–1905. DOI: 10.1007/s11367-021-01958-2

Valdivia, S., Schluep, M., Murcia, D., & Wehrli, A. (2024). ISO 59014 on sustainability and traceability of secondary materials recovery – Principles and requirements contributing to a circular economy. *Proceedings of the 2024 International Conference Electronics Goes Green 2024+ (EGG)* (pp. 1–7). Berlin: Fraunhofer IZM. DOI: 10.23919/EGG62010.2024.10631253

Vanichchinchai, A. (2021). Investigating the impacts of ISO 9001 certification on lean manufacturing and supply chain relationship: An empirical analysis. *International Journal of Lean Six Sigma.* Advance online publication. DOI: 10.1108/IJLSS-10-2020-0164

Veroba, G., & Azmi, N. (2021). Front End Work Process Digital Transformation: Challenges and Opportunities. *Day 2 Wed, October 13, 2021.* DOI: 10.2118/205606-MS

Wallace, D. W., III. (2021). *R*esilient Maintenance Infrastructure: Dynamic Repair Network Designs to Effectively Manage Supply Chain Disruptions *(Master's thesis). Air Force Institute of Technology.* https://scholar.afit.edu/etd/5052

Walters, L. (2020). A Supplier Risk Matrix Approach to ISO 9001:2015 Compliance: *A Case Study,* 10, 65-81. DOI: 10.15239/j.brcacadjb.2020.10.01.ja03

Wella, W., & Chia, L. (2020). The Implementing ISO 9001 in Manufacture Industry: Case Study PT Softex Indonesia. *International Journal of New Media Technology (IJNMT*), 6(2), 92–97.** DOI: 10.31937/ijnmt.v6i2.1248

Xue, L. (2024). Exploring the Impact of Contingency Strategies and Organizational Resilience on Institutional Adaptability and Sustaining Educational Quality in Chinese Higher Education. *International Journal of Academic Research in Business & Social Sciences, 14*(6). Advance online publication. DOI: 10.6007/IJARBSS/v14-i6/21917

Zamlynskyi, V., Heretskiy, R., Firsa, D., & Stepanenko, S. (2023). Strengthening economic security through the zero-waste concept in sustainable business. *Ukrainian Journal of Applied Economics and Technology*, *8*(4), 139–149. DOI: 10.36887/2415-8453-2023-4-22

Zhang, F., & Gong, Z. (2021). Supply Chain Inventory Collaborative Management and Information Sharing Mechanism Based on Cloud Computing and 5G Internet of Things. *Mathematical Problems in Engineering*, *2021*, 1–12. DOI: 10.1155/2021/6670718

Zhang, M., & Huo, R. (2022). Assessing the logistic system maturity level in integrated supply chains under Logistic 4.0 paradigm. *Bulletin of the National Technical University "Kharkiv Polytechnic Institute" (Economic Sciences), No. 3*, 86–92. http://dx.doi.org/DOI: 10.20998/2519-4461.2022.3.86

Zhang, Y. (2024). Risk management, operational efficiency and corporate governance in the banking industry: Basis for corporate resiliency framework. *International Journal of Research Studies in Management*, *12*(9). Advance online publication. DOI: 10.5861/ijrsm.2024.1230

Chapter 17

Blockchain in the Supply Chain: The Prelude to the New ISO 9001:2026

Omar A. Guirette-Barbosa
http://orcid.org/0000-0003-1336-9475
Universidad Politécnica de Zacatecas, Mexico & Broward International University, Mexico

Selene Castañeda-Burciaga
http://orcid.org/0000-0002-2436-308X
Universidad Politécnica de Zacatecas, Mexico & Broward International University, Mexico

ABSTRACT

The imminent publication of ISO 9001:2026 represents a significant transformation in quality management, marked by the integration of emerging technologies such as Blockchain into supply chains. This chapter examines how Blockchain is establishing itself as a strategic axis for traceability, transparency, and organizational resilience, anticipating the regulatory changes that the new version of the standard will impose. Through a comprehensive analysis of literature and case studies, it explores its capabilities for recording transactions in an immutable manner, preventing fraud, and optimizing decision-making. It also reflects on the role of Blockchain as a facilitator of business trust and as a differentiating factor in increasingly competitive and regulated markets. This work offers a detailed overview of the convergence between quality, technology, and strategic management, identifying opportunities and challenges for organizations that aspire to align their processes with next-generation international standards.

1. INTRODUCTION

1.1 Global significance & relevance

Quality management, historically linked to the standardization of processes and the minimization of variability, has evolved alongside technological advances and the growing complexity of global supply chains. The imminent arrival of ISO 9001:2026 signals a profound transformation aimed at addressing persistent challenges such as traceability, transparency, and real-time assurance (Hariyani et al., 2025). In this context, Blockchain is positioned not only as a tool but as a structural change enabler for the next generation of Quality Management Systems (QMS).

DOI: 10.4018/979-8-3373-4027-2.ch017

1.2 Limits of current approaches

The transformation of supply chains over the last two decades has been marked by the globalization of suppliers, the acceleration of product life cycles, and unprecedented pressure for transparency. Despite advances in ERP systems and barcode or RFID-based traceability solutions, the ability to guarantee the authenticity and integrity of records across all links in the chain continues to be an unresolved issue (Herrmann et al., 2021). Each link maintains its own databases and recording systems, which creates interoperability barriers and opportunities for manual manipulation or error, directly affecting the end consumer's perception of quality (Shwetha et al., 2020).

In this scenario, Blockchain emerges as a powerful response to the need for verifiable and immutable records. Its architecture, based on distributed ledgers and cryptographic validations, makes it possible to build a shared truth among all collaborators, reducing dependence on centralized intermediaries and strengthening distributed trust among all participants.

The concept of total traceability, so often mentioned in quality management, gains a concrete framework thanks to Blockchain: each transaction, from the origin of raw materials to the distribution of finished products, can be recorded, verified, and audited in a secure and transparent way. This ensures not only regulatory compliance but also provides significant strategic value by improving risk management capabilities and the ability to respond to incidents or nonconformities (Azevedo, Gomes, & Romão, 2023).

1.3 Justification

The technological acceleration of recent years has shown that the traditional model of periodic auditing is insufficient in hyperconnected and highly dynamic environments. Blockchain enables a paradigm shift toward continuous auditing, where records are not consulted ex post, but are generated and verified in real time. This offers an unprecedented ability to detect deviations, anticipate risks, and implement corrective actions immediately, with a direct impact on the reduction of nonconformities, an increase in consumer confidence, and an optimization of costs derived from incident management (Bósquez-Andrade & Torres-Palacios, 2024).

ISO 9001:2026, in its intention to align itself with the need for transparency and resilience of modern supply chains, recognizes and encourages the use of technologies that ensure data integrity and the ability to audit in real time. Blockchain fits naturally into this vision by providing a decentralized and distributed network that certifies the authenticity of each piece of data (Kumar & Mangaiyarkarasi, 2024). At a strategic level, the impact of Blockchain on supply chains goes beyond compliance: it redefines the way information is shared, aligns the incentives of participants, enables the design of smart contracts that automate quality controls in real time, and becomes the basis for predictive decisions (Oyeyemi et al., 2024).

1.4 Objective & how this chapter addresses the gaps

This chapter aims to analyze in depth this intersection between ISO 9001:2026 and Blockchain, exploring its principles, practical applications, implementation challenges, and the strategies for managing change that enable its sustainable adoption.

Additionally, selected case studies and a discussion of their strategic impact are presented, as well as recommendations and future lines of research for organizations seeking to implement Blockchain with quality objectives and regulatory alignment.

Working definition used in this chapter. Blockchain is a distributed ledger technology (DLT) that records time-stamped, cryptographically linked transactions across multiple nodes, enabling tamper-evident traceability and verifiable evidence across organizations.

2. PROBLEM STATEMENT

Supply chains are complex systems composed of multiple actors — suppliers, manufacturers, logistics providers, distributors, and retailers — who must coordinate not only the flow of goods but also the flow of information. Despite the sophistication of current management systems, persistent gaps remain in traceability and data integrity that can compromise quality management and regulatory compliance.

2.1 Gaps to address

2.1.1 Lack of comprehensive traceability.

The absence of comprehensive traceability means not just that a product cannot be tracked from origin to destination, but that the information associated with a specific batch may be fragmented across multiple systems. This becomes especially problematic when an incident or nonconformity occurs, and it is necessary to reconstruct the history of the product. Centralized systems, though robust, do not offer the level of tamper-proofing and distributed verification that Blockchain provides, leaving room for undetected errors or manipulations.

2.1.2 Risk of counterfeiting and fraud.

Counterfeiting is a growing threat in multiple industries, particularly pharmaceuticals, electronics, and food. The lack of an immutable record shared among all participants complicates the identification of the point at which fraudulent alteration occurred. Blockchain, by contrast, creates a historical record of each transaction that is extremely difficult to falsify, which acts as a deterrent and a powerful mechanism for ex post verification.

2.1.3 Lack of data synchronization.

Siloed data systems, typical of traditional supply chains, generate discrepancies that lead to operational inefficiencies and increase the risk of errors. The lack of real-time synchronization can result in the duplication of records, gaps in information, and delays in decision-making. The distributed nature of Blockchain fosters the construction of a single source of truth.

2.1.4 Regulatory compliance and audits.

Regulatory compliance in sectors such as food, pharmaceuticals, and aerospace demands detailed, reliable, and accessible records. Periodic audits, although necessary, are often insufficient in dynamic environments where conditions can change rapidly. Blockchain enables the possibility of continuous auditing, shortening verification times and strengthening the evidence presented to regulatory entities.

2.1.5 Vulnerability to disruptions.

Supply chains are exposed to disruptions due to natural disasters, geopolitical conflicts, or unexpected events (e.g., pandemics). In such scenarios, the visibility and integrity of data are critical for effective response. Blockchain strengthens resilience by providing a tamper-evident record that can continue to function even if one or more nodes fail.

2.1.6 Hidden costs and loss of trust.

The costs associated with nonconformities, product recalls, and disputes with suppliers often remain hidden until they translate into legal or reputational problems. Fragmented traceability and the inability to verify the origin and transformations of products undermine trust. Blockchain offers a new architecture to mitigate these risks by building verifiable trust through shared records.

Stakeholders. Industry. Core actors include manufacturers, tier-1/2 suppliers, logistics providers, distributors, and retailers. For these stakeholders, blockchain-enabled traceability addresses pain points such as fragmented records, slow incident response, and disputes over custody or quality status. Internally, Quality, Operations, IT, Compliance, and Internal Audit require reliable, tamper-evident evidence that can be queried in near real time without duplicating data entry.

Assurance ecosystem. Certification bodies, external auditors, and customers increasingly expect audit-ready, immutable records that demonstrate process control and product provenance across organizational boundaries

Regulators. Sector regulators (e.g., food, pharma, aerospace) focus on record integrity, timeliness, and accessibility for inspections and recalls. Permissioned ledgers with role-based access and clear governance provide a path to preserve confidentiality while improving visibility, making it easier to verify compliance and reconstruct events.

Society and end users. Consumers and communities' benefit from transparent product histories and faster, more precise recalls. Clear communication channels tied to verifiable supply-chain data can help rebuild trust after incidents and incentivize higher-quality practices throughout the network.

3. PURPOSE OF THE STUDY

Purpose. This chapter's purpose is to determine how and when blockchain strengthens ISO 9001:2026, ready quality systems by operationalizing three priorities, traceability, integrity, and continuous verification, across organizational boundaries. Building on the problem statement and the research questions set out in the Introduction, we integrate theory, method, and empirical evidence to specify the mechanisms, organizational conditions, and governance choices that translate into measurable quality outcomes.

Objectives: Synthesis: 1) Consolidate evidence (2020–2025) on blockchain-for-quality across food, pharma, automotive, aerospace, and mining; 2) Framework: link design choices (permissioned networks, smart contracts, off-chain storage with on-chain hashing, identity & access) to ISO 9001:2026 capabilities; 3) Evaluation lens: identify metrics—recall speed, nonconformity rate, audit preparation time, data completeness, and stakeholder trust; 4) Guidance: articulate actionable implications for managers, auditors, and regulators.

Scope and boundaries: Unit of analysis: enterprise and inter-enterprise processes where documented information, traceability, and evidence management are critical. Focus: permissioned/consortium ledgers with role-based access, event logging, and smart-contract quality gates. Evidence types: peer-reviewed studies with methods, high-credibility industry cases with reportable outcomes, and standards guidance. Exclusions: purely speculative token economies, crypto-financial topics not tied to quality evidence, and editorials without methods. Time window: 2020–July 2025. Geography: global, with emphasis on regulated supply chains.

Expected contributions and outcomes:

- Theoretical: connect change-management lenses to adoption variance in blockchain-enabled QMS, clarifying moderating roles of data governance and edge data quality.
- Methodological: transparent review protocol and extraction matrix enabling replication.
- Practical: a conceptual framework and a set of implementation patterns (e.g., smart-contract quality gates; off-chain payloads anchored on-chain) that reduce audit friction and recall latency. Assurance/policy: show how permissioned ledgers improve auditability while preserving confidentiality, informing regulators and certification bodies.

Beneficiaries and use cases: Primary beneficiaries: Quality, Operations, IT, Compliance, and Internal Audit teams; external: suppliers, auditors, and regulators. Representative use cases: a) supplier-certificate verification with tokenized attestations; b) cold-chain control with IoT oracles that trigger holds on excursions; c) calibration status enforcement for measurement equipment; d) batch genealogy and recall triage through end-to-end provenance queries. Together these use cases illustrate how blockchain capabilities map to ISO 9001:2026 clauses on documented information, operational control, and performance evaluation.

The convergence between Blockchain and ISO 9001:2026 is not accidental; it is the result of the evolving demands of supply chains and the need for credible, tamper-evident evidence. Regulatory frameworks increasingly emphasize traceability, record integrity, and continuous assurance, all areas where Blockchain provides architectural advantages.

Regulatory connection points: ISO 9001:2026 establishes a series of requirements that go beyond the maintenance of documented information, aiming to ensure the integrity and verifiability of records over time. Blockchain provides a mechanism to guarantee that each record, from the supplier's certificate to the final product's distribution, is part of an immutable, distributed chain that can be audited.

From periodic auditing to continuous auditing: Traditional audit models operate in cycles and rely on sampling, which can fail to capture isolated incidents or manipulations. Blockchain allows for a paradigm shift toward continuous auditing, where evidence is generated and verified in real time. This increases the capacity for early detection of deviations and the effectiveness of corrective actions.

4. IMPORTANCE AND JUSTIFICATION

The technological acceleration of recent years has shown that the traditional model of periodic auditing is insufficient in hyperconnected and highly dynamic environments. Blockchain enables a paradigm shift toward continuous auditing, where records are not consulted ex post, but are generated and verified in real time. This offers an unprecedented ability to detect deviations, anticipate risks, and implement corrective actions immediately, with a direct impact on the reduction of nonconformities, an increase in consumer confidence, and an optimization of costs derived from incident management.

Direct alignment with ISO 9001:2026. ISO 9001:2026, in its intention to align itself with the need for transparency and resilience of modern supply chains, recognizes and encourages the use of technologies that ensure data integrity and the ability to audit in real time. Blockchain fits naturally into this vision by providing a decentralized and distributed network that certifies the authenticity of each piece of data.

At a strategic level, the impact of Blockchain on supply chains goes beyond compliance: it redefines the way information is shared, aligns the incentives of participants, enables the design of smart contracts that automate quality controls in real time, and becomes the basis for predictive decisions.

Why legacy approaches fall short. Despite advances in ERP systems and barcode or RFID-based traceability solutions, the ability to guarantee the authenticity and integrity of records across all links in the chain continues to be an unresolved issue. Each link maintains its own databases and recording systems, which creates interoperability barriers and opportunities for manual manipulation or error, directly affecting the end consumer's perception of quality.

Regulatory salience and continuous assurance. Traditional audit models operate in cycles and rely on sampling, which can fail to capture isolated incidents or manipulations. Blockchain allows for a paradigm shift toward continuous auditing, where evidence is generated and verified in real time. This increases the capacity for early detection of deviations and the effectiveness of corrective actions.

By integrating Blockchain into supplier certification processes, organizations can verify the validity of certificates, **the calibration of measuring instruments**, and the compliance of processes in a decentralized manner. Smart contracts can automate the acceptance or rejection of lots based on predefined conditions.

5. METHODOLOGY

This study adopts a qualitative, descriptive, and analytical design based on documentary research and an integrative narrative literature review. The approach is explicitly aligned with: a) the priorities framed in Chapter 1 (traceability, integrity, continuous verification); b) the problem categories in Chapter 2 and c) the purpose and objectives stated in Chapter 3. The unit of analysis is the chain of evidence across organizational boundaries, i.e., how blockchain mechanisms and governance produce audit-ready records within ISO 9001:2026, ready Quality Management Systems (QMS).

Review scope. Time window: 2020–July 2025. Domains: regulated supply chains (food, pharma, automotive, aerospace, mining) and cross-industry studies on blockchain for quality/traceability. Technological focus: permissioned/consortium Blockchain networks, smart contracts, on/off chain data models with on chain hashing, identity and access (IoT), and ERP/MES integration. The scope operationalizes the RQs by examining when and how these design choices enable ISO 9001:2026 capabilities.

Sources and search strategy: We searched Scopus, Web of Science, IEEE Xplore, SpringerLink, ProQuest, and Google Scholar, complemented with standards/technical materials (e.g., ISO/TC 176 notes, GS1/EPCIS interoperability guidance) and high-credibility industry case reports. Example search strings: (blockchain or "distributed ledger" or DLT) and (quality or "ISO 9001" or auditing or "documented information"), (traceability or provenance) and (food or pharma or manufacturing) and (blockchain), ("continuous audit" or assurance) and (blockchain or "smart contract") and (governance or interoperability) and (blockchain and supply chain).

Inclusion and exclusion criteria: Include studies/reports that (a) describe implementation context; (b) specify blockchain design choices and integration patterns; (c) report outcomes or audit-relevant evidence (e.g., recall speed, nonconformity rate, audit preparation time, data completeness, stakeholder trust). Exclude opinion-only pieces without methods, crypto-financial discussions unrelated to quality evidence, and duplicates.

Data extraction and coding: We used a structured extraction matrix with the following fields: sector & context; ISO 9001:2026 clauses targeted (documented information, operation, performance evaluation, improvement); problem category (maps to statemen problem chapter 2); blockchain design (network type, data model, consensus, identity/access); edge data capture/oracles; governance (roles, node accountability). Two reviewers performed dual coding on a pilot set to calibrate categories; discrepancies were resolved by discussion and rule refinement. An audit trail captured search strings, screening decisions, and extraction notes. Synthesis and analysis: We conducted a thematic synthesis to outcome links. Findings are contrasted with legacy baselines and analyzed by sector and network type. This structure directly supports the framework and implications developed in subsequent chapters (6...12).

6. THEORETICAL FRAMEWORK

6.1 Concept origin & definition

A deep understanding of blockchain requires going beyond its popular definitions and exploring its underlying mechanics and concrete applications in contexts such as supply chains and quality traceability (Bager et al., 2022). Although these descriptions are useful for introducing the concept, they are insufficient to understand how Blockchain can transform quality management. For this reason, it is essential to delve into its architecture and the operational principles that underpin its ability to guarantee integrity, traceability, and transparency in production processes (Akram et al., 2024).

Essentially, Blockchain is a distributed ledger technology (DLT) in which records (transactions) are grouped into blocks linked cryptographically, creating an immutable sequence. Each block contains a "hash," a fingerprint generated by applying a cryptographic function to its contents. Any modification to the data would result in a different hash, allowing the detection of tampering (Li et al., 2022). Immutability is reinforced by the distributed nature of the network: records are replicated across multiple nodes, and any attempt to alter them would be rejected by the consensus mechanism (e.g., Proof of Stake or PBFT) unless the consensus of all network participants is achieved (Alhat, 2024).

This principle of immutability is achieved by structuring the data in such a way that each block contains the hash of the previous block, establishing a cryptographically secure link (Thilakavathy et al., 2023). Any attempt to modify data would alter the hash and break the chain, making tampering immediately detectable, provided the network's cryptographic protocols are properly managed (Wang, 2024).

6.2 Types of blockchain for supply chains

In supply chains, public, private, and consortium (permissioned) networks coexist, although their applicability and degree of control vary significantly (Franke & Fischer, 2023). Public blockchains offer maximum transparency and resilience to censorship but face constraints in privacy and scalability. By contrast, permissioned or consortium networks prioritize controlled participation, performance, and confidentiality—properties that align with inter-enterprise quality evidence and auditability in regulated sectors (Journal of Current Research and Review, 2024; Vadrevu, 2025). According to Oriekhoe et al. (2024), hybrid Blockchain combines elements of public and private modalities, allowing shared control among several actors, which favors inter-company collaboration without sacrificing security.

In the context of complex supply chains, Hossain and Shabnam (2025) highlight that these models have positioned themselves as the most viable when multiple companies that do not have full mutual trust are involved, as they allow each link to maintain control over its information while benefiting from shared transparency and traceability.

6.3 Key principles underlying effectiveness

The relevance of Blockchain for quality management and ISO 9001:2026 is based on a series of technical and operational principles (Muruganandham et al., 2022).

- Decentralization: unlike traditional databases, where information is stored on a single server or repository, Blockchain distributes identical copies of the record to all nodes in the network, eliminating the risk of a single point of failure and improving resilience to cyberattacks or disasters (Bettín-Díaz et al., 2021).
- Immutability: Once a transaction has been validated and included in a block, it cannot be modified without invalidating the entire chain, which gives the stored records exceptional probative value (Muruganandham et al., 2022).
- According to Das, Samal, and Mohanta (2024), the transparency and auditability of blockchain are manifested in the ability to record all transactions in a manner visible to authorized participants, enabling real-time audits and facilitating regulatory compliance.
- Regarding distributed consensus, Ahn, Yi, and Kim (2024) explain that transaction validation is achieved through mechanisms such as Proof of Work, Proof of Stake, or Practical Byzantine Fault Tolerance, which require the approval of most nodes, thus guaranteeing the veracity of the information.

Finally, Abayomi (2024) highlights that Blockchain's cryptographic security is based on robust encryption algorithms, which protect against unauthorized access and ensure data integrity against malicious modification attempts.

6.4 Comparison with previous traceability technologies

Chaabaoui et al., (2024) point out that traceability is not a new concept in supply chains, as technologies such as barcodes, RFID (Radio Frequency Identification) and, more recently, centralized ERP (Enterprise Resource Planning) management platforms have been used for decades. However, these systems have critical limitations: first, their dependence on a central intermediary, since in an ERP system the validity of the information depends on the integrity of the central database and those who administer it. Furthermore, as Wang, He, & Wu (2022) explain, there is vulnerability to tampering, as records can be modified retrospectively if one has the appropriate privileges, compromising the reliability of the information.

Finally, full interoperability remains limited, as integration between systems from different organizations is often partial and costly, hindering the smooth exchange of data (Chaabaoui et al., 2024).

Blockchain overcomes these limitations by offering a natively distributed, secure, and interoperable architecture. Instead of relying on a central authority, trust is transferred to the system design itself, where each node verifies and validates the information (Shaik, 2025).

6.5 Blockchain as a digital control framework

According to Alfuhaid et al., (2023), Blockchain not only functions as an information repository, but can also play the role of a digital control framework in the supply chain. This means that business rules, quality control procedures, and contractual conditions can be encoded as smart contracts, which are automatically executed when predefined conditions are met, reducing the need for manual supervision and minimizing the risk of noncompliance.

Yadav & Jasmin (2024) point out that, for example, a smart contract could release payment to a supplier only when, through IoT data, it is confirmed that the goods were transported under the agreed conditions and delivered correctly. This type of technological integration is in line with the expectations of the future ISO 9001:2026, where information integrity and real-time traceability will be essential pillars for ensuring quality (Onu et al., 2024).

In short, Blockchain is not only a technological innovation, but also a trusted infrastructure capable of radically transforming the way supply chains are managed (Bhasin, 2023; Liu et al., 2025). Its principles of decentralization, immutability, transparency, and security form the basis on which a new quality management paradigm (**also known as smart quality**) can be built, aligned with the most advanced regulatory requirements (Sawant, Poladia, & Shah, 2023).

7. LITERATURE REVIEW AND ANALYSIS

7.1 Supply Chains and Current Challenges

Contemporary supply chains have been configured as interconnected and dynamic global systems involving multiple actors in different geographical locations. Mohammed et al. (2023) point out that this complexity, while promoting supplier diversification and economies of scale, increases challenges related to quality, safety, and efficiency. In this regard, understanding these challenges, especially in the context of the upcoming ISO 9001:2026 standard, is key to assessing how emerging technologies such as Blockchain can contribute to their mitigation, improving traceability, transparency, and operational resilience.

Unlike traditional linear models, today's supply chains operate as non-hierarchical networks in which the flows of information, materials, and capital are bidirectional and even simultaneous. According to Drljača and Tolić (2025), this structure, while efficient, means that any disruption or loss of visibility at a specific point can trigger multiplier effects throughout the network. Recent examples, such as the COVID-19 pandemic, the Suez Canal blockade, and energy crises, have demonstrated the vulnerability of global chains to external and unforeseen events (Fuchs et al., 2021).

Lack of comprehensive traceability: One of the most persistent problems in supply chain management is fragmented traceability. Sangeetha (2020) explains that, although many companies have internal management systems, information is often divided and does not flow accurately between the different links, creating uncertainty and risk. In sectors such as pharmaceuticals and food, Potter (2022) and Pulita et al. (2024) highlight that this limitation can have serious consequences, from the distribution of contaminated (expired) products to the inability to execute an efficient recall in the event of detecting defects (non-compliant work), increasing the economic impact and risks to public health.

Documentary traceability based on centralized records has three key limitations:

- Delays in updating information: it can take hours or days for data to be reflected throughout the chain.
- Possibility of manipulation: with authorized access, records can be altered without leaving a trace, compromising the integrity of the evidence.
- Lack of shared visibility: each organization controls its own database, making it difficult to have a real-time overview.

In this regard, Blockchain offers the possibility of consolidating a single, shared, and reliable record that serves as a common reference for all actors, ensuring that the information supporting an audit or certification is verifiable and unquestionable (Kumar, 2022; Riaz et al., 2023).

Risk of counterfeiting and fraud: The problem of counterfeiting in global trade, which affects multiple sectors, has been widely documented. According to Subramaniam et al (2025), combining blockchain with technologies such as NFC offers a secure and tamper-resistant authentication mechanism that can be applied in industries as diverse as pharmaceuticals, automotive, and medical devices. In the pharmaceutical sector, recent research shows that blockchain not only improves traceability but also significantly reduces the risk of counterfeit drugs entering the supply chain (Pareek et al., 2024; Sharma & Rohilla, 2023).

These systems allow each stage a product goes through, from manufacturing to final delivery, to be recorded in an immutable way, acting as a digital seal that supports its authenticity (Khaleelullah et al., 2024; Devre et al., 2024).

Lack of data synchronization: Information asymmetry in supply chains, resulting from the use of heterogeneous systems such as ERP, CRM, and non-interoperable logistics platforms, causes delays and errors in data transfer, affecting the quality of decisions. Qiao & Zhao (2023) demonstrate that supply chain integration, through real-time information exchange, significantly reduces these problems, improving transparency and mitigating operational risks.

In addition, recent research indicates that a Blockchain enabled supply chain can effectively reduce quality information asymmetry, although it does not eliminate those related to demand or disruptions

(Li, 2022). In this sense, the incorporation of IoT together with blockchain facilitates shared visibility and reliable data, aligning with the integration requirements of the future ISO 9001:2026.

Regulatory compliance and audits: In regulated sectors such as food, pharmaceuticals, and aerospace, regulatory compliance requires maintaining accurate and auditable records for long periods of time, something that current systems often solve with manual and costly processes that slow down audits and create friction with certifying bodies (traditional document systems). According to Akram et al. (2024), the use of blockchain in pharmaceutical supply chain management allows for the creation of a distributed, immutable, and reliable record that improves traceability and facilitates regulatory verification.

A concrete example can be found in the food industry, where Regulation (EU) 178/2002 requires traceability "from farm to table." Meeting this requirement involves managing records from multiple sources, which is a significant challenge in non-integrated systems. Akram et al. (2024) point out that by providing a single, accessible, and secure record, blockchain could enable an auditor to confirm compliance almost instantly, reducing weeks of work to minutes.

Vulnerability to disruptions: In the field of supply chain resilience, Manzoor et al. (2024) highlight that the integration of Blockchain improves real-time visibility and resilience to disruptions, reducing shortages and inequalities in supply during crises. Complementarily, Ramkumar & Gopan (2025) argue that a Blockchain-based logistics framework facilitates product tracking and the immediate activation of risk mitigation protocols, optimizing the response to unforeseen events.

In the manufacturing sector, Zhou (2024) found that the use of blockchain enhances traceability, coordination, and collaboration among partners, contributing to a more agile response and operational continuity even under adverse conditions. Similarly, Sharma et al. (2021) show that, in the food industry, this technology acts as a catalyst to increase flexibility and shorten the supply chain, minimizing the impact of disruptions such as the COVID-19 pandemic.

Hidden costs and loss of trust: Deficiencies in traceability, synchronization, and visibility in supply chains generate significant hidden costs, such as excessive inventories, returns, litigation, and regulatory fines, but the most difficult damage to reverse is the loss of trust. Zariwala (2023) points out that Blockchain, by improving transparency and traceability, acts as a structural mechanism to strengthen trust between actors who do not have a history of direct collaboration.

This role of Blockchain as a trust builder is also confirmed in the agri-food chain, where its use has been shown to improve transparency, resilience, and sustainability, generating stronger relationships between suppliers and customers (Olech-Anyebe et al., 2024).

In summary, as Liu et al. (2025) point out, Blockchain's ability to create decentralized, secure, and verifiable records provides a technological foundation that not only optimizes processes but also transforms the management paradigm toward more reliable models aligned with standards such as ISO 9001:2026.

7.2 Convergence Between Blockchain and ISO 9001:2026

The imminent transition to ISO 9001:2026 represents a decisive milestone in the evolution of quality management systems (QMS). This new revision, closely linked to digitization trends and the Industry 4.0 paradigm, seeks to broaden the scope of the standard to explicitly integrate advanced data management, real-time traceability, and organizational resilience as strategic pillars (perhaps the most significant revision since the inclusion of the Plan-Do-Check-Act cycle in 1994, or the process management of the 2000 version). In this context, Blockchain is no longer perceived as an optional technological tool but rather as a structural enabler, capable of materializing several of the principles and requirements that the new standard is expected to incorporate.

Recent research has highlighted that the convergence between disruptive technologies, including the Internet of Things (IoT), artificial intelligence (AI), and Blockchain, and Quality Management gives rise to approaches such as Quality Management 4.0, where transparency, interoperability, and information integrity are essential for sustainable success (Binh et al., 2024; Damayanti, 2023).

The preliminary working draft of the ISO/TC 176 Technical Committee suggests a clear focus on digital information integrity and the incorporation of means to enable continuous verification of regulatory compliance. This implies that records must be reliable, auditable, and as far as possible, immune to unauthorized alterations. Blockchain, by its intrinsic design, meets these conditions and raises them to a standard that, until a few years ago, was unattainable by conventional methods (representing an ideal mechanism for these new requirements).

Regulatory connection points: ISO 9001:2026 will maintain its high-level structure (HLS), but will strengthen key sections where blockchain can play a decisive role:

- Rozario & Vasarhelyi (2018) highlight that the immutability of blockchain is a powerful tool for complying with Clause 7.5 on documented information, as it allows critical documents to be recorded and protected, ensuring their availability and preventing undetected alterations.
- In relation to Clause 8.5, Andrés & Lorca (2021) explain that smart contracts can automate processes and verify quality criteria before products move on to the next phase, reducing manual intervention and the risk of error.
- Regarding Clause 9.1, Popchev et al. (2022) point out that Blockchain, combined with IoT, facilitates the collection and secure storage of real-time performance data, which improves analysis and increases the reliability of evaluations.
- For Clause 9.2, Rozario & Thomas (2019) propose continuous auditing based on Blockchain, which reduces time and costs compared to on-site audits.
- Finally, for Clause 10.2, Prashanth et al. (2023) emphasize that the automatic and immutable recording of nonconformities streamlines root cause investigation and prevents evidence tampering. Clause 9.2 (Internal audit).

The standard establishes that the organization must conduct audits at planned intervals. With Blockchain, a continuous audit model is enabled in which records are verified automatically and permanently, drastically reducing the time and cost of on-site audits.

7.3 From periodic auditing to continuous auditing

The possibility of replacing periodic audits with a continuous audit model using Blockchain has been highlighted by various authors, who point out that this technology allows for real-time verification, increases transparency, and reduces the costs and time associated with audit processes by automatically recording and validating critical information from the management system, eliminating much of the omissions and delays present in traditional approaches (Arianpoor & Borhani, 2024; Wu & Liu, 2025; Li & Bai, 2022).

With Blockchain, on the other hand, every relevant transaction or event is immediately recorded in a shared digital ledger, allowing auditors to access the information they need to verify compliance or detect deviations at any time, eliminating the risk of pre-audit alterations thanks to the immutability of the records (Kokogho et al., 2025). Auditors can access the information necessary to verify compliance or detect deviations at any time. The risk of pre-audit "cleaning" disappears, as records cannot be altered retroactively.

This approach is in line with the ISO 9001:2026 trend toward operational transparency and the integration of technologies that facilitate remote monitoring.

Applied example. Supplier certification. Let's imagine a supply chain involving raw material suppliers on different continents. In the traditional model, the certification of these suppliers depends on on-site audits or documents sent by email or centralized platforms, which increases the risk of falsification, loss of information, or delays in updating (Amarnath, 2025).

In a blockchain-based system, each supplier records their certifications, test results, and previous audits on the chain. These records are available to all authorized members of the network. When a supplier updates their certification, the change is cryptographically validated and automatically notified to all interested parties.

An auditor could verify the validity of the certificate directly on the chain, without intermediaries and with a guarantee that it has not been altered (Puli et al., 2022; Priyadarshini et al., 2025; Reddy et al., 2025). This model not only streamlines document management but also increases confidence in the information received and reduces dependence on manual verification processes.

7.4 Key advantages in the context of ISO 9001:2026

The implementation of Blockchain in quality management offers multiple complementary benefits: (a) real-time evidence of compliance, as records comply with the traceability principle required by the standard without requiring manual consolidation of scattered data (Muthirevula et al., 2024); (b) reduced audit times, as validated and shared information eliminates the need to prepare extensive documentation packages prior to each audit (Talha et al., 2024); (c) integration with other ISO standards, as Blockchain interoperability allows the information to also be used to meet the requirements of standards such as ISO 14001 or ISO 45001 (Soori et al., 2024); and (d) greater resilience, as the decentralization of information protects records from physical disasters or cyberattacks (Omisola & Bihani, 2023).

In short, the convergence between Blockchain and ISO 9001:2026 is not fortuitous, but structural. The standard is moving toward a management model where information reliability and continuous verification are essential, and Blockchain offers the perfect technological framework to meet and exceed those requirements (Kramer et al., 2021; Xue et al., 2025).

To the extent that organizations understand this synergy and begin to adopt the technology before the standard comes into force, they will not only be prepared for certification but will also gain competitive advantages in an environment where transparency and trust become key differentiators (Proskurnina & Bilousko, 2023; Wiyono & Silitonga, 2025).

7.5 Strategic impact on Quality Management

Sahoo (2024) asserts that quality management in supply chains is undergoing a paradigm shift driven by the integration of Blockchain, as this technology strengthens traceability, security, and collaboration among stakeholders. Along the same lines, Akram et al. (2024) highlight that blockchain not only protects data integrity through its immutability, but also reinforces transparency in processes, reducing the risk of fraud or alteration of information. Likewise, Alabaddi et al. (2023) point out that this advance redefines strategic quality management models, integrating continuous verification as a structural element in business operations.

In the context of ISO 9001:2026, quality will no longer be evaluated primarily through periodic sampling and historical records, but will become a continuous, proactive process based on reliable real-time data. As Shiyanbola (2024) points out, this transition involves not only a technical change, but also a systemic redesign that integrates statistical control tools, continuous improvement, and real-time analytics, thereby strengthening the competitiveness and responsiveness of organizations.

Likewise, Dobrin et al. (2025) highlight that this approach allows companies to adapt more agilely to market conditions and customer demands, turning quality management into a strategic driver for organizational resilience and innovation. This ensures compliance with the ISO 9001 family of standards promoted by ISO itself, as well as increased sales, customer satisfaction, and performance (Guirette-Barbosa et al., 2025).

From a reactive model to a predictive model. Historically, Quality Management Systems have relied on reactive models, where the priority was to identify non-conformities, investigate their root causes, and apply corrective actions. According to Sreedharan et al. (2020), this approach, although proven effective, has the limitation that problems are detected after they occur, which can result in economic losses and a deterioration of customer confidence. Similarly, Pambreni et al. (2019) point out that, in highly regulated sectors, this delay in detection also increases risks to consumer safety and raises compliance costs, especially when product recalls are required.

With blockchain, a predictive and preventive model is enabled thanks to:

- Real-time traceability: information flows instantly between actors in the chain.
- Automatic alerts: smart contracts can trigger immediate actions when parameters are out of specification (e.g., transport temperature higher than allowed for refrigerated food).
- . Integration with data analysis and AI: historical patterns recorded on the blockchain can be analyzed to anticipate failures and optimize processes.

This transforms quality into a living system capable of anticipating risks before they affect the end customer.

Quality as a competitive advantage. In increasingly competitive markets, quality has evolved from being a simple requirement for operating to becoming a key strategic differentiator. Transparency and traceability not only strengthen consumer confidence but also directly influence customer loyalty. For example, Kim & Kim (2024) point out that organizational transparency increases trust and, consequently, customer loyalty, while more recent studies confirm that blockchain-based traceability increases consumers' willingness to pay a premium price for products whose authenticity and origin are verifiable.

In this sense, having certified traceability not only facilitates positioning in high value-added segments, but also opens doors to markets with strong regulatory requirements. Research by Sharma et al. (2024) highlights that the integration of blockchain into supply chain management mitigates the risk of counterfeiting and reinforces regulatory compliance, which is particularly relevant in sectors such as pharmaceuticals, food, and aerospace. Thus, having a blockchain system aligned with the principles of ISO 9001:2026 could become an indispensable criterion for accessing international contracts.

Companies such as Nestlé and Carrefour have demonstrated that blockchain-backed transparency not only improves trust but also has a positive impact on sales and brand perception (Chapter 8).

Cost reduction and operational efficiency. The integration of blockchain into quality management also generates tangible operational efficiencies:

- Reduction in audit time: having all records in an immutable and accessible database eliminates the need to compile scattered documentation. Walmart, for example, reduced the time it takes to track a batch from weeks to seconds (Kamath, 2018; Shankaran, 2024).
- Fewer complaints: Continuous monitoring and early detection of deviations reduce the number of defective products reaching the market (Choy, 2022).
- Optimized document management: Blockchain replaces multiple data repositories with a single, shared system, reducing duplication of information and the risk of human error (Choy, 2022).

This has a direct impact on profitability and frees up resources that can be invested in innovation and development.

Organizational resilience. An organization's ability to adapt and recover from disruptions is a critical success factor. Blockchain reinforces this resilience by:

- Providing complete visibility of the chain, allowing vulnerable points to be quickly identified.
- Ensuring data integrity even in crisis situations (server failures, cyberattacks, natural disasters).
- Facilitating inter-organizational coordination, as all participants work on a common and reliable record.

During the COVID-19 pandemic, companies that had already implemented Blockchain were able to maintain operational continuity by quickly validating alternative suppliers and documenting regulatory compliance without relying on on-site audits.

Integration with other management standards. ISO 9001:2026 will not be an isolated standard. The ISO trend is toward an integrated management system where different standards (ISO 14001, ISO 45001, ISO 27001) share compatible structures and requirements. Blockchain can serve as a centralized platform to support this ecosystem:

- In ISO 14001 (environment), to track the carbon footprint of products.
- In ISO 27001 (information security), to protect data confidentiality and integrity.
- In ISO 45001 (occupational health and safety), to document incidents and preventive measures.

The ability to interoperate between standards makes it easier for investment in Blockchain to have a broader and more lasting return.

From operational quality to Strategic Quality. One of the most significant changes brought about by blockchain is the shift from operational quality (focused on internal processes) to strategic quality (integrated into the business model). Quality is no longer a support area but has become a differentiating factor in the value proposition (Muruganandham et al., 2022). Examples such as Carrefour show how Blockchain traceability is used not only to comply with the law, but also as a marketing argument, strengthening the relationship with consumers who value verifiable information and transparency (Bettín-Díaz et al., 2021).

In short, the strategic impact of blockchain on quality management is transformational: it improves efficiency, reduces risks, strengthens trust, and opens new market opportunities. As ISO 9001:2026 incorporates stricter traceability and data verification requirements, organizations that integrate Blockchain will not only be complying with the standard but also positioning themselves as leaders in an increasingly demanding and digitized business environment (Andita & Nugraha, 2022).

7.6 Opportunities and Challenges of Implementation

The adoption of Blockchain in supply chains is not a simple technological project; it involves a profound change in the way quality, traceability, and the relationship between the actors involved in the flow of products and information are managed. While its potential is widely recognized, the implementation of Blockchain for purposes aligned with ISO 9001:2026 requires careful analysis of the opportunities it offers and the barriers that must be overcome for its successful integration (Kouhizadeh et al., 2021; Liu & Shen, 2020; Zekhnini et al., 2021).

7.6.1 Strategic Opportunities

The incorporation of Blockchain into quality management and supply chain traceability opens a range of opportunities that go beyond regulatory compliance.

Radical transparency as a competitive advantage. In a context where consumers value provenance, sustainability, and ethical production, Blockchain enables the sharing of verifiable information in real time. This translates into brand differentiation and the possibility of positioning oneself in premium market segments. Example: Carrefour has used blockchain to demonstrate to customers the origin and production conditions of its fresh products, which increased its sales and strengthened its brand image.

Simplified regulatory compliance. Audits, both internal and external, are simplified by having immutable records that are accessible from any authorized point. Companies can demonstrate compliance with regulatory requirements immediately, reducing the costs and time associated with audits. Example: Walmart reduced the time to trace the origin of a batch of mangoes from 6 days to 2.2 seconds, allowing it to respond more quickly to regulatory incidents.

Multi Standard integration. The same Blockchain infrastructure used for ISO 9001 can be used for other certifications such as ISO 14001, ISO 45001, and ISO 27001, optimizing resources and avoiding duplication in document management (highlighting the reliability of measurements in an ISO 17025 QMS).

Reduction of losses and fraud. The immutable data record prevents the falsification of documents and certifications, reducing the risk of fraud in transactions and product origin.

Synergy with IoT and artificial intelligence. The integration of Blockchain with IoT sensors allows critical data (temperature, humidity, location) to be captured automatically, while advanced analytics and artificial intelligence enable patterns to be identified and risks to be anticipated.

7.6.2 Implementation challenges

Despite its benefits, the adoption of Blockchain faces obstacles that can slow down or limit its effectiveness if not addressed strategically.

Initial investment costs. Although the costs of the technology have decreased, implementing blockchain still involves investments in infrastructure, systems integration, training, and technical support. This factor can be a significant barrier for small and medium-sized enterprises (SMEs).

Technical complexity and interoperability. Global supply chains use a wide variety of ERP, CRM, and logistics platforms. Integrating blockchain with these systems requires careful design and, in many cases, the development of custom applications or middleware to enable seamless communication between platforms (Ravi et al., 2024; Sever & Angin, 2021; Potru, 2024).

Cultural and organizational resistance. The shift from a centralized trust model to a distributed one requires a cultural reconfiguration. Some actors may be reluctant to share data openly, even within a secure and controlled environment.

Scalability. In public blockchain networks, transaction validation speed can be a limitation. Although private or consortium networks improve this aspect, they require a design that guarantees performance without sacrificing security.

8. CASE STUDIES

The food industry has been a pioneer in adopting blockchain, driven by the urgent need to ensure traceability, authenticity, and food safety. The growing complexity of global supply chains, coupled with strict regulations such as the Food Safety Modernization Act in the United States (FSMA 204) and Regulation (EU) 178/2002 in Europe, has led large corporations to integrate this technology not only to comply with more rigorous audits, but also to respond quickly to incidents of contamination or fraud.

Recent studies show that blockchain allows each link in the chain to be recorded immutably, enabling "farm-to-table" traceability and improving transparency, efficiency, and consumer confidence (Dakshayini et al., 2024; Tanwar et al., 2022). In addition, interoperability with IoT systems and Smart Contracts facilitates real-time verification of critical parameters, such as temperature and transport conditions, strengthening the ability to respond to food risks (Pisupati & Ulle, 2024).

Below are three real and documented cases of Blockchain implementation in the food industry, showing the context, deployment strategies, and measurable results obtained.

8.1 The Walmart case and food safety

Context: Walmart, one of the world's largest retailers, faced a recurring problem: the difficulty of tracing the origin of fresh produce during contamination incidents. Before implementing blockchain, identifying the farm of origin for a batch of mangoes could take 6 days, 18 hours, and 26 minutes, according to an internal study conducted in 2018 (Kamath).

Implementation: In collaboration with IBM Food Trust, Walmart adopted a private blockchain network based on Hyperledger Fabric to record critical information about fruits, vegetables, and fresh meat. Each batch is tagged with a code that connects to its record on the blockchain. Producers enter data about the origin, harvest date, and health certifications. Transporters add information about transport conditions (temperature, humidity).

Results: Traceability time was reduced to 2.2 seconds, enabling rapid recalls of contaminated products. Significant reduction in economic losses from food safety incidents. Improved consumer confidence thanks to the ability to verify origin using mobile apps.

8.2 The Carrefour case and transparency for consumers

Context: Carrefour, a French multinational retailer, was facing increasingly demanding consumers who wanted more information about the origin and sustainability of food products.

Implementation: Carrefour adopted Blockchain (IBM Food Trust) to record the history of fresh products such as chicken, tomatoes, eggs, and milk (Eletter et al., 2022). Consumers scan a QR code on the packaging and access detailed information: farm of origin, type of animal feed, production and transport dates. Producers and distributors update the information directly on the Blockchain.

Results: 11% increase in sales of products with Blockchain traceability in the first year of implementation. Greater loyalty among customers who value transparency and sustainability. Reduction in conflicts with suppliers thanks to immutable supply chain records.

8.3 The Nestlé case

Context: Nestlé, a global leader in food and beverages, implemented Blockchain technology to ensure complete traceability of its premium Zoégas coffee, made with 100% sustainably sourced beans. The company integrated the IBM Food Trust platform, which allows each batch to be tracked from its origin in plantations in Brazil, Rwanda, and Colombia to its arrival at the point of sale in Europe. This system records key data from all stages, including harvesting, processing, shipping, roasting, and packaging, enabling immediate verification of provenance and associated sustainable practices.

*Implementation:*According to Schilhabel et al. (2023), the use of blockchain in food supply chains not only improves traceability and visibility but also strengthens relationships with suppliers by offering transparency and verifiable trust in real time. Sustainability certifications issued by the Rainforest Alliance are added as verifiable documents on the blockchain.

Results: Reduction in fraud related to falsification of certificates of origin. Increased consumer confidence and strengthened brand image. Possibility of real-time auditing of the entire chain, from the field to the supermarket.

8.4 Strategic impact common to all three cases

These cases share clear strategic benefits:

- Reduction in traceability times: from days to seconds.
- Reduction in economic losses: through faster and more accurate recalls.
- Strengthening of trust: among consumers, auditors, and regulators.
- Preparation for ISO audits: the immutability and availability of information facilitate compliance with the future ISO 9001:2026 standard.

In addition, convergence with IoT, through sensors in transport and storage, has enabled automatic, real-time data capture, avoided human error and ensured the accuracy of records (Cha et al., 2023).

In conclusion, the use of Blockchain in the food industry has gone from being an experimental project to becoming an emerging standard for companies that want to combine operational efficiency, regulatory compliance, and radical transparency. Walmart, Carrefour, and Nestlé have demonstrated that the strategic integration of this technology is not only viable but also generates measurable and sustainable competitive advantages.

9. IMPLICATIONS

9.1 Managerial Implications

Strategic opportunities. The incorporation of Blockchain into quality management and supply chains offers a range of opportunities that go beyond regulatory compliance.

Radical transparency as a competitive advantage. In a context where consumers value provenance, sustainability, and ethical practices, transparency becomes a differentiating factor. Blockchain enables real-time access to verifiable information for consumers and stakeholders, creating an environment of trust that translates into increased sales and greater brand loyalty. Example: Carrefour has used blockchain to demonstrate to customers the origin and handling of certain products, which increased its sales and strengthened its brand image.

Simplified regulatory compliance. Audits, both internal and external, are simplified by having immutable and transparent records that can be consulted by auditors in real time. This not only facilitates compliance but also enables organizations to demonstrate compliance with regulatory requirements immediately, reducing the costs and time associated with audits. Example: Walmart reduced the time to trace the origin of a batch from days to seconds thanks to blockchain-based systems, allowing it to respond more quickly to regulatory incidents.

Multi-standard integration. The same Blockchain infrastructure used for ISO 9001 can be used to support other standards, such as ISO 22000 (food safety) or ISO 14001 (environmental management), by integrating a common data structure.

Re-conceptualizing "documented information." Under ISO 9001, evidence has traditionally been organization-bounded and stored in centralized repositories. A permissioned DLT reframes this as a shared, cryptographically anchored evidence layer spanning multiple firms. Authenticity, custody, and versioning become properties of network governance rather than of a single firm's IT, reshaping theories of record integrity and chain of custody.

From periodic to continuous, event-driven assurance. Classic assurance models emphasize periodic, sample-based verification within firm boundaries. Blockchain enables event-level verification across boundaries (e.g., lot releases, quarantine holds, calibration status) with immutable timestamps, extending continuous auditing/monitoring theory into inter-organizational settings.

Smart contracts as formal controls (compliance-by-design). In control theory, policies/procedures are enacted by people and IT workflows. Smart contracts translate rules (quality gates, segregation of duties, escalation thresholds) into executable logic, shifting emphasis from ex-post detection to ex-ante prevention and offering a programmable layer for internal control systems.

Information asymmetry and coordination costs. Drawing on agency theory and transaction-cost economics, permissioned ledgers can reduce verification/monitoring costs by making provenance and state changes verifiable to authorized parties. At the same time, they introduce new governance costs (node accountability, incentive alignment, data stewardship, dispute resolution) that must be theorized within inter-firm coordination frameworks.

9.2 Practical Implications

Key advantages in the context of ISO 9001:2026. The implementation of Blockchain in quality management offers multiple complementary benefits:

(a) real-time evidence of compliance, as records comply with the traceability principle required by the standard without requiring manual consolidation of scattered data (Muthirevula et al., 2024);
(b) reduced audit times, as validated and shared information eliminates the need to prepare extensive documentation packages prior to each audit (Talha et al., 2024);
(c) integration with other ISO standards, as Blockchain interoperability allows the information to also be used to meet the requirements of standards such as ISO 14001 or ISO 45001 (Soori et al., 2024); and
(d) greater resilience, as the decentralization of information protects records from physical disasters or cyberattacks (Omisola & Bihani, 2023).

In short, the convergence between Blockchain and ISO 9001:2026 is not fortuitous, but structural. The standard is moving toward a management model where information reliability and continuous verification are essential, and Blockchain offers the perfect technological framework to meet and exceed those requirements (Kramer et al., 2021; Xue et al., 2025).

To the extent that organizations understand this synergy and begin to adopt the technology before the standard comes into force, they will not only be prepared for certification but will also gain competitive advantages in an environment where transparency and trust become key differentiators (Proskurnina & Bilousko, 2023; Wiyono & Silitonga, 2025).

9.3 Theoretical Implications

Re-conceptualizing "documented information." Under ISO 9001, evidence has traditionally been organization-bounded and stored in centralized repositories. With a permissioned blockchains, evidence becomes a shared, cryptographically anchored layer spanning multiple firms. Authenticity, custody, and versioning shift from being properties of one firm's it to properties of inter-organizational governance, reframing theories of record integrity and chain of custody.

From periodic to continuous, event-driven assurance. Classic assurance models emphasize periodic, sample-based checks within a single organization. Blockchain enables event-level verification across boundaries (e.g., lot releases, holds, calibrations) with immutable timestamps, extending continuous auditing/monitoring theory to multi-actor, distributed settings and replacing "snapshot" bias with near-real-time traceability.

Smart contracts as formal controls (compliance-by-design). Traditional control theory assumes policies executed by people and IT workflows. Smart contracts encode quality gates, segregation of duties, and escalation thresholds as executable logic, shifting emphasis from ex-post detection to ex-ante prevention and introducing a programmable layer for internal control systems.

Information asymmetry and coordination. Drawing on agency theory and transaction-cost economics, permissioned ledgers reduce verification/monitoring costs by making provenance and state changes verifiable to authorized parties. They also introduce new governance costs (node accountability, incentive alignment, data stewardship, dispute resolution) that must be theorized within inter-firm coordination frameworks.

Socio-technical contingencies and boundary conditions. The performance of blockchain-enabled QMS is moderated by edge data quality (IoT, operators), identity assurance, and privacy/regulatory constraints (e.g., off-chain payloads with on-chain proofs). Network topology (consortium vs. private), ERP/MES integration maturity, and regulatory intensity act as boundary conditions explaining adoption variance and heterogeneous outcomes.

Dynamic capabilities for quality. Cryptographically anchored evidence strengthens organizational sensing (earlier anomaly detection), seizing (automated quality gates), and reconfiguring (faster CAPA learning loops). Thus, DLT functions not only as infrastructure but as an enabler of quality-oriented dynamic capabilities.

10. RECOMMENDATIONS

10.1 Strategies for overcoming barriers.

To maximize opportunities and minimize challenges, we recommend:

- Gradual implementation: start with a pilot project focused on a product or segment of the chain, evaluate results, and then scale up.
- Training and change management: train all stakeholders in the use of the technology and the strategic benefits of its adoption.
- Participation in industry consortiums: collaborate with other companies in the industry to develop shared standards and platforms that reduce costs and increase interoperability.
- Design of data governance policies: establish clear rules about what data is shared, with whom, and under what conditions.
- Appropriate selection of the type of blockchain: opt for private or consortium networks in environments where privacy and performance are critical.

10.2 Outlook for ISO 9001:2026

With the arrival of ISO 9001:2026, organizations that have already incorporated Blockchain will be better positioned to meet traceability, information integrity, and continuous verification requirements. Those that delay its adoption could face a more costly and complex transition, especially if their current processes rely on fragmented systems or manual records (Fonseca et al., 2019; Wang et al., 2021).

In conclusion, Blockchain offers unprecedented opportunities to transform quality management and traceability in supply chains. However, its implementation must be strategically planned, anticipating technical, economic, and cultural challenges. Forward-thinking companies will not only be able to comply with ISO 9001:2026, but also turn transparency, efficiency, and innovation into their main competitive advantages (Zimon et al., 2020).

11. FUTURE RESEARCH

The advancement of blockchain in supply chains and its convergence with ISO 9001:2026 should not be understood as a passing trend, but rather as a structural change in the way quality systems are conceived, managed, and audited. Although implementation is currently concentrated in large corporations and pilot projects in strategic sectors, technological evolution, regulatory pressure, and consumer demand anticipate a scenario in which adoption will be massive and crosscutting across multiple industries by 2030 (Cai et al., 2024).This chapter outlines possible paths for development, integrating technological, regulatory, economic, and social factors that will influence the degree and way Blockchain will consolidate itself as the de facto standard in quality management and traceability.

11.1 Towards global standardization of blockchain quality

The regulatory landscape shows clear signs that international organizations will tend to officially recognize Blockchain as a valid means of evidence of compliance. In the short term, ISO 9001:2026 is unlikely to explicitly require Blockchain, but it will demand levels of traceability, data integrity, and continuous verification that will be very difficult to achieve without this technology (Regueiro and Urquizu, 2024; Sawant, 2025; Trisnandar & Kurniawan, 2025).In the medium term, it is feasible that complementary standards or specific technical guidelines for the implementation of Blockchain in quality management will emerge, as was the case with specialized standards in environmental management and information security. This will allow for the establishment of uniform requirements for interoperability, security, and governance of inter-company Blockchain networks.

11.2 Full Integration with IoT, AI, and predictive analytics

The maturity of blockchain will be accompanied by its integration with other key technologies: Internet of Things (IoT): connected sensors will capture critical variables (temperature, humidity, location, vibration) in real time and automatically send the data to the blockchain, eliminating manual intervention (Yang et al., 2023).Artificial Intelligence (AI): analysis of historical and real-time data will enable the identification of risk patterns and the anticipation of non-conformities before they impact the customer (Omisola & Bihani, 2023).Predictive Analytics: Statistical and machine learning models will be fed with immutable data, increasing their reliability and reducing false positives (Owusu-Berko, 2025).

11.3 Blockchain as a commercial and contractual requirement

By 2030, blockchain traceability could cease to be a competitive advantage and become a requirement for market access. Large international buyers and government agencies could require their suppliers to demonstrate that they have an integrated blockchain system as a precondition for establishing business relationships (Fan, 2020). This trend is already evident in sectors such as: Food: to guarantee safety and authenticity. Pharmaceuticals: to combat counterfeit medicines and comply with regulations such as the European Falsified Medicines Directive. Mining and metals: to certify the ethical origin of mineral.

11.4 Democratization of technology and access for SMEs

According to Wong, et al., (2020), Blockchain adoption is currently concentrated in large corporations due to initial costs and technical complexity. However, the development of Blockchain-as-a-Service (BaaS) platforms will reduce these barriers, allowing small and medium-sized enterprises to access the technology through subscription models, without the need for their own infrastructure. Providers such as IBM, Microsoft, and AWS already offer scalable Blockchain solutions that could be integrated with ERP and CRM systems commonly used in SMEs, accelerating their mass adoption (Kumar, 2024).

11.5 Advances in data control and regulation

The immutable nature of Blockchain poses legal challenges, especially in relation to the right to be forgotten and the protection of personal data. In the future, hybrid architectures are expected to be developed in which sensitive information is stored off-chain and only encrypted references or hashes are kept on the blockchain. This will enable compliance with regulations such as the General Data Protection Regulation (GDPR) without sacrificing the traceability or integrity of the information (Wang et al., 2023).

11.6 Prospective scenarios for 2040Total Adoption Scenario

Blockchain becomes the universal standard for quality management and traceability. Most ISO 9001-certified management systems use globally interoperable Blockchain networks (Sunmola et al., 2021).Selective Adoption Scenario: The technology is mainly used in regulated and high-value sectors, while other sectors adopt more economical hybrid solutions (Ghode et al., 2021).Invisible Integration Scenario: Blockchain is so deeply integrated into the digital infrastructure that its use is transparent to the end user, functioning as a layer of security and trust underlying all quality processes (Abdelwahed & Soomro, 2025).

11.7 The role of research and academia

Academia will play a key role in generating methodologies and reference models that enable the evaluation of return on investment, risks, and best implementation practices. The training of professionals specialized in quality management and blockchain will be crucial for companies to adopt the technology effectively and sustainably.In summary, prospects indicate that blockchain will cease to be an emerging technology and become a structural requirement in quality management. Convergence with ISO 9001:2026 and other international standards will mark a new era where transparency, traceability, and data integrity will be as essential as process control is today (Mosa et al., 2024). Organizations that adopt this vision early on will not only be prepared to comply with regulations, but also to lead the transformation of their sectors toward more reliable, efficient, and sustainable models.

12. CONCLUSIONS

The evolution of Quality Management Systems towards ISO 9001:2026 represents much more than a documentary update; it constitutes a structural transformation towards a management model based on data integrity, real-time traceability, and continuous verification. In this scenario, Blockchain emerges not as a complementary technological option, but as the fundamental pillar that will enable the guiding principles of the new standard to be realized.

Throughout this chapter, it has been demonstrated that Blockchain:

- Resolves historical limitations of supply chains, such as information fragmentation, record manipulation, and lack of comprehensive visibility.
- Raises the standard of traceability to levels that were previously operationally unfeasible, reducing tracking times from days to seconds, as evidenced by real-life cases from Walmart, Carrefour, and Nestlé.
- Transforms the role of quality from reactive to predictive, integrating IoT and artificial intelligence to anticipate risks and make decisions based on reliable data.
- Facilitates regulatory compliance and opens business opportunities by becoming a seal of transparency and trust for customers, auditors, and regulators.

The convergence between Blockchain and ISO 9001:2026 is not a random phenomenon, but a natural response to a business environment characterized by globalized digital supply chains, informed consumers, and increasingly stringent regulations. In a context where trust becomes a strategic asset, Blockchain offers a technical and organizational framework that allows for the decentralization of trust and guarantees the authenticity of information without relying on a single intermediary.

However, its implementation is not without challenges:

- It requires initial investment in infrastructure and training.
- It demands a cultural redesign to encourage collaboration and data sharing among stakeholders.
- It involves careful management of privacy and data protection in an immutable environment.

Overcoming these barriers is not only a technical challenge, but also a strategic one. Organizations that do so early will not only comply with ISO 9001:2026 but will also set the competitive standard in their industries for the next decade.

Looking ahead, the trend is clear: Blockchain will cease to be a differentiator and become a basic operational requirement, just as having a certified management system is today. Academia, industry, and regulatory bodies will need to work together to establish regulatory frameworks, adoption methodologies, and interoperability standards that maximize its value and minimize its risks.

In conclusion, Blockchain is not simply a technology for recording data; it is the backbone of digital quality. Its widespread adoption will mark the beginning of an era in which transparency, traceability, and integrity of information are not promises, but unquestionable operational guarantees. Organizations that understand and act on this reality will not only be prepared for ISO 9001:2026 but will also be ready to lead the construction of more reliable, resilient, and sustainable supply chains globally (precisely the most representative changes that this new version of the standard seeks to achieve).

REFERENCES

Abdelwahed, N. A. A., & Soomro, B. (2025). Blockchain adoption effect on supply chain integration, innovation management, and performance. *Journal of Governance and Regulation*. https://doi.org/DOI: 10.22495/jgrv14i1art11

Ahn, J., Yi, E., & Kim, M. (2024). Blockchain consensus mechanisms: A bibliometric analysis (2014–2024) using VOSviewer and R Bibliometrix. *Information (Basel)*, *15*(10), 644. Advance online publication. DOI: 10.3390/info15100644

Akram, W., Joshi, R., Haider, T., Sharma, P., Jain, V., Garud, N., & Narwaria, N. S. (2024). Blockchain technology: A potential tool for the management of pharma supply chain. *Research in Social & Administrative Pharmacy: RSAP*. https://doi.org/DOI: 10.1016/j.sapharm.2024.02.014

Alabaddi, Z., Obidat, A., & Alziyadat, Z. (2023). Exploring the effect of blockchain technology on supply chain resilience and transparency: Evidence from the healthcare industry. *Uncertain Supply Chain Management*, *11*(2), 787–798. Advance online publication. DOI: 10.5267/j.uscm.2023.1.001

Alfuhaid, S., Amyot, D., Anda, A., & Mylopoulos, J. (2023). A mapping review on cyber-physical smart contracts: *Architectures, platforms, and challenges. IEEE Access : Practical Innovations, Open Solutions*, *11*, 65872–65890. DOI: 10.1109/ACCESS.2023.3290899

Alhat, P. (2024). *Blockchain technology*. International Journal of Scientific Research in Engineering and Management., DOI: 10.55041/IJSREM30694

Amarnath, J. L. (2025). Online blockchain based certificate generation and validation system for government organization. *International Journal of Scientific Research in Engineering and Management*, *9*(1), 1–6. DOI: 10.55041/IJSREM41957

Andita, A. D., & Nugraha, I. B. (2022). A blockchain-based traceability system to achieve the quality objectives in the production process of a manufacturing industry. 2022 *International Conference on Information Technology Systems and Innovation* (ICITSI), 194–199. https://doi.org/DOI: 10.1109/ICITSI56531.2022.9970822

Andrés, J., & Lorca, P. (2021). On the impact of smart contracts on auditing. *The International Journal of Digital Accounting Research*, *21*(6), 197–222. DOI: 10.4192/1577-8517-v21_6

Arianpoor, A., & Borhani, A. (2024). Blockchain-based continuous auditing for quality management systems. *Journal of Accounting and Organizational Change*, *20*(3), 421–440. DOI: 10.1108/JAOC-03-2023-0045

Azevedo, P., Gomes, J., & Romão, M. (2023). Supply chain traceability using blockchain. *Operations Management Research : Advancing Practice Through Research*, *16*(3), 1359–1381. DOI: 10.1007/s12063-023-00359-y

Bager, S., Düdder, B., Henglein, F., Hébert, J. M., & Wu, H. (2022). Event-based supply chain network modeling: Blockchain for good coffee. *Frontiers in Blockchain*, *5*, 846783. DOI: 10.3389/fbloc.2022.846783

Bettín-Díaz, R., Mejía, C., & Rojas, A. E. (2021). *A blockchain-based approach to support an ISO 9001:2015 quality management system*. ParadigmPlus., DOI: 10.55969/paradigmplus.v2n2a2

Bhasin, P. (2023). Blockchain-based supply chain management system. *International Journal for Research Publication and Seminars, 14*(5), 9–19. Advance online publication. DOI: 10.36676/jrps.2023-v14i5-02

Binh, A. D. T., Akbari, M., Le, H. T. C., Nguyen, L. C., & Truong, H. Q. (2024). Forging pathways to circular economy excellence: Integrating Industry 4.0 with quality management. *Sustainability (Basel), 16*(7), 3053. DOI: 10.3390/su16073053

Bósquez-Andrade, E., & Torres-Palacios, M. (2024). *Continuous auditing and real-time monitoring: detection, mitigation of business risks in hospitality industries*. Revista Metropolitana de Ciencias Aplicadas., DOI: 10.62452/q62zma54

Cai, J., Cao, Z., & Shang, J. (2024). Blockchain adoption in a green supply chain: Considering information asymmetry of consumers' privacy concern. *International Journal of Production Economics, 272*, 109459. DOI: 10.1016/j.ijpe.2024.109459

Cha, S., Meng, W., Li, W.-W., & Yeh, K.-H. (2023). A blockchain-enabled IoT auditing management system complying with ISO/IEC 15408-2. *Computers & Industrial Engineering, 178*, 109091. DOI: 10.1016/j.cie.2023.109091

Chaabaoui, S., Oughannou, Z., & Chaoui, H. (2024). A systematic review of blockchain applications in pharmaceutical supply chain traceability and security. *2024 10th International Conference on Optimization and Applications (ICOA)*, 1–7. https://doi.org/DOI: 10.1109/ICOA62581.2024.10754349

Choy, W., & Communications, M. (2022). T raditional Supply Chain Challenges During COVID-19 Spur Innovation in Blockchain Applications. .

da Fonseca, L. M. C. M., Domingues, J. P. T., Machado, P. B., & Harder, D. (2019). ISO 9001:2015 adoption: A multi-country empirical research. *Journal of Industrial Engineering and Management, 12*(1), 27. Advance online publication. DOI: 10.3926/jiem.2745

Dakshayini, M., Sushma, H. P., & Spoorthi, S. (2024). Blockchain based traceability system for food safety. *2024 International Conference on Emerging Technologies in Computer Science for Interdisciplinary Applications (ICETCS*), 1–6. https://doi.org/DOI: 10.1109/ICETCS61022.2024.10543664

Damayanti, R. (2023). Staff competence model in implementation of Quality Management 4.0 at telecommunications industry: Literature review. *In Proceedings of the International Conference on Industrial Engineering and Operations Mana*gement. https://doi.org/DOI: 10.46254/AP03.20220049

Das, S., Samal, T. K., & Mohanta, B. K. (2024). Addressing security in IoMT systems: A blockchain consensus approach. *2024 15th International Conference on Computing Communication and Networking Technologies (ICCCNT)*, 1–6. https://doi.org/DOI: 10.1109/ICCCNT61001.2024.10725986

Devre, S., Agrawal, G., Deore, S., Dahapute, A., & Patil, S. (2024). Medicine Supply Chain using Blockchain. *International Journal of Advanced Research in Science. Tongxin Jishu*, 128–133. Advance online publication. DOI: 10.48175/IJARSCT-22318

Dobrin, C., Girneata, A., Mascu, M., & Croitoru, O. (2025). Quality: a determinant factor of competitiveness – the evolution of iso certifications for management systems., 9, 1062-1073.

Drljača, M., & Tolić, A. (2025). Quality models for preventing the impact of supply chain disruptions in future crises. *Sustainability (Basel)*, *17*(8), 3293. DOI: 10.3390/su17083293

Eletter, S., Elrefae, G., Yasmin, T., Qasem, A., Alshehadeh, A., & Belarbi, A. K. (2022). Leveraging Blockchain-Based Smart Contracts in the Management of Supply Chain: Evidence from Carrefour UAE. *2022 International Arab Conference on Information Technology (ACIT)*, 1–5. IEEE. https://doi.org/DOI: 10.1109/ACIT57182.2022.9994083

Fan, Z., Wu, X., & Cao, B. (2020). Considering the traceability awareness of consumers: Should the supply chain adopt the blockchain technology? *Annals of Operations Research*, *309*(1), 837–860. DOI: 10.1007/s10479-020-03729-y

Franke, P. D., & Fischer, F. (2023). Will blockchain technology revolutionize supply chain management? *Sri Lanka Journal of Marketing*, *9*(1), 23–40. Advance online publication. DOI: 10.4038/sljmuok.v9i1.118

Fuchs, M., Rezac, M., & Sousek, R. (2021). The overall cumulative impact of Covid-19 and Brexit on European supply chains. *2021 New Trends in Aviation Development (NTAD)*, 37–41. https://doi.org/DOI: 10.1109/NTAD54074.2021.9746509

Ghode, D., Jain, R., & Soni, G. (2021). Challenges of adoption of blockchain technology in supply chain: *An overview. In Lecture Notes in Mechanical Engineering* (pp. 1–12). https://doi.org/DOI: 10.1007/978-981-16-5281-3_15

Guirette-Barbosa, O. A., Castañeda-Burciaga, S., Ramírez-Salazar, M. A., Cruz-Domínguez, O., Carrera-Escobedo, J. L., Velázquez-Macías, J. D. J., Lara-Torres, C. G., Celaya-Padilla, J. M., & Durán-Muñoz, H. A. (2025). Transforming Quality into Results: A Multivariate Analysis with Hotelling's T2 on the Impact of ISO 9001. *Systems*, *13*(4), 226. DOI: 10.3390/systems13040226

Hariyani, D., Hariyani, P., Mishra, S., & Sharma, M. (2025). *A literature review on transformative impacts of blockchain technology on manufacturing management and industrial engineering practices.* Green Technologies and Sustainability., DOI: 10.1016/j.grets.2025.100169

Herrmann, J., Tackenberg, S., Padoano, E., Hartlief, J., Rautenstengel, J., Loeser, C., & Böhme, J. (2021). An ERP Data Quality Assessment Framework for the Implementation of an APS system using Bayesian Networks., 194-204. https://doi.org/.DOI: 10.1016/j.procs.2022.01.218

Hossain, M., Shabnam, S., Ahad, M. A., Nurani, B., & Hoque, M. E. (2025). Blockchain technology in supply chain management: Enhancing transparency and efficiency. *OAlib*, *12*(874), 1–16. Advance online publication. DOI: 10.4236/oalib.1112874

Kamath, R. (2018). Food traceability on blockchain: Walmart's pork and mango pilots with IBM. The Journal of the British Blockchain Association. https://doi.org/DOI: 10.31585/jbba-1-1-(10)2018

Khaleelullah, S., Reddy, K. S., Reddy, A. S., Kedhar, D., Bhavana, M., & Naresh, P. (2024). Pharmashield: Using Blockchain for Anti-Counterfeit Protection. *2024 Second International Conference on Inventive Computing and Informatics (ICICI)*, 529–534. https://doi.org/DOI: 10.1109/ICICI62254.2024.00092

Kokogho, E., Onwuzulike, O. C., Omowole, B. M., Ewim, C. P.-M., & Adeyanju, M. O. (2025). *Blockchain technology and real-time auditing: Transforming financial transparency and fraud detection in the Fintech industry*. Gulf Journal of Advance Business Research., DOI: 10.51594/gjabr.v3i2.88

Kouhizadeh, M., Saberi, S., & Sarkis, J. (2021). Blockchain technology and the sustainable supply chain: Theoretically exploring adoption barriers. *International Journal of Production Economics*, *231*, 107831. Advance online publication. DOI: 10.1016/j.ijpe.2020.107831

Kramer, M. P., Bitsch, L., & Hanf, J. (2021). The impact of instrumental stakeholder management on blockchain technology adoption behavior in agri-food supply chains. *Journal of Risk and Financial Management*, *14*(12), 598. DOI: 10.3390/jrfm14120598

Kumar, A. (2022). *Blockchain technology A algorithm for drug serialization*. Trends Journal of Sciences Research., DOI: 10.31586/ujpp.2022.452

Kumar, C., & J, D. (2024). A comparative analysis of AWS and Azure in the context of blockchain technology. *International Journal of Research Publication and Reviews*. https://doi.org/DOI: 10.55248/gengpi.5.0324.07112

Kumar, R., Mangaiyarkarasi, V., Ramesh, G., Arvind, S., & Fallah, M., & M, N. (2024). Boosting Supply Chain Transparency with Blockchain and Smart Contracts. *2024 International Conference on IoT, Communication and Automation Technology (ICICAT*), 1351-1355. https://doi.org/DOI: 10.1109/ICICAT62666.2024.10923137

Li, C. (2022). Information asymmetry in supply chains and blockchain technology: An empirical examination. https://doi.org/DOI: 10.5204/thesis.eprints.236968

Li, Y., & Bai, C. (2022). Real-time assurance using blockchain-enabled continuous auditing: Framework and implementation. *International Journal of Accounting Information Systems*, *47*, 100565. DOI: 10.1016/j.accinf.2022.100565

Liu, W., Zhang, X., & Chen, H. (2025). Improving supply chain transparency through blockchain technology. *Optimizations in Applied Machine Learning*, *5*(1). Advance online publication. DOI: 10.71070/oaml.v5i1.89

Liu, Y., & Shen, B. (2020). Quality management and blockchain adoption in a supply chain. *IFAC-PapersOnLine*, *53*(5), 10732–10736. DOI: 10.1016/j.ifacol.2020.12.2853

Manzoor, R., Sahay, B. S., Gumte, K., & Singh, S. K. (2024). Blockchain-backed resilient strategies in a stochastic supply chain sourcing and distribution environment under disruption: Implications for B2B sector. *Journal of Business and Industrial Marketing*. Advance online publication. DOI: 10.1108/JBIM-10-2023-0589

Mohammed, A., Potdar, V., Quaddus, M., & Hui, W. (2023). Blockchain adoption in food supply chains: A systematic literature review on enablers, benefits, and barriers. *IEEE Access : Practical Innovations, Open Solutions*, *11*, 14236–14255. DOI: 10.1109/ACCESS.2023.3236666

Mosa, H., Saleh, A., Qusef, A., Altamimi, A., & Alnabhan, M. (2024). Leveraging blockchain for ethical sourcing and sustainability in supply chains: *A systematic review. 2024 25th International Arab Conference on Information Technology (ACIT)*, 1–7. https://doi.org/DOI: 10.1109/ACIT62805.2024.10877059

Muruganandham, R., Venkatesh, K., Devadasan, S., & Harish, V. (2022). TQM through the integration of blockchain with ISO 9001:2015 standard based quality management system. *Total Quality Management & Business Excellence, 34*(3-4), 291–311. DOI: 10.1080/14783363.2022.2054318

Muthirevula, G. R., Amarapalli, L., & Keezhadath, A. A. (2024). Blockchain for secure data lifecycle management in FDA-regulated environments. *Journal of AI-Powered Medical Innovations*. https://doi.org/DOI: 10.60087/Japmi.Vol.03.Issue.01.Id.010

Oh, L. K.Journal of Current Research in Blockchain. (2025). A comprehensive study on public and private blockchain performance. *Journal of Current Research in Blockchain, 2*(1), 13–27. Advance online publication. DOI: 10.47738/jcrb.v2i1.25

Olech-Anyebe, E. I., Olaniyi, E. O., & Kayode, A. D. (2024). From trust to circular economy: Evolution of blockchain's role in enhancing agro-food supply chain transparency, resilience, and sustainability. *Environmental and Sustainability Indicators, 24*, 100460. DOI: 10.1016/j.indic.2024.100460

Omisola, O., & Bihani, P. (2023). Blockchain in supply chain transparency: A conceptual framework for real-time data tracking and reporting using blockchain and AI. *International Journal of Multidisciplinary Research and Growth Evaluation*. https://doi.org/DOI: 10.54660/.IJMRGE.2023.4.1.1238-1253

Onu, P., Mbohwa, C., Pradhan, A., & Madonsela, N. (2024). The potential of smart contracts in blockchain-based supply chain management for automation and sustainable manufacturing: An in-depth analysis and perspectives. *2024 International Conference on Science, Engineering and Business for Driving Sustainable Development Goals,* 1–6. https://doi.org/DOI: 10.1109/SEB4SDG60871.2024.10629874

Oriekhoe, O. I., Ashiwaju, B. I., Ihemereze, K. C., Ikwue, U., & Udeh, C. A. (2024). Blockchain technology in supply chain management: A comprehensive review. *International Journal of Management & Entrepreneurship Research, 6*(1), 150–166. Advance online publication. DOI: 10.51594/ijmer.v6i1.714

Owusu-Berko, L. (2025). Advanced supply chain analytics: Leveraging digital twins, IoT and blockchain for resilient, data driven business operations. *World Journal of Advanced Research and Reviews*. https://doi.org/DOI: 10.30574/wjarr.2025.25.2.0572

Oyeyemi, B., Orenuga, A., & Adelakun, B. (2024). Blockchain and AI Synergies in Enhancing Supply Chain Transparency. *International Journal of Future Engineering Innovations*. https://doi.org/.DOI: 10.54660/IJFEI.2024.1.1.115-126

Pambreni, Y., Khatibi, A., Azam, S., & Tham, J. (2019). The influence of total quality management toward organization performance. *Management Science Letters, 9*(9), 1397–1406. DOI: 10.5267/j.msl.2019.5.011

Pareek, V., Saran, D., Sharma, L., Jakhar, P., & Kumar, S. (2024). Blockchain technology in pharmaceutical industry: A review of recent research articles on PubMed. *Scripta Medica, 55*(3), 357–369. Advance online publication. DOI: 10.5937/scriptamed55-47100

Pisupati, C. A., & Ulle, R. (2024). The impact of blockchain technology on transparency and traceability in the supply chain of the food industry. *International Journal for Research in Applied Science and Engineering Technology*, *12*(5), 488–494. Advance online publication. DOI: 10.22214/ijraset.2024.61563

Popchev, I., Radeva, I., & Velichkova, V. (2022). Auditing blockchain smart contracts. *In 2022 International Conference Automatics and Informatics (ICAI)* pp. 276-281. IEEE. https://doi.org/DOI: 10.1109/ICAI55857.2022.9960058

Potru, S. (2024). Blockchain integration in Salesforce CRM: A framework for enhanced supply chain traceability and stakeholder trust. International Journal of Scientific Research in Computer Science, *Engineering and Information Technology*. https://doi.org/DOI: 10.32628/CSEIT241061207

Potter, A. (2022). Supply chain traceability. The Fairchild Books Dictionary of Fashion. https://doi.org/DOI: 10.5040/9781501365287.2696

Prashanth, M. S., Srujana, S. V. U., & Aluvalu, R. (2023). Smart contract-based security auditing for web applications. *In 2023 Asia Conference on Power, Energy Engineering and Computer Technology (PEECT)* pp. 128-132. IEEE. https://doi.org/DOI: 10.1109/PEECT59566.2023.00029

Priyadarshini, R., Pandey, R., Ankit, K. C., Bhandari, D., Khadka, B., Barik, R., & Saikia, M. (2025). A faster, integrated, and trusted certificate authentication and issuer validation system based on blockchain. *IEEE Access : Practical Innovations, Open Solutions*, *13*, 27037–27049. DOI: 10.1109/ACCESS.2025.3539180

Proskurnina, N., & Bilousko, V. I. (2023). The trends of quality management to improve the competitiveness of an enterprise in the international market. *Bìznes Ìnform*, *5*(544), 209–214. DOI: 10.32983/2222-4459-2023-5-209-214

Puli, S., Reddy, K. V., Vinay, K., & Fatima, M. (2022). Blockchain based certificate validation. [IJSR]. *International Journal of Science and Research (Raipur, India)*, *11*(12), 962–966. Advance online publication. DOI: 10.21275/SR221219113003

Pulita, J. G., Pereira, C., & da Silva, A. L. (2024). How does traceability support stakeholders in food recall management? A case study of the beef chain. *Gestão & Produção*. https://doi.org/DOI: 10.1590/1806-9649-2024v31e3324

Qiao, R., & Zhao, L. (2023). Reduce supply chain financing risks through supply chain integration: Dual approaches of alleviating information asymmetry and mitigating supply chain risks. *Journal of Enterprise Information Management*, *36*(6), 1533–1555. DOI: 10.1108/JEIM-01-2023-0016

Ramkumar, P., & Gopan, V. (2025). Enhancing Supply Chain Resilience: Integrating Blockchain for Transparency and Risk Mitigation in Logistics. *2025 International Conference on Visual Analytics and Data Visualization (ICVADV*), 194-200. https://doi.org/DOI: 10.1109/ICVADV63329.2025.10961897

Ravi, V. K., Jampani, S., Gudavalli, S., Pandey, P., Singh, S. P., & Goel, P. (2024). Blockchain integration in SAP for supply chain transparency. *Integrated Journal for Research in Arts and Humanities*. https://doi.org/DOI: 10.55544/ijrah.4.6.22

Reddy, V. C. S., Jammu, K., Vaishnavi, G., Jeevan, J., & Ansari, A. A. (2025). Student certificates authentication and verification system using blockchain. *International Scientific Journal of Engineering and Management*, *4*(1), 1–6. Advance online publication. DOI: 10.55041/ISJEM02226

Regueiro, C., & Urquizu, B. (2024). Blockchain-based evidence trustworthiness system in certification. *Journal of Cybersecurity and Privacy*, *5*(1), 1. Advance online publication. DOI: 10.3390/jcp5010001

Riaz, R., Abrar, S., & Gul, M. J. (2023). Securing supply-chain network with blockchain. *En Proceedings of the International Conference on Emerging Technologies* (pp. 243–258). https://doi.org/DOI: 10.1007/978-3-031-28076-4_20

Rozario, A. M., & Thomas, C. (2019). Reengineering the audit with blockchain and smart contracts. *Journal of Emerging Technologies in Accounting*, *16*(1), 21–35. DOI: 10.2308/jeta-52432

Rozario, A. M., & Vasarhelyi, M. A. (2018). Auditing with smart contracts. *The International Journal of Digital Accounting Research*, *18*, 1–27. DOI: 10.4192/1577-8517-v18_1

Sahoo, S. (2024). Blockchain-enabled traceability systems for supply chain quality management: Empirical insights from pharmaceutical manufacturers. *International Journal of Quality & Reliability Management*. Advance online publication. DOI: 10.1108/IJQRM-03-2024-0091

Sangeetha, M. (2020). Blockchain based Information Architecture for Medical Product Supply Chain.

Sawant, A. (2025). Digital document verification using blockchain. *International Journal for Research in Applied Science and Engineering Technology*, *13*(4), 2794–2798. Advance online publication. DOI: 10.22214/ijraset.2025.68159

Sawant, S. R., Poladia, J. A., & Shah, S. (2023). Chaining success: How blockchain reshapes the landscape of supply chain. *2023 6th International Conference on Advances in Science and Technology (ICAST)*, 95–99. https://doi.org/DOI: 10.1109/ICAST59062.2023.10455024

Schilhabel, S., Sankaranarayanan, B., Basu, C., Madan, M., Glennan, C., & McSherry, L. (2023). Blockchain technology in the food supply chain: Influences on supplier relationships and outcomes. *Issues in Information Systems*. Advance online publication. DOI: 10.48009/3_iis_2023_127

Sever, Y., & Angin, P. (2021). Blockchain integration into supply chain operations. In *Handbook of Research on Blockchain Technology* (pp. 329–350). IGI Global., DOI: 10.4018/978-1-7998-6650-3.ch014

Shaik, N.Imran Ahmed Shaik. (2025). Security applications of blockchain: Emerging research and innovations. *World Journal of Advanced Research and Reviews*, *26*(2), 1183–1190. Advance online publication. DOI: 10.30574/wjarr.2025.26.2.1664

Shankaran, S. (2024). Maximizing operational efficiency: Utilizing blockchain for comprehensive tracking and visibility throughout the supply chain. *International Journal of Supply Chain and Logistics*. https://doi.org/DOI: 10.47941/ijscl.2403

Sharma, D., Mungal, V., Khairnar, A., Gavali, S., & Bhadange, P.Durgesh K. SharmaVishal J. MungalAmit P. KhairnarSwaraj D. GavaliProf. U. B. Bhadange. (2024). Decentralized Supply Chain Management Using Blockchain for Enhanced Security and Anti-Counterfeiting. *International Journal of Advanced Research in Science. Tongxin Jishu*, 178–183. Advance online publication. DOI: 10.48175/IJARSCT-22434

Sharma, M., Joshi, S., Luthra, S., & Kumar, A. (2021). Managing disruptions and risks amidst COVID-19 outbreaks: Role of blockchain technology in developing resilient food supply chains. *Operations Management Research : Advancing Practice Through Research, 15*(3), 268–281. DOI: 10.1007/s12063-021-00198-9

Sharma, N., & Rohilla, R. (2023). A multilevel authentication-based blockchain powered medicine anti-counterfeiting for reliable IoT supply chain management. *The Journal of Supercomputing, 80*(4), 4870–4913. DOI: 10.1007/s11227-023-05654-w

Shiyanbola, O. (2024). A systems-based framework for ISO 9000 compliance: Applying statistical quality control and continuous improvement tools in U.S. manufacturing. *International Journal of Advanced Multidisciplinary Research and Studies*. https://doi.org/DOI: 10.62225/2583049X.2024.4.6.4052

Shwetha, S., & Chandana, R. (2020). Enhanced refrigerator with quality and quantity monitoring (ER-QQM). 04, 128-130. https://doi.org/.DOI: 10.33564/IJEAST.2020.v04i11.024

Soori, M., Ghaleh Jough, F. K., Dastres, R., & Arezoo, B. (2024). Blockchains for industrial internet of things in sustainable supply chain management of Industry 4.0: *A review. Sustainable Manufacturing and Service Economics*. https://doi.org/DOI: 10.1016/j.smse.2024.100026

Sreedharan, V. R., Raju, R., & Srivatsa Srinivas, S. (2020). Examining the impact of total quality management and operational performance on organizational performance: *An empirical study. The TQM Journal, 32*(6), 1341–1361. DOI: 10.1108/TQM-04-2019-0102

Subramaniam, S., Azzuhri, S. R., Wah, T. Y., Mahmood, A., & Balakrishnan, V. (2025). A Holistic Anti-Counterfeiting Platform Using NFC and Blockchain Technologies. *Computers, Materials & Continua, 83*(3), 4257–4280. Advance online publication. DOI: 10.32604/cmc.2025.061560

Sunmola, F., Burgess, P. R., & Tan, A. (2021). A meta-review of blockchain adoption literature in supply chain. *Lecture Notes in Business Information Processing, 444*, 371–388. DOI: 10.1007/978-3-031-04216-4_32

Talha, M., Ellahi, E., Vinod, J., Mehta, S., Tripathi, S., & Prakash, R. (2024). *Blockchain in accounting: Transforming transparency and security in financial records*. Dandao Xuebao/Journal of Ballistics., DOI: 10.52783/dxjb.v36.142

Tanwar, S., Parmar, A., Kumari, A., Jadav, N., Hong, W.-C., & Sharma, R. (2022). Blockchain adoption to secure the food industry: Opportunities and challenges. *Sustainability (Basel), 14*(12), 7036. DOI: 10.3390/su14127036

Thilakavathy, P., Jayachitra, S., Aeron, A., Kumar, N., Ali, S. S., & Malathy, M. (2023). Investigating blockchain security mechanisms for tamper-proof data storage. 2023 *International Conference on Communication, Security and Artificial Intelligence* (ICCSAI), 926–930. https://doi.org/DOI: 10.1109/ICCSAI59793.2023.10421006

Trisnandar, R., & Kurniawan, F. (2025). A systematic literature review on document verification with blockchain. *2025 International Conference on Advancement in Data Science, E-learning and Information System (ICADEIS*), 1–6. https://doi.org/DOI: 10.1109/ICADEIS65852.2025.10933054

Vadrevu, P. K.Pavan Kumar Vadrevu. (2025). Scalable approaches for enhancing privacy in blockchain networks: A comprehensive review of differential privacy techniques. *Journal of Information Systems Engineering & Management, 10*(8s), 635–648. Advance online publication. DOI: 10.52783/jisem.v10i8s.1119

Wang, J., Liu, F., & Wu, J. (2021). A strategy tripod perspective on ISO 9001 adoption: Evidence from Chinese manufacturing firms. *IEEE Transactions on Engineering Management,* PP, 1–15. https://doi.org/DOI: 10.1109/TEM.2021.3093581

Wang, L., Guan, Z., Chen, Z., & Hu, M. (2023). Enabling integrity and compliance auditing in blockchain-based GDPR-compliant data management. *IEEE Internet of Things Journal, 10*(20), 20955–20968. DOI: 10.1109/JIOT.2023.3285211

Wang, L., He, Y., & Wu, Z. (2022). Design of a blockchain-enabled traceability system framework for food supply chains. *Foods, 11*(5), 744. Advance online publication. DOI: 10.3390/foods11050744

Wang, X. (2024). *Blockchain security and applications: A comprehensive analysis from hash functions to consensus algorithms.* Theoretical and Natural Science., DOI: 10.54254/2753-8818/31/20240862

Wiyono, S., Silitonga, T. H., & Heryanto, D. (2025). The influence of ISO 9001:2015 quality management system implementation on marketing performance at PT Timah Tbk. *Journal of Management Studies and Development, 4*(1), 770. DOI: 10.56741/jmsd.v4i01.770

Wong, L.-W., Leong, L.-Y., Hew, J.-J., Tan, G., & Ooi, K. (2020). Time to seize the digital evolution: Adoption of blockchain in operations and supply chain management among Malaysian SMEs. *International Journal of Information Management, 52*, 101997. DOI: 10.1016/j.ijinfomgt.2019.08.005

Wu, J., & Liu, Q. (2025). Integrating blockchain and AI for real-time auditing in Industry 4.0 environments. *Computers & Industrial Engineering, 189*, 109973. DOI: 10.1016/j.cie.2024.109973

Xue, J., Li, G., & Ivanov, D. (2025). Digital transformation in the blockchain era: Balancing efficiency and resilience in operations management. *International Journal of Production Economics, 109525*, 109525. Advance online publication. DOI: 10.1016/j.ijpe.2025.109525

Yadav, S., & Jasmin, D. (2024). Smart contracts on blockchain for transparent supply chain transactions. *2024 International Conference on IoT, Communication and Automation Technology (ICICAT)*, 1144–1149. https://doi.org/DOI: 10.1109/ICICAT62666.2024.10923250

Yang, C., Lan, S., Zhao, Z., Zhang, M., Wu, W., & Huang, G. (2023). Edge cloud blockchain and IoE enabled quality management platform for perishable supply chain logistics. *IEEE Internet of Things Journal, 10*(5), 3264–3275. DOI: 10.1109/JIOT.2022.3142095

Zariwala, K. (2023). Impact of blockchain technology on supply chain transparency, sustainability and profitability. *Sustainable Operations and Computers, 4*, 16–26. DOI: 10.1016/j.susoc.2023.04.001

Zekhnini, K., Cherrafi, A., Bouhaddou, I., Chaouni Benabdellah, A., & Raut, R. D. (2021). Barriers of blockchain technology adoption in viable digital supply chain. In *Lecture Notes in Networks and Systems* (pp. 225–238). Springer., DOI: 10.1007/978-3-030-94335-6_16

Zhou, Y. (2024). Blockchain Technology Improves the Resilience of Manufacturing Supply Chain: An Exploration Based on Grounded Theory. *Advances in Economics, Management and Political Sciences.* https://doi.org/DOI: 10.54254/2754-1169/2024.18266

Zimon, D., Tyan, J., & Sroufe, R. (2020). Drivers of sustainable supply chain management: Practices to alignment with ISO 9001 standard. *Sustainability*, *12*(6), 1–20.

KEY TERMS AND DEFINITIONS

Blockchain: A type of DLT that links blocks of transactions via cryptographic hashes, making retroactive alteration detectable and economically infeasible in properly governed networks.

CAPA & Quality Gate (ISO 9001): CAPA: Corrective and Preventive Action cycle to remove causes of nonconformities. Quality Gate: a formal checkpoint that must be passed (often automated via smart contracts) before advancing to the next process step.

Consensus: The protocol by which network nodes agree on the validity and order of transactions in distributed settings.

Continuous Auditing: Ongoing, event-driven verification of controls and records, replacing or complementing periodic, sample-based audits.

Distributed Ledger Technology (DLT): A database replicated across multiple nodes where entries are time-stamped and append-only, providing resilience and tamper-evident histories.

End-to-End Traceability: The ability to trace a product or batch from source to destination, including all intermediate events and transformations.

Hash (Cryptographic Hash): A fixed-length fingerprint of data; any change in input yields a different output, enabling integrity checks.

Identity & Access Management (IAM) / PKI: Mechanisms (certificates, keys, roles) that authenticate participants and authorize actions on a permissioned network.

Immutability: The property whereby recorded data cannot be altered without detection because each block references the previous block's hash.

Merkle Tree: A tree of hashes that enables efficient verification of large data sets or batch transactions with a single root hash stored on-chain.

On-Chain / Off-Chain (and On-Chain Proofs): Pattern where sensitive payloads remain off-chain while integrity proofs (hashes, pointers) are stored on-chain to balance auditability and confidentiality.

Oracle (IoT Oracle): A trusted bridge that submits external data (e.g., sensor readings, calibration status) to the blockchain for use by smart contracts.

Permissioned (Consortium) Blockchain: A ledger with controlled participation and role-based access, typically used for inter-organizational assurance in regulated supply chains.

Provenance: The verifiable history of an item (origin, transformations, custody) across the supply chain.

Public Blockchain: An open ledger where anyone can read/write under protocol rules, high transparency but limited suitability for confidential industrial data without additional privacy layers.

Smart Contract: Code executed on the ledger that enforces business rules (e.g., quality gates, holds/releases) automatically when defined conditions are met.

Compilation of References

Abbas, A., Ekowati, D., Suhariadi, F., Anwar, A., & Fenitra, R. M. (2024). Technology acceptance and COVID-19: A perspective for emerging opportunities from crisis. *Technology Analysis and Strategic Management*, *36*(11), 3551–3563. DOI: 10.1080/09537325.2023.2214642

Abdelwahed, N. A. A., & Soomro, B. (2025). Blockchain adoption effect on supply chain integration, innovation management, and performance. *Journal of Governance and Regulation*. https://doi.org/DOI: 10.22495/jgrv14i1art11

Accenture. (2024). Reinventing R&D in the age of AI. Accenture. https://www.accenture.com/us-en/insights/life-sciences/ai-biopharma

Adama, H., Popoola, O., Okeke, C., & Akinoso, A. (2024). Economic theory and practical impacts of digital transformation in supply chain optimization. *International Journal of Advanced Economics*. .DOI: 10.51594/ijae.v6i4.1072

Adekoya, O. A., Atlam, H. F., & Lallie, H. S. (2025). Quantifying the multidimensional impact of cyber attacks in digital financial services: A systematic literature review. *Sensors (Basel)*, *25*(14), 4345. DOI: 10.3390/s25144345

Adelakun, B. O.Beatrice Oyinkansola Adelakun. (2022). The impact of AI on internal auditing: Transforming practices and ensuring compliance. *Finance & Accounting Research Journal*, *4*(6), 350–370. Advance online publication. DOI: 10.51594/farj.v4i6.1316

Ahmad, H., Habidin, F., & Mustapha, I. (2025). The role of lean six sigma and discrete event simulations in achieving sustainability goals in logistics: reduce carbon emissions and minimizing waste. *International Journal of Innovation and Industrial Revolution*. .DOI: 10.35631/IJIREV.720005

Ahmad, M., Ahmed, I., & Jeon, G. (2022). A sustainable advanced artificial intelligence-based framework for analysis of COVID-19 spread. *Environment, Development and Sustainability*, *24*(10), 1–16. DOI: 10.1007/s10668-022-02584-0

Ahmed, S. A., & Ruth, D. (2024). *The benefits of ISO 9001 certification for small to medium-sized engineering firms*. Performance Improvement Journal., DOI: 10.56811/PFI-24-0010

Ahn, J., Yi, E., & Kim, M. (2024). Blockchain consensus mechanisms: A bibliometric analysis (2014–2024) using VOSviewer and R Bibliometrix. *Information (Basel)*, *15*(10), 644. Advance online publication. DOI: 10.3390/info15100644

Ainurrofiq, I., & Amir, M. T. (2023). Application of e-culture in a hybrid working model: A case study in the banking industry in Indonesia. *International Journal of Interdisciplinary Organizational Studies, 18*(2), 93–115. Advance online publication. DOI: 10.18848/2324-7649/CGP/v18i02/93-115

Aithal, P. S. (2016). The concept of ideal strategy and its realization using white ocean mixed strategy. *International Journal of Management Sciences and Business Research, 5*(4), 171–179.

Akerlof, G. A. (1970). The market for "Lemons": Quality uncertainty and the market mechanism. *The Quarterly Journal of Economics, 84*(3), 488–500. DOI: 10.2307/1879431

Akram, W., Joshi, R., Haider, T., Sharma, P., Jain, V., Garud, N., & Narwaria, N. S. (2024). Blockchain technology: A potential tool for the management of pharma supply chain. *Research in Social & Administrative Pharmacy: RSAP.* https://doi.org/DOI: 10.1016/j.sapharm.2024.02.014

Aktürk, E. B. (2024). The role of social quality in enhancing total quality management: An assessment through corporate social responsibility and business ethics. *Business & Management Studies: An International Journal, 12*(4), 1106–1122. DOI: 10.15295/bmij.v12i4.2477

Al Balushi, M. (2024). The impact of quality management systems on organizational resilience. *International Journal of Quality & Reliability Management.* Advance online publication. DOI: 10.1108/IJQRM-05-2023-0169

Alabaddi, Z., Obidat, A., & Alziyadat, Z. (2023). Exploring the effect of blockchain technology on supply chain resilience and transparency: Evidence from the healthcare industry. *Uncertain Supply Chain Management, 11*(2), 787–798. Advance online publication. DOI: 10.5267/j.uscm.2023.1.001

Albert, S., Ashforth, B. E., & Dutton, J. E. (2000). Organizational identity and identification: Charting new waters and building new bridges. *Academy of Management Review, 25*(1), 13–17. DOI: 10.5465/amr.2000.2791600

Albion, M. J., & Gagliardi, R. (2011). A study of transformational leadership, organizational change and job satisfaction. *Journal of Organizational Change Management, 2*(1), 23–32. https://research.usq.edu.au/item/9y5v9/a-study-of-transformational-leadership-organisational-change-and-job-satisfaction

Alfuhaid, S., Amyot, D., Anda, A., & Mylopoulos, J. (2023). A mapping review on cyber-physical smart contracts: *Architectures, platforms, and challenges. IEEE Access : Practical Innovations, Open Solutions, 11*, 65872–65890. DOI: 10.1109/ACCESS.2023.3290899

AlHamad, A., Kurdi, A., Alshurideh, M., & Alrawabdeh, W. (2022). Impact of business process management and lean operations on cost of quality. [IJBAS]. *International Journal of Business Analytics and Security, 1*(1), 173–192. DOI: 10.54489/ijbas.v1i1.141

Alhat, P. (2024). *Blockchain technology*. International Journal of Scientific Research in Engineering and Management., DOI: 10.55041/IJSREM30694

Almeida, F., Silva, M., & Pinto, M. (2021). Chatbot application in document management: A natural language processing approach. *Computer Science Proceeded, 181*, 1080–1087. DOI: 10.1016/j.procs.2021.01.291

Al-Mohareb, M. (2025). The impact of cyber governance quality on dividend policy in mitigating cybersecurity breaches. *Risks*, *13*(2), 34. DOI: 10.3390/risks13020034

Al-Salah, A., Al-Harbi, F., & Al-Mutairi, S. (2025). Revolutionizing industrial management: A review of artificial intelligence applications in manufacturing operations. *Al-Noor Journal of Engineering Management and Computer Science*, *1*(2), 19–28. DOI: 10.71229/njemcs.v1i2.3

Alsalman, F. A., & Chyad, S. A. (2025). Impact of Emotional Intelligence on Leadership and Team Dynamics in Agile Software Engineering Projects. *IEEE Access : Practical Innovations, Open Solutions*, *13*, 74217–74228. DOI: 10.1109/ACCESS.2025.3563424

Altice Labs. (2023). *5G-AUTO - Desenvolvimento e teste de tecnologia V2X 5G para condução autónoma.* https://www.alticelabs.com/innovation/rdi-projects/5g-auto/

Altice Labs. (s.d.). *Our History.* https://www.alticelabs.com/history/

Altice Portugal. (2024, October). *Altice Portugal divulga resultados referentes ao terceiro trimestre de 2024.* https://institucional.meo.pt/media/comunicados/2024/novembro/altice-portugal-divulga-resultados-referentes-ao-terceiro-trimestre-de-2024

Amaral, A. M. D. S. (2022). O papel dos líderes na comunicação interna dos processos de gestão de mudança: o caso da implementação do SIGDN na Marinha Portuguesa (Dissertação de Doutoramento). Instituto Politécnico de Lisboa, Escola Superior de Comunicação Social, Lisboa.

Amarnath, J. L. (2025). Online blockchain based certificate generation and validation system for government organization. *International Journal of Scientific Research in Engineering and Management*, *9*(1), 1–6. DOI: 10.55041/IJSREM41957

Amazon Web Services. (2023). Nestlé centralizes its IoT data on AWS IoT Core to improve customer experiences. *AWS Case Studies*. https://aws.amazon.com/solutions/case-studies/nestle-aws-iot-case-study/

Amin, M. W., & Wang, J. (2024). Social media ostracism and creativity: Moderating role of emotional intelligence. *BMC Psychology*, *12*(1), 484. DOI: 10.1186/s40359-024-01985-2 PMID: 39272175

ANACOM. (2024, February 23). *4,7 milhões de subscritores de pacote de serviços em 2023.* https://www.anacom-consumidor.pt/-/4-7-milhoes-de-subscritores-de-pacote-de-servicos-em-2023

Andita, A. D., & Nugraha, I. B. (2022). A blockchain-based traceability system to achieve the quality objectives in the production process of a manufacturing industry. 2022 *International Conference on Information Technology Systems and Innovation* (ICITSI), 194–199. https://doi.org/DOI: 10.1109/ICITSI56531.2022.9970822

Andrés, J., & Lorca, P. (2021). On the impact of smart contracts on auditing. *The International Journal of Digital Accounting Research*, *21*(6), 197–222. DOI: 10.4192/1577-8517-v21_6

Andrianandrianina Johanesa, T. V., Equeter, L., & Mahmoudi, S. A. (2024). Survey on AI applications for product quality control and predictive maintenance in Industry 4.0. *Electronics (Basel)*, *13*(5), 976. DOI: 10.3390/electronics13050976

Annabi, A. (2024). The Digital rights (future perspectives and horizons). *International Journal of Advanced Research in Humanities and Law, 1*(2), 1–14. DOI: 10.63053/ijrel.7

Anttila, J., & Jussila, K. (2021). ISO 9004 - A stimulating quality management standard for the creative leaders of contemporary sustainable organizations. *Production Engineering Archives, 27*(2), 148–155. DOI: 10.30657/pea.2021.27.19

Aras, S., Yayla, A. A., & Yıldız, E. (2023). Digital maturity assessment: A systematic literature review. *Systems, 11*(4), 213. DOI: 10.3390/systems11040213

Arbaiza, L. (2016). A Human Centered Approach in Executive Education at ESAN Graduate School of Business in Peru. In *Human Centered Management in Executive Education* (pp. 82-95). Palgrave Macmillan UK. https://link.springer.com/chapter/10.1057/9781137555410_5

Arianpoor, A., & Borhani, A. (2024). Blockchain-based continuous auditing for quality management systems. *Journal of Accounting and Organizational Change, 20*(3), 421–440. DOI: 10.1108/JAOC-03-2023-0045

Arinola, A. F., & Olalekan, A. (2023). Artificial intelligence & internal audit quality of commercial banks in Nigeria. *International Journal of Management and Economics Invention, 9*(4), 123–134. DOI: 10.47191/ijmei/v9i4.05

Asachi, G. (2021). Total Quality Management vs. Six Sigma. *IOSR Journal of Engineering (IOSRJEN), 11(07)*, pp. 05–15

Assante, M. J., & Tobey, D. H. (2011). Enhancing the healthcare artificial intelligence workforce. *IT Professional, 13*(1), 12–15. https://ieeexplore.ieee.org/abstract/document/5708280?casa_token=yxPpApYJEIsAAAAA:Vzm7QYPYm-3qn8bzBT0whOlsDDnJTKe9pgzEAVZ8wxvVE4z1QGx1HMT3Gzd92vo_VC6tXW5bMzE. DOI: 10.1109/MITP.2011.6

Ates, A., & Acur, N. (2022). Making obsolescence obsolete: Execution of digital transformation in a high-tech manufacturing SME. *Journal of Business Research, 152*, 336–348. DOI: 10.1016/j.jbusres.2022.07.052

Atienza-Barba, M., del Río, M. D. L. C., Meseguer-Martínez, Á., & Barba-Sanchez, V. (2024). Artificial intelligence and organizational agility: An analysis of scientific production and future trends. *European Research on Management and Business Economics, 30*(2), 100253. DOI: 10.1016/j.iedeen.2024.100253

Attalah, I., Nylund, P. A., & Brem, A. (2023). Who captures value from hackathons. Innovation contests with collective intelligence tools bridging creativity and coupled open innovation. *Creativity and Innovation Management, 32*(2), 266–280. DOI: 10.1111/caim.12552

Attanayake, A., & Ratnayake, R. (2024). Transitioning to Circular Economy in Power Distribution Utilities: A Framework Integrating ISO 9001 Quality Management Standards. *2024 IEEE International Conference on Industrial Engineering and Engineering Management*, 760-764. DOI: 10.1109/IEEM62345.2024.10857066

Avolio, B. J., & Bass, B. M. (2002). *Developing Potential Across a Full Range of Leadership*. Lawrence Erlbaum Associates.

Avolio, B. J., Kahai, S. S., & Dodge, G. E. (2014). E-leadership: Re-examining transformations in leadership source and transmission. *The Leadership Quarterly*, *25*(1), 105–131. DOI: 10.1016/j.leaqua.2013.11.003

Avruscio, G., Ragazzo, S., Ceccato, D., Adamo, A., Napoli, C., Cacco, L., Scalzotto, F., Canciani, M., Cognolato, M., Fedele, A., Scipioni, A., & Tocco Tussardi, I. (2022). Implementation of a quality management system according to ISO 9001:2015 standards in an Angiology Unit: an Italian experience. *Annali di igiene : medicina preventiva e di comunità*. Advance online publication. DOI: 10.7416/ai.2022.2501

Azevedo, P., Gomes, J., & Romão, M. (2023). Supply chain traceability using blockchain. *Operations Management Research : Advancing Practice Through Research*, *16*(3), 1359–1381. DOI: 10.1007/s12063-023-00359-y

Bager, S., Düdder, B., Henglein, F., Hébert, J. M., & Wu, H. (2022). Event-based supply chain network modeling: Blockchain for good coffee. *Frontiers in Blockchain*, *5*, 846783. DOI: 10.3389/fbloc.2022.846783

Bagga, S. K., Gera, S., & Haque, S. N. (2023). The mediating role of organizational culture: Transformational leadership and change management in virtual teams. *Asia Pacific Management Review*, *28*(2), 120–131. DOI: 10.1016/j.apmrv.2022.07.003

Bagno, R. B., & de Faria, A. F. (2022). *O Modelo das Duas Rodas: Uma Referência para o Sistema de Gestão da Inovação em Pequenas e Médias Empresas*. Editora UFV. DIGI Portugal. (s.d.). *Quem somos*. Disponível em: https://www.digi.pt/quem-somos

Baker, A., Weisgrau, J., & Philyaw, K. B. (2022). *Feedback loops: Mapping transformative interactions in education innovation*. Digital Promise., DOI: 10.51388/20500.12265/155

Baker, J. (2012). The technology-organization-environment framework. In Dwivedi, Y. K., Wade, M. R., & Schneberger, S. L. (Eds.), *Information systems theory: Explaining and predicting our digital society* (Vol. 1, pp. 231–245). Springer., DOI: 10.1007/978-1-4419-6108-2_12

Balabanova, Y., Lukyanova, A., & Shatskaya, E. (2024). Digital transformation in human resources management and its impact on the performance of enterprises. Вестник Северо-Кавказского федерального университета, 0(2), 24–30. DOI: 10.37493/2307-907X.2024.2.3

Baldwin, C. Y., Bogers, M. L. A. M., Kapoor, R., & West, J. (2024). Focusing the ecosystem lens on innovation studies. *Research Policy*, *53*(3), 104949. DOI: 10.1016/j.respol.2023.104949

Banaszak, I., Dworczak, P., & Stępień, S. (2023). Digitalization of pharmaceutical supply chains: Challenges and strategic responses. *Sustainability*, *15*(4), 3412. DOI: 10.3390/su15043412

Bankoff, K. P., Muñoz, R., Pasini, A., & Pesado, P. (2022). Quality Management Systems and Blockchain in the 4.0 Era: A Literature Review. DOI: 10.1007/978-3-031-34147-2_10

Barber, B. M., & Odean, T. (2001). Boys will be boys: Gender, overconfidence, and common stock investment. *The Quarterly Journal of Economics*, *116*(1), 261–292. DOI: 10.1162/003355301556400

Başaran, B. (2021). The past, present and future ISO 9001 quality management system standard. Business and Management Studies. *International Journal (Toronto, Ont.)*, *9*(1), 227–247. DOI: 10.15295/bmij.v9i1.1756

Bass, B. M. (1985). *Leadership and Performance beyond Expectations*. Free Press.

Bass, B. M., Avolio, B. J., Jung, D. I., & Berson, Y. (2003). Predicting unit performance by assessing transformational and transactional leadership. *The Journal of Applied Psychology*, *88*(2), 207–218. DOI: 10.1037/0021-9010.88.2.207

Bastas, A., & Liyanage, K. (2018). ISO 9001 and Supply Chain Integration Principles Based Sustainable Development: A Delphi Study. *Sustainability (Basel)*, *10*(12), 4569. DOI: 10.3390/su10124569

Baumeister, R. F., & Leary, M. R. (1997). Writing narrative literature reviews. *Review of General Psychology*, *1*(3), 311–320. DOI: 10.1037/1089-2680.1.3.311

Bechtel, J., Kaufmann, L., & Kock, A. (2023). The interplay between dynamic capabilities' dimensions and project portfolio success. *International Journal of Project Management*, *41*(6), 102469. DOI: 10.1016/j.ijproman.2023.102469

Bedi, K., Singh, P., Kohli, N., Kaur, H., Angra, P., & Cheema, G. (2024). Effectiveness of IoT (Internet of Things) in Real Time Supply Chain Monitoring and Management. *2024 Second International Conference Computational and Characterization Techniques in Engineering & Sciences*, 1-5. DOI: 10.1109/IC3TES62412.2024.10877555

Bendhi, M. (2025). Supply Chain Transparency: Real Time Analytics for Product Tracking, Bottleneck Detection, and Logistics Optimization. *International Journal of Scientific Research and Management*. .DOI: 10.18535/ijsrm/v13i04.ec02

Bendig, D., Schulz, C., Theis, L., & Raff, S. (2023). Digital orientation and environmental performance in times of technological change. *Technological Forecasting and Social Change*, *188*, 122272. DOI: 10.1016/j.techfore.2022.122272

Benraouane, S. (2024). *AI management system certification according to the ISO/IEC 42001 standard*. Routledge., DOI: 10.4324/9781003463979

Bento, F., Tagliabue, M., & Lorenzo, F. (2020). Organizational silos: A scoping review informed by a behavioral perspective on systems and networks. *Societies (Basel, Switzerland)*, *10*(3), 56. DOI: 10.3390/soc10030056

Berson, A., & Stieglitz, R. (2013). *Leadership Conversations: Challenging High Potential Managers to Become Great Leaders*. Jossey-Bass Publishing.

Besio, C., & Pronzini, A. (2025). Algorithmic responsibility without accountability. *Systems Research and Behavioral Science*, *42*(4), 576–589. DOI: 10.1002/sres.3028

Bettín-Díaz, R., Mejía, C., & Rojas, A. E. (2021). *A blockchain-based approach to support an ISO 9001:2015 quality management system*. ParadigmPlus., DOI: 10.55969/paradigmplus.v2n2a2

Bhasin, P. (2023). Blockchain-based supply chain management system. *International Journal for Research Publication and Seminars*, *14*(5), 9–19. Advance online publication. DOI: 10.36676/jrps.2023-v14i5-02

Bhuiyan, M., Faraji, M., Rashid, M., Bhuyan, M., Hossain, R., & Ghose, P. (2024). Digital Transformation in SMEs Emerging Technological Tools and Technologies for Enhancing the SME's Strategies and Outcomes. *Journal of Ecohumanism*. DOI: 10.62754/joe.v3i4.3594

Binh, A. D. T., Akbari, M., Le, H. T. C., Nguyen, L. C., & Truong, H. Q. (2024). Forging pathways to circular economy excellence: Integrating Industry 4.0 with quality management. *Sustainability (Basel)*, *16*(7), 3053. DOI: 10.3390/su16073053

Birkinshaw, J., & Gibson, C. B. (2004). Building an ambidextrous organisation. *Advanced Institute of Management Research Paper*, (003).

Bloom, N., Barrero, J. M., Davis, S., Meyer, D., & Mihaylov, E. (2023, August 28). Survey: remote work isn't going away — and executives know it. *Harvard Business Review*. https://hbr.org/2023/08/survey-remote-work-isnt-going-away-and-executives-know-it

Bolman, L. G., & Deal, T. E. (2017). *Reframing Organizations: Artistry, Choice, and Leadership*. Jossey-Bass. DOI: 10.1002/9781119281856

Bósquez-Andrade, E., & Torres-Palacios, M. (2024). *Continuous auditing and real-time monitoring: detection, mitigation of business risks in hospitality industries*. Revista Metropolitana de Ciencias Aplicadas., DOI: 10.62452/q62zma54

Boukarras, S., Ferri, D., Borgogni, L., & Aglioti, S. M. (2024). Neurophysiological markers of asymmetric emotional contagion: Implications for organizational contexts. *Frontiers in Integrative Neuroscience*, *18*, 1321130. DOI: 10.3389/fnint.2024.1321130

Boukarras, S., Filho, E. R., & Sanchis, A. (2022). Bringing social interaction at the core of organizational neuroscience. *Frontiers in Psychology*, *13*, 1034454. DOI: 10.3389/fpsyg.2022.1034454

Bouveret, A. (2018). Cyber risk for the financial sector: A framework for quantitative assessment. *IMF Working Paper*, *18*(143), 1–37. DOI: 10.5089/9781484360750.001

Brankley, L., Tuğrul, A., Anderson, J., & Knight, D. (2017). *A manufacturing sector's experience of integrating EPD alongside product, management system and responsible sourcing certification for public procurement*. En *LCM 2017 Conference* – Lifecycle Management, Luxemburgo.

Braojos, J., Weritz, P., & Matute, J. (2024). Empowering organisational commitment through digital transformation capabilities: The role of digital leadership and a continuous learning environment. *Information Systems Journal*, *34*(5), 1466–1492. DOI: 10.1111/isj.12501

Braun, V., & Clarke, V. (2006). Using thematic analysis in psychology. *Qualitative Research in Psychology*, *3*(2), 77–101.

Bravi, L., & Murmura, F. (2021). Evidence about ISO 9001:2015 and ISO 9004:2018 implementation in different-size organisations. *Total Quality Management & Business Excellence*, *33*(11–12), 1366–1386. DOI: 10.1080/14783363.2021.1954900

Bravim, M., Lira, T., De Freitas, R., & Xavier, T. (2020). A evolução nos estudos da gestão da qualidade baseado na norma iso 9001:2015: um estudo bibliométrico: the evolution in quality management studies based on iso 9001: 2015 standard: a bibliometric study. *Brazilian Journal of Production Engineering* - BJPE, 88-106. https://digitalcommons.unl.edu/cgi/viewcontent.cgi?article=10411&context=libphilprac&utm_source=chatgpt.com

Bravim, M., Lira, T., De Freitas, R., & Xavier, T. (2020). A evolução nos estudos da gestão da qualidade baseado na norma iso 9001:2015: um estudo bibliométrico: the evolution in quality management studies based on iso 9001: 2015 standard: a bibliometric study. *Brazilian Journal of Production Engineering*, 88-106. http://DOI: 10.17632/4d3m89f2s8.1

Brock, W. (2012). Synthesizing a systems perspective and organizational change: Principles of a whole-systems metrics model. *Organization Development Journal, 30*(3), 17–28.

Browder, R. E., Dwyer, S. M., & Koch, H. (2024). Upgrading adaptation: How digital transformation promotes organizational resilience. *Strategic Entrepreneurship Journal, 18*(1), 128–164. DOI: 10.1002/sej.1483

Brynjolfsson, E., & McAfee, A. (2017). *Machine, Platform, Crowd: Harnessing Our Digital Future*. W. W. Norton & Company.

Brynjolfsson, E., & McAfee, A. (2017). *Machine, platform, crowd: Harnessing our digital future*. W. W. Norton.

Budur, T., Demirer, H., & Rashid, C. A. (2023). The effects of knowledge sharing on innovative behaviours of academicians; mediating effect of innovative organization culture and quality of work life. *Journal of Applied Research in Higher Education*. Advance online publication. DOI: 10.1108/JARHE-08-2022-0257

Buisson, B., & Silberzahn, P. (2010). Blue ocean or fast-second innovation? A four-breakthrough model to explain successful market domination. *International Journal of Innovation Management, 14*(03), 359–378.

Burke, W. W. (2017). *Organization Change: Theory and Practice*. Sage Publications.

Burnes, B. (2019). The origins of Lewin's three-step model of change. *The Journal of Applied Behavioral Science*. Advance online publication. DOI: 10.1177/0021886319892685

Burns, J. M. (1978). *Leadership*. Harper & Row.

Burrell, D. N. (2019). An exploration of the critical need for formal training in leadership for cybersecurity and technology management professionals. In *Human Performance Technology: Concepts, Methodologies, Tools, and Applications* (pp. 1420-1432). IGI Global. https://www.igi-global.com/chapter/an-exploration-of-the-critical-need-for-formal-training-in-leadership-for-cybersecurity-and-technology-management-professionals/226624

Burrell, D. N. (2025). Cyber-Psychological System Failures that Translate Deep-Fake and other Social Engineering Attacks in Ways that Hamper Organizational Resilience. *Bulletin of the Transilvania University of Braşov. Series VII: Social Sciences• Law*, 409-422.

Burrell, D. N. (2023). Dynamic evaluation approaches to telehealth technologies and artificial intelligence (AI) telemedicine applications in healthcare and biotechnology organizations. *Merits*, *3*(4), 700–721. https://www.mdpi.com/2673-8104/3/4/42. DOI: 10.3390/merits3040042

Burrell, D. N., Aridi, A. S., & Nobles, C. (2018). The critical need for formal leadership development programs for cybersecurity and information technology professionals. In *International Conference on Cyber Warfare and Security* (pp. 82–91). Academic Conferences International Limited., https://books.google.com/books?hl=en&lr=&id=eHpTDwAAQBAJ&oi=fnd&pg=PA82&dq=+Leadership+training+and+darrell+norman+Burrell&ots=9VOX4c0qw0&sig=Imkq77BTHWaCkNlmn-jeO8xJ6g4#v=onepage&q=Leadership%20training%20and%20darrell%20norman%20Burrell&f=false

Burrell, D. N., Johnson, M. B., & Lim, J. (2023). Leveraging artificial intelligence to advance strategic performance management in volatile environments. *Review of Applied Socio-Economic Research*, *25*(1), 14–26. DOI: 10.2478/raft-2023-003

Burrell, D. N., Lewis, E. J., & Richardson, K. (2023). Adaptive marketing, management strategy, and technology innovation in beverage and hospitality markets. *International Journal of Innovation in the Digital Economy*, *14*(1), 1–10. DOI: 10.4018/IJIDE.324096

Burton, S. L. (2022). *Cybersecurity leadership from a Telemedicine/Telehealth knowledge and organizational development examination (Order No. 29066056)*. ProQuest Dissertations & Theses Global.

Burton, S. L. (2023). Cybersecurity risk: The business significance of ongoing tracking. In Burrell, D. N. (Ed.), *Transformational Interventions for Business* (1st ed., pp. 245–268). Technology, and Healthcare., DOI: 10.4018/979-8-3693-1634-4.ch015

Burton, S. L. (2024). Securing tomorrow: Synergizing change management and cybersecurity in the digital era. *Holistica Journal of Business and Public Administration*, *15*(1), 1–20. DOI: 10.2478/hjbpa-2024-0001

Bux, A., Zhu, Y., & Devi, S. (2025). Enhancing organisational agility through knowledge sharing and open innovation. *Sustainability*, *17*(15), 6765. DOI: 10.3390/su17156765

Cai, J., Cao, Z., & Shang, J. (2024). Blockchain adoption in a green supply chain: Considering information asymmetry of consumers' privacy concern. *International Journal of Production Economics*, *272*, 109459. DOI: 10.1016/j.ijpe.2024.109459

Cameron, K. S., & Quinn, R. E. (2011). *Diagnosing and Changing Organizational Culture: Based on the Competing Values Framework*. John Wiley & Sons.

Camilleri, M. A. (2024). Responsible AI governance and ethical decision-making for sustainable performance and growth. *Expert Systems: International Journal of Knowledge Engineering and Neural Networks*, *41*(6), e13406. DOI: 10.1111/exsy.13406

Campanella, F., Del Giudice, M., Thrassou, A., & Vrontis, D. (2020). Ambidextrous organizations in the banking sector: An empirical verification of banks' performance and conceptual development. *International Journal of Human Resource Management*, *31*(2), 272–302.

CAPA–– Centre for Aviation. (2025, May 8–9). *CAPA Airline Leader Summit: Airlines in Transition 2025*. Athens, Greece. *Author*. https://ait25.capaevents.com/

Capgemini Research Institute. (2025). The strategic edge: How digital continuity drives business outcomes in aerospace and defense. *Capgemini*. https://www.capgemini.com/wp-content/uploads/2025/06/Final-Web-Version-Report-Digital-Continuity-in-AD.pdf

Carvalho, A. M., Luis, J. M., & Sousa, R. (2023). Operational excellence, organizational culture, and agility: Bridging the gap between quality and adaptability. *Total Quality Management & Business Excellence, 34*(11-12), 1598–1628. Advance online publication. DOI: 10.1080/14783363.2023.2191844

Carvalho-Ishikura, R. (2024). *Impact of ISO 9001 implementation on financial results: A case study on publicly traded companies*. Scientific Journal of Applied Social and Clinical Science., DOI: 10.22533/at.ed.216432431014

Cavagnetto, S., & Gahir, B. R. U. C. E. (2013). Shades of purple strategy. *CRIS-Bulletin of the Centre for Research and Interdisciplinary Study*, *1*, 77–92.

Cavazotte, F., Moreno, V., & Hickmann, M. (2012). Effects of leader intelligence, personality and emotional intelligence on transformational leadership and managerial performance. *The Leadership Quarterly, 23*(3), 443–455. https://www.sciencedirect.com/science/article/abs/pii/S1048984311001615?casa_token=AK7Eh88E1u0AAAAA:9RUv4pWWEAlfrtLC7Tna7n6Cj82goWBd7lFuzIS5GxPzp2aKO11YLm4mYcNUHfaBmKsLCdhywx8. DOI: 10.1016/j.leaqua.2011.10.003

Cavusoglu, H., Mishra, B., & Raghunathan, S. (2004). The effect of internet security breach announcements on market value: Capital market reactions for breached firms and internet security developers. *International Journal of Electronic Commerce, 9*(1), 70–104. DOI: 10.1080/10864415.2004.11044320

CDC. (2016). *National and State Healthcare-Associated Infections Progress Report*. Center for Disease Control. Retrieved from https://stacks.cdc.gov/view/cdc/70275

Ceitil, M. (2023). *Gestão e desenvolvimento de competências, (2º Edição)*. Edições Sílabo.

Ceko, E. (2023). On the Relationship Between ISO Standards and Sustainable Development. *Problemy Ekorozwoju / Problems of Sustainable Development*, 18(2), 148–158. DOI: 10.35784/preko.3953

Celeny, D., Maréchal, L., Rousselot, E., Mermoud, A., & Humbert, M. (2024). Prioritizing investments in cybersecurity: Empirical evidence from an event study on the determinants of cyberattack costs. SSRN Electronic Journal. DOI: 10.2139/ssrn.4717020

Chaabaoui, S., Oughannou, Z., & Chaoui, H. (2024). A systematic review of blockchain applications in pharmaceutical supply chain traceability and security. *2024 10th International Conference on Optimization and Applications (ICOA)*, 1–7. https://doi.org/DOI: 10.1109/ICOA62581.2024.10754349

Chaikovskaya. L. (2021). Accounting of Intangible Assets and Their Reflection in Corporate Reporting in Conditions of Digital Transformation. *Intellectual property law* .DOI: 10.18572/2072-4322-2021-2-19-22

Chakravorti, B. (2017). *The Digital Planet 2017: How competitiveness and trust in digital economies vary across the world*. Tufts University.

Chandran, V. (2024). Operational Excellence: Process optimization for competitive edge. *International Journal for Multidimensional Research Perspectives*. .DOI: 10.61877/ijmrp.v2i10.203

Chang, L. (2023). Innovative Marketing Strategies in China's Telecommunication Sector: Adapting to the Digital Age. *Journal of Marketing Communications*.

Cha, S., Meng, W., Li, W.-W., & Yeh, K.-H. (2023). A blockchain-enabled IoT auditing management system complying with ISO/IEC 15408-2. *Computers & Industrial Engineering*, *178*, 109091. DOI: 10.1016/j.cie.2023.109091

Chatwani, N. (2019). Organisational agility. *Springer International Publishing, Cham, doi, 10*, 978-3.

Cheng, X., Hsu, C., & Wang, T. (2022). Talk too much? The impact of cybersecurity disclosures on investment decisions. *Communications of the Association for Information Systems*, *50*(1), 481–485. DOI: 10.17705/1CAIS.05022

Chen, R., Ren, X., He, L., & Huang, J. (2024). Editorial: AI as intelligent technology and agent to understand and be understood by human minds. *Frontiers in Psychology*, *15*, 1461881. DOI: 10.3389/fpsyg.2024.1461881

Chepeliuk, M. (2024). Transformation of Ukrainian business in the face of global challenges. *Ukrainian Journal of Applied Economics and Technology*, *2024*(4), 187–191. DOI: 10.36887/2415-8453-2024-4-28

Chiarini, A., & Cherrafi, A. (2023). Artificial intelligence and quality management: A systematic literature review and research agenda. *The TQM Journal*, *35*(5), 1050–1071. DOI: 10.1108/TQM-08-2022-0259

Chiarini, A., & Cherrafi, A. (2023). Integrating ISO 9001 and Industry 4.0: An implementation guideline and PDCA model for manufacturing sector. *Total Quality Management & Business Excellence*, *34*(15–16), 1629–1654. DOI: 10.1080/14783363.2023.2192916

Chin, R., & Benne, K. D. (1969). *General Strategies for Effecting Changes in Human Systems*. Human Relations Center, Boston University.

Chorazy, E. (2020). Coke and health. *Decoding Coca-Cola*, 207-225.

Chowdhary, Y., & Kumar, B. (2023). Advancement and benefits associated with ISO 9000 series. *Asian Journal of Pharmaceutical Research*. DOI: 10.52711/2231-5691.2023.00008

Chowdhury, A. (2025). A systematic review of risk-based procurement strategies in retail supply chains: sourcing flexibility and vendor disruption management. *American Journal of Advanced Technology and Engineering Solutions*. DOI: 10.63125/jr03rv07

Chowdhury, M. T., Sarkar, A., Paul, S. K., & Moktadir, M. A. (2020). A case study on strategies to deal with the impacts of covid-19 pandemic in the food and beverage industry. *Operations Management Research*, *15*(1-2), 166–178.

Choy, W., & Communications, M. (2022). T raditional Supply Chain Challenges During COVID-19 Spur Innovation in Blockchain Applications. .

Chumba, P., Sang, H., Kibett, J., & Kirui, J. (2019). Relationship between ISO 9001 Certification and the Number of Non Conformities Identified during System Audits in Selected Public Universities in Kenya. *EngRN: Operations Research*. DOI: 10.2139/ssrn.3517114

Cieslak, V., Bouaziz, A., & Davenport, T. (2025). An integrative review of employee resistance to digital transformation. *Cogent Business & Management*, *12*(1), 2442550. DOI: 10.1080/23311975.2024.2442550

Clegg, C. W. (2000). Sociotechnical principles for system design. *Applied Ergonomics*, *31*(5), 463–477. DOI: 10.1016/S0003-6870(00)00009-0 PMID: 11059460

Cooper, H. M. (1988). Organizing knowledge syntheses: A taxonomy of literature reviews. *Knowledge in Society*, *1*(1), 104.

Costa, E., & da Silva Oliveira, T. (2020). Comunicação organizacional: Uma ferramenta estratégica de compatibilização de interesses. *Revista Alterjor*, *22*(2), 397–409. DOI: 10.11606/issn.2176-1507.v22i2p397-409

Costa, M. B. S. D. (2021). *Especificidades da Comunicação em Organizações da Administração Pública–o caso da Câmara Municipal de Penacova (Tese de Mestrado)*. Faculdade de Letras da Universidade de Coimbra.

Creswell, J. W., & Poth, C. N. (2018). *Qualitative inquiry and research design: Choosing among five approaches* (4th ed.). SAGE Publications.

Ćwiklicki, M., Wojnarowska, M., & Pilch, K. (2020). Diffusion of ISO 9001 quality management system in service and manufacturing organizations. *The TQM Journal*, *32*(6), 1059–1077. DOI: 10.1108/TQM-10-2019-0252

da Costa, H. C. M. (2021). Liderança e Motivação no Contexto Organizacional (Dissertação de Doutoramento). Instituto Politécnico do Porto, Porto.

da Fonseca, L. M. C. M., Domingues, J. P. T., Machado, P. B., & Harder, D. (2019). ISO 9001:2015 adoption: A multi-country empirical research. *Journal of Industrial Engineering and Management*, *12*(1), 27. Advance online publication. DOI: 10.3926/jiem.2745

da Silva Duque, J. I. (2020). A Influência da Motivação Para O Serviço Militar No Comprometimento Organizacional: O Efeito Moderador do Vínculo Contratual dos Militares da Força Aérea Portuguesa (Dissertação de Doutoramento). Universidade de Lisboa, Lisboa.

Da Silva, C. P., Paschoalotto, M. A. C., & Endo, G. Y. (2020). Liderança organizacional: Uma revisão integrativa brasileira. *Revista Pensamento Contemporâneo em Administração*, *14*(1), 146–159. DOI: 10.12712/rpca.v14i1.36370

Daft, R. (2015). *Management*. South-Western College Publishing.

Daher, M. M., & Ziade, F. (2023). Technology, workforce, and the future of sustainable work. In El-Chaarani, H., El Dandachi, I., El Nemar, S., & Abiad, Z. E. L. (Eds.), *Navigating the Intersection of Business, Sustainability and Technology* (pp. 79–97). Springer., DOI: 10.1007/978-981-99-8572-2_6

Dahmen, P. (2023). Organizational resilience as a key property of enterprise risk management in response to novel and severe crisis events. *Risk Management & Insurance Review, 26*(2), 203–245. DOI: 10.1111/rmir.12245

Dakshayini, M., Sushma, H. P., & Spoorthi, S. (2024). Blockchain based traceability system for food safety. *2024 International Conference on Emerging Technologies in Computer Science for Interdisciplinary Applications (ICETCS*), 1–6. https://doi.org/DOI: 10.1109/ICETCS61022.2024.10543664

Damayanti, R. (2023). Staff competence model in implementation of Quality Management 4.0 at telecommunications industry: Literature review. *In Proceedings of the International Conference on Industrial Engineering and Operations Mana*gement. https://doi.org/DOI: 10.46254/AP03.20220049

Das, S., Samal, T. K., & Mohanta, B. K. (2024). Addressing security in IoMT systems: A blockchain consensus approach. *2024 15th International Conference on Computing Communication and Networking Technologies (ICCCNT),* 1–6. https://doi.org/DOI: 10.1109/ICCCNT61001.2024.10725986

Data Insights Market. (2025). Digital transformation in aviation market demand dynamics: Insights 2025–2033. *Data Insights Market.*DOI: 10.1057/9781403920249_5

Davenport, T. H., & Ronanki, R. (2018). Artificial Intelligence for the Real World. *Harvard Business Review, 96*(1), 108–116.

De Bock, K. W., Coussement, K., De Caigny, A., Słowiński, R., Baesens, B., Boute, R. N., Choi, T.-M., Delen, D., Kraus, M., Lessmann, S., Maldonado, S., Martens, D., Óskarsdóttir, M., Vairetti, C., Verbeke, W., & Weber, R. (2024). Explainable AI for operational research: A defining framework, methods, applications, and a research agenda. *European Journal of Operational Research, 317*(2), 249–272. DOI: 10.1016/j.ejor.2023.09.026

De Carolis, A., Sassanelli, C., Acerbi, F., Macchi, M., Terzi, S., & Taisch, M. (2025). The Digital REadiness Assessment MaturitY DREAMY framework to guide manufacturing companies towards a digitalisation roadmap. *International Journal of Production Research, 63*(15), 5555–5581. Advance online publication. DOI: 10.1080/00207543.2025.2455476

de Paula Pereira, G., de Medeiros, J. F., Kolling, C., Ribeiro, J. L. D., Morea, D., & Iazzolino, G. (2024). Using dynamic capabilities to cope with digital transformation and boost innovation in traditional banks. *Business Horizons, 67*(4), 317–330. DOI: 10.1016/j.bushor.2024.03.006

De Paula, D., Marx, C., Wolf, E., Dremel, C., Cormican, K., & Uebernickel, F. (2023). A managerial mental model to drive innovation in the context of digital transformation. *Industry and Innovation, 30*(1), 42–66. DOI: 10.1080/13662716.2022.2072711

Deloitte. (2017). Predictive maintenance and the smart factory. Deloitte Insights. https://www2.deloitte.com/us/en/insights/focus/industry-4-0/using-predictive-technologies-for-asset-maintenance.htm

Deloitte. (2022). State of AI in the Enterprise, 5th Edition: Thriving in the era of pervasive AI. Retrieved from: https://www2.deloitte.com/us/en/insights/focus/cognitive-technologies/state-of-ai-and-intelligent-automation-in-business-survey.html

Deloitte. (2023). The state of AI in the enterprise. Deloitte Insights. https://www2.deloitte.com/us/en/insights/focus/cognitive-technologies/state-of-ai-and-intelligent-automation-in-business-survey.html

Devre, S., Agrawal, G., Deore, S., Dahapute, A., & Patil, S. (2024). Medicine Supply Chain using Blockchain. *International Journal of Advanced Research in Science. Tongxin Jishu*, 128–133. Advance online publication. DOI: 10.48175/IJARSCT-22318

Dias, A. S., Abreu, A., Navas, H. V., & Santos, R. (2020). Proposal of a holistic framework to support sustainability of new product innovation processes. *Sustainability*, *12*(8), 3450.

Dobrin, C., Girneata, A., Mascu, M., & Croitoru, O. (2025). Quality: a determinant factor of competitiveness – the evolution of iso certifications for management systems., 9, 1062-1073.

Dove, R. (2001). *Response ability: The language, structure, and culture of the agile enterprise*. John Wiley & Sons.

Drankova, N. A., & Denisova, Y. V. (2023). Successful supplier audit practices taking into account the risk-based approach. *Izvestiia Samarskogo Nauchnogo Tsentra Rossiiskoi Akademii Nauk*, *25*(4), 13–22. DOI: 10.37313/1990-5378-2023-25-4-13-22

Dreković, E., Radosavljević, M., & Bejtović, M. (2021). Analysis of limitations of ISO standards implementation from the external stakeholders' point of view. *Facta Universitatis, Series: Economics and Organization*. .DOI: 10.22190/FUEO210402010D

Drljača, M., & Tolić, A. (2025). Quality models for preventing the impact of supply chain disruptions in future crises. *Sustainability (Basel)*, *17*(8), 3293. DOI: 10.3390/su17083293

du Plessis, M. (2023). Trait emotional intelligence and flourishing: The mediating role of positive coping behaviour. *SA Journal of Industrial Psychology*, *49*, 2063. DOI: 10.4102/sajip.v49i0.2063

Dutta, P. K., Ricciuti, M., Bogrekci, I., & Suseelan, S. (Eds.). (2025). *Digital transformation in aviation industry operations: Innovations and sustainable solutions* (1st ed.). Routledge., DOI: 10.4324/9781003494720

Dvorak, J., & Razova, I. (2018). Empirical Validation of Blue Ocean Strategy Sustainability in an International Environment. *Foundations of Management*, *10*(1), 143–162.

Dzameshie, D. O. (2012). Leadership in project management: The behaviors of successful male project managers in information technology (Order No. 3499910). Available from ProQuest Dissertations & Theses Global. (962412637). https://www.proquest.com/openview/fb508641a440199ee731c3179ef0def9/1?pq-origsite=gscholar&cbl=18750

Eagle, K. A., Montoye, C. K., Riba, A. L., DeFranco, A. C., Parrish, R., Skorcz, S., Baker, P. L., Faul, J., Jani, S. M., Chen, B., Roychoudhury, C., Elma, M. A., Mitchell, K. R., & Mehta, R. H. (2005). Guideline-based standardized care is associated with substantially lower mortality in Medicare patients with acute myocardial infarction: The American College of Cardiology's Guidelines Applied in Practice (GAP) Projects in Michigan. *Journal of the American College of Cardiology*, *46*(7), 1242–1248. DOI: 10.1016/j.jacc.2004.12.083 PMID: 16198838

Egbumokei, P. I., Dienagha, I. N., Digitemie, W. N., Onukwulu, E. C., & Oladipo, O. T. (2024). Driving operational excellence in the LNG industry: Leveraging Six Sigma principles for continuous improvement. *International Journal of Multidisciplinary Research and Growth Evaluation*, *5*(4), 1298–1310. DOI: 10.54660/.IJMRGE.2024.5.4.1298-1310

Eich, D. (2012). *Root Down and Branch Out: Best Practices for Leadership Development Programs*. CreateSpace Independent Publishing., https://www.amazon.com/Root-Down-Branch-Out-Development/dp/1468034782

Ejjami, R. (2024). Leveraging AI to enhance marketing and customer engagement strategies in the French market. *International Journal for Multidisciplinary Research*, *6*(3), 120–131. DOI: 10.36948/ijfmr.2024.v06i03.23147

Eletter, S., Elrefae, G., Yasmin, T., Qasem, A., Alshehadeh, A., & Belarbi, A. K. (2022). Leveraging Blockchain-Based Smart Contracts in the Management of Supply Chain: Evidence from Carrefour UAE. *2022 International Arab Conference on Information Technology (ACIT)*, 1–5. IEEE. https://doi.org/DOI: 10.1109/ACIT57182.2022.9994083

Elia, G., Solazzo, G., Lerro, A., Pigni, F., & Tucci, C. L. (2024). The digital transformation canvas: A conceptual framework for leading the digital transformation process. *Business Horizons*, *67*(4), 381–398. DOI: 10.1016/j.bushor.2024.03.007

Elkington, J. (2018). *Green Swans: The Coming Boom in Regenerative Capitalism. Fast*. Company Press.

Elkins, R. (2015). *Business: Golden Nugget Methods for High Effectiveness - Leadership, Management & Communication*. CreateSpace Independent Publishing Platform., https://www.amazon.com/Management-Effectively-Personnel-Conflict-Resolution/dp/1515041441

Ellström, D., Holtström, J., Berg, E., & Josefsson, C. (2022). Dynamic capabilities for digital transformation. *Journal of Strategy and Management*, *15*(2), 272–286. DOI: 10.1108/JSMA-04-2021-0089

Empresas, M. E. O. (n.d.) *5G API Sprint*. https://www.meo.pt/empresas/5g-api-sprint?blog=5g-api-sprint-programa-inovacao-aplicacoes-diferenciadoras

Endrejat, P. C., & Burnes, B. (2024). Draw it, check it, change it: Reviving Lewin's Topology to facilitate organizational change theory and practice. *The Journal of Applied Behavioral Science*, *60*(1), 87–112. DOI: 10.1177/00218863221122875

Engelmann, A. (2023). Algorithmic transparency as a fundamental right in the democratic rule of law. *Brazilian Journal of Law. Technology and Innovation*, *1*(2), 169–188. DOI: 10.59224/bjlti.v1i2.169-188

Enyejo, J. O., Fajana, O. P., Jok, I. S., Ihejirika, C. J., Awotiwon, B. O., & Olola, T. M. (2024, November). Digital Twin Technology, Predictive Analytics, and Sustainable Project Management in Global Supply Chains for Risk Mitigation, Optimization, and Carbon Footprint Reduction through Green Initiatives. *International Journal of Innovative Science and Research Technology*, *9*(11), 609–630. Advance online publication. DOI: 10.38124/ijisrt/IJISRT24NOV1344

Eom, S.-J., & Lee, J. (2022). Digital government transformation in turbulent times: Responses, challenges, and future direction. *Government Information Quarterly*, *39*(2), 101690. DOI: 10.1016/j.giq.2022.101690

Erdal, B. S., Laugerette, A., Fair, K. H., Zimmermann, M., Demirer, M., Gupta, V., O'Donnell, T., & White, R. D. (2023). AI algorithm deployment and utilization: Strategies to facilitate clinical workflow implementation and integration. *medRxiv.* DOI: 10.1101/2023.09.19.23295729

Ernst, B. A., Banks, G. C., Loignon, A. C., Frear, K. A., Williams, C. E., Arciniega, L. M., Gupta, R. K., Kodydek, G., & Subramanian, D. (2021). Virtual charismatic leadership and signaling theory: A prospective meta-analysis in five countries. *The Leadership Quarterly*, *32*(5), 101541. DOI: 10.1016/j.leaqua.2021.101541

Errida, A., & Lotfi, B. (2021). The determinants of organizational change management success: Literature review and case study. *International Journal of Engineering Business Management*, *13*, 18479790211016273. Advance online publication. DOI: 10.1177/18479790211016273

Esteva, A., Robicquet, A., Ramsundar, B., Kuleshov, V., DePristo, M., Chou, K., Cui, C., Corrado, G., Thrun, S., & Dean, J. (2019). A guide to deep learning in healthcare. *Nature Medicine*, *25*(1), 24–29. DOI: 10.1038/s41591-018-0316-z

European Medicines Agency. (2023). Artificial intelligence workplan: A strategy for EMA. EMA. https://www.ema.europa.eu/en/about-us/how-we-work/big-data/artificial-intelligence-workplan-strategy-ema

Executive Digest. (2025, May 22). *Altice Labs obtém nova patente europeia para otimização de redes de fibra ótica.*_https://executivedigest.sapo.pt/noticias/altice-labs-obtem-nova-patente-europeia-para-otimizacao-de-redes-de-fibra-otica/

Eyieyien, O., Paul, P., & Ijomah, T. (2024). *Strategic approaches for successful digital transformation in project management across industries.* International Journal of Frontiers in Engineering and Technology Research., DOI: 10.53294/ijfetr.2024.7.1.0037

Faciane, M., Fan, S., & Dwyer, R. (2021). *Returning to Solvency Through Quality Improvement.* International Journal of Applied Management and Technology., DOI: 10.5590/IJAMT.2021.20.1.01

Famoti, O., Omowole, B., Nzeako, G., Shittu, R., Ezechi, O., Ewim, C., & Omokhoa, H. (2025). A Digital Transformation Framework for U.S. E Commerce Supply Chains. International Journal of Scientific Research in Computer Science, *Engineering and Information Technology*. .DOI: 10.32628/CSEIT251112202

Fantozzi, I., Santolamazza, A., Loy, G., & Schiraldi, M. (2025). Digital Twins: Strategic Guide to Utilize Digital Twins to Improve Operational Efficiency in Industry 4.0. *Future Internet*, *17*(1), 41. DOI: 10.3390/fi17010041

Fan, Z., Wu, X., & Cao, B. (2020). Considering the traceability awareness of consumers: Should the supply chain adopt the blockchain technology? *Annals of Operations Research*, *309*(1), 837–860. DOI: 10.1007/s10479-020-03729-y

Fatma, N., Ponda, H., & Kuswara, R. (2020). Analisis preventive maintenance dengan metode menghitung mean time between failure (MTBF) dan mean time to repair (MTTR) (*studi kasus pt. Gajah tunggal tbk).*17, 87-94. DOI: 10.30996/heuristic.v17i2.4648

Félix, F. J. D. (2020). *Comunicação Estratégica e Integrada: A visão de 23 renomados autores de 5 países*. Editora Rede Integrada.

Ferouali, S. E. (2021). Governance of the digital transformation in Moroccan universities: Case study of Cadi Ayyad University-Marrakech. *Journal of Economics. Finance and Management Studies*, *4*(9). Advance online publication. DOI: 10.47191/jefms/v4-i9-22

Ferreira, I. N. S. (2024). *Supply Chain and Procurement Performance Assessment - a Case Study at Altice Portugal.* [Relatório de Estágio, Universidade Europeia].

Ferreira, R. J. (2020). Integração do cliente no processo de inovação: Estudo de caso na Altice Portugal [Dissertação de mestrado, Iscte - Instituto Universitário de Lisboa]. Repositório Iscte. http://hdl.handle.net/10071/21264

Ferrell, O. C., Fraedrich, J., & Ferrell, L. (2019). *Business ethics: Ethical decision making and cases* (12th ed.). Cengage Learning.

Fiedler, F. E. (1972). How Do You Make Leaders More Effective? *Organizational Dynamics*, *1*(2), 2–18. https://www.sciencedirect.com/science/article/abs/pii/0090261672900083. DOI: 10.1016/0090-2616(72)90008-3

Figueiredo, A. (2025, abril). *Estamos prontos para liderar a próxima fase da transformação tecnológica em Portugal* [Publicação no LinkedIn]. https://www.linkedin.com/feed/update/urn:li:activity:7333161873338531840/

Fitz-Enz, J., & Mattox, J. (2014). *Predictive analytics for human resources*. John Wiley & Sons. DOI: 10.1002/9781118915042

Fivetran. (2025). Fivetran report finds nearly half of enterprise AI projects fail due to poor data readiness. https://www.fivetran.com/blog/report-enterprise-ai-projects-fail-data-readiness

Flyvbjerg, B., Holm, M. K. S., & Buhl, S. L. (2003). How common and how large are cost overruns in transport infrastructure projects? *Transport Reviews*, *23*(1), 71–88. DOI: 10.1080/01441640309904

Fonseca, L., Cardoso, M. C., & Nóvoa, M. H. (2021). Motivations for ISO 9001 quality management system implementation and certification mapping the territory with a novel classification proposal. *International Journal of Quality and Service Sciences*, *13*(4), 585–603. DOI: 10.1108/IJQSS-02-2021-0031

Fontanela, C., Burtet, G., Pereira, R., & Marroco, A. (2021). *Open innovation: the role of scientific and technological parks in the transformation of traditional industries.* [Brazilian Journal of Development]. DOI: 10.34117/bjdv7n6-160

Forbes Technology Council. (2024). Why AI projects fail: Lessons for enterprise leaders. Forbes. https://www.forbes.com/councils/forbestechcouncil/

Fowler, S. (2018). Toward a new curriculum of leadership competencies: Advances in motivation science call for rethinking leadership development. *Advances in Developing Human Resources*, *20*(2), 182–196. DOI: 10.1177/1523422318756644

Frank, A. G., Dalenogare, L. S., & Ayala, N. F. (2019). Industry 4.0 technologies: Implementation patterns in manufacturing companies. *International Journal of Production Economics*, *210*, 15–26. DOI: 10.1016/j.ijpe.2019.01.004

Franke, P. D., & Fischer, F. (2023). Will blockchain technology revolutionize supply chain management? *Sri Lanka Journal of Marketing*, *9*(1), 23–40. Advance online publication. DOI: 10.4038/sljmuok.v9i1.118

Fuchs, M., Rezac, M., & Sousek, R. (2021). The overall cumulative impact of Covid-19 and Brexit on European supply chains. *2021 New Trends in Aviation Development (NTAD)*, 37–41. https://doi.org/ DOI: 10.1109/NTAD54074.2021.9746509

Gabarro, J. (2007). When a New Manager Takes Charge. *Harvard Business Review*, *85*(1), 104–117. https://hbr.org/2007/01/when-a-new-manager-takes-charge

Gaidhani, Y., Ramesh, J. V. N., Singh, S., Dagar, R., Rao, T. S. M., Godla, S. R., & El-Ebiary, Y. A. B. (2025). AI-driven predictive analytics for CRM to enhance retention, personalization and decision making. *International Journal of Advanced Computer Science and Applications*, *16*(4). Advance online publication. DOI: 10.14569/IJACSA.2025.0160456

Galanakis, C. M., Rizou, M., Aldawoud, T. M., Uçak, İ., & Rowan, N. J. (2021). Innovations and technology disruptions in the food sector within the covid-19 pandemic and post-lockdown era. *Trends in Food Science & Technology*, *110*, 193–200.

Galles, K. (2021, August 10). *Strategies to scale innovation from a Stanford researcher*. Qualia Blog. https://blog.qualia.com/scale-change-management/

Galloway, S. M. (2016). What makes a leader transformational? *Leadership Excellence*, *33*(5), 20–21.

Gamit, A. M., Santos, A. R., Armas, K. L., & Villegas, M. N. (2024). Implementation of ISO 9001:2015 in state universities and colleges: A quality management, organizational performance, and legal framework. *Corporate Law & Governance Review*, *6*(4), 94–102. DOI: 10.22495/clgrv6i4p9

Gamit, R., Prajapati, R., & Gohil, A. (2024). ISO 9001 and competitiveness: Empirical evidence from Indian manufacturing firms. *Journal of Business Excellence*, *18*(1), 42–56. DOI: 10.1504/IJBEX.2024.100602

Gandellini, G., & Venanzi, D. (2011). Purple ocean strategy: How to support SMEs' recovery. *Procedia: Social and Behavioral Sciences*, *24*, 1–15.

Garay-Gallastegui, L. M., Achurra-González, F., Delgado Ruiz, G., & Sánchez-González, J. L. (2024). The role of analytical techniques in the industrialization of digital profiles and the operationalization of business strategy: The case of BBVA. *Innovative Marketing*, *20*(2), 90–101. DOI: 10.21511/im.20(2).2024.09

Garcia, M. (2025, August b1). Cybersecurity in aviation: Analyzing the surge in airline and airport breaches. *Aerospace Global News*. https://aerospaceglobalnews.com/news/airline-airport-aviation-cyberattacks-2025/

Gartner. (2023). Gartner Survey Finds More Than Half of Organizations Have AI in Production. Retrieved from: https://www.gartner.com/en/newsroom/press-releases/2023-08-22-gartner-survey-finds-more-than-half-of-organizations-have-ai-in-production

Garza-Reyes, J. A., Kumar, P., Chen, F., & Wang, Y. (2017). Editorial: Seeing green: Achieving environmental sustainability through Lean and Six Sigma. *International Journal of Lean Six Sigma*, *8*(1), 2–11. DOI: 10.1108/IJLSS-01-2017-0005

Gascó-Hernández, M., Gil-García, J. R., & Luna-Reyes, L. F. (2022). Unpacking the role of technology, leadership, governance and collaborative capacities in inter-agency collaborations. *Government Information Quarterly, 39*(3), 101710. DOI: 10.1016/j.giq.2022.101710

George, S., Kate, J., & Frank, E. (2025). Strategic AI applications in multi-project management for biopharmaceutical innovation.

Ghode, D., Jain, R., & Soni, G. (2021). Challenges of adoption of blockchain technology in supply chain: *An overview. In Lecture Notes in Mechanical Engineering* (pp. 1–12). https://doi.org/DOI: 10.1007/978-981-16-5281-3_15

Giacosa, E., Alam, G. M., Culasso, F., & Crocco, E. (2023). The paradox of digital surveillance in the workplace. *Journal of Innovation & Knowledge, 8*(2), 100357. DOI: 10.1016/j.jik.2023.100357

Gibson, C. B., & Birkinshaw, J. (2004). The antecedents, consequences, and mediating role of organizational ambidexterity. *Academy of Management Journal, 47*(2), 209–226.

Gilley, J. W., & Gilley, A. M. (2003). *Strategically integrated HRD: Six transformational roles in creating results-driven programs* (2nd ed.). Perseus Publishing.

Glikson, E., & Woolley, A. W. (2020). Human trust in artificial intelligence: Review of empirical research. *The Academy of Management Annals, 14*(2), 627–660. DOI: 10.5465/annals.2018.0057

Glogovac, M., & Ruso, J. (2020). ISO 9004 maturity model for quality in Industry 4.0. *International Journal of Quality & Reliability Management, 37*(8), 1101–1117. DOI: 10.1080/14783363.2020.1865793

Glogovac, M., Ruso, J., & Anđelković, A. (2022). Leadership for Quality 4.0: Improvement, learning and innovation. *Total Quality Management & Business Excellence, 33*(11–12), 1197–1214. DOI: 10.1080/10429247.2022.2108668

Goldberg, J. R. (2006). Making the transition from technologist to manager. *Biomedical Instrumentation & Technology, 40*(6), 465–468. https://array.aami.org/doi/full/10.2345/i0899-8205-40-6-465.1. DOI: 10.2345/i0899-8205-40-6-465.1 PMID: 17190088

Goldman, S. L., Nagel, R. N., & Preiss, K. (1995). *Agile competitors and virtual organizations: Strategies for enriching the customer*. Van Nostrand Reinhold.

González, M. (2024). *Integración de Inteligencia Artificial en la Inteligencia de Negocio: potencial de los datos no estructurados para la toma de decisiones estratégicas*. UCV-Scientia., DOI: 10.18050/revucv-scientia.v16n2a5

Graf, D. G., & Burrell, D. N. (2024). Utilizing resistance feedback for software implementation in healthcare. *Health Economics and Management Review, 5*(1), 106–116. DOI: 10.61093/hem.2024.1-08

Grand View Research. (2024). Aviation cyber security market size, share & trends analysis report by component (hardware, software, services), by type (endpoint security, cloud security), by deployment (cloud-based, on-premises), by application, by region, and segment forecasts, 2024 - 2030. *Author*. https://www.grandviewresearch.com/industry-analysis/aviation-cyber-security-market-report

Graves, L., Dalgarno, N., Hoorn, R. V., Hastings-Truelove, A., Mulder, J., Kolomitro, K., & Kirby, F. (2023). Creating change: Kotter's change management model in action. *Canadian Medical Education Journal, 14*(3), 136–139. DOI: 10.36834/cmej.76680

Gray, J., Ross, J., & Badrick, T. (2022). The path to continual improvement and business excellence: Compliance to ISO standards versus a business excellence approach. *Accreditation and Quality Assurance, 27*(4), 195–203. DOI: 10.1007/s00769-022-01503-0

Greiman, V. A. (2013). *Megaproject management: Lessons on risk and project management from the Big Dig*. John Wiley & Sons. DOI: 10.1002/9781118671092

Große, C., & Sundberg, L. (2025). Generative AI and digital resilience: A research agenda. *Journal of Risk Research*, 1–26. Advance online publication. DOI: 10.1080/13669877.2025.2539105

Guduru, A. (2025). Reinventing supply chain dynamics: The rise of intelligent AI Agents. *World Journal of Advanced Engineering Technology and Sciences, 15*(2), 721–729. DOI: 10.30574/wjaets.2025.15.2.0581

Gueorguiev, T. (2025). An approach to integrate Artificial Intelligence in ISO 9001-based quality management systems. *Measurement. Sensors, 38*, 101787. DOI: 10.1016/j.measen.2024.101787

Guirette-Barbosa, O. A., Castañeda-Burciaga, S., Ramírez-Salazar, M. A., Cruz-Domínguez, O., Carrera-Escobedo, J. L., Velázquez-Macías, J. D. J., Lara-Torres, C. G., Celaya-Padilla, J. M., & Durán-Muñoz, H. A. (2025). Transforming Quality into Results: A Multivariate Analysis with Hotelling's T2 on the Impact of ISO 9001. *Systems, 13*(4), 226. DOI: 10.3390/systems13040226

Gupta, R., Biswas, D., Ronty, A., Kapali, S., & Khan, M. (2024). Empowering Digital Transformation: The Strategic Role of Artificial Intelligence in Enterprise Innovation. *European Journal of Theoretical and Applied Sciences*. .DOI: 10.59324/ejtas.2024.2(6).16

Gurin, P., Dey, E. L., Hurtado, S., & Gurin, G. (2002). Diversity and higher education: Theory and impact on educational outcomes. *Harvard Educational Review, 72*(3), 330–366. DOI: 10.17763/haer.72.3.01151786u134n051

Gutiérrez Broncano, S., González-Sánchez, M., & Villanueva-García, D. (2024). Hybrid strategy and its effect on the market performance of family-business SMEs: The mediating role of innovation. *The International Journal of Organizational Analysis*. Advance online publication.

Gutiérrez-Broncano, S., Linuesa-Langreo, J., Rubio-Andrés, M., & Sastre-Castillo, M. Á. (2024). Can hybrid strategy improve SME performance? The role of innovation and adaptive capacity. *European Journal of Innovation Management, 27*(9), 173–197.

Hadji, S., Gholizadeh, P., & Naghavi, N. (2022). Diagnosing of human resource performance management based on lack of ambidextrous learning themes: A case study of public Iranian banking system. *International Journal of Ethics and Systems, 38*(3), 484–509.

Hagl, C., Kanitz, R., Gonzalez, K., & Hoegl, M. (2024). Change management interventions: Taking stock and moving forward. *Human Resource Management Review, 34*(1), 101000. DOI: 10.1016/j.hrmr.2023.101000

Hakimi, M., Zarinkhail, M. S., & Musawi, S. Z. (2024). Exploring the fusion of enterprise architecture, blockchain, and AI in digital governance: A systematic review. *International Journal Software Engineering and Computer Science*, *4*(2), 45–61. DOI: 10.35870/ijsecs.v4i2.2832

Hall, K., & Taylor, J. (2024). Standardizing technical understanding to support a robust, archivable and accessible digital thread Supported by ISO 10303 STEP and IEC/ISO 81346 standards. AIAA SCITECH 2024 Forum. DOI: 10.2514/6.2024-0480

Hall, P. (2005). Interprofessional teamwork: Professional cultures as barriers. *Journal of Interprofessional Care*, 19(sup1), 188-196.

Hammouchi, H., Cherqi, O., Mezzour, G., Ghogho, M., & El Koutbi, M. (2019). Digging deeper into data breaches: An exploratory data analysis of hacking breaches over time. *Procedia Computer Science*, *151*, 1008–1015. DOI: 10.1016/j.procs.2019.04.141

Hänel, A., Seidel, A., Frieß, U., Teicher, U., Wiemer, H., Wang, D., Wenkler, E., Penter, L., Hellmich, A., & Ihlenfeldt, S. (2021). Digital Twins for High-Tech Machining Applications—A Model-Based Analytics-Ready Approach. *Journal of Manufacturing and Materials Processing*, *5*(3), 80. Advance online publication. DOI: 10.3390/jmmp5030080

Hanson, B. (2013). The leadership development interface: Aligning leaders and organizations toward more effective leadership learning. *Advances in Developing Human Resources*, *15*(1), 106–120. DOI: 10.1177/1523422312465853

Hariyani, D., Hariyani, P., Mishra, S., & Sharma, M. (2025). *A literature review on transformative impacts of blockchain technology on manufacturing management and industrial engineering practices*. Green Technologies and Sustainability., DOI: 10.1016/j.grets.2025.100169

Harrison, R., Fischer, S., Walpola, R. L., Chauhan, A., Babalola, T., Mears, S., & Le-Dao, H. (2021). Where do models for change management, improvement and implementation meet? A systematic review of the applications of change management models in healthcare. *Journal of Healthcare Leadership*, *13*, 85–108. DOI: 10.2147/JHL.S289176

Hartigan, R. (1974). Training and development toward leadership. *Occupational Health Nursing*, *22*(9), 12–16. https://journals.sagepub.com/doi/abs/10.1177/216507997402200903. DOI: 10.1177/216507997402200903 PMID: 4859571

Hassan, R. R., Talib, M. A., Dweiri, F., & Roman, J. (2024). An artificial intelligence (AI) framework to predict operational excellence: UAE case study. *Applied Sciences (Basel, Switzerland)*, *14*(6), 2569. DOI: 10.3390/app14062569

Haugan, G. T. (2002). *Project planning and scheduling*. Management Concepts.

Haug, N., Dan, S., & Mergel, I. (2024). Digitally induced change in the public sector: A systematic review and research agenda. *Public Management Review*, *26*(7), 1963–1987. DOI: 10.1080/14719037.2023.2234917

Heifetz, R. A. (2003). Adaptive work. *DEMOS COLLECTION*, 68-78.

Heifetz, R., Grashow, A., & Linsky, M. (2009). *The Practice of Adaptive Leadership: Tools and Tactics for Changing Your Organization and the World*. Harvard Business Press.

Henien, S., Aronow, H. D., & Abbott, J. D. (2020). Quality management in the cardiac catheterization laboratory. *Journal of Thoracic Disease, 12*(4), 1695–1705. DOI: 10.21037/jtd.2019.12.81 PMID: 32395312

Henrichs, E., & Krupitzer, C. Towards a Self Adaptive, Real-Time Monitoring System for Food Quality Assessment. 2024 IEEE International Conference on Autonomic Computing and Self-Organizing Systems Companion (ACSOS-C) (2024): 178-179. DOI: 10.1109/ACSOS-C63493.2024.00056

Herath, H. M. D. K., & Gamlath, M. (2025). Impact of digital transformation on financial performance of licensed commercial banks in Sri Lanka pre and post COVID-19 pandemic. *Sri Lanka Journal of Social Sciences, 47*(2), 145–163. Advance online publication. DOI: 10.4038/sljss.v47i02.9019

Herrmann, J., Tackenberg, S., Padoano, E., Hartlief, J., Rautenstengel, J., Loeser, C., & Böhme, J. (2021). An ERP Data Quality Assessment Framework for the Implementation of an APS system using Bayesian Networks., 194-204. https://doi.org/.DOI: 10.1016/j.procs.2022.01.218

Hiatt, J. (2023). ADKAR: A model for change in business, government and our community. *Prosci*. https://www.prosci.com/resources/articles/adkar-model-overview

Hiatt, J. M. (2006). *ADKAR: A model for change in business, government, and our community*. Prosci Learning Center Publications.

Hirst, C. (2024). *Mudança sem tretas: Um guia de 8 passos para líderes*. Escolar Editora.

Hladio, M., & Edwards, R. (2017). *Developing Leaders: Why Traditional Leadership Training Misses the Mark*. Morgan James Publishing.

Hoch, J. E., Bommer, W. H., Dulebohn, J. H., & Wu, D. (2016). Do ethical, authentic, and servant leadership explain variance above and beyond transformational leadership? A meta-analysis. *Journal of Management, 42*(1), 125–157. DOI: 10.1177/0149206316665461

Hoffmann, E. (2007). Consumer integration in sustainable product development. *Strategic Direction, 24*(1), sd.2008.05624aad.005. Advance online publication. DOI: 10.1108/sd.2008.05624aad.005

Hong, P., & Luo, K. (2024). Coca-Cola's global marketing strategy: A Go-Stop signal framework analysis. *Proceedings of the 3rd International Conference on Financial Technology and Business Analysis*, 159-163.

Honorato, G., & Peroni, R. (2024). *Convergences between ESG and circular economy: A comparative analysis of implementation practices in Brazil*. Revista Gestão da Produção, Operações e Sistemas., DOI: 10.15675/gepros.3039

Hooper, K., & Lunn, S. (2024). A scoping review of transparency and explainability in AI ethics guidelines. *The International FLAIRS Conference Proceedings*, 37(1), 135–143. DOI: 10.32473/flairs.37.1.135594

Hornstein, H. A. (2015). The integration of project management and organizational change management is now a necessity. *International Journal of Project Management, 33*(2), 291–298. DOI: 10.1016/j.ijproman.2014.08.005

Hossain, M., Shabnam, S., Ahad, M. A., Nurani, B., & Hoque, M. E. (2025). Blockchain technology in supply chain management: Enhancing transparency and efficiency. *OAlib*, *12*(874), 1–16. Advance online publication. DOI: 10.4236/oalib.1112874

Hugo, A. (2024). Impact of Digital Technologies on Enhancing Supplier Collaboration and Performance in Sweden. *Global Journal of Purchasing and Procurement Management*, *3*(2), 1–12. DOI: 10.47604/gjppm.2752

Huy, Q. N. (1999). Emotional capability, emotional intelligence, and radical change. *Academy of Management Review*, *24*(2), 325–345. DOI: 10.2307/259085

IBM. (2021). IBM global AI adoption index 2021. IBM Institute for Business Value. https://newsroom.ibm.com/IBMs-Global-AI-Adoption-Index-2021

Ikram, M., Shen, Y., Ferasso, M., & D'Adamo, I. (2021). Intensifying effects of COVID-19 on economic growth, logistics performance, environmental sustainability and quality management: Evidence from Asian countries. *Journal of Asia Business Studies*, *15*(5). Advance online publication. DOI: 10.1108/JABS-07-2021-0316

Ikram, M., Zhang, Q., & Sroufe, R. (2020). Future of quality management system (ISO 9001) certification: Novel grey forecasting approach. *Total Quality Management & Business Excellence*, *32*(16–17), 1666–1693. DOI: 10.1080/14783363.2020.1768062

IMD. (2025, May). *What Is Disruptive Innovation? 10 real-world examples.* https://www.imd.org/blog/innovation/what-is-disruptive-innovation/

International Labor Organization. (2021). The impact of artificial intelligence at work: risks and opportunities in industrialized environments. Geneva: ILO. Retrieved from: https://www.ilo.org/global/publications/WCMS_823260/lang--es/index.htm

International Organization for Standardization. (2022). ISO/IEC 27001:2022, *Information security management systems.* ISO. https://www.iso.org/standard/82875.html (Accessed September 2, 2025)

International Organization for Standardization. (2022*). The ISO Survey of Management System Standard Certifications* – 2021. https://www.iso.org/the-iso-survey.html

Ivakhnenkov, S. (2023). Artificial intelligence application in auditing. *Scientific Papers NaUKMA. Economics*, 8(1), 54–60. DOI: 10.18523/2519-4739.2023.8.1.54-60

Jain, R., Kralovic, S., Evans, M., Ambrose, M., Simbartl, L., Obrosky, S., Render, M., Freyberg, R., Jernigan, J., Muder, R., Miller, L., & Roselle, G. (2011). Veterans Affairs Initiative to Prevent Methicillin-Resistant Staphylococcus aureus Infections. *The New England Journal of Medicine*, *364*(15), 1419–1430. DOI: 10.1056/NEJMoa1007474 PMID: 21488764

Jain, V. (2024). Creating a Roadmap for Digital Transformation. *Journal of Artificial Intelligence & Cloud Computing*, *3*(6), E255. Advance online publication. DOI: 10.47363/JAICC/2024(3)E255

Jaiyeoba, H. B., Jamaludin, M. A., Busari, S. A., & Amuda, Y. J. (2025). The implications of Maqasid al-Shari'ah for integrated sustainability practices among businesses: A qualitative inquiry. *Qualitative Research in Financial Markets*, *17*(3), 511–531. DOI: 10.1108/QRFM-09-2023-0222

Jansen, J. J., Van Den Bosch, F. A., & Volberda, H. W. (2006). Exploratory innovation, exploitative innovation, and performance: Effects of organizational antecedents and environmental moderators. *Management Science, 52*(11), 1661–1674.

Jarvis, C., Gulati, A., McCririck, V., & Simpson, P. (2013). Leadership matters: Tensions in evaluating leadership development. *Advances in Developing Human Resources, 15*(1), 27–45. DOI: 10.1177/1523422312467138

Jensen, M. L. (2011). Nurturing self-knowledge: The impact of a leadership development program. *OD Practitioner, 43*(3), 30–35. https://openurl.ebsco.com/EPDB%3Agcd%3A9%3A954665/detailv2?sid=ebsco%3Aocu%3Arecord&id=ebsco%3Agcd%3A63991047&bquery=IS%201086-2609%20AND%20VI%2043%20AND%20IP%203%20AND%20DT%202011&page=1&link_origin=scholar.google.com&searchDescription=OD%20Practitioner%2C%202011%2C%20Vol%2043%2C%20Issue%203&crl=f

Jeremić, N., & Luka, S. (2024). *Artificial intelligence – challenges of use in auditing*. Revizor., DOI: 10.56362/Rev24107043J

Jesus, C. (2024, August 14). *Agilidade, inovação e segurança: os alicerces do futuro do setor das telecomunicações*. Forbes Portugal. https://www.forbespt.com/agilidade-inovacao-e-seguranca-os-alicerces-do-futuro-do-setor-das-telecomunicacoes/

Jobin, A., Ienca, M., & Vayena, E. (2019). The global landscape of AI ethics guidelines. *Nature Machine Intelligence, 1*(9), 389–399. DOI: 10.1038/s42256-019-0088-2

Joel, O., Oyewole, A., Odunaiya, O., & Soyombo, O. (2024). *Navigating the digital transformation journey: strategies for startup growth and innovation in the digital era*. International Journal of Management & Entrepreneurship Research., DOI: 10.51594/ijmer.v6i3.881

Johannesen, D. T. S., Lindøe, P. H., & Wiig, S. (2020). Certification as support for resilience? Behind the curtains of a certification body—A qualitative study. *BMC Health Services Research, 20*(1), 1–13. DOI: 10.1186/s12913-020-05608-5

Jones, G. (2012). *Organizational Theory, Design, and Change*. Pearson Publishing.

Jones, L. A. (2021). Unveiling human factors: Aligning facets of cybersecurity leadership, insider threats, and arsonist attributes to reduce cyber risk. *SocioEconomic Challenges, 5*(4), 43–63. DOI: 10.61093/sec.5(4).44-63.2021

Jun, S., & Lee, S. (2023). Transformational leadership and followers' innovative behavior: The roles of commitment to change and perceived organizational support. *Behavioral Sciences (Basel, Switzerland), 13*(4), 320. DOI: 10.3390/bs13040320

Kafi, M. A., & Akter, N. (2023). Securing financial information in the digital realm: Case studies in cybersecurity for accounting data protection. *American Journal of Trade and Policy, 10*(1), 15–26. DOI: 10.18034/ajtp.v10i1.659

Kafoe, A. S. (2024). Holistic Competitive Strategy: Embracing A Holistic Approach To Establishing A Competitive Edge. *Revista Academiei Fortelor Terestre, 29*(4).

Kafoe, A. S. (2025). Conquering the Competitive Landscape: A Fusion of Defensive and Offensive Strategies for Sustainable Growth. In *Organizational Readiness and Research: Security, Management, and Decision Making* (pp. 53-100). IGI Global Scientific Publishing.

Kahneman, D., & Tversky, A. (1979). Prospect theory: An analysis of decision under risk. *Econometrica*, *47*(2), 263–291. DOI: 10.2307/1914185

Kahyaoglu, S., & Aksoy, T. (2021). Artificial intelligence in internal audit and risk assessment. In Kahyaoglu, S. (Ed.), *Digital Business Strategies in Blockchain Ecosystems* (pp. 179–192). Springer., DOI: 10.1007/978-3-030-72624-9_8

Kai, Z., Hui-tao, H., Yuan, Y., & Sun, P. (2023). Can adopting lean startup strategy promote the sustainable development of new ventures? the mediating role of organizational iterative learning. *PLoS One*, *18*(8), e0290849.

Kamath, R. (2018). Food traceability on blockchain: Walmart's pork and mango pilots with IBM. The Journal of the British Blockchain Association. https://doi.org/DOI: 10.31585/jbba-1-1-(10)2018

Kandil, S., Marzbani, F., & Shamayleh, A. (2024). Beyond Blockchain: Enhancing Data Sharing in Supply Chains through Horizontal Federated Learning in IoT Enabled VMI Systems. 2024 Advances in Science and Engineering Technology International Conferences (ASET), 01-07. DOI: 10.1109/ASET60340.2024.10708671

Kane, G. C., Palmer, D., Phillips, A. N., Kiron, D., & Buckley, N. (2015). *Strategy, not technology, drives digital transformation*. MIT Sloan Management Review and Deloitte University Press.

Kant, S., & Ashuro, T. (2025). Effect of eco-logistics practices on organizational performance with mediating role of MSE competitiveness in Ethiopia. In *Eco-Logistics and Sustainable Supply Chain Innovations* (pp. 39–60). IGI Global.

Kapoor, A., & Vangala, S. (2024). The role of cross-functional collaboration in digital transformation success: A study across agile enterprises. *ResearchGate*. https://www.researchgate.net/publication/377458921

Karan, A., Jayaprakash, V., & Ghosh, M. (2022). Review on statistical methods applied in pharmaceutical quality control and quality assurance. *Journal of Pharmaceutical Chemistry*, *8*, 1–4. DOI: 10.14805/jphchem.2022.art122

Karayel, T., Aktas, B., & Akbıyık, A. (2025, January 20). Human factors in remote work: Examining cyber hygiene practices. *Information and Computer Security*, *33*(1), 96–116. DOI: 10.1108/ICS-11-2023-0215

Karimi, S., Raeesi Vanani, I., & Dashti, F. (2023). The role of transformational leadership in developing innovative work behaviors: The mediating role of employees' psychological capital. *Sustainability (Basel)*, *15*(2), 1267. DOI: 10.3390/su15021267

Kark, K. (2018, March 11). IT spending: From value preservation to value creation. WSJ CIO. https://deloitte.wsj.com/cio/it-spending-from-value-preservation-to-value-creation-1520830927

Kartha, C. P. (2022). An empirical investigation of the impact of ISO 9001 certification: A comparative study. *International Journal of Business Excellence*, *26*(3), 362–378. DOI: 10.1504/IJBEX.2022.124457

Kasana, D., Smithwick, J., Dodd, J., Cavalline, T. L., & Mayo, G. (2023). Successful change management strategies for unforeseen events: Impact of COVID-19 on facility management. *Journal of Management Engineering*, *39*(4), 04023016. Advance online publication. DOI: 10.1061/JMENEA.MEENG-4870

Kaswan, M. S., & Rathi, R. (2020). Green Lean Six Sigma for sustainable development: Integration and framework. *Environmental Impact Assessment Review*, *83*, 106396. DOI: 10.1016/j.eiar.2020.106396

Keifer, S. C. (1996). Scope creep... not necessarily a bad thing. *PM Network*, *10*(5), 33–35.

Kennedy, F., Carroll, B., & Francoeur, J. (2013). Mindset not skill set: Evaluating in new paradigms of leadership development. *Advances in Developing Human Resources*, *15*(1), 10–26. DOI: 10.1177/1523422312466835

Kerzner, H. (2017). *Project Management Metrics, KPIs, and Dashboards: A Guide to Measuring and Monitoring Project Performance*. John Wiley & Sons., DOI: 10.1002/9781119427599

Khaleelullah, S., Reddy, K. S., Reddy, A. S., Kedhar, D., Bhavana, M., & Naresh, P. (2024). Pharmashield: Using Blockchain for Anti-Counterfeit Protection. *2024 Second International Conference on Inventive Computing and Informatics (ICICI)*, 529–534. https://doi.org/DOI: 10.1109/ICICI62254.2024.00092

Khan, M., Khan, N., Ahmed, S., & Mahfooz, A. (2012). Connotation of organizational effectiveness and factors affecting it. *International Journal of Business and Behavioral Sciences*, *2*(9), 21–30. https://d1wqtxts1xzle7.cloudfront.net/54315801/20-libre.PDF?1504327628=&response-content-disposition=inline%3B+filename%3D20_PDF.pdf&Expires=1770159723&Signature=EKcfp1JMA9DNucDH6pma3d0-WpEcBzcqoC8lxsE-iPclP~UE5o9MM7aGtT4jK7fds6xQnuXgH7ntNIZKMTb23DPVLBhySuQDTMfGToronWxpu-JWs7Fn82zpJHkHfvpehNUHflMj0ugMRJODo9DAYTQ1a7EAAEZ9F~NMJV2vP3wdJpGuO~AGbfqKiQBU9Y9waTDEU6FahOsP9T9sNfF2kxpo4UGej0NXN7aRldfbY~DgzbGGgk2wtnBZgA~KF6hxfu-MVIiB3Io9aQaWbSOFdRf6rZ87arhTCdEMdk3hPhgfmzjS6qZHjSTB9phWsBp2-IBjpYKfiuY92pEFMh2dUA__&Key-Pair-Id=APKAJLOHF5GGSLRBV4ZA

Khan, S., Kabanov, I., Hua, Y., & Madnick, S. (2022). A systematic analysis of the Capital One data breach: Critical lessons learned. *ACM Transactions on Privacy and Security*, *26*(1), 3. Advance online publication. DOI: 10.1145/3546068

Kiarie, D. (2020). The evolution of quality management and customer-centric approaches. *International Journal of Qualitative Research*, *14*(4), 957–972. DOI: 10.24874/IJQR14.04-17

Kılıç, M. (2021). Ethico-juridical dimension of artificial intelligence application in the combat to COVID-19 pandemics. In *Artificial Intelligence and Ethics in the Pandemic Era* (pp. 299–317). Springer., DOI: 10.1007/978-981-33-6811-8_16

Kim, W. C., & Mauborgne, R. (2005). *Blue ocean strategy: How to create uncontested market space and make the competition irrelevant*. Harvard Business School Press.

Klasmeier, K. N., & Lehmann-Willenbrock, N. (2024). Temporal dynamics of shared leadership, team workload, and collective team member well-being: A daily diary study. *European Journal of Work and Organizational Psychology*, *33*(3), 263–275. DOI: 10.1080/1359432X.2023.2263200

Klimoski, R. (2016). Critical success factors for healthcare artificial intelligence leaders: Not just technical competence. *People and Strategy, 39*(1), 14-18. Retrieved from https://www.researchgate.net/profile/Richard-Klimoski/publication/325347163_Critical_Success_Factors_for_Cyber_Security_Leaders_Not_Just_Technical_Competence/links/5b0716d4aca2725783deaa2f/Critical-Success-Factors-for-Cyber-Security-Leaders-Not-Just-Technical-Competence.pdf

Kokogho, E., Onwuzulike, O. C., Omowole, B. M., Ewim, C. P.-M., & Adeyanju, M. O. (2025). *Blockchain technology and real-time auditing: Transforming financial transparency and fraud detection in the Fintech industry.* Gulf Journal of Advance Business Research., DOI: 10.51594/gjabr.v3i2.88

Kondra, A. Z., & Hinings, C. R. (1998). Organizational diversity and change in institutional theory. *Organization Studies, 19*(5), 743–767. DOI: 10.1177/017084069801900502

Kondratieva, H. (2025). Formation of organizational sustainability in organizations in the context of sustainable development goals. *Economic scope.* DOI: 10.30838/EP.196.244-248

Kostopoulos, G., Vrochidis, S., Moumtzidou, A., Kompatsiaris, I., & Kompatsiaris, Y. (2024). Explainable artificial intelligence based decision support systems: A survey. *Electronics (Basel), 13*(14), 2842. DOI: 10.3390/electronics13142842

Kotter, J. P. (2012). *Leading change.* Harvard Business Review Press.

Kouhizadeh, M., Saberi, S., & Sarkis, J. (2021). Blockchain technology and the sustainable supply chain: Theoretically exploring adoption barriers. *International Journal of Production Economics, 231*, 107831. Advance online publication. DOI: 10.1016/j.ijpe.2020.107831

Kouzes, J., & Posner, B. (2017). *The Leadership Challenge: How to Make Extraordinary Things Happen in Organizations.* Harvard Business Review Publishing.

Kovtunenko, Y., Kovtunenko, D., Hryhoriuk, H., & Kucherenko, Y. (2024). Global transformations as the background of the emergence of threats and opportunities for management. *Economics. Finances. Law., 3/2024*(3), 22–24. DOI: 10.37634/efp.2024.3.4

Kowalczyk, A. (2024). *Quality management system according to standard ISO 9001:2015.* Problemy Techniki Uzbrojenia., DOI: 10.5604/01.3001.0054.7510

Kramer, M. P., Bitsch, L., & Hanf, J. (2021). The impact of instrumental stakeholder management on blockchain technology adoption behavior in agri-food supply chains. *Journal of Risk and Financial Management, 14*(12), 598. DOI: 10.3390/jrfm14120598

Kraus, S., Durst, S., Ferreira, J. J. M., Veiga, P., Kailer, N., & Weinmann, A. (2022). Digital transformation in business and management research: An overview of the current status quo. *International Journal of Information Management, 63*, 102466. DOI: 10.1016/j.ijinfomgt.2021.102466

Kraus, S., Ferraris, A., & Bertello, A. (2023). The future of work: How innovation and digitalization reshape the workplace. *Journal of Innovation & Knowledge, 8*(4), 100438. DOI: 10.1016/j.jik.2023.100438

Kucharska, W., & Bedford, D. A. D. (2020). Love your mistakes! - They help you adapt to change. How do knowledge, collaboration and learning cultures foster organizational intelligence? *Journal of Organizational Change Management, 33*(7), 1329–1354. DOI: 10.1108/JOCM-02-2020-0052

Kumar, C., & J, D. (2024). A comparative analysis of AWS and Azure in the context of blockchain technology. *International Journal of Research Publication and Reviews*. https://doi.org/DOI: 10.55248/gengpi.5.0324.07112

Kumar, A. (2022). *Blockchain technology A algorithm for drug serialization*. Trends Journal of Sciences Research., DOI: 10.31586/ujpp.2022.452

Kumari, S., & Lele, V. (2023). Synergy of CRM and Industry 4.0: Advancing Supply Chain Management and Customer Experience via Digital Innovations. *International Journal of Industrial Engineering*, *10*(1), 20–25. Advance online publication. DOI: 10.14445/23499362/IJIE-V10I1P104

Kumar, R., Mangaiyarkarasi, V., Ramesh, G., Arvind, S., & Fallah, M., & M, N. (2024). Boosting Supply Chain Transparency with Blockchain and Smart Contracts. *2024 International Conference on IoT, Communication and Automation Technology (ICICAT)*, 1351-1355. https://doi.org/DOI: 10.1109/ICICAT62666.2024.10923137

Kumar, S., & Khanduja, D. (2021). *Cost of poor-quality reduction in auto sector: an exploration with Six-Sigma*. International Journal of Six Sigma and Competitive Advantage., DOI: 10.1504/IJSSCA.2021.120249

Kupiek, M. (2023). Revisiting organizational change management (OCM): A context-sensitive and dynamic approach of change. In Kupiek, M., & Brandmeier, R. A. (Eds.), *The Digital Transformation of Georgia* (pp. 139–158). Springer., DOI: 10.1007/978-3-031-26451-1_7

Kurniawati, P., Nursalam, N., & Neolaka, M. (2022). Analysis of the Implementation of ISO 9001:2015 Quality Management System to Improve Organizational Performance (Study in the Regional Human Resource Development Agency in NTT Province). *Journal of Governance, Taxation and Auditing*. DOI: 10.38142/jogta.v1i2.445

Lacy-Nichols, J., Scrinis, G., & Carey, R. (2019). The evolution of Coca-Cola Australia's soft drink reformulation strategy 2003–2017: A thematic analysis of corporate documents. *Food Policy*. Advance online publication. DOI: 10.1016/j.foodpol.2019.101793

Langemeyer, I. (2019). Mindfulness and the psychodynamics in high-reliability-organizations: Critical-psychological considerations for a research on high-tech work. *Annual Review of Critical Psychology*, *16*, 1237–1257.

Langley, A. N. N., Smallman, C., Tsoukas, H., & Van de Ven, A. H. (2013). Process studies of change in organization and management: Unveiling temporality, activity, and flow. *Academy of Management Journal*, *56*(1), 1–13.

Larsson, S., & Heintz, F. (2020). Transparency in artificial intelligence. *Internet Policy Review*, *9*(2). Advance online publication. DOI: 10.14763/2020.2.1469

Laser, J. (2022). Criteria to appraise top executives for ambidextrous leadership. *Journal of organizational effectiveness: people and performance*, *9*(3), 449-470.

Lawlor, D., Sher, M., & Khaleelee, O. (2023). Systems psychodynamics and the impact of digitalisation, AI and virtual working on the eco-system. In *Systems Psychodynamics* (pp. 239–256). Routledge. DOI: 10.4324/9781003368663-18

Lawrence, P. R., Lorsch, J. W., & Garrison, J. S. (1967). Organization and environment: Managing differentiation and integration.

Lawton-Misra, N., & Pretorius, T. (2021). Leading with heart: Academic leadership during the COVID-19 crisis. *South African Journal of Psychology. Suid-Afrikaanse Tydskrif vir Sielkunde, 51*(2), 205–214. DOI: 10.1177/0081246321992979

Lazibat, T., & Damić, M. (2022). Determinants, barriers and outcomes of ISO 9001 implementation in SMEs. *Poslovna izvrsnost - Business excellence*, 16(1), 93–115. DOI: 10.22598/pi-be/2022.16.1.93

Lenning, J., & Gremyr, I. (2021). Unleashing the potential of internal audits: A review and research agenda. *Total Quality Management & Business Excellence, 33*(9–10), 994–1010. DOI: 10.1080/14783363.2021.1911635

Leonardi, P. M., Huysman, M., Steinfield, C., & Gruber, T. (2013). Enterprise social media: Definition, history, and prospects for the study of social technologies in organizations. *Journal of Computer-Mediated Communication, 19*(1), 1–19. DOI: 10.1111/jcc4.12029

Lepeley, M. T., von Kimakowitz, E., & Bardy, R. (Eds.). (2016). *Human Centered Management in Executive Education: Global Imperatives, Innovation and New Directions*. Springer., https://link.springer.com/content/pdf/10.1057/9781137555410.pdf DOI: 10.1057/9781137555410

Leslie, J. (2009). What you need, and don't have, when it comes to leadership talent. Center for Creative Leadership. Retrieved from https://www.ccl.org/wp-content/uploads/2015/05/leadership-gap-what-you-need-research-paper-center-for-creative-lea

Lester, D. L., & Parnell, J. A. (2006). The Desktop Manager. S.A.M. *Advanced Management Journal*, 71(4), 43-49,3. https://libres.uncg.edu/ir/uncp/f/The%20Desktop%20Manager.pdf

Levytska, S. (2024). Risks of the auditing services quality. *Fìnansi Ukraïni*, *2*(2), 101–118. DOI: 10.33763/finukr2024.02.101

Li, C. (2022). Information asymmetry in supply chains and blockchain technology: An empirical examination. https://doi.org/DOI: 10.5204/thesis.eprints.236968

Linden, R. (2010). *Leading Across Boundaries: Creating Collaborative Agencies in a Networked World*. Jossey-Bass Publishing.

Lin, Q., Wang, S., & Chen, G. (2022). The relationship between distributed leadership and teacher innovativeness: The mediating roles of teacher autonomy and professional collaboration. *Frontiers in Psychology, 13*, 948152. DOI: 10.3389/fpsyg.2022.948152

Liu, S., & Liu, C. (2025). Mapping the Digitalization Across Fashion Value Chain: A Meta analysis of Applications, Challenges, and Opportunities. *Making Waves Toward a Sustainable and Equitable Future*. DOI: 10.31274/itaa.18752

Liu, C., & Babar, M. A. (2024). Corporate cybersecurity risk and data breaches: A systematic review of empirical research. *Australian Journal of Management*, *49*(1), 31–62. DOI: 10.1177/03128962241293658

Liu, W., Zhang, X., & Chen, H. (2025). Improving supply chain transparency through blockchain technology. *Optimizations in Applied Machine Learning*, *5*(1). Advance online publication. DOI: 10.71070/oaml.v5i1.89

Liu, Y., & Shen, B. (2020). Quality management and blockchain adoption in a supply chain. *IFAC-PapersOnLine*, *53*(5), 10732–10736. DOI: 10.1016/j.ifacol.2020.12.2853

Li, Y., & Bai, C. (2022). Real-time assurance using blockchain-enabled continuous auditing: Framework and implementation. *International Journal of Accounting Information Systems*, *47*, 100565. DOI: 10.1016/j.accinf.2022.100565

Li, Y., Chen, C., & Yuan, Y. (2025). Evolving the job demands resources framework to JD-R 3.0: After-hours connectivity and psychological distress. *Acta Psychologica*, *253*, 104710. DOI: 10.1016/j.actpsy.2025.104710

Li, Y., & Goel, S. (2025). Artificial intelligence auditability and auditor readiness for auditing artificial intelligence systems. *International Journal of Accounting Information Systems*, *56*, 100739. DOI: 10.1016/j.accinf.2025.100739

Lou, B., & Wu, L. (2021). AI on Drugs: Can Artificial Intelligence Accelerate Drug Development? Evidence from a Large-Scale Examination of Bio-Pharma Firms. *Management Information Systems Quarterly*, *45*(3), 1451–1482. DOI: 10.25300/MISQ/2021/16565

Loufek, B., Vidal, D., McClintock, D. S., Lifson, M., Williamson, E., Overgaard, S., McNaughton, K., Lipford, M. C., & Pardi, D. S. (2024). Embedding internal accountability into health care institutions for safe, effective, and ethical implementation of artificial intelligence into medical practice: A Mayo Clinic case study. *Mayo Clinic Proceedings. Digital Health*, *2*(4), 574–583. Advance online publication. DOI: 10.1016/j.mcpdig.2024.08.008

Luna-Pérez, A., Martínez-Mendoza, S. M., Hernández-Acevedo, R. E., Santos-Pineda, L. Á., Vasquez-Martinez, M., Bartolo-Alemán, M. H., Martínez-López, M., Silva-Montes, G., Morales-Castillo, V., & Cordova-Mireles, D. A. (2023). The internal audit process as a tool for the certification of management systems. *Asian Journal of Current Research*. DOI: 10.56557/ajocr/2023/v8i18218

Lyandau, Y., & Biryukov, E. (2022). Digital Transformation of Organization as Way to Raise the Level of Digital Maturity of Industry 4.0. *Vestnik of the Plekhanov Russian University of Economics*. DOI: 10.21686/2413-2829-2022-6-11-16

Lyu, B., Yi, R., Fan, G., & Zhang, Y. (2023). Stakeholder network for developing open innovation practice of China's manufacturing enterprises. *Heliyon*, *9*(3), e13192. DOI: 10.1016/j.heliyon.2023.e13192

Madhani, P. M. (2020). Enhancing supply chain efficiency and effectiveness with Lean Six Sigma approach. *International Journal of Project Management and Productivity Assessment*, *8*(1), 40–65. DOI: 10.4018/IJPMPA.2020010103

Maghroor, H., Madanchi, F., & O'Neal, T. (2024). The Role of Generative AI in Supply Chain Resilience: A Fuzzy AHP Approach. *Proceedings of the International Conference on Industrial Engineering and Operations Management*. DOI: 10.46254/NA09.20240049

Mahdikhani, M. (2023). Total quality management and Lean Six Sigma impact on supply chain research field: Systematic analysis. *Total Quality Management & Business Excellence, 34*(15–16), 1921–1939. DOI: 10.1080/14783363.2023.2214506

Majstorović, V. D., & Babić, V. (2025). Development of business standardization and the new ISO 9001:2026 model. *Advances in Production Engineering & Management, 20*(1), 45–56. DOI: 10.14743/apem2025.1.456

Majumdar, S. M. (2024). Quality Management System implementation at construction projects. *International Journal of Scientific Research in Engineering and Management, 8*(12), 1–7. DOI: 10.55041/IJSREM39978

Makhafola, L., van Deventer, M. J., Holmner, M. A., & Van Wyk, B. (2025). A scoping review of digital literacy, digital competence, digital fluency and digital dexterity in academic libraries' context. *Journal of Academic Librarianship, 51*(3), 103053. DOI: 10.1016/j.acalib.2025.103053

Malekpour, M., Caboni, F., Nikzadask, M., & Basile, V. (2024). Taste of success: A strategic framework for product innovation in the food and beverage industry. *British Food Journal, 126*(13), 94–118.

Mandal, P. (2020). The Changing Marketplace. *International Journal of Business Strategy and Automation*. https://doi.org/DOI: 10.4018/ijbsa.2020070103

Mangla, N., & Singh, K. (2024). Cultural intelligence as a strategic approach to change management & the mediating role of learning organization. *Journal of Global Business and Commerce*. https://doi.org/DOI: 10.1007/s42943-024-00092-8

Manzoor, R., Sahay, B. S., Gumte, K., & Singh, S. K. (2024). Blockchain-backed resilient strategies in a stochastic supply chain sourcing and distribution environment under disruption: Implications for B2B sector. *Journal of Business and Industrial Marketing*. Advance online publication. DOI: 10.1108/JBIM-10-2023-0589

Maqbool, S. (2023). Digital transformation, ISO 9001 and dynamic capabilities: A systematic review. *Total Quality Management & Business Excellence, 34*(3–4), 267–285. DOI: 10.1080/14783363.2021.2012117

March, J. G., & Lee, S. H. (2022). Exploration and exploitation in organizational learning: A temporal perspective. *Strategic Management Journal, 43*(4), 789–812. DOI: 10.1002/smj.3398

Marhenke, U. (2025). AI Is Here. But Is the Legal Profession Ready for It? In *Liquid Legal–Sustaining the Rule of Law: Artificial Intelligence, E-Justice, and the Cloud* (pp. 233–245). Springer Nature Switzerland. DOI: 10.1007/978-3-031-78596-2_11

Martins, Y., Da Silva, C., Sampaio, P., & Gabriel, L. (2021). ISO 9001:2015 and risk-based thinking: scientific research insights. *Total Quality Management & Business Excellence, 33*(11-12), 1326–1343. DOI: 10.1080/14783363.2021.1954898

Matos, F., Vairinhos, V., Anes, A., Matos, M., & Vale, J. (2022). Relating organizational knowledge with ISO 9001:2015: An empirical approach. *European Conference on Knowledge Management*, 23(2), 812–821. DOI: 10.34190/eckm.23.2.812

Matos, F., Vairinhos, V., & Velez, P. (2022). Competence development in the age of AI: Implications for ISO 9001 organizations. *Journal of Intellectual Capital*, *23*(5), 1068–1085. DOI: 10.1108/JIC-09-2021-0241

Maxwell, J. (2013). *The 5 levels of leadership: Proven steps to maximize your potential.* Center Street Publishing.

McGettrick, A., Cassel, L. N., Dark, M., Hawthorne, E. K., & Impagliazzo, J. (2014, March). Toward curricular guidelines for cybersecurity. In *Proceedings of the 45th ACM technical symposium on Computer science education* (pp. 81–82). ACM., https://dl.acm.org/doi/abs/10.1145/2538862.2538990 DOI: 10.1145/2538862.2538990

McGregor, D. (1960). *The Human Side of Enterprise*. McGraw-Hill.

McKinsey & Company. (2022). The State of AI in 2022—and a Half Decade in Review. Retrieved from: https://www.mckinsey.com/capabilities/quantumblack/our-insights/the-state-of-ai-in-2022-and-a-half-decade-in-review

McKinsey & Company. (2024). The state of AI in early 2024: Gen AI adoption spikes and starts to generate value. McKinsey & Company. https://www.mckinsey.com/capabilities/quantumblack/our-insights/the-state-of-ai

McLaren, T. A. S., van der Hoorn, B., & Fein, E. C. (2023). Why vilifying the status quo can derail a change effort: Kotter's contradiction, and theory adaptation. *Journal of Change Management*, *23*(1), 93–111. DOI: 10.1080/14697017.2022.2137835

Meier, A. K., & Kock, A. (2024). Agile R&D units' organisation and its relationship with innovation performance. *R & D Management*, *54*(3), 496–512. DOI: 10.1111/radm.12655

MEO. (2025). *História*. https://institucional.meo.pt/meo/historia

MEO. (2025, February). *MEO lidera em velocidade e qualidade da internet móvel em Portugal.* https://institucional.meo.pt/media/comunicados/2025/fevereiro/meo-lidera-em-velocidade-e-qualidade-da-internet-movel-em-portugal

MEO. (2025a, April). *Comunicado de Resultados MEO - 4T 2024*. https://conteudos.meo.pt/institucional/documentos/pt/media/comunicados/2025/Abril/Comunicado-Resultados-MEO-4T-2024.pdf

MEO. (n.d.) *Inovação para liderar o futuro*. https://institucional.meo.pt/inovacao/inovacao-para-liderar

Meredith, J. R., & Shafer, S. M. (2022). *Project management: A managerial approach* (11th ed.). John Wiley & Sons.

Minglana, J., Tobias, R. R., & Roxas, R. (2021). Artificial intelligence applications in quality management system: A bibliometric study. *TENCON 2021 - IEEE Region 10 Conference (TENCON)*, 947–952. DOI: 10.1109/TENCON54134.2021.9707340

Miranda, R. (2023, May 9) *Inovação aberta: vantagens e desafios da colaboração entre empresas e startups.* Linkedin. https://pt.linkedin.com/pulse/inovação-aberta-vantagens-e-desafios-da-colaboração-entre-miranda-1f MJV Team. (2022, December 19). *Tudo sobre mudança organizacional: conceitos e boas práticas.* https://www.mjvinnovation.pt/blog/tudo-sobre-mudanca-organizacional-conceito-e-boas-praticas/

Mitchell, G. (2012). The construct of organizational effectiveness: Perspectives from leaders of international nonprofits in the United States. *Nonprofit and Voluntary Sector Quarterly*, *42*(2), 324–345. https://journals.sagepub.com/doi/full/10.1177/0899764011434589?casa_token=uc8mXBA3TBMAAAAA%3AfpXBbFtfdxJZNbZE4dcawl9l7uzWstMslGC47qsLJFAkaBECMf53n8DeEz9gfxTxFN2rrQAtbzs_yw. DOI: 10.1177/0899764011434589

MITRE Corporation. (n.d.). MITRE ATLAS: Adversarial Threat Landscape for Artificial-Intelligence Systems. MITRE. https://atlas.mitre.org/ (Accessed September 2, 2025)

Mizrak, F. (2024). Effective change management strategies: Exploring dynamic models for organizational transformation. In N. George & L. Jamil (Eds.), *Perspectives on artificial intelligence in times of turbulence: Theoretical background to applications* (1st ed., pp. 135-162). IGI Global. https://doi.org/ DOI: 10.4018/978-1-6684-9814-9.ch009

Moghadasnian, S. A., & Rajol, M. (2025). Artificial intelligence in airline business management a paradigm shift in the industry. *Journal Business of Data Science Research*, *4*(1), 6–12. https://www.researchgate.net/profile/Seyyedabdolhojjat-Moghadasnian/publication/392270838_

Moghaddasi, H. (2021). The role of information management in the process of digital health confrontation with COVID-19. *Biomedical Journal of Scientific & Technical Research*, *38*(2), 6123–6132. DOI: 10.26717/BJSTR.2021.38.006123

Mohammed, A., Mustapha, R., & Haruna, K. (2024). An Improved Collaborative Supply Chain Framework. *Kasu Journal of Computer Science*, *1*(1), 28–40. DOI: 10.47514/kjcs/2024.1.1.003

Mohammed, A., Potdar, V., Quaddus, M., & Hui, W. (2023). Blockchain adoption in food supply chains: A systematic literature review on enablers, benefits, and barriers. *IEEE Access : Practical Innovations, Open Solutions*, *11*, 14236–14255. DOI: 10.1109/ACCESS.2023.3236666

Mohd Hanif, A. H., & Jaafar, A. G. (2023). A Review: Application of Big Data Analytics in Airlines Industry. *Open International Journal of Informatics*, *11*(2), 196–209. DOI: 10.11113/oiji2023.11n2.254

Möller, D. P. F. (2023). Cybersecurity in Digital Transformation. In *Guide to Cybersecurity in Digital Transformation. Advances in Information Security, 103*. Springer., DOI: 10.1007/978-3-031-26845-8_1

Montealegre, R., & Keil, M. (2000). De-escalating information technology projects: Lessons from the Denver International Airport. *Management Information Systems Quarterly*, *24*(3), 417–447. DOI: 10.2307/3250968

Montenegro Gutiérrez, E., & Aragón Casas, L. G. (2023). Improving customer satisfaction through the ISO 9001 quality management system and quality control design: A case study. Proceedings of the 21st *LACCEI International Multi-Conference for Engineering, Education and Technology.* DOI: 10.18687/LACCEI2023.1.1.692

Montoya, A. (2024). Troubling environmental governance: Citizen legal experiments with transboundary commons. *Oxford Development Studies*, *52*(4), 396–412. DOI: 10.1080/13600818.2024.2395008

Morandín-Ahuerma, F. (2022). What is Artificial Intelligence? *International Journal of Research Publication and Reviews*. DOI: 10.55248/gengpi.2022.31261

Mosa, H., Saleh, A., Qusef, A., Altamimi, A., & Alnabhan, M. (2024). Leveraging blockchain for ethical sourcing and sustainability in supply chains: *A systematic review. 2024 25th International Arab Conference on Information Technology (ACIT)*, 1–7. https://doi.org/DOI: 10.1109/ACIT62805.2024.10877059

Mouazen, A. M., Hernández-Lara, A. B., Abdallah, F., Ramadan, M., Chahine, J., Baydoun, H., & Bou Zakhem, N. (2024). Transformational and transactional leaders and their role in implementing the Kotter change management model ensuring sustainable change: An empirical study. *Sustainability (Basel)*, *16*(1), 16. Advance online publication. DOI: 10.3390/su16010016

Muhl, E. (2024). The challenge of wearable neurodevices for workplace monitoring: An EU legal perspective. *Frontiers in Human Dynamics*, *6*, 1473893. DOI: 10.3389/fhumd.2024.1473893

Mujtaba, B. (2024). Clarifying ethical dilemmas in sharpening students' artificial intelligence proficiency: Dispelling myths about using AI tools in higher education. *Business Ethics and Leadership*, *8*(2), 107–127. DOI: 10.61093/bel.8(2).107-127.2024

Mullapudi, L. B. (2025). Optimizing supply chain management with real-time data integration platform. *International Journal on Computer Science and Engineering*, *13*(5), 40–48.

Mumford, E. (2000). A socio-technical approach to systems design. *Requirements Engineering*, *5*(2), 125–133. DOI: 10.1007/PL00010345

Mumford, T. V., Zaccaro, S. J., Harding, F. D., Jacobs, T. O., & Fleishman, E. A. (2000). Leadership skills for a changing world: Solving complex social problems. *The Leadership Quarterly*, *11*(1), 11–35. DOI: 10.1016/S1048-9843(99)00041-7

Muncaster, P. (2023, January 9). Global cyber-attack volume surges 38% in 2022. *Infosecurity Magazine*. https://www.infosecurity-magazine.com/news/global-cyberattack-volume-surges/

Muneeb, D., Khattak, A., Wahba, K., Abdalla, S., & Ahmad, S. Z. (2023). Dynamic capabilities as a strategic flexibility enabler: Organizational responsiveness to COVID-19. *Journal of Asia Business Studies*, *17*(4), 824–849.

Murikah, W., Nthenge, J. K., & Musyoka, F. (2024). Bias and ethics of AI systems applied in auditing – A systematic review. *Scientific African*, *23*, e02281. DOI: 10.1016/j.sciaf.2024.e02281

Muruganandham, R., Venkatesh, K., Devadasan, S., & Harish, V. (2022). TQM through the integration of blockchain with ISO 9001:2015 standard-based quality management system. *Total Quality Management & Business Excellence*, *34*(3–4), 291–311. DOI: 10.1080/14783363.2022.2054318

Muruganandham, S., Kumar, S., & Singh, A. (2022). Application of artificial intelligence in quality management and predictive maintenance. *Journal of Manufacturing Technology Management*, *33*(8), 1352–1371. DOI: 10.1108/JMTM-02-2021-0065

Murugan, S. (2024). A Study On Organizational Structure Of Nestle. *International Research Journal of Modernization in Engineering Technology and Science*. Advance online publication. DOI: 10.56726/irjmets48778

Muthirevula, G. R., Amarapalli, L., & Keezhadath, A. A. (2024). Blockchain for secure data lifecycle management in FDA-regulated environments. *Journal of AI-Powered Medical Innovations*. https://doi.org/DOI: 10.60087/Japmi.Vol.03.Issue.01.Id.010

Nagy, G., & Szentesi, S. (2024). Green logistics: Transforming supply chains for a sustainable future. *Advanced Logistic Systems –. Theory into Practice*, *18*(3), 29–42. DOI: 10.32971/als.2024.026

Nakat, Z., & Bou-Mitri, C. (2021). COVID-19 and the food industry: Readiness assessment. *Food Control*, *121*, 107661.

Naslund, D., & Norrman, A. (2019). A performance measurement system for change initiatives: An action research study from design to evaluation. *Business Process Management Journal*, *25*(7), 1647–1672. DOI: 10.1108/BPMJ-11-2017-0309

National Institute of Standards and Technology. (2023). *Artificial intelligence risk management framework (NIST AI 100-1)*. U.S. Department of Commerce., DOI: 10.6028/NIST.AI.100-1

National Institute of Standards and Technology. (2024). *Artificial intelligence risk management framework: Generative artificial intelligence profile (NIST AI 600-1)*. U.S. Department of Commerce., DOI: 10.6028/NIST.AI.600-1

Navarro, J. G. (2024). Marketing in the United States -- statistics & facts. https://www.statista.com/topics/8972/marketing-in-the-united-states/#topicOverview

Nelson, R. E., Stevens, V. W., Khader, K., Jones, M., Samore, M. H., Evans, M. E., Douglas Scott, R.II, Slayton, R. B., Schweizer, M. L., Perencevich, E. L., & Rubin, M. A. (2016). Economic Analysis of Veterans Affairs Initiative to Prevent Methicillin-Resistant Staphylococcus aureus Infections. *American Journal of Preventive Medicine*, *50*(5, Suppl 1), S58–S65. DOI: 10.1016/j.amepre.2015.10.016 PMID: 27102860

Neves, S. C. L. D. (2022). O modelo de competências de liderança nas Forças Armadas (Dissertação de Mestrado em Ciências Empresariais), Instituto Superior de Economia e Gestão, Lisboa Santos, A. F. C. D. (2021). A Gestão Estratégica de Recursos Humanos no Setor Público e os Sistemas de Avaliação de Desempenho. O Sistema Integrado de Gestão e Avaliação do Desempenho na Administração Pública (SIADAP). Relatório de Estágio em Administração Público-privada, Coimbra.

Nicholaus, K. (2024). 14 reasons why 70 to 80% of AI projects fail: Decoding the high failure rate of AI projects. Medium. https://medium.com/@kennethnicholaus

Nikolakis, N., Catti, P., Chaloulos, A., Van De Kamp, W., Coy, M., & Alexopoulos, K. (2024). A methodology to assess circular economy strategies for sustainable manufacturing using process eco-efficiency. *Journal of Cleaner Production*, *141289*, 141289. Advance online publication. DOI: 10.1016/j.jclepro.2024.141289

Nithisathian, K., Wall, W. P., Thanitnan, C., & Pongsittisak, D. (2020). Black Ocean Strategy: A Preliminary Literature Review. *Journal of Management and Innovation*, *7*(2), 121–140.

Nithisathian, K., & Walsh, J. (2013). Understanding Purple Ocean Strategy. *International Journal of Management Research*, *3*(1), 42–57.

Niyommaneerat, W., Suwanteep, K., & Chavalparit, O. (2023). Sustainability indicators to achieve a circular economy: A case study of renewable energy and plastic waste recycling corporate social responsibility (CSR) projects in Thailand. *Journal of Cleaner Production*, *391*, 136203. Advance online publication. DOI: 10.1016/j.jclepro.2023.136203

Northouse, P. G. (2017). *Leadership: Theory and Practice* (8th ed.). Sage Publications.

NOS. (2025). *A nossa história. Conheça os principais marcos da NOS.* https://www.nos.pt/pt/institucional/a-nos/o-nosso-adn/historia

NOS. (2025). *O nosso ADN: Inovação.* https://www.nos.pt/pt/institucional/a-nos/o-nosso-adn/inovacao

Nunes, F. (2025, June 3). *Entrada da Digi em Portugal coloca reclamações à Anacom em rota de crescimento.* https://eco.sapo.pt/2025/06/03/entrada-da-digi-em-portugal-coloca-reclamacoes-a-anacom-em-rota-de-crescimento/

Nunhes, T., Campos, T., Francisco, F., & Oliveira, O. (2021). Contributions of Annex SL to Corporate Sustainability. DOI: 10.3389/frsus.2021.745350

O'Reilly, C. A.III, & Tushman, M. L. (2013). Organizational ambidexterity: Past, present, and future. *The Academy of Management Perspectives*, *27*(4), 324–338.

OECD. (2020). *OECD Principles on Artificial Intelligence*. Organisation for Economic Co-operation and Development.

Oh, L. K.Journal of Current Research in Blockchain. (2025). A comprehensive study on public and private blockchain performance. *Journal of Current Research in Blockchain*, *2*(1), 13–27. Advance online publication. DOI: 10.47738/jcrb.v2i1.25

Olech-Anyebe, E. I., Olaniyi, E. O., & Kayode, A. D. (2024). From trust to circular economy: Evolution of blockchain's role in enhancing agro-food supply chain transparency, resilience, and sustainability. *Environmental and Sustainability Indicators*, *24*, 100460. DOI: 10.1016/j.indic.2024.100460

Oliveira, T., & Martins, M. F. (2011). Literature review of information technology adoption models at firm level. *Electronic Journal of Information Systems Evaluation*, *14*(1), 110–121.

Olutimehin, D. O., Falaiye, T. O., Ewim, C. P.-M., & Ibeh, A. I. (2021). Developing a framework for digital transformation in retail banking operations. *International Journal of Multidisciplinary Research and Growth Evaluation*, *2*(1), 608–622. DOI: 10.54660/.IJMRGE.2021.2.1.608-622

Omisola, O., & Bihani, P. (2023). Blockchain in supply chain transparency: A conceptual framework for real-time data tracking and reporting using blockchain and AI. *International Journal of Multidisciplinary Research and Growth Evaluation*. https://doi.org/DOI: 10.54660/.IJMRGE.2023.4.1.1238-1253

Omisola-Shiyanbola, A. (2024). A systems-based framework for ISO 9000 compliance: Applying statistical quality control and continuous improvement tools in U.S. manufacturing. *International Journal of Advanced Multidisciplinary Research and Studies*, *4*(6), 4052. DOI: 10.62225/2583049X.2024.4.6.4052

Onikoyi, I. A. (2017). Impact of product innovation on organizational performance (A Survey of Nestle Nigeria Plc). *Journal of Marketing and consumer Research, 37*(1), 21-39.

Onu, P., Mbohwa, C., Pradhan, A., & Madonsela, N. (2024). The potential of smart contracts in blockchain-based supply chain management for automation and sustainable manufacturing: An in-depth analysis and perspectives. *2024 International Conference on Science, Engineering and Business for Driving Sustainable Development Goals,* 1–6. https://doi.org/DOI: 10.1109/SEB4SDG60871.2024.10629874

Onwubuariri, E. R., Adelakun, B. O., Olaiya, O. P., & Ziorklui, J. E. K.Ebere Ruth OnwubuaririBeatrice Oyinkansola AdelakunOmolara Patricia OlaiyaJoseph Elikem Kofi Ziorklui. (2024). AI-driven risk assessment: Revolutionizing audit planning and execution. *Finance & Accounting Research Journal*, *6*(6), 1069–1090. Advance online publication. DOI: 10.51594/farj.v6i6.1236

Open Worldwide Application Security Project. (2024). OWASP top 10 for large language model applications v1.1. OWASP. https://owasp.org/www-project-top-10-for-large-language-model-applications/ (Accessed September 2, 2025)

Organisation for Economic Co-operation and Development. (2019). Recommendation of the Council on Artificial Intelligence. OECD Legal Instruments. https://legalinstruments.oecd.org/en/instruments/OECD-LEGAL-0449

Organisation for Economic Co-operation and Development. (2023). OECD framework for the classification of AI systems. https://www.oecd.org/digital/artificial-intelligence/

Oriekhoe, O. I., Ashiwaju, B. I., Ihemereze, K. C., Ikwue, U., & Udeh, C. A. (2024). Blockchain technology in supply chain management: A comprehensive review. *International Journal of Management & Entrepreneurship Research*, *6*(1), 150–166. Advance online publication. DOI: 10.51594/ijmer.v6i1.714

Orlov, A., Riad, R., Subbarayudu, Y., Kapoor, T., Kumar, P., Kansal, L., Bhardwaj, N., Kumar, Y., & Lakshmi, P. (2024). Circular Economy in Manufacturing: Optimization using Lean Six Sigma. *E3S Web of Conferences*. DOI: 10.1051/e3sconf/202458101016

Orwa, O., & Ragui, M. (2024). *International Quality Standard 9001: 2015 And Sustainability of Iso Certified Deposit Taking Saccos in Nairobi City County*. International Journal of Business Management, Entrepreneurship and Innovation., DOI: 10.35942/ytd95805

Osho, G., Omisola, J., & Shiyanbola, J. (2024). An Integrated AI-Power BI Model for Real-Time Supply Chain Visibility and Forecasting: A Data Intelligence Approach to Operational Excellence. *International Journal of Advanced Multidisciplinary Research and Studies*. https://www.multiresearchjournal.com/admin/uploads/archives/archive-1744730594.pdf?utm_source=chatgpt.com

Osório, A. L., Camarinha-Matos, L. M., Dias, T., Gonçalves, C., & Tavares, J. (2021). Open and collaborative micro services in digital transformation. En *PRO-VE 2021: Smart and Sustainable Collaborative Networks 4.0* (pp. 393–402). Springer. DOI: 10.1007/978-3-030-85969-5_36

Owusu-Berko, L. (2025). Advanced supply chain analytics: Leveraging digital twins, IoT and blockchain for resilient, data-driven business operations. *World Journal of Advanced Research and Reviews*, *25*(2), 1777–1799. DOI: 10.30574/wjarr.2025.25.2.0572

Oyeyemi, B., Orenuga, A., & Adelakun, B. (2024). Blockchain and AI Synergies in Enhancing Supply Chain Transparency. *International Journal of Future Engineering Innovations*. https://doi.org/.DOI: 10.54660/IJFEI.2024.1.1.115-126

Ozek, A., Seçkin, M., Demircioğlu, P., & Bogrekci, I. (2025). Artificial Intelligence Driving Innovation in Textile Defect Detection. *Textiles*, *5*(2), 12. Advance online publication. DOI: 10.3390/textiles5020012

Packard, T., & Jones, L. (2015). An outcomes evaluation of a leadership development initiative. *Journal of Management Development*, *34*(2), 153–168. DOI: 10.1108/JMD-05-2013-0063

Pambreni, Y., Khatibi, A., Azam, S., & Tham, J. (2019). The influence of total quality management toward organization performance. *Management Science Letters*, *9*(9), 1397–1406. DOI: 10.5267/j.msl.2019.5.011

Paoletti, M. (2024). ISO/IEC standards and design of an artificial intelligence system. *2024 IEEE 13th International Conference on Artificial Intelligence Systems (ICAIS),* 39–43. DOI: 10.1109/ICAIS59948.2024.10472957

Papagiannidis, E., Mikalef, P., & Conboy, K. (2025). Responsible artificial intelligence governance: A review and research framework. *The Journal of Strategic Information Systems*, *34*(2), 101885. DOI: 10.1016/j.jsis.2024.101885

Pareek, V., Saran, D., Sharma, L., Jakhar, P., & Kumar, S. (2024). Blockchain technology in pharmaceutical industry: A review of recent research articles on PubMed. *Scripta Medica*, *55*(3), 357–369. Advance online publication. DOI: 10.5937/scriptamed55-47100

Parmar, J. (2022). Artificial intelligence in high-tech manufacturing: A review of applications in quality control and process optimization. *International Journal of Innovative Research in Engineering & Multidisciplinary Physical Sciences*, *10*(6), 55–61. DOI: 10.37082/IJIRMPS.v10.i6.231961

Parviainen, P., Tihinen, M., Kääriäinen, J., & Teppola, S. (2017). Tackling the digitalization challenge: How to benefit from digitalization in practice. *International Journal of Information Systems and Project Management*, *5*(1), 63–77. DOI: 10.12821/ijispm050104

Patel, J., Patel, D., & Meshram, D. (2023). *Artificial Intelligence in Pharma Industry- A Rising Concept. 1*(2).

Pazhayattil, A. B., & Konyu-Fogel, G. (2023). An empirical study to accelerate machine learning and artificial intelligence adoption in pharmaceutical manufacturing organizations. *Journal of Generic Medicines*, *19*(2), 81–91. DOI: 10.1177/17411343221151109

Pelletier, C., & Cloutier, L. M. (2019). Conceptualising digital transformation in SMEs: An ecosystemic perspective. *Journal of Small Business and Enterprise Development*, *26*(6–7), 855–876. DOI: 10.1108/JSBED-05-2019-0144

Pereira, A., Henriques, R., & Barata, J. (2021). An ArchiMate-based approach to ISO 9001:2015 quality management: Shifting to IT-enabled documented information. *2021 IEEE 23rd Conference on Business Informatics (CBI),* 2, 125–133. DOI: 10.1109/CBI52690.2021.10063

Pereira, A., Monteiro, A., & Silva, T. (2021). Conversational agents for document retrieval: Enhancing organizational knowledge access. *Information Systems Frontiers*, *23*(3), 743–756. DOI: 10.3390/app15010223

Peteraf, M., Di Stefano, G., & Verona, G. (2013). The elephant in the room of dynamic capabilities: Bringing two diverging conversations together. *Strategic Management Journal*, *34*(12), 1389–1410.

Pisupati, C. A., & Ulle, R. (2024). The impact of blockchain technology on transparency and traceability in the supply chain of the food industry. *International Journal for Research in Applied Science and Engineering Technology*, *12*(5), 488–494. Advance online publication. DOI: 10.22214/ijraset.2024.61563

Pitelis, C. N., Teece, D. J., & Yang, H. (2024). Dynamic capabilities and MNE global strategy. *Journal of Management Studies*, *61*(7), 3295–3326. DOI: 10.1111/joms.13021

Pitelis, C. N., Teece, D. J., & Yang, H. (2024). Dynamic capabilities and MNE global strategy: A systematic literature review-based novel conceptual framework. *Journal of Management Studies*, *61*(7), 3295–3326.

Plachkinova, M., & Maurer, C. (2018). Teaching case: Security breach at Target. *Journal of Information Systems Education*, *29*(1), 11–20.

Plekhanov, D., Franke, H., & Netland, T. H. (2023). Digital transformation: A review and research agenda. *European Management Journal*, *41*(6), 821–844. DOI: 10.1016/j.emj.2022.09.007

Popchev, I., Radeva, I., & Velichkova, V. (2022). Auditing blockchain smart contracts. *In 2022 International Conference Automatics and Informatics (ICAI)* pp. 276-281. IEEE. https://doi.org/DOI: 10.1109/ICAI55857.2022.9960058

Porfirio, J. A., Carrilho, T., Felício, J. A., & Jardim, J. (2021). Leadership characteristics and digital transformation. *Journal of Business Research*, *124*, 610–619. DOI: 10.1016/j.jbusres.2020.10.058

Porter, M. E. (2008). The five competitive forces that shape strategy. *Harvard Business Review*, *86*(1), 78–93.

Porter, M. E. (2023). Changing patterns of international competition. In *International Strategic Management* (pp. 61–86). Routledge.

Porter, M. E., & Kramer, M. R. (2011). Creating shared value: How to reinvent capitalism—and unleash a wave of innovation and growth. *Harvard Business Review*, *89*(1/2), 62–77.

Potru, S. (2024). Blockchain integration in Salesforce CRM: A framework for enhanced supply chain traceability and stakeholder trust. International Journal of Scientific Research in Computer Science, *Engineering and Information Technology*. https://doi.org/DOI: 10.32628/CSEIT241061207

Potter, A. (2022). Supply chain traceability. The Fairchild Books Dictionary of Fashion. https://doi.org/DOI: 10.5040/9781501365287.2696

Pramila, T. P. (2025). Emotional Intelligence and Effective Leadership in the Digital Era. *Leadership Studies in the Turbulent Business Ecosystem*, 61

Prashanth, M. S., Srujana, S. V. U., & Aluvalu, R. (2023). Smart contract-based security auditing for web applications. *In 2023 Asia Conference on Power, Energy Engineering and Computer Technology (PEECT)* pp. 128-132. IEEE. https://doi.org/DOI: 10.1109/PEECT59566.2023.00029

Prazian, M. (2023). Resilience for Better Sustainability. ISO 28000: 2022 vs 2007. *Comparative Analysis. Nuclear and Radiation Safety*, *1*(97), 67–70. DOI: 10.32918/nrs.2023.1(97).08

Pritchett, P. (2014). *Red Ocean vs. Blue Ocean*. Pritchett LP.

Priyadarshini, R., Pandey, R., Ankit, K. C., Bhandari, D., Khadka, B., Barik, R., & Saikia, M. (2025). A faster, integrated, and trusted certificate authentication and issuer validation system based on blockchain. *IEEE Access : Practical Innovations, Open Solutions*, *13*, 27037–27049. DOI: 10.1109/ACCESS.2025.3539180

Project Management Institute. (2017). *A Guide to the Project Management Body of Knowledge (PMBOK® Guide)* (6th ed.). Project Management Institute.

Project Management Institute. (2021). *A guide to the project management body of knowledge (PMBOK® guide)* (7th ed.). Project Management Institute.

Prosci. (2020). Best practices in change management (11th ed.). Prosci Inc. https://www.prosci.com/resources/articles/best-practices-in-change-management

Proskurnina, N., & Bilousko, V. I. (2023). The trends of quality management to improve the competitiveness of an enterprise in the international market. *Bìznes Ìnform*, *5*(544), 209–214. DOI: 10.32983/2222-4459-2023-5-209-214

Público. (2019, May 10). *Ganhar clientes de televisão "é o grande desafio deste ano" para a Altice*. https://www.publico.pt/2019/05/10/economia/noticia/ganhar-clientes-televisao-desafio-ano-altice-1872200

Público. (2025, março 3). *Queixas caem nas telecomunicações, mas sobem nos serviços postais em 2024*. https://www.publico.pt/2025/03/03/economia/noticia/queixas-caem-telecomunicacoes-sobem-servicos-postais-2024-2124608

Puli, S., Reddy, K. V., Vinay, K., & Fatima, M. (2022). Blockchain based certificate validation. [IJSR]. *International Journal of Science and Research (Raipur, India)*, *11*(12), 962–966. Advance online publication. DOI: 10.21275/SR221219113003

Pulita, J. G., Pereira, C., & da Silva, A. L. (2024). How does traceability support stakeholders in food recall management? A case study of the beef chain. *Gestão & Produção*. https://doi.org/DOI: 10.1590/1806-9649-2024v31e3324

Purwanto, A., Fahmi, K., & Sulaiman, A. (2023). Linking of transformational leadership, learning culture, organizational structure and school innovation capacity: CB SEM AMOS analysis. *Journal of Information Systems and Management*, *2*(3), 1–8. DOI: 10.4444/jisma.v2i3.306

Pylypchuk, O., Holitsyn, O., & Vasilkova, N. (2025). International standards of the ISO 9000-9004 series in the system of marketing management. *Marketing and Digital Technologies*, *9*(1), 130–139. Advance online publication. DOI: 10.15276/mdt.9.1.2025.7

Pyun, J., Kim, D., & Rha, J. (2023). *Understanding the EU Directive on Corporate Sustainability Due Diligence and Examining Strategic Responses*. Korean Production and Operations Management Society., DOI: 10.32956/kopoms.2023.34.4.495

Qian, X. (2023). Strategic adaptation in beverage companies: A focus on health trends. *Journal of Consumer Behavior Studies*, *13*(4), 123–138.

Qiao, R., & Zhao, L. (2023). Reduce supply chain financing risks through supply chain integration: Dual approaches of alleviating information asymmetry and mitigating supply chain risks. *Journal of Enterprise Information Management*, *36*(6), 1533–1555. DOI: 10.1108/JEIM-01-2023-0016

Quigley, D. D., Wiseman, S. H., & Farley, D. O. (2011). *Improving Customer Service and Access in a Surgical Practice* (Working Paper WR-857-RWJF). RAND Corporation.

Quinn, S., Ivy, N., Barrett, M., Feldman, L., Witte, G., & Gardner, R. (2021). *Identifying and estimating cybersecurity risk for enterprise risk management (NIST IR 8286A)*. National Institute of Standards and Technology., DOI: 10.6028/NIST.IR.8286A

Rad, P. F. (2002). *Project estimating and cost management*. Management Concepts.

Rafi, T. (2022, June 9). Why sustainability is crucial for corporate strategy. *World Economic Forum*. https://www.weforum.org/stories/2022/06/why-sustainability-is-crucial-for-corporate-strategy/

Raghavan, M., Barocas, S., Kleinberg, J., & Levy, K. (2020). Mitigating bias in algorithmic hiring: Evaluating claims and practices. *Proceedings of the 2020 Conference on Fairness, Accountability, and Transparency,* 469–481. DOI: 10.1145/3351095.3372828

Rahman, M., Honey, U., Rangari, S., & Wu, F. (2025). Blockchain-Based Supply Chain Management for Ensuring the Quality and Traceability of Fresh Produce: *An Illustrative Analysis. 2025 IEEE 15th Annual Computing and Communication Workshop and Conference (CCWC),* 00038-00044. DOI: 10.1109/CCWC62904.2025.10903802

Rahman, H., Hossain, M., Mintoo, A. A., & Islam, S. (2025). A systematic review of intelligent support systems for strategic decision-making using human-AI interaction in enterprise platforms. *American Journal of Advanced Technology and Engineering Solutions*, *4*(2), 33–47. DOI: 10.63125/a5yh1293

Rajagopal, A. (2022). The Agile Mind-Set. In *Agile Marketing Strategies: New Approaches to Engaging Consumer Behavior* (pp. 189–224). Springer International Publishing. DOI: 10.1007/978-3-031-04212-6_7

Rajagopal, A. (2023). Gaming Without Rules: Role of Agility in Tourism Marketing. In *Paradigm Shift in Business: Critical Appraisal of Agile Management Practices* (pp. 179–194). Springer Nature Switzerland. DOI: 10.1007/978-3-031-40439-9_9

Rakić, B., Ubavić, V., Živanović, V., & Babić, D. (2024). *Implementation of integrated ISO standards (ISO 9001, ISO/IEC 27001 and ISO/IEC 27701): Proof of quality and safe business processes and services*. Urbanism and Sustainable Development., DOI: 10.46793/Urbanizam24.277R

Ramese, W. K. D., Jayasooriya, S. D., & Lakmal, A. H. (2024). Adopting ISO 9001:2015 & ISO 21001:2018 EOMS to the Sri Lankan higher educational institutions: A review of literature. *KDU Journal of Multidisciplinary Studies*, *6*(1), 145–157. Advance online publication. DOI: 10.4038/kjms.v6i1.118

Ramirez, B., & Ramirez, J. (2018). *Douglas Montgomery's Introduction to Statistical Quality Control: A JMP® Companion*. SAS Institute Inc. Retrieved from https://support.sas.com/content/dam/SAS/support/en/books/douglas-montgomerys-introduction-to-statistical-quality-control/68860_excerpt.pdf

Ramkumar, P., & Gopan, V. (2025). Enhancing Supply Chain Resilience: Integrating Blockchain for Transparency and Risk Mitigation in Logistics. *2025 International Conference on Visual Analytics and Data Visualization (ICVADV)*, 194-200. https://doi.org/DOI: 10.1109/ICVADV63329.2025.10961897

RAND Corporation. (2024). *The root causes of failure for artificial intelligence projects and how they can succeed: Avoiding the anti-patterns of AI*. DOI: 10.7249/RRA2680-1

Rand, G. K. (2000). Critical chain: The theory of constraints applied to project management. *International Journal of Project Management*, *18*(3), 173–177. DOI: 10.1016/S0263-7863(99)00019-8

Rasmussen University. (2023). *What is Organizational Change Theory and How Can it Empower You?* https://www.rasmussen.edu/degrees/business/blog/what-is-organizational-change-theory/

Ravi, V. K., Jampani, S., Gudavalli, S., Pandey, P., Singh, S. P., & Goel, P. (2024). Blockchain integration in SAP for supply chain transparency. *Integrated Journal for Research in Arts and Humanities*. https://doi.org/DOI: 10.55544/ijrah.4.6.22

Reaiche, C. (2022). Module 6. Quality management and its key concepts. In *Strategic Project Management*. JCU Pressbooks. https://jcu.pressbooks.pub/pmriskquality/chapter/module-6-quality-management-and-its-key-concepts/

Reddy, V. C. S., Jammu, K., Vaishnavi, G., Jeevan, J., & Ansari, A. A. (2025). Student certificates authentication and verification system using blockchain. *International Scientific Journal of Engineering and Management*, *4*(1), 1–6. Advance online publication. DOI: 10.55041/ISJEM02226

Regueiro, C., & Urquizu, B. (2024). Blockchain-based evidence trustworthiness system in certification. *Journal of Cybersecurity and Privacy*, *5*(1), 1. Advance online publication. DOI: 10.3390/jcp5010001

Reinartz, W., Wiegand, N., & Imschloss, M. (2019). The impact of digital transformation on the retailing value chain. *International Journal of Research in Marketing*, *36*(3), 350–366. DOI: 10.1016/j.ijresmar.2018.12.002

Reis, F. (2020). *Manual de Gestão das Organizações*. Edições Sílabo.

Reiter, I., Ozman, M., Goglio-Primard, K., Dalmasso, C., & Garraffo, F. (2024). Managing multi tiered innovation ecosystems. A governance perspective. *Research Policy*, *53*(1), 104905. DOI: 10.1016/j.respol.2023.104905

Rever, H. (2007). *Quality in project management—a practical look at chapter 8 of the PMBOK® guide*. Paper presented at PMI® Global Congress 2007—Latin America, Cancún, Mexico. Project Management Institute.

Reyes, I. O., & Barillo, E. A.IMELDA O. REYESEFREN A. BARILLO. (2024). Challenges encountered in the implementation of ISO 9001:2015 risk management system DNV-GL. *International Journal For Multidisciplinary Research, 6*(2), 16380. Advance online publication. DOI: 10.36948/ijfmr.2024.v06i02.16380

Rezki, N., & Mansouri, M. (2023). Improving supply chain risk assessment with artificial neural network predictions. *Acta logistica*. DOI: 10.22306/al.v10i4.444

Riahi, R., & Islam, M. S. (2024). Employees' information security awareness (ISA) in public organisations: Insights from cross-cultural studies in Sweden, France, and Tunisia. *Behaviour & Information Technology*. Advance online publication. DOI: 10.1080/0144929X.2024.2311734

Rialti, R., & Filieri, R. (2024). Leaders let us get agile: Observing agile leadership in successful digital transformation projects. *Business Horizons, 67*(4), 439–452. DOI: 10.1016/j.bushor.2024.04.003

Riaz, R., Abrar, S., & Gul, M. J. (2023). Securing supply-chain network with blockchain. *En Proceedings of the International Conference on Emerging Technologies* (pp. 243–258). https://doi.org/DOI: 10.1007/978-3-031-28076-4_20

Ribeiro, S. (2024, November 8). *Impacto da Digi? "nós competimos com quadidade", diz CEO da Meo.* Negócios.pt https://www.jornaldenegocios.pt/empresas/telecomunicacoes/detalhe/impacto-da-digi-nos-competimos-com-qualidade-diz-ceo-da-meo

Rickett, L. K., & Smith, D. (2026). Major cybersecurity breaches: Shaping corporate cybersecurity policies and closing the gaps. *Journal of Corporate Accounting & Finance*, jcaf.70032. Advance online publication. DOI: 10.1002/jcaf.70032

Riedl, C., & Woolley, A. W. (2020, October 28). Successful remote teams communicate in bursts. *Harvard Business Review*. https://hbr.org/2020/10/successful-remote-teams-communicate-in-bursts

Rioseco Pais, J. G., & Ponce, L., & colegas. (2024). Digital skills for sustainability in Latin America. *Sustainability, 16*(22), 9876. DOI: 10.3390/su16229876

Robertson, G., & Lapiņa, I. (2023). Digital transformation as a catalyst for sustainability and open innovation. *Journal of Open Innovation, 9*(1), 100017. DOI: 10.1016/j.joitmc.2023.100017

Rojo-Gallego-Burin, A., Montes, F., Perez-Arostegui, M., & Stevenson, M. (2020). Ambidextrous supply chain strategy and supply chain flexibility: The contingent effect of ISO 9001. *Industrial Management & Data Systems, 120*(9), 1691–1714. DOI: 10.1108/IMDS-01-2020-0038

Rose, K. H. (2014). *Project Quality Management: Why, What, and How* (2nd ed.). J. Ross Publications.

Rothenberger, K. E. (2016). A quantitative study of perceptions about leadership competencies of IT project managers (Order No. 10132045). Available from ProQuest Dissertations & Theses Global. (1810428469). https://www.proquest.com/openview/3ebc148fa5e7ce38741c0a1462cfefc8/1?pq-origsite=gscholar&cbl=18750

Roux, M., & Härtel, C. E. (2018). The Cognitive, Emotional, and Behavioral Qualities. *Individual, Relational, and Contextual Dynamics of Emotions*, 59.

Roux, M., & Härtel, C. E. (2018). The cognitive, emotional, and behavioral qualities required for leadership assessment and development in the new world of work. In *Individual, relational, and contextual dynamics of emotions* (pp. 59–69). Emerald Publishing Limited. DOI: 10.1108/S1746-979120180000014010

Rozario, A. M., & Thomas, C. (2019). Reengineering the audit with blockchain and smart contracts. *Journal of Emerging Technologies in Accounting, 16*(1), 21–35. DOI: 10.2308/jeta-52432

Rozario, A. M., & Vasarhelyi, M. A. (2018). Auditing with smart contracts. *The International Journal of Digital Accounting Research, 18*, 1–27. DOI: 10.4192/1577-8517-v18_1

Rustam, A. R., & Widiastutik, R. N. (2024). Pendampingan audit mutu perusahaan (ISO 9001). *Jurnal ABM Mengabdi, 11*(1), 46. Advance online publication. DOI: 10.31966/jam.v11i1.1407

Saarikko, T., Westergren, U. H., & Blomquist, T. (2020). Digital transformation: Five recommendations for the digitally conscious firm. *Business Horizons, 63*(6), 825–839. DOI: 10.1016/j.bushor.2020.07.005

Sacavém, A., de Bem Machado, A., dos Santos, J. R., Palma-Moreira, A., Belchior-Rocha, H., & Au-Yong-Oliveira, M. (2025). Leading in the digital age: The role of leadership in organizational digital transformation. *Administrative Sciences, 15*(2), 43. DOI: 10.3390/admsci15020043

Sachdeva, P., & Mitra, A. (2025). Embracing Emotional Intelligence in Digital Workspaces: A Qualitative Case Study of Organizational Culture Dynamics. In *Emotional Intelligence in the Digital Era* (pp. 238-249). Auerbach Publications.

Sadikin, A., Wibowo, H., & Rahman, R. (2022). Artificial intelligence and ISO 9001: Theoretical perspectives and future challenges. *Computer Science, 197*, 601–610. DOI: 10.1016/j.procs.2021.12.178

Saeedikiya, M., Salunke, S., & Kowalkiewicz, M. (2024). Toward a dynamic capability perspective of digital transformation in SMEs: A study of the mobility sector. *Journal of Cleaner Production, 439*, 140718. DOI: 10.1016/j.jclepro.2024.140718

Saeed, S., Altamimi, S. A., Alkayyal, N. A., Alshehri, E., & Alabbad, D. A. (2023). Digital transformation and cybersecurity challenges for businesses resilience: Issues and recommendations. *Sensors (Basel), 23*(15), 6666. DOI: 10.3390/s23156666

Sahoo, S. (2024). Blockchain-enabled traceability systems for supply chain quality management: Empirical insights from pharmaceutical manufacturers. *International Journal of Quality & Reliability Management*. Advance online publication. DOI: 10.1108/IJQRM-03-2024-0091

Sambamurthy, V., Bharadwaj, A., & Grover, V. (2003). Shaping agility through digital options: Reconceptualizing the role of information technology in contemporary firms. *Management Information Systems Quarterly, 27*(2), 237–263. DOI: 10.2307/30036530

Samiee, S., & Chirapanda, S. (2019). International marketing strategy in emerging-market exporting firms. *Journal of International Marketing, 27*(1), 20–37.

Sampene, A. K., & Nyirenda, F. (2024). Evaluating the effect of artificial intelligence on pharmaceutical product and drug discovery in China. *Future Journal of Pharmaceutical Sciences, 10*(1), 58. Advance online publication. DOI: 10.1186/s43094-024-00632-2

Sánchez Lizárraga, M. A., Limón Romero, J., Tlapa Mendoza, D., & Báez López, Y. (2020). ISO 9001 standard: Exploratory analysis in the manufacturing sector in Mexico. *Dyna*, *87*(213), 202–211. DOI: 10.15446/dyna.v87n213.83230

Sangeetha, M. (2020). Blockchain based Information Architecture for Medical Product Supply Chain.

Sankaran, S. (2025). Enhancing Trust Through Standards: A Comparative Risk-Impact Framework for Aligning ISO AI Standards with Global Ethical and Regulatory Contexts. *ArXiv, abs/2504.*16139. *L* arXiv.2504.16139.DOI: 10.1109/ACDSA65407.2025.11166403

Santos, L. A. B. D. (2021). As Forças Armadas Portuguesas no mercado de trabalho: análise crítica do atual modelo de prestação de serviços militar em regime de contrato. http://hdl.handle.net/11067/6054

Sarfraz, A., Sarfraz, Z., Sarfraz, M., Abdul Razzack, A., Bano, S., Makkar, S. S., Thevuthasan, S., Paul, T., Sana, M. K., Azeem, N., Félix, M., & Chérrez-Ojeda, I. (2022). Industry 4.0 technologies for the manufacturing and distribution of COVID-19 vaccines. *Journal of Primary Care & Community Health*, *13*, 21501319211068638. Advance online publication. DOI: 10.1177/21501319211068638

Sawant, S. R., Poladia, J. A., & Shah, S. (2023). Chaining success: How blockchain reshapes the landscape of supply chain. *2023 6th International Conference on Advances in Science and Technology (ICAST)*, 95–99. https://doi.org/DOI: 10.1109/ICAST59062.2023.10455024

Sawant, A. (2025). Digital document verification using blockchain. *International Journal for Research in Applied Science and Engineering Technology*, *13*(4), 2794–2798. Advance online publication. DOI: 10.22214/ijraset.2025.68159

Scarlat, C., & Panduru, D. A. (2021). The Purple Ocean: Revisiting the Blue Ocean Strategy. *Journal of Eastern Europe Research in Business and Economics*, *2021*, 165416. Advance online publication. DOI: 10.5171/2021.165416

Schein, E. H. (2010). *Organizational Culture and Leadership* (4th ed.). Jossey-Bass.

Schilhabel, S., Sankaranarayanan, B., Basu, C., Madan, M., Glennan, C., & McSherry, L. (2023). Blockchain technology in the food supply chain: Influences on supplier relationships and outcomes. *Issues in Information Systems*. Advance online publication. DOI: 10.48009/3_iis_2023_127

Schwalbe, K. (2019). *Information Technology Project Management* (9th ed.). Cengage Learning.

Searles, K. (2024, January 3). Case study: L'Occitane. *Internet Retailing*. https://internetretailing.net/loccitane-en-provence-building-loyalty/

Semenova, S., Shpyrko, O., Androsenko, O., Afanasieva, I., Kolumbet, O., & Vorchakova, I. (2024). The essence of goodwill in disclosing the intangible value of business in the context of digital transformation. *Financial and credit activity problems of theory and practice*. DOI: 10.55643/fcaptp.4.57.2024.4449

Senanayake, N., & Naveen, R. (2021). Process performance evaluation in mechanical engineering industries in accordance with ISO 9001. *IOP Conference Series. Materials Science and Engineering*, *1057*(1), 012067. DOI: 10.1088/1757-899X/1057/1/012067

Senna, P. P., Monteiro, D. S., Lacerda, D. P., & Alencar, M. H., & colaboradores. (. (2023). Development of a digital maturity model for Industry 4.0. *Computers & Industrial Engineering*, *183*, 109645. DOI: 10.1016/j.cie.2023.109645

Sever, Y., & Angin, P. (2021). Blockchain integration into supply chain operations. In *Handbook of Research on Blockchain Technology* (pp. 329–350). IGI Global., DOI: 10.4018/978-1-7998-6650-3.ch014

Shadraconis, S. (2013). Organizational leadership in time of uncertainty: Is transformational leadership the answer. LUX: *A Journal of Transdisciplinary Writing and Research,* 2(1), 1-15. https://scholarship.claremont.edu/lux/vol2/iss1/28/

Shahzad, M. A., Jianguo, D., & Junaid, M. (2023). Impact of green HRM practices on sustainable performance: Mediating role of green innovation, green culture, and green employees' behavior. *Environmental Science and Pollution Research International*, *30*(38), 88524–88547. DOI: 10.1007/s11356-023-28498-6

Shaikh, F. A., & Siponen, M. (2023). Organizational learning from cybersecurity performance: Effects on cybersecurity investment decisions. *Information Systems Frontiers*, *26*(3), 1109–1120. DOI: 10.1007/s10796-023-10404-7

Shaik, N.Imran Ahmed Shaik. (2025). Security applications of blockchain: Emerging research and innovations. *World Journal of Advanced Research and Reviews*, *26*(2), 1183–1190. Advance online publication. DOI: 10.30574/wjarr.2025.26.2.1664

Shaker, A. S., Al-Shiblawi, G. A., Union, A. H., & Hameed, S. (2023). The role of information technology governance on enhancing cybersecurity and its reflection on investor confidence. *International Journal of Professional Business Review*, *8*(6), e01605. DOI: 10.26668/businessreview/2023.v8i6.1605

Shankaran, S. (2024). Maximizing operational efficiency: Utilizing blockchain for comprehensive tracking and visibility throughout the supply chain. *International Journal of Supply Chain and Logistics.* https://doi.org/DOI: 10.47941/ijscl.2403

Sharma, D., Mungal, V., Khairnar, A., Gavali, S., & Bhadange, P.Durgesh K. SharmaVishal J. MungalAmit P. KhairnarSwaraj D. GavaliProf. U. B. Bhadange. (2024). Decentralized Supply Chain Management Using Blockchain for Enhanced Security and Anti-Counterfeiting. *International Journal of Advanced Research in Science. Tongxin Jishu*, 178–183. Advance online publication. DOI: 10.48175/IJARSCT-22434

Sharma, M., Joshi, S., Luthra, S., & Kumar, A. (2021). Managing disruptions and risks amidst COVID-19 outbreaks: Role of blockchain technology in developing resilient food supply chains. *Operations Management Research : Advancing Practice Through Research*, *15*(3), 268–281. DOI: 10.1007/s12063-021-00198-9

Sharma, N., & Rohilla, R. (2023). A multilevel authentication-based blockchain powered medicine anti-counterfeiting for reliable IoT supply chain management. *The Journal of Supercomputing*, *80*(4), 4870–4913. DOI: 10.1007/s11227-023-05654-w

Sharma, R., & Haralayya, B. (2025). Corporate governance and AI ethics: A strategic framework for ethical decision-making in business. *Journal of Information Systems Engineering & Management*, *10*(30s), 233–247. DOI: 10.52783/jisem.v10i30s.4775

Shenhar, A. J., & Dvir, D. (2007). How projects differ, and what to do about it. In Morris, P. W. G., & Pinto, J. K. (Eds.), *The Wiley guide to project, program, and portfolio management* (pp. 1265–1286). John Wiley & Sons.

Shi, C., Agbaku, C., & Zhang, F. (2021). How Do Upper Echelons Perceive Porter's Five Forces? Evidence From Strategic Entrepreneurship in China. *Frontiers in Psychology, 12*. Advance online publication. DOI: 10.3389/fpsyg.2021.649574

Shivale, N., Patwal, P., & Mahalle, D. (2025). Enhanced Traceability and Transparency in Medical Supply Chain Management Using Blockchain-Based Customized Smart Contracts. *Journal of Information Systems Engineering & Management, 10*(10s), 478–489. Advance online publication. DOI: 10.52783/jisem.v10i10s.1410

Shoira Azimovna, K. (2024). Ethical governance of artificial intelligence in quality management systems. *International Journal of Ethics and Systems, 40*(1), 19–35. DOI: 10.1108/IJOES-06-2023-0112

Shostak, L., & Pavlova, S. (2024). Formation of the potential of a business model in the context of digitalization. *Intellect, XXI*(3, 2024). Advance online publication. DOI: 10.32782/2415-8801/2024-3.15

Shrivastava, N. K. (2012). Project risk management—Another success-boosting tool in a PM's toolkit. Paper presented at PMI® Global Congress 2012—North America, Vancouver, British Columbia, Canada. Project Management Institute.

Shwetha, S., & Chandana, R. (2020). Enhanced refrigerator with quality and quantity monitoring (ER-QQM). 04, 128-130. https://doi.org/.DOI: 10.33564/IJEAST.2020.v04i11.024

Silvério, J., & Pestana, G. F. (2022). Integrated Risk Monitoring in the Quality Management System. *En A. Rocha, H. Adeli, G. Dzemyda, & F. Moreira (Eds.), Information Systems and Technologies – WorldCIST 2022* (*Vol*. 470, pp. 3–12). Lecture Notes in Networks and Systems. Springer. DOI: 10.1007/978-3-031-04829-6_1

Simão, V., Bonina, N., Lima, G., & Gonçalves, O. (2020). Comparative analysis between ABNT NBR ISO 9001:2015 and ABNT NBR ISO 31000:2009: The risk mindset in quality management systems. *Sistemas & Gestão*, 14(3), 310–322. https://link.springer.com/chapter/10.1007/978-3-030-14969-7_22

Singh, C. L. (2024). Implications of AI and metaverse in media and communication spaces. *SN Computer Science, 5*(1098), 1–15. DOI: 10.1007/s42979-024-03415-x

Skogstad, A., Einarsen, S., Torsheim, T., Aasland, M. S., & Hetland, H. (2007). The destructiveness of Laissez-faire leadership behavior. *Journal of Occupational Health Psychology, 12*(1), 80–92. DOI: 10.1037/1076-8998.12.1.80 PMID: 17257068

Snyder, H. (2019). Literature review as a research methodology: An overview and guidelines. *Journal of Business Research, 104*, 333–339. DOI: 10.1016/j.jbusres.2019.07.039

Solace. (n.d.). Customer Success Story: JDE. Solace. Retrieved August 13, 2025, from https://solace.com/resources/case-studies/customer-success-story-jde--casestudy

Solodkovska, G., & Avksientiev, Y. (2024). *Digital transformation of the global service market: trends, challenges, and prospeCTS*. Business Navigator., DOI: 10.32782/business-navigator.77-61

Somasundaram, M., Junaid, K., & Mangadu, S. (2020). Artificial intelligence (AI) enabled intelligent quality management system (IQMS) for personalized learning path. *Procedia Computer Science*, *172*, 438–442. DOI: 10.1016/j.procs.2020.05.096

Soori, M., Ghaleh Jough, F. K., Dastres, R., & Arezoo, B. (2024). Blockchains for industrial internet of things in sustainable supply chain management of Industry 4.0: *A review. Sustainable Manufacturing and Service Economics*. https://doi.org/DOI: 10.1016/j.smse.2024.100026

Sørensen, P. (2017). What research on learning transfer can teach about improving the impact of leadership-development initiatives? *Consulting Psychology Journal*, *69*(1), 47–62. https://psycnet.apa.org/buy/2016-55619-001. DOI: 10.1037/cpb0000072

Sousa, M. J., & Rocha, Á. (2019). Leadership styles and skills developed through game-based learning. *Journal of Business Research*, *94*, 360–366. DOI: 10.1016/j.jbusres.2018.01.057

Spence, M. (1973). Job market signaling. *The Quarterly Journal of Economics*, *87*(3), 355–374. DOI: 10.2307/1882010

Sreedharan, V. R., Raju, R., & Srivatsa Srinivas, S. (2020). Examining the impact of total quality management and operational performance on organizational performance: *An empirical study. The TQM Journal*, *32*(6), 1341–1361. DOI: 10.1108/TQM-04-2019-0102

Sreenivasan, A., & Suresh, M. (2024). A comparative analysis of lean start-up and design thinking and its integration. *Asia Pacific Journal of Innovation and Entrepreneurship*, *18*(2), 172–194. DOI: 10.1108/APJIE-09-2023-0181

Sreenivasan, A., & Suresh, M. (2024). Start-up sustainability: Does blockchain adoption drive sustainability in start-ups? A systematic literature review. *Management Research Review*, *47*(3), 390–405. DOI: 10.1108/MRR-07-2022-0519

Srinivasan, A., & Kurey, B. (2014, April). Creating a culture of quality. *Harvard Business Review*. https://hbr.org/2014/04/creating-a-culture-of-quality

Stanford University. (n.d.). *A guide to innovation management*. Stanford Online. https://online.stanford.edu/guide-innovation-management

Stefanova-Stoyanova, V., & Danov, P. (2022). Comparative Analysis of Specialized Standards and Methods on Increasing the Effectiveness and Role of PDCA for Risk Control in Management Systems. *2022 10th International Scientific Conference on Computer Science (COMSCI)*, 1-4. DOI: 10.1109/COMSCI55378.2022.9912583

Stephen, G. (2025). Leveraging AI for Strategic Decision-Making in Biopharmaceutical Program Management: A Framework for Risk and Opportunity Analysis. *International Journal of Management Technology*, *12*(4), 1–26. DOI: 10.37745/ijmt.2013/vol12n4126

Stetsenko, S. P., Tytok, V. V., Emelianova, O. M., Bielienkova, O. Y., & Tsyfra, T. Y. (2021). The interrelation of digital technologies and organizational and economic mechanisms in construction: Adaptation to change management. *International Review. Special Issues*, *1*(Part I), 21–31. DOI: 10.37943/AITU.2021.40.39.006

Steyn, H. (2001). An investigation into the fundamentals of critical chain project scheduling. *International Journal of Project Management, 19*(6), 363–369. DOI: 10.1016/S0263-7863(00)00026-0

Stoumpos, A. I., Kitsios, F., & Talias, M. A. (2023). Digital transformation in healthcare: Technology acceptance and its applications. *International Journal of Environmental Research and Public Health, 20*(4), 3407. Advance online publication. DOI: 10.3390/ijerph20043407

Stravinskienė, I., & Serafinas, D. (2020). The Link between Business Process Management and Quality Management. *Journal of Risk and Financial Management, 13*(10), 225. Advance online publication. DOI: 10.3390/jrfm13100225

Strifler, L., Barnsley, J. M., Hillmer, M., & Straus, S. E. (2020). Identifying and selecting implementation theories, models and frameworks: A qualitative study to inform the development of a decision support tool. *BMC Medical Informatics and Decision Making, 20*(1), 91. Advance online publication. DOI: 10.1186/s12911-020-01128-8

Strupczewski, G. (2021). Defining cyber risk. *Safety Science, 135*, 105143. DOI: 10.1016/j.ssci.2020.105143

Subramaniam, S., Azzuhri, S. R., Wah, T. Y., Mahmood, A., & Balakrishnan, V. (2025). A Holistic Anti-Counterfeiting Platform Using NFC and Blockchain Technologies. *Computers, Materials & Continua, 83*(3), 4257–4280. Advance online publication. DOI: 10.32604/cmc.2025.061560

Suebsuwong, P. (2023). Beyond Technology: Digital Transformation in Aerospace and Aviation. In Karakoc, T. H., Atipan, S., Dalkiran, A., Ercan, A. H., Kongsamutr, N., & Sripawadkul, V. (Eds.), *Research Developments in Sustainable Aviation. ISSASARES 2021. Sustainable Aviation*. Springer., DOI: 10.1007/978-3-031-37943-7_32

Sumbal, M. S. U. K., Tariq, A., Amber, Q., Janovská, K., & Ferraris, A. (2024). Tech revolution unleashed: Navigating the winds of digital transformation in the fast lane. *Journal of Innovation & Knowledge, 9*(4), 100551. DOI: 10.1016/j.jik.2024.100551

Sunmola, F., Burgess, P. R., & Tan, A. (2021). A meta-review of blockchain adoption literature in supply chain. *Lecture Notes in Business Information Processing, 444*, 371–388. DOI: 10.1007/978-3-031-04216-4_32

Sun, S. (2009). Organizational culture and its themes. *International Journal of Business and Management, 3*(12), 137–143. DOI: 10.5539/ijbm.v3n12p137

Suredranath, R. (2025). A systematic approach to AI security governance: Leveraging ISO 42001. *International Journal of Innovative Science and Research Technology, 10*(4), 394–401. DOI: 10.38124/ijisrt/25apr394

Tagscherer, F., & Carbon, C.-C. (2023). Leadership for successful digitalization: A literature review on companies' internal and external aspects of digitalization. *Sustainable Technology and Entrepreneurship, 4*(2), 100039. DOI: 10.1016/j.stae.2023.100039

Tahrir, M., & Barus, M. D. B. (2023). The effectiveness of implementing the quality management system ISO 9001:2015 in supervising road and bridge projects in South Sulawesi Province. *International Journal of Economic. Technology and Social Sciences (Injects)*, *3*(2), 375–380. Advance online publication. DOI: 10.53695/injects.v3i2.857

Talha, M., Ellahi, E., Vinod, J., Mehta, S., Tripathi, S., & Prakash, R. (2024). *Blockchain in accounting: Transforming transparency and security in financial records*. Dandao Xuebao/Journal of Ballistics., DOI: 10.52783/dxjb.v36.142

Tanveer, U., Hoang, T. G., Ishaq, S., & Khalid, R. U. (2025). Public private partnerships as catalysts for digital transformation and circular economy. Insights from developing countries. *Technological Forecasting and Social Change*, *219*, 124270. DOI: 10.1016/j.techfore.2025.124270

Tanwar, S., Parmar, A., Kumari, A., Jadav, N., Hong, W.-C., & Sharma, R. (2022). Blockchain adoption to secure the food industry: Opportunities and challenges. *Sustainability (Basel)*, *14*(12), 7036. DOI: 10.3390/su14127036

Tapscott, D., & Tapscott, A. (2016). *Blockchain Revolution: How the Technology Behind Bitcoin and Other Cryptocurrencies is Changing the World*. Penguin.

Tazvivinga, K., & Samuels, A. (2024). Digital transformation and its role in FMCG supply chain resilience. *International Journal of Business Ecosystem & Strategy* (2687-2293). DOI: 10.36096/ijbes.v6i5.606

Teece, D. J. (2019). A capability theory of the firm: An economics and (strategic) management perspective. *New Zealand Economic Papers*, *53*(1), 1–43.

Teece, D. J., Peteraf, M., & Leih, S. (2016). Dynamic capabilities and organizational agility: Risk, uncertainty, and strategy in the innovation economy. *California Management Review*, *58*(4), 13–35. DOI: 10.1525/cmr.2016.58.4.13

Teece, D. J., Pisano, G., & Shuen, A. (1997). Dynamic capabilities and strategic management. *Strategic Management Journal*, *18*(7), 509–533. DOI: 10.1002/(SICI)1097-0266(199708)18:7<509::AID-SMJ882>3.0.CO;2-Z

Thakur, V. (2024). Collaborative supply chain network: Confusion or way ahead. *International Journal of Multidisciplinary Research and Growth Evaluation*. DOI: 10.54660/.IJMRGE.2024.5.4.688-694

Thamrin, H. M. (2012). The influence of transformational leadership and organizational commitment on job satisfaction and employee performance. *International Journal of Innovation, Management and Technology*, *3*(5), 566–572. https://www.ijimt.org/show-39-520-1.html

Thilakavathy, P., Jayachitra, S., Aeron, A., Kumar, N., Ali, S. S., & Malathy, M. (2023). Investigating blockchain security mechanisms for tamper-proof data storage. 2023 *International Conference on Communication, Security and Artificial Intelligence* (ICCSAI), 926–930. https://doi.org/DOI: 10.1109/ICCSAI59793.2023.10421006

Thordsen, T., Bick, M., Müller, S., & Becker, W. (2023). A decade of digital maturity models: Much ado about nothing? *Information Systems and e-Business Management*, *21*(4), 947–976. DOI: 10.1007/s10257-023-00656-w

Tim, Y., & Leidner, D. E. (2023). Digital resilience: A conceptual framework for information systems research. *Journal of the Association for Information Systems, 24*(5), 1184–1198. DOI: 10.17705/1jais.00842

Tircovnicu, G. I., & Hategan, C.-D. (2023). Trends in enterprise risk management research: A bibliometric analysis. In Grima, S., Thalassinos, E., Cristea, M., Kadłubek, M., Maditinos, D., & Peiseniece, L. (Eds.), *Digital Transformation, Strategic Resilience, Cyber Security And Risk Management, 111* (pp. 1–20). Emerald Publishing Limited., DOI: 10.1108/S1569-37592023000111A001

Tiss, S., & Orellano, M. (2023). A Maturity Model of Digital Transformation in Supply Chains: A Multidimensional Approach. *2023 27th International Conference on Information Technology (IT),* 1-7. DOI: 10.1109/IT57431.2023.10078510

Topuz, E. (2022). Integration of ecotoxicity assessment with product design for circularity management. *Integrated Environmental Assessment and Management, 18*(2), 305–307. DOI: 10.1002/ieam.4580 PMID: 35262254

Tornatzky, L. G., & Fleischer, M. (1990). *The processes of technological innovation.* Lexington Books.

Toroslu, A., Schemmann, B., Chappin, M. M. H., Castaldi, C., & Herrmann, A. M. (2023). Value capture in open innovation. A literature review and a research agenda. *Industrial Marketing Management, 114,* 297–312. DOI: 10.1016/j.indmarman.2023.08.012

Trequattrini, A. L., Cuozzo, B., & Manfredi, S. (2022). *Intangible assets management and digital transformation: evidence from intellectual property rights-intensive industries.* Meditari Accountancy Research., DOI: 10.1108/MEDAR-03-2021-1216

Trisnandar, R., & Kurniawan, F. (2025). A systematic literature review on document verification with blockchain. *2025 International Conference on Advancement in Data Science, E-learning and Information System (ICADEIS)*, 1–6. https://doi.org/DOI: 10.1109/ICADEIS65852.2025.10933054

Trist, E. L., & Bamforth, K. W. (1951). Some social and psychological consequences of the longwall method of coal-getting. *Human Relations, 4*(1), 3–38. DOI: 10.1177/001872675100400101

Trzeciak, M. (2024). Factors of success in the change management process of IT programs. *Journal of Organizational Change Management, 37*(1), 58–74. DOI: 10.1108/JOCM-04-2023-0110

Tsado, L. K. (2016). *Analysis of healthcare artificial intelligence threats and vulnerabilities: Skills gap challenges and professional development* (Doctoral dissertation, Texas Southern University). https://www.proquest.com/openview/815feaa0609c2434c71526139576fc7e/1?pq-origsite=gscholar&cbl=18750

Turner, J. R., Baker, R., Schroeder, J., Johnson, K. R., & Chung, C. H. (2018). Leadership development techniques: Mapping leadership development techniques with leadership capacities using a typology of development. *European Journal of Training and Development, 42*(9), 538–557. Advance online publication. DOI: 10.1108/EJTD-03-2018-0022

Tushman, M. L., & O'Reilly, C. A. (2006). *Winning through innovation: A practical guide to leading organizational change and renewal.* Harvard Business Press.

Tzempelikos, N. (2021). Business-to-Business Marketing in the Light of the Evolution of the Business Environment. *Journal of Business-To-Business Marketing*, *28*(2), 101–104. DOI: 10.1080/1051712X.2021.1920696

Uddin, M. H., Ali, M. H., & Hassan, M. K. (2020). Cybersecurity hazards and financial system vulnerability: A synthesis of literature. *Risk Management*, *22*(3), 239–309. DOI: 10.1057/s41283-020-00063-2

Uffindell, R. (2025, May 21). UK Science Funding HQ Hit by 5.4m cyber assaults as attacks increase 600%. *Techerati*. https://www.techerati.com/news-hub/uk-science-funding-hq-hit-by-5-4m-cyber-assaults-as-attacks-increase-600/

Uhlir, K. (2025, February 17). Decentralized leadership: How it drives organizational agility & innovation. *CEON Foundation*. https://ceonfoundation.org/decentralized-leadership/

Ukwandu, E., Ben-Farah, M. A., Hindy, H., Bures, M., Atkinson, R., Tachtatzis, C., Andonovic, I., & Bellekens, X. (2022). Cyber-security challenges in aviation industry: A review of current and future trends. *Information (Basel)*, *13*(3), 146. DOI: 10.3390/info13030146

Ullah, A. (2025). The Effect of Artificial Intelligence (AI) on Customer Satisfaction: A Review of Bangladesh Perspective. *International Journal of Science. Technology in Society*, *13*(2), 54–60. Advance online publication. DOI: 10.11648/j.ijsts.20251302.13

Urbani, R., Ferreira, C., & Lam, J. (2024). Managerial framework for evaluating AI chatbot integration: Bridging organizational readiness and technological challenges. *Business Horizons*, *67*(5), 595–606. DOI: 10.1016/j.bushor.2024.05.004

Urban, M. C., Swaegers, J., Stoks, R., Snook, R. R., Otto, S. P., Noble, D. W., Moiron, M., Hällfors, M. H., Gómez-Llano, M., Fior, S., Cote, J., Charmantier, A., Bestion, E., Berger, D., Baur, J., Alexander, J. M., Saastamoinen, M., Edelsparre, A. H., & Teplitsky, C. (2024, February). When and how can we predict adaptive responses to climate change? *Evolution Letters*, *8*(1), 172–187. DOI: 10.1093/evlett/qrad038

Vadrevu, P. K.Pavan Kumar Vadrevu. (2025). Scalable approaches for enhancing privacy in blockchain networks: A comprehensive review of differential privacy techniques. *Journal of Information Systems Engineering & Management*, *10*(8s), 635–648. Advance online publication. DOI: 10.52783/jisem.v10i8s.1119

Valdivia, S., Schluep, M., Murcia, D., & Wehrli, A. (2024). ISO 59014 on sustainability and traceability of secondary materials recovery – Principles and requirements contributing to a circular economy. *Proceedings of the 2024 International Conference Electronics Goes Green 2024+ (EGG)* (pp. 1–7). Berlin: Fraunhofer IZM. DOI: 10.23919/EGG62010.2024.10631253

Valdivia, S., Backes, J., Traverso, M., Sonnemann, G., Cucurachi, S., Guinée, J., Schaubroeck, T., Finkbeiner, M., Leroy-Parmentier, N., Ugaya, C., Peña, C., Zamagni, A., Inaba, A., Amaral, M., Berger, M., Dvarionienė, J., Vakhitova, T., Benoît-Norris, C., Prox, M., & Goedkoop, M. (2021). Principles for the application of life cycle sustainability assessment. *The International Journal of Life Cycle Assessment*, *26*(9), 1900–1905. DOI: 10.1007/s11367-021-01958-2

Van Giffen, B., Beitinger, G., Ludwig, H., Schiano, B., Schmidt, K., & vom Brocke, J. (2025). The culture clash of AI adoption in lean quality management: Resolving the tensions at Siemens Electronics Works Amberg. *Information Systems Journal*, isj.70006. Advance online publication. DOI: 10.1111/isj.70006

Vanichchinchai, A. (2021). Investigating the impacts of ISO 9001 certification on lean manufacturing and supply chain relationship: An empirical analysis. *International Journal of Lean Six Sigma*. Advance online publication. DOI: 10.1108/IJLSS-10-2020-0164

Vazirizade, S. M., Alikhani, M., & Shams, M. (2020). Using NLP and machine learning for document classification and knowledge management in organizations. *Journal of Information Science*, *46*(5), 635–650. DOI: 10.1177/0165551519893281

Veroba, G., & Azmi, N. (2021). Front End Work Process Digital Transformation: Challenges and Opportunities. *Day 2 Wed, October 13, 2021*. DOI: 10.2118/205606-MS

Vettriselvan, R. (2025). Empowering Digital Education: The Future of Value-Based Learning in the Digital Era. In *Empowering Value Co-Creation in the Digital Era* (pp. 199-228). IGI Global Scientific Publishing.

Vettriselvan, R., Velmurugan, P. R., & Varshney, K. R. EP, J., & Deepika, R. (2025). Health Impacts of Smartphone and Internet Addictions Across Age Groups: Physical and Mental Health Across Generations. In *Impacts of Digital Technologies Across Generations* (pp. 187-210). IGI Global Scientific Publishing.

Vial, G. (2019). Understanding digital transformation: A review and a research agenda. *The Journal of Strategic Information Systems*, *28*(2), 118–144. DOI: 10.1016/j.jsis.2019.01.003

Visão. (2020, March 24). *Receitas da Altice Portugal sobem 1,7% em 2019 para 2.110 milhões de euros*. Visão. https://visao.pt/atualidade/economia/2020-03-24-receitas-da-altice-portugal-sobem-17-em-2019-para-2-110-me/

Vodafone. (2024). *Ainda mais velocidade: Fibra da Vodafone Portugal atinge 50 Gbps em teste pioneiro*. Disponível em: https://www.vodafone.pt/press-releases/2024/9/ainda-mais-velocidade-fibra-da-vodafone-portugal-atinge-50-gbps-em-teste-pioneiro.html

Waheed, A., & Zhang, Q. (2022). Effect of CSR and ethical practices on sustainable competitive performance: A case of emerging markets from stakeholder theory perspective. *Journal of Business Ethics*, *175*(4), 837–855. DOI: 10.1007/s10551-020-04679-y

Walawalkar, A., Swamy, R. M., & Kuttimarks, M. S. (2024). Improving organizational performance with ISO 9001 QMS audits. *International Journal for Research in Applied Science and Engineering Technology*, *12*(6), 456–465. DOI: 10.22214/ijraset.2024.65667

Wallace, D. W., III. (2021). *R*esilient Maintenance Infrastructure: Dynamic Repair Network Designs to Effectively Manage Supply Chain Disruptions *(Master's thesis*). *Air Force Institute of Technology*. https://scholar.afit.edu/etd/5052

Walters, L. (2020). A Supplier Risk Matrix Approach to ISO 9001:2015 Compliance: *A Case Study,* 10, 65-81. DOI: 10.15239/j.brcacadjb.2020.10.01.ja03

Wang, J., Liu, F., & Wu, J. (2021). A strategy tripod perspective on ISO 9001 adoption: Evidence from Chinese manufacturing firms. *IEEE Transactions on Engineering Management,* PP, 1–15. https://doi.org/DOI: 10.1109/TEM.2021.3093581

Wang, L., Guan, Z., Chen, Z., & Hu, M. (2023). Enabling integrity and compliance auditing in blockchain-based GDPR-compliant data management. *IEEE Internet of Things Journal, 10*(20), 20955–20968. DOI: 10.1109/JIOT.2023.3285211

Wang, L., He, Y., & Wu, Z. (2022). Design of a blockchain-enabled traceability system framework for food supply chains. *Foods, 11*(5), 744. Advance online publication. DOI: 10.3390/foods11050744

Wang, X. (2024). *Blockchain security and applications: A comprehensive analysis from hash functions to consensus algorithms.* Theoretical and Natural Science., DOI: 10.54254/2753-8818/31/20240862

Warner, K. S. R., & Wäger, M. (2019). Building dynamic capabilities for digital transformation: An ongoing process of strategic renewal. *Long Range Planning, 52*(3), 326–349. DOI: 10.1016/j.lrp.2018.12.001

Watkins, M. D. (2013). *The First 90 Days: Proven Strategies for Getting Up to Speed Faster and Smarter.* Harvard Business Review Publishing., https://d1wqtxts1xzle7.cloudfront.net/63499530/The-First-90-Days-Proven-Strategies-For-Getting-Up-To-Speed-Faster-And-Smarter-Updated-And-Expande20200601-70801-hsk65w-libre.pdf?1591079475=&response-content-disposition=inline%3B+filename%3DThe_First_90_Days_Proven_Strategies_for.pdf&Expires=1770162233&Signature=XMjEd1kPmeF8x-WkKnyhWFpvkdEhVcW4XBgaS0-Q18VaaTIceUCQMZX01QwrtvermcefFdLG7eZzPFAYRwK0wGNnebrJUMzvYJMe1EZmUMFtjr53ej6lnF-0kO64KzvbkXaw7VwH51QSVS1XrxiLfoOhMQiCiYOIAZg6Ek~EjmtCxcxKtuo4FNSsBXG67qYaRRrM4q4JO6r73Ne02ZtsrhDBEUQxv9mMnyYsuo8nJfe25j0ZsSB99sqaRHsTvoth6dEdL7IMETXLIoAwcqbACBxuxTXzaRgtUvS0MDMVcUET49XJudKJOojZMfseq9~H0zmV645ORuZgTAsuKPcA6g__&Key-Pair-Id=APKAJLOHF5GGSLRBV4ZA

Weber, E., Krehl, E.-H., & Büttgen, M. (2022). The digital transformation leadership framework: Conceptual and empirical insights into leadership roles in technology-driven business environments. *Journal of Leadership Studies, 16*(1), 6–22. DOI: 10.1002/jls.21810

Wee, C. H. (2017). Think Tank—Beyond the Blue Ocean Strategy. *Visions of Strategy*, 2017.

Weick, K. E., & Quinn, R. E. (1999). Organizational change and development. *Annual Review of Psychology, 50*(1), 361–386. DOI: 10.1146/annurev.psych.50.1.361 PMID: 15012461

Wella, W., & Chia, L. (2020). The Implementing ISO 9001 in Manufacture Industry: Case Study PT Softex Indonesia. *International Journal of New Media Technology (IJNMT*), 6(2), 92–97.** DOI: 10.31937/ijnmt.v6i2.1248

Westerman, G., Bonnet, D., & McAfee, A. (2014). *Leading digital: Turning technology into business transformation.* Harvard Business Review Press.

Whittemore, R., & Knafl, K. (2005). The integrative review: Updated methodology. *Journal of Advanced Nursing, 52*(5), 546–553.

Wilden, R., & Gudergan, S. P. (2015). The impact of dynamic capabilities on operational marketing and technological capabilities: Investigating the role of environmental turbulence. *Journal of the Academy of Marketing Science*, *43*, 181–199.

Wiyono, S., Silitonga, T. H., & Heryanto, D. (2025). The influence of ISO 9001:2015 quality management system implementation on marketing performance at PT Timah Tbk. *Journal of Management Studies and Development*, *4*(1), 770. DOI: 10.56741/jmsd.v4i01.770

Wójcik, P., Obłój, K., Wąsowska, A., & Wierciński, S. (2020). Corporate acceleration process: A systems psychodynamics perspective. *Journal of Organizational Change Management*, *33*(6), 1163–1180. DOI: 10.1108/JOCM-05-2019-0136

Wolniak, R. (2021). *Internal audit and management review in ISO 9001:2015. Silesian University of Technology Scientific Papers, Organization and Management.* Series., DOI: 10.29119/1641-3466.2021.151.49

Wong, L.-W., Leong, L.-Y., Hew, J.-J., Tan, G., & Ooi, K. (2020). Time to seize the digital evolution: Adoption of blockchain in operations and supply chain management among Malaysian SMEs. *International Journal of Information Management*, *52*, 101997. DOI: 10.1016/j.ijinfomgt.2019.08.005

World Economic Forum. (2021, March 23). Principles for Board Governance of Cyber Risk. *Author.* https://www.weforum.org/publications/principles-for-board-governance-of-cyber-risk/

World Economic Forum. (2022). *Global Technology Governance Report 2022.* WEF.

Wu, J., & Liu, Q. (2025). Integrating blockchain and AI for real-time auditing in Industry 4.0 environments. *Computers & Industrial Engineering*, *189*, 109973. DOI: 10.1016/j.cie.2024.109973

Xiong, M., & Wang, H. (2022). Digital twin applications in aviation industry: A review. *International Journal of Advanced Manufacturing Technology*, *121*(9-10), 5677–5692. DOI: 10.1007/s00170-022-09717-9

Xue, J., Li, G., & Ivanov, D. (2025). Digital transformation in the blockchain era: Balancing efficiency and resilience in operations management. *International Journal of Production Economics*, *109525*, 109525. Advance online publication. DOI: 10.1016/j.ijpe.2025.109525

Xue, L. (2024). Exploring the Impact of Contingency Strategies and Organizational Resilience on Institutional Adaptability and Sustaining Educational Quality in Chinese Higher Education. *International Journal of Academic Research in Business & Social Sciences*, *14*(6). Advance online publication. DOI: 10.6007/IJARBSS/v14-i6/21917

Yadav, S., & Jasmin, D. (2024). Smart contracts on blockchain for transparent supply chain transactions. *2024 International Conference on IoT, Communication and Automation Technology (ICICAT)*, 1144–1149. https://doi.org/DOI: 10.1109/ICICAT62666.2024.10923250

Yakushova, E., Cherepovskaya, N., Litvin, I., Chemodanova, O. N., & Gainochenko, T. M. (2022). Transformation of hospitality industry under the COVID-19 crisis. In *Strategies and Trends in Organizational and Project Management* (pp. 145–157). Springer., DOI: 10.1007/978-3-030-94245-8_11

Yang, C., Lan, S., Zhao, Z., Zhang, M., Wu, W., & Huang, G. (2023). Edge cloud blockchain and IoE enabled quality management platform for perishable supply chain logistics. *IEEE Internet of Things Journal, 10*(5), 3264–3275. DOI: 10.1109/JIOT.2022.3142095

Yang, L., Lau, L., & Gan, H. (2020). Investors' perceptions of the cybersecurity risk management reporting framework. *International Journal of Accounting & Information Management, 28*(1), 167–183. DOI: 10.1108/IJAIM-02-2019-0022

Yazo-Cabuya, E. J., Ibeas, A., & Rey-Caballero, R. (2025). Multi-criteria decision making for risk management in quality management systems. *Sustainability (Basel), 17*(3), 1092. DOI: 10.3390/su17031092

Yin, R. K. (2018). *Case study research and applications: Design and methods* (6th ed.). SAGE Publications.

Yu, Y., Hu, X., Rajaganapathy, S., Feng, J., Abdelhameed, A., Li, X., Li, J., Liu, K., Yang, L., Taner, N., Fiero, P., Boroumand, S., Larsen, R., Goyal, M., Otley, C., Zong, N., Halamka, J., & Tao, C. (2025). Launching Insights: A Pilot Study on Leveraging Real-World Observational Data from the Mayo Clinic Platform to Advance Clinical Research. *ArXiv, abs/2504.16090*. /arXiv.2504.16090.DOI: 10.48550

Zamlynskyi, V., Heretskiy, R., Firsa, D., & Stepanenko, S. (2023). Strengthening economic security through the zero-waste concept in sustainable business. *Ukrainian Journal of Applied Economics and Technology, 8*(4), 139–149. DOI: 10.36887/2415-8453-2023-4-22

Zariwala, K. (2023). Impact of blockchain technology on supply chain transparency, sustainability and profitability. *Sustainable Operations and Computers, 4*, 16–26. DOI: 10.1016/j.susoc.2023.04.001

Zekhnini, K., Cherrafi, A., Bouhaddou, I., Chaouni Benabdellah, A., & Raut, R. D. (2021). Barriers of blockchain technology adoption in viable digital supply chain. In *Lecture Notes in Networks and Systems* (pp. 225–238). Springer., DOI: 10.1007/978-3-030-94335-6_16

Zhang, M., & Huo, R. (2022). Assessing the logistic system maturity level in integrated supply chains under Logistic 4.0 paradigm. *Bulletin of the National Technical University "Kharkiv Polytechnic Institute" (Economic Sciences), No. 3*, 86–92. http://dx.doi.org/DOI: 10.20998/2519-4461.2022.3.86

Zhang, F., & Gong, Z. (2021). Supply Chain Inventory Collaborative Management and Information Sharing Mechanism Based on Cloud Computing and 5G Internet of Things. *Mathematical Problems in Engineering, 2021*, 1–12. DOI: 10.1155/2021/6670718

Zhang, H., Ding, H., & Xiao, J. (2023). How organizational agility promotes digital transformation: An empirical study. *Sustainability (Basel), 15*(14), 11304. DOI: 10.3390/su151411304

Zhang, L., Carter, R. A.Jr, Greene, J. A., & Bernacki, M. L. (2024). Unraveling challenges with the implementation of universal design for learning: A systematic literature review. *Educational Psychology Review, 36*(1), 35. DOI: 10.1007/s10648-024-09860-7

Zhang, S. (2024). Research on the application of AI technology in auditing. *Economic Management & Global Business Studies, 3*(2), 41–50. DOI: 10.69610/j.emgbs.20240831

Zhang, Y. (2024). Risk management, operational efficiency and corporate governance in the banking industry: Basis for corporate resiliency framework. *International Journal of Research Studies in Management, 12*(9). Advance online publication. DOI: 10.5861/ijrsm.2024.1230

Zhang, Z., Zhao, Y., & Xu, W. (2021). AI-based visual inspection in automotive manufacturing. *Journal of Manufacturing Systems*, *60*, 555–564. DOI: 10.1016/j.jmsy.2021.03.009

Zhao, Y., Cai, B., Cozzani, V., & Liu, Y. (2024). Failure dependence and cascading failures: A literature review and investigation on research opportunities. *Reliability Engineering & System Safety*, *256*, 110766. DOI: 10.1016/j.ress.2024.110766

Zheng, L. (2023). The evolution of reformulation strategies in carbonated beverages. *International Food Research*, *45*(2), 211–227.

Zhou, Y. (2024). Blockchain Technology Improves the Resilience of Manufacturing Supply Chain: An Exploration Based on Grounded Theory. *Advances in Economics, Management and Political Sciences.* https://doi.org/DOI: 10.54254/2754-1169/2024.18266

Zimon, D., Tyan, J., & Sroufe, R. (2020). Drivers of sustainable supply chain management: Practices to alignment with ISO 9001 standard. *Sustainability*, *12*(6), 1–20.

Zineb, A., Zineb, F., Ismael, E. O., & Ikram, M. (2022). Effects of COVID-19 on population, economic growth, logistics performance, and quality management in Africa: Grey relational analysis. *International Journal of Grey Systems*, *2*(3), 18–33. Advance online publication. DOI: 10.52812/ijgs.56

Zoppelletto, A., Orlandi, L. B., Zardini, A., Rossignoli, C., & Kraus, S. (2023). Organizational roles in the context of digital transformation: A micro-level perspective. *Journal of Business Research*, *157*, 113563. DOI: 10.1016/j.jbusres.2022.113563

Zuluğ, A., Ceylan, E., & Elmas, B. (2022). Pandemic impact on food industry: Consumer behavior change analysis. *Journal of Food Science and Technology*, *15*(3), 187–202.

About the Contributors

Darrell Norman Burrell is a visiting scholar at the Samuel DeWitt Proctor Institute for Leadership, Equity, and Justice at Rutgers University, where he is currently focusing his research on sustainability, health equity, and inclusive leadership. His work as a visiting researcher at the Pellegrino Center for Clinical Bioethics at the Georgetown University Medical Center in Washington, D.C., and as a post-doctoral public health researcher at the University of Maryland School of Pharmacy in Baltimore, MD, has provided him with a unique perspective on issues related to health disparities, health technology access, telehealth, adolescent health, and health literacy. For more than 12 years, he has also served in various roles as a doctoral faculty member, dissertation chair, and research panel participant at Marymount University, the Florida Institute of Technology, Capitol Technology University, the University of Liverpool in the U.K., and The Chicago School of Professional Psychology in Washington D.C. Dr. Burrell is a Certified Diversity Professional and a Certified Executive Coach. Dr. Burrell is an alumnus of the Presidential Management Fellows Program www.pmf.gov with the U.S. Federal Government and U.S. Nuclear Regulatory Commission, where he managed and developed leadership and diversity programs for professionals in Public Health, Environmental Health, Emergency Response, Technology, and Engineering. Academically, Dr. Burrell has three doctorate degrees and six graduate degrees, including a Master of Research in Artificial Intelligence Biotechnology Applications and Healthcare, along with additional graduate degrees in (H.R. Management, Management, Health Leadership, Sales and Marketing Management, Higher Education Administration, and Interfaith Action and Conflict Management). Dr. Burrell received his first doctoral degree in health education (DHEd), focusing on environmental public health and executive leadership coaching, at A.T. Still University in 2010. Dr. Burrell completed his 2nd doctorate, a Doctor of Philosophy (Ph.D.) in Cybersecurity Leadership at Capitol Technology University. In 2022, Dr. Burrell completed his 3rd Doctor of Business Administration (DBA) in Supply Chain Management at Capitol Technology University. He has over 20 years of management, teaching, and training experience in academia, government, and private industry. Dr. Burrell has over 200 peer-reviewed publications and more than 1200 Google Scholar citations. Dr. Burrell can be reached at

***

A. K. Subramani holds a Ph.D. in Business Administration from Manonmaniam Sundaranar University, Tirunelveli, India, and has over 19 years of teaching experience. He has published 80 research articles in international journals, including two in the ABDC-A category, ten in ABDC-B, two in ABDC-C, 38 in Scopus-indexed journals, and ten in Web of Science-indexed journals. He has also presented papers at various national and international conferences. He has completed more than 36 courses through the Swayam online platform in human resource management, business analytics, and intellectual property rights. He has earned several NPTEL Star recognitions, including Evangelist, Motivated Learner,

Enthusiast, and Discipline Star. He serves as a peer reviewer for reputable journals published by Inderscience and Emerald. His research interests include human resource management and organisational behaviour. He has been honoured with the Teaching and Research Excellence Award and the Distinguished Teacher Award – Management.

Sivadi Balakrishna is currently working as an Associate Professor in the Department of Advanced Computer Science and Engineering at Vignan's Foundation for Science, Technology & Research (VFSTR), Vadlamudi, and Guntur. He pursued a Full-time Ph. D in the Department of Computer Science and Engineering, at Pondicherry University (A Central University) in 2020, Puducherry, India. He received his Bachler of Technology (B.Tech) in the Department of Computer Science and Engineering from Jawaharlal Nehru Technological University (JNTU) in 2010 and Master of Technology (M.Tech) in the Department of Computer Science and Engineering from Jawaharlal Nehru Technological University (JNTU) in 2013, Kakinada, AP, India. He has qualified NET (National Eligibility Test) in Dec-2018, which was conducted by UGC. He has 13+ years of teaching and research experience. He taught various advanced courses in the field of AIML and Data Science such as Artificial Intelligence, Machine Learning, Big Data Analytics, Intelligent Application Development, Cloud Computing, Deep Learning, Fundamentals of Image Processing, and many more. He has supervised one Ph.D scholar and currently, three Ph.D scholars are working under his supervision. He has published more than 50 research articles in International journals and contributed chapters to several books. He has also presented papers at several International conferences. His current research interests are Machine Learning, Data Analytics, Computer Vision, and Artificial Intelligence. He may contact at: drsivadibalakrishna@gmail.com

Sharon L. Burton stands out as an eminent figure in cybersecurity leadership, information security, business, and education with a distinguished career spanning over 25 years at the intersection of academia, industry, and government. Her exper-tise is grounded in a robust foundation of technical acumen and strategic oversight, enabling her to fortify information security and enhance organizational resilience effectively. Dr. Burton's academic credentials include a Ph.D. in Cybersecurity Leadership, a DBA in Quality Systems Management, two MBA degrees (Human Resources Management, and Management, alongside multiple certifications in in-formation security management, project management, change management, strate-gic workforce planning, and Lean Six Sigma Black Belt, among others. A prolific thought leader, Dr. Burton has contributed over 110 publications to the field, including peer-reviewed journal articles, book chapters, and conference pro-ceedings, showcasing her dedication to advancing knowledge and practice in cyber-security and leadership. Her work is recognized and indexed in prestigious data-bases such as SCOPUS (56943042000), ORCID (0000-0003-1653-9783), and Web of Science (B-2916-2019). Dr. Burton's commitment to education and mentorship is evident in her roles as a doctoral dissertation chair, adjunct faculty, and senior executive consultant, where she has significantly impacted STEM education and supported the next generation of cybersecurity professionals. She can be reached at 302-547-8010 or Burtons6@erau.edu or sharonlburton2@comcast.net.

Marisa Cleveland With more than two decades in the education and publishing industries, Dr. Marisa Cleveland is adamant about supporting efforts toward the betterment of the human condition. Cleveland is the executive director for The Seymour Agency and co-author of the leadership book, There Is No Box. Cleveland holds an Ed.D. in Organizational Leadership from Northeastern University, and an M.A. in Educational Administration and a B.A. in Speech Communication from George Mason University.

Simon Cleveland is a professor of project management Purdue at University Global. Dr. Cleveland is a graduate of George Mason University with Bachelor of Science degree in Business, of the George Washington University with a Master of Science degree in Project Management, of the City University of Seattle with a Master of Arts degree in Leadership, with a Ph.D. in Information Systems from Nova Southeastern University, and with a Ed.D. in Organizational Leadership from Northeastern University. He is also certified as a project management professional (PMP), Six Sigma Black Belt (SSBB) expert, and Information Technology Infrastructure Library (ITIL) foundations expert. Dr. Cleveland is the author of over 60 peer-reviewed publications in journals and conferences, and is a three-time recipient of the prestigious Dr. Harold Kerzner Scholarship which is awarded by the Project Management Institute Educational Foundation. Professionally, Dr. Cleveland has worked as both technology manager, program manager and PMO Director for organizations such as MD Anderson Cancer Center, Department of Homeland Security, NASA, Accenture, and AOL.

Oscar Cruz Domínguez obtained a Ph.D. in industrial engineering at CIATEC. He is currently a researcher professor at Universidad Politécnica de Zacatecas and Instituto Tecnológico Superior de Fresnillo. His research field considers the use of artificial intelligence for industrial applications.

Alieu Stephen Kafoe is a doctoral research student at Marymount University in Arlington, Virginia, USA. He is also the co-owner and chief operating officer of Pivotal Initiatives, LLC, a company he co-founded in Minnesota, USA. In this role, he serves as the EOS integrator and Chief Operating Officer, responsible for implementing the Entrepreneurial Operating System (EOS) within the company's operations and ensuring efficient and effective management. He is a business consultant providing expertise in quality and process control, supply chain operations, and logistics. Mr. Kafoe's expertise in business intelligence, supply chain management, and competitive strategy is not merely theoretical. He has made significant academic contributions through various publications, including book chapters titled "Supply Chain Resilience Strategy for Healthcare Organizations: Crucial Steps in Addressing the Impact of Natural Disasters" and "Conquering the Competitive Landscape: A Fusion of Defensive and Offensive Strategies for Sustainable Growth, "published by IGI Global; as well as peer-reviewed journal articles: “Holistic Competitive Strategy: Embracing a Holistic Approach to Establishing a Competitive Edge” and “ Enhancing Organizational Agility in Traditional Corporations: A Strategic Intervention Model based on Galbraith’s Star Model and Consumer Psychology Insights,” published by Land Forces Academy Journal. With over 22 years of experience in the food, beverage, and process automation industries, Mr. Kafoe has held significant leadership positions, including Chief Operating Officer, Director of Brewing Operations, and Sales Director. His expertise spans quality assurance, project management, product innovation, and supply chain operations, demonstrating strong leadership skills and the ability to succeed in diverse roles.

Vinodh N is currently pursuing his PhD as a Research Scholar at Saveetha School of Management, SIMATS, Saveetha University, Chennai. Concurrently, he serves as an Assistant Professor in the MBA Department at St. Joseph College of Engineering, Chennai, Tamil Nadu, India. He earned his Master of Philosophy (M.Phil) degree from Sri Venkateshwara University, Tirupati, and holds an MBA from Madras University, Chennai. With over fifteen years of teaching experience across various esteemed educational institutions in Chennai, Mr. He exemplifies a strong commitment to academia and scholarly research. His contributions to the field are underscored by his publications in SCOPUS indexed journals.

Daniel Ngueya is a doctoral student at Marymount University, specializing in digital transformation and artificial intelligence strategy in regulated industries. His research focuses on the intersection of enterprise innovation, responsible AI governance, and organizational change. Drawing on both theoretical frameworks and real-world case studies, Daniel explores how AI implementation can fail or succeed depending on alignment between technology, governance, and human systems. His work aims to bridge academic research with practical leadership insight for digital decision-makers.

José De Jesús Reyes-Sánchez, Ph.D. in senior management, has six master's degrees, in education, in management, professional soccer technique, in physical preparation, in professional soccer, in physical rehabilitation sciences, in sports sciences, as well as in coaching and integral well-being, who is a research professor at the TECNM Instituto Tecnológico Superior De Fresnillo, with more than 20 years of teaching experience, PRODEP profile and coordinator of the academic body with vast experience in conferences and workshops, currently novelist and writer.

Gabriela R. Romo, PhD in teaching-learning strategies, specializes in language teaching, particulary English. Collaborator in projects that significantly improve active language learning in transversality with other subjects such as Arts and Humanities in young people of the University of Zacatecas, where is currently a research professor. Her research areas have been related to Pedagogy. With more than 20 years of experience in the educational field and her greatest interest is designing strategies that actively involve young people in enriching learning not only with the language, but also with its culture, customs and daily life.

Amalisha Sabie-Aridi, Ph.D., MBA, CMP-UNGGA, is an esteemed scholar, educator, and executive leader whose career spans over a decade of exceptional contributions to higher education, project management, organizational strategy, and leadership development. As a distinguished graduate professor and doctoral committee chair at multiple institutions, including Marymount University and Washington University of Science & Technology, she has guided countless doctoral candidates and shaped innovative curricula across disciplines such as technology, business, leadership, and project management. Dr. Sabie-Aridi's prolific scholarly output includes over 80 peer-reviewed publications covering diverse fields such as organizational behavior, artificial intelligence strategy, healthcare management, strategic leadership, diversity and inclusion, and cybersecurity. She is renowned for integrating research excellence with practical expertise drawn from her tenure as a senior project manager and executive operations leader, notably in high-stakes environments like NASA Engineering Inc. Internationally recognized, she holds honors including UN Global Goodwill Ambassador.

Vijender Kumar Solanki, Ph.D. is an Associate Professor in Computer Science & Engineering, Stanley College of Engineering and Technology For Women (Autonomous), Hyderabad, TS, India. He has more than 15 years of academic experience in network security, IoT, Big Data, Smart City and IT. Prior to his current role, he was associated with Apeejay Institute of Technology, Greater Noida, UP, KSRCE (Autonomous) Institution, Tamilnadu, India & Institute of Technology & Science, Ghaziabad, UP, India. He has authored or co-authored more than 125 research articles that are published in journals, books and conference proceedings. He has edited or co-edited 24 books in the area of Information Technology.. He received Ph.D in Computer Science and Engineering from Anna University, Chennai, India in 2017 He is Editor in International Journal of Machine Learning and Networked Collaborative

Engineering (IJMLNCE) ISSN 2581-3242, Associate Editor in International Journal of Information Retrieval Research (IJIRR), IGI-GLOBAL, USA, ISSN: 2155-6377 | E-ISSN: 2155-6385 . He is guest editor with IGI-Global, USA, InderScience & Many more publishers. He can be contacted at spesinfo@yahoo.com .

Index

A

B

C

D

E

F

H

I

L

M

O

P

Q

R

S

T

www.ingramcontent.com/pod-product-compliance
Lightning Source LLC
LaVergne TN
LVHW060253011026
849161LV00011B/2706